D1611293

Loyal Hearts Proclaim

Lower Dauphin High School:
The First Fifty Years

Cover and Book Design by E. Nan Edmunds
Yesteryear Publishing

LOYAL HEARTS PROCLAIM

Lower Dauphin High School:
The First Fifty Years

by

Judith I. Witmer

LOYAL HEARTS PROCLAIM
Lower Dauphin High School: The First Fifty Years

ISBN 978-0-9837768-4-0

Published in the United States by Yesteryear Publishing.

LOYAL HEARTS PROCLAIM Lower Dauphin High School: The First Fifty Years is available through the Hummelstown Historical Society and can be purchased on their website **www.hummelstownhistoricalsociety.org** using PayPal, directly from the Historical Society during business hours or during an event, or by mail at 32 West Main Street, Hummelstown, PA 17036. Checks are to be made payable to LDAA (Lower Dauphin Alumni Association). The book is also available for purchase through **www.amazon.com**.

Disclaimer:

The idea for this book was first conceived in 2008 when the Lower Dauphin Alumni Association began to plan for Lower Dauphin's Golden Jubilee to take place in 2010. We wanted a record—all in one place—of everything from football to fads. However, in the excitement, little did we realize the almost impossibility of such a task.

Like most schools, Lower Dauphin did not keep records of all of the resources we now believe were important to those who attended Lower Dauphin. There were no lists of homecoming themes, yearbook editors, class advisors, clubs, or courses; no history of school pranks or of the falcon mascot; no collection of the *Falcon Flash* newspaper or *Media* magazine; no list of the faculty nor any record of traditions through the years; and, regardless of what many may assume, yearbooks are inconsistent—and often, incomplete—in their coverage of school life. Finally, as is appropriate, we had no access to private files or student records.

Primary sources were used in nearly all cases—copies of the *Falcon Flash, Falconaire, Know Your Schools, The Sun* and other area newspapers, programs from performances, letters, interviews, notes, photos, and personal collections, including those of David C. Smith and William Minsker, as well as the author's archival materials and those of the Lower Dauphin Alumni Association.

Because of all of these factors—and the length of time which can fade memories as well as photographs, it must be recognized that our sources may not be completely accurate. However, with the careful and serious research, we likely have **the most comprehensive record—in one book—that any high school has ever produced**.

Yesteryear Publishing
www.yesteryearpublishing.com

Table of Contents

Summit Achievers

Special sections throughout the book will honor twelve alumni exemplifying Summit Achievement. These accomplished professionals, six men and six women, reflect the many success stories of Lower Dauphin graduates in various fields. As might be expected, most of these high achievers were graduated in the first decade of Lower Dauphin; in addition, there is one example from the 1970s, three from the 1980s, and one from the 1990s.

We proudly salute these men and women —— Summit Achievers all!

Loyal Hearts Proclaim

Early History of Lower Dauphin School District

Overview and Highlights of the Decades

Academics

The Arts

Sports

Publications

School Governance and Policies

Traditions and Events

Pranks

Unofficial Student Organizations

Faculty, Administration, and Staff

Testimonials and Tributes

Lower Dauphin Alumni Association and the Golden Jubilee

Golden Jubilee

2009 Events

2010 Events

 # The Author

Dr. Judith Thompson (Ball) Witmer has been involved with Lower Dauphin High School and the District since the spring of 1960 when she came to Hummelstown at the invitation of Mr. David J. Emerich to interview for a teaching position in a junior-senior high school that was at that time under construction. Many new "jointures" were then forming and others in the state, including her own hometown of Curwensville, had recently established these new educational entities with their surrounding townships and/or nearby similar small towns. Although she had been offered a position in Mechanicsburg, the attraction to Lower Dauphin was the opportunity to have a role in building something new. The choice was one she never regretted.

While at Lower Dauphin Judith (then Ball) taught ninth grade English for the first three years at which time Mr. Emerich asked her to accept an assignment that would include British Literature and Public Speaking in the senior high. There she was able to initiate a number of innovative courses, most notably the award-winning English Enrichment, a team-taught, three-year course for self-selected students, and during the heyday of mini courses she taught "The Lesser Known Plays of Shakespeare." She was the director/producer of six musicals and served in other capacities in five others. She also directed a number of dramatic productions and served as advisor to seven yearbooks and assisted in several more.

She initiated student-centered Commencement and Baccalaureate programs which occurred from the early 1960s until the end of the 1980s. She also originated the inclusion of alumni in some graduation programs and as speakers for others, as well as the practice of Junior Class Marshals. She further introduced the reception event for graduating classes following Baccalaureate.

As an administrator Dr. Witmer was the Director of the Coalition of Essential Schools, a plan for a model school-within-a-school using an integrated curriculum designed by a faculty task force on school improvement. She initiated a Student Advisory Board; the Senior Awards Family Night; Elementary and Secondary Parent Advisory Boards; a revamped Superintendent's Forum for Students; Spirit Club; an alumni network to serve in resource and partnership capacities which became the Lower Dauphin Alumni Association; was editor of "Know Your Schools;" and established FIELDS, a community task force to plan a sports complex.

In recent years Dr. Witmer served as the co-chair for fund-raising for the new library in Hummelstown, chairman and commemorative book editor of the Publications Committee for Hummelstown's Bicenquinquagenary, and currently serves as committee co-chair to raise funds to build the new Field House for Lower Dauphin School District. She is active in the Lower Dauphin Falcon Foundation, and continues as an ex officio in the Lower Dauphin Alumni Association which she founded in 1989.

Dr. Witmer holds a Bachelor of Arts degree in British Literature from Penn State University, a Masters in Science and Humanities, and a Doctorate in Administration from Temple, in addition to post-doctoral credits from Harvard. Her dissertation was the first qualitative study to be honored by the Association for Moral Education at that institution and she was offered a faculty position at Temple. Not wanting to relocate to Philadelphia, she chose to return to Lower Dauphin, agreeing to accept a faculty adjunct position with Temple, and two years later was accepted at Widener School of Law. However, the sitting superintendent of the Lower Dauphin School District asked that she accept a position as assistant to the superintendent, in which she remained until leaving LDSD in 1992. She established her own consultancy with clients such as the Department of Education, Milton Hershey School, and Penn State Harrisburg. She currently serves as the Director of the Capital Area Institute for Mathematics and Science at Penn State.

Judith Witmer has authored many books, listed below, as well as more than fifty published articles, in addition to book chapters, monographs, programs, speeches for national clients, scripts, newsletters, book reviews, eulogies, and evaluations.

The Class: A Journey with the Boomers (in progress)

Growing Up Silent: Life in the 1950s; Not All Tailfins and Rock and Roll, 2012.

The Bicenquinquagenary of Hummelstown, 2012.

All the Gentlemen Callers: Letters from a 1920s Steamer Trunk, 2011.

Jebbie: Vamp to Victim; a Tale of Elder Abuse, 2010.

Team-Based Professional Development: A Process for School Reform, co-authored with Dr. Steven Melnick, 2007.

I Am From Haiti: The Story of Rodrigue Mortel, MD, 2000. (French edition, Je Suis D'Haiti, 2002.)

The Keystone Integrated Framework, a Case Study in Curriculum Integration, 1998.

The Keystone Integrated Framework: A Compendium, 1997.

Moving Up! A Guide for Women in Educational Administration, 1995. (second edition in 2006)

A Style Manual for Publications. Bureau of Special Education, PDE, 1994.

How to Establish a Service-Learning Program. co-authored with Dr. Carolyn S. Anderson '65, 1994.

Dedication

In loving memory of Harold Lee Snyder, Class of 1964

Members of the Class of 1964 were freshmen in the fall of 1960 when Lower Dauphin first opened its doors. Among that class of nearly 300 students was Harold Lee Snyder from Hummelstown. He was part of many coteries of friends who were separated into nine sections, many of which held more than 35 students. Harold and his best friends, Byron Wyld and John Burtner, along with Luke and Dale and George, were full of fun, mixed with trepidation and bravado, an interesting combination, but not unusual for fourteen-year-olds. Harold, by then accustomed to being the tallest boy in the class, was well-positioned to be a leader, but instead was a conciliator, popular with boys and girls alike. One could not help but notice his gentle demeanor, well-spoken, reserved, and unfailingly polite. He was, without realizing it, the kind of person who came to exemplify the evocative Lower Dauphin student.

That first day of school, as I was introducing course material and trying to put the students at ease, full of apprehension myself and only a handful of years older than those who sat facing me, I noticed the hint of a smile from the tall, lanky boy in the center of the room. I glanced at him and he made eye contact, the beginning of a friendship that was to be lasting.

Harold was cast in the first ninth grade play and continued on stage in the Lower Dauphin musicals, only a sophomore in his first featured role. However, it was to be in a more specialized role that he would make his mark in Lower Dauphin history. The November 1963 issue of the *Falcon Flash* made the following announcement:

> *The Lower Dauphin Falcon mascot was introduced at the pep rally. Harold Snyder, who takes the part of our mascot, appeared in the falcon costume made by Mr. Fickes and home economics students.*

The costume was constructed as a one-piece suit covered with fabric cut with pinking shears to look like feathers, layered alternately blue and white. Completing the costume was a large, heavy, airless papier-mâché headpiece in which the wearer almost smothered. It took a special person to carry off this role and Harold did so with elan.

He maintained this enthusiasm throughout his life, making lifelong friends from all walks of life. At ease in his own skin, he had a keen sense of humor and a perceptive mind.

While he didn't know he was to be honored in this book, Harold Snyder had been chosen from the book's inception as the person to whom it would be dedicated because he exemplified what Lower Dauphin has always produced: well-educated, productive citizens who remain loyal to family, friends, and their Alma Mater. Thus, *Loyal Hearts* proclaim that this book be dedicated to the memory of "Howie."

Acknowledgements

Wade and Jean Deimler Seibert '65, without whom this book likely would not have seen publication. Their love and support go far beyond a friendship of more than fifty years.

E. Nan Edmunds, designer extraordinaire, has seen this author through a half dozen books to date. Even to say this publication would not have been possible without her cannot fully honor the time and talent she has devoted to this publication.

Kathleen Imhof Weber '74 has been invaluable in locating information and her positive support throughout this project is incalculable.

Randy Umberger '65 is credited with garnering all of the sports records and reviewing the author's narratives on sports. His knowledge of LD is boundless and his patience with my many questions was limitless.

Elizabeth Musser Radle '62 and Susan I. Petrina '65 served as initial yearbook researchers and more recently as part of the marketing committee for the book, spending countless hours in planning strategies and pouring over hundreds of photos, most of which were less than perfect candid shots.

Marie Weber assisted with the preparation of the music department history, including the high school musicals, students' participation in MENC and PMEA festivals, her file of the high school orchestra and string orchestra concert programs and information on many of the musicians.

Bill Minsker provided his collection of the *Falcon Flash*, dating from the mid-1960s to 1992.

David C. Smith holds an enviable collection of memorabilia and stories which he willingly offered for our use.

Kathy Saltzer Peffer '73 has loaned material to this project, particularly a collection of various renderings of the Falcon mascot. She and Rick Smith '83 convinced us of the benefits of Facebook and a website, which Rick set up.

Wendell Poppy's meticulous work on the chart of LDSD administrators was a labor of devotion.

Ken Staver granted long interviews to both Bill Minsker and this author.

Kathleen Convery '64 prepared two stunning scrapbooks from the Golden Jubilee which were most helpful.

Joe Quigley was a master storyteller for Team 70 and escapades of the Class of 1970.

George Emerich '62 provided personal stories of the establishment of the new school since he had a front row seat in the household of the Supervising Principal.

The following donated programs and other material which was very useful: Ed and Faye Parmer '67, Jeannine Lehmer '69, Marilyn Menear '66, Jan Brightbill '72. Barry Richcreek provided photographs for Team 70.

Ann Landis Kopp '65 provided personal material, much of which is being designated for the next book, *The Class*.

Lena Russell and Karen Burk, LD faculty, were helpful in trying to find past issues of publications.

Tom Taylor's personal interest and skills at researching the sports records are very much appreciated.

The LD library staff donated PTA and LDHS scrapbooks to the Association who will preserve them.

All who wrote the Reflections for their own classes are noted with a byline.

Those many who responded to questions of identification and clarification.

The yet-to-be confirmed committee who will assist in the distribution of *Loyal Hearts Proclaim*.

 # Foreword

As I write this, the Lower Dauphin football team and field hockey team have just completed a very successful season, with field hockey earning its sixth state championship and the football team earning its way to a place in the state semi-finals.

Winning championships is not unusual for Lower Dauphin, and if you are wondering if this year is the most successful for these two teams, you would learn that accurate and official records have been maintained at the school for all sports, as well as for academics.

However, you will find no listings of the annual spring musicals, fall band competitions, longstanding or more recent clubs, or for many other school activities. Hence, there has been a need for a more complete historical account of Lower Dauphin High School in all areas.

In *Loyal Hearts Proclaim*, you will find these listings, along with commentary noting that the 1995 football team was the runner-up state champion and that the field hockey teams have won five prior championships, as well as who was prom queen in a particular year, what class "pulled off" the best prank, when and how Media magazine began, the names of every teacher over the first fifty years, Valedictorians and Salutatorians, Class Presidents, why "black olives" strikes terror in the heart of the Class of 1966, what is an "Un-hook Day," and thousands of other facts of all areas of Lower Dauphin High School history.

The author of the book, Judith (Ball) Witmer was one of the original teachers when the school opened in 1960, later becoming principal of academics. Her passionate interest in the students of the district has led her to devote countless hours amassing the information contained in this book, as it was a daunting task compiling memories from so many people, checking facts, recording the information, writing the text, and organizing it into a readily accessible form while relating it to what was happening in the world around us at the time.

Dr. Witmer's support for the school and its students extends much further than recording its history, however, in that she has generously donated the proceeds of this endeavor to the Lower Dauphin Alumni Association to help record LDHS history as it happens and to preserve its importance.

May each reader experience many fond memories of your years at Lower Dauphin as you read and reminisce about your past, perhaps writing about your own experiences for posterity.

Russel E. Cassel, President
Lower Dauphin Alumni Association

Loyal Hearts Proclaim:

Lower Dauphin High School: The First Fifty Years

"Time It Was and What a Time It Was"

Lower Dauphin High School has had a rich history and heritage, both from those who conceived the idea and created a new high school with such care and love and from those who had opportunities in creating a school that is often held as the exemplar of what high schools can be.

One can only imagine the formidable task facing the Joint Board in the 1950s as they set on a course that was new to the experience of all members. There was a strong foundation from Hummelstown High School, but that could have been an impediment had those who planned the school not been as wise as they must have been to not mold this new school in the shape of the one that was ending, regardless of its successful history and community support for its schools. One can only imagine being alumni of Hummelstown High School serving on a planning committee whose success would arise from the death knell for their alma mater.

However, rather than focus on Hummelstown, founders for the new high school viewed this as an opportunity to create something different with a staff comprised of (1) seasoned faculty, many of whom had spent their careers at Hummelstown High School, and (2) newly minted college graduates eager to begin their careers. We do not know if the seasoned faculty collectively decided to embrace the new staff or whether individually they had the wisdom to not try to direct the inexperienced newcomers, most of whom would not even have known one another until the first day of school.

Administrators—and board members who made the final decision on hiring—were faced with filling approximately three-fourths of the teaching positions, having to rely mainly on the recommendation from the supervising principal who had only an interview and a college transcript—and perhaps resumes from some applicants—by which to assess a candidate.

From the beginning there was camaraderie among the staff despite the fact that, unlike in most professions, faculty members are, for the most part, isolated in their classrooms. What was unusual, however, is that there was an uncommon energy in this new school not usually seen in educational institutions. Perhaps part of it was the youth of the staff or the fact that the school was arranged by sections of the building known as "wings," and that those areas became small work-related enclaves. This arrangement made it possible for a small group of teachers to become acquainted with one another in each wing.

As a result, a rapport developed through a common purpose, more sensed than named. The staff collaborated on ways to engage the students socially as well as educationally and soon a number of informal clubs and events began to appear, based on student interest or a teacher who had an interest or hobby s/he wanted to share. From the beginning students were encouraged to participate in after-school clubs and in 1967 an activity period was scheduled at the end of each day, allowing more to participate.

More important, teachers were supported in new endeavors. They were trusted in their judgment and encouraged to try new approaches to learning. With six classes a day, many with up to 37 students in a class, innovation was welcomed. The result was academic excellence. The pace was set and we never looked back.

Loyal Hearts Proclaim is the story of this process, its results, and as much general information as can be contained in a limited space, even at the monumental length this book is. This is a labor of dedication and a desire to collectively claim and preserve the elements of school life during the first fifty years of the high school—the factors that many believe have made the difference between other schools and Lower Dauphin High School.

Loyal Hearts Proclaim was written in the expectation that each of you will rediscover your classmates, relive an event that was memorable, recall an incident you may have forgotten, and revisit your own youth. This journey will be different for each of you and it was our intent to present the information in ways that will lead you to view the history through your own lens of memory and within your own timeframe. We further advise all of you reading this to remind both your families and future high school classes to keep good records of events so that they in turn can honor the well-documented memories of their own experiences.

Loyal Hearts Proclaim stands as a testament to the "singular sensation" that is Lower Dauphin High School where each graduate has been part of a glorious and distinctive history that has generated Falcon Pride in 12,440 alumni through 2010. We trust you will find pleasure as you read and reflect that, "in short, there's simply not a more congenial spot for happily-ever-aftering than here in (our own) Camelot."

JTH

Early History of
Lower Dauphin
School District

The Foundational History: An Overview

Background of the District

The location of what we know as Lower Dauphin School District is in Dauphin County in the southeastern portion of the Commonwealth of Pennsylvania. The overall area consists of five large sub-divisions which are bordered on the north by Blue Mountain, the east by Lebanon County, the west by West Hanover, Lower Paxton, and Swatara Townships, and the south by the Susquehanna River. The Swatara Creek flows through the center of the district, joins Beaver Creek, flows south to Middletown and empties into the Susquehanna River. The district covers an area of 90 square miles.

Background of the Area in Which Lower Dauphin High School is Situated

After the Civil War Hummelstown was incorporated as a borough on August 25, 1874. In 1887 water mains were installed, a water works was built, and the already established electric company was moved to its site to use water instead of steam and coal for power. In 1908 a filter plant and pumping station were built.

The first school building of record in Hummelstown was a log structure built circa 1764 on Hanover Street. In 1790 the school was moved to another log structure located just west of the Zion Lutheran Parish House, where classes were conducted until the building was destroyed by fire in 1817.

In 1845 the community was divided into three school districts, with a school building located in each district: (1) near the corner of Railroad Street and Walnut Alley; (2) near the corner of Hanover Street and Walnut Alley; and (3) in "Grovesville," near the intersection of East Main Street and Quarry Road.

The first high school is said to have been started in 1858. In 1920 *The Hummelstown Sun* is reported to have displayed a copy of the Second Annual Commencement program of the then Hummelstown Male and Female High School; 23 graduates were named. The next school was a consolidation of the others, a three-story building along East Main Street, which later formed part of the E.B. Smith Hardware. A complete high school course was introduced in the Hummelstown schools in 1875.

On March 3, 1892, with elaborate ceremonies, the first modern consolidated school building in rural Dauphin County was formally dedicated at the corner of High and Water Streets. This building in later years became known as the Price Building.

In 1926 the Junior-Senior High School moved into a new building at the corner of John and Short Streets. In 1930 a gymnasium-auditorium, a science laboratory, and another classroom were added. The gymnasium was equipped with a folding stage which could be removed for basketball games.

Creating Lower Dauphin Junior-Senior High School

Lower Dauphin, like hundreds of other jointures at the time, was created during an era in which our country became committed to education, to progress, and to improvement in the lives of Americans. The vision of the times was more than Sputnik and competing with the Russians; rather, it was the sense that America should prepare the next generations for the future. What was to become Lower Dauphin High School began as a dream, a desire by the citizens of three townships and a borough to provide for the young people of their communities, through a collaborative effort, that which they could not provide individually.

In 1952 the Hummelstown School Board invited the school boards of Conewago, Londonderry, and South Hanover Townships to discuss the possibility of a jointure. A Joint Board was formed and Articles of Agreement signed. Initially, plans called for an addition to Hummelstown High School that would be known as the Hummelstown Area Junior-Senior High School.[1] Had that occurred, students today would be wearing maroon and white, calling themselves "Bulldogs" and vying to uphold the proud traditions and legendary sports successes of Hummelstown High School.

There were many meetings, both jointly and separately, among the townships. There is also some evidence that both East Hanover and Conewago had wanted to be part of Derry Township schools— at least they were indecisive. The final decision was made by the state who ordered them to join Lower Dauphin. There were other set-backs with political and financial situations which were able to be resolved.

It was not until June 1955 that the Board decided to build a new high school with a new name that would be its own. Thus the plan for Lower Dauphin Junior-Senior High School was conceived, and the name of the Joint Board was changed to the Lower Dauphin Joint School Board, accepting the challenge to create a totally new school system with an identity for the residents of all representative constituencies. In October 1955 the site for the new school was approved by the Board. The land, then in Derry Township, would later be annexed to the Borough of Hummelstown.

In April 1956 East Hanover was accepted as the fifth member of Lower Dauphin. Rumor has it that there had been opposition from some residents of East Hanover because of the impact of Route 81. They had not wanted an exit there as it divided the township; however, they were persuaded of the need for an exit for emergency vehicles, even though some believe that there was also a reason to prepare an easy access for what would become Penn National Racetrack which opened in 1972. Regardless of the possible politics, there were many who just wanted the township to remain rural and saw no reason to cross Route 22 to become a part of the new school jointure. Roads were an issue on the other side of Hummelstown as well; in the early 1960s there was no overpass over Route 422, thus causing a traffic concern for the townships south of the high school.

In July 1956 the State first approved a two-story building for the classrooms, but the following April the Joint Board adopted the one-story Unit School Plan which would give more teaching space and would reduce the overall construction cost. Each of five separate "units" was to have nine classrooms surrounding a service core in the center to be used as small auditoriums and study and experimental rooms for advanced students. To the right of each activity room would be a reference room. In April 1958 the annexation of the building site to the borough was approved.

---

[1] A timeline of the formation of the jointure can be found in the *Lower Dauphin High School Dedication program, March 19, 1961.*

All of this came none too soon for the childhood population explosion (later known as the Baby Boom) was making the merging of various districts necessary. As Jean Deimler Seibert '65 recalls, "I well remember my seventh grade study hall which was one row of seventh graders situated in Mr. Hoover's Senior Math class; while he taught math, we were expected to study."

Interviews for the position of Supervising Principal of the new school were announced on March 6, 1959: "Applicants included Dr. John Springer, Middletown; Dr. B. F. Van Horn, New Enterprise; Dr. Paul L. Glazert, Harrisburg; Dr. Charles Clark, New Castle; Dr. George P. Bluhm, Mansfield; Dr. Charles M. Micken of Atlantic Highlands, NJ. Other applicants may be considered in the future, in addition to the present supervising principal, David J. Emerich." Interviews were held March 7 "in the Hershey Community Building in order that it not be situated in any of the member boards' territories. Candidates will be reimbursed for sixty percent of their travel expenses."

A month later (April 7, 1959) bids for construction were opened. The total projected cost of the structure, fees, site, furniture and equipment, and incidental expenses was $2,981,903.65. Three weeks later Mr. David J. Emerich was elected as Supervising Principal and on May 9, 1959 a groundbreaking ceremony took place on what had been known as the Book Farm, purchased for $30,000. Mr. Kenneth Staver remembers attending the groundbreaking: "I came up from Kutztown where I was teaching vocational agriculture because I wanted to get a sense of the area and the people. I was out there in the cornfield when they broke ground and I talked to Mr. Emerich. He said to me, 'If you want to work here, send in an application,' so I did, and they hired me." Mr. Staver adds, "People made fun of the school early on, such as asking me, 'Is the corn still growing in the halls down there?' and other schools calling Lower Dauphin students farmers."

According to Mr. Marshall B. Mountz, a member of the Joint Board, the original plans for a stadium, to be built on the school site at the cost of $105,000, were halted because the Board declared that a stadium would not be built until the library shelves were filled. Mr. Mountz also stated that the board chose auditorium seats made of wood because they would last longer than upholstered seats. In his remarks at the 1990 annual general meeting of the Lower Dauphin Alumni Association, Mr. Mountz commented that his proudest recollection about his participation in the creation of the Lower Dauphin School District was the building of a quality facility at a cost the rural townships could support.

Mr. Samuel C. Grubb, also a Joint Board member who addressed an annual meeting of the Lower Dauphin Alumni Association, stated that the vision the original Board had in the 1950s for the school district required a shift in the thinking of residents, parents, staff, and students alike, for the experience of most of those living in the area was a graduating class of approximately 50 students. For many students of Hummelstown High School, it was hard to say good-bye to the "Bulldogs" and to the proud traditions and legendary sports successes. However, the new school held many promises!

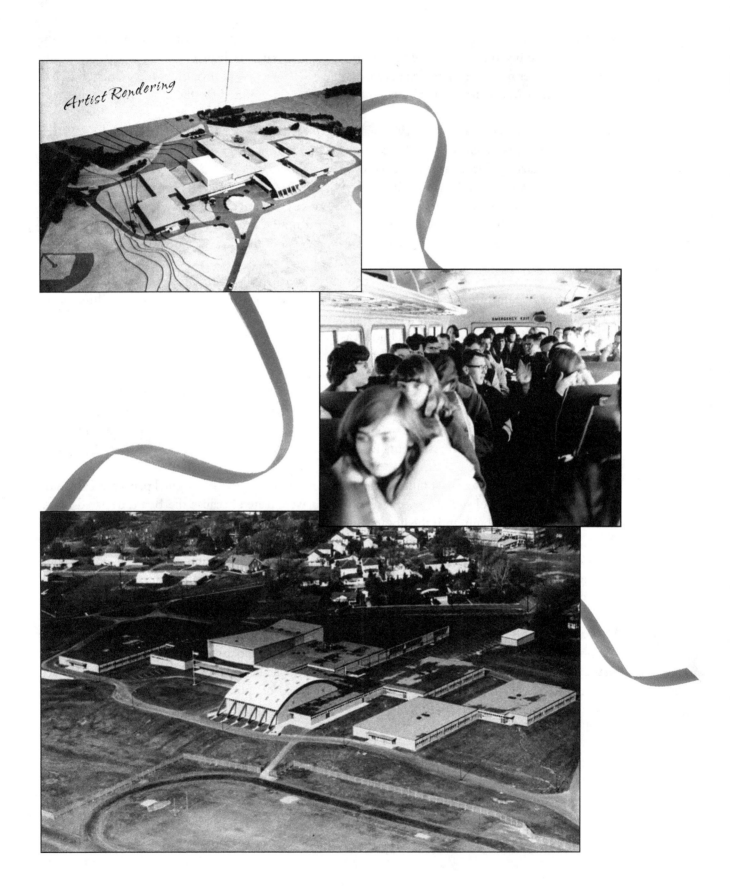

Artist Rendering

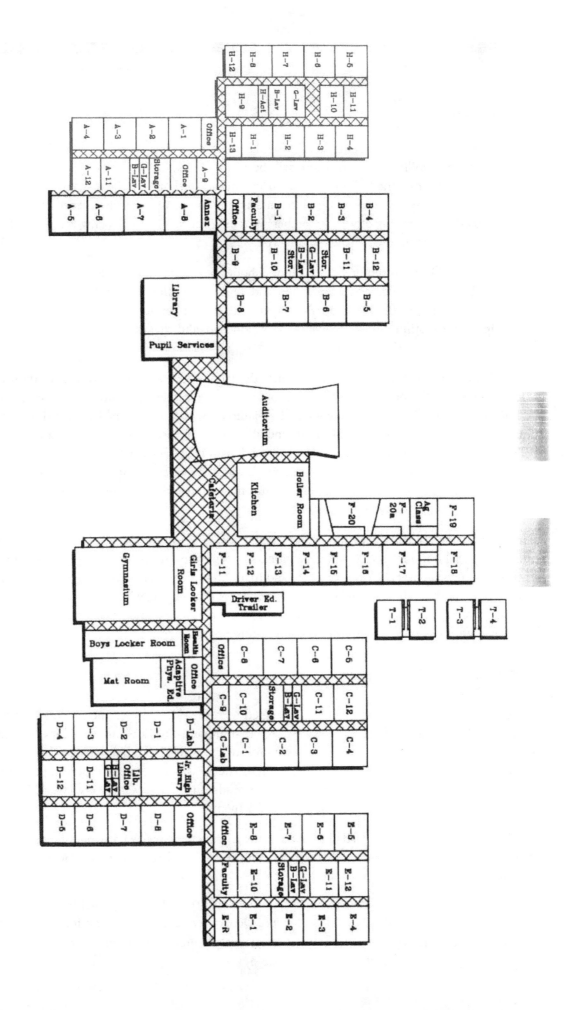

Opening Day

There were some anxious moments as opening day drew near. The May 13, 1960 *Hummelstown Sun* noted, "In all probability the gymnasium will be ready for use at the opening of school. For some time the completion of the building was held up by the steel strike which delayed the delivery of the skylights, but now that they are in place and the roofing completed the interior can be finished." George Emerich '62, among others, remembers watching the steel girders being transported from the railroad station through town to the building site.

The new Lower Dauphin Junior-Senior High School opened its doors on September 12, 1960, only a few days behind schedule. It was a rainy day and neither the cafeteria nor the gymnasium was quite complete. According to the Harrisburg newspaper of September 13, "The roof leaked and much of the equipment was still in railroad cars." "But, we opened, and that is the important thing," David J. Emerich, Supervising Principal, said.

Physical education met in the cafeteria because the gymnasium floor wasn't finished. Industrial arts teachers tossed well-worked lesson plans into drawers while they concentrated on teaching theory because their shops were either unequipped or jammed with contractors' supplies. The band could not start rehearsals because the bass drum and all percussion instruments had not arrived and were believed to be on freight cars. P. M. Seitzinger said even if he had percussion instruments the band "would not be able to march at any of this year's football games because the uniforms will not be completed in time." Mr. Emerich himself had not moved into his new office space, still occupying a basement office in the square in Hummelstown.

For many of the students who had begun their education in one-room schools, Lower Dauphin offered many educational, social, and recreational opportunities. In the fall of 1960, nearly two-thirds of the teaching staff were in their twenties and many were first-year teachers. Mr. Emerich had had to interview and hire 70 new teachers to fill needed positions. None will forget the gracious and very efficient Miss Frances Rathfon who was the first to greet nervous candidates in the below ground level, makeshift office in a building on the square of Hummelstown.

Building a New School Culture

The excitement and enthusiasm of youth combined with the skilled experience and dedication of the staff from Hummelstown High created a synergy that propelled the students to achieve scholastically and to succeed personally. The spirit of a joint endeavor was felt in all quarters as school colors were chosen, a mascot was decided upon, and an alma mater was composed. Mr. Staver, fifty years later, noted that Glenn Ebersole, president of the first graduating class, was a very strong influence on bringing the student body together, as was John Clements.

While a concerted effort was made by staff and many students, however, it would be naïve to believe that there were no incidents and that every student was thrilled to be part of a new school. As one student reflected,

> My only visits to Hummelstown prior to coming to Lower Dauphin Junior-Senior High School in the fall of 1960 were going to Hauer's Department Store once a year for school clothes. I remember riding the bus home from East Hanover Elementary School for the last time in May of

1960 and worrying about starting at "the new school" that coming fall and thinking about getting lost or not being able to do the schoolwork or never seeing my friends, or even possibly getting crushed to death in the hallways while changing classes.

No one talked about these fears, but they were real. And they happened. The worse was the bullying we as "outsiders" had to endure from the kids from Hummelstown who thought Lower Dauphin was just another building for Hummelstown High School, *and they were going to make sure it would remain theirs.*

At one of the first football games at the stadium that fall I was jumped by and had to fight two eighth graders from Hummelstown as they taunted me, calling me "farmer" and many other worse terms. This was a real physical confrontation, and it continued, even though I had defended myself during that first encounter. The one "bully" later became my best friend once we got to know each other, but the other boy continued the bullying for the remainder of junior high up until we became juniors in high school. One day when we were in Metal Club he called me out to the F-wing lavatory. I went out, and a pair of glasses, a broken nose, two black eyes, and a fractured jaw later, the bully stayed clear of me for the remainder of my high school days.

Mr. David Emerich led this new venture known as Lower Dauphin as the Supervising Principal, with Mr. Curtis Taylor as High School Principal; Mr. H. Victor Crespy was the twenty-eight-year-old Junior High Principal. Ken Staver remembers, "After three years Mr. Crespy left. He didn't like it all that well here even though he was top-notch. We could not have had a better principal, but he wanted to move on or perhaps return to New Jersey. He was highly respected and just a wonderful fellow." A surprise farewell party was held by the faculty at his leaving.[2]

Most of the faculty and students quickly became involved in school-sponsored clubs and/or extracurricular activities and specialty clubs to match every interest, such as is found described in a fall 1961 issue of the school newspaper: "The Modern Theatre Club is discussing the current musicals on Broadway, the most recent discussion being 'West Side Story.' ...the club has a special problem of an all-female membership and will have some difficulty in finding plays suited for them."

Also in the fall of 1961, Mr. Emerich reported that "...school spirit was a major concern during the first year of the school's operation because of melding students from two rival schools into one cohesive body. Last year's winning football team and an all-school operetta did a lot to make the students pull together and the guidance department did the rest." There was even a faculty basketball team (with its own faculty cheerleaders) that was good enough to win against visiting celebrity and college teams.

The first yearbook, the *1961 Falconaire,* noted, "After one year's flight the Lower Dauphin Falcons show promise of living up to their namesake in every way. By bringing home a championship trophy of their first flight, the Falcon football team was an important factor in binding the school together and establishing a school spirit—a Falcon spirit."

What was not widely known, however, is that initially many players on the team who would have been playing for Hershey High School their senior year were not all pleased to come to Hummelstown/Lower Dauphin. Glenn Ebersole said that had it not been for Mr. Cleon Cassel's encouragement and the welcome from the former Hummelstown team members, things might

[2] Mr. Crespy earned a doctorate and became Superintendent of Freehold Regional School District, 1975-1987, from which he retired.

have been different. As George Emerich remembers, "Before the Hershey game of that 1960 Championship season, Glenn addressed the team by tearing his Varsity Football Letter from Hershey H.S. to shreds, demonstrating his loyalty to his new school and team. In fact, at our 50th team reunion, in 2009, he stood to tell everyone, once again, that he had never had a more rewarding team experience than with that group of guys!"

The 1961 yearbook was dedicated "To a man who has worked untiringly for the successful start of our new high school… To one whose qualities of friendliness, sincerity, and sportsmanship have won a place of high respect, admiration, and affection among the student body: Mr. Curtis S. Taylor, the Principal of Lower Dauphin High School." There were 65 students on the first yearbook staff; on the 2010 *Falconaire* staff there were 12.

An inexperienced, but savvy, Parent-Teacher Association became very active generating news articles and starting a scrapbook. They provided a school banner for the marching band (with the rod purchased by "a civic organization"), created a special fund to pay for lunches for students who could not afford them, established a $100 scholarship for a student entering the teaching profession, and produced an Occupational Profile of parents of students in the high school:

Occupation	Fathers	Mothers (One-third unemployed)
Professions	3%	8%[3]
Managerial	5%	
Clerical	5%	22%
Sales	5%	10%
Mechanical and Trades	30%	
Labor (manual)	8%	4%
Agriculture	8%	
Manufacturing	20%	45%
Service	9%	11%
Armed Forces	2%	
Railroad	5%	

There were 606 fiction books and 446 non-fiction books on the library shelves when the school opened, with "limited" service offered by the library beginning in January 1961. The first "big" dance was the Christmas Ball on December 17, 1960 with music by the Fred Harry Orchestra for students in grades 10-12. The first graduating class had two National Merit Finalists: Carol Flocken and John Hall.

The first prom was called simply the Junior-Senior Dinner Dance and was held on May 5, 1961 at the Palmyra American Legion (a popular venue during the early years). The menu featured a fruit cup, chicken and ham, and cherry pie, with music by the Jerry Leffler Orchestra.

[3] The percentages for Mothers are based on the two-thirds who were employed

The first senior class officers included the following:

President:	Glenn Ebersole
Vice President:	Louis Cobaugh
Secretaries:	Helen Stephen and Gloria Shertzer
Treasurer:	Linda Verdelli
Faculty Advisors:	Miss Janet Ausmus and Mr. Conrad Stanitski
Class Motto:	Onward Ever, Backward Never
Class Colors:	Royal Blue and White (The class chose to adopt the school colors as their own.)

At the end of the second year of LDHS, the *Falcon Flash* ran an article by Mr. Emerich, summarizing the progress, "…Looking back in review a feeling of satisfaction and pride exists due to the many things we have accomplished in so short a time. Our school has become well known in Eastern Pennsylvania and has established a fine reputation scholastically. Attainment of this must be credited to the remarkable attitude and spirit of cooperation displayed by the school board, parents, teachers, students, and other members of the staff. A noticeable factor is the desire of so many to meet their responsibility, coupled with pride and satisfaction of doing a job well. I sincerely want to express my appreciation to everyone who is a part of the Lower Dauphin Joint School for their individual efforts in helping us develop to this point. I am sure we can continue to grow by putting forth renewed energy in the coming years."

The January 23, 1964 issue of *The Press and Journal* reported that Conewago was asked by Derry Township to merge with it; Conewago is said to have offered the rationale that their leaving the jointure would give Lower Dauphin the additional space it needed for expansion and also save transportation costs. A month later Derry admitted that it could not accept Conewago Township in a merger because of a contractual agreement with Lower Dauphin. Conewago was then faced with building a consolidated elementary school of its own. Conewago's indecision on these matters over the years delayed acceptance of the full jointure state mandate.

In 1964 an additional wing was added to the west side of the high school at a cost of $254,000. Known as H-wing, it was located next to A-wing and far removed from F and G wings.

September 4, 1964, *The Hummelstown Sun* wrote, "Lower Dauphin's Falcons remain birds without a nest as they again play their home games in the Hershey Stadium. We fans wait patiently for the day (or night) when we can see them on the home field. Some would settle for Saturday afternoon games in the daylight."

In 1965 a feasibility study was conducted as to playing football on our own field. Dr. Fitterer, a member of the School Board, was quoted in *The Sun* that this would positively affect school spirit. "Until the boys play a game on their own field there will be no unity of purpose," he maintained. Plans called for bleachers, ticket booths, a refreshment stand, and some arrangements for restroom facilities, all for under $20,000. The following year a citizen's advisory group recommended that the board purchase land for the construction of an elaborate athletic area, including facilities for night football.

In June 1966 a "Citizens Committee of Fifteen," with the support of 4,000 signatures representing the borough and four townships, formally protested a record $2.5 million budget, offering twenty specific points proposing a reduction of costs, one of which was the purchase of the former Stoner residence to be refurbished to serve as the district's center. The school district real estate tax was then reduced by three mills. Even so, angry residents climbed the stage to take the microphone to "blast the board." (*Patriot*, June 9, 1966). In September the Board petitioned Dauphin County Court for authorization to elect regional school directors rather than electing directors "at large."

The Hoerner Years

The need for a leader with experience in developing a consolidation plan as required by the state department of education led to the hiring of Dr. Henry R. Hoerner to do the study. His report was submitted to the Joint Board on May 15, 1966. The following year Conewago again made the news and created a problem for the School Board with its decision by the township supervisors to retain $4 of the $10 resident tax permitted by law.

Two weeks after the consolidation report was accepted, the School Board offered Dr. Hoerner the first superintendency of Lower Dauphin School District, a consolidation now of the high school and all levels of education in the district. Hoerner accepted and, at age 33, became the youngest superintendent in the state. While the Board may not initially have known his background, they soon learned that (1) Dr. Hoerner had been born in Hummelstown and had attended the Price Elementary School before his family moved to northern Dauphin County and (2) Hoerner had done his student teaching in the East Hanover Township Elementary School. Mr. Emerich was named Administrative Assistant for Business Affairs.

The consolidated district's administration office was located to 5 West Main Street but fast outgrew the space. A new office center was needed and the district had its eye on the Elsie Mumma Farm at the east end of town for its central office and also for a new high school and playing fields.

As Dr. Hoerner tells the story, "When I approached Miss Mumma I was told the farm was not for sale to the school district; however, a few days later I received a telephone call from her and she asked if Mr. Henry Hoerner, Sr., formerly of South Hanover Township, was any relation of mine. I told her he was my father, after which she invited me to come back to her house to discuss the sale of the property."

What had changed? "We must go back to 1936 and the terrible flood of that year," Dr. Hoerner continued. "Water had backed up into Hummelstown and Miss Mumma's cows were stranded on a patch of high ground near where the district administrative center is now. The animals refused to cross the flood waters and were in danger of starving. When my father saw the dilemma, he went home, got two mules and a lot of rope and returned. Swimming out to the stranded cows and using the rope and the mules, he pulled each cow to safety.

Miss Mumma had not forgotten my father's helping her and she offered to sell the land to me for the district. Thus, we acquired the major portion of the land that now holds the middle school, the administration center, and the turf playing fields. In addition, because initially the state aid ratio to Lower Dauphin had been so high and the board had almost immediately established a capital reserve fund, the district was able to pay cash for all improvements and never borrowed a dime for the next 19 years."

The July 22, 1969 *Evening News* announced that the Lower Dauphin School Board planned to build a $3.6 million senior high school to relieve overcrowded conditions with 80 acres—64.06 from the Mumma Farm, 15.66 from Milton Hershey School, and 1.6 from Weis Markets. This land would later house the middle school, administration offices, and playing fields.

Dr. Horner believed that with this kind of support and programs the staff would see no need to form a teachers' union. He was right. For many years Educators of Lower Dauphin (ELD) was an independent association, not affiliated with the Pennsylvania State Education Association. However, one of the several times ELD was upset was in May 1973 when an article on the teacher merit raise program and other aspects of teaching in the Lower Dauphin School System, written by Dr. Hoerner and appearing in the "Metro East" section of the *Harrisburg Evening News,* brought on an upheaval at the high school.

Dr. Hoerner, like others, however, continues to credit the early success of the Lower Dauphin School District to the first joint school board: Wilmer Brubaker, Paul Deimler, Mervin Etnoyer, Paul Felty, Paul Fitterer, William Gaudette, Sr., James Helsel, and Melvin Mateer, along with early board members Fred Bolton, Roy Brightbill, and Daniel Derr.

The Staver Years

Mr. Kenneth Staver, then a guidance counselor,[4] credits the success of Lower Dauphin High School to several factors, in addition to the student leadership mentioned above, "In the Class of 1963 were a good half dozen students who were 'out of this world.' These included Bobby Gibble, Joyce Keener, Fred Shope, Carol Flocken, and Vivian Lewin.[5] Mrs. Lewin was a driving force with this class and the high school in general in bringing things together." He then looked directly at this author and said, "The next class like that was your Class of 1965."[6]

He further noted, "The full support of Hummelstown (in all ways) was critical to the district's success." Additional factors were that the officers at Olmsted Air Force Base paid tuition to send their children to Lower Dauphin and this district began to be viewed as "the best school" to attend. He added, "Our vocational agriculture program was another factor, particularly the leadership training it provided to those like Russ Cassel, Jay Brandt, and countless others. It was a loss when we no longer could financially justify continuing the program."

Another factor was providing activity buses, transportation for those who lived in the townships; in fact, these buses were crucial to both the athletic and music programs. This also helped the supportive teachers who were willing to offer enriched, specialized programs both as part of their curriculum and in extra-curricular activities. Further positive factors were the formal study and travel experiences such

---

[4] In a series of interviews with Mr. William Minsker and separately with the author of this book.

[5] The Harrisburg Evening News did a feature article on Fred Shope who built and launched a rocket and another on Vivian Lewin and Robert Gibble as National Merit Scholars; Gibble advanced to winning a Merit Scholarship to Princeton and the Commencement address by Lewin, who matriculated at Oberlin, was published in the Harrisburg newspaper. Joyce Keener, who was graduated from Bennington, became an author, movie producer and artist.

[6] Many referred to the Class of 1965 as being the class of this author because I had been (1) the English teacher for many of them during their ninth, eleventh, and twelfth grades as well as (2) their class advisor.

as managed by David Smith and the AIFS program; field trips to see great art and architecture and performances; unusual offerings such as archeology, longitudinal studies, and the early years of English Enrichment; and the personal mentoring many teachers provided, such as an annual Christmas Open House the author hosted for alumni home from college as well as Mr. Staver's inviting these students to visit the school and talk to students about their various colleges they were attending.[7]

In a conversation initiated by Mr. Staver on September 15, 2009 after he had read the articles the Lower Dauphin Alumni Association had running in *The Sun* relative to the then upcoming Golden Jubilee in 2010, he asked the author of this book what the Association was doing in the Golden Jubilee celebration regarding the school musicals, because "it was the musicals that played a crucial role in setting the direction for the kind of high school Lower Dauphin would become."

He noted that Jane Mellin Smith, the vocal music teacher, was determined to do a musical comedy the first year with students who were just getting to know one another in a school community where musicals had never before been performed, even though doing so would be a risk. Many citizens from the town and the townships were quite skeptical of such an undertaking as a school musical and had no idea that they would enjoy such a stage production. However, both Mr. Emerich and Mr. Taylor saw the value of this endeavor and supported Mrs. Smith.

Mr. Staver continued with a smile, "Here she was, a 'fiery little thing' who just charged ahead. It was all her influence that made this happen. She never had the space needed for music classes or a chorus rehearsal. She taught from a cart and never had a classroom or any permanent space. She even held classes in the cafeteria—we were so crowded for space, even from the beginning.

"Doing a musical was the catalyst in elevating the culture of the school. It brought something to this area that hadn't been before. More importantly, what came out of all of this was the fact that it was the musical that first year that put music and art on the same table as English and Latin." Then, again addressing this author, he said, "What you did in your classroom and enrichment activities and what Jane did with the musicals gave us the foundation for the pursuit of a liberal arts education for the students. This is what led to scheduling chorus and band during the day as singletons, as areas as important as any other subject. Then when Marie Bergan Weber came in the 1970s and created an orchestra literally from scratch, she added to the importance of music and culture for the district."

And then, unexpectedly, came these words from this estimable member of the Greatest Generation who was directly addressing this author, a member of the Silent Generation, "High school students in the 1960s and 1970s had the most extraordinary female teachers, such as you—educated women who at any other time in history would have entered other professions. These students were very lucky."

In the mid-1970s Mr. Staver was appointed Dean of Students, not a job he had sought, but the result was that he made a major positive difference in the lives of many young people. He recalled, "The 1970s was really a tough time and we made mistakes. I had to register people for the draft and most of the kids didn't want to register … and the kids didn't want to have Army recruiters in to tell them what to do their senior year.

---

[7] This program was as critical as the numerous college visits the guidance counselors arranged for students, for at this time there were few methods by which to learn about what various colleges had to offer; further, many parents were not in a position—nor had the experience—to arrange individual college visitations, a practice then uncommon.

"One of the greatest things about LD was that if we made a mistake—and we made some—the parents for some reason would still be on our side. We began to send notices home in the middle of the nine-week period called Progress Reports. Parents would come in and say, 'Staver, I don't know what in the heck is wrong with you. Why do you give a poor kid eight report cards a year and the good kids four?' Then Bill Minsker started sending cards home when students were doing well: **Something good is happening at Lower Dauphin,** on which the teacher would write positive comments about the student. I don't know how many other teachers did this, but it sure helped.

"Next the School Board decided it wanted attendance to be 96% or above, and I asked for a Home and School Visitor. This was not approved initially. They then wanted me to take the kindergarten roster and show the rate of graduation from those who attended kindergarten and those who did not. (Before Dr. Hoerner's arrival only Hummelstown had kindergarten.) That was hard to do, because there is a difference between withdrawals and the drop-out rate.

"We then got a Home and School Visitor but after a short tenure in the position he said the job was all negatives, and that he preferred not to continue, so the Board said I should do it. I put together a plan by which all of the secretaries who did attendance at all of the buildings communicated with one another to try to identify if a particular student's poor attendance was a student or family problem. This communication helped us with the families. At that time we had our own buses and I also asked the bus drivers to start to notice situations when students got on the bus, such as a student's anger level. This was also helpful, although it didn't really solve the problem. We then hired a school psychologist and that was a positive move, along with the skills of the school nurse, Anna Barton. One of the best things we did with this situation was to create an in-school suspension room. Mark French made that work."

In 1985 Mr. Staver was also named Student Advocate who would represent students at expulsion hearings before the school board.

"Open lunch for the Senior High in the mid-70s is another example of a good idea that didn't work. There was no place in town to have lunch and be back within half an hour. Kids came straggling in, and we couldn't allow that. Most of these problems were resolved, but they were difficult to deal with at the time and we were learning as we went.

"The main problem, however, was that we were overcrowded. Sometimes in trying to solve that situation we came up with stop-gap measures that turned out to be beneficial, such as the years there were nine sections in seventh grade and teachers and rooms for only eight. I was told to solve the problem, so I created a section with students who tested with average intelligence but had low reading scores. We found the right teacher with Bud Heiss, who had support from Virginia Ax and Bill DeLiberty. We also had no special education program and no staff for special needs children. We were fortunate that we had people willing to help with this until we developed a formal program.

"Another factor we had to consider is that there were no additional higher education facilities in the county at that time. Hershey Junior College closed its doors in June 1965, disappointing many of our students, some of whom then turned to the new Harrisburg Area Community College. Then Penn State's taking over at Olmsted after it closed in the mid-1960s turned out to be a positive for us, but the Dauphin County Vo-Tech didn't open until 1970, so opportunities were limited until that time.

"The last 50 years have brought many changes that have affected the district with all the growth and development north, south, east and west, but none as great as the Milton S. Hershey Medical Center which changed demographics for Lower Dauphin. We were a very rural community, and it is still a very rural section down in the southern end," Mr. Staver concluded.

On to the Future

The issue of Lower Dauphin's building its own athletic fields continued when an organizational meeting of the Lower Dauphin Sports Complex Committee was held March 19, 1991 to discuss the need for playing fields in general and a stadium in particular. Chaired by Dr. Judith T. Witmer, then a district administrator, the committee agreed to prepare a proposal for the School Board.

The "audions" and "general labs" long ago were converted into small classrooms and in the late 1980s the junior high became a middle school. An additional increase in population in the later years of the 1980s and 1990s was the boom in housing developments, wiping out most of the corn fields of our district. And it was the large presence of the Milton S. Hershey Medical Center staff, many of whom resided in the Lower Dauphin School District, that then elevated the cultural and intellectual being of our district.

Talk of renovations began in 1990, resulting in a building project dispute in early February 1991, and in April the *Sun's* headline was "Lower Dauphin Axes High School Project." Cuts that spring also included the cancellation of field trips, attendance at conventions and workshops, and elimination of the Mentor Program. Even a proposal from an East Hanover resident with a request from a local committee to expand outdoor facilities was rejected.

By May the Board was faced with difficult decisions on the renovations at which "a distressed Board President, David Duncan" noted that the district "can't afford this project, but can't afford not to do it." Mr. Roy Brightbill added, "…the condition of the building is appalling." Shortly thereafter Dr. Sauers resigned. By fall building administrators were asking the Board for changes in the building plans as they had had no input to that date. On December 3, 1991, Dr. Jeffrey A. Miller became Superintendent.

By 1995, under the leadership of Dr. Miller, grades 6-8 moved into a newly built middle school. The original building then became strictly a high school. Renovations were completed wing by wing. Each wing was leveled down to gravel and steel I-beams and then reconstructed, according to Dr. Miller. "This new school has air conditioning, all heating and plumbing has been replaced, and the lockers—much smaller—have locks that are built in." With the redesign, the Lower Dauphin Alumni Association was granted permission to build an alumni showcase and to incorporate the mosaic donated by the Class of 1988, both of which are now designated as the Alumni Lobby.

In a technology update in December 1996, the following advances were addressed: "Fiber optic cable has been laid among the high school, middle school, and DAC to connect the three buildings to the same file servers. Coaxial cable is being installed to allow cable television access to every classroom. Telephone lines and phones are to be installed in every classroom. Internet access will be provided by the Intermediate Unit and telephone lines will be connected; email and video conferencing capabilities will be completed so that every employee in the district will have an email address and

Lotus installed as the networking software. Forty-eight laptops were distributed to staff. Also in November the Thespian Society was the first to perform in the high school's brand new auditorium."

As the school population continued to grow, so did building expansion. Guided by Dr. Sherri L. Smith, Superintendent since August 2003, the 1000-wing was opened in 2004 and is a two-story addition with classroom space, a weight-room and training space and is also home to the district's computer and network servers. The cafeteria also underwent a major addition in 2004, greatly expanding the seating. The glassed-in enclosure was finished in 2010 and converts the smaller cafeteria into a usable large-group instruction space.

The auditorium has remained at the same location and was renovated with upholstered seating and a new sound system. The central area of the building is now the high school office rather than Guidance Services which now is located in the space once housing the library. The library, completely new, is now located at the end of the 300-wing, formerly B-wing. In 2010 part of the library was converted to a computer lab. The gymnasium also was renovated; the folding doors, that had provided the ability to divide the space into three areas for classes, were removed and a new floor and bleachers were installed.

We have had our share of defining moments related to our national history as well. The Class of 1964 most remembers the death of JFK, the Class of 1979 remembers TMI, the Class of 1986 remembers the loss of the space shuttle Challenger, and the Class of 2002 marks 9/11 as its defining moment when the world changed. Classes who were here during those times have said the events they experienced made them realize they lived in an unpredictable world and, as a result, they learned the value of lasting friendships and shared experiences that bonded them to a time and place in history.

Lower Dauphin High School has earned an enviable reputation through its half century history. We have produced Olympians and screenwriters, collegiate national champions and Broadway producers, corporate executives and Merit Scholars, Emmy-winning authors and nationally recognized artists. We are lauded for our field hockey team and honored for many innovative academic programs. Our spring musicals have been outstanding, and we win Gold Keys in scholastic writing, art, and architecture. We excel in band competitions and are well-represented in Harrisburg area all-star teams. We serve in government and as volunteers to better humanity. We make our mark in the world, and we return for Homecoming.

Importantly, we have attained the goal of the school's early planners. We have grown under the nurture of the staff. Every graduate should agree with Sara Marian Seibert Lucking '02 who wrote, "For a brief time, we all share the experience of arriving, with our teachers and fellow students, at our destination, the culminating year of our high school experience. We will remember this time forever, no matter where our paths may take us in the future."

Regardless of that future, however, we all found a home in our Alma Mater and we proudly proclaim, "We are L.D.!"

Members of the Original Junior-Senior High School Faculty

Marian J. Achenbach

Janet M. Ausmus

Judith T. Ball (Witmer)

Virginia Ax

Anna Barton

Joan M. Beers

Henry G. Benner

Bernard J. Bernitsky

James H. Bishop

Isaiah Bomboy

Rosalie E. Bowers

Gerald W. Brittain

James Burchfield

Frank A. Capitani

Cleon S. Cassel

John Croll Jr.

William F. DeLiberty

Jane Durborow

A. Jean Eckman

Richard P. Falstick

Robert R. Fickes

Homer L. Gelbaugh, Jr.

John L. Geopfert

Beatrice E. Hallman

William C. Harrell

John (Jack) Harry

Donald F. Heistand

Carl E. Herr

Barbara Hess

Nancy L. Hicks

Warren E. Howard

William K. Kahler

Ruby G. Landis

Patricia M. Lanshe

Sandy K. LeGay

Mary Lewin

Cornelia M. Merwin

James M. Middlekauf

Dennis P. Musket

Barney J. Osevala

Kenneth H. Paden

G. William (Bill) Peck

Gordon E. Putt

M. Edward (Max) Richards

Max V. Ritter

Kathryn W. Sandel

Louise K. Schaffner

Joseph G. Schan

Prowell M. Seitzinger

Robert D. Shankweiler

Jane Mellin Smith

Arthur L. Sowers

Carl L. Stanitski

Conrad L. Stanitski

Douglas A. Stauffer

Kenneth W. Staver

Mary Jane Strite

Leslie Dean Taylor

Elizabeth B. Will (Richards)

Richard O. Wolfe

Katherine M. Young

Helen E. Yount

Kathryn K. Zeiters

Original Administration:

David J. Emerich, Supervising Principal
Curtis S. Taylor, High School Principal
H. Victor Crespy, Junior High School Principal

Italicized names indicate those of whom we are aware are deceased as of September 2013.

Lower Dauphin Junior-Senior High School PTA

To the current reader the most astonishing information about the first Parent-Teacher Association is its membership the year it was formed. Total parent membership was 662 (244 men and 418 women) and 41 teachers/administrators from a possible 65. This organization was very active in the formative years of Lower Dauphin Junior-Senior High School, including keeping scrapbooks. These scrapbooks came into the hands of the Lower Dauphin Alumni Association through the thoughtfulness of the LD library staff in 2010 when they culled their holdings. These books are currently housed in the Alumni Archival Room in the Hummelstown Area Historical Society Library.

The PTA formed in July 1960 when Mrs. Elmer Peters, President of Lower Dauphin Area Council of the Parent-Teacher Associations, invited the presidents of the five local units comprising the joint school to send a representative to an organizational meeting. The first elected president was Mr. William Gaudette who served in that office for three years.

Minutes of the initial meeting show that approximately 400 persons attended. The financial report for the first year of operation showed receipts of $600 in memberships ($1 per membership) and expenditures of $540. Among their first projects was the purchase of a banner for the band. By the 1963-64 school year membership had increased to 818, astonishing for a secondary school.

On September 1, 1961 the PTA sponsored a covered dish social for the faculty. They also began a Study Group program, the first of which was a panel discussion on "You—and the Teenage Driver." Following topics were "Understanding Your Teenager" and "Testing and Your Child" as well as a series of Challenges:

… in Extra Curricular Activities: "Let's Go Clubbing"

… in our Personal Budget: "Father's Wallet and the High School Student"

… in Americanism: "Are We Conscious of Communist Brainwashing Against Lax American Loyalty?"

… in Guiding Our Children's Leisure Time: "What TV Programs Would You Be Watching Tonight?"

They also sponsored dances in the junior and senior high school. Announcements included the information that devotions would be part of the program.

Notably this group of citizens was a positive force in developing a good relationship between school and community and garnered news media attention for the school. This organization continues its support in the Lower Dauphin Middle School.

The Alma Mater

The year was 1960; the July afternoon was hot and muggy in the city of York. Mr. Prowell M. Seitzinger was sitting on a hill outside of York Hospital overlooking the city. He was, in his own words, "simply passing time." No spark of musical inspiration had struck him, nor had he become a spontaneous compositional genius; yet it was then and there that Mr. Seitzinger composed Lower Dauphin's now historic and traditional "Alma Mater." Mr. Seitzinger had just accepted the position of Band Director of the then new high school. He knew that the fledgling school was just opening, so he made the correct assumption that they would need an alma mater. The only other thing he really knew about the school was its name, so he began with the words "Lower Dauphin," and composed from there. He credits Elaine Sulkey Harris, Class of 1963, with providing the very meaningful lyrics for his music.

A well-known musician and recognized as such by his peers, Seitzinger was not a newcomer to the art of composing. By the time he came to write the "Alma Mater" music, he had already worked with the famous Glenn Miller Orchestra, traveled the country playing in thirty-nine different states, and had ten copyrighted songs of his own.

A man who truly loved music, Prowell Seitzinger later remembered his days as the Lower Dauphin Band Director with fondness and nostalgia and never forgot any of the chords to the "Alma Mater." When asked in an interview in 1998 what his secret was for creative success, he responded, "Have tenacity, stick to it, and don't imitate. Do things your way and you will go far."[1]

Alma Mater

Lower Dauphin, Onward Falcons, Victory over all;
Praises to thee, Alma Mater,
Echo through the hall.

Ever striving toward our goals,
Eager, brave, and true;
Help us keep our standards high for the White and Blue.

Seeking friendships, gaining knowledge,
Honor is our aim;
We will proudly serve thee always, loyal hearts proclaim.

—Music by Prowell Seitzinger, Band Director
—Lyrics by Elaine Harris Sulkey '63

---

[1] 1990 *Falconaire*

The Shield and Class Rings

Lower Dauphin High School Shield

According to the *Hummelstown Sun* in June 1960, the Joint School Board Directors of the newly formed Lower Dauphin High School "adopted a school seal which is gold, in the shape of a shield, and contains five stars, an arrow, the book of knowledge, and tools." The December 1965 issue of the *Falcon Flash* provided details:

> The five stars represent the joining of the four townships (Conewago, East Hanover, Londonderry, and South Hanover) and the borough of Hummelstown; the keystone reflects the Pennsylvania relationship; the open book of knowledge/learning emphasizes the school's mission; the plow and pick reflect the agrarian and laboring aspects of the area; and the arrow pays tribute to the native American influence of the school district. The original seal was hand-drawn by Robert Fickes, the high school art teacher, with assistance from Virginia Stroman '61.[1] They also painted the cheerleader megaphones, with Ginny providing the lettering and Mr. Fickes the drawing of the falcon mascot.

Lower Dauphin Class Ring

Early rings included this shield. Elizabeth Musser Radle '62 recalls, "I can remember ordering my ring as a Junior and we had them before Christmas of the year 1960. I know there were three sizes of the top of the class rings themselves: large (for the boys), a medium size ring which is the one I purchased, and a petite size. There were four color stone choices—red, blue, white, and green. On one side of the band was the shield and the other side was the falcon with the year of graduation under it. Around the outer side of the stone was inscribed Lower Dauphin High School."

In some high schools, class rings can be ordered as soon as a student begins class as a freshman and in most other schools by the sophomore year. Since the purpose of a ring was to serve as an identifier, to tie classmates together through their four years in school, earlier was thought to be better for this purpose. While in some high schools ring ceremonies were part of the tradition, by mid-century the ring orders were simply delivered to the schools or mailed to the students.

Many high schools in the first two-thirds of the twentieth century either had a specific ring style that had been designed for that school or a class would vote for a particular style for all its members. Today, however, most schools do not have a specific ring which all students wear, and often no two students in the school will have identical rings. Typically modern day high school class rings feature the wearer's birthstone rather than the school color/stone.

Generally high school graduates wear their class rings for only a few years before and after graduation. At that time the high school ring is usually replaced with a college/university class ring or simply removed and placed in storage as a keepsake. Rings are often brought out of storage and worn for class reunions, that is, if it hasn't been lost to a "steady" girlfriend or boyfriend or sold for its gold.

[1] *Falcon Flash*, V. 6, no. 8, March 1967

The Falcon Mascot

The falcon bird has always been the mascot of Lower Dauphin High School (See related story on the Falcon Missile), although there was no actual replica of this mascot in the person of a student role-playing by wearing the costume of a falcon bird until the fall of 1963. According to the *Falcon Flash* in its November issue, "The Lower Dauphin Falcon Mascot was introduced to the students at the pep rally. Harold Snyder '64, who takes the part of our mascot, was dressed in a beautiful falcon costume made by Mr. Robert Fickes and the Home Ec. students." The bird's name was "Royal." Harold Snyder remembers the headpiece as being almost airless and that he had difficulty not passing out when cheering during those warm fall evenings at the football games. In the fall of 1964, Susan Petrina '65 served as the mascot, confirming that there were few breathing holes in the papier-mâché head.

A new Falcon Mascot with a new name ("Falcon Pride") debuted in the fall of 1972 and was portrayed by Sandy Zitsch and Patti Hall. Jim Neidinger, of the *Falcon Flash*, wrote the following account in the October 1972 issue of the transition of names and the farewell to Royal.

> Ever since this school has been in its infancy, there has been one loyal member who has come to every football game, pep rally, and major spirit event. His picture has appeared in the yearbook countless times and his name is used over and over again by the students and fans of all Lower Dauphin. For over a decade he has served us faithfully and has never received anything in return. He has now left us and stepped down for youth to take his place. This one great fan is our "old faithful" Lower Dauphin Falcon. During the Susquenita Pep Rally the old bird waved good-bye to his fans and the new bird spread his proud wings to make his first impression. His original name of Royal was changed to Falcon Pride, a more fitting name. What would be a just reward for the old Falcon? Could his royal head be placed in a trophy case? Surely there must be a proper end for such an old friend. Good-bye, old Falcon, Mr. Royal.

Craig College '74, also a writer for the *Falcon Flash*, critiqued this brand new Falcon costume which was described as being top-heavy, "with fur/feathers down to the trunk of the body, and 'regular people clothes' to cover the rest of the body." The review continued with a bit of exaggeration in the following suggestions, "...for the real connoisseur of flashy Falcon costume the complete garb is unavailable. Couldn't someone complete the costume? Maybe Falcon socks, or Falcon pants, or Falcon patches to decorate or Falcon scarves, or Falcon formals, Falcon bow ties, Falcon athletic shoes...."

In October 1976 the *Falcon Flash* ran an article with the title, "The Lost Falcon." The Falcon bird mascot had disappeared and a notice was placed in the daily bulletin. Later that day Mr. Royal Dimond (no relation to the original mascot Royal) received word that someone had found the Falcon in the girls' locker room with a major concussion (smashed head). The bird's head was rushed to emergency surgery in F-14 where Mr. Fickes "carefully mended the Falcon's bruises, and Terri Stare (one of the mascots) 'flew' the body to the cleaners." All was well.

Apparently there was a new mascot in the early 80s as well as a school newspaper article noting that a new mascot was purchased through the efforts of the Classes of 1981 and 1982, Student Council, and Booster Club. Recently a new costume has made an appearance, in colors close to the avian coloring of a falcon.

The Falcon Missile

The **Falcon Missile** was a gift to Lower Dauphin High School by the Olmsted Air Force Base as a tribute to the power of the **Falcon Bird, Lower Dauphin's mascot.** The Olmsted Air Force Base, now the Harrisburg International Airport at Middletown, saw its first military use by the United States Army Signal Corps in 1898. The first known use of the field by military aircraft is when Middletown Airfield opened in 1917 as a supply depot and maintenance center for the Signal Corps aircraft. The first airplanes landed at the Middletown Air Deport in 1918. The facility is named in honor of 1st Lieutenant Robert Stanford Olmsted, U. S. Army Air Service, and Olmsted Air Force Base held a huge presence in this area until its closure in 1969.

In the late 1950s when the founders of Lower Dauphin had been in search of a mascot, they selected the Falcon Bird because of its association with the Air Force and its Academy. However, some persons mistakenly thought that the Falcon Missile was the school's mascot. Even the Harrisburg *Evening News* of October 27, 1961, in a write-up of football, said, "Lower Dauphin's Falcons, named after a space-age missile, orbited to their first victory in the CAC with the decision."

It was about this time that an authentic Falcon Missile was gifted to the school by the Air Force at the Olmsted Base in nearby Middletown. It was accepted with ceremony and prominently displayed in the lobby outside the entrance to the auditorium, but it was never the mascot of the school. Possibly because some students also mistakenly thought the Falcon Missile was the school's mascot they would take the missile and hide it. It was always found—until it disappeared in 1984 and was never returned.

In 2005 the Lower Dauphin Alumni Association contacted the Lower Dauphin Rocket Club asking if the club members would build a replica with material paid for by the Association. The young men agreed to do this for their Alma Mater and the replica was presented to the school by the Alumni Association and rededicated at Homecoming 2006. Accepting were Randy Umberger, assistant principal, and Thomas Taylor, son of the late Curtis Taylor who was principal of Lower Dauphin High School when the original missile was presented to LDHS.

Members of the Lower Dauphin Missile Agency who participated in the construction of the Falcon Missile replica are Joe Skitka, Brian Yovoich, Keil Reese, Brian Pagano, Mike Hilbert, Jake Goerl, and Adam Wilson, all Class of 2006.

For 50 years at the time of this writing the Falcon Bird Mascot has served as a symbol of the excellence of Lower Dauphin in athletics, academics, arts, and activities. The Falcon Missile is a part of the tradition surrounding the Lower Dauphin Falcons. Long may they soar!

For more details on the mascot and the theft of the missile, see Section IX. Pranks and for the complete story of the search for the Falcon Missile, contact the author of *Loyal Hearts Proclaim.*

The saga of the missing Falcon Missile became the basis for a play that was performed at the 2012 Lower Dauphin Falcon Foundation Gala in January of 2012. See the introduction to this play in the Appendix on page 491. For a copy of the script for *The Disappearing Falcon*, contact the playwright. (Good entertainment for a class reunion.)

Summit Achiever Barry Stopfel '65

"Oh, the places we will be asked to go." (bls 10/10/95)

The Reverend Barry L. Stopfel '65 may be remembered by those who don't know him only as an Episcopal Priest who in 1991 was ordained as an "out" gay man by Bishop Walter C. Righter, a cleric later tried for heresy by an ecclesial court for performing this ordination.

However, Barry Stopfel is so much more.

As a child Barry was talented in a way that local people honored. When only 11, he already was a gifted preacher, a charismatic member of the fundamentalist Brethren Church. Then the 1960s happened and he drifted away from the church and didn't return for 20 years.

Barry did not set out to make any kind of history, but make history he did, although doing so is only a part of this brilliant, gentle man. In some ways, Barry Stopfel is representative of his time; in another he is atypical, a leader, but seen by some as a pariah (an exile and recluse, not, as is commonly misunderstood, an outcast).

Similar to Joyce Keener, Barry Stopfel spent his childhood in a conservative family and church. Similar to Don Frantz, Barry found his early calling in the theatre. Like both, he was creative, but in a less noticed way. He sometimes felt he stumbled into situations without realizing he was embroiled. Unfailingly well-mannered, soft-spoken, tender, and loyal, he probably didn't recognize that he was hearing a different drummer.

Like Keener, Stopfel is a published writer; like Frantz, he was enamored of "show business," even working a summer at the Mt. Gretna Playhouse; like Keener, he was in marketing (he at Hershey Resorts, American Express, and the Joffrey Ballet). Like both Keener and Frantz, Stopfel, too, worked in entertainment. Frantz at Hershey Park, Keener at public television in Hershey, Stopfel at Hershey Entertainment. Frantz was creative in bringing the first corn maze to the US, Keener with delivering the first movie premier to her Alma Mater, Frantz a Broadway producer, and Stopfel, marketing director for the Joffrey Ballet. All moved among luminaries, Barry even to the White House and dinner with the Reagans. Keener and Seinfeld, Nick Poppy and Comedy Central, Frantz and the Lion King, and Barry and the Joffrey: Success and the City.

Barry Stopfel followed undergraduate studies in broadcasting and film, planning to make socially relevant films to change the world. Then four students were killed at Kent State. He remembers hearing the news, sitting on the steps of the library at Columbia and "giving up." He came home and entered advertising with HERCO and remained six years. He then returned to NYC where he worked in financial services.

When the AIDS epidemic began to decimate NYC, he volunteered to try to persuade the media to cover "this strange new epidemic" while joining those who were caring for persons suffering from AIDS, "touching them with cool compresses and rubbing olive oil into kaposi sarcoma lesions because health care professionals were too afraid," he recalls. Inspired by Rev. Paul Moore, an Episcopal priest who was "mad as hell" that the city itself was ignoring the malady that was killing young gay men, Barry turned to the Episcopal Church, entering the ministry and earning an M.Div. from Union Theological Seminary. ———*And, of course, the rest is history.*

*Overview and
Highlights of the Decades*

Events Through the Decades: Nationally and at LDHS

The 1960s

November 10, 1960	First football championship
April 1961	Bay of Pigs Invasion
August 28 – September 2, 1962	Hummelstown Bicentennial
August 28, 1963	Martin Luther King's "I Have a Dream"
November 22, 1963	Assassination of President John F. Kennedy
1966	Penn State's College of Medicine Founding
August 16, 1967	Death of Elvis Presley
February 27, 1968	Carol Channing hoax
April 4, 1968	Assassination of Martin Luther King, Jr.
June 5, 1968	Assassination of Robert Kennedy
July 21, 1969	Neil Armstrong – first walk on the moon

The 1970s

June 20 – 23, 1972	Hurricane Agnes
1973-74; 1977	Energy Crises
August 9, 1974	Resignation of President Richard M. Nixon
September 26, 1975	Hurricane Eloise, schools closed
March 28, 1979	Three Mile Island Nuclear Incident

The 1980s

December 8, 1980	Assassination of John Lennon
March 30, 1981	Attempted Assassination of President Ronald Reagan
May 13, 1981	Attempted Assassination of Pope John Paul II
December 31, 1985	Death of Ricky Nelson in airplane crash
February 1986	Explosion and loss of the Challenger

The 1990s

1990s	Launching of the World Wide Web
1993	Lower Dauphin's first Field Hockey State Championship
December 1995	Lower Dauphin's runner-up as State Football Champs
August 31, 1997	Death of Princess Diana
October 12, 1997	Death of John Denver, piloting his own plane
December 19, 1998	Impeachment of President William Clinton by the House

The 2000s

September 11, 2001	Terrorist Attacks: NYC, Pentagon, and Flight 93
May 21, 2008	East End Restaurant explosion, Hummelstown

The Impact of Ten Defining Events

Assassination of President John F. Kennedy ♦ ♦ ♦ November 22, 1963

The assassination of President Kennedy is without parallel the event that had the most impact on high school teachers and students in the 1960s. The following is a personal account of that unforgettable day:

On Friday afternoon, November 22, 1963, I was overseeing a study hall in B-1 when near the end of the period there was a light tap at the door. I opened it to find Sally Walters, a senior. She motioned me to step outside the room as she proceeded to whisper the frightening information coming out of Dallas, Texas. "The President has been shot," she said solemnly, adding that she had been sent to notify all faculty in B-wing. It was understandable that such news be delivered personally and not announced over the PA system and I thought later of that wise choice made by Mr. Curtis Taylor, the high school principal. Sally appeared to be calm, entrusted with her heavy burden, but no doubt was in as much shock as those to whom she had been instructed to deliver her staggering news.

Shortly thereafter we were called to report to the auditorium. Word of the shooting had begun to spread, but not all students had yet heard the details. Teachers were exchanging glances of disbelief, sorrow, and fear, for none of us had ever faced a national event of such import. We were filled with our own thoughts as well as how we would handle the students. Of course, none of us had any more information than what Sally Walters had delivered, and we were hoping for more information at the assembly.

The principal didn't need to ask for silence. We already had been struck dumb by the gravity of the situation. Mr. Taylor, with overwhelming sadness evident in his face, announced that the president had been "mortally wounded." (Later many of the students said they had not known what "mortally wounded" meant and were left in even more perplexity. As Dr. Janet Calhoon '66 recalls, "There was a scheduled school assembly that day, but I don't recall the subject. Walking home that day were two girls walking in front of me asking what 'mortally wounded' meant; they truly did not know and did not grasp that the president was dead.") Mr. Taylor gave us the information that he had and asked us to pray for the country. As no other news was available and it was near the end of the day, the students were asked to go to their lockers and get what they needed to take home, as no one yet knew what the next steps would be. Grief-stricken, the faces of most of the adults were ashen. We just looked hopelessly at one another, or bowed our heads. The silence was deafening until Mr. Seitzinger raised his baton and, as the students stood to leave, we all were startled to hear the full force of a rousing John Philip Sousa march, as disquieting as the news of the death of our president.

The Berlin Crisis　　•　•　•　　June 4 – November 9, 1961

This was the last major politico-military European incident of the Cold War regarding the occupational status of Berlin and post-World War II Germany when the USSR issued an ultimatum demanding the withdrawal of Western armed forces from West Berlin, culminating with the city's de facto partition with the East German erection of the Berlin Wall. Mr. Roy Campbell, a faculty member, was called to service as a member of the Reserves. Also as a result of this crisis, an issue was raised at the school board meeting regarding fallout shelters and/or the evacuation of the school in case of aerial attacks. Supervising Principal David Emerich reported that the state was developing a plan but until that plan was put into effect, "the plan for the school will be to take shelter as effectively as possible in the building." (*The Sun*, October 6, 1961)

The Vietnam War Moratorium　•　•　•　　1969

Among the many events of the 1970s that had a major impact on youth, both in college and in high school, were massive demonstrations against the involvement of the United States in the Vietnam War. Taking the lead from a call by Jerome Grossman (April 20, 1969) for a general strike if the war was not concluded by October, David Hawk and Sam Brown took the idea and called for a less radical moratorium, naming it the Vietnam Moratorium Committee.

Held across the United States on October 15, 1969, the event was a success with the participation of millions worldwide. A month later the first nationwide Moratorium was held on November 15, 1969, through a second massive march on Washington, DC. This event attracted over 500,000 demonstrators and included many performers and activists on stage at a rally across from the White House. While most demonstrators were peaceful, late in the day conflict broke out at DuPont Circle, and the police sprayed the crowd with tear gas. More than 40,000 people gathered to parade silently down Pennsylvania Avenue to the White House, where protesters walked single file all evening, each calling out the name of a dead soldier as each protestor passed on the sidewalk directly in front of the White House. For some time to come, campus activists continued to hold monthly "Moratoria" on the 15th of each month.

The following account was written by Lower Dauphin student Joe Quigley '71 who, with two friends, decided to attend the Moratorium rally held in DC on April 24, 1971:

> We arrived sometime in the morning, parking near the Museum of Natural History. Everywhere we went there were hippies handing out socialist papers. We had never seen anything like it. The three of us were patriotic and although hardly anyone wanted the war we were not anti-American.

> We walked to the Washington Monument where what we saw made us realize there had been a major gathering the night before as there were huge piles of bottles, some 15 feet in diameter and four to five feet in height. The crowd itself was a mix of every sort of person with most of them the typical longhaired, bellbottomed-blue-jeaned-with tie-dyed tee shirt protester.

There were also entertainers such as Peter, Paul, and Mary who performed "Blowing in the Wind" and "Give Peace a Chance." One observer of the time described the voices of the protesters thus, "Their gentle, clear voices and consistent adherence to treating everyone with dignity and respect amplified their belief far beyond any shouting or violence. It was an American protest at its best."

From there we walked to the Lincoln Monument where the march formed with a huge stream of people who then marched to the front of the White House, then down Pennsylvania Avenue to the Capital. They were singing songs like "We Shall Overcome" and Arlo Guthery's "What are We Fighting For?" along with chants laced with profanity.

One of the most memorable scenes we witnessed was at one of the fountains into which someone had poured a box of Ivory Snow detergent; the suds were at least 10 feet high. The people were grabbing arms-full of the suds and throwing them around. There were soapsuds everywhere.

By the time we got to the Museum of Art we were exhausted and tired of all the people, so we headed back to the Mall and the car. On the way out we saw what looked like a homeless man passed out on the grass. He looked dead. I've always wondered if he was.

Hurricane Agnes ◆ ◆ ◆ June 20-23, 1972

Hurricane Agnes and its resulting flooding from June 20 through June 23, 1972 caused an estimated $2.1 billion damage to the eastern United States. Official flood stage at Harrisburg is 17 feet and Agnes reached between 32 and 35 feet. Many in Hummelstown were without water and electricity and either left town or moved in with others who lived on higher ground. With the destruction of 68,000 homes and 3,000 businesses, leaving 220,000 Pennsylvanians homeless, President Nixon declared Pennsylvania a disaster area. Hurricane Agnes was the nation's most costly natural disaster at the time. June 2012 marked the 40th year anniversary of the event.

(Editor's note: At first it seemed quite odd that there was nothing in the school scrapbooks about this major event, only a clipped article a month later of an article in the local paper (*The Sun*, July 19, 1972) on the school board meeting in which the board approved flood damage repairs as a result of the hurricane. It is likely that the board had not met in June—perhaps because of the hurricane—and also that there were no articles about the hurricane's effect on the school at the time because it was not in session.)

Energy Crisis of the 1970s

In the 1970s in response to the U.S. decision to re-supply the Israeli military during the Yom Kippur War, the Arab countries placed an embargo on oil to the United States. This Energy Crisis hit schools and other institutions hard; LD turned off the hall lights, leaving all in semi-darkness. Classroom and hallway temperatures were reduced to 68 degrees (the temperature fell much lower in some classrooms "at the end of the line") and to 60-62 degrees in the gymnasium. In classrooms only one or two rows of lights were allowed to be turned on, and on clear days, teachers were told to open the blinds and turn off the lights. Students were not permitted to exit the building to travel from one wing to another in order to not lose heat with the doors being opened. Field trips were drastically cut as were the number of activity buses. There was also a call for students to car pool or to take the school bus.

Falcon Flash Editor Ray Kennedy discussed the energy crisis in the November 21, 1973 issue, "One idea is to shorten the school day. This does not really seem practical. The amount of energy saved by a shorter day does not seem to warrant this change since the building would still have to be heated. Another alternative is to close the schools completely during the month of January. At first we might say 'great' or as one person said to me, it would be nice to have a month vacation in winter, one month in summer, and the third month spread throughout the year."

Milton Shapp closed all schools in Pennsylvania from January 26 to January 31, 1977 due to an energy crisis, mainly caused by a natural gas shortage caused by low pressure in pipelines due to unusually cold weather. This severe weather was noted as the worst in the country's history, allegedly caused by a mysterious Arctic wind covering half the United States.

Hurricane Eloise ◆ ◆ ◆ September 26, 1975

School closed because of flooding which occurred September 23-26 as a result of Hurricane Eloise. The high water mark for 1975 was 24 feet, seven feet above the designated flood stage of 17 feet on the Susquehanna River in Harrisburg. The Harvey Taylor Bridge and Market Street Bridge were closed. There was a lot of rain that fall with many events having to be postponed, including the band's sponsored competition, "Super Sounds." The Class of 1976 wrote this account in their yearbook, the style of which was a journal of their senior year:

- Sept. 22. I think the rain has affected everyone. No one remembered his play lines and blocking was utter chaos.

- Sept. 23. It's still raining. If it's not cold or roasting hot, then it's cold and raining. All cross country runners must learn to endure liquid sunshine.

- Sept. 24. Rained heavily today—hockey practice in the cafeteria.

- Sept 24. It is still raining. The auditorium roof leaked during "Story Theatre."

- Sept. 25. Super Sounds was washed out again; don't know if we'll even have it. Heard the (Hershey) stadium's a swamp.

- Sept. 26. School canceled. This is our second major flood in 3 years — short 100 years! Fun Night wiped out, too.

- Sept. 28. Went to town this morning by boat. Seriously. *La lluvia en Espana cae principalmente sobre las pampas.*

TMI ♦ ♦ ♦ March 1979

On Wednesday, March 28, 1979, the worst fears held by the critics of nuclear power were realized when at Three Mile Island, less than ten miles from Hummelstown, a series of events began by which the core of a nuclear reactor came very close to meltdown. Area residents were alerted that morning by an announcement that broke into the regular radio programming that there had been an "incident" at Three Mile Island. No details were available, but listeners were told there was no immediate danger. Residents were, however, advised, as a precaution, to "stand by, close the windows, and stay indoors."

Mid-morning at the high school a guidance counselor rapped on the door of each classroom, motioned the teacher to come to the door, and advised that all windows be closed because of a problem about which he was not at liberty to elaborate. While the teachers waited to know more information, they were again reminded just how isolated their classrooms were without radios, televisions, or telephones, and how they themselves were without recourse, not able to leave because of their responsibility for the students.

Later in the morning, it was announced by radio and television stations that while no schools were officially closing because of the incident at nearby Middletown, any parents who wanted to pick up their children at local schools could do so. At Lower Dauphin High School teachers were told to release any students whose names would be called over the public address system. At this point the faculty realized something serious was occurring and rumors began to float. School was not dismissed early nor was the school closed at that time, so faculty and students remained in their classes.

The next six days were anxiety-laden for everyone in the country, but especially so in the area around the nuclear power plant at Three Mile Island. Emergency evacuation centers were being identified at destinations fifty miles from the reactor and routes to these centers were hastily being planned, even as to which towns in this area should evacuate in what order. Most of the citizenry didn't know what to do and did not know whose advice to follow. Some were reluctant to leave their homes for fear of looting and some packed up their valuables and left town as soon as they could, hoping for the best. Others remained, believing the assurances of the media and government sources and dismissing the warnings from relatives outside the area who voiced far more dire concerns for what the local media insisted on calling an "incident."

Only later was it fully known that the rest of the country was getting news information far more frightening than what was being broadcast to central Pennsylvanians. The local tactic was to keep the population calm and, while no one would ever admit to withholding information, the residents were not being told how potentially dangerous the situation was. Official announcements from the government and, in particular, the Nuclear Regulatory Commission, were delivered with composure, providing assurances that everything was under control. In reality, Middletown, the town closest to TMI, was fast emptied of its citizenry as people fled in fear.

Later, the Class of 1982 recalled, "In 9th grade we had the eyes of the world watching our little community. To this day I tell people the truth that I was at track practice at the time TMI was releasing the radioactive gases just a few miles away." The Class of 1985 wrote, "The TMI accident was particularly close to home for me as my dad was known to be a radiation safety expert in the community. He often made presentations to classes on radiation. When on the day of the accident my mother showed up and removed me early from my class at Conewago Elementary School, it set off quite an increased level of panic at the school."

Space Shuttle Challenger • • • January 28, 1986

The tragedy of the 1980s that had the most impact on students and teachers was the loss of the Space Shuttle Challenger. Wade Alexander, a senior in 1986, describes this event, "As we returned from the holiday season into 1986, the reality of winter weather, the seemingly long stretch of the third marking period, and the routine of school activities took precedence. Then, on January 28, 1986, when the Space Shuttle Challenger exploded 73 seconds into flight killing all seven crew members, part of our innocence also slipped away. Indeed, 'the whole world cried' and mourned the loss of the Challenger's astronauts. This event taught us or reminded us that outcomes in life are not always fair, easy, or easily explainable."

World Wide Web, 1990s

The 1990s brought LD its first state championship in field hockey and a second place in the state football championship. On the national scene and international scene, however, the most important event to impact the lives of students was the launching of the World Wide Web, a collection of interconnected documents and other resources, linked by hyperlinks and URLs; not to be confused *with* the Internet, it is an application that runs *on* the Internet. The WWW was incremental and most who freely use it don't think in terms of a date when they began using it. For most, it was just "there" and they use it much as earlier generations used typewriters and encyclopedias. Not one of the Class Reflections addresses the miracle of the Internet and the World Wide Web, as it simply has become part of life.

September 11, 2001

The defining event of this decade was September 11, 2001, forever after identified by the term 9/11, the day of a series of four coordinated terrorist suicide attacks by al-Qaeda upon the United States, specifically on the Twin Towers in New York City, the Pentagon, and the interrupted attack, intended for either the Capitol Building or the White House, that ended in a crash in Shanksville, Pennsylvania. The members of the Class of 2002 (in their Reflections) have said it made them realize they live in an unpredictable world and, as a result, they realize the value of lasting friendships and shared experiences that have bonded them.

The horribleness of this event is still almost too overwhelming to talk about. The last vestige of any innocence or sense of security was shattered for anyone who was old enough to realize what was meant by this previously unthinkable attack.

Pennsylvania Governors during the first 50 years of LDHS

David Lawrence	1959 – 1963
William Scranton	1963 – 1967
Raymond Shafer	1967 – 1971
Milton Shapp	1971 – 1979
Richard Thornburgh	1979 – 1987
Robert Casey	1987 – 1995
Tom Ridge	1995 – 2001
Mark Schweiker	2001 – 2003
Edward Rendell	2003 – 2011

United States Presidents during the first 50 years of LDHS

Dwight D. Eisenhower	1953 – 1961
John F. Kennedy	1961 – 1963
Lyndon B. Johnson	1963 – 1969
Richard M. Nixon	1969 – 1974
Gerald Ford	1974 – 1977
Jimmy Carter	1977 – 1981
Ronald Reagan	1981 – 1989
George H. W. Bush	1989 – 1993
William Clinton	1993 – 2001
George W. Bush	2001 – 2009
Barack Obama	2009 –

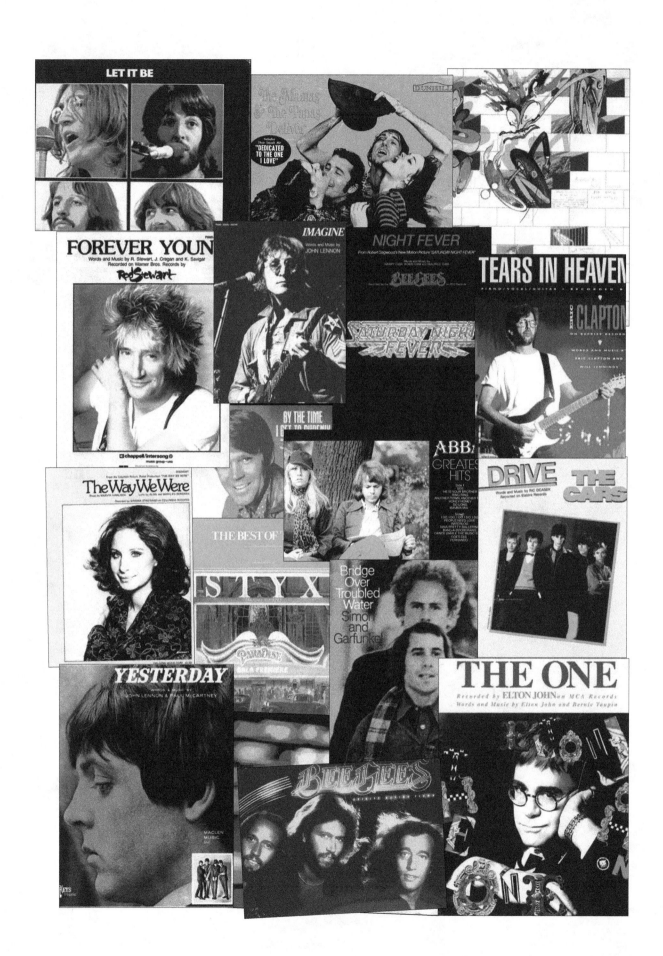

Billboard's Top Three Songs: 1960–2010

Theme from A Summer Place – Percy Faith

He'll Have to Go – Jim Reeves

Cathy's Clown – Everly Brothers

Tossin' and Turnin' – Bobby Lewis

I Fall to Pieces – Patsy Cline

Michael – Highwaymen

Stranger On the Shore – Acker Bilk

I Can't Stop Loving You – Ray Charles

Mashed Potato Time – Dee Dee Sharp

Sugar Shack – Jimmy Gilmer and the Fireballs

Surfin' USA – Beach Boys

The End of the World – Skeeter Davis

I Want to Hold Your Hand – Beatles

She Loves You – Beatles

Hello, Dolly – Louis Armstrong

Wooly Bully – Sam the Sham and the Pharaohs

I Can't Help Myself – Four Tops

(I Can't Get No) Satisfaction – Rolling Stones

The Ballad of the Green Berets – Sgt. Barry Sadler

Cherish – Association

(You're My) Soul and Inspiration
Righteous Brothers

To Sir With Love – Lulu

The Letter – Boxtops

Ode to Billie Joe – Bobby Gentry

Hey Jude – Beatles

Love is Blue – Paul Mauriat

Honey – Bobby Goldsboro

Sugar, Sugar – Archies

Aquarius/Let the Sunshine In
Fifth Dimension

I Can't Get Next to You – Temptations

Bridge Over Troubled Waters
Simon & Garfunkel

(They Long to Be) Close to You – Carpenters

American Woman/No Sugar Tonight
Guess Who

Joy to the World – Three Dog Night

Maggie May/(Find a) Reason to Believe
Rod Stewart

It's Too Late / Feel the Earth Move
Carole King

The First Time Ever I Saw Your Face
Roberta Flack

Alone Again (Naturally) – Gilbert O'Sullivan

American Pie – Don McLean

Tie a Yellow Ribbon – Tony Orlando and Dawn

Bad, Bad Leroy Brown – Jim Croce

Killing Me Softly with His Song – Roberta Flack

The Way We Were – Barbra Streisand

Seasons in the Sun – Terry Jacks

Love's Theme – Love Unlimited Orchestra

Love Will Keep Us Together – Captain & Tennille

Rhinestone Cowboy – Glen Campbell

Philadelphia Freedom – Elton John

Silly Love Songs – Wings

Don't Go Breaking My Heart – Elton John
and Kiki Dee

Disco Lady – Johnnie Taylor

Tonight's the Night (Gonna Be All Right)
Rod Stewart

I Just Want to Be Your Everything – Andy Gibb

Best of My Love – Emotions

Shadow Dancing – Andy Gibb

Night Fever – Bee Gees

You Light Up My Life – Debby Boone

My Sharona – Knack

Bad Girls – Donna Summer

Le Freak – Chic

1980

Call Me – Blondie
Another Brick in the Wall – Pink Floyd
Magic – Olivia Newton-John

1981

Bette Davis Eyes – Kim Carnes
Endless Love – Diana Ross and Lionel Richie
Lady – Kenny Rogers

1982

Physical – Olivia Newton-John
Eye of the Tiger – Survivor
I Love Rock 'n' Roll
Joan Jett and the Blackhearts

1983

Every Breath You Take – Police
Billie Jean – Michael Jackson
Flash Dance (What a Feeling) – Irene Cara

When Doves Cry – Prince
What's Love Got to Do With It – Tina Turner
Say, Say, Say – Paul McCartney
and Michael Jackson

Careless Whisper – Wham!
Like a Virgin – Madonna
Wake Me Up Before You Go-Go – Wham!

1986

That's What Friends Are For – Dionne and Friends
Say You, Say Me – Lionel Richie
I Miss You – Klymaxx

1987

Walk Like an Egyptian – Bangles
Alone – Hart
Shakes You Down – Gregory Abbott

1989

Look Away – Chicago
My Prerogative – Bobby Brown
Every Rose Has Its Thorn – Poison

Faith – George Michael
Need You Tonight – INXS
Got My Mind Set on You – George Harrison

1990

Hold On – Wilson Phillips
It Must Have Been Love – Roxette
Nothing Compares 2 U – Sinead O'Connor

1991

I Do It for You – Bryan Adams
I Wanna Sex You Up – Color Me Badd
Gonna Make you Sweat – C + C Music Factory

1992

End of the Road – Boyz II Men
Baby Got Back – Sir Mix-a-lot
Jump – Kris Kross

1993

I Will Always Love You – Whitney Houston
Whoomp! (There It Is) – Tag Team
Can't Help Falling in Love – UB40

1994

The Sign – Ace of Base
I Swear – All-4-One
I'll Make Love to You – Boyz II Men

1995

Gangsta's Paradise – Coolio
Waterfalls – TLC
Creep – TLC

1996

Macarena – Los Del Rio
One Sweet Day – Mariah Carey and Boyz II Men
Because You Loved Me – Celine Dion

1997

Candle in the Wind 1997 – Elton John
Foolish Games/You Were Meant for Me – Jewel
I'll Be Missing You – Puff Daddy and Faith Evans

1998

Too Close – Next
The Boy is Mine – Brandy and Monica
You're Still the One – Shania Twain

1999

Believe – Cher
No Scrubs – TLC
Angel of Mine – Monica

2000

Breathe – Faith Hill
Smooth – Santana, featuring Rob Thomas
Maria, Maria – Santana,
featuring The Product G&B

Hanging By a Moment – Lifehouse
Fallin' – Alicia Keys
All for You – Janet Jackson

2002

How You Remind Me – Nickleback
Foolish – Ashanti
Hot in Herre – Nelly

2003

In Da Club – 50 Cent
Ignition – R. Kelly
Get Busy – Sean Paul

Yeah! – Usher, featuring Lil Jon and
Ludacris
Burn – Usher
If I Ain't Got You – Alicia Keys

We Belong Together – Mariah Carey
Hollaback Girl – Gwen Stefani
Let Me Love You – Mario

2006

Bad Day – Daniel Powter
Temperature – Sean Paul
Promiscuous – Nelly Furtado, featuring
Timbaland

2007

Irreplaceable – Beyonce
Umbrella – Rihanna, featuring Jay-Z
The Sweet Escape – Gwen Stefani,
featuring Akon

Low — Flo Rida, featuring T=Pain
Bleeding Love – Leona Lewis
No One – Alicia Keys

2009

Boom Boom Pow – The Black Eyed Peas
Poker Face – Lady Gaga
Just Dance – Lady Gaga

2010

Tik Tok – Kesha
Need You Now – Lady Antebellum
Hey, Soul Sister – Train

Highlights from the Early Years

Early Academic Highlights

The expectations for Lower Dauphin Junior-Senior High School were set high and students rose to these expectations. The 1960s and 1970s were a time for experimentation in new courses, new teaching methods, and a great deal of support for teachers to provide enrichment activities. These initial successes provided the basis for the strong academic reputation that has been a hallmark of the school, as well as attracting faculty who wanted to be a part of the success and be supported in their willingness to provide many electives and courses not typically offered in high schools. (See Overview of Special Academic Programs in Section III.) The following notations are not comprehensive, but are given as an example of our beginnings.

1960s

- 1961-62 enrollment of grades 7–12 was 1,350
    - 12th – 136 students
    - 9th – 316
    - 11th – 145
    - 8th – 287
    - 10th – 210
    - 7th – 256

- "A Secret Highly Guarded by the Faculty" about student grouping in classes revealed that the high school's most carefully guarded secret is kept under lock and key and if the jointure were a military institution instead of a school, the secret probably would be stamped "Confidential" and placed in a safe instead of a desk drawer:

    "…The 10 sections in the ninth grade were numbered 9-1, 9-2, 9-3 to 9-10. The 30 best pupils were placed in 9-1 and the slowest pupils were placed in 9-10 while the others were placed according to their ability in the group between. The advantage of the grouping system was that each pupil competed with pupils of like ability. …but the system had its drawbacks," Mr. Bomboy, a guidance counselor, said. "Many of those in the advanced class considered themselves the cream of the scholastic crop while those in the lower classes often avoided mentioning which class they were in because they felt it branded them as slow students."

    As a result the following year the students were still placed in homogeneous groups but with no numbers assigned to each group. The students still had a vague idea of which group they are in but they don't know which group was above them or below them so there was not as much quibbling about being moved to another section. Ironically, it was kept from the faculty in which township or borough each studdent lived.

- The Public Speaking class taught by Mr. Douglas Stauffer had an opportunity to speak through a microphone and record their voices at Olmsted Air Force Base in December 1960.

- A progress report by Mrs. Sandel, the librarian, in December 1960 noted that "books on the shelves, most from Hummelstown High School, include 606 fiction books and 446 non-fiction. Individual units (known as 'wings') libraries have encyclopedias." Limited service would be available in the library beginning in January 1961.

- The following is the First Honor Roll for First Marking Period of the First Year of Lower Dauphin Junior-Senior High School:

    - Distinguished Honors:
        - 12th – John Hall
        - 11th – Sandra Longreen
        - 10th – Robert Gibble, Carol Kasbee, Vivian Lewin, Marilyn Shertzer
        - 9th – none
        - 8th – Karl Bell, Bethanne Bojanic, Jean Deimler, John Enders, Carol Kauffman, Sandra Kreiser, William Stump, Stephanie Zeiters, Carol Zerfoss
        - 7th – Linda Lash, Lester Ratcliff

    - In the 1st year of the Grand Champion Science Fair there were 135 exhibits. Fred Shope earned top honors; the reserve grand champion was Mary Ann Umberger. Other winners included Judith Sharp, Ann Seaman, and Karl Bell.

- The first Commencement featured an invited speaker, Dr. Michael Duda, President of California State College.

- The fall of 1961 saw the first student handbook.

- In October 1961 LD had 23 tuition students, four of whom were from military personnel at Olmsted Air Force Base. During school year 1965-1966 the school board ruled that pupils of parents who are being transferred to other AF bases may have their children continue to attend LD if an affidavit is submitted that an adult will be responsible for the student.

- The "First Annual" Physical Education Demonstration was held April 28, 1962.

- Robert Gibble '63 became a National Merit Winner.

- Vivian Lewin's Commencement Address was quoted in Paul Beers' column in *The Patriot*, June 12, 1963.

- The October 3, 1963 issue of *The Falcon Flash* reported the results of a questionnaire sent to the faculty asking for recommended reading: *Silent Spring, The Story of Philosophy, The Elements of Style, The Art of Thinking, How to Win Friends…, The Bible, The Meaning of Communism, Soldier of Peace, Carol Heiss: Olympic Quest, Lord of the Flies, Black Like Me, Death Be Not Proud, The Old Man and the Sea, To Kill a Mockingbird, The Good Years, A Child is Waiting, Hawaii, Fires of Spring, Travels with Charlie, The Agony and the Ecstasy, The Family of Man, The Power Elite, Makers of the Modern World,* and *Successful Wrestling.*

- Betty Wert, Harold Snyder, and Karl Bell represented LD at the Youth Forum in Harrisburg.

- The British Literature classes attended *Hamlet* with Richard Burton shown in Electrovision in the State Theatre in Harrisburg on September 23, 1964. On November 10, this class also attended *Macbeth* with Maurice Evans and Dame Judith Anderson at the ticket price of ninety cents.

- In early 1964 the Keystone Farmer Degrees were conferred on three LD Future Farmers of America members: Russel Cassel, Kenneth Zell, and Doug Hancock. A later news article noted that Keystone (Pennsylvania) Farmers Degrees were earned by 20% of the Lower Dauphin FFA students while the national average was 2%.

- Both regional ACES (Americans for the Competitive Enterprise System) winners were from LD, Bethanne Bojanic and Russel Cassel.

- Two members of the Class of 1965 received letters of commendation from the National Merit Scholarship Corporation: Jean Deimler and Lynn Sandel.

- In the fall of 1965 the student population in the district was 3,905, just a few short of the magic number of 4,000 set by the state for the ideal size of new districts.

- Linda Lash '66 was the first LD student to skip her senior year to enroll in college, after spending part of her junior year in England.

- In the winter of 1969 the developer of the ITA (Initial Teaching Alphabet) system of reading, Sir James Pittman, presented two programs at LD. While studies showed that students had no difficulty switching from this system to "regular" reading, some of the Lower Dauphin teachers noted that the emphasis on phonetics led some children to never learn to spell conventionally.

- In January 1967 an announcement was made that the district would be using teacher aides the following school year.

- In the summer of 1967 LD began a federally sponsored science program (Title I, ESEA) for the purpose of improving science education programs in school districts. Ground-breaking at the time, the program offered a platform for inquiry-based, hands-on science education at all levels. It engaged teachers as well, both in learning new techniques and having time to create science units K-12. The Senior High developed curriculum for atomic and nuclear physics, optics, electricity and electronics; ecology, advanced biology, and units for the non-academic students; and chemistry units in atomic structure and change. The program director was Mr. David C. Smith.

- *The Patriot* published a double page spread on area exchange students, including LD's first, Kate Prodromidou, from the Greek Island of Crete.

- Letters of Commendation (National Merit Scholarship) went to 1968 seniors Yolande McCurdy, James Messinger, and Ann Rhoads. The following year Anne-Marie McCurdy was awarded a Merit Scholarship.

- The first Outstanding Business Student Award was initiated in the fall of 1968; the first winner was Denise Luttrell.

- On November 11, 1969 the *Evening News* included an article on Ken Leskawa, a junior who was doing original research at Hershey Medical Center under Dr. E. A. Davidson. The following year Ken scheduled all his required courses in the morning, freeing him at noon to work on his research at the medical center.

1970s

- On April 10, 1970, Ken Leskawa won first place in the chemistry division of the 13th annual Capital Area Science Fair. The following year he took first place again. (He matriculated at Upsala breezing through his studies and, as a freshman, tutoring other students in calculus and working on an independent scientific research project usually reserved for juniors and seniors.)

- In the summer of 1970 Karen Shertzer '70 won the first prize in *Seventeen* magazine short story contest, selected from 3,000 manuscripts.

- In the fall of 1970 the school offered new courses in English: "The totally elective program offers 27 different quarterly and semester courses in all areas of literature, public speaking, journalism, grammar and composition. ... an innovative new English program that is the most extensive of its type in the state."

- On October 1970 the National Shakespeare Company performed "Hamlet" and "Much Ado About Nothing" on the LD stage. A near capacity crowd filled the auditorium.

- An article on the Elective Program in the spring of 1971 stated that there were more than 40 courses available to students in English with plans for nine more.

- On April 13, 1971 *The Evening News* announced that Mr. William Minsker had gained permission to seek to buy a used voting machine; to his surprise, the company donated two used ones in good condition. "It's tremendous, just tremendous," Minsker exclaimed. "These machines are to be used for the course on politics and will be used also for the mock elections. The machines add to the interest of the course, and this in turn stimulates the kids' desire to learn," he added. "That's what I am after—kids enjoying learning."

- The fall of '71 brought National Merit Commendations to Toni Bibb, Joan Hassel, and Carol Larsen.

- In January 1972 the LD English Department was chosen by the Pennsylvania Department of Education (PDE) to participate in a pilot project of poets in a residency in the school.

- In the summer of 1972 LD was selected by PDE to pilot a program, "Environmental Impact of Electrical Generation: Nuclear vs. Conventional." A newspaper article reported that if the program was successful it may be included as a regular course selection. The purpose of the course was awareness of nuclear reactors and their effects.

- Sometime during the 1972-73 school year the (now) renowned poet Daniel Hoffman gave a presentation in the classroom of Margaret DeAngelis (then Yakimoff). The room in A-wing provided a connecting door to the principal's office and a view of a newly-planted tree. Its installation had consumed two class periods of observation, with the teacher making the best of the situation in suggesting ways to "write about trees." The arrangement for this guest poet was likely made under the Poets-in-the-Schools program. According to Miss Yakimoff, "Daniel Hoffman talked about Edgar Allen Poe as his critical study, *Poe Poe Poe Poe Poe Poe Poe*, had been published not long before. He read a poem he'd written about the poet. Its last line was the repetition of Poe's name seven times, as in the book's title. Each uttering of the name was louder, and by the sixth or seventh one, Hoffman was on his feet, nearly shouting. Looking back, I can say that this was probably my first exposure to poetry as performance art."

- Mary Zeager wrote the following in the *Falcon Flash*, February 1973: "The lights went out in H-5 in December on the day the class planned to videotape its production of the Christmas program that had been long in the making. The producer (Chuck Leh), the director (Greg Fogleman), and our filmmaking teacher accepted the invitation of the graciously cooperative British Literature teacher to move the program into the brighter world of B-1."

- In spring 1973 several students went to Kennedy Space Center for the historic launching of SKYLAB, the largest aircraft ever put into space. These included Ed Neiswender, Cindy Seesholtz, Cathy Druffner, Martin Ferris, Carole Crist, and Karl Appleyard.

1980s

- In the fall of 1980 a headline in *The Patriot* (Oct. 28) was "Pupils Go to the Woods," but not for a course on survival. Rather it was English Enrichment, "one of the most innovative and productive programs at Lower Dauphin," initiated by Judith Witmer and Ron Zeigler in 1971. The students were divided into groups of three and had to plan their day, establishing a campsite, building fires and shelters, preparing their own meal, and writing a reflective journal piece in the style of Thoreau's "Why I Went to the Woods."

- In 1985 Venus Klinger was named a National Merit Scholarship winner and Junior Ann Schwentker was selected to attend the prestigious Governor's School for the Sciences.

- In 1986 Junior Matthew Williams won a Scholastic Gold Key for his short story. Jen Szymborski garnered a Blue Ribbon and Gold Key while Matt Royer's pencil work earned him a Gold Key. Peter Ward and Matthew Williams were selected to attend the Governor's School for the Arts. Ann Schwentker was named a Presidential Scholar, one of only 141 students in the nation so named.

Early Extra-Curricular Highlights

♦ The **first** class play was *Publicity Mad*.

♦ The **first** Spring Concert program, listing all music numbers, was the subject of a column in *The Sun*.

♦ The **first** musical admission price was $1 to help defray costs.

♦ June 2, 1961 saw the formation of the **first** National Honor Society.

♦ Linda Verdelli and Carol Flocken were announced in the Harrisburg paper as the top honor students.

♦ In the fall of 1964 LD students appeared on WGAL's Dance Party.

♦ In January 1966 the Service Club, under the guidance of Mrs. Venus M. Connelly, presented a talent assembly: Participants included Karen Neagle doing a Russian ballet, Dodie Crousore singing "Moon River" and "Goldfinger," and Wanda Gingrich presenting a free exercise routine. Vocal acts featured show tunes including Marilyn Hallman singing "Hello, Dolly," Sharon Patrick, "The Sound of Music," and Stephen Ginder, "Maria." Barbara Grubb did an interpretive dance to *West Side Story*, Jack Brandt a piano solo, "Deep Purple," and the Crousore sisters, Nancy and Sandy, a comedy act featuring the song "Let the Sun Shine In." Two folk song duets highlighted the program: Connie Campbell and Rogie Carroll singing "Cruel War" and Linda Kassman and Ruth Comitz accompanying themselves on guitars and singing "The First Time Ever." The master of ceremonies was John Williams.

♦ May 9, 1966 *The Patriot*: Linda Kassman and Ruth Comitz met backstage with Peter, Paul, and Mary when they performed recently at the Hershey Arena.

♦ *The Sun*, May 10, 1968: The featured speaker at the Second Annual All Sports Banquet on May 28, 1968 will be the popular young head coach of the Penn State Nittany Lions, Joe Paterno.

♦ The *Press and Journal*, February 9, 1972: A new system of activity bus passes has gone into effect at LDHS. Anyone in an activity has a special pass containing his picture and activity destination. Students who stay after school for remedial work are given special bus passes by their teachers. These are collected by the drivers and returned to the teacher the next day. This is intended to discourage loitering in the building after school. It will also give the school a better idea of how many buses are needed on a given day.

Early Facility Highlights

♦ *The Patriot*, December 22, 1960: The LD building was cited for outstanding design of a school within a school by AIA. In each corridor are sub-wings called units which contain 8 classrooms, office, library and conference room, an audion classroom, a general education laboratory where gifted students can do advanced work, and a service core.

♦ *The Sun*, September 1, 1961: The high school will be taxed to capacity when it opens for school September 5.

♦ The School Board voted that the building will not be used on Sundays except for Baccalaureate.

♦ In the spring of 1962 the board approved an addition to the school.

♦ *Falcon Flash*, Vol. III, No. 1, October 3, 1963: Work on a new school addition is being started this September. It will adjoin the high school and will be parallel to B wing.

♦ "The School of Today," an editorial by Mr. Emerich, Supervising Principal, was featured in the same issue of the *Falcon Flash*.

♦ September 8, 1964, *The Evening News:* New Addition (H-wing) opens for a capacity of 1800 with 1600 students entering.

♦ October 1, 1964, *Press and Journal:* Regarding complaints from some parents about the food served in the cafeteria, Mr. Emerich says getting the youngsters to eat what they don't like is better than having them eat nothing at all.

♦ *The Patriot*, November 2, 1964: After solving its overcrowded classroom problem, the LD Joint School Board now faces the task of finding room for its athletic program and may be forced to build a new gymnasium.

♦ In the fall of 1964, new equipment was purchased for the gymnasium, including the uneven parallel bars and "the health ball."

♦ LD's first new tree was planted on Arbor Day, 1965 with Bill Pinkerton, Student Council President, presenting the tree to Mr. Emerich.

♦ The outdoor athletic area was enlarged using funds left from the addition built during the summer of 1965. This included two basketball courts, two tennis courts, and a parking area.

♦ *The Patriot*, June 7, 1965: The issue of a football stadium is being revived. Dr. Fitterer is a strong proponent and stated the school badly needs a stadium to promote unity, cohesiveness, and school spirit. While no one disagrees with him, it is still considered too expensive for a five-year-old school. The joint committee will investigate a new approach to financing a stadium.

♦ *The Sun*, October 4, 1965: A feasibility study was voted on for playing football on our own field, Dr. Fitterer believing this will positively affect school spirit, more than any other effort.

- The *Press and Journal*, October 20, 1966: A citizen's advisory group recommended that the board purchase land for construction of an elaborate athletic area, including facilities for night football. The board asked Mr. Bowser to resubmit the proposal with cost estimates.

- *The Evening News*, July 22, 1969: The Lower Dauphin School Board plans to build a $3.6 million senior high school to relieve overcrowded school conditions.

- In Spring 1971 the School Board purchased 15¾ acres around Conewago Elementary School for $16,000.

- The school requested annexation of the Mumma farm since it is in Derry Township.

Early Governance and Operations Highlights

Like many new institutions Lower Dauphin High School went through growing pains, but in retrospect the early years were marked by finding our way and learning about who we were, perhaps not even realizing just how amazing we were.

- On August 30, 1963, *The Sun* reported, "Lower Dauphin High School will abide by the ruling of the United States Supreme Court that the reading of ten verses of the Bible and the repeating of the Lord's Prayer is unconstitutional." After lengthy discussion they agreed that a reading, followed by silent meditation, would replace the Bible reading. Faculty member Mrs. Judith T. Ball was assigned the readings."

- In the fall of 1964 a column in the *Falcon Flash* written by Patty Pheasant noted that something new had been added to the lunch hour: "Music will be played on a trial basis. Susan Petrina and Karen Kalbach are in charge of selecting the music."

- Teachers were to leave their keys in their mailbox at the end of each school day.

- In the spring of 1967 the School Board heard an evaluation and recommendations report of the cafeteria operations. One recommendation was that workshops be conducted for the managers.

- In 1968 a videotape recorder began to be used to record wrestling matches and basketball games: "The small TV camera picks up the scene and the signal is fed through the machines on the table. The playback is via the small TV set on the table."

- In May of 1968 LD's projected budget topped $3 million.

- The July 22, 1969 *Evening News* announced that "the Lower Dauphin School Board planned to build a $3.6 million senior high school to relieve overcrowded school conditions. $275,000 will be designated for purchase of a site in the coming school year."

- In 1969 Mr. William DeLiberty, Asst. Principal of the Junior High, designed a Substitute Teacher Handbook and Mr. Barney Osevala, Assistant at the High School, prepared a Student Teacher Handbook. Mr. Curtis Taylor, Principal, worked with a Student Council Committee to design a new Student Handbook. Mr. Ike Bomboy, Junior High Principal, worked on a new Teacher Appraisal Plan: "One goal is for the principal to become a coach and counselor rather than a judge."

- The Guidance Department was very active in building cohesiveness with their newsletters and their work with the students.

  - During school year 1962-1963 they published a "book of facts," which included a variety of information about school activities; the following is a sample:

    - 96 clubs were in place, 31 of them in senior high

    - 13% of students were on the honor roll

    - 157 Junior High girls tried out for cheerleading

- A complete cheerleading uniform costs $45
- There were eight varsity cheerleaders.

▶ Average cost of lunch was 45 cents.

▶ Average cost of books per pupil was $16.50.

▶ Visual aid equipment included seven 16 mm sound projectors, six filmstrip projectors, two opaque projectors, one micro-projector, twelve record players, and ten tape recorders.

▶ The Guidance Department had catalogues from about 150 colleges.

▶ All 7th graders would have dental exams.

▶ All 11th graders would have physical exams.

▶ All students would have eyesight, height, weight checked every year.

▶ In fewer than 2 months of school there had been 17 pencil accidents.

▶ 77 manual typewriters and 16 electric were available for student use. There were also six adding machines, three calculators, two duplicating machines, and three transcribing and recording machines, and five different makes of typewriters.

▶ Band uniforms costs $60 each. (Ten years earlier in another Pennsylvania town, the cost of new uniforms was $70 each.)

▶ The main band is known as the "A" band.

▶ The library contained approximately 6,000 volumes (recommendation size for a school this size three years after opening was 10,000 volumes).

▶ The major library problem was lost and stolen books.

▶ Big Band Sound, Bob Aulenbach's Band, performed at a benefit concert in March 1963.

▶ A multi-page guidance newsletter provided much information for students.

◆ *The Sun*, August 26, 1970: The School Board adopted a student dress code, saying, "The Board considers student dress and grooming to be the primary responsibility of students and their parents." They further noted that "Students should be encouraged to form and participate in a variety of extra-curricular organizations as a means of broadening their educational experiences; however, the Board considers that only those organizations that conduct their activities on school premises, with authorization by the building principal and under faculty supervision, are the responsibility of the School District. Non-school organizations may not conduct their activities on school premises without expressed authority of the building principal...."

◆ The first mention of drugs was early in 1970: "On March 17, 1970, *The Evening News* reported that Dr. Hoerner told the Crestview Manor Civic Association parents that there is 'no evidence of drug abuse.' He said that media attention tends to give rise to many rumors on the local scene."

- In October 1970 the School Board signed a landmark agreement with the teachers' bargaining agency under Act 195 which gives public employees the right to organize and bargain collectively. By December a collective bargaining agreement was signed.

- New regional educational services named Intermediate Units came into existence July 1971; these are to replace the former County Units.

- *The Sun*, March 29, 1972: A Fashion Bridal Show was sponsored by the Class of 1972, with prom and bridal gowns provided by the Irene Shop of Hershey. Models included Vicki Peters, Karen Fenner, Carol Bubb, and Sue Howard.

- *The Sun*, July 26, 1972: The Lower Dauphin High School majorettes will sponsor a bikini car wash on Saturday, July 29, from 9 to 5. Proceeds would be used for a novelty presentation during the football season. The following week there was a photo to prove this car wash was a success.

- And who will ever forget locker inspections?

- 1987 saw the first strike in LD history when the bus drivers did not drive on Monday, September 14. As of September 22, there was still no bus service.

The following fund-raising activities are representative of clubs and classes:

- The Band sold metal racks (for four quarts of milk) to be placed inside the milk boxes into which milk was delivered.

- Senior Class sold Stanley Bubble Bath; they also sold Christmas candles and Prom peanuts.

- Future Nurses sold all-occasion napkins.

- Cheerleaders sold subs.

- FHA sold cookbooks.

- GAC sold shakers.

- Band sold candy.

- Junior Industrial Development Club sold donuts.

- Junior Class in the spring of 1965 sold Easter candy to raise funds for their prom.

- The National Honor Society in 1965 sold booklets for 25 cents titled "Off to College."

- Car washes abounded.

- FBLA sold candy, peanuts, and candles to support a trip to the World's Fair.

- Class of '66 sold fruit cakes.

- Concert Choir held a pancake breakfast and sponsored a "Miss Pancake Day" with Rhonda Schell serving as hostess for the day. (*The Sun*, November 18, 1966)

- The American Technology Club sold shirts.

- Class of '69 sold Bachman pretzels.

- The 1966 Student Council sold "friendship bonds" priced at 25 cents and $1.00 to fund a foreign exchange student to come to LD.

- Circa 1966 the Booster Club sold small brown plastic coin purses in the shape of a football with the game schedule printed on them.

- International Club would be sponsoring a Slave Day on November 23. (*The Sun*, November 18, 1966)

- The Class of 1973 sponsored donkey basketball.

- Class of 1972 held a fashion show of prom and bridal gowns.

- In 1972 Spanish Club sold stationery and candy apples.

- The Class of 1977 spent much of their time fund-raising with cushions, candles, magazines, Donkey basketball, M & Ms, Christmas wrapping paper, and calendars.

- FFA sold citrus fruit and mums annually for years.

- In 1980-81 the band boosters held a pizza sale and sub sale.

- Booster Club sold carnations for Valentine's Day in 1981.

Early Social Highlights

1960s

- The first big dance, The Christmas Ball, was held December 17, 1960 with music by the Fred Harry Orchestra and was open to grades 10-12.

- The first after-prom party, sponsored by the Junior Chamber of Commerce, was announced in the Harrisburg paper in spring 1961: "After lengthy discussion and altercation, the Lower Dauphin Joint School Board approved."

- A Homecoming Dance in honor of the Youth Festival Queen was held in the cafeteria October 28, 1961. This is an indication that the first Homecoming Queen likely was selected as a result of the need for a representative to the regional Youth Festival. Prices for the semi-formal dance were "35 cents Stag, 65 cents Drag."

- The "Annual" School Board and Faculty Dinner was held December 14, 1961. [LD was always initiating the "first annual" something or another.]

- The Mardi Gras Ball on March 3, 1962 was a costume dance held by the L.D. Choir.

- By 1964 the admission price for the Homecoming Dance had increased to $1.

- The front page article in the March 1966 issue (Vol. V, no. 5) of the *Falcon Flash* was the Junior Prom. Page two featured an article by Kitch Lee on "Apathy." Page three's column "The Falcon's Tracks" chastised the boys for not inviting girls to the Junior Prom with this header, "…Event of all Events"—the social occasion of a lifetime—The Junior Prom!" The article continued, "Please note that we use the past tense…for sadly enough, the Juniors of 1966 have their enthusiasm dampened by some extremely apprehensive prospects. You see, the Junior Class has a problem—perhaps the most grave and serious ever to befall the young damsels of any school…namely, this difficulty is the Junior boys! Now, you may ask, 'What's so new about that?' Well, granted, more often than not they are confusing our lives, but this time they have apparently out-done themselves. In short, these fine examples of chivalry and gallantry have taken it upon themselves not to invite the girls to the Prom!"

- On April 4, 1966 the Joint Board of the Lower Dauphin School District rejected a proposal from the PTA to hold a post-prom party, saying students should not be encouraged to stay out until 5 a.m. and that midnight was late enough for high school juniors.

- The regional Youth Festival, November 27, 1964 featured "The Lettermen" and Vonda Kay Van Dyke, Miss America 1965. The 1965 Festival offered "The Four Seasons" along with LD's own "Young Troubadors" and the 1966 Festival featured the "Highwaymen."

1970s

- Fun Nights were initiated by the Class of 1970 and continued at least through 1981.

- In the spring of 1970 Student Council sponsored a Sweetheart Dance.

- An Arts Festival was planned for May 27-29, 1970 with a drama festival, film, and art exhibit including sculpture and photography. Ken Leskawa served as chairman of this new event.

- *Falcon Flash,* February 1971: *Media* magazine sponsored a dance that was canceled two days before the event. (The advisor had agreed to be a sponsor after students had trouble finding other teachers to chaperone the dance. The advisor's condition was that only LD students could attend and he confirmed this with the principal. Student Council then disputed the ruling and the principal canceled the dance.)

- On March 24, 1971 the Senior Class sponsored a Film Festival.

- In April 1971 the Cheerleaders sponsored a dance, "The Varsity Drag," with music by Cold Steel.

- The May Festival '71 included food, games, and a dance featuring Cobby Tweebo.

- In the Fall of 1971 Student Council held a Back-to-School Welcome dance with music by Gulliver.

- The following year's Welcome Back-to-School dance on September 8, 1972 bore the name "New Beginnings," with music by "Hot Ice."

- A "Fun Night" was scheduled April 7, 1973 as part of Sam Campbell Month.

Early Student Highlights

♦ In the fall of 1962 Fred Shope and Ralph Espenshade launched a rocket, following a record-breaking rocket Ralph had launched in April 1960, one that had traveled 15,000 feet at a speed exceeding 760 mph, breaking the sound barrier and resulting in a sonic boom. ("Reporter at Large," Paul Beers, *The Patriot*, September 26, 1962)

♦ On May 21, 1965 the seniors set a precedent by presenting a special "seniors only" talent show assembly … given for the entire senior high student body. Featured was "The Sand Box" by Edward Albee, a one-act play under the direction of Barry L. Stopfel. (Twenty years later, Mrs. Kathryn Sandel wrote to this author, "Looking back, you must feel great satisfaction with your part in drama and Commencement activities at L.D. I am recalling "The Sandbox" by Edward Albee which was likely the first dramatic attempts to raise the literary level of students (and teachers) there."

♦ The Library Club held a paperback book fair on December 6, 1965, selling 1,320 books from a display of 530 titles. The top seller was *Kids Say the Darndest Things*, followed by *Sweet Sixteen*. In 1967 1,522 books were sold at the fair with the most popular title being *Here Comes Charlie Brown*.

♦ In the spring of 1969 *The Evening News* ran a lengthy article on "This Generation: Students Speak Up on Decency." As part of their investigation, reporters interviewed LD students. This followed a "decency movement" sparked by a recent decency rally in Miami that had protested a rock concert in which Jim Morrison, leader of "The Doors," exposed himself before a teenage audience.

The following are comments resulting from interviews:

▸ "I think the decency movement is a good idea," said Don Hixon, 17, of Hummelstown. "Television and movies have to be controlled. You can't even see a movie with a girl without being embarrassed. Movies may be restricted at the theatre, but they're showing restricted movies on TV."

▸ "The parents can't seem to do anything about it, so I think it's about time the kids did. To stop Doors-type stuff the musicians' union should have some kind of standard. Groups could be dropped from the union and punished or fined."

▸ "Overexposure in public places is getting too much. It started out in 'Hair' and now 'Che.' I think they're shooting for kids since teens don't have much experience. By sensationalism they think they can become popular."

Miniskirts and dress in general received a lot of mention by these students:

▸ "Too short dresses I'm completely against," said Bob Wolfe, 16, of Grantville. "The standards of teens have completely changed. Any type of drug at all I'm completely against unless it can be used for good. A drug used by the doctor is okay, but when it gets into the hands of teen-agers, I'm completely against it."

- Tempering Wolfe's negatives, Kim Brightbill, 15, of Hummelstown, said, "I think people should be able to dress the way they want to as long as it's half decent. I have a miniskirt I wear when I'm not here. If I could, I'd wear it to school. I like long hair if the person wearing it keeps it neat. It's a person's individual right to do what he wants."

- Speaking out on sex, Jeff Rider, 16, of Middletown said, "Miniskirts—it's just a temptation really. We boys like to see it, but it's the reason for all these births out of wedlock. Morally, living together is wrong, though to a couple doing it, it might be right if their standards are that low. It's wrong – it's against God's will to do it. I figure it's up to each person whether they take drugs, so long as a wild man on drugs doesn't come up to you on the street and hit you over the head."

- Darlene Parmer, 18, of Deodate, reacted against the idea of a dress code, saying, "I can't agree with that. People should dress the way they want to. But when they go all-out and walk around nude, I'm against that. If there are laws against certain clothes, I'll break them. I wear miniskirts at home, but not in public. I don't have the legs for them. Her companion, Linda Bender, 17, also of Deodate, said, "I think what this country needs most is to get back to God again. I don't think the hippies' ideas are going to work out – free love and this business with dope and all. At the Doors' concert I would have gotten up and gone out. Laws don't help things—people will just try and break them."

- Lucinda Wagner, 15, of Hershey, said, "I like beards and moustaches, but I don't like miniskirts. I think the boys are trying to look more like the girls. I don't believe in nudity on the stage. I don't wear actual miniskirts. I don't believe in free love and all that. I think the hippies are lowering themselves. Drugs? I don't think you have to take anything that gets you high. It's immature to take them. You only hurt yourself, and future children are affected."

The Personality of Classes, a Sampling of the First 25 years

The Introduction to the 1991 *Falconaire* stated, "Lower Dauphin, our school … can you imagine it in twenty years — without us? After all, we are the school."

The Class of 1961

The Class of 1961 will always hold the banner of being the first graduating class of Lower Dauphin High School. Imagine, if you will, being a senior in the fall of 1960 and not knowing at least half of your classmates. It is greatly to their credit that they rose to the challenge set before them by Mr. David J. Emerich, Supervising Principal, of taking the leadership, setting aside old rivalries, and creating a whole new culture in the newly formed school.

In the fall the new school was willing to take all comers on the football field and the football team brought home the championship. There were fine athletes who came together from both Hummelstown and Hershey High Schools, but the magic was in the coaching which created a team out of former rivals. Mike Shifflet, a sophomore, made the first touchdown ever for the Falcons on the last play of the first game.

Even without a school newspaper (which did not start in the high school until the following year), but with strong academic and sports program, the fledgling school district quickly made its mark as an "up and comer." Without this strong example of a senior class willing to set the standard and wear new colors and follow a new mascot, the strong identity of Lower Dauphin would not have occurred. Class of 1961, we salute you.

The Class of 1965

Nationwide the Class of 1965 was noted for its many achievements and the Lower Dauphin Class of 1965 was no exception. Taking a back seat to no one, they were multitudinous in number (colleges were becoming jam-packed with this raft of baby boomers), they were bright (the best class ever in the experience of many high school teachers), and they had a veneer of confidence. They seemed to know that they would soon be taking charge of the world and, over the next fifty years, they did.

They describe themselves thus: "We were the generation who grew up with television. We grieved the death of President Kennedy. We eventually went to war with Vietnam. We were raised to have opinions and we let them be known. We had the draft and the lottery numbers—but they were for military duty and not for professional sports or fortune. We fell in love, drove too fast, and danced the night away—yet had our school work ready for the next day."

Born of the Greatest Generation, whose parents fully expected great things from them, they were described by *Time* magazine in 1965 as being "on the fringe of a golden era of introspection with a fixation on self. Boomers were said to be idealists, later in life surprising even themselves."[1]

This was said about the Class of 1965 in 1999: "I do hope you all realize what wonderful, special,

---

[1] Strauss & Howe, *Generations*

joyous, creative people you were and still are. Perhaps the sheer numbers of you led to your carving out individual niches; however, I rather think it was a caring for one another that was the key. That caring is still there, as evidenced by your continuing close contact with one another."

The Class of 1969

This class was part of what William McLoughlin calls America's "Fourth Awakening."[2] Beginning in 1967 with the "Vietnam Summer" and counterculture euphoria, the awakening peaked in 1970 with Kent State, the first Earth Day, and the "Days of Rage" on university campuses. However, high school lives of this class were filled with sports, plays, dances, and helping to create a student musical during their junior year with "It's a Big, Wide, Wonderful World," entirely written and directed by members of the choir.

Mr. Linnane recalls this class with great fondness, "You even have your own theatre group. I've never seen a group who could throw together such grand performances in so short a period of time. Your ability to bring laughter and entertainment to your classmates was always impressive. … Your one outstanding quality is your enthusiasm for things you believe to be worthwhile. For your senior prom the school cafeteria was transformed into a most attractive ballroom through the efforts of Jeannine Lehmer, Don Frantz, Linda Goepfert, Kathy Schock, Carol Kreider, and others. The pathway to the ballroom led one through two huge stone portals on either side of a drawbridge which opened to reveal a candlelight vision of coats of arms, banners, and a Queen's throne and four attendants' chairs directly out of Camelot."

In August 1969 Jeannine Lehmer was head majorette and featured twirler for the Big 33 half-time show. The Lower Dauphin Band was the invited band to play the pre-game and half-time music. Jeannine then directed the 1970 Big 33 half-time performance. Don Frantz, drum major, went on to work for Disney, later becoming a Broadway Producer.

Hauers was still a presence on the square in Hummelstown, as were Grant's Sunoco, Fazio's Sporting Goods, Porter's Market, E. B. Smith Hardware, Rudy's Drycleaning, and Hocker's Drug Store.

The Class of 1971

The Dartmouth valedictorian in 1971 declared, "I have made no plans because I have found no plans worth making," and the *Berkeley Daily Californian* observed, "All too many people are just waiting for life rather than living." A back-to-nature movement and diet fads triggered what one writer called "the century's Second Golden Age of Food Quackery,"[3] although this did not include the infamous Lower Dauphin Dandy in the school cafeteria.

Seniors remember that during their sophomore year there was still racial tension that caused an altercation at the Hershey Ballroom in HersheyPark. They also recall the 1971 Valentine's Day Dance with George Stauffer voted as Cupid, as well as the "Waisted" Evening Dance where admission was based on one's waist measurement.

---

[2] Strauss and Howe, *Generations*, p. 299.

[3] Strauss and Howe, *Generations*, p. 311.

However, the main event of their year was not dances but winning the Capital Area Conference (CAC) Football Championship with an Undefeated and Untied record of 11 wins and no losses. This was followed by the Wrestling Team earning another undefeated CAC championship. In the spring track had its best season to date when Joe Quigley broke the 10 year high hurdles record with a 16.0. Other record-breakers were Mike Slough, Rick Goss, and the relay team of Kevin Patrick, Kim Witmer, Bruce Cox, and Mike Slough. Mike is also called one of the best sprinters in LD history. To round it out to a near perfect year, LD won the 1971 Baseball League Championship despite the fact that there were only four seniors. And all of this at a time when jeans were not acceptable attire and hall monitors wore LD armbands.

The Class of 1973

The fall of 1972 marks the first time the band is called "Big Blue," having increased its size to 160 members. Another first was the opening of the Home Economics' food course to co-ed classes.

Archaeology class, in its second year, began an investigation of the grounds that surround the Mumma farm house in the Hummelstown borough. The farm house stands on land which had been purchased by the School District as a site for the construction of a new high school.

Homecoming boasted ten floats and the queen candidates circled the track in chariots drawn by students in togas. Randy Lehman ran from the high school to the stadium to light the Olympic torch.

Media magazine had not yet been launched and creative writing had only the occasional showcasing in the *Falcon Flash*, while the newly formed Thespian Society presented its maiden production, "Balcony Scene."

Wrestling claimed the CAC Championship again and earned three berths in States with Ed Neiswender, Tom Mutek, and Mark Stauffer. Coach Futchko reached his 100th win with JV Basketball, and Kim Witmer set a school high mark during the Mechanicsburg basketball game and finished with a career total of 1,048 points.

The Track Team captured its second consecutive undefeated season. According to *The Flash*, Randy Lehman destroyed the school record in the two-mile run and also was the League Meet Champion; Kim Witmer never lost a 440 yard dash and won the League Meet 440 easily; and Mike Gallagher also enjoyed an undefeated season in the 880 yard run while winning the 880 League Meet Championship and a school record in the 880. Jim Kulina continued to break records in baseball, posting three shut-outs and LD's first no-hitter ever.

The Class of 1974

There were 75 members in the 1973-1974 Booster Club and AIFS trips were popular where a student could go to Russia with Mr. Smith for $599, Spain with Mrs. Barbush for $499, Germany with Mr. Schan for $459, and Italy with Mrs. J. Witmer (substituting for Mr. Zeigler) for $479.

Craig College observed in *The Flash*, "Well, here it is October 12, school has been underway several weeks, the water has been shut off twice, the lavs are again unofficial smoking lounges, and everyone is inured in the scheme of things for another year."

There was a lot of rain that fall and a headline read "Cross Country swims to a win in soaking, flooding rain." Basketball finished at 15-9, the second best record in school history. A copy of the *Falconaire* sold for $8.00 and *The Flash* announced that cheerleading uniforms now matched the football team's new uniforms for away games.

Unsupervised honor study halls were established in the auditorium and cafeteria and were thought to be operating smoothly while a new "Release Time" was initiated so that seniors with morning study halls need not report until the time of their first class and students with afternoon study halls could leave school early.

There was also an energy crisis that winter, leading Ray Kennedy to comment, "Speed limits are to be reduced, public lighting reduced as well…to force frugality in our use of energy." Energy use was cut in three major areas of room temperature, lighting, and transportation. Classrooms were set at 68° and the gym at between 60° and 62°. The wing halls were dark and on clear days, lights were out in classrooms and the blinds up. Field trips were canceled except those directly related to the curriculum, and the number of activity buses cut.

The Class of 1977

The 1977 yearbook theme was a play on their double digit class year. They used the phrase "77 Up" and the iconic soft drink "7-Up." For the first time sponsorships were offered to parents, asking $60 for a full page.

A new energy crisis occurred and Governor Milton Shapp closed all schools in Pennsylvania from January 26 to January 31, 1977. The crisis was said to have been caused by the natural gas shortage created by low pressure in pipelines due to terrible cold weather, the worst ever in the history of the U.S. All this cold was reported to be caused by a mysterious Arctic wind which covered half the country.

The cold, however, did not keep some students from taking advantage of the new Smoking Policy, approved by the School Board on February 7 which permitted senior high students (with parental permission) to smoke in certain areas outside the school, namely outside the auditorium in the area facing B-wing and the porch outside of H-wing before and after school, during the student's lunch period, and between classes.

Trivia this year included a person who was marking lockers with a wavy line and the initials MM, whom the school paper dubbed the Mad Marker; a *Falcon Flash* which listed jumpsuits, clogs, berets, knickers, and peasant skirts as popular items, and the disbanding of the Kazoo Band.

That spring Todd Eby was honored by the Harrisburg Old Timers Athletic Association for leading the CAC East Champions with a .390 batting average and led the club in extra base hits and runs batted in. He was the fourth LD winner, preceded by Paul Pintarch in 1970, Don Gourley in 1972, and Jim Kulina in 1973. Pam Malvin set school and CAC records in track in the mile and two-mile in dual meets.

The 1977 Class History, found in their yearbook, is among the few to mention the theme of their float entries for Homecoming (Junior Year, "Hall of the Presidents" and Senior Year, "2004 Olympiad," both designed by Doug Topper), but they could not get together to write a Class Reflection or to remember the theme of their Senior Year (Fall of 1976) Homecoming.

The Class of 1981

In the fall of 1980 *Know Your Schools* reported that there was strong student support for strict administration of school attendance and disciplinary policies that had emerged as a central theme of student discussion at the Superintendent's Forum.

Whit Hill was named to the French Horn I position in the 1981 All-State Orchestra.

In January Helen Woltman wrote an editorial on "Equal the Score for Women," "…Because women have been discriminated against for so long, they are currently striving to eliminate chauvinistic inequalities between the sexes."

Tim Goss was the high scorer in most, if not all, of the basketball games.

In May two members of Lower Dauphin Thespian Troupe earned honors in the Bucks County Drama Festival with Conni Weller as Best Actress and Best Director.

The end of year article in the *Flash* featured a self-congratulatory article on the gifts the class had given of themselves to the school. They prided themselves on being a difficult class.

Falcon baseball captured the CAC Crown, the first since 1972 and wrestling captured its second consecutive CAC Championship.

The Class of 1984

Described by the *Falcon Flash*, the Class of 1984 seemed to suffer an identity crisis and described itself as "not as proud or productive as other classes."

Excerpts from the school newspaper captured their zeitgeist:
- Freshman Year: Upset with a starting line-up of eighth graders on the JV basketball team.
- Junior Year: Morale is low. Class Council members are griping. "We need more unity," "They just don't care about our class!" "Well, what can we do?" (The Class)… seemed to have a gray cloud hovering above its head…. Stricken with bad teacher-student relations, they hold gloomy reports on conduct.
- Upset with their dwindling class treasury.
- Little participation in Class Council meetings, except for the yearbook picture.
- "Some problems haven't begun to surface because there is still the prom to plan. The band, the location, the expenses, and the theme of the prom in addition to the choice of the class color and motto are a few decisions that are still to be placed on this class's head. Did you

ever hear of a class without a prom? You might next year if the Junior Class members don't put an effort into helping their class."

- ▸ (They) Laugh at the thought of selling candy or magazines.
- ▸ Senior Year: Class Advisors institute the first Senior Class Council homeroom.
- ▸ As seniors few are in starting positions in football, basketball, and wrestling.
- ▸ 146 seniors are absent on January 13, 1984; the Falcon Missile is taken and ransomed; this appears to be the work of the seniors.
- ▸ Bob Early defends the class by saying it has the largest selection of proud, fast, and clean cars.
- ▸ April 1984 issue of *Falcon Flash*: the seniors congratulate themselves on their class trip.
- ▸ June 1984 *Falcon Flash*: "The purpose of Senior Night to show all of the 'doubters' in the school that the Class of 1984 does have more than it has been given credit for."

The Class of 1986

Kevin Strawser raised the question in the *Falcon Flash* as to "Why" (1) there was an "intermediate school," (2) passing time between classes was being extended to five minutes, and (3) a high number of courses were being dropped for the following year.

The marching band garnered a standing ovation, a first with 1,000 people on their feet, as it left the field after completing its competition. Drum majors, Thomas Ball and Kathy Smee, held the 1st place trophy high as the band, screaming non-stop, jumped off the bleachers and ran onto the field to greet them. Early in the season Mr. Turnball had told the band that they were championship material and this win proved it. Later in the season this band took second place in state competition after performing a dazzling show filled with balloons and fireworks, accentuated with patriotic music, leaving many saying that it gave them chills just to watch. In May the band won LD's first ever Grand Championship trophy with the highest score overall in their division.

T. J. Mann (pen name) in a balanced editorial noted that the smoking area had become the center of controversy. Another article claimed the smoking porch was a failure.

The Future Farmers of America organization again was honored at the state convention.

Guest speakers in Behavioral Sciences advised the class to focus on the good things in life and to be sure to attend "all your class reunions!"

The sell-out musical, *Camelot*, also garnered standing ovations and accolades as the finest ever.

The Spring Forum topics included class weighting of grades, hall passes (top priority), the disruptive summoning of students via the PA system's loud speaker, parking passes, required grade point averages for extra-curricular activities, heterogeneous grouping of social studies classes. Also of concern was reported low faculty morale and in some cases unprofessional behavior such as teachers talking about other teachers and students in front of classes.

The *Flash* gave this send-off to the class, "In five or ten years think back on your senior year with fond memories. Dwell on the good thoughts not the bad. Remember how we as a class came together to form one of the most outstanding senior classes in the history of Lower Dauphin."

The Class of 1993

… is noted for its recognition of Falcon Pride. "Pride is the first thing that comes to mind when we think of Lower Dauphin. The spirit can be sensed floating through the halls and completely engulfing the entire school. There is an overwhelming sense of caring more about the school in general and it helped to make this year a more memorable one." This is also the year the community pep rally was renewed. "Falcon Pride is Alive!"   ——1993 *Falconaire*

The Class of 2008

…selected for its showcasing some of the less expected sections of the yearbook, the 2008 *Falconaire* listed the best-selling cookies in the cafeteria, selling approximately 700 per day:

1. Chocolate chip   *3.* Double chocolate

2. M & Ms   *4.* Sugar

"50% of the 400 students surveyed said they look forward to Grilled Cheese Day, and a cafeteria cashier said that regular lunch sales dramatically increase on this day. Coming close behind is sweet and sour chicken. The sandwiches are not technically grilled but baked in the ovens."

The Class of 2008 also noted a section in the yearbook as (out of school) Special Interests:

- ▸ Showing livestock
- ▸ Showing horses through participating in events such as show jumping
- ▸ Showing quarter horses, in both western and English riding
- ▸ Alternate Rock Band, the Pink Yard Flamingos
- ▸ Dance Schools (Hershey, McCann, Movement Laboratory, Richie, One Broadway, Company Dance, and CPYB)
- ▸ Asphalt Modified Racing
- ▸ Motocross Racing
- ▸ Karate
- ▸ Gymnastics.

The yearbook featured some of the clubs by describing their Defining Moment, a refreshing way to showcase the clubs rather than the same tired verbiage. Congrats!

- ▸ The Marching Band's Defining Moment was winning "Best Percussion" at Championships.

- The Defining Moment for National English Honor Society was forming with 86 members, an organization for students who believe in the power of literature, the pleasure of good writing, and the excitement of language studies and by participating in monthly meetings, author talks, writing workshops, and the first ever district wide book drive. (Where were you when the library purged its books?)
- The Fellowship of Christian Athletes notes their Defining Moment as taking the lead on activities such as Winterfest, Summerfest, After-Prom Party, and See You at the Pole events.
- Defining the reemerging Science Club was its Haunted Hallway on Falcon Fright Night.

The Class of 2009

The Class of 2009 found themselves with an unusual distinction in that eighty-seven of them had siblings in the high school.

The Class of 2010

The Class of 2010 rose to the honor and the responsibility of being the Golden Class, marking fifty years of LDHS, celebrating the event through Homecoming, football programs, various noting of their high school heritage; institutionalizing the Falcon Nation; and producing a spectacular yearbook.

Class Notes

Class Advisors

1961	Janet Ausmus, Conrad Stanitski		1987	Bernard Bernitsky, David Dickson
1962	Louise Kiscadden, Douglas Stauffer		1988	Melody Lovelidge
1963	Janet Ausmus, Barney Osevala		1989	Victoria Pine, William Smith
1964	Helga Rist, Leslie Taylor		1990	Steven Futchko, C. Richard Miller
1965	Judith (Ball) Witmer, Gerald Brittain		1991	Michelle Govora, Ronald Zeigler
1966	Judith P. Martin, Barney Osevala		1992	Barbara Atkinson, Rudolph Sharpe
1967	Aleda Myers, Joseph G. Schan		1993	Jean Hynicker, Melody Lovelidge
1968	Tom Campbell, Emily Keller		1994	Dodie Etter, Jim Seacrist
1969	Judith P. Martin, John Croll		1995	Barbara Atkinson, Sheron Marshall
1970	Judith P. Martin, Joseph G. Schan		1996	Mark Painter, Lori Fischer
1971	Kathryn Taylor, Thomas Campbell		1997	Craig Cassel, Phil Green
1972	Jacquelyn Douglass, William W. Linnane		1998	Marsha Costabile, Christina Wolfe
1973	Barbara Atkinson, Edward F. Romano		1999	Darby Dimpsey, Barb Weigan
1974	Audrey Conway, Thomas Campbell		2000	Rebecca Cassel, Dave Machamer
1975	Jacquelyn Douglass, Allen Risser		2001	Dodie Etter, Sheron Marshall
1976	Audrey Conway, Steven Messner		2002	Teri Eytchenson, Bret Sparks
1977	Barbara Atkinson, Charles Cole		2003	Darby Fischl, Amy Miller
1978	Susan Ewing, Edward F. Romano		2004	Teri Eytchenson, Tom Hanninen
1979	Laura Shaw, Randy Umberger		2005	Diane McCullough, Cindy Gelanis-Jones
1980	Audrey Conway, C. Richard Miller		2006	Michelle McGinnis, Barb Kuhlen
1981	Susan Ewing, Stephen Futchko		2007	Beth Kirman, Dawn Koons
1982	Anne Ehrhart Bocian, Randy Umberger		2008	Karen Burk, Kiley Strohm
1983	Dodie Etter, James Seacrist		2009	Diane McCullough
1984	Barbara Atkinson, Stephen Futchko		2010	Michelle McGinnis, Barb Kuhlen
1985	Anne Bocian, Stephen Futchko			
1986	Barbara Atkinson, Linda Chavez			

Class Presidents

1961	Glenn Ebersole		1994	Jennifer Jones
1962	Everett Hertzler		1995	Richard Shertzer
1963	Gerald Wampler		1996	Samantha Rush
1964	Randall Kahler		1997	Jaime Bolen
1965	Michael Hubler		1998	Jessica Jiao
1966	Verna Jean Miller		1999	Adriane Gross[2]
1967	John Fureman		2000	Kyle Whitman
1968	Joseph Hipple		2001	Nicole Kennel
1969	Scott Gleim		2002	Elizabeth Smolick
1970	Michael Orsini		2003	Rachel Myers
1971	Carol Rhoad[1]		2004	Carson Parr
1972	Marshall Scott Reichenbaugh		2005	Kim Pintarch
1973	Mark Osevala		2006	Colin Matichak
1974	Kerry Fies		2007	James Miller
1975	Thomas Reichenbaugh		2008	Kari Skitka
1976	Wynn Willard		2009	Laura Cromwell
1977	Richard Cook		2010	Lauren Carberry
1978	Susan Reichenbaugh			
1979	Patrice Alexander			
1980	Charles Ritrovato			
1981	Steven J. Painter			
1982	Ronald D. Orsini			
1983	William F. Cusack			
1984	Kurt E. Geib			
1985	Patti Jo Schan			
1986	Todd McTavish			
1987	Thomas Salus			
1988	Jenifer J. Petrina			
1989	Jamie Ferguson			
1990	Sharon Kuntz			
1991	Erin L. Price			
1992	Jennifer L. Pringle			
1993	Brett W. Lovelidge			

[1] Following the untimely death of Carol Rhoad several years following graduation, the class appointed Tom Luttrell as their president.

[2] (This class kept essentially the same officers beginning in 7th grade)

Class Sizes

Class Year — No. of Class Members		Class sizes from smallest to largest	
1961 - 129	1991 - 218	1961 - 129	1996 - 267
1962 - 134	1992 - 206	1963 - 130	2001 - 268
1963 - 130	1993 - 201	1962 - 134	1989 - 273
1964 - 179	1994 - 210	1964 - 179	1970 - 274
1965 - 265	1995 - 220	1969 - 193	2003 - 277
1966 - 239	1996 - 267	1993 - 201	2004 - 277
1967 - 209	1997 - 260	1992 - 206	2005 - 277
1968 - 242	1998 - 250	1967 - 209	1971 - 279
1969 - 193	1999 - 248	1986 - 210	1982 - 279
1970 - 274	2000 - 234	1994 - 210	2010 - 283
1971 - 279	2001 - 268	1991 - 218	1978 - 286
1972 - 251	2002 - 252	1984 - 220	2006 - 286
1973 - 253	2003 - 277	1995 - 220	1981 - 287
1974 - 302	2004 - 277	1990 - 226	1980 - 289
1975 - 297	2005 - 277	1987 - 233	1975 - 297
1976 - 265	2006 - 286	2000 - 234	1977 - 297
1977 - 297	2007 - 297	1966 - 239	2007 - 297
1978 - 286	2008 - 305	1968 - 242	1974 - 302
1979 - 264	2009 - 319	1999 - 248	2008 - 305
1980 - 289	2010 - 283	1998 - 250	2009 - 319
1981 - 287		1972 - 251	
1982 - 279		2002 - 252	
1983 - 264		1973 - 253	
1984 - 220		1988 - 257	
1985 - 259		1985 - 259	
1986 - 210		1997 - 260	
1987 - 233		1979 - 264	
1988 - 257		1983 - 264	
1989 - 272		1965 - 265	
1990 - 226		1976 - 265	

Class Mottos

The purpose of a Class Motto is to bring together the members of a particular class to represent its unity and team spirit. At best a motto carries an inspiring message that motivates members of the class to follow ideals. A Class Motto is intended to bring about a commonality of identity, a belief, a demonstration of what the class wants to exemplify, and/or what the class may think is reflective of itself and its members.

The motto sometimes reveals the class personality, or can be simply a quotation that "catches the fancy" of enough class members to carry a vote. Some mottos are longer and are more like a creed while others are succinct. Many are quotations from well-known personages and some are written by a class member or a committee of class members. Some are inspiring, some are overly sentimental, a few are political, a few are song lyrics, and most are forgettable.

The following are, for the most part, traditional to the intended spirit of a Class Motto. Authors are identified where the class itself has noted them:

1961 *Onward ever, backward never.*

1962 *Growing toward tomorrow.*

1963 *With ropes of the past, we'll ring the bells of the future.*

1964 *Conduct and courage lead to honor.*

1965 *It's better to have tried and failed, than never to have tried at all.*

1966 *Today we follow, tomorrow we lead.*

1967 *In ourselves our future lies.*

1968 *It is given to us for this generation, to achieve real peace, if not for ourselves, for our children.*

1969 *The door to success is labeled: Push.*

1970 *The stage is set, the destiny disclosed, we cannot turn back, we can only go forward.*

1971 *Communication is the beginning of understanding.*

1972 *If a man does not keep pace with his companions, perhaps it is because he hears a different drummer. Let him step to the music he hears, however measured or far away.*

        Thoreau

1973 *Ask, and it shall be given you; seek, and ye shall find; knock, and it shall be opened unto you.*

1974 *I am not afraid of tomorrow, for I have seen yesterday and I love today.*

       William Allen White

1975 *Let us not look back in anger, nor forward in fear, but around in awareness.*

1976 *Having opened the door, shall we have the courage to go beyond?*

1977 *For yesterday is but a dream, and tomorrow is only a vision; but today well-lived makes yesterday a dream of happiness, and every tomorrow a vision of hope.*

1978   *We don't remember days; we remember moments.*

1979   *May you live your life today, so that every yesterday will become a vision of happiness and every tomorrow a vision of hope.*

1980   *Look back on the past to echo the happy times and into the future to herald great expectations.*

1981   *Yesterday is already a dream; and tomorrow is only a vision; but today, well-lived, makes every yesterday a dream of happiness, and every tomorrow a vision of hope.*

1982   *If you dream it, you can achieve it. If you strive for it, you can become it.*

1983   *If you know who you are and what you want and why you want it, and if you have confidence in yourself and a strong will to obtain your desires and a very positive attitude, you can make your life yours, if you ask.*

Susan Polis Schutz

1984   *Future, the inevitability of it; life, the constant struggle of it; knowledge, the beauty of it.*

Randall Ian Thames '84

1985   *Know Thyself, Socrates. Control Thyself, Confucius. Give Thyself, Christ.*

1986   *What lies behind us and what lies before us are tiny matters compared to what lies within us.*

Ralph Waldo Emerson

1987   *Behold, I have set before thee an open door and no man can shut it.*

Revelation 3:8

1988   *Today we may dream dreams, but tomorrow we live them.*

1989   *Dare to live the life you have dreamed for yourself. Go forward and make your dreams come true.*

1990   *Our dreams of today change the world of tomorrow.*

1991   *Learn from yesterday, live for today, dream for tomorrow.*

1992   *Don't walk in front of me ... I may not follow; don't walk behind me ... I may not lead; walk beside me and just be my friend.*

Often attributed to Albert Camus

1993   *Until you make peace with who you are, you'll never be content with what you have.*

1994   *To achieve all that's possible we must attempt the impossible; to be as much as we can be, we must dream of being more.*

1995   *The future belongs to those who believe in the beauty of their dreams.*

Eleanor Roosevelt

1996   *What lies behind us and what lies before us are tiny matters compared to what lies within us.*

Ralph Waldo Emerson

1997   *Having then gifts differing according to the grace that is given to us, let us use them.*

Romans 12:6

1998 *The world is but a canvas to our imaginations. Dreams are the touchstones of our characters.*
Henry David Thoreau

1999 *Yesterday is not ours to recover, but tomorrow is ours to win or lose.*
Lyndon B. Johnson

2000 *We are not permitted to choose the frame of our destiny. But what we put into it is ours.*
Dag Hammarskjold

2001 *It is not in the stars to hold our destiny, but in ourselves.*
William Shakespeare

2002 *Good friends we've had and good friends we've lost along the way…in this bright future you can't forget your past.*
Bob Marley

2003 *Take my hand and run with me out of the past called yesterday and walk with me into the future.*
Grateful Dead

2004 *I may not have gone where I intended to go, but I think that I have ended up where I intended to be.*

2005 *It's something unpredictable, but in the end it's right. I hope you have the time of your life.*

2006 *Celebrate we will 'cause life is short but sweet for certain.*
Dave Matthews

2007 *Pile up enough tomorrows and you'll find yourself with a bunch of empty yesterdays.*
The Music Man

2008 *Here's to the crazy ones. The misfits. The rebels. The trouble-makers. The round heads in the square holes. The ones who see things differently. They're not fond of rules, and they have no respect for the status quo. You can quote them, disagree with them, glorify or vilify them. But the only thing you can't do is ignore them. Because they change things. They push the human race forward. And while some may see them as the crazy ones, we see genius. Because the people who are crazy enough to think they can change the world are the ones who do.*

2009 *It well may be that we will never meet again in this lifetime, so let me say before we part, so much of me is made of what I learned from you, you'll be with me like a hand print on my heart, and now whatever way our stories end I know you have re-written mine by being my friend.*
Wicked, Stephen Schwartz

2010 *Live as if you were to die tomorow. Learn as if you were to live forever.*

Class Gifts

Class gifts to the school often are not recorded or remembered; therefore, this list likely is only a sampling.

Lower Dauphin Alumni Association, established 1989

Established Falcon Alumni Trust which annually awards a scholarship.

Created a large, walk-in Showcase as part of Alumni Lobby.

Purchased signage for the gymnasium: Falcon Pride!

Purchased (through a fund-raiser) seating for winter sports teams.

Established Sports Complex Committee to study the feasibility for playing fields.

Purchased and installed an Award Plaque honoring LDAA scholarship winners.

Established an archival fund to preserve historical documents and other memorabilia.

Sponsor Alumni Band and Alumni Cheerleaders.

Provided a Field Banner to be carried at sport events.

Replaced the original Falcon Missile with a replica.

Produced Lower Dauphin's Golden Jubilee, a Celebration of 50 Years.

Published *Loyal Hearts Proclaim: The First Fifty Years of Lower Dauphin High School.*

Class Gifts

1965	Initiated a class gift program by purchasing and donating art work from their class members
	Established two scholarships, one in the name of the class and one in honor of Dr. Judith T. Witmer.
1966	Announcement Board for the Gymnasium for Names of Players.
1970	Lectern for the auditorium.
1971	Strobe lights donated to the school their junior year.
1973	Watercolor of the high school building that hangs in the guidance office.
1976	A large mural in the gymnasium proclaiming "FALCONS, CLASS OF 1976".
1977	Academic trophy case designated to honor scholastic achievement.
1977	There is a sketch of a sculpture by Doug Topper shown in the yearbook as a class gift, but there is no evidence that it was created.
1977	An exterior sign noting "Home of the Falcons," was created through the efforts of the Senior High Student Council and the Adult Booster Club.

1979	A gift from the Class of 1979, a split rail fence was installed outside the front Entrance in August of 1977 under the supervision of Mr. Randy Umberger, Mr. Paul Lytle, Jr. and Chip Lytle. Rose bushes were to be planted around the fence in the spring to conclude the job.
1981	(unconfirmed) Sign board (no further description).
1981, 1982	Student Council and Booster Club combined efforts to pay for a new mascot costume.
1982	The class purchased a camera to be used for taking snapshots of their class, then donated the camera to the school.
1982	A painting by Craig Camasta of a falcon, gifted to the School Board.
1984	The yearbook notes Joe Roman's sketch depicting the ideals of "Falcon Pride" as a gift on behalf of the Class of 1984. This is confirmed by the October 1984 issue of *Know Your Schools* that reports at the student forum "Joe Roman '84 presented a sketch which depicts the ideals of "Falcon Pride."
1986	"Several flower planters and concrete picnic tables and benches for the circle were donated by the Class of 1986, upon the request of Mrs. J. Witmer." (*Falcon Flash*, October 1987)
1987	The electronic message board located in the cafeteria is a gift of the Class of '87, in response to the request by Mrs. Witmer.
1988	The Falcon Mosaic in the entrance to the Alumni Lobby was donated by the Class of 1988 to accompany the gift from the Alumni of a ShowCase in the Alumni Lobby
1993	A tree in the front courtyard in memory of deceased classmates.
2005	Sizable contribution for the purchase of the sign at the front of the building.
2006	Field Hockey scoreboard by parents of the 2005 Season Field Hockey Team.
2008	Rain Garden installed by the National Science Honor Society.
2008	New display cases for the lobby and a smaller display case in the lobby entry opposite the LDAA ShowCase.
2009	Large contribution toward the purchase of the flags on the exterior light poles.
2010	Large indoor blue mats marked "LD" at the entrances to the school.

Habbyshaw Winners

Outstanding Student of Each Senior Class

The Honorable William E. Habbyshaw was a Representative in the Pennsylvania General Assembly. He later became Chief Clerk in the PA House of Representatives, 1943-1954. Local citizens describe Mr. Habbyshaw as "quite a political mover and shaker, getting many things accomplished for the borough of Hummelstown."

The Honorable Mr. Habbyshaw, who also was described as philanthropic, was a member of the Hummelstown School Board in 1937. He is also listed as a member of the School Board in the 1941 and 1942 yearbooks. He had a nephew who was his namesake. William Habbyshaw the younger was graduated from Hummelstown High School in 1937.

Faculty in 1937 included Annie B. Nye who had come to Hummelstown in 1896 after a year at Conewago School and for whom the Nye Building is now named. Miss Janet Ausmus, who taught at Lower Dauphin in the early years, was also a teacher at Hummelstown High School at this time. One of Mr. Habbyshaw the younger's classmates was Jane Strite, also a former teacher of note both at Hummelstown and Lower Dauphin.

1961	Barry Broadwater		1986	Julia Petrina
1962	Alice Wiest		1987	Matthew Espenshade
1963	Michael Stauffer		1988	Andrew Knupp
1964	George Chellew		1989	Ernest Manders
1965	Karl Bell		1990	Corinne Fink
1966	Lester Ratcliff		1991	Carolyn Anderson
1967	Charles Staver		1992	John Botti
1968	Mary Baum		1993	Christian Manders
1969	Wendy Bolton		1994	Jennifer Jones
1970	Michael Orsini		1995	Jonathan Raser
1971	Carol Rhoad		1996	Brian Broadwater
1972	Dorothy McClure		1997	Nathan Irvin
1973	Mark Osevala		1998	Abigail Martin
1974	Sandra Naples		1999	Nora Graber
1975	Jerry Peacock		2000	Joel Martin
1976	Wynn Willard		2001	Jennifer Johnson
1977	Jeffrey Gesford		2002	Ryan Burk
1978	Susan Reichenbaugh		2003	Alisha Cain
1979	Jan Engle		2004	Joshua Todd Young
1980	Patricia Stare		2005	Kelley Burk
1981	Jeffrey Koppenhaver		2006	Sarah Ebright and Emily Gray
1982	Ronald Orsini		2007	Lauren Alloway and Aaron Magaro
1983	Lamar Eifert		2008	Suzanne Cake
1984	Cheryl Stoner		2009	Clayton Cooper
1985	April DeMuth		2010	John Groh

Falcon Mascots

Perhaps because the falcon mascot costume and mask totally cover the identity of the wearer, it is particularly difficult to identify the mascot. Many of those who served in this role did not list it with their activities in those years that yearbooks included seniors' activities. We did our best to track down the bird, but fell short of our prey. A sincere thank you to those who endured the discomfort of the early heavy papier-mâché head and some of the encumbrances of later costumes, including the "bird claws" of one of the versions.

1963 – 1964	Harold Snyder	1988 – 1989	Suzanne Bendull
1964 – 1965	Susan Petrina	1989 – 1990	Suzanne Bendull
1965 – 1966	Lee Seibert	1990 – 1991	possibly Josh Tison
1968 – 1969	Patricia Thompson	1991 – 1992	Justin Hugill
1969 – 1970	Kathy Petrina	1992 - 1993	unconfirmed
	/Tom Seaman	1993 – 1994	Ronald Herman
1970 – 1971	Becky Hughes	1994 – 1995	Jessica Whitcomb
	/Mary Frascella		/Samantha Barnhart
1971 - 1972	Becky Hughes	1995 – 1996	Samantha Barnhart
	/Kathy Gingrich	1996 – 1997	unconfirmed
1972 – 1973	Sandy Zitsch	1997 – 1998	Samantha Carnathan
	/Patti Hall	1998 – 1999	Samantha Carnathan
1973 – 1974	unconfirmed	1999 – 2000	Samantha Carnathan
1974 – 1975	unconfirmed	2000 – 2001	Allen Kliss
1975 – 1976	unconfirmed		/Jessie Lininger
1976 – 1977	Terri Stare	2001 – 2002	unconfirmed
1977 – 1978	various cheerleaders	2002 – 2003	unconfirmed
1978 – 1979	unconfirmed	2003 – 2004	unconfirmed
1979 - 1980	Booster Club members	2004 – 2005	unconfirmed
1980 – 1981	unconfirmed	2005 – 2006	Mike Reese
1981 – 1982	Coleen Sieg	2006 - 2007	Mike Reese
1982 – 1983	unconfirmed	2007 - 2008	Mike Reese
1983 – 1984	unconfirmed	2008 – 2009	Jon Tirado
1984 – 1985	Kevin Strawser	2009 – 2010	Luke Adams
1985 – 1986	Kevin Strawser	2010 – 2011	Luke Adams
1986 – 1987	Pete Valeri	2011 – 2012	Luke Adams
1987 – 1988	unconfirmed	2012 – 2013	Jesse Gault

Class Profiles

Each graduating class is unique. While each class goes through the same process of voting for class officers, planning for Homecoming, voting for class colors, motto, flower, and sometimes a class song, looking forward to graduation, decorating for the prom, and participating in extra-curricular activities, no two classes are quite alike, either in their own view or in the eyes of the faculty and administration. Classes often take on personalities and, if not, they have certain classmates with "personalities" that are forever after associated with a particular graduating class. Some classes are remembered for their many academic achievements and some for their athletic prowess. Some classes are competitive, others appear to lack ambition. Some classes are more memorable than others. Oddly enough, however, there is little agreement among the high school faculty as to which classes were the best, with the exception of a handful. Even today, siblings will say, "Everyone thought your class was so bad or good," and "Mr./Mrs./Ms. always liked your class better than ours."

Each class has charm and each has a personality. Not all have leadership. Some classes are remembered as being funny, or creative, or having outstanding musicians or a very special stage crew. Others are remembered for their sports championships. A few are remembered for not getting along very well among themselves, and one in particular spent most of its time in school—and after—being constantly on the defensive.

As part of the Golden Jubilee, each of the 50 graduating classes (1961-2010) was approached to provide information about itself in two ways: The first was called the Class Profile which was to include basic information about its homecoming, proms, queens, captains, school plays, editors, head majorettes, etc. The second was called the Class Reflection. This was to be a narrative, thus described to the class:

> "We would like to hear from each class as to the specialness or uniqueness of who you were in high school. We want to know what you think marks your class as different in and of itself: the pranks, high achievers, sports championships, great friendships, major current events, field trips, traumas, trends and fads, fashion finds and mistakes, unusual courses, initiating new programs, creating a new event. How was your generation shaped by history and by LD? What did you share as a class?"

We went to great lengths to find a person or a committee of the class to create their reflection. The editor met with some classes and corresponded with many others, tracking down any leads in classes in which it was difficult to get a response. Many of the submitted "Reflections" exceeded our expectations! Other classes did not respond at all—despite efforts by more than one Jubilee committee member to identify a point person for each class. We tried again and again to find someone in each class, but were unsuccessful. However, what we did receive is a rich description of life at Lower Dauphin, 1961-2010. Some of you found yourselves renewing friendships and forming various "breakfast clubs" or a presence on Facebook. We salute all of you who reunited and are now expanding those friendships and building even closer ties among your classmates and to your Alma Mater. We gratefully thank those who responded and we hope all of you enjoy reliving the moments herein described by a member or members of your class.

1960s Class Profiles

1961 Class Profile

Senior Prom Theme	Junior-Senior Dinner-Dance
Senior Prom Music	Jerry Leffler Orchestra
Senior Class Play	Publicity Mad
Cheerleading Captain	Linda McGarvey
Head Majorette	Barbara Olson
Drum Major	Ken Miller
Falconaire Editor	None identified

1962 Class Profile

Senior Prom Music	Mello-Macs
Teen/Festival Queen	Mary Ann Grubb
Junior Prom Theme	Junior-Senior Dinner Dance (1961)
Junior Prom Music	Jerry Leffler Orchestra
Senior Class Play	Tish
Junior Class Play	Kind Lady
Cheerleading Captain	Joyce Keener
Head Majorette	Barbara Olson
Drum Major	Ken Miller
Falconaire Editor	Ann Seaman
Falcon Flash Editor	Gail Walborn

1963 Class Profile

Homecoming Queen	Vicki Fackler
Junior Prom Theme	Combined with the Senior Prom
Junior Prom Music	Mello-Macs
Senior Class Play	The Curious Savage
Junior Class Play	Kind Lady
Cheerleading Captain	Joyce Keener
Head Majorette	Audrey Roland
Drum Major	Terry Mills
Falconaire Editor	Vivian Lewin and Fred Shope
Falcon Flash Editor	George Hall and Ralph Espenshade

1964 Class Profile

Homecoming Music	Bob Shipley, DJ
Homecoming Queen	Nancy Fabian
Senior Prom Theme	Bon Voyage
Senior Prom Music	Don Weidner
Teen/Festival Queen	Nancy Fabian
Junior Prom Theme	Moonlight and Roses
Junior Prom Music	Bob Aulenbach's Orchestra
Senior Class Play	Curtain Going Up
Junior Class Play	Gentlemen Prefer Blondes
Sr Yr Falcon Mascot	Harold Snyder
Cheerleading Captain	Judy Bell
Head Majorette	Audrey Roland
Drum Major	Terry Mills
Falconaire Editor	Susan Lawson
Falcon Flash Editor	Kathleen Convery

1965 Class Profile

Homecoming Music	The Del-Chords
Homecoming Queen	Jane Harper
Senior Prom Theme	Southern Nights[1]
Senior Prom Music	Gene Soles Orchestra
Teen/Festival Queen	Jane Harper
Junior Prom Theme	Tahitian Twilight
Junior Prom Music	Mello-Macs
Senior Class Play	By the Skin of Our Teeth
Junior Class Play	A Hillbilly Weddin
Sr Yr Falcon Mascot	Susan Petrina
Cheerleading Captain	Fran Fenner
Head Majorette	Patty Pheasant
Drum Major	Terry Mills
Falconaire Editor	Kathleen Verdelli
Falcon Flash Editor	Bethanne Bojanic

[1] aka Dining and Dancing at Colonial Greens

1966 Class Profile

Homecoming Theme	Sights and Sounds of Autumn
Homecoming Music	The DuValles
Homecoming Queen	Carol Gingrich
Senior Prom Theme	The Twelfth of Never
Senior Prom Music	Hal Herman Orchestra
Teen/Festival Queen	Carol Gingrich
Junior Prom Theme	Summer Place
Junior Prom Music	Chuck Hennigan Orchestra
Senior Class Play	Ten Little Indians
Junior Class Play	Our Town
Sr. Yr. Falcon Mascot	Lee Seibert
Cheerleading Captain	Terry Witters
Head Majorette	Patty Pheasant
Drum Major	Jack Brandt
Falconaire Editor	Harold Johns
Falcon Flash Editor	Verna Jean Miller and Elizabeth Sandel

1967 Class Profile

Homecoming Theme	A Royal Affair
Homecoming Music	The El Dantes
Homecoming Queen	Sharon Smoyer
Senior Prom Theme	Tender is the Night[2]
Senior Prom Music	Hal Herman Orchestra
Teen/Festival Queen	Sharon Barnhart
Junior Prom Theme	Wonderland by Night
Junior Prom Music	The Music Masters
Senior Class Play	Arms and the Man
Junior Class Play	Melody Jones
Head Majorette	Patricia Jeffries
Drum Major	Jack Brandt
Falconaire Editor	Sandra Mersing
Falcon Flash Editor	Elizabeth Sandel

1968 Class Profile

Homecoming Theme	Midnight Rhapsody
Homecoming Music	Peter and the Wolves
Homecoming Queen	Jane Youtz
Teen/Festival Queen	Kay Wert
Junior Prom Theme	Somewhere
Junior Prom Music	Mello-Macs
Senior Class Play	She Stoops to Conquer
Junior Class Play	Rebel Without a Cause
Cheerleading Captain	Jane Youtz
Head Majorette and Featured Twirler[3]	Jeannine Lehmer
Drum Major	Gary Wagner
Falconaire Editor	Hank Imhof
Falcon Flash Editor	Joyce Alwine and/or Yolande McCurdy

1969 Class Profile

Homecoming Theme	Ye Noble Knight
Homecoming Music	The Skyliners
Homecoming Queen	Bonnie Beissel
Senior Prom Theme	Reflections
Senior Prom Music	The Skyliners
Teen/Festival Queen	Jeannine Lehmer
Junior Prom Theme	Magic Moments
Junior Prom Music	Don Peebles Orchestra
Senior Class Play	The Boy Who Changed the World
Junior Class Play	Tom Jones
Sr Yr Falcon Mascot	Patricia Thompson
Cheerleading Captain	JoAnn Ricker and Bonnie Beissel
Head Majorette	Jeannine Lehmer
Drum Major	Don Frantz
Falconaire Editor	Rachel Wywadis
Falcon Flash Editor	Laurie Granzow

[2] Prom Program for Class of 1967: Penn Harris, dinner music provided by Jeanne Michelle

[3] In the 1967-68 school year the band front added an acrobatic majorette, Sandy Wenrich.

1970 Class Profile

Homecoming Theme	Mystic Depths (dance theme; $3 for couple)
Homecoming Music	The Counts
Homecoming Queen	Judy Fisher
Senior Prom Theme	Eve of Excalibur
Senior Prom Music	Nicky C and the Chateaux
Teen/Festival Queen	Linda Dunkle
Junior Prom Theme	Faraway Places
Junior Prom Music	Rudy Jiras and the Concords (or Intentions)
Senior Class Play	Curtain Going Up
Junior Class Play	Lock, Stock, and Lipstick
Sr Yr Falcon Mascot	Kathy Petrina and Tom Seaman
Cheerleading Captain	Linda Goepfert
Head Majorette	Sheila Miller
Falconaire Editor	Cindy Miller
Falcon Flash Editor	George Cruys
Media Editor	Kenneth Leskawa

1971 Class Profile

Homecoming Theme	Boulevarde de Paris
Homecoming Music	Del Chords
Homecoming Queen	Donna Gleim
Senior Prom Theme	Xanadu
Senior Prom Music	Truth, Justice, and the American Way
Teen/Festival Queen	Mary Ratcliff
Junior Prom Theme	Faraway Places
Junior Prom Music	The DelChords
Senior Class Play	
Junior Class Play	Up the Down Staircase
Falcon Mascot	Becky Hughes and/or Mary Frascella

Cheerleading Captain	Annette Basler and Bonnie Osevala
Head Majorette	Lynette Shipper
Falconaire Editor	Mary Frascella
Falcon Flash Editor	Beverly Hallman
Media Editor	Kenneth Leskawa

1972 Class Profile

Homecoming Theme	Octoberfest
Homecoming Music	Truth, Justice, and the American Way
Homecoming Queen	Barbara Higgins
Homecoming King	NA
Senior Prom Theme	Deja Vu
Senior Prom Music	Rich Clare Pentagon
Teen/Festival Queen	Debra Witters
Junior Prom Theme	Sign of the Times
Junior Prom Music	Chaumonts
Senior Class Play	
The Gondoliers	(Students of Drama I)
Junior Class Play	The Late Christopher Bean
Falcon Mascot	Becky Hughes
Cheerleading Captain	Karen Fenner
Head Majorette	Candy Tritch
Drum Major	Charles Dowell
Falconaire Editor	Becky Hughes
Falcon Flash Editor	Barbara Saylor

1973 Class Profile

Homecoming Theme	Olympiad: Ancient & Modern[1]
Homecoming Music	Haji
Homecoming Queen	Sherry Cooper
Senior Prom Theme	Reflections
Senior Prom Music	Saturday
Teen/Festival Queen	Marilyn Peterman
Junior Prom Theme	Now More Than Ever
Junior Prom Music	Rich Clare Pentagon
Senior Class Play	Ask Any Girl
Thespians[2]	Balcony Scene
Falcon Mascot	Sandy Zitsch and Patti Hall[3]
Cheerleading Captain	Barbara Verdelli and Michelle Wrzesniewski
Head Majorette and Featured Twirler	Candy Tritch
Drum Major	Charles Dowell
Falcon Flash Editor	Barbara Saylor
Media Editor	Sue Eshelman

1974 Class Profile

Homecoming Theme	Mardi Gras
Homecoming Music	The Big City Music Music (no show)
Homecoming Queen	Suzanne Wallish
Senior Prom Theme	Days of Future Past
Senior Prom Music	Rich Clare Pentagon
Teen/Festival Queen	Gina Heffley
Junior Prom Theme	Pieces of April
Junior Prom Music	Saturday
Senior Class Play	Tell Me That You Love Me, Junie Moon
Junior Class Play	You Were Born on a Rotten Day
Cheerleading Captain	Linda Poole
Head Majorette and Featured Twirler	Denise Lehmer
Drum Major	Russ Feeser
Falconaire Editor	Karen Emsweiler
Falcon Flash Editor	Ray Kennedy
Media Editor	Sue Eshelman

1975 Class Profile

Homecoming Theme	The Good Times: America's Golden Years
Homecoming Music	Favor
Homecoming Queen	Jody Reitz
Senior Prom Theme	Tomorrow's Yesterday
Senior Prom Music	Favor
Teen/Festival Queen	Vicki Finney
Junior Prom Theme	April Wine
Junior Prom Music	Saturday
Junior Class Play	Arsenic and Old Lace
Cheerleading Captain	Renee Sieg
Head Majorette	Michelle DeRosa
Featured Twirler	Denise Lehmer[4]
Drum Major	Russ Feeser
Falconaire Editor	Suzanne Mader
Falcon Flash Editor	Lisa Kindig
Media Editor	Karen Imhof

---

1 "Heralding the start of the activities will be Falcon cross-country runner Randy Lehman, who will carry a flaming torch from LD to the stadium. Other events will include a parade of national flags and a float contest. In keeping with the theme, 'Olympiad: Ancient and Modern,' the queen candidates will circle the stadium in chariots crafted by the Booster Club and drawn by toga-wearing 'slaves.' " The winning float by the Senior Class depicted the 1972 Olympics with the flags of several nations and the Olympic seal.

2 Thespians formed this year, chartered March 14, 1973, under advisor Karen Bowser

3 The first to wear the newly styled and newly christened "Falcon Pride," replacing "Royal."

---

4 Head Majorette for the Big 33 Game

1976 Class Profile

Homecoming Theme	Celebrate America
Homecoming Music	Nickleplate Road
Homecoming Queen	Sherry Paine
Senior Prom Theme	Until We Meet Again
Senior Prom Music	Journey's End
Teen/Festival Queen	Martha Costik
Junior Prom Theme	A Moment in Time
Junior Prom Music	Patch
Thespians[5]	A Winter's Tale Story Theatre
Cheerleading Captain	Sherry Paine
Head Majorette	Paula Bressi
Drum Major	Russ Feeser
Falconaire Editor	Gwendolyn Black
Falcon Flash Editor	Lisa Kindig
Media Editor	Janet Johnson

1977 Class Profile

Homecoming Theme	Senior float was "2004 Olympiad"
Homecoming Queen	Marilyn Heffley
Senior Prom Theme	We May Never Pass This Way Again
Senior Prom Music	Kicks
Teen/Festival Queen	Georgia Finney
Junior Prom Music	East Coast Invasion
Thespians	Our Town The Drunkard
Falcon Mascot	Suzanne Williams
Cheerleading Captain	Cheryl Wagner
Head Majorette	Diane Hetrick
Drum Major	Kristi Myers
Falconaire Editor	Pamela Shadel
Falcon Flash Editor	Beverly Rife
Media Editor	Herbert Schaffner

1978 Class Profile

Homecoming Theme	The World of Animation
Homecoming Music	Skyhorn
Homecoming Queen	Susan Reichenbaugh
Senior Prom Theme	The Times of Your Life
Senior Prom Music	Saturday
Junior Prom Theme	Cherished Interlude
Junior Prom Music	Aardvark
Thespians	Arms and the Man The Nut Factory
Cheerleading Captain	Susan Reichenbaugh
Drum Major	Kristi Myers and Walt Stine
Falconaire Editor	Melanie Boyer and David Early
Falcon Flash Editor	(poss. Brenda Menges)
Media Editor	Stephanie Hoover

1979 Class Profile

Homecoming Theme	Lost Horizons[6]
Homecoming Music	Orion
Homecoming Queen	Cindy Heisey
Senior Prom Theme	
Senior Prom Music	PUSH
Junior Prom Theme	Only Yesterday
Junior Prom Music	Orion
Thespians	Regarding Electra Dracula
Cheerleading Captain	Natalie Wagner
Featured Twirler	Cindy Heisey
Drum Major	Walt Stine
Falconaire Editor	Jan Engle
Falcon Flash Editor	Tina Taylor
Media Editor	Steve Bobb

---

[5] By this time all plays were being produced by the Thespians and were no longer considered Class Plays even though the yearbooks continued to refer to them as such.

[6] Dance theme was "Don't Let the Sun Go Down on Me"

1980s Class Profiles

1980 Class Profile

Homecoming Theme	A Night at the Movies
Homecoming Queen	Patricia Stare
Senior Prom Theme	Time Passages
Senior Prom Music	High Tide
Junior Prom Theme	New Beginnings Rise Each Dawn
Junior Prom Music	Raz
Thespians	Pillow Talk Dracula
Falcon Mascot	Booster Club Members
Cheerleading Captain	Pam Schug & Terri Frascella
Drum Majors	Steve Euker, Lynn Dunkleburger, and Laurie Petrina
Falconaire Editor	David Leaser
Falcon Flash Editor	Elaine Shizkowski
Media Editor	Brenda Grimm

1981 Class Profile

Homecoming Theme	The Times of Your Life
Homecoming Music	Joe Hojak Trio
Homecoming Queen	Peggy Hoover
Senior Prom Theme	The End is Just the Beginning
Senior Prom Music	Pair-a-dice
Junior Prom Theme	Always and Forever
Thespians	The Miracle Worker Ask Any Girl Pillow Talk
Falcon Mascot	
Cheerleading Captain	Helen Frascella and Linda Crater
Head Majorette	Kimberly Rogers
Drum Major	Madeleine Barrett and Carol Dillon
Falconaire Editor	Patricia Early
Falcon Flash Editor	Cheryl Menges
Media Editor	Ann Snyder

1982 Class Profile

Homecoming Theme	A Salute to Pennsylvania
Homecoming Music	Bondage
Homecoming Queen	Coleen Sieg
Senior Prom Music	Now and Then
Junior Prom Theme	The Best of Times
Junior Prom Music	Breezin'
Thespians	MASH A Murder is Announced
Falcon Mascot	Coleen Sieg
Cheerleading Captain	Lori Engle and Sandy Fasnacht
Head Majorette	Mitzi Swigart
Drum Major	Madeleine Barrett and Carol Dillon
Falconaire Editor	Coleen Sieg and Cindy Cassel
Falcon Flash Editor	Sharon Lyle
Media Editor	Tom Houtz

1983 Class Profile

Homecoming Theme	LD Gives Its Regards to Broadway[1]
Homecoming Music	Class Act
Homecoming Queen	Lisa Kurr
1983 Junior-Senior Prom Theme	Separate Ways
Senior Prom Music	Shark
Junior Prom Theme	Returned to combined proms
Junior Prom Music	Now and Then

[1] Dance theme: A Night on Broadway

Thespians	Cheaper by the Dozen	Prom Music	Direct Drive
Cheerleading Captain	Lisa Hereshko	Senior Prom Queen	Roxanne Hetrick
Head Majorette	Karen Ierley	Senior Prom King	Shaun Smith
Drum Major	Carl Law and Robin Hyde	Junior-Senior Prom Theme, 1984	A Night in Heaven
Falconaire Editor	Karen Bricker and Michelle Holubeck	Junior Prom Music	Maxwell
		Thespians	The Curious Savage
Falcon Flash Editor	Jodie Kramer	Falcon Mascot	Kevin Strawser
Media Editor	Jodie Kramer	Cheerleading Captain	Ann Deeney and P. J. Schan

1984 Class Profile

Homecoming Theme	A Trip Around the World
Homecoming Music	Off the Wall
Homecoming Queen	Tina Agostino
Junior-Senior Prom Theme, 1984	A Night in Heaven
Prom Music	Maxwell
Senior Prom Queen	Christina Schug
Senior Prom King	Craig Wallace
Junior-Senior Prom Theme, 1983	Separate Ways
Junior-Senior Prom Music	Shark
Thespians	The Fall of the House of Usher
Cheerleading Captain	Tina Agostino and Kim Allen
Drum Major	Robin Hyde
Falconaire Editor	Michelle Holubeck
Falcon Flash Editor	Randy Thames
Media Editor	Catherine Clark

Drum Major	Thomas Ball and Kathryn Smee
Falconaire Editor	Brenda Stoner
Falcon Flash Editor	Tammy Cryzer
Media Editor	Venus Klinger

1986 Class Profile

Homecoming Theme	Fairy Tales
Homecoming Music	The Pros
Homecoming Queen	Kimberly Cutler
Junior-Senior Prom Theme, 1986	Almost Paradise
Prom Music	Prime Time
Senior Prom Queen	Lisa Filippelli
Senior Prom King	Kevin Strawser
Junior-Senior Prom Theme, 1985	Take a Look at Us Now
Junior Prom Music	Direct Drive
Thespians	Harvey
Falcon Mascot	Kevin Strawser
Cheerleading Captain	Nikki Henson and Sonya Zearing
Drum Major	Thomas Ball and Kathryn Smee
Falconaire Editor	Deb Holubeck

1985 Class Profile

Homecoming Theme	Decades
Homecoming Queen	April DeMuth
Junior-Senior Prom Theme, 1985	Take a Look at Us Now

1987 Class Profile

Homecoming Theme	Cartoons and Comics
Homecoming Queen	Laurel Hershey
Junior-Senior Prom Theme, 1987	Tropical Getaway
Prom Music	Bill Rivera, DJ
Senior Prom Queen	Laynie Overby
Senior Prom King	Greg Hostetter
Junior-Senior Prom Theme, 1986	Almost Paradise
Prom Music	Prime Time
Thespians	A Night of Three One-Act Plays[2]
Falcon Mascot	Pete Valeri
Cheerleading Captain	Gail Reichenbaugh
Drum Major	Susan Motz and Greg Reinhardt
Falconaire Editor	Lynn Hamann
Falcon Flash Editor	Leslie Price
Media Editor	Matthew Williams

1988 Class Profile

Homecoming Theme	Oldies But Goodies on TV
Homecoming Music	Bill Rivera, DJ
Homecoming Queen	Jenifer Petrina
Junior-Senior Prom Theme, 1988	Sun Splash
Prom Music	Dan Steele, DJ
Junior-Senior Prom Theme, 1987	Tropical Getaway
Prom Music	Bill Rivera, DJ
Thespians	The Crucible
Cheerleading Captain	Tami Swartz and Deb Mehaffey
Drum Major	Wendy Farver and Greg Reinhardt

[2] One was written by student Dwayne Menges

Falconaire Editor	Dawn Singley
Media Editor	Pamela Schwentker

1989 Class Profile

Homecoming Theme	Great Hometown Adventures
Homecoming Music	Michael Gobrecht, DJ
Homecoming Queen	Kira Jones
Homecoming King	Ernie Manders
Junior-Senior Prom Theme, 1989	Bungle in the Jungle
Winter Formal	Michael Gobrecht, DJ
Junior-Senior Prom Theme, 1988	Sun Splash
Junior Prom Music	Dan Steele, DJ
Thespians	Noises Off
Falcon Mascot	Suzanne Bendull
Cheerleading Captain	Janelle Koppenhaver and Dorinda Norton
Drum Major	Wendy Farver and Chip Schell
Falconaire Editor	Christine Gross
Falcon Flash Editor	multiple division editors
Media Editor	Holly Feeney and Rebecca Simmons et al

1990s Class Profiles

1990 Class Profile

Homecoming Theme	Decades
Homecoming Music	Ron Mann, DJ
Homecoming Queen	Jodi Pringle
Homecoming King	Michael Pit
Junior-Senior Prom Theme, 1990[1]	An Everlasting Moment
Senior Prom Queen	Michelle Pheasant
Senior Prom King	Brian Bischof
Junior-Senior Prom Theme, 1989	Bungle in the Jungle
Falcon Mascot	Suzanne Bendull
Cheerleading Captain	Michele Donnelly and Gwen Hollenbush
Drum Major	Chip Schell
Falconaire Editor	Corinne Fink and Kerry McGuinness
Falcon Flash Editor	multiple division editors
Media Editor	Jeremy Fox

1991 Class Profile

Homecoming Theme	A Game of Imaginings
Homecoming Music	Ron Mann, DJ
Homecoming Queen	Michelle Gaudette
Homecoming King	Chris Wallish
Junior-Senior Prom Theme, 1991	Phantoms
Prom Music	Ron Mann, DJ
Senior Prom Queen	Carrianne Elliot
Senior Prom King	Elton Nestler
Junior-Senior Prom Theme, 1990	An Everlasting Moment
Winter Gala Theme	A Night to Remember
Winter Gala Queen	Jen Leib
Winter Gala King	Aaron Joyce
Thespians	Macbeth
Cheerleading Captain	Crystal Funck
Drum Major	Tom Runkle
Falconaire Editor	Christine Cassel and Erin Sokalsky
Falcon Flash Editor	Josh Tison
Media Editor	Carrianne Elliot and Jeremy Fox

1992 Class Profile

Homecoming Theme	Cartoons
Homecoming Music	Allen Norton, DJ
Homecoming Queen	Jennifer Pringle
Homecoming King	Jeremy Kuhlen
Junior-Senior Prom Theme, 1992	Candle on the Water
Senior Prom Queen	Megan Grubb
Senior Prom King	Howard Gorberg
Winter Formal Theme	A Night of Enchantment
Winter Formal Queen	Elizabeth Groves
Winter Formal King	Tim Byerly
Junior-Senior Prom Theme, 1991	Phantoms
Prom Music	Ron Mann, DJ
Thespians	Fahrenheit 451
Falcon Mascot	Justin Hugill
Cheerleading Captain	Tonya Meko, Katherine Klinger and Carrie Stahl
Drum Major	Tom Runkle and Jen Cunningham
Falconaire Editor	Tracy Gross and Dania Pazakis
Falcon Flash Editor	multiple division editors
Media Editor	Beth Grant and Heather Kohler

[1] This class held the first official school Graduation Party sponsored by the LD Care Club

1993 Class Profile

Homecoming Theme	Around the World
Homecoming Queen	Kim Andrasik
Homecoming King	Brett Lovelidge
Junior-Senior Prom Theme, 1993	The Sea of Love
Senior Prom Queen	Lindsee Bowen
Senior Prom King	Kevin Dillon
Junior-Senior Prom Theme, 1992	Candle on the Water
Thespians	Our Town
Cheerleading Captain	Andrea Leilli and Heidi Gray
Drum Major	Tish Saner
Falconaire Editor	Andria Zaia and Jill Trenn
Falcon Flash Editor	Brian Fox
Media Editor	multiple division editors

1994 Class Profile

Homecoming Theme	Music Styles
Homecoming Queen	Jennifer Jones
Homecoming King	Jason DeHart
Junior-Senior Prom Theme, 1994	Just for Tonight
Senior Prom Queen	Deanna Africa
Senior Prom King	Ed Gnall
Winter Formal Queen	Allison Collins
Winter Formal King	Ed Slatt
Junior-Senior Prom Theme, 1993	Around the World
Thespians	Arsenic and Old Lace
Cheerleading Captain	Destinie Smertnick and Michelle Shaffer
Drum Major	Sean Devine and Kerry McKeever
Falconaire Editor	Stephany Espenshade
Falcon Flash Editor	editors of individual issues
Media Editor	Michael Darowish

1995 Class Profile

Homecoming Theme	Disney Movies
Homecoming Queen	Leslie Miller
Homecoming King	Anthony Pazakis
Senior Prom Theme	A Time Soon Forgotten
Prom Music	Pablo, DJ
Senior Prom Queen	Rosina Spitler
Senior Prom King	Buddy Long
Junior Prom Theme,	Just For Tonight
Prom Music	Pablo, DJ
Falcon Mascot	Samantha Barnhart/ Jessica Whitcomb
Cheerleading Captain	Jessica Whitcomb and Carrie Champ
Drum Major	Keri McKeever and Julie Garner
Falconaire Editor	Jennifer Wolfe and Lori Knackstedt
Falcon Flash Editor	Anita Ketty
Media Editor	multiple division editors

1996 Class Profile

Homecoming Queen	Kristi Templin
Homecoming King	Dave Hoopes
Junior-Senior Prom Theme, 1996	Wonderful Tonight
Prom Music	Scott Mateer
Senior Prom Queen	Heather Rhoad
Senior Prom King	Brad or Brett Lechleitner
Junior-Senior Prom Theme, 1995	A Time Soon Forgotten
Prom Music	Pablo, DJ
Thespians	Steel Magnolia The Boys Next Door
Falcon Mascot	Samantha Barnhart
Drum Major	Kent Pierce and Chris Rutt

Falconaire Editor	Shanna Plouse	Falcon Mascot	Samantha Carnathan
Falcon Flash Editor	division editors	Cheerleading Captain	Jennifer Harvey
Media Editor	Gretchen Haupt and Lisa Black	Drum Major	Kent Pierce
		Falconaire Editor	Tony Frascella
		Falcon Flash Editor	Meagan Gold and Abigail Martin
		Media Editor	Jennifer Sheaffer and Jessica Ordich

1997 Class Profile

Homecoming Theme	One Moment in Time
Homecoming Queen	Cara Byerly
Homecoming King	Forrest Carlough
Junior-Senior Prom Theme, 1997	The Dance
Senior Prom Queen	Dawn Bedeaux
Senior Prom King	John Heistenrether
Junior-Senior Prom Theme, 1996	Wonderful Tonight
Prom Music	Scott Mateer
Thespians	Love and Kisses
Drum Major	Chris Rutt and Kent Pierce
Falconaire Editor	Michael McBeth and Jaime Bolen
Falcon Flash Editor	Abby Martin
Media Editor	Katie Wigdahl

1998 Class Profile

Homecoming Theme	Á Paris
Homecoming Queen	Rhea Graber
Homecoming King	Matt Bolton
Junior-Senior Prom Theme, 1998	Time After Time
Prom Music	Mixed Impressions
Senior Prom Queen	Natalie True
Senior Prom King	Al Lundy
Winterfest[2]	
Junior-Senior Prom Theme, 1997	The Dance
Thespians	Desire

1999 Class Profile

Homecoming Theme	Tropical Nights
Homecoming Queen	Brandy Espenshade
Homecoming King	Cody Ebersole
Junior-Senior Prom Theme, 1999	I Will Remember You
Prom Music	Digital DJ
Senior Prom Queen	Gabby Page
Senior Prom King	Jarrad Sipe
Junior-Senior Prom Theme, 1998	Time After Time
Prom Music	Mixed Impressions
Thespians	Anne Frank and Me
Falcon Mascot	Samantha Carnathan
Cheerleading Captain	Brandy Heckman and Cori Grierson
Drum Major	Lindsey Eide and Tess Price
Falconaire Editor	Sarah McCloskey and Brandy Heckman
Falcon Flash Editor	Megan Gold
Media Editor	Jessica Ordich

---

[2] This is Winterfest's first year as an event, not a dance

2000 Class Profile

Homecoming Theme	An Enchanted Evening
Homecoming Queen	Jena Fulton
Homecoming King	Tyler Edmundson
Junior-Senior Prom Theme, 2000	The Time of Your Life
Senior Prom Queen	Sommer Costabile
Senior Prom King	Chris O'Brien
Junior-Senior Prom Theme, 1999	I Will Remember You
Prom Music	Digital DJ
Falcon Mascot	Samanthan Carnathan
Cheerleading Captain	Jill Raffensberger
Falconaire Editor	Tracy Thorpe

2001 Class Profile

Homecoming Theme	Reflections of Time
Homecoming Queen	Kellie Kulina
Homecoming King	Justin Schildt
Junior-Senior Prom Theme, 2001	Mardi Gras
Prom Music	Soundwave
Senior Prom Queen	Nicole Zarefoss
Senior Prom King	Sam Naples
Junior-Senior Prom Theme, 2000	The Time of Your Life
Thespians	The Odd Couple
Falcon Mascot	Allen Kliss and Jessie Lininger
Cheerleading Captain	Kate Spaulding, Kara Swank, and Tera McCorkel
Drum Major	Jen Turgeon
Falconaire Editor	Samantha Carnathan
Falcon Flash Editor	Lindsey Johnson and Charissa Jelliff
Media Editor	Liz Melly

2002 Class Profile

Homecoming Theme	Treasures Under the Sea
Homecoming Queen	Rachel Daubert
Homecoming King	Dan Sassani
Junior-Senior Prom Theme, 2002	A Night Under the Rising Sun
Prom Music	DJ Rico
Senior Prom Queen	Missy Colter
Senior Prom King	Steve Hilbert
Junior-Senior Prom Theme, 2001	Mardi Gras
Prom Music	Sound Wave
Thespians	Murder by the Book
Cheerleading Captain	Beth Smolick, Caitie Stoehr and Renee Hyde
Drum Major	Brandon Anthony
Falconaire Editor	Sara Marian Seibert
Media Editor	Ann Zaino and Abby Snyder

2003 Class Profile

Homecoming Theme	A Moonlight Chariot Ride
Homecoming Queen	Jackie Barton
Homecoming King	Mike Podrasky
Junior-Senior Prom Theme, 2003	A Night Among the Stars
Senior Prom Queen	Alicia Cain
Senior Prom King	Brenton Haldeman
Junior-Senior Prom Theme, 2002	A Night Under the Rising Sun
Thespians	The Scarlet Letter
Cheerleading Captain	Lisa Green, Megan Stine, Nikke Kametz
Falconaire Editor	Tara Russo

2004 Class Profile

Homecoming Theme	A Cruise to Tropical Paradise
Homecoming Queen	Laura Seesholtz
Homecoming King	Carson Parr
Junior-Senior Prom Theme, 2004	Caught in a Dream
Senior Prom Queen	Nicole Wolfe
Senior Prom King	Derrick Halbleib
Junior-Senior Prom Theme, 2003	A Night Among the Stars
Prom Music	Soundwave
Thespians	Blythe Spirit
Cheerleading Captain	Hollyn Harner
Falconaire Editor	Roberta Murray and Michelle O'Donnell
Media Editor	Amanda Leer and Caitlin Downs

2005 Class Profile

Homecoming Theme[1]	Journey Around the World
Homecoming Queen	Laura Dupler
Homecoming King	Alex Sharkey
Junior-Senior Prom Theme, 2005	Midnight Masquerade
Prom Music	Soundwave
Senior Prom Queen	Kaitlin Santanna
Senior Prom King	Ryan Bowe
Junior-Senior Prom Theme, 2004	Caught in a Dream
Prom Music	Soundwave
Thespians	Jane Eyre
Cheerleading Captain	Jillian Perry
Falconaire Editor	Maggie Boyd and Nina Landis
Falcon Flash Editor	Andrew Sorgi, Tyler Angeloff and Kaitlin Santanna
Media Editor	Sarah Joyce

[1] Dance theme: Dancing in the Moonlight

2006 Class Profile

Homecoming Theme	Dancing Through the Decades
Homecoming Queen	Alexis Graham
Homecoming King	Tucker Berry
Junior-Senior Prom Theme, 2006	Classic Hollywood
Senior Prom Queen	Danielle Cordero
Senior Prom King	Justin Mack
Junior-Senior Prom Theme, 2005	Midnight Masquerade
Prom Music	Soundwave
Thespians	The Comet of St. Loomis
Cheerleading Captain	Joann Marshbank
Falconaire Editor	Becca Snyder
Media Editor	Laura Bierbower

2007 Class Profile

Homecoming Theme	Escape to the Far East
Homecoming Music	DJ
Homecoming Queen	Bryn Stevens
Homecoming King	Kevin Gearhart
Junior-Senior Prom Theme, 2007	A Starry Night in Paris
Senior Prom Music	Mixed Impressions
Senior Prom Queen	Melissa Reese
Senior Prom King	John Gacesa
Junior-Senior Prom Theme, 2006	Classic Hollywood
Thespians	Several One-Act Plays
Falcon Mascot	Mike Reese
Falconaire Editor	Megan Chirdon and Melissa Olson
Falcon Flash Editor	Chelsea White
Media Editor	Laura Bierbower

2008 Class Profile

Homecoming Theme	Party in Atlantis
Homecoming Music	Hot 92 DJ
Homecoming Queen	Kari Skitka
Homecoming King	William McGee
Junior-Senior Prom Theme, 2008	Arabian Nights
Senior Prom Queen	Chelsea Miller
Senior Prom King	John Wolgemuth
Junior-Senior Prom Theme, 2007	Escape to the Far East
Thespians	The Shadow Box
Winter Semi-Formal	Snowball Dance DJ, Freez
Falcon Mascot	Mike Reese
Cheerleading Captain	Abby McCann
Falconaire Editor	Kari Skitka and Sara Angle
Falcon Flash Editor	Jordan Costik
Media Editor	Laura Bierbower

2009 Class Profile

Homecoming Theme	Sweet Escape
Homecoming Queen	Marissa Goss
Homecoming King	Jared Bausch
Junior-Senior Prom Theme, 2009	Masquerade Ball
Prom Music	Hot 92
Senior Prom Queen	Sarah Labe
Senior Prom King	Nathan Kenyon
Junior-Senior Prom Theme, 2008	Arabian Nights
Thespians	A Midsummer Night's Dream
Falconaire Editor	Maura Sharkey and Marissa Goss
Falcon Flash Editor	Shawn Christ and Mike Hoffman
Media Editor	no publication this year

2010 Class Profile

Homecoming Theme	The Golden Years
Homecoming Music	Scott Payonk, DJ
Homecoming Queen	Dominique Zegretti
Homecoming King	Brandon Desrosiers
Junior-Senior Prom Theme, 2010	NYC: Big Lights, Big City
Prom Music	Intention or DJs Scooter and Puff
Senior Prom Queen	Kristina Sheibley
Senior Prom King	Joshua Miller
Junior-Senior Prom Theme, 2009	Masquerade
Prom Music	Hot 92, DJ "Scooter"
Thespians	The Visit
Falcon Mascot	Jon Tirado
Cheerleading Captain	Maeve Wilson, Alexis Barge, Angela Olson
Drum Major	Will Thompson
Falconaire Editor	Erin Cooney and Ellyn Hefflefinger
Falcon Flash Editor	Ashley Errickson
Media Editor	Chris Pearson

Class Reflections

This section is designed for each class to reflect, remember, and reminisce about the years the class members spent together in Lower Dauphin High School. Slightly more than half (54%) of the classes are represented here. As might be expected, the classes that were graduated in the 1960s responded in full force, with every class herein represented. We had a sixty percent actual response from the classes who were graduated in the 1970s and sixty percent of the classes from the 1980s heeded our call by writing remembrances, suggesting that interest in one's past generally begins to increase as persons reach the age of 40. Predictably, those who were graduated during the last twenty years of the first fifty years of Lower Dauphin High School were the least responsive to our request with four classes from the 1990s (and three of them from the earliest dates of 1990, 1991, and 1992) and only one from the 2000s classes showing an interest in recording its history for this publication.

No parameters of style or length were imposed on those who volunteered to speak about their classes. We asked only that the author (or a committee of writers, if they so chose) reflect on what it was that gave each class its own personality, its memories, its place in history, or its regrets. One of the most satisfying parts of compiling this fifty-year record is this collection of history written by those who lived it.

Reflections from the Class of 1961

William H. Calhoon, Jr.

The class of 1961 approached our senior year at Lower Dauphin with a lot of mixed emotions. At least some of us who had attended Hummelstown High School for 5 years felt a bit cheated or resentful. We were not going to be allowed the traditional senior class trip to Washington, D.C., we had not been allowed to carry-over any of our class funds, and we had not been given any say on the colors or mascot for the new school. No doubt those from all of the other districts shared some of these feelings as well.

At the same time there was the excitement of the new school with larger and better facilities and courses and activities not offered at Hummelstown High. Of course we also wondered about how all of us from the different districts would blend together and who our new friends might be.

While we didn't get to pick the mascot or colors it was neat having the same colors and mascot as the almost brand new Air Force Academy. And when Lower Dauphin obtained its own Falcon missile that was really cool. What really stands out though is that we all wanted to make it our school regardless of former rivalries or loyalties. We all made many new acquaintances and friends, we forged a FALCON spirit and of, course, the football team set a high standard of athletic accomplishment for all the teams that would follow.

By the end of the year the negative feelings had all given way to feeling that we had been very fortunate to have had all the opportunities of a new school.

Reflections from the Class of 1962

Carole Jane (Janie) Baker Wenrich

Once upon a time there was—and still is—a group of people who were classmates at Lower Dauphin High School. Some of us have known each other all of our school days beginning in first grade with Mrs. Emma Horner and Mrs. Sara Jane Seavers. Those of us who grew up in Hummelstown and its special closeness helped us to feel comfortable going into a jointure of many called Lower Dauphin High School.

As I look back, there were many new friendships developed with the students coming from the townships. There were bittersweet times at school as life can be for all of us, such as not doing well on a test, and losing a football game was the pits, especially if the other team happened to be Hershey. The different activities, clubs, and the wonderful Pep Rallies before the football games were awesome.

I remember it was really cool being friends with the principal's son and having his presence in homeroom. Also it was fun having a really neat guy in our classes who enjoyed dressing and wearing his hair as Elvis Presley styled his hair. Even though we girls liked this, our principal frowned on the impersonation very much.

I also remember two classmates and I stayed at my home overnight before a class trip coming up the next day and we decided we were going to lighten our hair. We went to the local drugstore and purchased hydrogen peroxide and went back to my home and after my parents were asleep we dumped the peroxide full strength on our hair. The next day two of us had orange hair but, because Janice was already a blonde, her hair lightened. We went on our class trip with our new hair colors! Yuck!

I met my husband Barry at LDHS and we were sweethearts for 44 years until his untimely passing on December 14, 2008. We were so young and looking forward to our new horizons when we became graduates of a really wonderful school and I have many fond memories.

Some of us have made lifetime friends in our school classmates and those friends are very cherished. The experience of my journey at Lower Dauphin High School was fantastic, living in Hummelstown has been a lifetime of happiness for me. RAH, RAH! Class of 1962!

Reflections from the Class of 1963

Michael Shifflet

To reflect back to what Lower Dauphin and the Class of '63 meant to me would be difficult without including Hummelstown. Being raised in Hummelstown was a great benefit to all who had the privilege of being part of this unique little community. The importance of Hummelstown and Lower Dauphin cannot be valued enough. In this day and age everyone talks about how "it takes a village to raise a child." Hummelstown was and to this day is just such a village.

I will always appreciate what Lower Dauphin, Hummelstown, and the people of the town did for me, people such as Robert Shaffer, Tony Orsini, and Meatball Evans, who were my first coaches. They taught not only the skills of the game but character as well. Every parent in Hummelstown looked after all the kids, not just their own. There is pride in Hummelstown, not just in the sports teams, or the school but in all the people of the town. This carried over to Lower Dauphin.

Unless you grew up in Hummelstown you wouldn't understand. Friends of mine, from other places, including Hershey, don't understand the uniqueness of this little town. Everyone in Hummelstown is appreciated and respected. As I get older, the respect for Hummelstown and the people grows stronger. I believe this pride and respect carried over to Lower Dauphin.

The beginning of Lower Dauphin wasn't easy. Five different areas were merged into one. The first football game, against Cumberland Valley, was played before school opened in mid-September. The starting team was all from Hummelstown, except for Glenn Ebersole. There were nine seniors, one junior and me, a 15-year-old sophomore. I remember the beginning of the season, Dick Summy, who was a friend of mine, couldn't play football anymore. So, I, the lonely sophomore, was moved to the quarterback position one week before that first game. I was accepted by all the seniors and the junior, George Emerich. I remember the first game as we scored on the last play of the game to win. Center Harry Menear called a quarter back sneak, and that was the winning play.[1] Way to go, Harry!

We went on to win the first CAC Championship for the new school, Lower Dauphin. It was so great seeing all those guys at the get-together in October 2009, as there is a very special bond between the guys on that first year championship team. I often tell people, if I could live one year of my life over it would be the first year at LD.

That first year was also difficult at times, but very rewarding. In a new school with students from Hummelstown, Hershey, and Middletown there was bound to be problems and differences of opinion. I remember seeing all the various school jackets being worn in the hallways and none for the school we were attending. That would soon change as we received our varsity jackets. We were all very proud of those jackets. Carl Espenshade actually wore his CAC Championship 1960 jacket to the reunion this year. Way to go, Carl! It was a tribute to all the students, teachers and administrators that the school functioned so well that first year.

Many of my friends were older because of my participation in the different athletic teams. Barry Broadwater, Tom Shaffer, and George Emerich were among my teammates. All the seniors on the football team and many people earlier in Hummelstown such as Dick Diebler, Pete Wagner, Craig Heister, Jerry Smith, and Rod Miller were people I remember from Hummelstown and Lower Dauphin. Lukey Warble and Jim Shearer were two good friends. Jim came to LD his junior year.

Elaine Harris wrote the words for the Alma Mater, what a tribute this is to the Class of '63 and Elaine. I remember Bob Gibble and Fred Shope, who sent a rocket in the air. They were always involved in science activities. Other classmates I remember are Galen and Jay Kopp, Sue and Linda McGarvey, Nancy Topping, and Joyce Keener.

There were many teachers who influenced me and other students. Bill Peck, who took some of us to Penn State to see a football game, is one such teacher. He kept talking about how beautiful the leaves are in the fall, and we still joke about it. I remember well the benefit basketball game for Mr. Peck several years later. Seeing him on a hospital bed watching the game was very hard for everyone in attendance. How sad to see such a young, remarkable man lying on a hospital bed. Mr. Peck had cancer and died soon thereafter, and was greatly missed by faculty and students alike. Joe Schan, the Staninski twins, Dennis Musket, Janet Ausmus, and Doug Stauffer had a great influence on me personally and educationally. I really felt they cared about me and all the students. We were not just

---

[1] Author's note: What Mike has not said it that it was he who made that touchdown, the first touchdown ever made by a Lower Dauphin football team.

a face to the teachers at LD. Coach Frank Capitani and Ben McClure also were very influential in my life.

I remember Isaiah Bomboy, Guidance Counselor, coming to Hummelstown High to help me with my schedule for the following year at LD. I kept asking him, "How many study halls does that give me?" He said to me, "You are not majoring in study halls." I took the easiest courses possible my sophomore year at LD. Mr. Bomboy and Miss Bowen would not allow me to continue with this schedule my junior year. I remember trying to get out of taking College Prep courses. Thanks to Mr. Bomboy and my parents for not allowing me to take the easy way out. Today, I think most schools and parents would allow the student to take the easy way out. If these people would have let me continue the way I was heading I would never have been prepared to go to college.

I still remember that conversation with Mr. Bomboy who said, "You can do the work if you apply yourself." I went home and told my parents what my guidance counselor had told me. They scheduled an appointment with Mr. Bomboy to get me out of College Prep Courses, or so I thought. I went home from school after the meeting and my parents' comment to me was "you can do the work if you apply yourself." Boy, was I surprised. If my parents and Mr. Bomboy would have listened to me I would not have gone to college or now have a Master's Degree. To them and everybody at Lower Dauphin and Hummelstown, I will always be grateful.

Reflections from the Class of 1964

Kathleen Convery

The year is 1960 and a new school is about to open in Hummelstown. Not only was the school new but the students were coming from very small schools to this large school with all new teachers and classmates. Oh, my, what an opening day on September 12, 1960, a cool, dreary day as we head to this new, overwhelmingly large school. Karen (Fair) Smith remembers being extremely nervous her first day. Karen had never ridden a school bus or eaten in a school cafeteria and all these classmates were strangers. Karen's years at LD turned into a good experience and she graduated as valedictorian of her class in 1964.

Harry Nusser remembers his first day and getting lost trying to find the rooms he was supposed to be in for his classes. Harry ended up having science class twice that day with the same teacher, Miss Young, he had had for science at Londonderry Elementary for seventh and eighth grades. Harry's most vivid memory of the first days at Lower Dauphin was the mad dash to the cafeteria, trying not to be at the end of the line.

Dale Broadwater believes that the first two or three years the loyalties to the township schools were hard to break. There was no union between and among the various segments of students. Additionally, Dale felt the friction between different sports during the same season, e. g., basketball and wrestling. However, by the fall of 1963, we were "THE SENIORS," and we had attended no other high school than LD. Finally, loyalties to neighboring schools no longer existed; we were "The Lower Dauphin Falcons." We were one in spirit. The class of '64 was now the leader of the student body and Dale remembers a united student body supporting all activities. Basketball players went to Thursday night wrestling matches and wrestlers went to Friday night basketball games.

Whether it was a play, musical, or sporting event the student body participated 100%. We wore old hats, brought drums, pans, and lids and Jeff Engle brought an old truck horn with a portable battery to sound off at sporting events. We had a cheering section that no school could rival and the cheering section made the pages of the year book.

Stu Wagner remembers lying under the wrestling mat trying to lose weight before the match and the two-a-day football practices before football season. Stu really feels it was the jocks, the students, and the support of the school that brought us all together as one. Stu has noted that he is glad that Lower Dauphin was the start of his adult life and he was very blessed.

Randy Kahler's thoughts are much like Dale Broadwater's. Dale and Randy were our only class presidents through the four years at LD. Dale for our freshman and junior years and Randy our sophomore and senior years. In his remarks at Commencement Randy noted that we were the first to experience four years at Lower Dauphin and that not having an experience at Hummelstown or Hershey allowed us to bond easier as a class and accept each other more readily.

When Randy attended the reunion for the 50th year of the 1960 Championship football team, the team members spoke of how close they had become as teammates that season (Randy was the only freshman on the varsity team) and how that championship season had given the school an identity as Lower Dauphin, bringing the school closer together even after the season ended.

Randy recalls three events from that season that really identified us as Lower Dauphin Falcons. The first was that the opening of school had been delayed one week; therefore, we played our first game before there was a Lower Dauphin High School. We beat Cumberland Valley in our first game (7-0) and everyone talked about the game that first week of school.

The second was during one of the football practices when the team broke the huddle and someone said "Go dogs" in reference to Hummelstown High bulldogs. Coach Osevala stopped everyone and told the team we were not the "dogs" or the Hershey Trojans but we were the "Falcons." From that moment on there were no more references to Hummelstown or Hershey.

The last event was in the locker room before the game with Hershey when Glenn Ebersole challenged the team to beat Hershey. Glenn had lettered in football at Hershey the previous year and brought his letter to the locker room where he placed it on the wall. He told the team if they destroyed Hershey the Falcons could destroy the letter, or words to that effect. We beat Hershey and the letter was destroyed immediately following the game. Later, Glenn took Randy aside and taught him a standup escape, a wrestling move that Randy used throughout his entire wrestling career, competing at the state championships in State College

Three years later Ted Klinger and Randy were talking with some of the teachers who remarked how little school spirit there was. Ted and Randy quietly decided to prove them wrong. They found some paper and paint then went to Randy's basement and made spirit signs which they hung in the school later that night. The next morning Randy and Ted were called to the principal's office where Mr. Taylor thanked them and said he wanted to keep the signs positive and in appropriate places. This was the beginning of the cheering section that Dale Broadwater referred to above.

Glenn Koons remembers Mr. Capitani in ninth grade gym the day the USSR sent a man into space. Glenn said that "Old Cap" made them line up in formation and march around the gym while Cap made a speech to his "troops" that he didn't believe the "Ruskies" were capable of doing such a thing and this was just propaganda. Glenn also remembers being back stage for the fall sports assembly when Mr. Taylor announced that JFK had been shot. Glenn went out the back stage door, jumped in his car and went home. He was just so stunned at what had just happened, as was the whole student body. Our classmates were in shock for days as we tried to comprehend what had taken place.

Glenn also remembers several of the teachers, among them Miss Strite. He feels some of the advice that Miss Strite gave to the students, about the work place and business, rang very true throughout his life. Glenn also felt that most students did not give Miss Strite the credit she was due, as she was a much greater teacher than many students realized. Glenn also recalls Mr. Leslie Taylor with fondness. Mr. Taylor was an avid hockey fan. Glenn worked at the Hershey arena. After a game one of the Bears players gave Glenn a hockey puck, which in turn Glenn gave to Mr. Taylor the next day at school. That puck remained on Mr. Taylor's desk as a paperweight until he retired.

Many teachers have left permanent impressions on all of us and Ellie (Kauffman) Fields will remember Mrs. Judith Ball, now Dr. Witmer. Ellie lived for English class with Dr. Witmer her freshman year at LD. Dr. Witmer encouraged Ellie to read books that were at a college level, and because of this influence Ellie is today a published poet. Even now if a book that Ellie is reading doesn't have an exquisite vocabulary, she finds that it does not hold her interest.

Miss Xanthopoulous, who had a different pair of glasses for every outfit she wore, was another teacher that Ellie was fond of, remembering how Miss Xanthopoulous would sit on the heaters and yell "People" to get our attention. Miss Xanthopoulous encouraged Ellie to think broadly. Ellie also mentioned Miss Ausmus, who was very enthusiastic about Latin and French. Then there was Senor Murdocca, who kept our fantasies alive and well. To this day Ellie still studies Spanish and takes her Biblica Espanol to church, because she believes the Scriptures in Spanish are much richer and provide a fresh understanding.

I fondly remember my years at LD. The teacher who had an influence on my life was Mrs. Ball (Dr. Judith Witmer). During my working years when I was asked to write technique books and flyers, my knowledge of English grammar helped tremendously. Another class that I have found very helpful was public speaking. Throughout my career I have been asked to conduct classes and seminars and being able to speak with assurance in front of others is very rewarding and gratifying.

My most difficult memory occurred just recently when I returned to LD and found out that one could no longer just walk into the school during the day; you have to be buzzed in through the front door near the office. How times have changed.

Randy Kahler remembers having four student Commencement speakers, no adults. Randy, as Class President, gave the opening remarks and three other students were also asked to speak including George Chellew, Karen Fair, and Joann Kettering. There was no announcement of a valedictorian or salutatorian. When Randy asked why, he was informed that our principal did not believe that it was fair and preferred that the three students with the highest grade point average be given the opportunity to speak.

Most of us in the class of 1964 are enjoying our retirement years and our experiences and memories are just a fleeting thought every now and then. Lower Dauphin will always be a place for memories, and relationships from a time some 50 years ago and as Stu Wagner said, "I think we are all very grateful for our years at Lower Dauphin." The Class of 1964 Remembers.

Reflections from the Class of 1965

Wade Seibert, Jean Deimler Seibert, Carolyn Sandel Anderson, and Clayton "Bo" Smith
(Edited by Ann Landis Kopp, Susan Petrina, Margie Park Cassel, Russel Cassel, and Mike Skinner)

The Class of 1965 has many memories; some are associated with Lower Dauphin, but others relate to life in the 1950s and 1960s. Born during the period of 1947 through January 1948, members of the Class of 1965 epitomize the Baby Boomers. With World War II over, our parents went back to work, bought homes, and created families. The Class was born into an era when many significant changes occurred in our lives and our families, as well as in the area and country. We were instilled with an attitude of great pride and love for our country because of the sacrifices of the "Greatest Generation" and an optimism that anything was possible if you worked hard and played fair.

One very important milestone was that on a rainy September 12, 1960, we found ourselves as 320 eighth graders at a brand new junior-senior high school. We came from four townships and a borough as well as a local parochial school, but quickly we became one as a class with spirit and commitment. The dances, musicals, plays, clubs, sports—and even time during cafeteria and study halls—gave us opportunities to develop friendships that have endured for 50 years. None of us could participate in every activity—but we learned to cheer and applaud and praise each other, as well as the members of other classes who were Falcons, as well. The combination of our rural and small town backgrounds, as well as our ages when we came together at Lower Dauphin, had a great bonding effect.

In our Senior Year, we staged the play, "The Skin of Our Teeth." Our prom was at the Colonial Country Club and featured a Southern Nights theme. That year our school won the Spirit Competition staged by a local radio station and we were awarded with a free dance. It was the first year that field hockey was recognized as a varsity sport at Lower Dauphin. We had wrestlers who made it to states. We were the only high school class to have three co-valedictorians. And we sold bubble bath as a fund raiser!

As for the period, there is much to remember as well. We were the generation who grew up with television. We grieved the death of President Kennedy. We eventually went to war with Vietnam. We were raised to have opinions and we let them be known. We had the draft and the lottery numbers—but they were for military duty and not for professional sports or fortune. And yet, we fell in love, drove too fast, and could dance the night away.

What Our World Was Like. *Life, Look,* and *Post* magazines chronicled our country and our world. Prior to computers and the Internet, magazine photographs and the articles informed us of the issues of the times, the events of the past, and the predictions of the future. Lyndon Johnson was our President and he oversaw a divisive war and new social programs for the elderly, minorities, and poor. Changes occurred all around us. For the first time, it was accepted that female as well as male high school graduates could continue their education beyond high school and become professionals or owners of their own businesses. We were a split generation. We had early influence of the fifties (e.g., know your place, wait your turn, be respectful of your elders), but lived in the sixties world where we had the opportunity to challenge the status quo and the world. It was truly a culture shock for some of us.

What We Valued. We loved our grandparents, many of whom moved from other parts of the state in order to provide better lives for their families. We revered "the new" and avoided "the old." We were raised to value change. We wanted to be different, we wanted to be recognized. There was optimism in America, and the desire to provide opportunities for all people. We were part of that culture—even if we did not know it at the time.

How We Lived. Our class was one of the first to attend modern elementary schools, but many of us started our education in one room school houses scattered throughout the school district. Many classmates still lived on family farms, but others lived in new housing developments that encircled Hummelstown. Still others lived in small towns of Grantville, Shellsville, Union Deposit, Hoernerstown, Sand Beach, and Deodate. Our homes had new televisions (colored televisions and stereos were items we all coveted), kitchen appliances, stereos, and living room suites when our families could afford them. Favorite colors were turquoise, burgundy, and pink in the 1950s and gold, avocado green, brown, and orange in the 1960s.

How We Learned. The administrators and School Board Directors were all men, with the exception of Director Mrs. Anna Staver. Our teachers either came from the former Hummelstown High School where they had taught for years or were recently graduated from colleges and eager to start their professions. We were attracted to the young teachers because of their enthusiasm, but we respected the senior faculty because of their experience. We used slide rules rather than calculators. We used manual, and in some cases, portable typewriters, rather than word processors. Researching a paper required manually looking in the card catalogue and using thick reference books. These sources were not available to us online. Spell check to us was looking up words in the dictionary. Boys had shop and girls took home economics. Audio-visual equipment was scarce and archaic compared to today. Cell phones did not exist—but there was a pay phone in the school lobby. We thought we were cool because we had a crystal ball suspending from the cafeteria ceiling.

What We Wore. Prom gowns, madras outfits, penny loafers, tennis sweaters, khaki slacks, and blue oxford shirts were bought at stores like Hauer's, Hostetter's, Pomeroy's, and Bowman's. Boat neck shirts, clam diggers, and spades with Cuban heels were worn by some to be cool. Other outfits that were important included letter sweaters and, sadly, military uniforms because of Vietnam. Girls' hemlines began to rise. Men wore cologne like Brut and English Leather and they carried combs. Women wore charm bracelets, engraved circle pins, and had bouffant hairdos. The hair dryer and hairspray were so important. The arrival of our gold class rings was a key event. Clearasil was a staple.

What We Bought. We loved chips and pretzels purchased in cans. Milk was still delivered to one's house. But new items foretold an era of convenience in cooking including instant tea, Tang, cake mixes, fluoride toothpaste, macaroni and cheese in a box, and pizza! Other new products were aluminum foil and deodorants in aerosol cans.

What We Drove. Gasoline was twenty-five cents a gallon. Cars were our passion, because they allowed us to leave, if only for a little while. It did not matter what the vehicle looked like, as long as it worked. The school parking lot was filled with cars, both new and old, including the Volkswagen Beetle, convertibles, farm trucks, a turquoise Thunderbird, a 1947 Mercury coupe and even, in some cases, the family vehicle. We anticipated being 16 so we could drive—passing our driver's test on Herr Street in Harrisburg.

Where We Went. The Class of 1965 entertained itself with visits to Hershey Park, Mt. Gretna, the Pennsylvania Grand Canyon, Gettysburg, Washington, DC, and the World's Fair in New York. The "rebels" cruised the Front Street-Second Street Circuit in Harrisburg in any car that sounded "hot." After the cruise, Bar-be-que Cottage or Dave's Dream was the final destination to hang out. We attended football games, wrestling matches, sock hops, and the fire hall dances. We drove to drive-in theatres. We ate at the Hob Nob, Towne and Country Restaurant, and enjoyed a lemon blend at the Rhoads Drug Store counter. We went to the area's first McDonald's restaurant on Progress Avenue in Harrisburg.

What Entertained Us. Television was our window to the world. Rock and Roll music had to be blaring! Portable radios were carried by everyone. The telephone allowed us to talk to each other. We loved the Beatles and also musical groups like the Temptations, the Beach Boys, the Rolling Stones, and the Supremes. We played Monopoly, Parcheesi, Scrabble, and Pinochle. As kids we had dolls, trains, paint-by-number pictures, and baseball cards—often purchased at Smith's Hardware Store or the Hershey Department Store. We watched Dick Clark's American Bandstand, Johnny Carson, and sports events on Channel 8.

Our class motto is "It is better to have tried and failed, than never to have tried at all." The theme seemed to mirror lives at that time, as well as the mood of the 1960s in America. And yet, the Class of 1965 is also known to this day as a class that retains an enduring spirit that comes from a journey that started on September 12, 1960.

Reflections from the Class of 1966

Martha ("Marty") Wrzesniewski Bossler and Beverly ("Beaver") Walmer Wyld

On a dreary September morning in 1960 what seemed to be a huge yellow bus wound its way around the wings of the new Lower Dauphin Junior-Senior High School campus. Students from five neighboring school districts were merging into one student body.

As we came through the doors at the E-wing entrance that morning, we scurried about, amid the chaos of a choir of voices shouting greetings to old friends and new. With the slamming of our new locker doors, the noise level reached a fever pitch. While trying to find our homerooms, we were asking, "Where do we go, what time is our first class and how do we get there?" So many questions and one that went unanswered was "What the heck is an Audion?"

Our class was going to be the first to attend Lower Dauphin from seventh grade through twelfth grade. This was a distinction we wore proudly. As seventh graders we thought that we were "all that and a bag of chips" until we learned we were at the bottom of the food chain. The eighth and ninth graders made sure we knew who was in charge. It didn't take long until we realized it wasn't us!

We were children born in the late forties to parents of the Greatest Generation. We were among the first wave of Baby Boomers. We grew up during the Cold War era, we played outside, rode our bikes without helmets, held our hand over our heart when we pledged our allegiance and bowed our heads during the morning prayer. We mastered the Dewey Decimal System, rode in cars without seatbelts, and our single black and white television at home had only three channels.

At the end of our first day of school we headed home, either by foot or on that big yellow bus, listening to Elvis sing "It's Now or Never" or Chubby Checker's "The Twist" on our transistor radios. We couldn't get home fast enough to watch American Bandstand.

Seventh grade was the start of a transition, changing boys and girls into young men and women. We watched the Pittsburgh Pirates win the World Series and witnessed the election of America's first

Catholic President. As a class, we watched America enter the manned space race when Alan Shepard completed the first sub-orbital flight. By the end of seventh grade, we had lived with the fear of war during the failed Bay of Pigs Invasion in Cuba and saw the founding of the Peace Corps. It was a busy, scary, but exciting, year.

Entering eighth grade, we were singing Bobby Vee's "Take Good Care of My Baby," were still trying to get acclimated, and talked about Mr. Cassel's paddle. I must confess, I lost my note to self to avoid "IT" and tested the rumors. Yep, with tears in my eyes, I will tell you the rumors were true! We participated in student council, sports, cheerleading, band, choir, and other school sponsored activities. The Cold War was still swirling around us, the Berlin Wall was erected and the Cuban missile crisis brought us to the brink of war.

Ninth grade put us on the top rung … we were the Freshmen. As the leaders of the pack, we ruled over the seventh and eighth graders. We wore our Ben Casey shirts, sang Tommy Roe's "Sheila" or maybe the Four Season's "Sherry" and watched Denny Rinesmith's dance moves at the Hummelstown Fire Hall. The Hob Nob was the place to go and be seen while enjoying one of their famous Hob Nob burgers. Sometimes we hung out at Rhoad's soda fountain, sipping a cherry Coke or vanilla milkshake. By the end of our Freshman year the World seemed to be taking a political breather.

Tenth grade put us back at the bottom of that proverbial ladder, being overseen by the classes of 1964 and 1965. Football, cross country, band, choir, wrestling, gymnastics, field hockey, and numerous other school and after school activities occupied our time. Life was fun. President John F. Kennedy made a visit to Berlin and gave his rousing "Ich bin ein Berliner" speech. Martin Luther King, Jr. delivered his "I Have a Dream" speech on the steps of the Lincoln Memorial and the LA Dodgers swept the NY Yankees in four games to become the 1963 World Series champions. Then on that fateful day, November 23, 1963, we were called to the auditorium where Mr. Taylor told us the President of the United States had been mortally wounded in Dallas. I can still remember the silence as we filed out to gather our belongings and went home. For days, in shock and disbelief, we watched the events unfold on television. And just when we needed a lift, the Beatles made their first American appearance on the Ed Sullivan show. Yeah, Yeah, Yeah, they wanted to Hold My Hand.

September 1964 and we were now Juniors. Some of us had gotten our first jobs and worked all summer, others had traveled, and one or two had even taken early college classes. That fall we listened as the Animals sang about "The House of the Rising Sun," Roy Orbison was singing about his "Pretty Woman," and who can forget Lorne Greene singing about "Ringo." They just don't write songs like that anymore. "Perry Mason," "Rawhide," and "The Fugitive" were on television and the St. Louis Cardinals beat the NY Yankees to win the 1964 World Series. Ford Motor Company introduced their '64 Mustang and the Civil Rights Bill of 1964 was passed. As a class we were starting to see some of our outstanding athletes and scholars develop. Buster Shellenhamer, Butch Crumling, Bill Crick, Mike Strite, Marsha Mountz, Paula Snyder, Beaver Walmer, Lester Radcliff, Linda Lash, Margaret Shemas, and Kitch Lee were just a few. As you can see, I didn't make the list.

At last our senior year arrived. As Seniors we were back on top; we ruled again! I remember riding to school in Bobby Carlson's big red car … no more yellow school bus for me … I was a Senior! Everything about school was taking on a new meaning. College boards, Channel 8 Dance Party, and Homecoming were the topics of discussion. We danced the night away to the Four Seasons, Tom Darlington and his Orchestra from Philadelphia and the Milton Hershey "Spartan" Dance Band.

That year the radio was playing "Eve of Destruction," "I Hear a Symphony," and "Over and Over" by the Dave Clark Five. The Los Angeles Dodgers beat the Minnesota Twins in the 1965 World Series and we were watching "I Dream of Jeannie," "Gunsmoke," and "The Man from U.N.C.L.E." on our new color television.

Does anyone else remember … John Knaub and his sweet gherkin pickles, wearing an angel blouse, black olives being served in the cafeteria, "Are you with me people," Mrs. Mandes and her civics class? Or what about Senior Hook Day, marbles being dropped in the auditorium during Senior Awards assembly, Karen Minnich cutting off her nylons during class, Mike Remsburg's cap gun going off in his pants pocket, how many sets of twins were in our class and JUST WHO did take the Falcon Missile from the lobby?

We were a class with things to do, places to go, and people to meet. The Class of 1966 produced educators, doctors, lawyers, a West Point graduate, artists, ministers, forest rangers, and maybe even a baker and a candlestick maker. Armed with a solid parental foundation and our journey through the hallowed halls of Lower Dauphin, we were enabled to leave and become a productive and diverse group of individuals, individuals to better improve and serve the lives of the people around us, our communities, and our country.

God Bless the Class of 1966!

Reflections from the Class of 1967

Jack Brandt

In 1967 some of us boldly claimed to know what life held for us, and even as we prepared to leave Lower Dauphin's halls, we looked forward to the successes which waited just on the other side of manageable challenges. Some of us had ideas about what to do after graduation, but those ideas were intertwined with indecision. Still others had yet to focus on a direction, but as a class we believed we could handle anything. After all, we had reached a milestone in our lives, we had succeeded in completing twelve or thirteen years of school, and with optimism, certainty, and bravado, we were ready to face the world.

We could not have begun to imagine the far-reaching forces of fate, the impacts that people and events would have on our lives. Some graduates enlisted in the military, while others gained first person knowledge of the Vietnam War draft lottery all too soon. Some of those did not return alive. As time marched across our lives, we were all affected by political, economic, social, and technological changes on a global scale.

There was drama on a much smaller scale in our daily lives at Lower Dauphin as well. Some short-term crushes turned to long term romances. There was "the thrill of victory, the agony of defeat" in athletic contests, the challenge and satisfaction of artistic production or performance in media, in theater, in music.

The crunch of fulfilling academic requirements was central—honing vocational skills, dreaming entrepreneurially while balancing accounts in business classes, preparing intellectually for moving to institutions of higher learning.

Whether the events that grabbed our attention were big or small, the one constant that almost everyone learned to treasure was friendship. My best friends and I were a group of four, and during lunch each day we talked. Among other things, we discussed music and literature, art and the theater—things that nourished our minds and spirits as much as food nourished our bodies. We reveled in the power of words, in emotional and intellectual responses to books, scripts, song lyrics, poems, speeches. Of course we talked about our classes: Memorizing and performing Hamlet's soliloquy (Act 3, Scene 1) for English class was more than a demanding course requirement. It was a brief chance to immerse ourselves in the mind of a tormented young Danish prince. The extemporaneous speeches in public speaking forced us to think fast and to organize ideas quickly. Whatever the substance of our talks, perhaps we were practicing for one of life's sweet pleasures: quiet conversation and food shared with close friends.

We weren't asked about our talks, nor did we tell others what we discussed, but we managed to annoy someone simply by being. In a letter submitted to and published by the *Falcon Flash*, we four were dubbed "the culture creeps"—by today's standards, a rather tame designation. At first offended by the title, we came to embrace it. This minor event was an early lesson with many to follow about accepting differences, about being slow to judge or to condemn.

Forty-five years later, we "culture creeps" have served in the hospitality and health care industries, in local and regional theater and in education. Members of the Class of 1967 have had an impact on local communities, on states, the nation and on the world. Even as we enter our sixties and look toward redefining ourselves in retirement, we will strive to continue our positive legacy.

Reflections from the Class of 1968

Alan Larsen

April 1968—The LDHS Class of 1968 is lapsing ever more quickly and firmly into party mode. Twelve years of school are drawing to a finish, while the weather is turning warmer and we're listening to all the Beach Boys "oldies" from way back in eighth and ninth grades.

Ah, this is the—BAM! As U2 would later sing, "Early morning, April four, a shot rings out..." Martin Luther King Jr. had been assassinated! OK, just let me catch my—BAM! BAM! Now Robert F. Kennedy had been assassinated! We're supposed to be thinking about that last chance to goof off before our first real jobs or going off to college and—the Vietnam War is escalating rapidly, and we or our friends are called on to fight in it. This isn't some Baby Boomer's idle recollection. If you visit the Vietnam War Memorial on the Mall in DC from time to time as I do, you will find on that Wall the name of Richard Criswell—that cheery, fresh-faced kid with whom we were sharing classes back then. These were the final months for us at LD, and they were seared into our consciousness, shaping who we became, individually and as a cohort.

But, let's rewind the film a bit, and see how these classmates got to this point. It was September of 1962, first day of 7th grade, in what we then called "Junior High." Everyone is meeting people from exotic places—Bachmanville, Shellsville. We're going to school in Hummelstown, not Middletown or Hershey where our big brothers or sisters went? And, now, we're LD Falcons, rather than H-town Bulldogs? This is the Tower of Babel!

But, you know, this may be OK. There is a big-time marching band we can join, and a lot of sports teams that play other schools (yeah, baby), and school dances with live bands, and all these 7th period clubs that do things we actually like! Not that there wasn't foreshadowing of what awaited our senior year: October of that first Junior High year—the Cuban Missile Crisis. November of eighth grade—President Kennedy assassinated. Every one of us remembers where and how we first heard the news. For me, it was Connie Jones bursting into Mr. Vernon Belser's history class, breathlessly announcing, "President Kennedy has been shot!"

But kids are resilient. Soon we were moving on to 9th grade. The good news was, we were big shots—in High School now. The bad news was, we weren't actually big shots—we were now the low kids on the totem pole once again, not the rulers of the halls we had been just a summer away at the end of eighth grade. But, hey—these girls are turning into very interesting young women. And these boys are finally growing up and aren't just geeky little guys with squeaky voices. This could be an interesting year.

As we moved through the next several high school years, we tended to drift apart from the more unified whole-class we had been in junior high, and into interest groupings across class lines. The band members, the football team, yearbook, stage crew, wrestling—ah, wrestling. Now, there was something that really brought the whole school together during our high school years. Coach Cleon Cassel's teams would pack the gym for matches. Every year, LD would be in strong contention for the league title, with numerous individual wrestlers going far into the State Championship sequence.

In football and basketball, it seemed that Middletown was always the team standing in our way. One of the biggest football victories in the entire history of LD (by then, what, all of seven years?) was when our guys beat M-town at Hershey Stadium 13-7, captured forever in a photo in our yearbook, the *Falconaire*. Unfortunately, one of the truly good basketball teams that LD has ever seen just couldn't get out of the league championship, succumbing to Middletown. The consolation is that the Middletown team went on to the State Championship game that year. Further consolation of a sort came years later in 1976 when I was living in Portland, Oregon. There a guy came out of the just-folded American Basketball Association to become the point guard who leads the Trailblazers to the 1977 NBA Championship with Bill Walton. And who was this guy? Dave Twardzik , the leader of that Middletown team that beat our guys. So, had Lower Dauphin not run into a "once-in-a-lifetime, they-have-a-future-NBA-champion" leading their team situation, who knows how far the LD guys would have gone our senior year.

Our high school years saw the birth and death of the *Flush Gazette*, the irreverent and definitely unofficial counterpart to the school newspaper, the *Falcon Flash*. It had the simultaneous virtues of ticking off the administration and ramping up school spirit. The identities of its authors and how it miraculously appeared in the hallways remain a secret to this day.

We can't revisit those great high school years without honoring our teachers. It's a little embarrassing, with at least a bit more maturity than we had back then, to think about how we goofed off in class, made wise-cracks, and generally failed to appreciate what a terrific education we were receiving at the hands of a crew of dedicated, superbly talented professionals. When I learned that Dr. Judith Witmer was seeking information in connection with this Jubilee celebration, I wrote to her to say, after all these years, thanks. I was able to speak for the entire Class of 1968, when I said in my note, "By now, I have seen enough to allow me to marvel at how fortunate we were to have teachers like you to send us off with the skills to succeed anywhere. You [those LD teachers] have touched thousands of lives."

So, it was quite a journey that brought us all to that springtime of 1968. It's now Commencement Day—the last time many of us would see each other. To enter the auditorium for the culminating ceremony, we walked the same halls as we had just a few years earlier when the Beach Boys "Good Vibrations" was the apt sound track for our 9th grade year. But now—with the assassinations and the escalating war, the dizzying redefinition of everything we thought we knew, at the very moment when seniors, those rulers of the hallways, usually are fully convinced they do actually know it all—the new soundtrack for us was Dylan's "The Times They are A-Changing." Against that backdrop, our class chose as its Commencement Theme, "The Answer is Blowin' in the Wind." Along with Yolande McCurdy and Ann Rhoads, I was honored to be asked to address the class at Commencement. As our adult leaders from the school and the community were launching us out into the world, I concluded my take on our chosen theme by saying, "If the answer is blowing in the wind, we are going to have to step outside to find it." I think that, as individuals and as a class, over what is now more years than seem possible, we have done just that. We stepped outside. We've had a lot of fun and done a lot of good—because of the values and skills we developed in those precious years roaming the halls of Lower Dauphin High School. Maybe "Good Vibrations" was a pretty good sound track after all.

Reflections from the Class of 1969

Craig Tritch

You haven't yet heard from the Class of '69 because they, like me, lived through the years of turmoil when this great nation nearly came undone. Spirited discussions in Mr. Croll's Problems of Democracy class contrasted harshly with the bucolic, peaceful lives that we all came from. American cities were in flames from race riots, students took to the streets to protest the Vietnam War, and those of us who remained loyal wondered why our government had lied to us.

In football our six seniors had to learn from losing, and yet lose with dignity. One of my teammates played with a broken arm until he broke his leg. Such efforts surely are worthy. Every LD athlete has the feeling of walking in the steps of giants who came before. Wrestlers could not imagine letting down our beloved coach. Every week Mrs. Ball (Witmer) faithfully placed our latest wins on her lectern for all of us to be proud. Some will never know what it's like to wait in a locker room and listen to the fans screaming at such a volume that the varsity wonders "Will they have anything left for us?" They did, and provided even more! No LD athlete ever took the floor, field, or mat without knowing that fathers and farmers, mechanics and mothers, lived and died with their efforts those nights.

No mentioning by name could ever do justice to the teachers (Bill Linnane), counselors (Pat Lanshe), coaches (Cleon Cassel), and superintendent (Doc) who had a profound impact on our lives. If they'd only known how much their guidance meant to us, each should receive an extra reward in heaven, or should have been more forceful in salary negotiations with Doc!

Our lives are marked by a few special events. The birth of our first child, the love of Mom and Dad, and Christmas morning when Santa Claus was sure to come are those special moments. Add to it the reunion with classmates and sad remembrance of those who are gone. We who walked the halls of LD and lived full and wondrous lives are blessed beyond measure.

Go Falcons!

Reflections from the Class of 1970

Michael Orsini and Linda Dunkle Orsini

Our Class of 1970 was the tenth graduating class, individuals who grew up together during the turbulent times of the 1960s. Our unforgettable LD years are remembered by the following:

- As 7th graders, helping LD to win our first school dance, sponsored by WCMB, for generating the most calls to the station demonstrating our school spirit.
- Mr. Falstick's "neck jobs" in 8th grade English class.
- "The Uninvited Guest," our 9th grade play, directed by Mr. Romano.
- Mr. Brittain and Mr. McLure teaching all of us to drive.
- The "high tech" language labs.
- "Hawaiian Paradise," our 9th grade dance.
- The Safe Driving Olympics competition.
- Mr. Sullivan and the Hello Dolly/Carol Channing hoax.
- Jean Stapleton visiting our school and speaking to us as sophomores.
- "Penny," the all school musical our junior year.
- Dr. Hoerner's summer Student Forums for student leaders at Meadowbrook.
- Mr. Nixon and Mr. Hummel directing band camp at Elizabethtown College, August 1969.
- The rise and fall of detention halls.
- The brand new Universal Gym.
- Six of our seniors, accompanied by Mr. David Smith, taking a European tour, including four weeks in Germany.
- The field hockey team attending preseason Capital Hockey Day Camp at CD East.
- Early morning band practices.
- A "new" drink, yellow Gatorade, for the football team.
- Moratorium Day, Oct. 15, 1969, a peaceful anti-war demonstration at HACC that was attended by several of our classmates.
- The many football pep rallies in the gym and dances that were sponsored by our Booster Club.
- At the Homecoming football game, student floats that glided around the stadium at halftime: Band, If Music is the Fruit of Love, Play On; Girls' Athletic Council, Eliminate the Spartans; Student Council, Apollo 11 Flight. Tickets for the dance were $3 per couple.
- The Powder Puff Football Team selling donuts to buy personalized powder blue jerseys.
- The band achieving their highest ranking ever by coming in 2nd place in the annual band competition at Middletown High School.
- The football team defeating Hershey for the first time since 1960. The student body was rewarded with a half day of school on Monday.
- The Hob Nob...the place to be on Friday night after the football game.
- Study halls in the cafeteria and sitting at most uncomfortable, new, fold-up cafeteria tables.

- The "Reading Room."
- Dimly lit auditorium study halls, used because of over-crowding.
- The Capital Area Conference championship wrestling team of 1970.
- The championship girls' basketball team, who went undefeated in league play.
- Our gymnastic teams sporting new uniforms.
- Fashion Board's assembly, with clothing provided by Pomeroy's Department Store.
- Snow, snow, snow…the winter of 1970. Our Easter vacation was cut short.
- Mr. Goepfert's handsome student teacher, Mr. Chubba Balaze.
- Square dancing in gym class.
- Courses, such as Industrial Arts, Home Economics, Highway Safety, Bookkeeping, Personal Typing, Vo Ag, Shorthand, and square dancing in gym class.
- The smell of the Chemistry labs.
- The 1969-70 debate team in its second year of competition, winning 10 matches in 17 debates.
- Mr. Claar shaving off his mustache.
- The Student Council's visits to the Easter Seal School.
- Fruit cakes, our senior year fundraiser, and bubble bath during our junior year.
- The big H-wing flood.
- 35 cent cafeteria lunches.
- The Varsity Club's pizza sales.
- The track team's 7-3 record as the best in school history.
- Our yearbook dedicated to Mr. McLure.
- May Day celebration that included Senior Day where seniors taught classes, a drama festival that presented Great Smokies, a May Day outdoor fair, and culminated by a May Day dance.
- The Senior Prom, "Eve of Excalibur," at the Penn Harris Motor Inn, followed by an After Prom Party at the school.
- The Commencement program, "Awake, Arise, Decide," which included projected slides, music, and narration.
- Nicknames: Biny, Bird, Dup, Eb, Eif, Rube, Wuss, Moon, DJ, Deacon, Gert, Nude, O'Be, Patch, Amoeba, Toad, Big Al, Stoney, Dino.
- Dr. Hoerner, in a school board address, lauding the 1970 graduating class as "exceptional, not only academically, but in extracurricular matters…not only in the way they participated, but in their behavior."
- In Memoriam: Larry Fackler and Ann Turel

The Class of 1970 also initiated many firsts at Lower Dauphin. The first:
- to attend an off-site pre-season football camp at Camp Log-n-Twig in the Poconos.
- Co-ed physical education classes, including archery and volleyball.
- Powder Puff football games.
- Championship season in field hockey with a record of 8-0-3.

- *Media*, a student literary publication of poems and short stories.
- "Fickle Finger of Fate" awarded by the *Falcon Flash*. It was given to persons demonstrating "excessive idiocy, a virtual absence of brains, and a general lack of coordination."
- Floats at halftime of the Homecoming game.
- To experience a "closed dance" policy regarding students from other schools.
- New Year's Eve Student Council Dance.
- Senior Fun Night with games, activities, music, food, and movies in the gym, cafeteria, and the auditorium.
- Ski Club and Racing Team sponsored by Mr. Filepas and Mr. Curry.
- Under the direction of the Varsity Club, to publish "The Hoop" and "The Mat," game day stat sheets and programs for basketball and wrestling.
- College Bowl assembly.
- To supply counselors for the fifth grade's Camp Hebron in May.
- Earth Day on April 22, 1970.
- Large format *Falconaire*.
- Class Night, which featured skits about our years at LD and the reading of the class's Last Will and Testament.
- White gold class rings.
- The first student-produced Commencement (slides of the class) and Baccalaureate programs ("For Heaven's Sake") designed by Mrs. Ball (Dr. Witmer).

Reflections from the Class of 1971

Joe Quigley, with Barb Walmer Miller and Tom Luttrell

Some of the best years of our lives have been spent with the Falcons going onward to victories in sports, scholastic achievements, and a better understanding of each other. Our class arrived at Lower Dauphin in September 1967. The majority of us came from the rural towns/townships surrounding the school: Hoernerstown, Grantville, East and South Hanover Township, parts of Conewago, Londonderry, and Lower Swatara Townships, and Middletown. We represent the families of Goss, Ricker, Luttrell, Harner, Gleim, Bell, Hickernell, Goodwin, Hock, Rhinesmith, Ratcliff, Rathfon, Howard, Popp, Leh, Lehmer, Mrakovich, Taylor, Tonkin, Kreiser, Day, Runkle, Sattazan, Walmer, Dupler, Campbell, Foreman, Crow, Stauffer, and Quigley, among many others.

There were also those "big city folk" from Hummelstown who were part of this great class: Osevala, Zeiters, Preble, Hutchinson, Brightbill, Nisley, Kulina, Basler, Coon, D'Agostino, Alleman, Grierson, Ernst, Slough, Plouse, Hornberger, Imhof, Frascella, DeRosa et al. But we all knew one thing—we had to get through the next four years and graduate in 1971.

Prior to graduation we experienced some wonderful occasions which created memories to last our lifetimes. These events began with our Freshman dance known as "Incense and Peppermints" with lighting provided through "blue-lights." A certain cheerleader arrived at the dance wearing white lingerie underneath a black blouse. Wow! Did that really light up!

During our Sophomore year, when many received driver's licenses, several class members attended dances which were held at the Hershey Ball Room, an elegant dance hall near the original location of the Hershey Country Club. At that time there was still racial tension as a result of the assassination of Dr. Martin Luther King which had occurred less than a year before. At one of those dances, a fight broke out with teen-agers from the Harrisburg area who wanted to dance with our dates. Police arrived to calm down the situation, but in the process they began spraying tear-gas. The place emptied out in a heartbeat. Other notable dances include the 1971 Valentine's Day Dance with George Stauffer voted as Cupid; the "Waisted" Evening Dance where you paid according to your waist measurement; and the Channel 8 Dance Party. During our Junior Year our class sponsored a dance called "Flashing Banana" for which we purchased strobe-lights and then donated them to the school.

During our junior year football season, we had been the first team to attend a real "football camp" at a distance from Lower Dauphin. We were away for one week at Camp Log 'n' Twig in Pike County. The following year we moved up by holding camp at Juniata College. Some may also remember the "Heckel and Jeckel" photo (of the Quigley twins) in the Lower Dauphin vs. Palmyra program at the time when both teams were 6 and 0.

Our senior year began with the most exciting event that had ever happened in the history of Lower Dauphin. We won the Capitol Area Conference (CAC) Football Championship on November 19, 1970 with an Undefeated and Untied record of 11 wins and no losses. At this writing our record has yet to be duplicated or surpassed. There have been other LD football teams with more wins who have participated in "playoffs" (which didn't exist in 1970), but those teams did not finish "Undefeated and Untied." After the culminating victory that evening, fans rushed the field and tore down the wooden goalposts. Many of us still have those souvenirs. Another sweet victory was that the team was honored with the CAC Sportsmanship Award. We did this despite an incident that had occurred late in the 1969 season leading several players choosing not to return for the 1970 season.

The 1971 Wrestling Team, coached by Mr. Cleon Cassel and Mr. Don Heistand, gave us another undefeated CAC Championship (13-0-1), and our Track and Field Team, led by Coach Ed Romano, attained the best record to that date with 8 wins and 3 losses. Several school records were broken.

In May 1971 we created what became known as the Great Pigeon Saga, emulating a similar prank by the Class of 1970. (See section on "Pranks" later in this book.) Our Class also inaugurated a widespread, organized Senior Hook Day on a spring day in 1971. (See "Senior Hook Days of Note.")

May 1971 also brought the infamous Falcon Rocket Crisis. (See "Pranks.") Joe also adds here, "The rocket was then taken by another class and has yet to be returned. Our advice to this group is that there is no glory in keeping it. It is better to return it and tell the story."

Finally we remember (1) wearing dress/khaki pants to school with no jeans during those years; (2) taking the bus to school and returning home on the activity buses. No personal cars for most of us; (3) hall monitors with felt LD armbands; and, finally—

June 4, 1971 —— **Graduation!**

Reflections from the Class of 1972

Jan Brightbill Heckenluber

Back in those carefree days of high school we really didn't look into the future. We never thought we would be parents or grandparents or that we would lose close friends, classmates, or family members. Some of our classmates suffered serious injuries or illnesses, were married or divorced, and some chose to move out of the area or the state. As we began to reflect on our high school days many of us laughed that we couldn't even remember what we were doing last week, let alone more than 30 years ago. Thanks to Connie, Beckie, Janice, Barry, Karen, Roxanne, and Paul for offering these reflections on our memorable days at Lower Dauphin.

We did not have computers. We used a manual typewriter and if you were lucky enough you had the chance to practice on an electric typewriter and most of the typing students were girls. A student was enrolled in college prep, business, general courses, or attended the new Vo-Tech school. We all sat in most classrooms in alphabetical order. The girls were expected to study home economics and the boys took wood shop. Not until we were Seniors were we able to choose to take one of these different courses. Gym class and health classes were not co-ed. Occasionally the physical education teachers allowed girls to play baseball or basketball with the boys. And who can forget the uniforms we had to wear for gym class? We would get demerits if we did not have the proper attire. And after gym class, you always had to take a shower with the teacher taking attendance.

There was no string orchestra and those, like me, who played the violin had to travel to Harrisburg to be involved with an orchestra. Beckie made the elite District Chorus, and I played violin in the District Orchestra at Central Dauphin High School. We still have the recording which featured "Camelot."

We would always start our day at school with a poem, silent prayer, and pledge to the flag. A different student took this job each day. We always had pizza or fish on Fridays. Student Council arranged for a soda and snack machine in the cafeteria. There was also a milk machine which offered milk at 5 cents per carton. And we even had a soft ice cream machine, which cost 10 cents a serving. Even though there was a strict dress code, the girls could wear pant suits. But by the time we were Seniors, we were allowed to wear jeans, no holes, and only on Fridays.

There were many sports and clubs to join. Every Friday during the fall we had a pep rally in the gym; the band would play and many students dressed up for the spirit days with hats and buttons which were sold by the student council or cheerleaders. After the games, many of us gathered at the Hob Nob, and when that closed, we headed to Burger King for hamburgers and fries.

Our boys' track team went undefeated in our Senior year and to this day is still the only class in L.D. history to hold this record. We did not have a girls' track team and one day as the girls' gym class was running around the track, Mr. Romano invited a few of us to the Cedar Cliff Relays. Deb ran barefoot in the race on a gravel track; and while the girls didn't do very well, it was an experience.

A Powder Puff football game was played between the Juniors and Seniors. Janice remembers Kevin telling her to be much tougher if she wanted to play football. The next play, she ended up plowing Kevin over and he said, "Now that's more like it!"

There was also a model club where the boys got together after school to glue model cars. Barry said he still laughs about how the teachers would always close the door to the classroom so the fumes from the glue wouldn't go into the hallway.

Our class started an Earth Day. Instead of taking a bus or driving, some of us rode bikes to school. Harry Saltzer roller skated to school from Middletown; he was late for school, and we all watched from our classrooms cheering him on as he approached the building. Mr. Osevala excused him for being tardy.

As we entered our Senior year, we had our pictures taken for the yearbook. There was also a dress code for these pictures which were taken at the Hershey Motor Lodge. Girls had to wear a dark blue top and the boys, a suit and tie.

One of our favorite days during the school year was when the Seniors took the place of a teacher. Beckie remembers taking Mrs. Conway's typing class, Jan was Mrs. Atkinson, and Harry Saltzer was Mr. Osevala, the principal.

Our graduation was held at the Hershey Theater. We closed our ceremony with "No Man Is An Island" directed by Mrs. Witmer. After all these years, I can still remember most of the words, "No man is an island; no man stands alone." As we left the graduation ceremony, we never even gave a thought that this was the last time our entire class would be together.

Then came the flood of 1972! Like the memories of the Class of 1972 have flooded our hearts, Hurricane Agnes flooded the Eastern seaboard as we all made our way into the wide world.

Reflections from the Class of 1973

Jim Neidinger

When I look back on our class, there is one unmistakable theme which always seems to permeate whatever we did. There were no cliques. No walls. We were one, or as close to it as one could hope. We belonged to each other. To this day we are friends and at times it feels like then.

Junior High

We had our own newspaper in Junior High, its inaugural issue coming in our seventh grade year and I designed the official Junior High emblem! Two of our favorite teachers in Junior High were Mr. Joseph Nutitas and Mr. Richard Zaepfel. Mr. Zaepfel was the brunt of a few practical jokes (See section on "Pranks.") Many female classmates would like to acknowledge our science teacher, Mr. Frank Neiswender, as our hunkiest teacher.

Senior High

Academics: Life in "The Sandbox" included contracting for our grades and our senior year saw a breakthrough when boys were allowed to take Home Economics classes. We had a student-produced Commencement program that included vocalists, instrumentalists, and dancers. Lower Dauphin School District also received the Freedoms Foundation George Washington Honor Medal Award.

Editorials: The *Falcon Flash* addressed the crossing guards near the school, smoking in the lavatories, the intense amounts of homework given, the unisex craze, the need for gym class reform, exercise gadget sales pitches in school assemblies, the need for more school facilities and additional classroom "wings," the need to be more welcoming to new students, the poor condition of our lavatories, the Vietnam War, the supposed inaccurate review of the musical "The Boyfriend," and ACES.

General: Our senior yearbook was dedicated to Mr. Steven Messner who was actively involved in advisory roles in the Student Council, Youth Festival, Science Fair, track meets, behavioral science, archaeology and the Mock Democratic Convention. The Senior Class Council dedicated a special page of our yearbook to Mrs. Barbara "Bobbie" Atkinson for her special involvement with our class. She was our advisor, our coach, our teacher and continues to be our friend.

Social: Voting for Homecoming Court was done in a real voting booth! The homecoming theme was based on the Olympics and heralding the start of the festivities was our cross country star, Randy Lehman. (See "Traditions of Homecoming.") Our favorite eating places were the Warwick for pizza, Rintz's Candy Store, Rhoads Pharmacy, Hocker's Drug Store, The Hob Nob, and the Red Barn in Palmyra. Wayne Jockers held the record for eating a Red Barn Barnbuster – in two bites. Good movies were "Butch Cassidy and the Sundance Kid," "Downhill Racer," "The Kremlin Letter," " The Molly Maguires," "Goodbye, Mr. Chips" and "Easy Rider."

Sports: It was a muddy year for football fans in Hershey Stadium. The seasonal rains that fell at an unusually heavy rate during the season made playing on the turf of the stadium more than an adventure as the players struggled for footing and the band struggled to keep the six-inch deep sucking mud from swallowing up their white bucks!

Kim Witmer's 1,000th point in basketball came on the floor of the Middletown gymnasium. He later set the school record at 1060. He also set school records for most points in a season (484), most points in a game (41), most field goals in a career (428), most field goals in a game (16), most free throws attempted in a season (215), and most free throws in a season (122). Our track team provided twenty-four consecutive victories!

Perfect seasons were accumulated by the following wrestlers: Wayne Jockers 12-0-0 in 1972-73; Tom Mutek 14-0-0 in 1971-72 and 13-0-0 in 1972-73; Ed Neiswender 13-0-0 in 1971-72 and 14-0-0 in 1972-73. Wrestling District Champions were Tom Mutek, Mark Stauffer and Ed Neiswender and State Runner Ups were Tom Mutek, Mark Stauffer and Ed Neiswender.

Jim Kulina pitched the first no-hitter in Lower Dauphin history by nesting Hershey 1-0 while Randy Lehman set a Capital Area Conference meet record in the two mile run with a 9:51.4. At the same meet Leo Hydrick edged out his nemesis J.C. Floyd with a high hurdle time of 15.3 and Kim Witmer and Mike Gallagher scored first with near record times in the 440 and 880 with 51.4 and 2:00.3 respectively.

We also had a gymnastics team and the girls' basketball team finished undefeated on their home court with a 10-4 league record and played in the District 3 playoffs in the Farm Show.

Kim Travitz was the first in a line of female statisticians for sporting events and paved the way for "The Wrestlerettes," a team of girls to perform duties at matches. With the addition of new head basketball coach, C. Richard Miller, a new spirit group emerged, "The Rowdies," whose job it was to cheer loudly and often, using ear-deafening megaphones, gallon jugs containing BBs, assorted noisemakers and vocals.

Music: The first public appearance by our class as members of the Band was during the BIG 33 game. There was something about performing for over 20,000 people as a ninth grader that cured your stage fright forever. Big Blue Band competitions included the controversial Middletown event, where the scores were changed after I noticed a discrepancy on the score sheet as the band returned home and we eventually vaulted over Hershey for a second place finish. We even had a Barbershop Quartet with Kent Myers, David Warfel, Kerry Fies '74, and me (Jim Neidinger).

Originals: We had three pilots among our ranks. Mitchell Funk, Stan Dobson, and Woody Menear. One of them was cited for performing aerobatics above the Hershey Airport airspace. On the original Earth Day of 1970, Mic Wrzesniewski and Candy Tritch rode their bicycles to LD from Londonderry Elementary School. The Class was challenged to suggest a school event in lieu of Senior Hook Day and the result was a pig roast and rock concert. (See "Senior Hook Days.") Another first was the mock Democratic Convention. (See "Special Projects and Events.")

Pixie Spacht Wright remembers, "Walking off-stage at rehearsal I sat on stack of painted cement blocks at the invitation of a stage crew member. The blocks were still wet and my new wool pants ruined. Accepting the apology, I later married this senior boy."

Reflections from the Class of 1974

Craig College

"When Life Was Sweet, I Knew Not Why"[1]

When the Class of 1974 arrived for junior high school we now owned a locker, moved from room to room to attend classes, and experienced our first after-school activities. We had more classmates than the 30 from Conewago Elementary, for example; others came from the big city (Hummelstown) or East and South Hanover and Londonderry Townships.

Life was sweet and we knew not why. The big issues were friends, hunting, the Farm Show, any sport against Hershey and Middletown High Schools. We were in the Capital Area Conference. Boys took "shop" and girls took "home ec." Study hall was held in the cafeteria because of overcrowding. To conserve energy, we could not open the exterior doors to take a shortcut to class to avoid the hallway crowds. Skip Hetrick and Dean Oellig drove to school in Skip's 1958 Studebaker pickup truck. The milkman delivered milk to a milk box in front of every home. We were cloistered in small town and small farm, USA.

Our teachers built the sweet life. In 7th grade English class, we produced a 70s "hippie" version of the "Legend of Sleepy Hollow." We hunted fossils at Swatara State Park in 8th grade. We square danced in 9th grade gym class. Mr. Minsker and Mr. Shirk took us to our first professional baseball game—the Phillies. Mr. Minsker's class read "The Prophet" by Kahlil Gibran—the first book that most purchased and one we still own. The first (and best) English Enrichment class followed for many of us. Field trips were a big part of the experience. The Health Careers class visited the Harrisburg state mental hospital and the clinical labs in the Hershey Medical Center. The Nuclear Science class visited the reactor at Penn State University. The American Institute of Foreign Studies (AIFS) sponsored a trip to Germany senior year—pastries, bratwurst, Munich's Hofbrau House, Jerry in a dress at a student dance.

Our classmates added a little spice. The Big Blue Band from Falconland was Falcon Pride incarnate—great music, intricate halftime shows, pumped up marching band competitions, majorettes, what a show. The Homecoming dance contract band failed to show so members of the Big Blue Band filled in—voila, tunes! We ran for Student Council, supported Youth Festival, and joined the Booster Club, Photography Club, the Falcon Flash, Choir, Future Secretaries/Homemakers/Farmers of America, and on and on. Spanish Club sold Costa's candy every year, sponsored a trip to Puerto Rico, and decorated a VW Beetle as a sombrero for Homecoming. Mr. Moore found his black VW parked on the steps of H-Wing. The Ag boys regularly foraged lunch at the Red Barn in Palmyra. Mr. Osevala unexpectedly joined them for their last raid.

The cheerleaders stoked school spirit. Steve Orsini was our Mr. Touchdown for a fund raiser sponsored by WKBO radio. The cheerleaders collected donations at every pep rally and football game. They dressed as raisins junior year, hid in Raisin Bran cereal boxes (Spire Electric refrigerator boxes), and popped out at the pep rally singing, "It's raisins that make the Falcon team victorious" (a take-off from the then popular California Raisins commercials). They bought their saddle shoes every year at Raub Shoe Store (now Gold's Gym). The cheerleaders would decorate lockers for the various teams and provided spirit banners in the cafeteria.

Our class motto is "I am not afraid of tomorrow, for I have seen yesterday and love today." Our yearbook cover featured Alfred, Lord Tennyson's "For I dipped into the future/Far as human eye could see/Saw the vision of the world/And all the wonder that would be." The yearbook also included verse and photography to remind us years later of *"when life was sweet and I knew not why."*

Reflections from the Class of 1976

Pam Sattazahn Zerphy

The Spirit of '76

The class of 1976 was the Class of the Bicentennial and in our own way we were part of a revolution in the Lower Dauphin School District. From the time we started elementary school our class was different from the classes that came after us. Some of our class members were the first to ever participate in an elementary school outdoor education program known more commonly as Camp Hebron. When our class seniors went back to Camp Hebron as counselors in 1976, the program had come full circle.

Lunch during our senior year consisted of a fairly decent hot meal, with the exception of the Lower Dauphin dandy. (What was in that thing?) If you didn't want to eat a hot balanced meal you could pick up a ready-made bag lunch, or go through the snack line. Best of all, there was a milkshake line. One additional privilege our class enjoyed was released lunch. With parental permission on file in the office, we were allowed to leave school grounds during lunchtime. Thank you, McDonalds, for opening one of Hummelstown's first fast food restaurants while we were in high school. School nutritionists, feel free to cringe.

Student Council funded many of its activities with the proceeds from the cafeteria vending machines. The soda and candy machines were turned off during the school day, but as soon as the final bell rang, Student Council turned on those machines. If you didn't grab your after school snack in the cafeteria, you could walk the couple of blocks down Water Street to Main Street to Rintz's. We feel truly sorry for anyone who has graduated without the benefit of a Rintz's cherry snow cone or Swedish fish.

After school activities revolved around school sports, cheerleading, band, and clubs. School dances were more prevalent but homecoming and the prom were the still the highlights. Our class didn't leave a football legacy, but we redeemed ourselves later with a championship wrestling team. Our band was larger than bands today. Band members held a tradition on the band bus when returning from a football game or competition. Just before entering Hummelstown, everyone on the bus sang the LD Alma Mater immediately followed by the singing of the Lord's Prayer.

Traditionally, girls were required to take home economics and boys took shop. On the more contemporary side were English Enrichment and Longitudinal Studies. English Enrichment was a three-year program that was team taught by two teachers. Longitudinal Studies included an exchange program with a school in England where LD students spent almost four weeks before coming back and hosting students from England.

We had a traditional spring musical, "Anything Goes," but our other productions really were anything goes. The senior class play, "Story Theater," based on Grimm's Fairy Tales and Aesop's Fables featured students wearing long johns and donning apparel to transform boys into old ladies, girls into roosters, boys into donkeys and an entire menagerie of characters. The performance of "The Winter's Tale" was the first time LD students attempted Shakespeare.

Perhaps the two most memorable events of the Class of 1976 were our class trip and our graduation itself. Having a class trip was not unusual. Other classes went on trips. They loaded onto buses, drove for a couple of hours, toured a city or some historic site and drove back to Hummelstown. Not our class. We wanted to go to Walt Disney World. Our class held non-stop fundraisers to come up with the money to fly to Florida. We spent two days in the Magic Kingdom and our final day at Cypress Gardens and Sea World. The trip was a series of firsts for many classmates: first time to fly, first time in Florida, first time at Walt Disney World, and oh yes, the legal drinking age in Florida was 18 years of age in 1976. Enough said.

Finally, we were coming to the end of our school days at Lower Dauphin. We anxiously anticipated that culminating moment when we would walk down the aisle to "Pomp and Circumstance," hear our names, walk across a stage and receive our diplomas. But wait! We were the Bicentennial Class. Our graduation theme was based on our nation's two hundredth birthday. Everything about it had to patriotic. Even the graduation gowns—honor society and class officers in red, girls in white, and boys in blue—had to proclaim, "We are the Bicentennial Class!" Everything had to be authentic including the music. We were informed "Pomp and Circumstance" was not a period piece and therefore we would not use it for graduation. The class that was graduating in the year that commemorated our nation's two hundredth birthday revolted. Students were in an uproar. Students who had waited 12 or 13 years to hear "Pomp and Circumstance" played for them began to talk about nothing else. Arguments broke out; people took sides. Little attention was paid to class work. Finally, the principal's voice came over the loudspeaker commanding, "All seniors to the auditorium!"

We were told this issue was about to be resolved once and for all. Mr. Osevala said any student who had something to say had to raise a hand, be recognized, and then would have the floor to make a statement. At the end, we would vote. An amazing thing happened that day. Students who hated public speaking stood up and said why they wanted "Pomp and Circumstance." Kids who were more comfortable on smokers' corner than in front of their class raised their hands to speak. Students that previously hadn't spoken more than a few words to each other bonded in a common cause and applauded each other. In fairness, some students also explained why another piece of music would be a better choice, but two hundred years ago we shed the king's rule and we became a democracy. And so it was. We voted and the majority ruled. The class of 1976 graduated in June at the Hershey Theater. Students walked down the aisle with smiles on their faces and "Pomp and Circumstance" as music to their ears. We were the Bicentennial Class.

Reflections from the Class of 1982

Ron Orsini

The world was smaller when we were in Lower Dauphin schools. This was the time before the Internet and social networking (in 1982 the founder of Facebook wasn't even born yet) and before there were more than four television stations and other electronic links to the rest of the world. Our life growing up was much more centered on our relationships and shared experiences at school, so LD had an indelible impact on our lives.

We shared some major cultural milestones in the years 1969-1982. We watched the very first Sesame Street episode in November 1969 (I remember thinking how neat it was that PBS went to the trouble to make a TV show just for us kindergartners), and then watched the astronauts walk on the moon. We participated in elections (my class was pictured in *The Sun* marching down Main Street in Hummelstown, me with my "Nixon Now" poster) and experienced the Bicentennial as top dog (6th graders!) in our elementary schools. Later on in 9th grade we had the eyes of the world watching our little community during the Three Mile Island incident. I tell people to this day when discussing the topic that I was at track practice at the time TMI was releasing the radioactive gases just a few miles away. This is followed by the requisite questions about glowing in the dark and webbed feet….

We also shared many experiences at LD that broadened our limited horizons: square dancing, roller skating PE classes, Camp Hebron, rope climbing, and those countless fundraisers just to name a few. Some of us even found our life's passion in extracurricular activities such as music, theater, and Longitudinal Studies. We learned to appreciate excellence in sports by our successes in the Capitol Area Conference and beyond with Coach Cassel's wrestling teams and Coach Kreiser's field hockey teams, and the character-building aspect of defeat with tough senior years in football, basketball, and track. It was always a challenge beating much larger Cumberland Valley and a thrill when we beat neighbors and rivals Hershey and Middletown. We also grew up a little faster with the tragic loss of two classmates at the beginning of our senior year, Stacey Fornwalt and Pat Foca.

We were fortunate to have some incredible teachers who everyday shared their passion for their subjects with us. Some of the best that immediately come to mind for me are Mrs. Atkinson in biology with her energetic style, even when we dissected frogs; Mr. Sharpe in junior high English (I still remember "To Kill a Mockingbird" and lines from "The Merchant of Venice"); Mrs. Witmer in Brit. Lit. and her weekly vocabulary quizzes; Mr. Etter in social studies challenging our critical thinking about historical and current events; and Mr. Romano, who was an exacting math teacher and first introduced us to computers, including cassette tape memory! Their passion left a lasting a mark on how to do your job well as what they were actually trying to teach us.

We were also fortunate to have our fellow classmates, placed together by fate to share in this experience. In hindsight, we weren't a very diverse group, but we learned from each other's differences nonetheless. We grew up together, learned social skills together (sometimes the hard way), laughed, got angry, and cried together for six and for some of us twelve years.

Lower Dauphin shaped how we think about the world. Our foundational values and world view were passed on to us by our parents and molded by our experiences, teachers, and friends. As we went off to college, moved away, and entered the workforce, the perspective we developed at LD was undoubtedly challenged and refined by later experiences, but we all shared that common foundation, remnants of which are still with us today.

Reflections from the Class of 1984

Ronda Stumpf

Thinking back twenty-five years now, it is hard to believe how far we have all come. It seems many who knew the members of the Class of 1984 probably didn't expect us to amount to much. In fact, I am not quite sure many of us expected to lead the successful lives we do now. I dare say we were known through the hallowed halls of LDHS as the "party class." We were a tight-knit group who knew how to have a good time. I am not saying we necessarily partied dangerously or even excessively, but many, many weekends were spent socializing and "just hanging together." Sure, there were some cliques, but despite most classes, we still tended to be all right all hanging out together.

We are possibly the class best known for most likely "borrowing" the time capsule, the class known for the most outrageous parties, and the class known for having some of the wildest pranks. Having said all that, if you are the reader, you are probably expecting to read that we didn't amount to much after high school. Well, there is where you would be mistaken.

Out of this class of "wild partying kids," came doctors, teachers, engineers, a pharmacist, librarian, business executives, architect, civil servants, militia, community leaders, and even a minister. We have classmates in states across the country and around the world. We are good citizens who are making meaningful contributions to our local communities and to the betterment of our world for our children and our grandchildren.

Every five years, we get together for our class reunion. Our class reunions are a time for reminiscing, catching up, sharing laughter and occasionally tears. I believe we have one of the largest turn-outs for reunions around. In fact, we even have classmates from other graduating years return to our class reunions, as well as students who left LDHS in elementary or middle school who join us. It is quite common for us to have classmates travel from as far as California, Florida, and even Europe to attend our celebratory reunions.

Our legacy remains strong, enduring friendships that have served the test of time. Many of us remain best of friends despite distance and time that separates us on a daily basis. A highlight every five years is reuniting for one more toast to the good ol' days and a nod to whatever the future has yet to hold. I feel blessed to be a member of the Class of 1984!

Reflections from the Class of 1985

Jeff Miller

Looking back, the class of 1985 was an interesting mix of classmates from various backgrounds and interests. There were the athletic jocks, the smoking and leather bound hoods, the studious nerds, future farmers, and of course people with a little of each in them. People had cliques and groups of friends but I don't remember many significant hostilities between groups. We were before the explosion of information and communication. I think having a business card in your wallet was considered advanced. It was definitely a more relaxed and comfortable pace of life. We didn't need play dates growing up. Being home "before dinner" was as supervised as it often got. Organized sports were contained primarily to school sponsored programs that were just one season long. Homework and tests seemed only an occasional event, not like the more demanding schedules of today.

One memorable event to anyone alive during the late 70's was of course the TMI accident. It was particularly close to home for me as my Dad, Kenneth Miller, was known to be a radiation safety expert in the community. He was well known for giving talks and demonstrations to classes over the years on radiation. When on the day of the accident my mother showed up and removed me early from my class at Conewago Elementary School, it set off quite an increased level of panic at the school.

An interesting event specific to our senior year was the near collapse of our class trip to Hunter Mountain, New York. One evening in our hotel room we heard yelling out the window. When we looked outside, the lower level roof was smoldering with smoke. It turns out students from another school were staying directly below us. Someone must have lit a towel on fire in their room and in a panic threw it out the window. It landed on the roof below and caught the underlying restaurant on fire causing thousands of dollars in damage. Next thing we knew we were being interviewed by State Police regarding the incident. Little did we realize or expect that after the interviews we would be accused of actually starting the fire. Before we knew it several of us were told we were being kicked out of the resort and were loaded on a van for an early departure home. Fortunately within minutes of our departure a student from the other school confessed to the incident and we were allowed to stay.

Not having grown up during the assassination of JFK, the attempted assassination of Ronald Reagan was a scary event affecting the nation on a heartfelt level. On a matter of national pride and achievement, I'll never forget the first liftoff of the Space Shuttle Columbia. Many students, myself included, actually stayed home from school to watch the liftoff live.

Reflections from the Class of 1986

Wade S. Alexander and Kathy M. Baker-O'Day

In general, 1986 was a simpler time for America. We seemed to confront national challenges with a united spirit. While we held differing views and preferences, we seemed more tolerant and respectful of opposing points of view. Global and domestic affairs seemed more stable or at least manageable. As a nation, time was distancing us from the war in Vietnam and Watergate while the Cold War was coming to an end. Most Americans wanted to live large and to dream big. The big hair, mullets, and seemingly "anything goes" wardrobe fashions suggested a desire for both acceptance and tolerance.

In 1986 the methods for learning and teaching were much different than what we use today. School districts were in the nascent stages of offering mainstream computer classes, we learned the basics of computer programming, and were taught typing, not keyboarding. The Internet, e-mail, and computer software products did not exist for commercial or classroom use. We did not have cell phones to make calls, to text messages, to check e-mail, or to direct us when lost. If we needed to make a call, we used the pay phone in the cafeteria or went to the office and asked for permission to use that phone.

Global and domestic affairs mattered to us, but we came of age before a constant stream of instant news. We were shaped by MTV (then known as Music Television), movies, and TV shows. In the 1980s MTV had one channel which broadcasted music videos and not "reality television." We strived for the coolness depicted on the television show "Miami Vice." We listened to various styles of music, and the theme song from the movie "St. Elmo's Fire" remains our class anthem.

We still had homecoming floats and most of us did not miss a school dance or other social activity. We enjoyed homecomings, proms, and other social opportunities. We found it hilarious when someone exploded a stink bomb in the lav. Being naïve to the gravity of such threats, when we experienced our first bomb threat, no one took it seriously. Instead, we used the time to socialize with classmates and considered ourselves lucky if we were sent home from school early.

The hallmark of our class is that we got along. While we had our squabbles, mostly everyone liked each other, and while we had our social cliques, we intermixed and socialized with each other. Our shared language consisted of "radical," "awesome," "no way," and "gag me with a spoon." We used these words as slang even as our teachers taught us to know better.

Many of our classmates participated in athletics, the band, the school musical, various clubs, and other activities. Some of us participated in extra-curricular activities where others found themselves under detention and other forms of discipline exercised by coaches and faculty. For all of us, however, high school was a rich social experience. Of course, some of us cared more about social exchanges to make favorable impressions on classmates and teachers than we did for our scholastic responsibilities and performance.

As we returned from the holiday season into 1986, the reality of winter weather, the seemingly long stretch of the third marking period, and the routine of school activities took precedence in our thoughts. However, on January 28, 1986, when the Space Shuttle Challenger exploded 73 seconds into flight killing all seven crew members, part of our innocence slipped away. While the world mourned the loss of the Challenger's astronauts, we were reminded that outcomes in life are not always fair, easy, or easily explainable.

By early March the talk of spring sports and the spring musical, along with thoughts of graduation, future plans, and other activities, ruled the hallway conversation. We began to grow into our post-high school identities in the comfort of familiar surroundings and people—a truly magical moment to be alive. Then, almost instantly, the Baccalaureate and Commencement activities were upon us. We conducted ourselves with decorum throughout these events. Our valedictorian and salutatorian spoke of our accomplishments and life to come while another classmate sang a song of farewell. We all relished our moment of walking across the graduation stage and a profound highlight in our graduation ceremony was honoring our classmate Joseph Youch with a standing ovation as he walked across the stage on his crutches to receive his diploma. Joe, loved by all of us, was a beacon of goodwill and decency through his extraordinary example of how to treat others.

As graduates, we have succeeded, and no doubt failed, in many facets of life. Though we have journeyed to life's differing stations and places, we remain united by the special moments of our time together at Lower Dauphin High School. Our class will continue to succeed in our chosen endeavors. The authors of these reflections want our LDHS 1986 classmates to know we are honored to be "captured in a moment" with each of you.

Our 1986 Falconaire is instructive. It opens with, "There is a phenomenon around ships at sea during storms in which a bright light or fire-like ball appears dancing at the top of the mast. The light, called St. Elmo's Fire, was thought by sailors to be a guardian over the ship during the terrors of a storm. … We believe that somewhere in each of the students, faculty, and other staff members that a similar fire grows at Lower Dauphin." It closes with, "Throughout the final year at Lower Dauphin, each of us experienced a variety of emotions. These ranged from joy, after a victorious match, to sorrow during the final days of school with the realization that we could never return to the halls of L.D. Now is the time to take the torch we carried together and go our separate ways. As we carry our candles through life, let us share the light we have with others and never forget the times we shared together under one light, both the joys and the sorrows." We hope this reflection on the Class of 1986 has shown a spark of that fire that will continue to burn.

Reflections from the Class of 1987

Brad Fischer and Tom Salus

Most of us arrived at Lower Dauphin as newly-minted seventh graders in the fall of 1981. Soon Conewago, Londonderry, South Hanover, East Hanover, and Hummelstown were merged into one. Our friendships grew through academics, sports, music, theater, student council and other activities and informal gatherings.

As teenagers, we focused mainly on what was happening in our school and with our friends. Our teachers reminded us to be aware of things going on outside the walls of Lower Dauphin, as one day soon we would be out in the real world. Significant world events from our high school years included the LIVE AID concerts in 1985, the Space Shuttle Challenger disaster in 1986, and President Reagan's famous challenge to Mikhail Gorbachev in 1987 to "Tear down this wall!"

The quality of LD musicals exceeded by far the typical high school show. Dedicated leadership and months-long commitment from staff and students were instrumental to the outstanding performance of "Oklahoma" in our senior year. Mike Carenzo, Chris Rhodes, and Gina Waters shined in the leading roles of Curly, Laurey, and Aunt Eller, and the entire performance was a success thanks to the performers, directors, choreographers and stage crew. In addition to the daytime show for an audience of students, "Oklahoma" ran for three straight nights to a packed auditorium.

We were inspired by many talented musicians who participated in the orchestra, chorus, concert choir and band. Some recall watching Suzann Motz at a band competition perform a brilliant saxophone solo that took our breath away.

We recall fabulous teachers who encouraged us to learn, think and write, and in hindsight we see that it prepared us well for our futures. Throughout our high school years our class was fortunate to receive guidance and direction from our faculty advisors, Messrs. Bernitsky and Dickson. As our senior year began, we bonded as we worked on college applications or looked ahead to the working world.

We have fond memories of our favorite hangout spots, like Jo-Jo's after sports practices, the Food Factory, Pizza Hut and McDonald's after football games, and the home of classmate Jody Dimpsey at almost any time. Many of us remember great times working on homecoming floats at classmate Kathy Wallish's family barn. In the summers, we worked at places like Hersheypark and Chocolate World to earn spending money.

We watched the powerful field hockey squad under legendary Coach Linda Kreiser compete in another state playoff run. The team was led by future Olympian (and our Homecoming Queen) Laurel Hershey and future collegiate star Stacey Gaudette, both of whom went on to become college field hockey coaches. The teams that played during our high school years helped solidify LD's reputation as one of the state's premier field hockey programs.

Some of us had the good fortune to play under Coach Al Hershey, a skilled soccer coach and an All-American player in his own right. We recall victories over rivals like Central Dauphin, a miraculous bicycle-kick save on the goal line, Jellybean, inside jokes and improvised song lyrics that entertained us on long runs. We also remember our good friend and soccer teammate who was killed in a car accident.

Although the wrestling team was not expected to win the league title in our senior year, Hall of Fame coach Cleon Cassel turned the team into a formidable group that continued the strong wrestling tradition at LD. The team was dubbed the best group of "no-names" in the mid-state by *The Patriot News*, and among the highlights of the wrestling season was a successful run to the state tournament by classmate Peter Valeri.

Our baseball team was led by Coaches Gourley and Collier and players Craig Eby, Tom Salus, Rick Wenner and others. The games were exciting, and the Falcons usually won, making it into the playoffs but having the playoff run end sooner than the team would have liked. The practices were memorable too, from chilly spring sessions on snow covered fields to lively games of pepper played during batting practice.

We remember that one day our school was invaded by "nerds." They wore mismatched clothing, hats, thick glasses and pocket protectors. Perhaps coincidentally, the same nerds crashed our 20-year reunion.

We remember the LD cafeteria, but probably not for the food. Lunch was a time to socialize with friends before afternoon classes. The cafeteria was also the place we witnessed a few food fights that seemed to ignite instantaneously and continue until the whole room had cleared. On the occasional Saturday evening, the cafeteria was home to a high school dance.

We remember our Senior Prom, as Prom King Greg Hostetter feigned tears of joy as he danced with smiling Prom Queen Laynie Overby. We also recall with great appreciation the dedication of Gail Reichenbaugh, who managed many projects that were important to our Class.

As our days at Lower Dauphin came to an end and we attended our graduation ceremony, we listened to a stirring rendition of our class song by Chris Rhodes and watched proudly as Peter Ward delivered his valedictory speech. For those of us who knew Peter in elementary school, and in some cases since before kindergarten, there was no surprise that he had earned the title of valedictorian for the class of 1987.

Looking back, we miss our days at Lower Dauphin and appreciate all that our Alma Mater gave to us.

Reflections from the Class of 1989

Denise Little

The class of 1989 held our 20th Class Reunion in the fall of 2009 as the 50th Anniversary of Lower Dauphin inaugurated its year of celebration. We had a great time at the Hershey Italian Lodge. Our class always seems to have a good turnout for our reunions. We really enjoy getting together and reliving old memories of our times at Lower Dauphin.

Our yearbook was titled "One Step Ahead." We spent our middle school and high school years in one building, 7th through 12th grade. We were greeted in middle school with our first bomb threat experience where the school was evacuated, and we ended as seniors with another bomb threat.

A new idea of having a Homecoming King was introduced during our senior year. The Homecoming Theme was "A Trip Around the World" and our class float was the winner.

We were children of the eighties, an MTV generation, full of big hair and big hair bands. New rock group Guns 'n' Roses hit the charts and won MTV's best new artist award for "Welcome to the Jungle." This song became the basis for our prom theme, Bungle in the Jungle.

Many classmates remember where they were when the space shuttle exploded. Classrooms were watching the historic event on television when the tragedy occurred.

The bus driver strike canceled classes for a day and thrilled parents had to drive kids to school.

When we arrived in middle school we were alarmed to find out we couldn't wear shorts to school, while the high school students could. We wore them in grade school, so why not for 7th and 8th grade only? So we petitioned and got the rule changed.

Many remember the sit-in in the hallway outside the office and library. A classmate was involved in an altercation with a teacher, and students were upset that no action was taken against the teacher. A protest also was held against the increase in school lunch prices and students started brown bagging their lunches.

As freshman we remember band camp as it used to be, 9:00 a.m. to 9:00 p.m. in the sweltering August heat for a week and being one of the last classes to be "initiated" by the seniors. We also remember winning second place in states our freshman year.

And who will ever forget our great trips—Wildwood and Rambo . . . .

Reflections from the Class of 1990

Chrissy Garber

In their own words...

Tina Amoroso-Crone: I will never forget the amazing staff who helped me through some tough years. Mr. French, Mrs. O'Brien, Mrs. Santana will always have a special place in my heart.

Angie Sunstrom (Attinger): Spending time with the friends I made then and am still friends with today.

Chris Bakota: Evacuating the school because of a bomb threat that two seventh graders called in from inside the school.

Kylan Booser: Hot August football two-a-days, Friday camo/jersey day and game night, and camaraderie with the guys on the team.

Caryn Borrell (Berkebile): Hanging out with band members and the Senior Prom with Nick.

Michelle Beyer: I will never forget Chrissy (Garber) and I doing the 10 yard markers during the football games.

Chris Blumenstein: Good memory of the Dr. Feelgood Machine.

John Bolden: Out with Gary and Kylan and always having fun times.

Chris Lee (Carnathan): My fondest moments I have to say was being a part of the band front for all those years... we were a close-knit family... I was very proud to be a part of band... Mr. Turnbull was the best director ever. I miss those times and would relive them again if I could...

Shawn Daniels: The 80's were a wonderful time!

Neill Dickson: Senior skip day, two carloads of us went to the beach for the day. Got a speeding ticket because the guys in my car said, "Don't worry; it's just a park ranger." Who knew that the MD State Troopers dressed just like park rangers?

Dave Dissinger: Well, I did a lot of pranks, some not so kind. Or if I didn't do them myself, I planted the ideas in someone else's head only to sit back and watch them get in trouble for doing what I had suggested. I'm not sure if I'm ready to confess everything, I might get hunted down.

Melissa Gahagan: Mr. Pantalone was by far my favorite teacher at LD. I will never forget everything he instilled in me. He has made me the person I am today.

Susanna Grubb: I'll say how much I enjoyed going to Camp Hebron as a junior and senior.

Rich Hershey: A memory that I haven't mentally blocked out . . . Chris Bakota and I skipped when we didn't have a report finished and went to the Hershey Library to finish it. How sad is that!

Kelly Seaman (Hoke): Love the times spent at basketball & football games and then a group of us would head to Friendly's after for huge sundaes.

Chris Hyde: I remember the great time I had playing sports and all that it taught me about life.

Jim Irwin: ...watching in horror as the brand new skis that I worked all summer to buy were just tossed into the back of the Ski Club van among all the others, getting scratched all to hell before ever hitting the snow.

Barry Keefer: ...those good old football days with the boys.

Sharrel Kint Van Wagner: It has been wonderful to get back in touch with many classmates, especially ones we've known since East Hanover!

Julie Hoyt (Koch): Met Curt during Mr. Rath's freshman Government class, sophomore year we had study hall together, junior year we started to date and by Christmas break our senior year we were married.

John Nolt: I remember eating baked goods and playing rummy for hours and hours with Matt Aungst and Shane Jenkins while we waited for results at indoor drumline competitions. I was and still am terrible at all card games. Good thing we weren't betting.

Mike Pit: One of my favorite memories is when Mr. French gave up on me.

Gary Schell: As long as I live I will never forget seeing a sloppy joe hurdling from the hand of Brett Musser or Jon Parmer, over one table towards me, only to splat on the back of its intended target, an underclassman.

Jen Shaffer (Smith): The bomb scare when we all had to sit outside for forever and about half the school left.

Tim Smith: I'll always fondly remember the class ordering Jo-Jo's pizza near the end of the day, and then getting them to deliver it to the end of "H" wing. Hot pizza, slow day at class, what a way to pass the winter!

Ty Stanton: The thing I remember most about high school is spending time with friends at school, in the library, and while playing basketball.

Ryan Woodring: Jumping in the car after classes to go to Ski Roundtop, finding whose parents were away for the weekend party, and the Cannonball 500 event we ran between all participating LD elementary schools.

Dan Youch: Favorite high school memory involved going to all you can eat pizza at some restaurant in Middletown on Thursday nights.

Chrissy Garber: Judging cows in the one agriculture class with Ms. Jones; helping set up the football field and doing the football chains with Michelle Beyer for the JV games; football jersey Fridays; the air guitar show; Jo-Jo's pizza after the school dances; carrying around a bag of flour (as a substitute for a baby) in Marriage & the Family class; playing softball… outfield; being completely sunburned for the Jr. Prom… and having our driver go through Wendy's drive-thru for a Frosty; going to see the Rocky Horror Picture Show with Billy, Michelle and Tommy after the Sr. Prom; helping to teach the class how to do algebra problems in Algebra I; the big hair and big hair bands; and finally seeing each other again in 2009 at our reunion with the Class of '89.

I've reconnected with a lot of old friends in the last two years—and I hope to continue rebuilding those old friendships.

Reflections from the Class of 1991

Nick Poppy

This writer is no greater authority on the collective experience of the two hundred-odd graduates of Lower Dauphin Senior High School's class of 1991 than any other member of the class. But when the call came to write this reflection, every other member of the Fightin' Ninety-First (no one ever called us that) had "gone to the grocery store," leaving me to remember what I can of our high school years. There are many ways to describe my memory, and "reliable" is not one of them, so I hope this is read in the spirit in which it was written, with fondness for a time and a place, and with some faint sense of recognition that yes, that was us. Also, I hope someone brings back some Utz potato chips from the store, because I'm out.

The LDHS class of 1991 bridged the eighties and nineties: two magical decades that our children will mock in future costume parties. Nineteen eighty-seven, 1988, 1989, 1990, 1991—they seem so distant, they can't possibly belong to us. (Seeing them written down, they hardly look like years. Where's the 2?) In that span, we saw the collapse of the Soviet Union, the fall of the Berlin Wall, the release of Nelson Mandela and the dissolution of apartheid, the death of Ayatollah Khomeini, the invasion of Kuwait by Iraq, the invasion of Iraq by the United States, and several amazing food fights. There was no spam email, because there was no email at all. Five people in the country had cellphones. We listened to mix tapes in our cars, and were allowed to smoke in designated areas of the school. Our jeans were washed in acid, because we were risk-takers, and we pegged those jeans tight to our ankles, to guard against snakes and vermin. They were different times.

And the hair. Dear lord, the hair. We had hair like no one had hair. Great, feathery moussed swoops that reached up, up, up into the sky, as if to touch the sun. Gelled cliffs that extended out from the brow like the brims of baseball caps. Forelocks that masked whole halves of faces. And the incomparable mullet—with its business up front, its party in the back—that so many of the guys sported. Future (and present) generations may laugh, but they have no idea. In those days, the backs of our young necks were always threatened by cold and the elements, and we did whatever we could to protect them. Oh, to be able to grow that kind of hair now.

Some 91-ers will remember the anxiety of an Algebra test, the fear of a Brit Lit paper, the bubbling terror of a Chemistry pop quiz. Others will remember Latin and Business and Home Ec and European History classes. Still others will remember that they had to go to different rooms with their friends whenever a bell rang. We all had to go to a lot of classes, where our teachers, bless their hearts, did what they could. Except for study hall. Nobody did anything in study hall.

School was never just about school, though. It was about making friendships, and trying to have boyfriend/girlfriend-ships, and surviving that truly wonderful stretch of human development known as puberty and adolescence. (Fortunately, the teenage years are always smooth and easy and not at all characterized by bad skin and wayward hormones, or high school would be a very difficult time and place.)

It was about the mortification at dropping one's tray in the cafeteria…and the peals of applause that invariably followed, you klutzes. Speaking of the cafeteria, what did we eat? One could buy cookies and corn chips and soft-serve, thus hitting all the major food groups. There were hamburgers and cheeseburgers and sausages and hot dogs and squares of something like pizza. There were tater tots and mashed potatoes and french fries and potato chips. There may have been a salad bar, but that's best left unremembered.

It was about sports. Anyone who ever suited up for Falcon athletics can tell you, our teams were very, very good. Excellent, in fact. The record may show some losses among the wins, but those were no doubt the result of poor officiating, or undiscovered dirty play on the part of our opponents (I'm looking at you, Hershey Trojans). Or, because we were nice people, sometimes our teams would let the other schools win, once in a while, just so they wouldn't feel bad about themselves. Our Junior Varsity soccer team may have gotten carried away with its generosity, but that's the kind of class we were.

Most of the other clubs and organizations at LD (Future Farmers of America, Spanish Club, Amnesty International, the Falcon Flash, and so on) were undefeated, because at the end of the day, we were champions.

Our band, our orchestra, our choirs and chorales spun sweet melodies that could soothe any savagery. Even today, who among us wouldn't wish for a Falcon ensemble from '91 to play us through various parts of our day? How marvelous that would be. I would even take one of the Battle of the Bands bands, whose tuneful metal was almost 100% identifiable as music.

Music so often defines a time. When Hollywood finally makes its blockbuster hit about the Class of 1991—and it will—the Grammy-winning soundtrack will have generous portions of Guns 'n' Roses and Poison, with a little Young MC and C&C Music Factory thrown in for good measure. C&C Music Factory? They had exactly one hit. "Everybody Dance Now" was a kind of electronic, hip-hoppy number that commanded "everybody" to drop what they were doing, feel the rhythm, and "dance." **Now**. And dance we did.

There were galas and formals and just plain dances; dances where we dressed up, and dances where we got down. A secret internal document I recently saw tells me that the theme of our Junior-Senior Prom was "Phantoms." I give our class credit for not going "Under the Sea," or siting our special night in some exotic foreign country, like Canada. But "Phantoms," I wonder what that was about. It wasn't, I don't think, a particularly scary prom. There were no buckets of pig's blood falling on anybody, no ominous, spectral twin girls in pink jumpers, no dinner rolls gamely buttering themselves. Besides, the Holiday Inn-Grantville has always had a strict anti-haunting policy.

Maybe it had to do with the Phantom of the Opera musical, which was popular then. Perhaps it was in reference to some other pop-cultural phenomenon, now lost to time. But I prefer to think that we chose "Phantoms" because phantoms were precisely what we were not. We needed to create ghosts, and dance among them, because we were so alive.

Reflections from the Class of 1992

Angie Eifert Key

Super Dogs and Super Memories: An Introduction to the Story of LD's Class of 1992

The class of 1992 has made significant contributions to the outstanding reputation of Lower Dauphin High School. Our class was gifted in many ways, and our legacy reflects academic, athletic, musical, and personal achievement. While we witnessed some wild events from 1986-1992, Lower Dauphin incubated us in our formative years and provided a captivating introduction to the story of our lives still being written. Connecting to classmates via Facebook helped compile this bird's eye view down memory lane.

Before the beautiful middle school was built, seventh and eighth grade at Lower Dauphin was housed in old "E" and "D" wings, respectively. Having just left the nurturing environment of elementary school, we experienced a bit of culture shock in our early years at the high school. Students were allowed to smoke cigarettes as they passed outdoors to class, and we endured sit-ins, bomb threats, bus strikes, and free-for-all food fights. One year, cafeteria lunches were raised from $1.05 to $1.25, and a massive protest ensued. For more than a week almost everyone (except the foreign exchange students and classmates whose parents taught at the school) packed a lunch, with hopes the embargo would result in compromise pricing. Those who bought a lunch were served bountiful portions, but were also greeted by deafening boos as they entered the cafeteria from the kitchen line. Students eventually lost the battle, and within two weeks, we resigned ourselves to fork over the extra 20 cents and once again we enjoyed the taco bar and questionably nutritious meals such as "super dogs" (two hot dogs smothered in melted cheese and strips of crispy bacon.) Despite the jump in cost, we still managed to afford the newly introduced Otis Spunkmeyer cookies, warmly served to foster addiction.

As we entered into our tenth grade year and beyond, the school drama calmed down substantially. With our jeans rolled tightly at our ankles, we began to soar through our high school experience as high as our flipped collars and sprayed bangs. Memories are mostly about relationships, and our class was tightly knit. During the prom at the Harrisburg Sheraton, we fell into a big circle and all danced to the lyrics of our class song by Billy Joel, "This is the time to remember, 'cause it will not last forever…" And as sappy as the scene sounds, the moment also epitomized our cohesiveness as a class.

Relationships with our teachers also contribute to our fond memories of our years at Lower Dauphin. We consumed the love and support of teachers like Mr. French, Ms. McLure, and the Etters. Though Mr. Seacrist challenged us in math, he also demonstrated his fun side by quizzing us on "How the Grinch Stole Christmas." Dr. Sharpe had the reputation of maximizing our potential (read: thrusting us to the stressful brink of our academic limits) in British Literature, but our beloved Mr. Cole had prepared us the year before with his rigorous American Literature course. If anyone ever walks down old "A" wing, which is currently the 200-wing, the faint chant of Mrs. Lovelidge's voice saying "a-s-d-f-j-k-l-semi" may still be heard as she taught us efficient keyboarding techniques. She and Mrs. Atkinson generously devoted their time to initiating Peer Helpers, and the class of 1992 participated in its inaugural year of volunteer service. In the sciences, a favorite chemistry teacher was Mr. Longreen, who would ask questions like, "So if pairs of electrons are shared, the bond is co---?" And we would answer in unison "valent." He always gave us the benefit of the doubt and made chemistry tolerable; the same way Mr. Smith, later changed to "Coach Smith" thanks to an impressionable professional development seminar, helped us appreciate biology. To this day, we are grateful for the dedication of the many teachers who guided us through academia.

Of course LD is not just about academics. The class of 1992 was and is highly talented! Our musicals always made an impression, along with the famous "Big Blue Band from Falconland." Traveling to pep assemblies we could hear the band playing its famous repertoire of rally cries as we entered the gym and sat by class. Cheerleaders boosted our school spirit and impressed us with their meticulously choreographed routines. In sports our class contributed to 14 straight years of field hockey championships under the legendary and unparalleled style of Coach Kreiser. Our boys and girls basketball teams also went far into playoffs, along with several track athletes, wrestlers, and golfers. In summary, our class was well-rounded and our teachers, advisors, and coaches have validated our reputation for high achievement.

Our creatively clever yearbook staff titled our *Falconaire* "The Story of Our Lives" to chronicle our high school experience. The privilege of growing into adulthood at LD provided us with warmhearted memories as we continue to write life's next chapters.

Post script: A nagging regret of mine has been the negligence of thanking my parents in our senior yearbook. If publication space allows, I would like to thank my mom and dad, Jan Heckenluber and Mac Eifert, for their relentless love and support.

Reflections from the Class of 1996

Nicole Cassel and Samantha Rush

The Class of 1996 had a reputation that preceded it. Senior High teachers had been warned about this somewhat apathetic class of troublemakers. At times, we did little to dispel this poor reputation, choosing a class t-shirt adorned with Grateful Dead bears and the class song "Hotel California."

We could, however, rally around a cause to leave our mark on Lower Dauphin High School. We were instrumental in the development of a merit-based lottery system for parking spaces and in the abolishment of the school's no-hat rule. We came together to pull off, arguably, the best senior class prank in school history when we decorated the front lawn with dozens of stolen lawn ornaments. Our class worked hard to be good citizens in the school and community. We adopted a highway, working on weekends to clear trash from Swatara Creek Road. We hosted an annual car wash to benefit the Children's Miracle Network. Our classmates were some of the first members of the Peer Helpers group.

The class of 1996 enjoyed much success in and out of the classroom. Most glaringly, this class excelled athletically. Our senior year brought Mid-Penn championships in wrestling, field hockey, football, and boys' soccer. The football team also won a district title and went to the state championship game. In the spring, our teams won league championships in softball and baseball. The baseball team compiled a record of 15-2 and maintained a national ranking in the top 15 for USA Today. Our classmates were leaders on the brand new, and very successful, club ice hockey team. The class of 1996 enjoyed being a part of the great history and tradition of Lower Dauphin High School.

Classmates remember…

- Watching Anderson Cooper and Lisa Ling get their start on Channel One.
- The blizzard of 95/96 causing so much school cancellation we thought we might not graduate on time.
- Our great teacher, friend, and mentor Mr. French and all that he did to help us on our journeys.
- The great rapport between Mr. French and Mr. Cole.
- Other favorite teachers: Mr. Bittenbender, Mr. Strohman, Mr. Smith, The Etters, Mr. Longreen, and Mr. Pantalone.
- Japanese class via satellite with Mr. Smith, our trusted guide, and the hilarious Mr. Tim Cook, our Japanese instructor.
- Building our Homecoming floats at the McKeever Farm, "Italy, The 50s" (which took 1st place), Peter Pan, and the Christmas float that never made it to the football game.
- The torrential rain at the Homecoming game our senior year when the Homecoming Court and Queen (Kristi Templin) got drenched at half-time.
- Our ever patient and helpful faculty advisor, Mrs. Fisher (formerly Ms. Mengel).

Reflections from the Class of 2002

Brooke Miller

There was a profound change of perspective for the class of 2002 that took place only two short weeks after school was back in session. Until that point, our young minds had a fairly naïve perspective due to our lack of experience in enduring any sort of hardship or tragedy. Each morning we came to LD and started our day by pulling into our assigned parking spot, followed by a short walk into school through the doors adjacent to the gym as well as the 900 wing. For those not so lucky, we had to saunter (with speed) from the lower lots by the band fields in order to make the first bell.

Once the school day began, there were the typical activities and classes that we had experienced as freshmen, sophomores, and juniors. We continued to pass notes to our friends in the hallway in between classes. We would enjoy the combination of the breakfast ring and Orange Julius recipes Mrs. Kuhlen had taught us during Foods II. Lunchtime was a social cocktail hour of sorts (without the cocktails) as we would excitedly rush to the cafeteria to meet our friends and enjoy the various goodies such as chocolate milkshakes, Little Caesar's pizza, and Otis Spunkmeyer cookies. While after school engagements varied from student to student, it is safe to say that by the beginning of their final year in high school, most seniors had found a comfortable niche which involved a balance of social, academic, and extracurricular endeavors.

Life proceeded with customary normalcy until September 11, 2001. Prior to this day, we were not trained to think about issues like international terrorism, the safety of our country, and the future of the United States in general. However, that day will forever stain the memories of those in the Class of 2002 as it served as a turning point, not only for the country of which we were so proud, but also for us as individuals. We no longer were naïve adolescents, but instead young adults who quickly became educated on worldwide affairs.

While it took time for some to grasp the details of the attacks that day, what became undoubtedly clear to us was that these random acts of terror and violence on such an extreme level were only the beginning. We no longer lived in a world where our safety and well-being could be taken for granted. The stark reality that this provided to us was more of an education that we ever could have learned through a textbook

[1] From "Expostulation and Reply," William Wordsworth

Summit Achiever Alan Sener '73

Alan Sener has worked in the motion picture, commercial television, and music video industries. He has performed in theaters throughout the world as part of the New York-based Louis Falco Dance Company. He is a Professor and Chair of the University of Iowa Department of Dance. Alan Sener has created over 80 dances for the stage, and teaches modern technique, improvisation, and choreography. He conducts master classes internationally and teaches annually in New York City for The Joffrey Ballet School Summer Programs. He is active as a freelance choreographer and performer, appearing in Martha Clarke's *In The Night*. One of his more recent works titled *Tongues in Trees*, with music composed by Payton MacDonald, was performed by the JACK Quartet in a premiere performance in the University of Iowa's dance department's 2010 fall gala. Upon request, Sener also restages the Louis Falco Repertory, a dance legacy with which he was entrusted as artistic director.

Alan was Louis Falco's long-term choreographic assistant and a former principal dance with the Louis Falco Dance Company. Shortly after Falco's death in March 1993, Alan began serving as the dance archivist for the Falco estate and supervised undergraduate and graduate students through courses of study in which Falco materials on paper were preserved, organized, and cataloged.

Working in conjunction with the Dance Collection of the New York Public Library for the Performing Arts, the documentation and preservation of existing film, video, and audio recordings of Louis Falco's career as a dancer and choreographer is well underway. Sener spent two years working with the Dance Collection of the New York Public Library to restore, preserve, catalog and document more than 70 videotapes in multiple formats, representing 26 separate pieces of Falco's choreography.

The Dance Collection of the New York Public Library holds copies of all videotaped recordings of Falco's choreography, including some that are available for public viewing. The others require permission to be viewed. In addition, copies of all videotapes are held in Sener's office at the University of Iowa and in a New York storage unit. As part of this mission, The Louis Falco Dance Project, Inc.—a nonprofit, tax-exempt foundation—was created to help facilitate this archiving process.

One of Alan's most emotionally moving pieces was his Eulogy of Interpretative Dance in Memory of his sister Judith (Judy) Louise Sener '63.

146

Academics

Curriculum

One would be hard pressed to find anywhere else the variety of programs offered at Lower Dauphin High School, particularly in the early years when most high schools had the typical tracked courses in College Prep, Business, and General. In the spring of 1968 a new method of scheduling based on individual ability and interest was instituted and managed through a data processing system, a very new idea at the time. "Arena" scheduling followed soon after. As might be expected, offering "singletons"—courses with only one section and one designated teacher—complicated the process of scheduling both classes and students, and it wreaked havoc for the person who did the scheduling, for this needed to be done "by hand." Nonetheless, development of new courses and new programs was encouraged in every subject area, and this brought richness to the depth of the course offerings, ranging from mini-courses which might be taught only once ever to programs that expected a two or three-year student commitment.

Special Academic Programs
Archaeology and Longitudinal Studies

Among the many unusual (for high school) and fascinating courses offered with the move to more electives and mini-courses in the early 1970s was the popular Archaeology course. Combining both class study and field digs, students were provided an unusual opportunity to understand local history and gain an appreciation for the meticulous work of library researchers and laboratory investigators, while trying their own hand at new discoveries.

In 1971 (reported in October 1972 *Know Your Schools*) the students uncovered an iron foundry in Union Deposit. Thrilled with this discovery they were primed for their major dig that occurred the following school year. The students had the unusual opportunity to investigate the grounds that surround an ancient farm house on land which had been purchased by the School District as a site for the construction of a new high school. The farmhouse originally belonged to the Mumma family and the last surviving occupant, Miss Elsie Mumma, agreed to sell the property to Dr. Henry R. Hoerner, Superintendent of Schools, whose father had once done her a major favor by rescuing her cows during a local flood.

For this excavation the students laid out a grid measuring 50' x 50' and conducted a test excavation of 10 square feet within the grid in order to dig down roughly 11 feet and examine every inch of soil. To their surprise they unearthed an air vent which did not lead into the cellar. Digging deeper, the students found a sub-cellar which they carefully excavated. The sub-cellar revealed a rectangular room about 8' x 16' with walls of hand-hewn limestone and a unique arched ceiling that was molded with cement of a kind used during the 1800s. While arched, there is no keystone at either side where the arch meets the wall. In the sub-cellar, students found apothecary bottles and wrought iron nails which date to the late 1700s but still in good condition. Reportedly this hidden sub-cellar could have been used by the underground railroad for hiding runaway slaves, or in earlier times to hide from Indians.

According to the *Middletown Press and Journal*, May 16, 1973 in an article about the elective course Archeology, plans were made to restore the Mumma farmhouse in part through a special three-year course, Longitudinal Studies, being established for this project. By fall plans were outlined for three phases of the course: (1) Restoration of the Mumma farmhouse, (2) A Bicentennial Festival, and (3) An Educational Exchange with Great Britain. The December 21, 1973 *Falcon Flash* noted that 52 sophomores would be selected for the three-year program.

Mr. (now Dr.) Steven Messner and Mr. Thomas Campbell selected the 52 students who would meet their credit requirements of World Cultures and American History through Longitudinal Studies and divided the class into committees that were given a problem or situation to solve. The class later reorganized to follow a corporate organizational model. By fall Longitudinal Studies and Archaeology Class were giving public tours to display their handiwork. Every December for a number of years the students held an Open House at the Mumma Farm.

The Cultural Exchange with Great Britain did occur when students went there for six weeks. There are confidential, personal reports of some situations there, but this is probably better left unsaid.

Coalition of Essential Schools

The Coalition of Essential Schools, founded by Theodore Sizer with whom Judith Witmer had studied during a summer at Harvard University, was a national school restructuring effort sponsored by the Pennsylvania Department of Education, in which a team of students would be assigned to a team of four teachers—combining traditional teaching methods with techniques designed for students to pursue knowledge in more depth. The four core subjects would be taught as they related to each other, essentially delivering an integrated curriculum. The philosophy behind the program is that each school would determine what information is "essential" in each subject and build the curriculum upon those essentials. The objective was to provide more diverse and personalized education.

Lower Dauphin High School's involvement was two years, from February 1989 to February 1991, with the following core planners, chaired by Dr. Witmer: Linda Chavez-Wilson (Spanish), Linda Hummel (Vocal Music), Debra McKee (Mathematics), David C. Smith (Science), Nan Willis (English), and Ron Zeigler (English). These were later joined by Jim Brandt (Social Studies), Jean Hynicker (French), Margaret DeAngelis (English), Kermit Katzaman (Science), Marjorie Carlson (Home Economics), Steve Kistler (Mathematics), Kathleen Jones (Vocational Agriculture) and Nancy Zeigler (English).

Following two years of planning and development with the support of Superintendent George Sauers, a pilot program was created to begin the fall of 1991 with 160 students (80 freshmen and 80 sophomores) to be taught by a team of four teachers using individualized instruction and an interdisciplinary curriculum. Instead, however, the Coalition was unexpectedly canceled by the School Board, upon recommendation of Dr. Sauers, when changes in the program, arbitrarily made by the superintendent and not discussed with the Coalition Committee, were rejected by the Coalition Committee.

According to the faculty newsletter, *The Insider*, February 1991, "The 14 members of the team have resigned from it. The resignation letter contained fourteen signatures because of the unacceptable conditions placed on the committee that the curriculum would not be refigured to be interdisciplinary while including all of the academic subjects. This mandated condition from the Board, of course, rendered it impossible to remain a Coalition School."

The account by the *Flash* (April 9) led with the headline, "Coalition has support, lacks funds" with a vote of 7-1, supported by Mrs. Manders, a School Board member. Mr. Joseph Brightbill, also of the Board, said he viewed the principles as "great" and "outstanding," but added that such a program could not be implemented in full when every cent of the budget was being watched.

Computer Programming

The first acknowledgement of computer programming in Lower Dauphin is found in Vol. 4 (1964) of the *Falcon Flash* in a feature article "Your Career with Computers," with information on programming as a career. This likely was the first time most students had ever heard of this career and likely most didn't even read the article, not realizing what was to come in a new Age of Technology. **This would turn out to be the only time the word "computer" occurred in the school publication of the 1960s.**

Even by the **1970s** little was known and less was understood about the potential of computers. However, the February 21, 1973 *Falcon Flash* reports that nine students were taking a course in basic computer language known then as FORTRAN (now Fortran), a language developed, according to Wikipedia, by IBM in the 1950s for scientific and engineering applications. It is the language used for programs that benchmark the world's fastest supercomputers.

The first course in computer programming was offered in the early **1980s** when Mr. Edward Romano taught a class to gifted elementary students in 1981. As the October 1981 issue of the *Flash* reports, "The first assignment given to the computer was figuring math problems. The students were awed by how quickly the machine provided the answers. More complicated processes were continually taught and soon the students were writing original programs.

In the fall of 1982 microcomputers arrived at LDHS for a course that was **filled** eight periods a day. The computer used was the Radio Shack TRS-80 model 3, described as "a good business computer with adaptations for advanced basic learning." In addition, there was a computer in the guidance department. LD had entered the modern age of technology.

In February 1983 *The Falcon Flash* ran a story, "Computer Craze Hits LD." It reported that Mark Peacock (LD '82), a freshman majoring in computer science at the University of Florida, was very pleased with the program at LD; however, Mark noted that in his program "the computer field is so competitive that 100-150 students share a terminal; often one can wait in line all day and not acquire the use of a terminal."

A year later, *Know Your Schools* (December 1984) was reporting that Lower Dauphin School District was beginning to create a computer curriculum. By March 1985 the district publication announced the recent acquisition of three word processors and four microcomputers in the Senior

High Business Department to begin the transition from manual or typewritten accounting and communicating into the modern electronic era of the business office. By October a Computer Aided Drafting (CAD) machine had been installed in C-4 where a course was taught by Mr. George Kunkle.

Two years later the Production Printing Class was processing and printing the *Falcon Flash*. Students formatted the newspaper on a computer, put it on a disk, then gave the disk to the printers where a series of processes resulted in the school newspaper.

Also that fall of 1987 an electronic message board, a gift from the Class of 1987 at the request of Mrs. Judith Witmer, was installed in the cafeteria. Students were permitted to post school-related messages confirmed by a coach or advisor. The keying in was handled by Bill Wrightstone who was selected because of his perfect attendance record and record of responsibility.[1]

Training in using computers was offered to the staff beginning in the mid-to-late 1980s. Classes quickly filled as the realization spread through the school community of the coming necessity to be what was being called "computer literate."

Driver Education (Adventures)

Where cars and learning to drive are involved, high school life can take many turns beyond the basic "right" and "left." Driver Education (both behind the wheel and classroom instruction) has been a part of the LD curriculum since the beginning, with Mr. Jerry Brittain as the first instructor. For whatever reason there were few mishaps in the first five years, but the first recorded incident in 1966 was every driver educator's nightmare.

One bright morning in the mid-1960s Mr. Ben McLure was asked by the principal to return a film to the Bureau of Motor Vehicles in Harrisburg (at that time located near the Capitol). He chose to go at a time when a more experienced student was to be behind the wheel, believing this city driving would be a valuable lesson for his charge, Ken Willis '66. Ken was in the driver's seat, following instructions left by Mr. McLure to "wait right here outside the building while I run in to return the film." In the brief time the teacher was completing the routine errand, a capitol police officer approached Ken and ordered him to move the vehicle immediately. Ken, fearful to raise questions because he had only a learner's permit, did as directed, planning to drive around the block and come back to pick up Mr. McLure. However, the street led Ken out of the city and the more he tried to find a way to "circle around and come back" the more confusing it became for this novice driver who had never been in the city before. He, of course, had no way to contact his teacher and certainly couldn't stop and ask directions because he neither knew where he was nor what specific directions to ask as he had not needed to pay attention to the fact that he had been at the Bureau of Motor Vehicles. Ken eventually found himself in Reservoir Park where he stopped the car. In the meantime, the police in Harrisburg were notified to look for a Driver Education car. Thus, Ken was found.

One of Mr. McLure's favorite comments from a student was in the early 1970s with the screaming "We are out of control" by Marty Ferris '73 during his first lesson. With dual controls in the car,

---

[1] *Falcon Flash*, October 2, 1987.

Marty was in no actual danger, but "new driver's terror" had overtaken him.

Mr. Heistand was known for parking the Driver Ed car in front of the school, sometimes blocking the buses. As a result, a good natured difference of opinion occurred between the teacher and some of the bus drivers who felt that the car being parked in front of the school was a bit of a hazard. One day when the car was there and Mr. Heistand had not yet come back outside with a student driver, someone (could it have been a bus driver?) filled the back seat area completely full of trash/scrap paper for Mr. Heistand to find.

Another memorable event with Mr. Heistand was the day he again left the motor running to warm up the car on a chilly day. As was his routine, he went inside the building to meet the first student driver of the day. Once the student arrived from his homeroom, teacher and student walked out the front door as prescribed. However, the Driver Education car was not there. It was nowhere in sight. No one had noticed anyone else getting in the car although a few people mentioned seeing the car sitting there during home room exercises. There was no explanation except to believe that the car had been stolen. Police arrived to investigate but could offer no explanation, advising the school to report the missing car. Evidently the thief had not noticed the car was very much identifiable by the lettering on the doors and rear of the car. Presumably, this is what caused the car to be set afire in Philipsburg, PA, two hours distance from Hummelstown. Also missing and never returned was a student who recently had moved to the Hummelstown area from this small town of Philipsburg in the center of the state.

In 1978 the Driver Education program got its own space in the form of a trailer that was installed between C and F wings. The reason—in addition to the crowded conditions—was to house a 40-unit Drivocator System, an instructional process that even generated a doctoral dissertation in 1971 after the Drivocator was first introduced in the late 1960s. However, Dwayne Menges '87 described the Drivocator from his own perspective thus,

> "The thing I hate most about driver's ed is that we have to press stupid little buttons to answer questions. If you are normal, you are often distracted during these films and miss the question. ...At random you pick button C. This means you have just made a left turn—into an ocean. The machine cannot be content to let you be wrong. It flashes a light to everyone else in the classroom, telling them you are wrong."

Probably what alumni most remember is the name given to the trailer, the H. E. Weishaupt Memorial Driver Training Institute and Trailer. Mr. McLure credits Mr. (now Dr.) Rudolph Sharpe with then coining the sobriquet, The Great White Trailer—Moby Trailer for short.

Moving ahead ten years, Shane Jenkins described his experience in the Moby Trailer as he invited the reader to "watch in horror as the killer sophomores from hell push all the film buttons at the same time; hear the raucous laughter emitting from their mouths as they watch the 1962 driver safety movie; feel your patience dwindle as they mistake the clutch for the parking lights for the seventh time that period." He adds, "In fairness to the sophomores, Mr. Heistand finds it more challenging to deal with licensed drivers taking driver training."

English Enrichment

English Enrichment was instituted in the fall of 1971, the brainchild of Judith (then Ball) Witmer, at the time a member of the English Department. After conceiving the concept, Mrs. Witmer approached Mr. Zeigler and together they created a team-taught three-year sequential program as a course to meet the needs of highly motivated, academically superior, self-directed students who also held various outside interests such as drama, music, sports, travel and/or service. The program was designed to be structured, yet with open dialogue as the norm, with students encouraged to question, comment, and even disagree. Further, it was created to develop a close interaction among its members and to encourage self-confidence in each student.

The primary rationale of the course, based on Mrs. Witmer's experience with the Class of 1965, sections of which she had taught as freshmen, juniors, and seniors, was that students will perform better and achieve faster with the same teacher who gets to know the students well. The added factor in English Enrichment was to have it taught by a team of two (preferably a male and female) not only to enrich the content, but also to provide a balance of style and personality and more than one mentor and evaluator of the student work. Using a humanities approach, based on an evening, no-credit elective Mrs. Witmer had taught in 1966, English Enrichment also focused on the development of better writing and general communication skills.

The structure was interdisciplinary, dealing with literature, art, music, philosophy, and religion using an enriched literary study to allow individual attention to composition and speech needs and encouraging better understanding of self through interaction of the group. Such a three-year experience leads to camaraderie not possible in a conventional program. The program produced some outstanding students who won national recognition, as well as being named in 1989 by the National Council of Teachers of English as a Center of Excellence. It later became the prototype for the gifted program in all disciplines at Lower Dauphin.[2]

One of the adventures with an Enrichment team included a Survival Project when the study of Thoreau's Walden became reality with the group spending five hours on the Kenneth Staver farm creating their own Walden existence. Students were to make a plan to survive in the woods for a season and to define their own nature philosophy. Working in pairs, they could take with them a theoretical $50 and whatever they could carry on their backs.

Another adventure led a group to Washington to visit the Shakespeare Library among other venues. Another class was invited for a week-end to West Point, guests of Craig College '74, a member of the original EE class. They stayed at the famous Thayer Hotel on site and were guests at the performance of *A Midsummer Night's Dream*, arriving home in time to attend a live performance of *Hamlet* with Dame Judith Anderson in the lead role.

Another group of sophomores toured the Philadelphia Museum of Art where they had the opportunity to see the 1492 exhibit which spotlighted the world's seven greatest cities at the time Columbus discovered America. Students and instructors agree that this was a most unusual and very special experience which greatly enriched their literary skills and took them on adventures undreampt of in their philosophies or by their peers. Mentoring continued even after graduation and friendships remain to this day.

---

[2] *Know Your Schools*, September 1989.

Independent Study

During the heyday of mini-courses, team-taught courses, and many innovational offerings at Lower Dauphin in the 1970s, an Independent Study program was made available to students who either could not schedule a particular specialty course because of a scheduling conflict or who had a desire to study an additional topic that might not be offered as part of the school curriculum. Independent Study also appealed to students who had time-management skills and internal motivation.

Further, the program depended upon faculty who were willing to give extra time to an individual student; this often meant the teacher either gave up his/her planning period to coach the student, stayed after school with the student, or worked with the student during the lunch period. This, of course, was long before online courses which have brought an entirely different dimension to studying independently.

Offering independent study in the 1970s is another demonstration of the dedication of the high school faculty, the willingness of students to branch out on their own, and the support of the administration of innovative approaches to learning. (*Know Your Schools*, September 1980)

The first trial course in studying independently was launched in the spring semester of 1966, as described by the local newspaper, *The Sun*, in its issue of March 3, 1966:

> A humanities course, initiated by Mrs. Judith T. Ball, senior English teacher, was begun recently for the benefit of students interested in the branches of learning concerned with man (languages, literature, and philosophy). Senior class college prep students have been meeting together on Monday evening from seven to nine o'clock for the non-credit course. Activities at the meetings vary from small group discussions to speeches and presentations by the students. Samples of topics addressed are "What kind of institutions and programs are reformers and critics attacking in society?" "Can man master himself?" "Why have men rebelled and revolted?" and "What is truth?"

Science Electives and the Summer of 1967

The summer of 1967 was a pivotal one and may have been the catalyst for the many and diverse changes at Lower Dauphin. One of these major changes occurred when Mr. David C. Smith was made Director of the Lower Dauphin School District Federal Project, Title I of the Elementary and Secondary Education Act, a milestone in public education. Lower Dauphin was awarded a Federal grant (as were many schools in the U.S. at this time) of $27,845 (close to $200,000 in today's dollars) to improve science education in grades K-12. More than 160 students and 50 teachers were involved in the project at LD and spent the summer working to develop a logical, sequential curriculum plan for K-12 science. A large number of course guides were developed and became the cornerstone of an outstanding science program in the district.

Following the development of new science curricula, the number of comprehensive science electives that became available to students by 1972 included genetics, histology, zoology, botany, limnology, organic chemistry, electronics, nuclear science, oceanography, and astronomy.[3] Limnology, team-

---

[3] *The Patriot-News*, circa 1972.

taught by Mr. Kermit Katzman and Mr. Paul Longreen, is the study of chemical and biological aspects of fresh water streams. Astronomy, taught by Mr. Jere Moser, utilized an eight-inch telescope that accommodated a camera for photographs of celestial phenomenon. Mrs. Nancy Kachniasz taught genetics. Later organic chemistry, qualitative analysis in chemistry, anatomy, and physiology were added.

Anatomy and Physiology

Among the many other electives was Anatomy and Physiology, designed for students who were interested in a detailed, comprehensive coverage of human structure and function. With emphasis on the human skeleton, human histology, and human physiology, the course is laboratory oriented and aimed toward students intending to pursue a career in nursing, medicine, dentistry, veterinary medicine, osteopathy, chiropractic medicine, pharmacy, medical technology, or related science fields. Each major concept deals with both normal and abnormal conditions (disease). As of the date of this writing, 55 students have enrolled for the 2011-2012 school year. This is the one remaining course of the electives established by David C. Smith in the early 1970s. Quite a tribute!

Oceanography

Another of the early—and continuing electives—was Oceanography, a highlight of which is an annual field trip to Wallops Island Marine Science Center in Virginia which provides study of both estuarine and coastal environments. The students engage in oceanographic research methods, water quality testing, basic navigation techniques, identification of specimens, beach profiling, ecology of sand dunes, and marsh organisms. Students conduct actual experiments and employ the methods they learned in their school classrooms. In a final examination at the end of the week, LD students typically outscore students from other schools.

Histology

This course is designed to present histological techniques in the preparation and identification of permanent glass slides of animal tissue. This semester course is divided into two nine week periods, the first of which emphasizes microscopic examination and identification of five types of tissue which compose a living organism. The second nine week period consists of laboratory preparation of permanent slides of various vertebrate (frog and rat) organs. The tissues are fixed in a preservative and processed into wax blocks then sliced with a micrometer, placed on glass slides and stained with specific organic stains to illustrate the tissue structure of the organs.

Around the same time changes in the science curriculum were being instituted, the LD activity period at the end of the day (2:35-3:30) was being studied as to better utilization, and the result was the addition of a more formal eighth period at the end of the day.[4] According to Mr. Kenneth Staver, "The primary purpose of the decision is to give teachers and pupils a chance to get together on a more favorable pupil-teacher ratio."[5] Time would be utilized for all special interest activities such as seminars and research in sciences, advanced studies in math, social studies, English or a

[4] *Falcon Flash,* September 1967.

[5] Undated unidentified news article

foreign language, along with special interest clubs such as future teachers, farmers, or businessmen. Other clubs such as chess club or sports club were also planned, along with the possibility of remedial and correctional instruction classes to help students. Transportation would be provided. This laid the groundwork for a variety of special courses to be offered in all fields.

The February 1967 issue of the *Falcon Flash* announced that there would be no more activity (eighth) period study halls, 2:35—3:30. The article stated, "Rather, students had the option to leave school at 2:35 or to stay for advanced and enrichment courses, as well as activities and clubs. Further, students could find remedial help or make-up missed work either at their own request or by being assigned by their teacher(s). This late eighth period could also be used for student detentions assigned by the administration. Transportation is provided."

The students liked the informality of the courses. By October, however, the activity buses were running as much as half an hour late every day, the students were looking for reasons to leave at 2:35, and the faculty members were exhausted. While philosophically sound, the practical issues revealed that continuing such a demanding schedule was not feasible.

The Reality Room

Mr. William Minsker

Beginning with the 1969-1970 school year, "The Reality Room" came into being after two young teachers were assigned a team-teaching situation for the 9th grade government course. During the summer months of 1969 they worked with a selected group of rising 9th grade students to create and pilot a new approach to the teaching of the course.

Through much experimentation during that summer, an individualized, multi-faceted, multi-media approach to the course work and teaching was created; this involved two classes meeting in C11-12 as one group with Mr. Paul Shirk and Mr. William Minsker instructing in a team-teaching style.

Throughout the course, a series of "track programs" was offered to provide a wide variety of supplemental and review materials to reinforce the basic content materials. Preceding the beginning of each two or three-day track program, students were given the responsibility of selecting which "track" they would follow. Track 1 was the most advanced and detailed, and it was designed to challenge students who were striving for the highest grades in the course. Track 2 was designed for average students, and Track 3 was created to reinforce the basic content materials for the students who were having difficulty with the coursework.

Each track had both required and elective activities for student engagement, consisting of readings, worksheets, filmstrips, small group discussions, and individual activities such as poster creations and surveys. During these track program activities, Mr. Minsker and Mr. Shirk worked with students individually and in small groups. All students, no matter which track was chosen, received a full range of grades, based on their performance on each activity. A weighted scale was then determined based on the track.

Track programs were used to supplement and reinforce major sections of the government course including Pressure Groups and Political Parties, Rights and Responsibilities, The Nomination and Election Process, Voting in Elections, American Legal System, Federal Government, State Government, and Local Government. A unit of study followed each of these programs.

It had been decided during the summer to select a name for room C11-12 which would emphasize the relevance of the program's focus on Government. From a number of various choices came the name "The Reality Room." This name remained in continuous use, first with rooms C11-12, and then with rooms A11-12, for the 9th grade Government program through the 1992-1993 academic year.

The Sand Box

The World Cultures Learning Laboratory was first established in 1969 as a three track program for 333 tenth grade students with the purpose of enabling student development of value discrimination, identification and development of leader and follower roles, and facility with decision-making processes. It was team-taught and the content was delivered through six learning areas and a resource center. One of the first of the three teachers involved with the development of the program in jest dubbed it "The Sandbox" and the name stuck.

The process led students to involve themselves with various areas of study and various approaches to learning in each of the six study areas. According to Mr. Steven Futchko, one of the instructors, "One group of youngsters might be involved in a discussion session, in another area the kids may be viewing slides, another group may be listening to tapes, and perhaps a fourth area is reviewing something with an instructor. It's not so much that we have come up with anything new and startling in and of itself, it's just that we've put it all together and come up with a very workable process. I used to think the only feasible way of teaching kids anything was to stand up in front of a class, give them lecture notes for more than 40 minutes, assign them a reading for homework and eventually give them a test. But now my views have changed."

All students enrolled in the world cultures program were assigned to all three teachers, rather than to individual teachers. H-10, the room designated for the laboratory, was an Audion, a double room with a folding partition. This allowed enough room for setting up the various study areas. The study areas were labeled zones, and the student had a choice of four out of six zones in the study of any one unit area. For example, in a ten-week study of China, a student could move through the four out of six zones that he had selected.

The program allowed for an instructor-student ratio of 1:10 to be realized utilizing regularly assigned student teachers from Penn State Harrisburg and Shippensburg University and was funded with approximately $750 in capital equipment.

Vocational Agriculture Program
Lower Dauphin Future Farmers of America, 1960-1993

The Vocational Agriculture Program and its accompanying Future Farmers of America (FFA) is one of Lower Dauphin High School's most successful and highly regarded programs. Considered a premier offering, vocational agriculture was an inherent part of the planning for this new high school. Located at the end of F-wing, "Vo Ag" was more than a program; it was a vocation, a lifestyle, and a home for those enrolled.

The Lower Dauphin FFA was at the heart of the school for more than thirty years with a vast number of accomplishments that resulted in many successful alumni. The program was designed to teach students the intricate processes and development in agriculture and related fields. The Mission Statement became more than a creed; it was words to live by for its members: *Learning to do, Doing to learn, Learning to live, Living to serve.*

In the 1960s Mr. Staver quietly designed a curriculum aimed at those who were academically strong and with a sincere commitment to agriculture; he identified members in the Class of 1965 who could carry both college prep and vocational curricula through their years in high school and, without fanfare, enrolled them in the challenging courses.[6] These students became the adult leaders in their field and in their communities.

Over the years students involved in this high school program achieved both state and national proficiency awards and recognition for their projects. The agricultural specialties included animal care, crop and plant management, horticulture, and farm management. FFA also promoted strong leadership skills through the student management of individual and national chapters. Students had many opportunities to meet, interact, and learn with students from other chapters at national meetings.

Among its numerous honors, both to the club and many of its individual members, was the designation in 1985 as Pennsylvania's top FFA unit and its being recognized with a National Chapter Gold Emblem plaque.

The unfortunate truth is that there are fewer and fewer family farms; as the business of the country continues to change, so does farming; thus farming, once the heart of every American home, now is big business. As we have fewer students interested in learning the basic skills of farming, a once flourishing program is now a memory but remains an essential and splendid part of our school's history.

---

[6] This was mentioned by Paul Beers in *The Evening News* in a profile of one of these students, Russel Cassel

Special Off-Campus Academic Programs

American Institute for Foreign Study

Founded in 1964, the American Institute for Foreign Study (AIFS) is one of the oldest, largest and most respected cultural exchange organizations in the world. With global offices in six countries, AIFS organizes cultural exchange programs for more than 50,000 participants each year. The company offered its first program in 1965 and Lower Dauphin students first participated in 1969 with two months in Europe that offered four weeks study and classes at the University of Salzburg, Austria. This group also saw London, Paris, Vienna, Berlin (East and West, crossing over the Berlin Wall at Checkpoint Charley), Brussels, Cologne, Munich and many little villages. This pioneer group, led by Mr. David C. Smith, Director of Foreign Studies, consisted of Julie Staver, Wendy Bolton, Sarah Kuntz, Wendy Saylor, Bob Matthews, Martin Beam, Joe Hoffman, Frank Graybill, Rick Landis and Carol Rhoad, along with three students from Derry Township and one each from Lancaster and Camp Hill. The cost per student was $812.86.

Trips were offered annually for academic credit and included Italy ($479) in 1972, Spain ($449) and Germany ($459) in 1973, and Russia in 1974 ($599). Other countries traveled to since 1967 include Puerto Rico, France, Switzerland, Costa Rico, Ireland, England, Scotland, Netherlands, Austria, Greece, China, and India. Several special tours were the Sound of Music Program in Austria and the Lake District in England. Among the Lower Dauphin chaperones through the years were Linda Chavez Wilson, Burr Rhodes, Ron Zeigler, Candy Romano, Ana Barbush, William Linnane, Flora Werner, Jean Hynicker, Joe Schan, Barbara Atkinson, Henry Hoerner, Barney Osevala, Melody Lovelidge, Irvin Curry, William Minsker, Barb Wiegand, Aleda Gruber, Judith Witmer, Steve Futchko, Ron Zeigler and, more recently, Craig and Becky Cassel.

Mr. Smith also served as AIFS Campus Principal at St. Andrews University for three summers and Cambridge University for one summer and worked a two week AIFS cruise on the Mediterranean. He also directed US Educators to AIFS campuses in England, Italy and Spain. Another stint was leading US teachers and their students to Australia and New Zealand. In 1982 Mr. Smith received the Ambassadors Award from AIFS for contributions made to international education.

Capital Area School for the Arts (CASA)

The Capital Area School for the Arts (CASA) was founded in 2001 through a partnership between the Capital Area Intermediate Unit (CAIU) and Open Stage of Harrisburg. CASA offers intensive instruction in visual art, dance, music, theatre, and film and video to qualified high school students in the CAIU (over 150 students from 24 different high schools). Located on the first floor of Strawberry Square, the school uses the city of Harrisburg as its "classroom," affording its students access to the numerous resources located downtown, and utilizing a yearly theme based on the urban environment. CASA continues to be the significant and innovative provider of multi-disciplinary arts education to school entities throughout the area. CASA is an outgrowth of various arts magnet schools offered over the past many years from various entities and offers an option to students whose interest and talent lies in the arts of visual art, dance, film and video, music, and theatre.

Capital Classroom

Capital Classroom was a program begun in 1977 as an internship program for eligible high school seniors to participate in an authentic eight-week experience in a specific career field. While not limited to the nearby Penn State College of Medicine, the college was a popular draw as students were welcomed and could find various levels of health care to explore.

Medical Center Internships

Penn State Hershey Medical Center internships have always been very popular, but limited for high school students. The time usually involved leaving school at the end of the last period and spending several hours in a laboratory or in shadowing a willing medical professional. While the guidance counselors were adept at finding "slots" for students, there was a better chance of acceptance for students who had personal contacts at the facility.

More recently, the Pennsylvania Youth Apprenticeship Program, a two year experience, has been offered to Lower Dauphin and Derry Township high school juniors in various supervised clinical experiences at the Medical Center. The program also provides seminars on various health care careers and related clinical topics. During the students' senior year each selects two clinical areas of interest in which he/she is supervised by a preceptor and by which the students gain in-depth knowledge of health careers.

Outdoor Education (Camp Hebron)

In the spring of 1969 Lower Dauphin embarked on a popular program called Outdoor Education which placed fifth graders at Camp Hebron to study environmental science. High school students were used as counselors. Fifth graders loved it, as did most of the high school counselors. High school teachers found it difficult to have a number of students out for a week at a time, for four weeks. It decimated some of the high school classes. However, the program's popularity made it a permanent program. The first year, only one elementary school participated but by the second year, all elementary schools scheduled what came to be known as "Camp Hebron." Mike Lebo, a fifth grade student, when asked how the counselors held up, replied that his counselor, Robert Wolf '70, was just about a nervous wreck by the end of the week. Bob had 13 energetic fifth grade boys in his cabin. According to Mike, "Bob had to take a few aspirin before he got on the bus to go home." Camp Hebron is now an institution and almost a rite of passage for the high school students who serve as counselors.

Writing Seminar

In either October 1981 or on March 30, 1982 (there is a conflict in dates in different sources used for this book) a busload of Lower Dauphin students were transported to Palmyra High School to participate in a writing seminar conducted by Stephen King. This was one of a number of special programs Palmyra held in its large theatre-style classroom and to which they invited other area schools. While he was popular, Stephen King was not the household name he would later become. Nonetheless, this was an outstanding opportunity for the students.

Special Curriculum Experiences

Language Labs

Once upon a time in Falconland there was a language laboratory, an installation used in the teaching and learning of a modern foreign language. Initiated in schools in the 1950s and 1960s as the newest teaching device, these laboratories originally consisted of reel-to-reel audio tapes, later using cassettes. They allowed for a teacher to listen to and to manage student audio, then provide individualized analysis. Lower Dauphin's language lab was a novelty when the high school first opened with a traditional system of a master console (for the instructor) which was electrically connected to a number of rows of student booths or carrels which typically contained a student tape recorder and headset with a boom arm microphone.

The teacher operated the tape transport controls, allowing for easy distribution of the program material. Once the master program had been transferred onto the student recorders, the teacher would then hand over control of the decks to the students. By pressing the record key in the booth, the student would simultaneously hear the playback of the program while being able to record his or her voice in the pauses, using the microphone.

The problem with the labs is that there were frequent problems ranging from tape running off the reel and parts that frequently wore out as well as bulbs in the control panel in continual need of replacement. Since the student tapes were not normally changed from one class to the next but were recorded over each time, these tapes eventually wore thin, leading to poor sound and tangling.

Service maintenance also became a problem as the technicians usually served many schools and were not on call. Thus, if several stations malfunctioned, much of the entire laboratory was out of action until service could be restored. Further, because of classroom space and/or scheduling, the rooms sometimes had to be used for other purposes, such as study halls which led to students "playing" with the equipment and breaking parts.

Increasing enrollment during the 1970s compounded the problem in many ways and most schools, including Lower Dauphin, converted the lab to a regular classroom, going the way of the audions and general labs.

School-to-Work, Work Experience, and Cooperative Learning

Some type of Cooperative Education Program has been in existence since 1974 to provide job experiences for students who wish to participate in an internship or who are employed in a career-related field. Typically a work experience program is available to senior students who plan to enter the job market immediately following graduation. All work site placements must be pre-approved and admission into this program is based upon prior school attendance, academic standing, and discipline record.

Similar to this was a program begun in 1977 and known as Capital Classroom This was an internship program for eligible high school seniors to provide an eight-week experience in a specific career field.

Senior Day

This program has a sporadic history beginning in the early 1960s as a day when seniors take on the duties of the adults, serving as a teacher, secretary, classroom aide, principal, or custodian for a day. In some situations this is more a shadowing than an actual work experience. (See "Senior Day" in Traditions and Events section.)

Americans for the Competitive Enterprise System

This association of enterprises/businesses is known for the program it offers to high school juniors to visit (a daylong field trip) local businesses and industries. In the early days of Lower Dauphin High School every junior registered for the place s/he wished to visit and faculty accompanied groups of students. Faculty had no choice as to which business they would be assigned.

Mini Courses, Uncommon Subjects, and Short-lived Classes

Beginning in the 1970-71 school year Lower Dauphin High School offered an extensive selection of courses, including what were called "mini courses," compressed nine-week, special topic courses. Students suddenly had opportunities unheard of prior to this experimental time in education during the 1970s. Following is a list of those courses that are best remembered.

Adolescent Literature
Advanced Biology
American Poetry
Archaeology, Introduction[1]
Architectural Studies
Athletic First Aid
Arts and Crafts in America
Astronomy
Athletic First Aid
Basic Electronics
Basic Fundamentals of Movement
Behavioral Sciences, Introduction
Behavior: Practical Choices for Living
Bible as Literature
Black Literature
Botany
Business English
Camping and Outdoor Education
Ceramics
Comic Literature
Communications
Comparative Political Systems
Comparative Religions
Computer Aided Design (CAD)
Computer Math
Consumer Decisions
Dance, from Square Dancing to Soul
Democracy, Living in a
Digital Techniques
Drama I (Stagecraft)
Drama II (Acting)
Drama III
Effective Debate
Electrical Power and the Environment

Electronic Circuits
Electronics, Basic
English Enrichment I, II, III
Family Role in Society
Federal, State, and Local Studies
Filmmaking[2]
Genetics (Human)
Geology
Grammar and Composition
Histology
Historical Problems, U. S. General Intro
History of Arts and Crafts
How Our Economy Works
Human Biology
Humanities
Humanities in Three Cities: Athens, Florence, New York
Human Reproduction and Sexuality
Independent Study
Intermediate Electronics
Invertebrate Zoology
Japanese offered in 1995 and 1996
Jewelry Making
Karate and Self-Defense
LD Studies: A Look at Urbanization
Library Club, 1960s and renewed 1971
Limnology
Literature for Pleasure
Literature of the American West[3]
Local Government Studies[4]
Local Perspectives on U. S. History
Longitudinal Studies
Man, A Study
Marine Biology

Mass Communications[5]
Microprocessors
Minority Literature
Minorities in the United States
Modern Literature[6]
Mythology
Net Set, The
Novel, Introduction to
Nuclear Science
Nursing Mathematics
Oceanography
Office Procedure/Office Machines
Officiating in Boys Sports
Officiating in Girls Sports
Organic Chemistry
Parasitology
Practical Politics
Pre-College Oceanography Program[7]
Psychology, Introduction to
Public Speaking I and II
Qualitative Analysis in Chemistry
Reading Advancement
Reality Room Social Studies
Russian
Sandbox, The
Science Fiction and the Supernatural
Science Research
Science and You

Semiconductor Devices
Shakespeare I, The Tragedies
Shakespeare II, The Comedies
Shakespeare III, The Histories
Short Story I
Short Story II
Slimnastics
Soap Operas as Literature
Space Science
Sports Officiating
U. S. Foreign Relations
U. S. History, New Beginnings from
American Conflicts
Vertebrate Zoology

[1] The course began in the fall of 1970. (Tom Campbell, the teacher commented "...the school likes to give the teacher a chance to run a course in some special area of interest, aside from the regular required courses.")

[2] Students do an original one-minute commercial, a 3 ½ minute animated cartoon, a 30-second drama, film loops and a final project of 100 feet of film.

[3] known as Cowboy Lit.

[4] open to only those appointed as school board student representatives

[5] one of the early forays into very specialized courses, with the study of news, television, and advertising; filmmaking was 50% of the class course

[6] The class attended "Love Story" movie in the spring of 1971 to discuss the transfer of a novel to a movie.

[7] Study in Lewes, Delaware and Wallops Island

In March 1972 the *Falcon Flash* listed some of the above as being additions and changes to courses for the year 1972-73, but there is no easy way to determine which were new in 1971 or which were taught only once. This extension and enrichment of offerings was taken seriously and many students at the time discovered these courses "prepped" them for their college courses, courses their peers from other schools had not experienced. The high school newspaper also provided these additional details:

> Grammar & Composition Review will be extended to one semester. Students taking Business English must also take Grammar and Composition. Supernatural and Science Fiction Literature has been lengthened to one semester. Public Speaking II has been shortened to one quarter. The combined course, Zoology and Botany, will be separated, each being one semester long.

Two years later, in March 1974 the school newspaper offered praise for the number of elective courses available, noting that all LD students had more than 250 electives from which to choose their course of study. At this time the system of multiple electives had been in place for four years, beginning with Social Studies Department and closely followed by the English Department. Among the new courses being offered in the fall of 1974 were Recreational Activities, Dancing, and Jewelry-making as electives.

Later in the mid-1980s Mr. Zeigler tried a new strategy in his ninth grade English by inviting parents of his students to not only observe but evaluate their children's efforts at presenting oral and visual exhibitions of research papers. This approach was prompted by what came to be known as Outcomes Based Education.

The high school also offered several special programs that were cutting edge. Teachers were encouraged to develop courses and submit them for review and approval. Scheduling was a challenge, but the result was invigorating for both staff and students.

Special Project Rooms

There were also rooms in the high school that found special designation throughout the years. With space always being an issue, many of the special rooms were phased out as programs and/or purposes changed.

Audions and General Labs

From the very beginning, the new high school was recognized as a school of advanced design by the American Institute of Architects. One of the special features, reported by the *Harrisburg Patriot* on December 22, 1960, was its sub-wings of self-contained units, each with eight classrooms, an office, library area initially stocked with a set of encyclopedias, conference room, faculty room, an audion classroom, and a general laboratory for individual student work, as well as a service core.

The original intent of the audions was for small performances and practices for public speaking. There was a pull-out stage in each audion. The general labs were intended to be areas for special projects. While these were innovative ideas, by the second year of Lower Dauphin it was evident that more classrooms were needed and the Audions and General Labs gradually were transferred to other uses.

Model Office

In school year 1963-64, students in the Clerical/Secretarial Class were engaged in "on the job" activities in a model office set up in one corner of Miss Strite's classroom. Here the students sampled various office tasks: typing various forms, taking direct dictation, putting telephone calls through, filing, recording a letter to be transcribed from a machine, using a calculating machine, and answering requests placed through the public address system. This experimental office gave the students experience in responsibility, proper dress and manners for work, and interaction with "clients."

Reading Room

Mention is made of this room in the March 1970 *Falcon Flash*, with a comment by new teacher Mr. Michael Filepas who said the Reading Room (recalled as a section of the library or a part of one of the audions) should be smaller in order to make room for another classroom. He disliked what he viewed as favoritism "that seems to exist in the school system." The Reading Room did not survive for long as space in the 1970s became a premium with increasing enrollment.

English Resource Center

With the advent of mini-courses and the resulting 42 courses in the English Department, space (A-10) was awarded in the fall of **1971** for the English Resource Center as a central location for textbooks, syllabi, blue curriculum guides, audiovisual aids, reference materials and professional information necessary in providing a 42-course English program—all of which had been inundating A-2 classroom. According to *Know Your Schools*, October 1971, "With the obstacle course in A-2 eliminated, teachers can now readily secure materials and plan programs in the roomy resource center.... Reading lamps, chairs, and a small rug provide a quiet atmosphere for planning by teachers who generally find their classrooms occupied by other classes during their planning periods."

School Store

In the December 1986 issue of the *Falcon Flash* appeared an editorial bemoaning the close of the school store because the space was needed for storage. The article also noted the lack of any space for the newspaper. The staff had seen Hershey's newspaper office, "...their very own newsroom. Hershey's newspaper is on about the same budget as we are now, yet they have their own room, telephone, two typewriters, and a computer. The *Flash* has a red folder and three desk drawers in an old desk, and a typewriter that eats ribbons."

There was a rebirth of the store in the fall of 2004 with this announcement in the school newspaper, November 9: "School store brings business to Falcon Marketing Class with hoodies, t-shirts, hats and school supplies now being sold in the first ever school store." (The writer obviously was not aware that this was not by any means the first school store in LDHS.)

The Blue Room

The Blue Room was, indeed, painted a soft blue color, befitting its intention as a place for groups of students to meet with guidance counselors, either on specific focused topics or as students with a common need or problem. The room was private and a safe space, with an adult counselor for support and facilitation. In 1988 the Blue Room also became the facility for the development of the Student Assistance Program which provided help for students with substance abuse or emotional problems. When not engaged for counseling sessions, the room was available to groups such as the Fashion Board whose advisor was Dr. Jacqueline Douglass, one of the several guidance counselors in the high school

Coalition of Essential Schools

During the planning for this national school restructuring initiative in 1989, the Coalition of Essential Schools was assigned to a small conference room where resources for the project could be kept, meetings could be held and a typewriter and telephone were available.

Publications

The student publications received space consideration because of need, particularly the school newspaper, for space in which to work and store materials; however, even the *Falcon Flash* occasionally found itself housed in the classroom of the advisor. The disadvantage of having an activity housed in a classroom, aside from space for the typewriter, supplies, and past issues, was the varying degrees of disruption to the classes being held in the room, noise of typing, and any consultation needed with other staff members or the advisor. Despite the handicap, both the *Falcon Flash* and *Media* magazine were consistent in high quality and in meeting deadlines.

From a contest entry, Shelby Jones '12 remembers, "Hidden within the 200 Wing, behind an unmarked door and a blind-covered window, there is a secret room. Once a janitor's closet, this room has become a haven for the *Falconaire* staff and a production room for the entire student body. …Within the closet-size space, there are four computers, seven desks, and one book shelf holding all fifty editions of the Lower Dauphin *Falconaire*. When the yearbook period is in full gear, the sounds of keyboards clicking under the conversation of staff members pitching new ideas can be heard from outside the heavy door.

Electronics Club and Technical (Stage) Crew

It is reputed that one or both of these groups at various times in the history of the school were able to carve out special, hidden space for their use.

Some of the other departments and special projects were also assigned space as it became available, but, as with most schools, as the population increased, space for anything except direct instruction became a premium.

Commencement

High School Graduation Traditions

By the end of the nineteenth century many high school graduations had evolved into elaborate ceremonies, often lasting several days. These were closely reported on the front pages of the local paper, with pictures of each graduate, a tradition still maintained today in towns with local newspapers. End-of-year events often spanned as many as ten days, during which a broad program of scholarly, social, and ceremonial activities took place, including a promenade or ball, baccalaureate services, a literary, a class play, and culminating in a graduation ceremony that included musical selections and declamations by several seniors. The ceremonies did not vary much from place to place or even from year to year, at least up through the 1970s.

It is difficult for high school students of the twenty-first century to understand the significance high school graduation once held at a time in which less than one percent of the population was educated beyond eighth grade. Those who were graduated were viewed as very special and the town honored this achievement. Graduation from small town high schools in particular had an underlying poignancy, which has been lost in a faster-paced world where one's friends and experiences are far more extensive.

From the 1890s until the 1990s in small towns, high school graduation brought a sense that something—perhaps childhood—was finished for each graduate. Then, as now, nostalgia was not a concept most young people understood as they looked toward their own futures, but the memories, which later would change to nostalgia, would never leave most of them.

1911 was the first year that academic caps and gowns were used in high schools; now, a hundred years later we can't help but wonder how much longer the tradition will hold, with disposable robes and throw-away mortar boards.

Lower Dauphin's First Commencement featured three student speakers: Gloria Shertzer, Linda Verdelli, and Carol Flocken, with invited main speaker Dr. Michael Duda, President of California State College of Pennsylvania.

In June 1980 the city paper (Metro East section, June 3-4) did a feature article on our special Commencement Programs:

> "Lower Dauphin seniors won't stage a T-shirt parade at graduation—the class of '79 did that—or sell apples in the audience—'77 graduates thought of that—but they will dip into the past to make commencement as fresh and unique as others have been. …It is the 13th year since LD broke away from a traditional commencement format and allowed students to create the program with each class creating distinctly different formats from a chosen theme.

"An Echo of the Past, A Herald of the Future" ... is this year's program, using guest speakers from past classes in a scripted dialogue with current graduates. Also featured will be a quartette of four sisters of the Snavely family, three of whom are alumni and one a graduating senior. The '79 theme was "Yesterday, Today, and Tomorrow," a recap of the 1970s decade.

"There is an unwritten competitive spirit as each class strives to top the preceding year's program, often discussed at the Christmas Open House Mrs. Witmer hosts for them each year in her home. As many as 50 former students will attend to reminisce and even years later, 'It's the first thing they talk about when I see them today,' she says.

"The programs, which began with a speaking choir in '67, have progressively become more sophisticated and technically complex. Last year's is a good example as it began with the Three Mile Island portrayal. The stage rose, revealing a reactor control console, illuminated by lights. The panel exploded and President Carter emerged on stage in a cloud of smoke from a fire extinguisher he was carrying. It ended with a T-shirt parade with the words "I survived," ironically selected in the fall before TMI, as the theme for the yearbook implying the seniors had survived high school. To complete the entire decade, more than 200 slides had been created from *Time* magazine.

"The Class of '77 ("The Way We Were") retold with music, slides, acting scenarios, and costumes, the way things were in double digit years of the century: '11, '22, '33, '44, '55, '66, and '77. Work on the 1981 program began with two junior girls spending their summer writing an original song for "Celebrate—A Song of Myself," based on the poem by Walt Whitman. In 1990 students were asked to report if their parents had been graduated from Lower Dauphin and the list of 52 families was included in the graduation program."

Class Day Traditions

The practice of holding Class Day for a graduating class is thought to have begun at Harvard and spread to other colleges in the mid-nineteenth century. Union College, Schenectady, New York, held its first Class Day in 1863 and the practice continued until 1968, with each senior class gathering a day or two before Commencement to celebrate Class Day. Morning exercises at a church were followed by afternoon exercises on campus. Elected Class Day officers included president, poet, orator, historian, prophet, address, and marshal. Afternoon exercises included the class history, prophecy, dedication of the class tree, and songs. Sometime after 1876 ivy was substituted for the planting of a tree.

Class Day was held regularly with the exception of 1890 and the years of the Second World War.

Later, Class Day was held in a church, and featured the class poet, class historian, and class prophecy. By the late 1960s, however, Class Day fell victim to a general indifference to tradition and few colleges or high schools still hold this special day. In some schools Class Night was celebrated as the time for providing a program and reading its Last Will and Testament.

At LDHS the Class of 1970 claims it was the first to hold a Class Night, which featured skits about their years at LD and the reading of the Class's Last Will and Testament. This was revived by the Class of 1984. In the spring of 1987 a new tradition began, when Judith Witmer, the Commencement Advisor, instituted a Senior Awards Family Night which included a covered dish supper for graduating seniors and their families.

Commencement Themes: The First 28 years

1961 Onward Ever, Backward Never

1962 Growing Toward Tomorrow

1963 The Past Our Heritage, the Future Our Challenge

1964 Pathways to Life[1]

1965 Every One to Whom Much is Given, Of Him Will Much Be Required

1966 To Know One's Self is the True: To Strive with One's Self is the Good; To Conquer One's Self is the Beautiful

1967 *Nils mortalibus arduum est* (Nothing is too high for the daring of mortals)[2]

1968 The Answer is Blowin' in the Wind

1969 You Can't Go Home Again[3]

1970 Awake! Arise! Decide!

1971 To everything there is a season

1972 E Pluribus Unum (From the Many, One)[4]

1973 Let There Be Peace on Earth

1974 The Past is Only the Beginning[5]

1975 ...but around in awareness[6]

1976 The World Turned Upside Down[7]

1977 The Way We Were[8]

1978 Moments to Remember[9]

1979 Yesterday, Today, and Tomorrow[10]

1980 An Echo of the Past, A Herald of the Future: The Twentieth Class

1981 Celebrate: A Song of Myself[11]

1982 The Class of 1982: Cohesive! Changing! Competitive! Conquering![12]

1983 The World is Yours; Therefore, Build Your Own World

1984 1984: The Prophecy and the Reality[13]

1985 What Really Happened to the Class of 85/65?[14]

1986 Sunrise, Sunset, Swiftly Fly the Years[15]

1987 This is the Time: For Reflection, for Excellence, for Commencement[16]

1988 Desiderata

---

[1] At this point Judith Witmer began a long tenure as the Commencement Advisor.

[2] This marks the first year for a program by the students; this was also the first choralogue (speaking choir)

[3] The first program to use slides

[4] A choralogue; this is also the year the honor of junior clas marshals was instituted

[5] Vignettes commemorating the highlights of school life

[6] A choralogue

[7] An American Bicentennial pageant

[8] Vignettes from the Double Number Decades ('00, '11, '22, '33, '44, '55, '66, '77)

[9] Vignettes from the class history

[10] A 1970s retrospective

[11] A choralogue based upon Whitman's "Leaves of Grass"

[12] A visual presentation and speakers: four brothers (three alumni; the fourth, class president and valedictorian). This year the advisor initiated a senior reception hosted by the junior class following Baccalaureate.)

[13] A mini-production in three parts: choralogue, dramatization, and vignette, based on Orwell's book *1984*

[14] The Silver Anniversary of LDHS, including an alumni choir and participation by the Class of 1965

[15] A combination of slides and parent participation

[16] This year marked the end of student produced Commencement programs.

Representative Commencement Programs

In **1976** the Commencement and Baccalaureate Services were patriotic in theme and featured historical events of 1776. The students realized they were an historic class and even parents who otherwise frowned on long hair worn by young men were very tolerant, allowing these top-ranked students to let their hair grow in order to wear it in the style of 1776. Authenticity was a hallmark of Lower Dauphin Commencement programs and this year was no exception. The class created a Bicentennial pageant titled "The World Turned Upside Down" that included music of the period and spotlighted events and personages who gave birth to the nation. The Baccalaureate program, "Many Churches, One Faith: Many States, One Nation," also featured original material from the American colonial period.

The **1977** Commencement program, "The Way We Were," presented vignettes of each decade, from 1911 through 1977, with interlude piano music and a piano solo in the segment, "A High School Literary," from 1911.

The class of **1980** marked the occasion of the 20th graduation by reliving two decades of school history with a student-researched, written, and produced slide show that required months of work to prepare. It was the 13th year that LD allowed students to create the program with each class creating distinctly different formats from a chosen theme.

The theme for Commencement **1983** was "The World is Yours," a program using slides to demonstrate how all of the influences on the life of a student help that senior build his or her own world.

Writing a script for the **1984** Commencement was in full swing by January. The program was a take-off on George Orwell's classic futurist novel written in 1949 as to what society might be like in 1984. "The Prophecy and the Reality," made its point through a series of vignettes portraying life as Orwell feared it might be contrasted to life as the Class of 1984 was living it.

Commencement **1985** was based on the premise that it was those who were graduated in the mid-60s who would have the most impact on the world in which the graduates of 1985 would make their way. The program used audio-taped messages from the Class of '65 to the Class of '85. Responses to the messages from 1965 class members were delivered by members of the Class of 1985. An Alumni Choir, representing the men of the choirs of the past 25 years (30 voices), performed, and the president of the school's first Student Council took part in the presentation of diplomas.

1986. Commencement 1986 included participation by parents of the graduates.

16th Annual
Lower Dauphin
Senior High School

Commencement

JUNE 1, 1976

For Heaven's Sake

Baccalaureate
June 4, 1978
7:30 p.m.

21st Annual Commencement
Lower Dauphin High School
June 5, 1981 8:00 p.m.

CELEBRATE

- A Song
of Myself

Twenty - Fifth Annual Commencement
Lower Dauphin High School

WHAT REALLY HAPPENED
TO THE CLASS OF

85

June

Commencement
1987

Hershey Theatre
June 5, 1987
7:30 p.m.

LOWER DAUPHIN SENIOR HIGH SCHOOL

COMMENCEMENT

IN THE

THIRTY- THIRD YEAR

FRIDAY, JUNE ELEVENTH
NINETEEN HUNDRED AND NINETY THREE
HUMMELSTOWN, PENNSYLVANIA

Hershey Community Theatre   8:00 p.m.

Valedictorians

1961	Carol Flocken
1962	Alice A. Weist
1963	Robert O. Gibble
1964	Karen L. Fair
1965	Bethanne Bojanic, Jean L. Deimler, and Karl Bell
1966	Lester B. Ratcliff
1967	Charles P. Staver
1968	Yolande deB. McCurdy
1969	Wendy G. Bolton
1970	Carole R. Engle
1971	Kerry L. Basehore
1972	Joan E. Hassel
1973	Tanya A. Heatwole
1974	Craig E. College
1975	Gregory G. College
1976	Wynn A. Willard
1977	Herbert R. Stoner
1978	Melanie A. Boyer
1979	Jay M. Steinruck
1980	Mark R. Harpel
1981	Elizabeth A. Snowden
1982	Ronald D. Orsini
1983	Charles R. Stoner
1984	Gretchen J. Lehman
1985	Brenda S. Stoner
1986	Heidi Jean Lehman
1987	Peter M. Ward
1988	Eric Behrens
1989	Matthew B. Royer
1990	Susanna Grubb
1991	Christine L. Cassel
1992	Dania N. Pazakis and Michelle R. Lander
1993	Christian D. Manders
1994	Thomas Hummel
1995	Jonathan Raser
1996	Jodi L. O'Donnell
1997	Kristen Ann Potter
1998	Abigail K. Martin
1999	Nora J. Graber
2000	Joel David Martin
2001	Jennifer E. Johnson
2002	Ryan C. Burk
2003	Christopher I. Alloway
2004	Lindsay Hitz
2005	Erin Meyer
2006	Kiel Reese
2007	Brent Geist
2008	Gwendolyn Hauck
2009	Catherine Meador
2010	Lindsay Yingst

Salutatorians

1961	Gloria Shertzer
1962	Sandra Longreen
1963	Frederick Shope
1964	George Chellew
1965	Carolyn Sandel
1966	Margaret Shemas
1967	Mary Elizabeth Sandel
1968	Alan Larsen
1969	Anne Marie McCurdy
1970	Julia Staver
1971	John Wert
1972	Carol Larsen
1973	Loren Reinhold
1974	Paul Stoner, Jr.
1975	Mary Berger
1976	Daniel Stokes
1977	Linda Auch
1978	Craig Cooper
1979	John Saufley
1980	Elaine Shizkowski
1981	Debra Lesher
1982	Glenn Book
1983	Lisa Kurr
1984	Robert Buse
1985	Angela Breidenstine
1986	Lori Magaro
1987	Todd Gould
1988	Lea Ann Knapik
1989	Ernest Manders
1990	Susan Shuman
1991	Jeremy Fox and Jonathan Manders
1993	Renee Hoffman
1994	Michael Darowish
1995	Richard Shertzer
1996	Corinne Isom
1997	John Ranck
1998	Nathan Kunisky
1999	Jill Pierce
2000	Sommer Costabile
2001	Jennifer Good
2002	Amanda Brown and Christopher Sobona
2003	Nathan Martin
2004	Greg McWhirter
2005	Erica Bates
2006	Laura James
2007	Andrew Santeusanio
2008	Stephanie Meador
2009	Allen Welkie
2010	John Groh

Commencement Speech Excerpts

Valedictorian

1967   Charles Staver (Agricultural Scientist)
Only the courageous came through.

1969   Anne Marie McCurdy (Homemaker)
… It is from this point that we go on, not powered by what we have done, but by what we can do.

1970   Carol Engle (Researcher, Director of Aquaculture)
The choice is before us, whether to deny reality and hide from it, or meet it face to face….

1971   Kerry Bashore
Life is precious, Life is time. It must not be wasted.

1971   Joan Hassel (Pediatrician)
… we have the power to better mankind … to build and not to destroy.

1973   Tanya A. Heatwole (Pastor)
We are seeking a true and lasting peace. We search and strive for all that is good in life.

1974   Craig E. College (Director, Installation Management, Pentagon)
*… America is wracked by the devastations of moral and social decay,
    a country slowly being strangled …*

1975   Gregory E. College (Actuary)
… we, as she (our country), are strong, ready, and willing, for we fear not the future.

1976   Wynn Willard
*In a world turned upside down, America was emerging onto the earth explosively,
    its ideas erupting …*

1977   Herbert Stoner (Pastor of Adult Education)
For each one who compromises his existence, the world moves one step closer to chaos and destruction.

1980   Mark Harpel
Trends of the last few decades have pointed towards an egocentric society.

1981   Elizabeth Snowden (Optometrist)
We celebrate tonight while those in Atlanta are living in fear of an unknown assailant.

1982   Ronald D. Orsini (Managing Director)
… all of us are influential in shaping the lives of young people with whom we come in contact.

1983   Charles Stoner (USAF, ret.)
… we touch and affect many people.

1984 Gretchen Leaman (Physician)
...it is the human mind that holds the potential for creativity, originality, and appreciation of the world's beauty.

1986 Heidi Leaman
Our class will continue to ... strive for world peace.

1987 Peter Ward
A complete life consists of a combination of personal achievement and service.

1988 Eric Behrens (Manager of Academic Computing)
What will determine your real self-worth, and your real value to humanity, is your integrity.

1989 Matt Royer (Attorney)
Life is continuous—there will always be crops to plant and fruit to harvest.

2010 Lindsay Yingst, The Fiftieth Class
...in one way or another we've changed each other's lives.

Salutatorian

1965 Carolyn Sandel (Assistant Superintendent)
Those who refuse to use potential within and around them offend this timeless code of noblesse oblige.

1970 Julia Staver (Veterinarian)
Remember what we all are—the family of mankind. All of us are worthy in some regard.

1972 Carol Larsen (Chemist)
Each person must choose his own standards; he must sometimes choose the road less traveled.

1973 Mark Osevala (Physician)
We have been taught that fighting accomplishes very little. We have a message tonight. Listen well.

1974 Paul S. Stoner, Jr. (Flight Surgeon, NASA)
In the first year of our lives was Sputnik. In our senior year the United States put a man on the moon.

1976 Daniel Stokes (Director of Music)
... the first Americans fought not for themselves alone, but for all mankind.

1977 Linda Auch (Physical Therapist)
We examine the past to learn from it, not to judge it.

1984 Robert Buse
If we do not fight to maintain or better our free world, we may one day be bound by oppressing chains. ...

1986   Lori Magaro (Marketing and PR Director)
Create a better society. Make it our world, one worth living in.

1987   Todd E. Gould (CEO, AbilSoft Corporation)
… always remain optimistic … following our journey as we find our place in the world of the future.

2010   John Groh, The Fiftieth Class
…Facebook can teach us a lot about high school.

Alumna

Jean Deimler Seibert, '65, Attorney

… As you leave this evening, do not be led to believe that you will never associate again with your fellow students, faculty, or administration from your high school years. Thirty-eight graduates from my own class, including my husband and I, are married to each other.

… You, the Class of 1991, have a wonderful style about you—you are a group with strong friendships and my wish for you is that your heroes will become your friends and your friends will remain your heroes.

Alumni, Parent and Faculty Commencement Speakers

1980   Julia Staver '70
Glenn Ebersole, first Class President, awarded diplomas

1982   Steven, Thomas, and Dr. Michael Orsini, '74, '72, and '70

1983   Dr. Linda and Dr. Douglas Goepfert, '70 and '73

1984   Dr. David Leaman, Parent

1985   Dr. Carolyn Sandel '65
Barry Broadwater, first Student Council President, awarded diplomas

1986   Dr. Judith T. Witmer, Faculty and Parent

1987   Lieut. Commander M. Scott Reichenbaugh '72

1988   George Cruys '70

1989   Nancy Hivner '72

1990   Capt. Craig E. College '74

1991   Jean Deimler Seibert '65

1992   Jerry Peacock '75

1993   Joyce Keener '63

1994   Linda Kreiser '70

1995   Gilbert Petrina '85

1996   Vincent Pantalone, Faculty

1997   Dr. Ernest C. Manders '89

1998   Kerry L. Basehore '71

1999   Kevin M. Strawser '86

2000   Ann Rhoads '68

2001   Dr. Gretchen Leaman Brandt '84

2002   Dr. Gary L. Kirman '78

2009   Stephen Kistler, Faculty

One Season Following Another

Alumni who are now parents of high school students may find some of their own reactions to graduation of their children captured in the following:

Graduations are strange events, their main purpose being to award a high school diploma, an indication of having attained a certain proficiency of skills. This diploma could be given the last day of school in homeroom, but our American society has developed a tradition of a high school graduation as a ceremony. It has become our culture's "rite of passage to adulthood." By being such, it takes on much more significance and much more emotion. It becomes an occasion filled with pride and hope, visions and dreams, goals and aspirations. And, graduates, it is your night!

Graduation is a time of pride — pride that you have completed your public education, for high school is the one challenge you have conquered together. But more than that, most of you can take pride in special, individual successes both in the classroom and out. You have proven yourselves on the playing fields, on the stage, in competitions and contests. As such, you have felt exhilaration, joy and excitement. You have tasted victory.

You also have learned how to strive for more successes, for upon the fields of friendly strife are sown the seeds that upon other fields on other days will reap more fruits of victory, be it Penn State, Widener or Shenandoah.

This pride once began as basic hope and caring, for pride cannot be built without a foundation, without support which began in your infancy when you depended upon your parents totally. We nurtured you and did our best to insure a secure and loving environment. We hauled you to lessons and practices because it mattered—it mattered to you and it mattered to us. The first ill-fitting baseball uniform in which you thought you were major league, the dance recital, the church children's choir, elementary school mass band night in which you blared your instruments in unison, scout meetings, retreats, fifth grade chorus. That pride grew as you attained skill and competence.

Middle School gave you more opportunity to spread your wings, stretch your legs and flex your muscles. You found yourselves a part of a Lower Dauphin team.

You worried if you would be good enough to make the team or be in the band, for being the best in South Hanover didn't assure you first chair in Middle School orchestra. We parents worried right along with you and found ourselves as spectators in the rain and blazing sun, wanting to be there to support you and wanting to be there to share your delight in wearing the blue and white. Even then we watched as some of you became known for your special skills.

By high school we sang the Alma Mater with you and our identification with L.D. was re-kindled. Your high school successes brought pride to yourselves, your school, and to your parents. Who but a parent would get up at the crack of dawn to travel to a play-off just to stand in the rain to watch his daughter strike a ball into a cage? Who except a parent would ride a bus, full of shouting teen-agers for four hours and spend four days in the cold winds of Wildwood to watch a total of ninety minutes of band performances? Who but a parent would postpone buying something for himself so that you could have a week at a specialty sports camp or a better musical instrument or even the prom dress that your heart was set on?

Most of those choices were made quietly and privately and the decisions were made because we remembered the sacrifices made by our own parents. Who among the parents here tonight can't remember their own mothers and fathers doing their best, and agreeing with an eager-faced son that, "Yes, maybe we can send you to camp this summer," or smiling against their own better sense of style and allowing their daughter to choose that dreadful pink gown. Our parents wanted for us, took pride in our successes, and cheered us on. We continued the same, and made our sacrifices because of our pride in you. We delight in your achievements, some because of reflected glory, some because of seeing you achieve a position we at your age had wanted, and all because we are so very proud for you.

Along with pride in your accomplishments, we have shared your visions and your dreams, perhaps for an even longer time than you have had these dreams and visions. When you picked up your first ball we had dreams of Hershey stadium, and as you banged on the pans in the kitchen we saw glimmers of District Band. When you began to strut with a broom handle, we bought batons; when your fingers found the piano keys, we arranged for lessons; when you posed a pedantic question, we dreamed of Yale, and when you first recited a poem, we saw Broadway. We encouraged you to "dip into the future, far as human eye could see" and we "saw the vision of yourself and all the wonder you could be."

We see in you tonight, ourselves at your age, and we remember our own visions and dreams. We want as much, if not more, for you. We dream with you and share your visions, for it is your eyes now which see and the sight of your eyes grants beauty to the earth. It is your ears which hear, and the hearing of your ears gives its song to the world. It is your mind which thinks, and the judgment of your mind is the only searchlight that can find the truth. It is your will which now chooses and the choice of your will is the only edict you must respect.

Keep this vision, singing of life immense in passion, pulse, and power. This vision of life is yours. With your heart, hand, and mind you hold the power to mold each golden moment, each shining, hour, into new designs and infinite possibilities.

Your parents and your teachers have tried to instill in each of you a zest for living, a desire to achieve, a passion for excellence. We have given you an indelible foundation of edifying experiences and the precious gift of knowledge. We trust that in your world of tomorrows you will carry with you what you have garnered from the world of yesterday: integrity, self-reliance, initiative. Use these in your journey to strive, to seek, to find, and not to yield!

Godspeed to each of you!

Commencement 1986

Class Marshals

The practice of using Class Marshals from the Junior Class for graduation ceremonies was initiated with the 1972 Commencement to honor the two juniors with the highest academic standing in their class.

1972   Tanya Heatwole and Douglas Goepfert

1973   Dennis Shope and Mark Vigilante

1974   Gregory College and Jerry Peacock

1975   Wynn Willard and Susan Berger

To celebrate our nation's Bicentennial, the Class of 1976 presented a Bicentennial historical pageant and included an "honor guard" of Class Marshals from the Junior Class to escort the processional of the graduates. These marshals included the top five male and the top five female honor students.

1976   Linda Auch   Dennis Bobb

           Jean Ball   Michael Dunkel

           Kathy Burns   Jeffrey Gesford

           Sharon Miller   John Kiessling

           Lisa Rhoad   Herbert Stoner

The practice of Junior Class Marshals was continued through 2008 after which it was suspended.

1977	Craig Cooper and Sherri Gesford	1993	Thomas Hummel and William Elliott
1978	Jan Engle and Kerry Hartman	1994	Jon Raser and Richard Shertzer
1979	Elaine Shizkowski and Mark Harpel	1995	Corinne Isom and Jodi Lynn O'Donnell
1980	Elizabeth Snowden and Jeff Koppenhaver	1996	Kristen Potter and John Ranck
1981	Ronald Orsini and Glenn Book	1997	Nathan Kunisky and Abigail Martin
1982	Lisa Kurr and Charles Stoner	1998	Nora Graber and Megan Potter
1983	Mary Krause and Gretchen Leaman	1999	Sommer Costabile and Joel Martin
1984	April DeMuth and John Tantum	2000	Jennifer Good and Jennifer Johnson
1985	Heidi Leaman and Matthew Morrison	2001	Ryan Burk and Christopher Sobona
1986	Peter Ward and Suzann Motz	2002	Nathan Martin and Chad Hollenbach
1987	Eric Behrens and Tricia Gaudette	2003	Lindsay Hitz and Greg McWhirter
1988	Matthew Royer and Kevin Ward	2004	Erin Meyer and Erica Bates
1989	Andrew Espenshade and Susanna Grubb	2005	Kiel Reese and Laura James
1990	Christine Cassel and Christine Quimby	2006	Brent Giest and Ben Labe
1991	Dania Pazakis and Michelle Lander	2007	Stephanie Meador and Gwendolyn Hauck
1992	Christian Manders and Renee Hoffman	2008	Allen Welkie and Catherine Meador

Sampling of Senior Portraits Through the Decades

1960s

'65   '65   '65   '67

1970s

'74   '74   '77   '79

1980s

'86   '87   '88   '88

1990s

'91   '91   '97   '97

2000s

'00   '01   '05   '11

Summit Achiever Brad Stroman '67

Brad Stroman combines his passion for making art with his concerns for our environment by incorporating a Japanese Zen philosophy known as wabi-sabi. His award-winning work is exhibited in both solo and juried group exhibitions garnering acclaim from environmentalists and art lovers alike. Currently represented by galleries in Pennsylvania, Colorado, Utah, New Mexico, North Carolina, South Carolina, and Ohio, Brad's unique paintings are included in nearly100 private and corporate collections both nationally and internationally.

In high school he took advantage of every opportunity to schedule time in the art room, even figuring out a way to escape taking chemistry his senior year so he could create art. It all paid off as he won a regional award for graphic design in his senior year. Inspired by his high school art teachers' commitment to visual arts education, he made the decision to pursue the same field of study to become an art teacher himself.

While teaching, his own art took many turns in its development, from detailed wildlife drawings in scratchboard, graphite, and colored pencil (even working for a graphics poster company out of Woodstock, VT) to oil landscapes of the area to finally Zen inspired nature paintings in acrylics which he is most known for today. It was his continued concern for our environment and a visit to the natural beauty of Sedona, AZ and the Grand Canyon that guided him into this unique style of painting.

Two of his works recently hung beside some of America's greatest artists known for their inclusion of nature in their work including American Impressionists and contemporary artists such as Thomas Hart Benton, Thomas Cole, Winslow Homer, Maxfield Parrish, Andrew Wyeth and Jamie Wyeth. It is among these giants that Brad Stroman stands. The 2010 survey exhibition was held at the Hudson River Museum, New York and presented over 60 original works by American artists from the Hudson River School to present day. The selection committee used one of Brad's paintings as the frontispiece image for the exhibition catalog. Stroman describes his experience, "Upon entering the two-tiered gallery space my breath was taken away. There surrounding me were works by American painters who, over the years, achieved well-deserved acclaim in the field of art. Among the exhibited 80 works were paintings done by the masters. Then it dawned on me... I was there too. It was the most humbling experience of my artistic career."

Brad recently relocated to Black Mountain, NC where he resides today with his wife. He supports both local and national environmental groups, often donating portions of gallery proceeds to these worthy causes. He maintains a painting studio in the River Arts District in Asheville, North Carolina.

More recent exhibitions include the following:

2012: "Earth Art" solo exhibition, Ellis-Nicholson Gallery, Charleston, SC and Solo Exhibition, Convergence Gallery, Santa Fe, New Mexico

2011: First Place in 2-D Category, Southern Appalachian Artist Guild National Juried Exhibition, Blue Ridge, GA

2010: "Black Mountain Fever," Lynden Gallery, Elizabethtown, PA; and Selected Works, The Artisan, Black Mountain, NC

The Arts

The Arts

The Power of the Arts

Fall 1991. Their faces were painted orange and blue. To the casual observer they appeared to be an informal pep squad or cheering section for the football game against their arch rival. They sat near the center of the home side in the stadium, and while they cheered for the Trojans to trample the Falcons, their real purpose was to create a disturbance. As their number increased, it was evident that they had come not to cheer for Hershey, but to agitate against Lower Dauphin, both its team and its marching band.

Tension mounted when this large group of odd-hued faces closed ranks and prepared to heckle their visitor's performance. It was obvious that the motley spirit-mongers were ready to do battle against the enemy. As the Big Blue Band from Falconland took the field, the orange marauders started their prepared counterpoint. The chanting and jeers rose to a crescendo as the program began. A few adults nearby were tentatively trying to quell the burgeoning booing, uneasy in their unexpected role of student monitors.

Just then something happened. As the band moved into its selection from "Phantom of the Opera" the student uproar, rather than increasing as the adults had feared, subsided. The hauntingly beautiful strains of Andrew Lloyd-Webber wafted through the spectators, touching all who watched and listened. Despite themselves, the pranksters were charmed by the music. The garish orange and blue faces paled in contrast to the more subtle splendidness of the white masks worn by the young band members on the field. A hush fell upon the spectators. In response to the music of the night, twice during the performance the crowd (rowdies included) stood in tribute to the creative skill of the musicians. The instigators were transformed from harassers to admirers. Such is the power of music. And of all the arts.

It is the arts which make us human and one is not truly educated or civilized without an understanding of the arts. Encounters with music, drawing, photography, and writing illuminate life and lead us through all its mystery, misery, wonder, pity, and delight. The arts can liberate us by awakening the spirit that lies within each person.

More importantly, the arts are the means through which human beings "talk," both to ourselves and to each other. Through the arts we express fears, hopes, and longings. The arts enable us to express love, order, and beauty. They are our universal way to make sense of our culture—and to preserve it. The arts allow us to demonstrate who we are and, thus, are the central force in human existence. Today, in the face of high tech or primal fears, the arts provide the essential avenue for human acceptance, understanding, and transcendence. Without arts education we would not be fully educated.

However, because engaging in the arts is visceral, engaging both cognitive and creative powers, records of achievement are not available in the way that general academic prowess is noted. Thus, the difficulty in paying tribute to the arts in this social history of Lower Dauphin High School is that chronicles are not kept in the way scores and "opponents" are noted by sports. There is no master list of who won arts awards, who attended the Governor's School for the Arts, or who became nationally recognized artists and musicians. However, thanks to Mrs. Marie Weber, we do have lists of all who represented LD at county, district, regional, and state music events, even though that is too long a list to include here. She also has more knowledge than most faculty do about those students who are the musicians. This information is now on record as it should be and both the school and the Alumni Association will have copies of these lists. Perhaps someone reading this can devise a better way to keep and display such records electronically.

Music: From the Marching Field

BAND—SOMETHING THAT BINDS, TIES TOGETHER, OR ENCIRCLES

The Big Blue Band from Falconland and its individual members have distinguished themselves in the top ranks of competition again and again over the years. In fact, the Band has won so many awards that there is not enough space here to list them all.

In the fall of 1960 the Lower Dauphin Marching Band was comprised of 60 marching players from eighth to twelfth grade and ten band front members. Under the leadership of Director Prowell M. Seitzinger and Drum Major Kenneth Miller, the goal for the band's first year was performing pre-game and half time at the football games. Mr. Seitzinger designed many of the drills that were performed on the field, with a new drill every week and new music to accompany the drill, unlike the later trend to create a marching band production that would serve for the season. This energetic, newly formed band also provided pep music in the stands during the games to accompany routines by the cheerleaders. Band uniforms, of course, were not available until partway into the fall season so the band members wore blue slacks and white tops.

The first music concert, "An Evening of Festive Music," was performed on December 19, 1960 with The Concert Band, Choir, Glee Club, Balladeers, Falconettes,[1] Falconaires, Band Front, and German Chorus. A silver offering was taken for the purpose of purchasing music. All proceeds from the silver offering taken at the Spring Concert were earmarked to purchase additional uniforms for the Marching Band. There was no separate orchestra, only Concert Band; however, Emily Trefz placed first chair at District Orchestra and in the summer of 1965 she appeared as a flutist at the Saltzburg Festival in Austria.

A Band Parents organization was formalized the first year with Mr. John Musser as President, building on the strength of the organization of which he had been president at Hummelstown High School. Under Mr. Musser's leadership the band gained financial support, with chaperones and a foundation that made it possible for the band to compete in major tournaments. Band parents also served as an unconditional cheering section that has continued to accompany the band to games and competitions.

---

[1] The first ensemble to use the term "Falconettes" was a vocal group. Later the term was used for a dance routine troupe in the marching band, and later yet for another vocal group.

The first band competition the LD Marching Band entered was the Olmsted Tournament, then in its 13th year, held February 13, 1961. As a new band they scored respectably and by the second year the band was earning high ratings, such as the "Excellent" they earned for a Class A Band in the annual Thanksgiving Parade in Harrisburg on December 1, 1962.

While some people laugh at cartoons depicting high school bands selling fruit cakes and turkeys, fund-raising is serious business for a band that wants to compete in parades and tournaments. By the second year of its existence, the LD Marching Band was selling Christmas trees following Thanksgiving in 1962. During the 1962-63 school year they sold Kool School Stools and through this vigorous fund-raising the Band was able to compete in the Cherry Blossom Festival in Washington, DC in the spring of 1963.

In the fall of 1963 the band took top honors for the second year in the Harrisburg marching contest of 20 bands with a rating of "Superior." The same year ninth grader Dayton Holmes took first honors at District Band on drums and a dance troupe of twenty girls, named the Falconettes, was added to the band. Band members continued what became a tradition for several years of selling Christmas trees ($1.50 each) for their trip to the Cherry Blossom Festival. (April 1964 *Falcon Flash*.) Another fund-raiser for this spring event in Washington was a concert by Bob Aulenbach's Big Band. The band's third fund raiser was very inventive: they performed a concert outside the local Standard Theatre in early March of 1964 where "The Music Man" was playing, and collected cash donations.

In July 1964 the School Board approved the plan that both band rehearsals and "sectionals" would be scheduled during the school day. This was quite a challenge to the administration as well as an adjustment for the faculty when students were excused from class to attend rehearsals.

Also during the summer of 1964, after the resignation of President Musser, the Band Parents organization was having difficulty finding a member who was willing to take the presidency. *The Sun* reported in its September 18, 1964 issue, "It's Either Or Else for L.D. Band Parents." The article explained the importance of the band parents and asked for a good showing at the meeting to decide whether or not to continue as an organization. This situation was also covered in a prominent article in the Middletown *Press and Journal*. Both newspapers called for support, although the articles were, upon closer inspection, identical. The Middletown paper gave the writer (Emory Fernback) of the submitted article a byline. Evidently the Band Parents were able to find leadership, as on April 3, 1965 the organization sponsored a ham dinner. That fall the Marching Band took second place out of 35 marching bands at the Ephrata County Fair parade.

Majorettes were an important part of high school bands and on the 1964 squad were thirteen majorettes and as many Falconettes. The February 21, 1966 edition of the Harrisburg *Evening News* printed an article about the Small Twirling Corps Championship being held with three counties in which LD was represented by Nadine Lutz, Patty Pheasant, Jeannine Lehmer, and Linda Shope.

In May of that same year the Concert Band took 2nd place at the Olmsted Air Force Base Band Concert. The *Press and Journal* wrote, "One of the highlights of the band's performance was its "free choice" number, a special arrangement of "Shangri-La" by their band director, Prowell Seitzinger. Another feature which was particularly effective was their finale using an entrance march, featuring a drum quartette performing a routine designed by David Kromer, a student drummer. With the closing of the Air Force base this event marked the final contest.

LD's own Spring Band Concert (1966) featured the entire band front in various numbers with highlights of the program focusing on the percussion section, one which showcased Jack Brandt as a tympani soloist.

In August 1966 six majorettes from LD participated in the half-time program of the Big 33 football game (a classic sporting event originating in 1957): Patty Pheasant, Linda Shope, Pat Jeffries, Wendy Deimler, Corinne Davies, and Jeannine Lehmer. In the fall of 1966 Lower Dauphin Band rated an "Excellent" in the annual Thanksgiving/Christmas Parade.

The following summer (1967) new graduate Tom Hughes toured Europe with the School Band of America, part of the People to People Program, after an audition and having represented LD at regional, state, and mid-east conferences.

During this same summer the local paper also did a feature article on the band front, noting "Heading the high-stepping Falconettes will be Head Majorette Jeannine Lehmer, Line Captain Sandy Wenrich, Choreographer Janice Wenrich, and Colorguard Captain Carol Grubb." The same article announced that in the fall Mr. Seitzinger would be heading the elementary music program and Mr. William Nixon would be taking the baton for the high school band. In September 1967 while LD did not win the Festival of High School Bands, the drum major featured in the newspaper was LD's own Don Frantz. At the eighth annual Spring Concert Mr. Seitzinger was honored as a guest conductor.

The first band camp was held at Elizabethtown College in the summer of 1968. According to band director William Nixon, "We learned a lot more than just the music." Thus began a long tradition of band camps at the college, and later on site at the high school.

In February 1969 the School Board accepted the low bid of the George Evans Company to provide uniforms for 100 musicians, 15 color guard, one band director, as well as 120 clear plastic raincoats and fabric to make 12 majorette uniforms. The Spring Band Concert that year featured twirling by the majorettes and a solo by Jeannine Lehmer who gave her stunning farewell performance to the "Original Dixieland Concerto." The Choral Concert used a storyline theme, "With a Li'l Bit O' Luck" with selections from Broadway shows. (Who could have known that one of the graduating seniors would later become a Broadway producer?)

In August of that year the LD Band was selected as the pre-game and halftime entertainment for the Big 33 Game at which Jeannine was also soloist. In September the band took second place in the third annual Festival of Bands at Middletown, a competition that was established after the closing of Olmsted.

In the early 1970s the Band Color Guard added Guide-on Flags as band competitions became popular. In the summer of 1970 Mr. David Hummel assumed the position of band director and in the fall of 1971 the Marching Band took a second at Sounds of Champions at Shikellamy High School. The band itself compiled the highest music score of all bands participating and finished just .8 points out of first place. They also were invited to

perform at half time at Susquehanna University's Homecoming.

In October 1971 the following description captured the excitement of the marching band's performance, "Majorettes are under the direction of the former head majorette, Jeannine Lehmer. You'll see LD strutting onto the field with Candy Tritch as head majorette. Then acrobatic majorette Denise Lehmer will stun you as she goes through her routine of flips and back bends."

By the fall of 1972 there were Color Guard, Rifle Squad and Flash Flags as part of the marching band—all adding variety. There also was a band slogan which led the troops into competition, "Do It for Bear," the affectionate nickname given to the director. Further, at this time the band greatly increased in number, from 115 to 160, leading Mr. Ben McLure to coin the term "Big Blue." From that point forward the band was introduced as "The Big Blue Band from Falconland."

Candy Tritch, Head Majorette both her junior and senior years, led the exhibition for "Super Sounds of '72" which featured this twirler with two batons and a show routine.

An article in the fall of 1973 stated, "The Big Blue Band from Falconland" is rumored to be even better than last year's—if that is possible."

The November 1974 issue of *Know Your Schools* noted, "The Senior High Marching Band experienced one of its best seasons ever this year. The group began the year with a triumphant exhibition as they took part in the Miss America Parade in Atlantic City where they were judged first runner-up out of 20 bands, representing Maryland, New Jersey, Pennsylvania, and Delaware. 150,000 people watched as the LD students performed courageously in a torrential downpour." Perhaps the 1975 *Falconaire* best describes the band competitions:

> The tension of a competition, the pep talks and nervous chatter, drew the group even closer together. One thought was mirrored in each person's mind, "Will our best be good enough?" Then the uncertainty as they stood, one body, filled with anxious anticipation… oh, please…**and in First Place** …maybe we should have taken second or third … **receiving the Grand Champion's Trophy** … all that work, what if it's not us … **Lower Dauphin.** Here was the source of final unification."

LD Marching Bands, under the direction of Thomas Turnbull in the fall of 1979, continued to compete and did very well for many years, with Winter Guard, formed in 1980, performing indoors with taped music and featuring silks, swing flags, rifles, and majorettes. The December 1981 *Flash* announced that the first Winter Drumline had formed as a competitive group. In 1983 Winter Drumline and Winter Guard placed third at a competition at Cumberland Valley. The following winter the Winter Drumline competed at Central Dauphin's Winter-Ram-A.

Peripherals to the band in 1984-85 were the Silks, Swing Flags, Rifles, Twirlers, and Main Guard. In the spring of 1984 the band competed in Norfolk, Virginia where Concert Band took second place and the band took third in overall standing for the festival.

A headline in *The Patriot*, October 29, 1985 announced, "Band outdoes predecessors! Big Blue accepted a 4th First Place award, performing its best show of the season, following its rewriting band history the week before when it won its 3rd First Place. An area disc jockey declared on the air that if he had a band he would want it to be just like Lower Dauphin's. He explained, "This year, the band has designed no ordinary show. It is one that builds to a crescendo of exciting patriotic music which leaves everyone in the audience with a majestic feeling of Americanism."

In the fall of 1985 at the state championship, Cavalcade of Bands Association, the band scored the highest of any band in LD History. Joelle Bendull reported in the November *Falcon Flash*, "This was the night Big Blue shattered the history books for the second time, the night they took first place in music and second place overall at the State Championship. The band was literally caught off guard when they heard '…and the winner of the High Music Award is Lower Dauphin!' This meant we had the highest and best music score and that assured us a high place in the final standings. As the countdown began and the tension mounted, we waited, ecstatic when third place was announced as Cedar Crest. We knew we now were assured of second place."

To top off its fall season, at their final game, the stands were crowded at half-time for the band's dazzling performance, resulting in the **first ever standing ovation** for an LD band and leaving many in the stands to say the magnificent performance gave them chills. Further accolades came in the form of a full page "Congratulations" in *The Sun*.

In May 1986 the Marching Band claimed its first ever "Grand Championship" at Wildwood, NJ competition, with the field show winning second place (one point away from first place) and eight trophies. Further, the percussion, captained by Doug Rosener, placed first with the highest score out of all three divisions. However, Big Blue went out with the highest score overall in their division with Drum Majors Thomas Ball and Kathy Smee accepting the Grand Championship Trophy.

And then they did it again! Big Blue earned the highest score ever by a Lower Dauphin Band at States in the fall of 1986. In the spring of 1987 at the KIDA Championships, the Majorettes won First Place; at the Williamsburg Music Festival the Band placed first in Concert Band, Jazz Band, Marching Band, Majorette Unit, Color Guard Unit, and Percussion Unit. They also were deemed the highest scoring Marching Band in Music, Drum Major, Band Front, and Percussion.

In 1988 in the UDA Band competition, Big Blue took first place. In the Tournament of Music Festival at Myrtle Beach they earned first Place in Concert Band, Jazz Band, Wind Ensemble,

Parade Band, Marching Band, Percussion, and Color Guard.

New band uniforms were paraded on October 20, 1989 and at the International Azalea Band Festival Field Show, the band took "Best" in Silks, Drum Major, Auxiliary Units, Field Shows, Music, Parade Best Auxiliary, Drum Line, and Twirlers. Indoor Guard took second place and The Lower Dauphin Marching Band was named **Overall Grand Champion.**

The fall of 1991 brought a memorable performance by the Marching Band with show-stopping solos by Scott Gilbert, Tom Runkel, Sean Devine, and a spectacular finale with a billowing white curtain drawn over the entire band. Mr. Turnbull described the overall product "a powerhouse of sound." (See further description above in the introduction to the Arts section.) In the winter of 1992 Indoor Percussion became the 1992 KIDA State Champions.

The fall of 1992 Tish Saner was named Best Drum Major at the state championship. In 1993 the twirlers (Indoor Unit) won the KIDA Championship and the Drumline remained undefeated.

In 1994 the Big Blue went to Walt Disney World where the Concert Band, Jazz Band, Indoor Twirlers, Indoor Percussion, and Indoor Drumline competed. The Marching Band also performed as the guest band in the Walt Disney World Parade. In that same year, following 17 weeks of competitions at various tournaments, LD's Indoor Drumline was chosen as the 1994 National Champion. The Band then competed in all of the following Music Festivals for the next four years: 1995, Wildwood, New Jersey; 1996, Ocean City, Maryland: 1997, Toronto, Canada; and 1998, Williamsburg, Virginia.

In the fall of 1999, Mr. Turnbull assumed the duties of Choral Director and Ms. Jill Wenrich became Band Director until the end of 2004 at which time Mr. Jonathan Pinkerton returned to his Alma Mater.

In 2003 Big Blue was selected to perform in Governor Rendell's Inauguration Parade.

The band was consistent in its competition, even with some bumps along the way through personnel changes and different music education philosophies. The November 30, 2005 *Flash* sums it up: "While personnel may change, the hard work and quality performances of the LD Marching Band remain consistent. The students had to learn how to march in different sets as well as learning the selected music. The band had already won first place at Lebanon High School and specialty awards at three out of five competitions, as well as second in three other competitions." Wins continued with the Drumline placing first in the Atlantic Coast Championships in early November.

Greg Reinhardt, 1987 Drum Major, summarized the experience of being in the marching band, as being "a family, albeit of immense proportions. It is a team, the largest in the school. Over a hundred members spend an immense proportion of their lives in a coordinated effort to present a ten-minute show. It takes devotion, loyalty, and, above all, a commitment to excel."

Lower Dauphin Band Memories

——from one who has been there since the beginning

My association began with the Lower Dauphin Marching Band in the summer of 1960. As a member of the Hummelstown High School Band I automatically became a member of Lower Dauphin's Marching Band. This was the beginning of a long association with the band.

Over the years the band has changed their format, but the love of music and the dedication of students to this activity have not changed. Music has always been part of my life and when my sister (70's) was in the band my parents and I were very active in the Parent Association which supported the organization.

When my daughter was involved in the band I, as my parents before me, supported this group in every way I could. At the time of my daughter's commitment to outdoor band which competed,

the music department established an Indoor Guard, Drum Line, and a Majorette program. These students primarily were supported by the Band Parents Association and chaperoning became a part of my life. Even after my daughter graduated I was still active with the Band Boosters. It was an activity that I enjoyed and didn't want to give up. With the formation of the Lower Dauphin Alumni Association, it was important to me to contact former band members and organize an Alumni Band. This group is still a favorite at Homecoming and is a way to let the students know that they do not need to put their instruments away. Thanks to Mr. Hutchinson, Middle School Band Director, the Alumni Band has increased in membership.

Now you will see me at my granddaughters' competitions as I continue my involvement with Marching Bands. It has been an honor to be a Marching Member, a Band Booster, Parent Chaperone and Alumna of the Lower Dauphin Band.

Elizabeth (Betty) Musser Radle '62

Drum Majors

Being a drum major for a marching band isn't just something that happens. It is learned and developed over time. In addition to conducting the field shows, drum majors are commonly responsible for the marching band's rehearsals, teaching the drill charts, and in general being the leader. The showmanship of drum majors is especially important when the marching band takes the field. They not only set the pace for the show, but also set the tone for the quality of the overall performance.

For drum majors to do all of these things, they must have an understanding of music and be a skilled field conductor capable of loud, clear commands. Most importantly, they must be able to inspire the band's performance through their own ability. This can cover many areas—theatre experience, musicianship, and, for some, mastery of the baton, particularly tossing it very high in the air and, of course, catching it without missing a beat, as was the specialty of the drum major shown here.

Fifteen percent of the years are still unconfirmed in the following list of Lower Dauphin drum majors, even though all avenues were sought to compile this list. With changes in band personnel, the yearbook rarely identifying drum majors, and senior directories not being included in every yearbook, in addition to drum majors being often overlooked in general, identifying these music leaders was particularly difficult. We are open to adding any missing names which will then be placed in the Lower Dauphin Alumni Association archives.

Class	Drum Major
1961	Kenneth Miller
1962	Kenneth Miller
1963	Terry Mills
1964	Terry Mills
1965	Terry Mills
1966	Jack Brandt
1967	Jack Brandt
1968	Don Frantz
1969	Don Frantz
1970	none
1971	none
1972	Charles Dowell
1973	Charles Dowell
1974	Russel Feeser
1975	Russel Feeser
1976	Russel Feeser
1977	Kristi Myers
1978	Kristi Myers and Walter Stine
1979	Walter Stine
1980	Steve Euker, Lynn Dunkleburger and Laurie Petrina
1981	Madeleine Barrett and Carol Dillon
1982	Madeleine Barrett and Carol Dillon
1983	Carl Law and Robin Hyde
1984	Robin Hyde

1985	Thomas Ball and Kathryn Smee
1986	Thomas Ball and Kathryn Smee
1987	Susan Motz and Greg Reinhardt
1988	Wendy Farver and Greg Reinhardt
1989	Wendy Farver and Joseph (Chip) Schell
1990	Joseph (Chip) Schell
1991	Tom Runkle
1992	Tom Runkle and Jen Cunningham
1993	Tish Saner
1994	Sean Devine and Kerry McKeever
1995	Kerry McKeever and Julie Garner
1996	Kent Pierce and Christopher Rutt
1997	Kent Pierce and Christopher Rutt
1998	Kent Pierce, Lindsey Eide and Tess Price
1999	Lindsey Eide and Tess Price
2001	Jen Turgeon
2002	Brandon Anthony
2006	Amy Dunlap and Ashley Shirk
2010	Will Thompson

Head Majorettes

The position of a traditional head majorette began to change in the mid-1970s, and 1983 was the final year for head majorettes leading the Big Blue Band bandfront.

Year	Head Majorette
1961	Barbara Olson
1961	Barbara Olson
1963	Audrey Roland
1964	Audrey Roland
1965	Patty Pheasant
1966	Patty Pheasant
1967	Patricia Jeffries
1968	Jeannine Lehmer
1969	Jeannine Lehmer
1970	Sheila Miller
1971	Lynnette Shipper
1972	Candy Tritch
1973	Candy Tritch
1974	Denise Lehmer
1975	Michelle DeRosa, with Denise Lehmer as Featured Twirler
1976	Paula Bressi
1977	Diane Hetrick
1979	Cindy Heisey, Featured Twirler
1981	Kimberly Rogers
1982	Mitzi Swigart
1983	Karen Ierley

No head majorettes after 1983

Music of Note: Chorus and Orchestra

"Perhaps one of Lower Dauphin's finest features is the talent and musical ability that is found in a major part of the entire student body." 1994 *Falconaire*

We regret that the only music archives we have for chorus and orchestra, in addition to a number of scores, are the music concert programs from 1977 to 2009, donated by Mrs. Marie Weber, and catalogued with the LDAA archives. There are also a number of programs in private collections that have been and others that will be donated to the Lower Dauphin Alumni Association; these will become part of a catalogued collection at the Hummelstown Historical Society. Orchestra and Chorus did not receive the same kind of "flashy press" that the Marching Band did because orchestra and chorus groups were not as public as the band in either parades or competitions. Thus, we pay tribute as we can, recognizing the fine musicianship generated by these programs as well as reminisces of the concerts and those who were engaged in the music program.

BORN TO PERFORM

"It starts deep inside, the calm before the storm, building excitement that can come only from music. The only thing to do is set it free by applying energy, heart, soul, and mind into every move, bringing it under control." 1987 *Falconaire*

Chorus

A chorus was formed when the school first opened its doors and has always been popular with students and the public. The first special choral ensemble, in addition to the formal choirs and choruses, was one of mixed voices called the Falconaires (1960-1961). The first Girls' Chorus with 75 voices was formed and directed by Mrs. Emily Trefz in the fall of 1962. The first Girls' Nonette was created in the fall of 1963 with Connie Wolfe, Elizabeth Kienzle, Elsie Badman, Jean Deimler, Bonnie Weaver, Lauren Haskin, Millie Goss, Edith Badman, and Anna Dibeler. This group in the fall of 1964 included Pat Johnson, Edith Badman, Faye Zeiders, Connie Wolfe, Elizabeth Keinzle, Jean Deimler, Lauren Haskin, Barbara Grubb, and Maryellen Wiest. Carol Kauffman was the accompanist. There was also a Girls Trio.

The Nonettes were featured in the 1964 Christmas program with both traditional music as well as the newer popular music such as "I'll Be Home for Christmas" and "Let It Snow." Members of this group included Wanda Girvin, Beth Kanode, Rogie Carroll, Janice Furman, Marilyn Hallman, Cathy Reed, Connie Campbell, Linda Shope, and Sandy Bixler. During the same time a male chorus known as the Imperials included Terry Folk, Ray Heisey, Richard Stare, Steven Ginder, Jack Brandt, Chris Lidle, Richard Wise, Al Schock, and Don Frantz.

New to the Nonettes in the fall of 1966 were Pat Shearer, Sandy Tschudy, Janice Fureman, Inez Puzuks, Marilyn Hallman, Sandra Frantz, Karen Espenshade, and Lois Baum with Joanne Kettering at the piano. The Imperials continued with Greg Detweiler, Gary Sarno, Richard Wise, Terry Folk, Steve Ginder, Jacob Heisey, Jack Brandt, and Don Frantz.

At the November 11, 1967 football game between LD and East Pennsboro, the half-time program was delivered by the LD choir and marching band as a salute to Veteran's Day. This had never before been done by any other school in this area.

The Class of 1968, disappointed that there had been no musical since 1965, determined to revive the high school musical. A team of band officers organized, wrote, and produced "It's a Big, Wide, Wonderful World," under the direction of band president Elaine Bell and the choir director, Mr. William Nixon. Several soloists were featured along with choreography to accompany the music. Admission was free.

A Stage Band was formed sometime during the 1970s—at least this is when photos of a stage band appear in the yearbook. The inconsistency of content in yearbooks leads to the impossibility of a complete record of performances and of various music groups, but singing groups likely were formed as the talent and interest warranted. Rarely do the yearbooks provide text with the group photos of musical groups and we have tried to follow trends and/or report when information is provided; for example, in the April 20, 1983 spring concert program is found the listing of a men's chorus and a men's trio, and in the fall of 1983, there is mention of the Senior High Chorus as being the major vocal performing group in the high school. The Chorus itself has been consistent; it is the smaller ensembles that ebb and flow. According to the 1984 *Falconaire*, the following groups performed in addition to the central chorus: Senior High Ensemble, Freshman Chorus, and Ninth Grade Girls Ensemble.

In school year 1986-87 Senior High School Choir was comprised of freshmen and sophomores and the Concert Choir consisted of juniors and seniors. In the April 28, 1992 Spring Concert Program Men of the Choir and Women of the Choir are featured.

In 2001, the concert showcased a combined Senior High Chorus and Concert Band. The January 23, 2006 headline in *Flash* announced, "LD's holiday concert gets standing ovation. Kudos to choral director Lynlee Copenhaver, orchestra conductor Marie Weber, and concert band director Jonathan Pinkerton.

In 2008 there was a litany of special groups including Men's Ensemble, Women's Ensemble, Octet, Sign Language Chorus, and Mixed Chorus.

Choral Directors

Mrs. Jane Mellin Smith was the first choral director as well as the music classroom teacher who set the bar high for this fledgling high school and is credited with bringing musicals to our stage. Upon her unexpected departure in the fall of 1962 to pursue her dream of stage performance, Mrs. Smith was followed for a short term by Mrs. Emily Trefz, then by Miss Margaret Gluck who also did not remain long. Mr. William Nixon expanded his duties from band and served as vocal music teacher for several years, followed by Louise Poorman, and then Sandra McConaghay. Energetic and talented perfectionist Linda Whitenight arrived in the fall of 1969 as junior high vocal music teacher, later bringing a classicist element—and longest tenure—to the vocal music program in the senior high. Mr. Turnbull moved into the position of choral director in the fall of

1999, followed by Ms. Lynlee Copenhaver in the fall of 2001. In the fall of 2007 Ms. Elizabeth Colpo became vocal director, raising the expectations even higher and bringing new perspectives to the repertoire.

Orchestra

The precursor to the formation of an orchestra program was a pilot elementary program that began in the early 1970s with instruction by Miss Cathy Smith and Mrs. Kay Luckenbill. With the hiring of Miss Marie Bergan in the summer of 1976, an outstanding program was soon to be the result. Officially the orchestra program began in the high school and junior high school in the fall of 1976. Marie Bergan Weber essentially built the orchestra program from the ground up and when she retired from the district she left a lasting legacy. Much as Linda Kreiser created a field hockey dynasty, so Mrs. Weber invested her career almost single-handedly into a first class orchestra program at all levels, culminating in the High School Orchestra, various ensembles, and a legendary list of students who not only won honors in high school but many of whom continued the passion first instilled in them under the conducting baton of Marie Weber.

In the fall of 1976 qualified students from both junior and senior high schools were selected to be members of the orchestra. One year later the orchestra performed its first concert in the senior high in November 1977. The following spring there was both an orchestra and a string ensemble ready for the concert. Three years later a violincello quartette and a string orchestra were added to the program, along with the string ensemble. Soon to follow in the Christmas program of 1980 was a string octet. Chamber music and other ensembles began in the late 1980s and these various ensembles were showcased depending upon the number and skill level of the musicians, and by the spring of 1982 there was in place a violin quartet, followed the next spring by a string sextet. A middle school string orchestra then made it possible for a combined string orchestra with the high school by December 1983.

On the printed concert programs are listed the students who have achieved various distinctions such as principal in a section of the orchestra, Tri-M Honor Society, Harrisburg Youth Symphony, Honors Orchestras, and County, District, and State Orchestras. By 1997 acknowledgements of membership in organizations and honor orchestras and bands and choruses increased to twelve in which Lower Dauphin students have participated. The current orchestra director is Miss Melody Brubaker, a graduate of the Class of 2004 and a former student of Mrs. Weber.

In 1981 Mrs. Weber became the Orchestra Conductor for the Musicals, a position she still holds.

Perhaps the words of Charles Ives, which Mrs. Weber cited in a statement of belief, best describes this extraordinary teacher herself: "The future of music may not lie entirely in music itself, but rather in the way it encourages and extends, rather than limits, the aspirations and ideals of the people, in the way it makes itself a part with the finer things that humanity does and dreams of."

MENC and PMEA Festival Participants

State, All-Eastern, any National Level

1966	Thomas Hughes/baritone horn, ASB	1997	Christopher Rutt/French horn, ASO
1967	Elaine Bell/flute,[1]ASB	1997	Natalie True/violin, AEO
1973	Tanya Heatwole, ASC	1998	Natalie True/violin, ASO
1977	Andrea Yannone/violin, ASO	1999	Elizabeth O'Hara/viola, ASO
1977	Will Foley/trombone, ASB	1999	Jesse Hoffman/string bass, ASO
1979	Andrea Yannone/violin, ASO	2000	Elizabeth O'Hara/viola, ASO
1980	Andrea Yannone/violin, ASO	2001	Wyatt True/violin, ASO
1980	Elizabeth Snowden/'cello, ASO	2001	Elizabeth O'Hara/viola, AEO, AEO
1981	R. Whit Hill/French horn, ASO	2002	Melody Brubaker/violin, ASO
1983	Gretchen Leaman/violin, AEO, ASO	2002	Joy Adams/viola, ASO
1983	Melissa Brown/alto, AEC, ASC	2002	Stephen Werner/tenor, ASC
1984	Gretchen Leaman/violin, ASO	2002	Meredith Mecum/soprano, ASC
1984	Peter Ward/violin, ASO	2003	Stephen Werner/tenor, AEC
1984	Heidi Leaman/violin, ASO	2004	Derek Alley/percussion, ASB
1985	Peter Ward/violin, ASO	2004	Douglas Lemke/string bass, ASO
1986	Peter Ward/violin, ASO	2005	Andrew Vinton/tenor, ASC
1987	Peter Ward/violin, AEO, ASO	2005	Zachary Samilo/tuba, ASB
1987	Kevin Ward/violin, ASO	2006	Corinna Mazzitti/alto, ASC
1990	Scott Gilbert/oboe, ASO	2008	Kaysey Davis, flute, ASB
1990	Tom Runkle/bass, ASC	2010	Ella Smith, soprano, ASC
1991	Scott Gilbert/oboe, AEO		
1991	Tom Runkle/bass, AEC	**ASB** – All-State Band
1992	Scott Gilbert/oboe, NHSHO, ASB	**AEC** – All-Eastern Chorus
1992	Sandy Stiles/bass clarinet, ASB	**ASC** – All-State Chorus
1992	Tom Runkle/bass, ASC	**AEO** – All-Eastern Orchestra
1993	Alaine Fink/piano, (soprano), ASC	**ASO** – All-State Orchestra
1994	Alaine Fink/piano, ASC	**NHSHO** – National High School Honors Orchestra
1996	Emily Shertzer/oboe, ASB		
1996	Natalie True/violin, ASO		
1997	Natalie True/violin, ASO		

[1] While we are including here only State, Eastern, and National selections, Elaine is a example of those who attained many music honors, in her case by attending District band annually from 1965-1968, qualifying for Regionals in 1967 and 1968 as well as all State in December of 1967,

Please note: This information is based on the available programs that were in the files. Any missing names are due to clerical error and are not intentional.

The Visual Arts

Visual Arts has always been a major part of the education at Lower Dauphin High School. Art Rooms had been built for that focus and the first two art teachers, Mr. Robert Fickes and Mr. Arthur Sowers, set the expectations high, establishing from the beginning that the visual arts was not recreation but a fully recognized discipline and that there was a process and a product. Junior High students all sampled arts classes, but Senior High students were self-selected and reflected the attitude of the instructors, that art, while enjoyable, was a serious vocation. Classes never lacked for students.

Art programs in schools are even more difficult than music programs to fully describe. The faculty is not as "public" as their music program colleagues and most achieve their professional recognition through their own art work. Among the Lower Dauphin art faculty who have had exhibitions and are recognized by the public as practicing artists are Mr. Brad Stroman, Ms. Sally McKeever, Ms. Mary Walsh, Mr. Sowers, and Mr. Fickes.

Perhaps the best nationally-known professional artist among them is Brad Stroman '67 who has mounted showings at various art galleries throughout the United States and who is noted in more detail elsewhere in this Lower Dauphin history. Several other talented students whose works are held in public or private collections and who come readily to mind are Joyce Keener, Lynne Taylor, Joe Roman, David Early, Pam Rainey, and Craig Camasta; we are sure there are many more and invite you to add their names here—or to our website—as a reminder.

Other contributions of LD's art department include supporting the National Art Honor Society which was formed in the school year 1981-82. In 1985 there were 13 members who at that time were noted in the *Falconaire* as taking their annual field trip to DC where they visit art galleries, displays, and monuments. Some of the Society's services include designing musical posters, calendar covers, and programs for special events. At Christmas the society members paint a window in a downtown business. They have also painted a wall mural in the former Hummelstown library as well as visiting elementary schools during art month and teaching an art project. Several students have been selected to attend the Governor's School for the Arts and many have won gold keys at various levels from county to national.

The importance of the visual arts was recognized early when the Class of 1965 purchased work of their classmates as a gift to the school and thus the first mounted work was displayed—and remained for many years—on the walls in the lobby outside the auditorium. This was followed by the first Art Show held the following year on May 17, 1966, sponsored by the Service Club. Forty entries were submitted: oil paintings, water colors, pottery, pencil drawings, sculpture, and jewelry. Judges were Mr. Harold Geesaman, Mr. Robert Nissley, and Mr. Sowers, all artists themselves. A silver pin was awarded to Larry Miller '67 for most outstanding work as well as best in the oil painting category.

In the spring of 1967 senior C. Bradley Stroman was chosen the winner of WGAL's Best Graphics and Design Award. One hundred junior and senior high schools from 20 county schools entered the exhibit and from a total of 2,530 pieces 704 were accepted. Two of Brad's pieces made it to the finals. His "zither in stereo," the painting of a sound, won a gold key and was sent to NYC for national judging.

What was billed as the First Annual Arts Festival, organized by Ken Leskawa '71, was held May 27, 28, and 29, 1970 with a drama festival of one-act plays, a student-produced film and slide show, and an exhibition of art, sculpture, and photography. There was also an art show of the work of junior and senior high students on May 12-14, 1971 arranged by the art teachers, Mr. Fickes, Ms. Mary Walsh, and Mr. Sowers.

In March 1971 Ed Nisley '71 earned a Gold Key for photography in the Scholastic Awards competition. The following year Mike Abraham '72 was awarded a Gold Key for textile design. Wayne Carl Lee '71 won the poster design for the 1971 Capital Area Youth Forum.

As a reflection of interest of the time, art classes in the fall of 1971 were learning decoupage and home economics classes were working with macramé.

In the spring of 1973 Randy Bennett '74 received the Honor Award for his color photograph "Infinity" in the National Scholastic Art/Kodak competition in New York City.

The February 1984 edition of the *Falcon Flash* reported that Gold Keys from the Scholastic Awards were awarded to seniors Cathy Clark, John Crater, Kim Jerpe, Gabrielle Maisels, Memory Smith, and freshmen Joel Shuman and Matthew Williams.

The long-standing National Art Honor Society has continued to provide recognition for achievement in the arts, expanding the classroom to field trips to national and regional museums, and service to the community. Students and citizens alike recognize that Lower Dauphin provides an outstanding curriculum taught by practicing artists.

Appropriately the 2010 *Falconaire* sums it up, "A strong arts program has always been a tradition at Lower Dauphin. Students have a variety of choices through the program, and specializations include courses in fine art, pottery, and photography. Before entering into a specific area of study, all LD students must take an introductory course to the arts; they then can select their interest as a hobby or as an avenue to a future career."

Artisans: Stage Crew and Set Design
Stage Crew: Behind the Scenes

From the 1987 *Falconaire*:
While other people are sleeping in on their Saturday mornings and are out on week-nights, a small group of very dedicated students are hard at work making sure that all Lower Dauphin productions run smoothly. There are many jobs that the Stage and Technical Crew must do, many of which they learn from Mr. Moser who gives much time and input to the members, teaching them the various aspects of behind-the-scenes theatre productions. Sorting through old sets and carrying in new supplies is one of our first jobs for any event. Then, there is set building and painting on which we spend weeks and months making sure everything is sturdy and visually appealing to the audience. Next are the rehearsals, where the crew works to reset the many lights, arrange the plot lighting and adjust sound equipment. The light, sound, and backstage tech crew members must be in constant communication through headsets. We also do musical concerts and other special events by pulling curtains, resetting lights, and moving sound reflectors, to name a few tasks.   —Amy Jo Mumma, Crew Member

Matthew J. Williams, 1987 Class Poet
PA Governor's School for the Arts
Poem Written for Commencement

The Web We Weave

As children we worked like spiders –
    lightly brushing legs
    across newly green blades of grass –
    tightly knitting a close, cloud-colored web –
    the center of our existence.

Building outward from our family and close friends –
    we continued to feed upon the central strength –
    while gradually widening the distance between
    strands of our sticky, cotton-candy lifeline.

Age and teardrop rains and changing winds
    beat down our fragile work –
    and as we entered our teen years,
    the weaving process began anew –
    stronger from former experience.

Each thread woven across the far-reaching
    support cables encompassed a greater area –
    knowledge – and each achievement caught
    in our net was wrapped and stored – as a fly –
    in the wispy white veil of memory.

Now looking up from our protective mesh,
    we feel the whispered wind once more,
    rippling across our four years' work.

At our backs stretch the thick support wires to the center –
    like phone lines to our past – and before us,
    spun thinly in each direction, lie yet
    unwoven lines, holding the future of
    the web we weave.

Musicals: A Rich Tradition

It is said that no one ever forgets the shared experience of performing in a high school musical, whether as a lead, a member of the chorus or orchestra, a member of the technical crew or a walk-on — walk-ons that, in the mid-1980s used members of the wrestling and football teams and in the 1990s began including cameo roles by the school superintendents.

Musicals were an important part of the school from its beginning, and while the auditorium might not have lent itself to a "pit" orchestra, the students who joined forces made musicals a wonderful legacy for others to continue.

According to Supervising Principal David J. Emerich, "…school spirit was a major concern during the first year of the school's operation. …an all-school operetta did a lot to make the students pull together."

Mr. Kenneth Staver, former Dean of Students, attests that two occurrences the first year had the most impact on Lower Dauphin's foundation for success: (1) the championship football team and (2) the music program begun by Mr. Prowell Seitzinger and Mrs. Jane Mellin Smith. During the ensuing years there were other contributing factors, but Mr. Staver was very clear that it was the music that made the difference. The music program later was expanded and enhanced by Mrs. Marie Bergan Weber's remarkable skill in developing the "string program," which grew into several important orchestral performance groups at the high school, as well as successful programs in the elementary schools.

Those who were in the chorus the first two years of LD will remember Mrs. Smith who was charged with creating a choir from students all of whom were new to the school. Faced with much the same challenge as the first football coaches had in building a team, she decided that the best way to engage adolescents was to "find a barn and do a show." Mr. Staver recalls that many local citizens were skeptical about a large stage performance, but imagine the excitement when the students heard *they* were going to "be in a musical."

What a brave decision to make when such trappings as musicals were not usual in high schools at that time. However, Jane Mellin Smith had the skill and, like the Pied Piper, where she led, the kids—and adults—followed. There was no money for costumes, so Mrs. Smith chose a show that was suitable for high school and could be performed in contemporary dress and without an orchestra, instead using two pianos, with Roberta Espenshade '63, a student, and Mrs. Judith Ball (later, Witmer), a faculty member, as accompanists. With Mr. Robert Fickes as scenery designer, *Good News*, set on a college campus, amazed everyone, and its success brought attention to the importance of music in a curriculum. There was no turning back. The admission price to the musical was $1. used toward the purchase of choir gowns the following year.

That spring of 1961 we were on fire with accomplishment: Lower Dauphin with a championship football team, a winning season in wrestling, and a musical debut—we had arrived!

The following year the musical was *The Boy Friend* and chaos would erupt at times in the ninth grade faculty room when Mrs. Smith would race in with her cart and have the place in an uproar. By the time she rushed back out, Mr. William (Bill) Peck, math teacher, would be almost convulsive with laughter, as in laying plans for that year's show, Jane had flown into the room, stated her needs and within five minutes had assigned a role to everyone who happened to be in there for lunch: music, posters, publicity, and ticket sales. Betsy Will (later Richards), home economics teacher, supervised the making of the costumes with her Junior High Costume Design Club and parents who were identified in the program only as Mrs. Stopfel, Mrs. Shaffner, and Mrs. Porr.

Soon students and faculty were walking through the halls, humming a song from the show, "I could be happy with you." After this production, Jane Mellin Smith left Lower Dauphin but the tradition of the stage remained.[1]

Many who participated in later musicals have no idea of the "make-dos" of the first several years at LD. Costumes were contrived, created first by Miss Will's students and volunteer mothers, and later fashioned by Mrs. Jarmilla Brinkmann, among other wardrobe mistresses. At one point a wardrobe closet was built across the back of Mrs. Brinkman's room for this purpose. Bob Fickes (without any real budget) was a magician with his creation of sets, as well as the posters, lighting and sound. The orchestra consisted of two pianos and a hired drum (Lester Stucky), the latter being added the last week of rehearsal, the former being provided in the first two years by a student and a teacher. This tradition was still in place by 1965 during "The Red Mill" with accompanists Carol Kauffman '65, Stephanie Zeiters '65, and Barbara Coble '66.

In 1968 members of the high school choir—on their own—presented "It's a Big, Wide Wonderful World," entirely written, directed, and produced by the band officers under the guidance of Elaine Bell, band president, with Susan Nissley as chair of the script committee and Don Frantz (now a Broadway producer) as set designer. As Elaine recalls, "I remember many hours sitting in the school cafeteria brainstorming and developing the script and selecting the music. We wanted Larry Robertson to sing "There's a kind of hush all over the world," but I couldn't convince him to do it. It was great fun and nerve-wracking and anxiety-producing at times. We even had a real car on stage!"

Don Frantz '69 recalls, "I did have a minor role in 'The Red Mill,' (...bless Miss Gluck's heart), but I don't remember a thing about the plot or the music. I do, however, have fond memories of "South Pacific" when I was in seventh grade. Mrs. Trefz pulled me into the senior high choir a few years early because (a) I was a tenor at the time and (b) I read music well. I remember being in awe of the senior leads and loving the whole production. It was a thrill just to be in the show's chorus. Sorry I can't say the same about 'Red Mill.'"

The 1979 *Falconaire*'s coverage of *Carousel* began, "Plagued with postponements such as blizzards and radiation......."

Every cast has its own stories to tell, of backstage romance, of costume disasters, of microphones malfunctioning (the first 20 or so years there was no amplification, in the early 80s floor microphones were used and actors had to be careful not to dance too close to them, and body mics were unknown

---

[1] August 7, 1964. Jane Mellin, Former Lower Dauphin High School music teacher will be one of the featured players in the forthcoming of Gretna Playhouse production of the musical, "She Loves me," which opens a two-week engagement. Miss Mellin gave up her local teaching position two years ago to go into professional theatre. She has been prominent in New York theatrical and television circles, including the "Lamb's Gambol for John Wayne" at the Waldorf-Astoria and the Blackjack Club, and last summer (1963) was a featured performer at St. John Terrell's Music Circus in Lambertville, NJ. Author's note: Jane, now Jane St. John, most recently appears in "What Goes Around," an official selection of both the 2012 NYC Downtown Short Film Festival and the 2010 Manhattan Film Festival.

until the 1990s). Snow storms during the winters wreaked havoc with rehearsals, rescheduled sporting events pulled away the athletes, and the occasional "walk-out" of a dismayed director or set designer created a brief panic.

One of the most upsetting delays, noted in the March 1972 edition of the *Falcon Flash*, was caused when in the late winter of 1972 the administration scheduled a company of actors (The Tadpole Players) to perform three plays on three separate dates, the last of which was scheduled two weeks before the opening date of "Camelot." This delayed the stage crew in their building of sets, driving to distraction everyone connected with the production.

On the other hand, in the early 1980s Mrs. Judith Witmer, then the musical director, was awarded a grant to provide dancing classes (25 girls and at least a dozen boys) conducted by choreographer Richard Wilson and she also included athletes in the productions, most notably as the Dogpatchers in "L'il Abner," crapshooters in "Guys and Dolls," teen-agers in "Bye Bye Birdie," and knights in "Camelot."

In 1982 the musical was featured in the news because of the casting of the roles of the "Crapshooters" in *Guys and Dolls* half of which were filled not by veteran LD Thespians, but by novice performers who previously had shown their talents as seasoned veterans of varsity athletic competitions: Ted Baumann, football (All Conference All Star) and baseball; Craig Camasta, wrestling (twice a sectional runner-up and thrice a district qualifier, as well as being awarded a Gold Key for art in the Scholastic Arts Program); Bernie Deluca, basketball and baseball (later becoming a professional dancer); Tony Dobson, football and baseball; Mike Graham, football and track; Dan Jenakovich, football and baseball (most valuable offensive player); Rick Martin, basketball; and Rick Salus, cross country, wrestling, track.

Despite or because of many other situations—both positive and otherwise and likely known only to each cast, orchestra, or technical crew, Michelle Mattson wrote in the December 1984 edition of *Falcon Flash*, "…. Musicals of Lower Dauphin differ from other school musicals. The scenery and costumes are all made by our students and helping faculty. An effort is made to use our male athletes, which gives the athlete a different opportunity to perform in an area he does not think he can succeed in. Another difference is seen in dance classes, building confidence in the inexperienced students, to allow more students to audition because there are dance roles to fill, and to become more familiar with the production."

The 47 musicals (as of 2010) produced at Lower Dauphin High School in the first fifty years rest on a long, rich history of many faculty with notable longevity in various capacities. Steven Kisler served as stage manager for 34 shows. Linda Whitenight Hummel was choral director for 31 years. "Hello Dolly" in 2010 marked 30 shows for Marie Bergan Weber as orchestra conductor. Jere Moser did sound and lighting as technical director for 24 years. Rudolph Sharpe spent a total of 17 years at the helm: ten as director, then seven as producer-director. The current director, Kevin Strawser '86, noted his 14th year in that capacity and Debbie Gable Heary '86 marked 11 years as producer. Judith T. Witmer worked with at least 11 musicals: two years as one of two pianists who comprised the "orchestra" in the early years, a year as producer, several years as either drama coach or rehearsal pianist, and six years as producer and director.

Accolades

Accolades to Marie Weber

Mrs. Marie Weber continues to serve as the high school musical pit orchestra conductor, with a tenure longer than any other person affiliated with the musicals. Often working under adverse conditions she never wavered in her professionalism and without her consistent dedication the musicals could not have attained the level of quality we have sometimes taken for granted.

"Once again, I wanted to take a moment to drop you a line and let you know how much I appreciated the work you did with this year's musical production of 'Oliver.' This musical has such great music in it, but the music is nothing if it's not performed wonderfully. Your pit crew performed it wonderfully."

Jeffrey A. Miller, EdD, Superintendent

" 'Annie Get Your Gun' is just another example of the fine quality of service you have provided to our school district. The orchestra was superb. ... Many of us feel that your employment as a music teacher was one of the best decisions we ever made."

Dr. Henry R. Hoerner

"You can be justifiably proud of what you have accomplished with the string program here at Lower Dauphin. Our orchestra is certainly one of the best—if not the best—high school orchestras in Central Pennsylvania. Also, please convey to the members of the pit orchestra that they did a marvelous job. I know that most people don't know or care about the tribulations they endure, but I do and am proud of the way they responded."

Jere L. Moser, Asst. Principal

"I was treated Thursday night to a truly astonishing performance of 'Brigadoon.' To say I was astounded at the very high quality of your work is an understatement. I sat where I could watch the conductor, and believe that much credit should be given to her for the energy and sensitivity to the music which was evident throughout."

Mary Ann Morse

Accolades to Rudolph Sharpe

Dr. Rudolph Sharpe recalls the many letters he received following his productions:

"Your interpretation of 'Carnival' was in our opinion, far superior to a high school play. Lower Dauphin can be proud of your accomplishments."

Mayor and Mrs. Marian Alexander

"Having seen several musicals on stage in New York, I was impressed by the professional quality of 'The Music Man.' You must be proud of the talented students."

Beverly Shaffer

"The L. D. musicals seem to get better each year. The involvement of the large number of students who play supporting roles provides the same thrill of success, and for many students the musical is the highlight of their high school years."

Dr. Henry R. Hoerner

" 'The Sound of Music' was one of the finest presentations at Lower Dauphin."

Beatrice Grove

" 'The Sound of Music' was superb!"

C. Donald Barbush

"The sets were tremendous, the acting was superb, and the music was totally enchanting. I commend you for a sensational achievement!"

William W. Linnane

"This production will be, without a doubt, the one by which all others will be measured. Every performer delivered with aplomb, and the total effect was superb."

Judith Witmer

" 'The Music Man' was among the best I have seen. You are a master at having students achieve the maximum of their potential."

Landry Appleby

"There were many times I felt like leaping on stage and joining you. To the singers in 'Rock Island Railroad' — it was those few moments where the entire audience was yours!"

Julie Sicher

Accolades to Kevin Strawser

Kevin Strawser is the only musical director to also have been *in* the musicals at Lower Dauphin—from seventh grade to taking lead roles in his junior (Albert Peterson in "Bye, Bye, Birdie") and senior (King Arthur in "Camelot") years. Only one alumnus, Thomas Ball, a classmate of Kevin's and also with leading roles (Conrad Birdie and Lancelot) in the same two musicals, has more longevity (seven years) in LD musicals. Kevin is currently Artistic Director for the Hershey Trolley Works and also continues as an actor in local theatre. He would be the first to admit that changes in technology have led to a sophistication in productions not possible before the 1990s. His own background with a degree in theatre has served him well as he joins the ranks of those who built the musicals at LD.

Mr. Strawser wrote in the "Hello, Dolly" 2010 playbill: "Every year I sit down to write these notes and the first thing that comes to mind is the level of dedication and effort each student puts forth while working on the musical. I am always impressed by it, and I used to be surprised by it, but not any more. Our expectations are very high and the students rise to meet, then exceed, those expectations. I suppose we could expect less and make the musical process easier, but my fear is that they would then meet those expectations, too. When January rolls around, I dust off my directing chair and psych myself up for the impending rehearsal period and every year, without fail, the students pull me through with their desire to produce a great show."

Accolades to Judith Witmer

In 1986, Mr. Wilson, well-respected regional choreographer, wrote the following letter:

"Camelot"—and to think that I thought it would be just another high school production. Well, was I ever wrong! Within my 34 years of working with the high schools, I am rarely surprised. I usually know what the finished product will be—I expect it and it occurs. Because I have come to know how much dedication you put into your productions, I allowed "Camelot" would be good and that you would get the most out of your actors and actresses and the most out of the general presentation. I was not prepared for what I did not know you did. In all of my 34 years, what happened at Lower Dauphin this year only happened twice in my working with productions, and I must admit that "Camelot" surpassed what I previously had thought was the best. Your Camelot will be an almost impossible feat to follow.

Others in the show and in the audience added,

"I have never been so moved by a high school production."

"Because you believed in me and the others, Camelot was an experience beyond all others."

"… a musical that people will **always remember.**"

"You have been, and continue to be, a most positive influence."

"You saw something in me that no one else did and I am grateful for the chance you have given me as the student producer."

And from the athletes who participated, "Thank you for letting us be part of this."

Remarks from Don Frantz, February 2013, speaking to LD students

"There were no closer friendships made in my high school years than on the boards lying across the stage floor in front of you. I trust the boards have retained their power and although they may not know it yet, tonight's merry band of players will never forget their dance partners. During the course of an Alan Menken score, we are witnessing the beginning of lifelong friendships and what joy that brings.

"Theater brightens you. It begins when you turn out all the lights except one and then invite a young person to step into the glow. Theater grows you. For 2 ½ hours a young artist slips into the clothes of another person from another time and the world becomes bigger. Theater transforms you. Belle whispers, "I love you," and a Beast morphs into a Prince. Similarly, when an audience applauds, the faces become prettier, minds bolder, and wills more confident.

"Young Thespians are pacing backstage, as I did years ago. They are ready to do their best. It is very real to me that in high school theatre there is a show inside the show which has the power to guide someone throughout their entire life. These very boards, lights, audiences and fellow actors transformed me.

"I am thrilled at the talent and polish on Broadway, but in some way, it is at the end of the journey. Here, on this stage we see the beginning of the journey and it is far more compelling. And so, tonight will be my most favorite turn, watching the players and listening to a 'Tale as Old as Time.'

Don Frantz '69, Associate Producer, the original "Beauty and the Beast," Broadway

Notes from Musical Alumni

Your letter reminded me of the many precious memories about the school, and especially you, Judy Sener, and Barry Stopfel. Happy Fiftieth Anniversary, Lower Dauphin High School.

Jane Mellin Smith (St. John)

While I will not be able to attend to sing in the alumni chorus, I wanted to thank you and Jane and let you know that your love of music inspired me towards a career in teaching and music.

Roberta Espenshade Centurion '63

I still have my costume.

Lena Lausch Vigilante '80

I was in four musicals and I would love to be a part of this.

Darla Ebersole Hoffer '81

I look forward to echoing the auditorium again as my lasting impression of LDHS can be summed up in one word: "Coconuts."

Mark Stare '83, "South Pacific"

The musical was my life in high school and my proudest achievements to that date!

Debbie Gable Heary, '86

There's No Business Like Show Business and as we gather to sing from the LD Musicals of 50 years, we have a common thread and pride in the part that we played in making these a great success. Thank you to everyone for making this a wonderful experience and remember to keep a song in your heart.

Betty Musser Radle '62

Notes from "The Pit"

Many students have commented that one of the benefits of being in the orchestra for the school musical is that both the students and conductor get to know each other better. For a period of time we spend many hours together in the small space fondly known as "the pit." Many things happened in this area, most of which the audience—and much of which not even those on stage—ever realized....

Because the music for the pit orchestra is written for professional Broadway instrumentalists/musicians, it becomes a catalyst for high school students to rise to a higher level of playing. It also provides instrumental challenges which may be problematic for some students as the parts were intended for professionals. Some of the other issues are the reed books, which require the woodwind players to play multiple instruments, which some students can do. For "Beauty and the Beast" the trombone player was required to play the tuba as well as bass trombone. In addition, when necessary, we have used professional musicians who challenge the students to "play up" to their level and, again, results in the student improvement from the process.

Another challenge occurs when the books are written in manuscript as opposed to printed music. An additional challenge for the conductor is that the conductor's score is a glorified piano part, i.e., piano conductor's score rather than a full score which means when the conductor hears a wrong pitch or pit members question notes in their parts, there is not a full score to check the pitch(es), so that the conductor needs to determine from the piano score which note is each musician's.

Among challenges that affect everyone is that the tempi of the dances (which are usually the most difficult numbers of the shows) are set by the recording that the choreographer uses for rehearsals, a tempo set by the music director and performed by professional Broadway musicians. Since the dancers and pit begin rehearsals at the same time, the pit is not ready to record the dances for the choreographer's rehearsals. Thus, when we begin combined rehearsals with cast and pit, we are all faced with "danceable" by the cast competing with "playable" by the high school musicians.

Challenges of the musical for the conductor include following leads or soloists who perform with molto rubato in that the conductor attempts her best to follow the lead and hopes that the orchestra is alert and following. I recall a year when the rubatos were so excessive that one of the pit members gave me a large orange hand (such as are seen at sporting events) with which to conduct. Another year an ensemble of females decided to accelerate to the extreme where a song that was in a fast 2 suddenly became a fast one. Over the years, there have been leads that have forgotten words or changed the order of the verses. In the song *Gabriel Blow Your Horn* from "Anything Goes," when one of the leads who missed the entrance, which was followed immediately by a chorus response, I had to make a decision whether to restart the song and hope that everyone on the stage knew what was happening or keep going and have the chorus sing, "Yes we hear that horn."

We kept going.

The same type of "second guessing" is what happens when a verse is reversed—i.e., 2nd verse is sung first, wondering whether to keep going or go back. There have been leads who cut measures out or shortened notes, which always was a challenge to let the pit know where we were. There was a lead

in "Once Upon a Mattress" who not only cut out or omitted numerous measures of interlude, but also accelerated throughout the song. There was another lead during the performance of "Carnival" who sang something that was not from the show or anything that I recognized; I brought the pit back to the volume that was almost inaudible and playing a "boom – chick" pattern until the singer found the correct song and melody. "Beauty and the Beast" added the challenge of the mask and the passarelle where in some instances the cast was blocked by having their backs to the conductor. There were other years when leads have gotten laryngitis or were absent and we either had to use an understudy who had not rehearsed with the pit and was going to perform in the performance or/in the case of laryngitis, the understudy sang from back stage. All of these surprises "kept me on my toes."

Before the auditorium was renovated and the sound system was updated, we had spots in the auditorium where the microphones would "cut out." Luckily I had established a signal of tapping on my chest to inform the pit that the volume had to be almost inaudible, so that the vocalist could be heard in the auditorium.

The pit has changed over the years and when I started, we had no real pit at all, so we used panels lined with egg cartons spray-painted black until the auditorium renovation when an actual pit was constructed.

There have been curious interactions with the audience members as well, such as asking the bass player to move or lower his instrument, requesting the conductor to sit lower, even adjusting the conductor's stand lights during intermission; for example, one year a parent had tickets for consecutive nights and the first night asked the director to request the orchestra conductor to conduct with a dimmer or no lights on the score. The second night during intermission the person entered the pit, wending his way through the instruments and adjusted the conductor's stand and lights!

Other personal memorable moments include the year when the lights were turned out as I was going down the steps from back stage into the pit; I missed the steps and sprained my ankle badly. Another year on the day before previews I ended up in the emergency room. Finally there was the year that on the day of previews, I was ill through the previous night, continuing into morning. Regardless of any of these mishaps, I have no understudy and the show must go on.

Marie Bergan Weber

Musicals

1961 Good News

Jane Mellin Smith, Director, Producer, Choral Director, and Choreographer

Judith (Ball) Witmer and Roberta Espenshade, Piano Accompanists

Cynthia Aldrich '62 and Mrs. Smith, Choreographers

Robert R. Fickes, Sets

1962 The Boy Friend

Jane Mellin Smith, Director, Producer, Choral Director, and Choreographer

Carol Kasbee and Charles McKee, Student Choreographers

Judith (Ball) Witmer and Roberta Espenshade, Piano Accompanists w/ Lester Stucky, drummer

Elizabeth (Will) Richards, Costumes, along with the Jr. High Design Club and several mothers

Robert R. Fickes, Joyce Keener '63 and Les Eckert '62, Sets

Judy Sener and Anna Dibeler, Stage Managers

1963 South Pacific

Emily Trefz, Director, Producer, Choral Director, and Choreographer

"Mitch" Grand, Carol Kauffman, Roberta Espenshade, Accompanists

Robert R. Fickes, Set Design and Construction

Costumes, Emily Trefz & Julia Espenshade

1965 The Red Mill

Margaret Gluck, Choral Director, Costuming

Mrs. Lewis Mandes, Dialogue Coach

Carol Kauffman '65, Stephanie Zeiters '65, and Barbara Coble '66, Accompanists

Robert R. Fickes, Set Design and Construction

1968 It's a Big, Wide Wonderful World

(Student-written and produced program)

William Nixon, Faculty Advisor

Elaine Bell '68, Director

Sue Nisley '68, Chair, Script Committee

Don Frantz '69, Set Design and Construction

Linda Funck '68 & Janice Fureman '68, Costumes

1969 Penny

William Nixon, Director and Choral Director

Judith T. (Ball) Witmer, Producer and Drama Coach

W. Richard Claar, and Wm. L. Linnane, Drama Coaches

Robert R. Fickes, Set Design and Construction

Arthur L. Sowers, Sound & Lights

Anne Broadwater, Shirley Witmer, and Marjorie Carlson, Costumes

1970 Plain and Fancy

William Nixon and Richard Claar Co-Directors and Producers

Linda Whitenight, Vocal Director

William Nixon, Choral Director

David Hummel, Orchestra Conductor

1971 Bye Bye Birdie

Richard Claar, Director and Producer

1972 Camelot

Rudolph Sharpe, Director and Producer

Louise Poorman, Choral Director

David Hummel, Orchestra Conductor

Robert R. Fickes, Sets; Richard Claar, Sound & Lights; Marjorie Carlson, Costumes

1973 The Boy Friend

Rudolph Sharpe, Director

Jere Moser, Production Manager

Louise Poorman, Choral Director

David Hummel, Orchestra Conductor

Kermit Katzaman, Lights and Sound

Jarmila Howell, Costumes

1974 Oklahoma

Rudolph Sharpe, Director and Producer
Louise Poorman, Choral Director
David Hummel, Orchestra Conductor
Laura Shaw, Choreography
Robert R. Fickes, Sets
Kim McClurg '74, Stage Manager
Jarmila Brinkman, Costumes

1975 Once Upon a Mattress

Rudolph Sharpe, Director and Producer
Louise Poorman, Choral Director
David Hummel, Orchestra Conductor
Stephen P. Kistler, Stage Manager
Robert R. Fickes, Set Design and Construction
Jere Moser, Technical Director

1976 Anything Goes

Rudolph Sharpe, Director and Producer
Louise Poorman, Choral Director
David Hummel, Orchestra Conductor
Stephen P. Kistler, Stage Manager
Robert R. Fickes, Set Design and Construction
Jere Moser, Technical Director

1977 Carnival

Rudolph Sharpe, Director and Producer
Sandra McConaghay, Choral Director
Laura Shaw, Choreographer
David Hummel, Orchestra Conductor
Stephen P. Kistler, Stage Manager
Doug Topper '77, Ken Stehman,
Mary Walsh, Set Design
Jere Moser, Technical Director
Jarmila Brinkman, Costumes

1978 The Music Man

Rudolph Sharpe, Director and Producer
Linda Hummel, Choral Director

Laura Shaw, Choreographer
David Hummel, Orchestra Conductor
Stephen P. Kistler, Stage Manager
Mary Walsh and Ken Stehman, Set Design
Jere Moser, Technical Director
Jarmila Brinkman, Costumes

1979 Carousel

Rudolph Sharpe, Director and Producer
Linda Hummel, Choral Director
Laura Shaw, Choreographer
David Hummel, Orchestra Conductor
Stephen P. Kistler, Stage Manager
Jere Moser and Ken Stehman
Technical Director
Jarmila Brinkman, Costumes

1980 The Sound of Music

Rudolph Sharpe, Director and Producer
Linda Hummel, Choral Director
Thomas Turnbull, Jr., Orchestra Conductor
Laura Shaw, Choreographer
Stephen P. Kistler, Stage Manager
Jere Moser, Ken Stehman, Stephen Kistler,
Set Design
Jere Moser, Technical Director
Jarmila Brinkman, Costumes

1981 Annie Get Your Gun

Judith T. Witmer, Director and Producer
Linda Hummel, Choral Director
Laura Shaw, Choreographer
Marie Bergan, Orchestra Conductor
Stephen P. Kisler, Stage Manager
Ken Stehman and Brad Stroman, Sets
Jere Moser, Technical Director
Jarmila Brinkman, Costumes

1982 Guys and Dolls
Judith T. Witmer, Director and Producer
Linda Hummel, Choral Director
Richard M. Wilson, Choreographer
Marie B. Weber, Orchestra Conductor
Stephen P. Kisler, Stage Manager
Brad Stroman and Ken Stehman, Sets
Jere Moser, Technical Director
Rich Dunham & Tom Backenstose '83,
Lighting and Sound
Jarmila Brinkman, Costumes

1983 South Pacific
Judith T. Witmer, Director and Producer
Linda Hummel, Choral Director
Richard M. Wilson, Choreographer
Marie B. Weber, Orchestra Conductor
Stephen P. Kisler, Stage Manager
Brad Stroman and Ken Stehman, Sets
Jere Moser, Technical Director
Lighting Design: Tom Backenstoes '83
Sound: William Vogelsong '83
Jarmila Brinkman, Costumes

1984 Li'l Abner
Judith T. Witmer, Director and Producer
Linda Hummel, Choral Director
Richard M. Wilson, Choreographer
Marie B. Weber, Orchestra Conductor
Stephen P. Kisler, Stage Manager
Mark Scalese, Ken Stehman, Set Design
Jere Moser, Technical Director
Jarmila Brinkman, Costumes

1985 Bye Bye Birdie
Judith T. Witmer, Director and Producer
Linda Hummel, Choral Director
Richard M. Wilson, Choreographer
Marie B. Weber, Orchestra Conductor
Joseph Snavely, Stage Manager
Mark Scalese, Robert Wagner, Sets
Jere Moser, Technical Director
Jarmila Brinkman, Costumes

1986 Camelot
Judith T. Witmer, Director and Producer
Linda Hummel, Choral Director
Richard M. Wilson, Choreographer
Marie B. Weber, Orchestra Conductor
Stephen P. Kisler, Stage Manager
Mark Scalese, Joel Edmunds, Sets
Jere Moser, Technical Director
Nan Edmunds, Costumes

1987 Oklahoma!
Beverly Sweger, Director
Linda Hummel, Choral Director
Marie B. Weber, Orchestra Conductor
Stephen P. Kisler, Stage Manager
Mark Scalese, Joel Edmunds, Set Design
Nan Edmunds, Costumes

1988 My Fair Lady
Rudolph Sharpe, Director and Producer
Linda Hummel, Choral Director
Marie B. Weber, Orchestra Conductor
Richard Wilson, Choreographer
Stephen P. Kisler, Stage Manager
Ron Zeigler, Joel Edmunds, Matt Royer '89, Sets
Jere Moser, Technical Director
Nan Edmunds, Costumes

1989 Once Upon a Mattress
Rudolph Sharpe, Director and Producer
Linda Hummel, Choral Director
Richard M. Wilson, Choreographer
Marie B. Weber, Orchestra Conductor
Stephen P. Kisler, Stage Manager
Joel Edmunds & Ron Zeigler, Set Design

Jere Moser, Technical Director
Nan Edmunds, Costumes

1990 The Music Man

Rudolph Sharpe, Director and Producer
Linda Hummel, Choral Director
Richard M. Wilson, Choreographer
Marie B. Weber, Orchestra Conductor
Stephen P. Kisler, Stage Manager
Joel Edmunds & Ron Zeigler, Set Design
Jere Moser, Technical Director
Nan Edmunds, Costumes

1991 Anything Goes

Rudolph Sharpe, Director and Producer
Linda Hummel, Choral Director
Richard M. Wilson, Choreographer
Marie B. Weber, Orchestra Conductor
Stephen P. Kisler, Stage Manager
Mary Walsh, Joel Edmunds, Stephen Kistler,
Set Design
Jere Moser, Technical Director
Nan Edmunds, Costumes

1992 Carnival

Rudolph Sharpe, Director and Producer
Linda Hummel, Choral Director
Richard M. Wilson, Choreographer
Marie B. Weber, Orchestra Conductor
Stephen P. Kisler, Stage Manager
Mary Walsh & Joel Edmunds, Sets
Jere Moser, Technical Director
Nan Edmunds, Costumes

1993 Hello Dolly

Rudolph Sharpe, Director and Producer
Linda Hummel, Choral Director
Colleen Schmidt, Choreographer
Marie B. Weber, Orchestra Conductor
Stephen P. Kisler, Stage Manager

Mary Walsh & Joel Edmunds, Set Design
Jere Moser, Technical Director
Nan Edmunds, Costumes

1994 Guys and Dolls

Rudolph Sharpe, Director and Producer
Linda Hummel, Choral Director
Colleen Schmidt, Choreographer
Marie B. Weber, Orchestra Conductor
Stephen P. Kisler, Stage Manager
Mary Walsh & Mark Painter, Set Design
Jere Moser, Technical Director

1995 Damn Yankees

Doug Royer '89, Director
Phil Green, Producer
Linda Hummel, Choral Director
Colleen Schmidt, Choreographer
Marie B. Weber, Orchestra Conductor
Stephen P. Kisler, Stage Manager
Doug Royer & Mark Painter, Sets
Jere Moser, Technical Director

1996 Brigadoon

Doug Royer, Director
Phil Green, Producer
Linda Hummel, Choral Director
Nanette Kimmel, Choreographer
Marie B. Weber, Orchestra Conductor
Stephen P. Kisler, Stage Manager
Doug Royer & Mark Painter, Set Design
Jere Moser, Technical Director

1997 Crazy For You

Kevin M. Strawser '86, Director
Debbie (Gable) Heary '86, Producer
Linda Hummel, Choral Director
Nanette Kimmel, Choreographer
Marie B. Weber, Orchestra Conductor

Stephen P. Kisler, Stage Manager
Mark Painter & Mary Walsh, Sets
Jere Moser, Technical Director

1998 Oliver

Kevin M. Strawser, Director
Debbie Heary, Producer
Linda Hummel, Choral Director
Nanette Kimmel, Choreographer
Marie B. Weber, Orchestra Conductor
Stephen P. Kisler, Stage Manager
Scott Baker, Sets
Matthew Mitchell '91, Technical Director

1999 Meet Me in St. Louis

Kevin M. Strawser, Director
Debbie Heary, Producer
Linda Hummel, Choral Director
Nanette Kimmel, Choreographer
Marie B. Weber, Orchestra Conductor
Stephen P. Kisler, Stage Manager
Kevin Strawser, Sets
Matthew Mitchell, Technical Director
Debbie Heary, Costumes

2000 No, No Nanette

Kevin M. Strawser, Director
Pamela (Schwentker) Waters '88, Producer
Linda Hummel, Choral Director
Nanette Kimmel, Choreographer
Marie B. Weber, Orchestra Conductor
Stephen P. Kisler, Stage Manager
Kevin Strawser, Sets
Matthew Mitchell, Technical Director

2001 Good News

Kevin M. Strawser, Director
Pamela Waters, Producer
Linda Hummel, Choral Director
Nanette Kimmel, Choreographer

Marie B. Weber, Orchestra Conductor
Stephen P. Kisler, Stage Manager
Kevin Strawser, Set Design
Matthew Mitchell, Technical Director
Chantal Atnip, Costumes

2002 The Wizard of Oz

Kevin M. Strawser, Director
Pamela Waters, Producer
Linda Hummel, Choral Director
Nanette Kimmel, Choreographer
Marie B. Weber, Orchestra Conductor
Lynlee Copenhaver, Voice Coach
Stephen P. Kisler, Stage Manager
Kevin Strawser, Sets
Matthew Mitchell, Technical Director
Chantal Atnip, Costumes

2003 Anything Goes

Kevin M. Strawser, Director
Debbie Gable Heary, Producer
Linda Hummel, Choral Director
Nanette Kimmel, Choreographer
Marie B. Weber, Orchestra Conductor
Lynlee Copenhaver, Voice Coach
Stephen P. Kisler, Stage Manager
Kevin Strawser & Steve Kistler, Sets
Tim Banis, Technical Director
Lori Friedlander, Lights

2004 Once Upon a Mattress

Kevin M. Strawser, Director
Debbie Heary, Producer
Linda Hummel, Choral Director
Nanette Kimmel, Choreographer
Marie B. Weber, Orchestra Conductor
Lynlee Copenhaver, Voice Coach
Stephen P. Kisler, Stage Manager
Kevin Strawser & Stephen Kistler, Sets

Michael James, Technical Director
Beth Ackerman Wappman '86, Make-up

2005 How to Succeed in Business
Kevin M. Strawser, Director
Debbie Heary, Producer
Linda Hummel, Choral Director
Nanette Oates, Choreographer
Marie B. Weber, Orchestra Conductor
Lynlee Copenhaver, Voice Coach
Stephen P. Kisler, Stage Manager
Kevin Strawser & Stephen Kistler, Sets
Michael James, Technical Director
Tim Deiling, Lights
Brian Peda, Sound
Beth Wappman, Make-up

2006 The Music Man
Kevin M. Strawser, Director
Debbie Heary, Producer
Linda Hummel, Choral Director
Nanette Oates, Choreographer
Jonathan Pinkerton '99, Orchestra Conductor
Lynlee Copenhaver, Voice Coach
Stephen P. Kisler, Stage Manager
Kevin Strawser & Stephen Kistler, Sets
Michael James, Technical Director
Tim Deiling, Lights
Beth Wappman, Make-up

2007 Kiss Me, Kate
Kevin M. Strawser, Director
Debbie Heary, Producer
Linda Hummel, Choral Director
Nanette Oates, Choreographer
Marie B. Weber, Orchestra Conductor
Lynlee Copenhaver, Voice Coach
Stephen P. Kisler, Stage Manager
Kevin Strawser & Stephen Kistler, Set Design

Michael James, Technical Director
Beth Wappman, Make-up

2008 Thoroughly Modern Millie
Kevin M. Strawser, Director
Debbie Heary, Producer
Linda Hummel, Choral Director
Nanette Oates, Choreographer
Marie B. Weber, Orchestra Conductor
Elizabeth Colpo, Voice Coach
Stephen P. Kisler, Stage Manager
Kevin Strawser, Stephen Kistler, Larry Freeman, Sets
Michael James, Technical Director
Beth Wappman, Make-up

2009 The Pajama Game
Kevin M. Strawser, Director
Debbie Heary, Producer
Elizabeth Colpo, Choral Director
Nanette Kimmel, Choreographer
Marie B. Weber, Orchestra Conductor
Stephen P. Kisler, Stage Manager
Kevin Strawser, Stephen Kistler, Larry Freeman, Sets
Michael James, Technical Director
Debbie Heary & Chris Keck, Costumes
Beth Wappman, Make-up

2010 Hello Dolly
Kevin M. Strawser, Director
Debbie Heary, Producer
Elizabeth Colpo, Choral Director
Nanette Kimmel, Choreographer
Marie B. Weber, Orchestra Conductor
Stephen P. Kisler, Stage Manager
Michael James, Technical Director
Drenda Cordeiro & Jon Tirado, Costumes
Beth Wappman, Make-up

Lower Dauphin High School

Proudly Presents

DISNEY'S
BEAUTY
AND THE
BEAST

February 28, March 1, and 2, 2013
7:00 p.m.
March 3, 2013
3:00 p.m.

Music by *Alan Menken*
Lyrics by *Howard Ashman & Tim*
Book by *Linda Woolverton*

Lower Dauphin
High School
Presents

BYE BYE
BIRDIE

April 11, 7:30PM
April 12, 8PM
April 13, 8PM

LOWER DAUPHIN HIGH SCHOOL
PRESENTS

GUYS &
DOLLS

LOWER DAUPHIN HIGH SCHOOL AUDITORIUM
HUMMELSTOWN, PA.

APRIL 1ST   7:30 PM
APRIL 2ND 3RD   8:00 PM

LOWER DAUPHIN HIGH SCHOOL PRESENTS
RODGERS AND HAMMERSTEIN'S

SOUTH
PACIFIC

LOWER DAUPHIN HIGH SCHOOL AUDITORIUM
HUMMELSTOWN, PA.

THURSDAY APRIL 7 7:30 PM
FRIDAY   APRIL 8 8:00PM
SATURDAY APRIL 9 8:00PM

CAMELOT
LOWER DAUPHIN HIGH
SCHOOL

APRIL 10, 7:30 APRIL 11, 12, 8:00

Lower Dauphin High School
Proudly Presents

Hello,
Dolly!

Lower Dauphin High School
Auditorium

March 4, 5, 6 2010
7:00 p.m.

ANNIE YOUR
GET GUN
ADMIT ONE
STUDENT

CAMELOT
$3.00 Adults
APRIL 10, 7:30
APRIL 11 8:00

SOUTH
PACIFIC
APRIL 7 @ 7:30
ADMISSION
RESERVED 3.50

Lower Dauphin Senior High School
presents

LI'L
ABNER

Thursday, April 5 7:00
Friday, April 6   8:00
Saturday, April 7

Lower Dauphin High School
Proudly Presents

Anything
Goes

March 27, 28, & 29, 2003

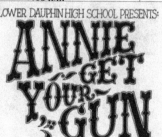

LOWER DAUPHIN HIGH SCHOOL PRESENTS:

ANNIE
GET
YOUR
GUN

Produced and Directed by .... Mrs. Judith T. Witmer
Musical Direction by .... Mrs. Linda W. Hummel
Technical Direction by .... Mr. Jere L. Moser
Orchestra Conducted by .... Miss Marie C. Bergan
Choreography & Dance Instruction by ... Mrs. Laura L. Shaw
Costuming by .... Mrs. Jarmila Brinkmann
Set Design by .... Mr. C. Bradley Stroman
Set Construction by .... Mr. Kenneth K. Stehman
Stage Management by .... Mr. Stephen P. Kistler
Make-Up and Publicity by .... Miss Nanette P. Willis

Student Stage Manager .... Wendy M. Whitehaus
Student Assistant Manager .... Karen E. Williams
Treasurer .... Linda J. Teets

Class Plays and Thespian Productions

The dates here listed for the plays are as close as could be ascertained because names of plays often do not appear in the yearbooks, and programs are difficult to obtain. It also was impossible to confirm names of all directors.

Class	Senior Class Play	Junior Class Play
1961	Publicity Mad Douglas Stauffer	*none*
1962	Tish Douglas Stauffer	Kind Lady (Class of '63) Douglas Stauffer
1963	The Curious Savage Douglas Stauffer	Gentlemen Prefer Blondes ('64) Douglas Stauffer
1964	Curtain Going Up Judith T. Ball, Director	Hillbilly Weddin' ('65) Helen Yount, Helene Kramer, Dir. Robert R. Fickes, Scenery/Lighting Judith T. Ball, Publicity/Tickets
1965	The Skin of Our Teeth Judith T. Ball, Director Robert R. Fickes, Scenery/Lighting	Our Town (Class of '66) Robert R. Fickes, Director
1966	Ten Little Indians Judith T. Ball, Director Robert R. Fickes, Scenery/Lighting	Melody Jones ('67) M. Jane Strite & Katherine Zeiters Robert R. Fickes, Scenery/Lighting
1967	Arms and the Man Judith T. Ball, Director Robert R. Fickes, Scenery/Lighting	Rebel Without a Cause ('68) Emily Keller, Director
1968	She Stoops to Conquer Judith T. Ball, Director Robert R. Fickes, Scenery/Lighting	Tom Jones ('69)
1969	The Boy Who Changed the World David Fullen, Director	Lock, Stock, and Lipstick ('70) William Linnane
1970	Curtain Going Up Edward Blandy, Director	Up the Down Staircase ('71) Alan Risser, Director
1971	*unconfirmed*	The Late Christopher Bean Kathryn Taylor
1972	The Gondoliers	*unconfirmed*

1973	Ask Any Girl Rudy Sharpe	You Were Born on a Rotten Day Audrey Conway and Karen Bowser
1974	Tell Me That You Love Me, Junie Moon Karen Bowser and Rudy Sharpe	Arsenic and Old Lace ('75) Karen Bowser and Nanette Willis
1975	*unconfirmed*	

Beginning with the Class of 1976, the Thespian Society began producing the plays, cast with all grades. However, a Thespian Club had been chartered in the fall of 1972 and participated in competition plays, the first of which was "Balcony Scene" presented in the auditorium for a public appearance and in April at the Harrisburg Community Theatre where Marguerite (Megg) Berger won best supporting actress award at the 13th annual Drama Festival. The short-lived Drama I class also did plays, three of which were "Mystery of Mouldy Manor," "The Gondoliers," and "Sorry, Wrong Number," in 1973. Evidence was also found with a poster "Funky Winkerbean," which may have been a production. The first officers of Thespians were Bob Nisley, acting president; Nadine Yancheff, scribe; Malia Dillon, secretary, Peggy Baker, vice president.

1976	Story Theatre; A Winter's Tale; The Stuck Pot
1977	The Drunkard
1977	Our Town (Ronald Zeigler, Director; Judith Witmer, Musical Director; David Gates, Producer; Jere Moser, Light and Sound; Robert Fickes, Art)
1978	Arms and the Man; The Nut Factory
1979	Regarding Electra; Dracula
1980	Pillow Talk; It Happens Every Summer
1981	The Miracle Worker; Ask Any Girl
1982	MASH; A Murder is Announced
1983	Cheaper by the Dozen
1984	The Fall of the House of Usher
1985	The Curious Savage
1986	Harvey
1987	A Night of One-Act Plays
1988	The Crucible (Ronald Zeigler, Director)
1989	Noises Off (Ronald Zeigler)
1990	Winnie the Pooh and The Best Christmas Pageant Ever (Ronald Zeigler)
1991	Macbeth (Ronald Zeigler)
1992	Fahrenheit 451 (Ronald Zeigler)
1993	Our Town (Ronald Zeigler)
1994	Arsenic and Old Lace (Ronald Zeigler)
1995	*unconfirmed*
1996	The Boys Next Door; Steel Magnolias
1997	Love and Kisses – the first play to be produced in the newly renovated auditorium in the fall of 1996 – (Sharon Hillegas)
1998	Desire
1999	Anne Frank and Me (Sharon Hillegas)

2000	Fame	2007	One-Act Plays: A Christmas Carol and from All in the Timing: Sure Thing; Words, Words, Words; Universal Language (Kevin M. Strawser)
2001	The Odd Couple		
2002	Murder by the Book (Margaret Becker)		
2003	The Scarlet Letter	2008	The Shadow Box (Kevin M. Strawser)
2004	Blythe Spirit	2009	A Midsummer Night's Dream (Kevin M. Strawser)
2005	Jane Eyre		
2006	The Comet of St. Loomis (Kevin M. Strawser)	2010	The Visit (Kevin M. Strawser)

Musical Careers and Avocations

The purpose of this section of the book is to indicate the variety of pathways taken by alumni who were active in the music programs at LD. While we can't begin to know—let alone acknowledge—all who have continued their careers or their pastimes in music, we here provide a sampling, based mainly on recommendations by those who have kept in touch with the alums. Some of the following information was found online which again suggests that all alumni should let the Lower Dauphin Alumni Association know their whereabouts and respond when we update our directory.

Dr. Thomas Hughes '67 is an Associate Professor of Music, Organ, and Music Technology for the School of Music at Texas Tech. He has taught at the Sydney Conservatorium of Music and has worked in curriculum design, distance education, and electronic music, among other areas. He is in demand as an educational technology consultant and provides workshops worldwide. A special topic of interest for him is cognitive function in musicians, and advanced teaching with distance education involving biofeedback. He is also an active concert artist organist.

Dr. Greg Detweiler '69 is an Associate Professor of Choirs, Conducting, and Choral Activities at Morehead State University and conducts the Chamber Singers and Concert Choir, groups that have toured in Europe, Costa Rica, and Canada. He is in demand as a clinician, guest conductor, and adjudicator and has been a member and performed with the Atlanta Symphony Orchestra Chorus, the Atlanta Chamber Chorus, and the Soldiers' Chorus of the U.S. Army Field Band. He has studied choral conducting and technique with many luminaries, including Robert Shaw.

Dan Stokes '76 is the Director of Music Ministries of the Christ Church United Methodist in Louisville, Kentucky where he serves as organist and choir director. Dan is viewed as a gifted musician and leader of a music ministry involving 640 participants in 16 ensembles, including the 135-member Chancel Choir. He is also in demand for recitals in various venues, particularly enjoying discovering vintage pipe organs and learning the idiosyncrasies of each.

Andrea Yannone '79 serves as the school administrative manager at the San Francisco Ballet and has been the "Keeping Score" program manager of the San Francisco Symphony.

R. Whit Hill '81 has performed with the Harrisburg Symphony, the Rochester Philharmonic, the Heidelberg Schloss-Spiele Orchestra, and the Chicago Civic Orchestra. He is currently on faculty of Boston Conservatory of Music. He is a member of various ensembles including the Chameleon Arts Ensemble, as well as numerous organizations throughout Boston and New England including the Boston Philharmonic, Boston Modern Orchestra Project, Emmanuel Music, Rhode Island Philharmonic, Albany Symphony, and New Hampshire Music Festival.

Jesse Garrett '85 (formerly Brian Englehart) is a country singer and recording artist in Nashville.

Dr. Douglas Rosener '86, Associate Director of Bands at Auburn University, has performed with many professional orchestras including the Altoona Symphony, the Boulder Philharmonic, the Sinfonia of Colorado, the Colorado Ballet Company Orchestra, and the Colorado Music Festival Orchestra. He has recorded CDs with the North Texas Wind Symphony, North Texas Chamber Players, and his percussion ensemble compositions and arrangements have been published.

Kevin Strawser '86 has earned a place on the list from a different pathway as a theatre major at Indiana University of Pennsylvania and currently director of LD's musicals.

Thomas Ball '86 also has followed a different path in the music industry. Following graduation from Lebanon Valley College, Tom began performing nationally in concert on college campuses and was a showcase performer five times with the National Association of Campus Activities, including selection as solo performer at the national convention. He returned to Hershey and is now president and owner of Thomas Ball Entertainment which provides special event and corporate entertainment.

Corinne Fink Adkins '90 has been Good Shepherd's Director of Music Ministry since 2005. She also is staff accompanist at Duquesne University, maintains a private piano studio, holds the keyboardist position with the Westmoreland Symphony, and is with the Pittsburgh Chapter of American Guild of Organists. She has been accompanist for the Pittsburgh Civic Light Opera, the Point Park Ballet Academy, and the River City Youth Chorale. Corinne notes that one of her most spiritually moving concerts was playing the organ in the Basilica of St. Francis in Assisi.

Scott Gilbert '92 uses music as an avocation. While he currently is news and programming consultant at Sunbury Broadcasting Corporation and Media Relations Specialist at Penn State Milton S. Hershey Medical Center, he continues as an oboist with the Hershey Symphony.

Alaine Fink '94, pianist, is on the faculty at Pittsburgh 6-12 School for Creative and Performing Arts (CAPA) and Duquesne University. She is the organist at St. Paul's United Methodist Church in Allison Park. She is an active chamber musician and accompanist, having collaborated in recital with principal members of the Pittsburgh Symphony, Philadelphia Orchestra, Cleveland Orchestra and vocalists from the Metropolitan Opera. She is featured on an album, *Trumpet Masterworks*, with Grammy-award-winning trumpet player George Vosburgh.

Sean Devine '94 is a member of the OC Times barbershop quartet which won the Barbershop Harmony Society's international competition in 2008. The same year they won the 2008 CARA

Recording Award (Contemporary A Cappella) for Best Barbershop Song and Best Barbershop Album for their sophomore release, *Let's Fly*. Sean is a 2002, 2005, and 2008 International Chorus gold medalist, and serves as lead section leader with the Masters of Harmony, the 8-time gold medalist chorus. He also serves as Director of Development with Harmony Foundation International.

Christopher E. Rutt '97 became a member of the Crossmen Drum and Bugle Corps after playing mellophone with the Cadets of Bergen County which won the DCI World championship in 1998. He also is one of the founding members of the theatrical production *Blast!* He has performed in *Blast II, Shockwave* in London, on Broadway, at Disneyland, and the Epcot Center and is the featured French horn soloist for the current US National Tour. He is also a drill writer, marching band consultant, and freelance French horn musician in the New York City Area.

Natalie True '98, a music teacher in a private school in New Orleans, also has broad theatre experience as an actor, violinist, pianist, and music director with several production companies, winning nominations for Best Musical Direction for "The Fantasticks" (2011), "Goodnight Moon" (2012), and "Bloody, Bloody Andrew Jackson" (2013). Among her many other credits are "Chicago," "Rent," "The Sound of Music," "Cabaret," "Footloose," and "Into the Woods" as musical director, pianist, or keyboardist.

Wyatt True '01, an active performer on both modern and baroque violin, has presented recitals throughout the United States and Europe and has performed with the Boulder Philharmonic, Fort Collins Symphony, Cheyenne Symphony, l'Orchestre Symphonique d'Orléans, Oregon Mozart Players, and the Oregon Coast Music Festival. A certified Suzuki instructor, Mr. True also coaches chamber music ensembles. Additional interests include learning and memory, performance psychology, and the mind-body relationship.

Elizabeth O'Hara '01 is a professional violist and violin/viola instructor in the Washington, DC Area. She is establishing herself as an illustrious chamber musician and with numerous large ensembles such as the Amadeus Orchestra, Youth Orchestras in Puerto Rico, and several symphony orchestras. She is also operating a rapidly growing private studio in the Ballston neighborhood of Arlington, VA. She is the violist of the Fairfax Chamber Ensemble and co-founder of the Vivace String Quartette and the Altra Strings who performed for Dream Works.

Joy Adams Deminski '02 teaches instrumental strings at Great Valley School District and is a founding member, violist, and current manager of the Appassionata String Quartet. ASQ, which has won various awards, provides a variety of music for weddings, corporate events, private parties and other special occasions.

Meredith Mecum '03 is a soprano soloist who was awarded Second Place in the New York Lyric Opera Competition, Second Place in the first annual Ades Vocal Competition at Manhattan School of Music, and an Encouragement Award from the Gerda Lissner Foundation Competition. Recent performances include Donna Anna ("Don Giovanni") with the Banff Centre Opera, Mimi ("La Boheme") and Contessa ("Le Nozze di Figaro") with New York Lyric Opera. She can be heard on the Albany Records recording of John Musto's "Later the Same Evening."

Stephen Werner '03 was a finalist for the X Factor, a finalist for American Idol, lead singer for K-Pop Boy Band: A'Star1, lead singer for "Reign: LIVE! At the Avalon," as well as playing the role of Simba in "The Lion King" cast that toured the US, China, and Korea. He also was a winner in the US Danceport Championship and was featured on various magazine covers.

Doug Lemke '04 is a classical double bass performer with a master's from Penn State, and a graduate performance certificate from Hartford School of Music. He is assistant principal in double bass with the Connecticut Virtuosi Chamber String Orchestra and is a professor of double bass at the Virtuosi Music Academy. He continues as a member of the Pennsylvania String Quartet (with other founding members, LD classmate Melody Brubaker and Joy Adams '03).

Recent Musicians in Summer Stock

Students and recent alumni who are highly talented and interested in performing find opportunities open to them in our local area which is near the state capital as well as Hershey Park. While no lists or records are kept, receiving such information as this book neared press time in the summer of 2013 we are reminded of the caliber of the skill and training Lower Dauphin's music program provides and we offer these names from the Summer of 2013 as representative of those who continue performing.

Hershey Trolley Works lists the following students and alumni who perform in their venue:

Students:	**Alumni:**
Rachael Bitner	Zach Hixon
Rachel Chambers	Mary Katerman
Mary Kate Hoag	Aaron Magaro
Kelsey Kindall	Katie Roksandic
Brendan McAlester	Cori Mazzitti Vinton
Danny Snyder	Andrew Vinto
Brandon Wiestling	

In addition, a relatively large number of Lower Dauphin students performed in local musicals:

▸ Cassie Zinkan as Liesl in "The Sound of Music," in the Harrisburg Christian Performing Arts Center.

▸ Rachel Bitner, Kelsey Kindall, Ocean Campbell, Michael Gainer, Maddie McCann, Emily McKissick, and Brendan McAlester in "Titanic," also at the Harrisburg Christian Performing Arts Center.

▸ Kaylor Long in "The Music Man" at the Hershey Area Playhouse

Further, LD's vocal music teacher, Elizabeth Colpo, played Little Sally and alumna Megan Nazar had a featured role as Soupy Sue in Theatre Harrisburg's "Urinetown, the Musical."

Summit Achiever Don Frantz '69

One would be hard-pressed to enumerate all of the creative ideas emanating from the mind of Don Frantz, celebrated and talented worldwide entertainment entrepreneur, CEO of Beijing Oriental Broadway and Owner, President, and Producer of Town Square Productions in New York City.

Don is the brilliant architect of many theatrical concepts that delight audiences at Walt Disney World, Busch Gardens and SeaWorld, Super Bowls, World Expos and Broadway productions, including *The Lion King, Beauty and the Beast, A Tale of Two Cities,* to whose preview performance he invited a large number of Lower Dauphin students as his guests, and now *Disenchanted,* recently receiving accolades in pre-Broadway tryouts in Orlando.

Don developed and produced the award winning "KATONGA" for Busch Gardens, Tampa and is the Producer/Creative Director for "BELIEVE," the new vision for Seaworld's killer whale show to be produced in Orlando, San Diego, and San Antonio. Don is a three-time winner of the Guinness Record for the World's Largest Maze and developed a new outdoor family game called the "Amazing Maize Maze" in Pennsylvania that has entertained over 5,000,000 players since 1993 and instigated a maze fad around the world.

An alumnus of Lebanon Valley College, Don earned an MFA in Theater Management from UCLA and then served on the faculty of the Department of Theater, Film and Television. He also authored the book *A Celebration of the Broadway Musical, Beauty and the Beast* (Hyperion Press). Don's high school classmates may remember him as the creator and producer of their high school musical revue, and his college classmates recall that he single-handedly created and produced the original spring festival, now known as Valley Fest, at Lebanon Valley College.

Highlights of his additional enterprises include building a puppet show for Burger King; spots as a magician in the Cher Show and Entertainer of the Year awards program; a dancer for Mark Wilson Productions; a magic tour to China in 1980 as one of the first Americans to go there since 1949; producer of live entertainment shows at Disney World; creator of SpectroMagic, the nighttime parade that closed the Magic Kingdom; manager of the conceptual development of Andrew Lloyd Webber's "EQ" and "Noah's Ark"; director of the entertainment at the 1984 World's Fair; collaborator with Bruce Springsteen's "The Steelworkers Project," creative director of Liberty Week-end events at the 100th Anniversary of the Statue of Liberty, and entertainment director for Universal Studios.

In association with Elliott Forrest, Don debuted "Walkin' Broadway™" in 2004, a celebrity, musical audio tour of the Broadway theatre district.

Currently he is the operations consultant of a new 1300-seat theatre and responsible for yearly ten-week programing for the Songlei Musical Theatre Company of Beijing; co-producer of Mandarin "Fame" and consultant for musical theatre training and production for the Central Academy of Drama of Beijing; consultant on the Musical Theatre Center for the Shanghai Theatre Academy in Shanghai; and design consultant for the Shanghai Expo Inner Mongolian Pavilion; producer/director for Inner Mongolian Expo Parade; producer/author/director of "The Promise," a one-act musical at Expo; and producer/creator/director of "Golden Trees," an outdoor spectacle in Alashan, Inner Mongolia for the Grassland Foundation of Inner Mongolia.

Sports

Sports

In the Beginning...

There was Hummelstown before there was Lower Dauphin and since Lower Dauphin High School is located in Hummelstown it is fitting to preface this sports history with the foundation that was established long before anyone ever dreamed of a consolidated high school. And so we replicate here information that may or may not be accurate but that was produced as a record of Hummelstown High School. I do not recall how this fell into my hands many years ago, but a hand-stamped address bears the name of Gerald R. Zinn, 325 W. 2nd Street, Hummelstown, PA and begins on page 100 of whatever this printed record was.

Hummelstown Legacy

Official school records show that Hummelstown High School's first Bulldog football team was formed in 1924. In 35 seasons after 1924, and before it was merged into the Lower Dauphin system, Hummelstown compiled an over .502 average on a 161-157-22 record. While this may not seem auspicious, the record includes two successive undefeated seasons and numerous titular honors. Hummelstown took four Overall and six Class B crowns in the Lower Susquehanna Conference. It also finished as the Class B runner-up on two occasions.

In addition, Hummelstown posted an all-time 24-10-6 record in Lower Dauphin League tilts, capturing seven titles and tying for two others. The record does show, however, that Bulldogs of that era suffered some of their losses to strong teams like Harrisburg Central, Lebanon, Carlisle, and York clubs. Few teams of this caliber were on the schedule after 1924.

Bulldog scoring records reveal the school four times copped team high scoring honors in Dauphin County. Hummelstown also produced a Super Gridnaut in Tony Orsini, who is among the area's 15 top all-time scorers.

L. Bruce Henderson, first as a coach and later as a principal, probably did more to establish football firmly at Hummelstown High than anyone. He coached the first Bulldog team to win a Lower Dauphin title in 1933, later helping the school get lights for night football. He was one of Hummelstown's most winning coaches.

Mike Intrieri, former Steelton High athlete, became the Bulldogs coach in 1944 and 1945, filling in for Stan Bulota who was in military service. Until then, Intrieri had been coach at Lebanon Valley College, which had to suspend its football program during World War II. Intrieri must be credited with being Hummelstown's most successful coach. In his two-year tenure, his clubs won 17 games and lost only three for a .850 average. Intrieri produced a runner-up for the LSC "B" title in his first season and a champion in the second term.

Some still say that Jack Goepfert produced the greatest Bulldog elevens in 1954 and 1955, years in which Hummelstown went undefeated. In those campaigns, the Maroon and White-clad teams amassed a total of 638 points to 64 for all opponents, a 10-1 ratio.

Sports History

While it may be hard to believe in what some would call our sports-driven culture of the modern life, interscholastic sports are less than a century in age. Luther Gulick is credited for establishing the New York Public Schools Athletic League (PSAL) in 1903, but similar leagues in cities weren't recognized until around 1915. The premise for schoolboy sports is sound—to encourage a healthy, strong body and mind through competitive exercises. Initial events were known as "Class Athletics" in grades five through eight and included track and field, swimming, baseball, football and basketball.

Originating in student organizations in the 1880s, sports first became popular through intercollegiate competitions, although many public schools had major reservations about the effect of time and energy devoted to sports and effects on the school, including the small number of boys involved, the quality of coaches, interference with school work, injuries, lack of "carry over" value, and the emphasis on winning. The major concern, however, may have been the worry over the reputations of schools and the perceived need for adult control. Thus, state high school athletic associations started to be formed in the late nineteenth century and into the early twentieth, including the Pennsylvania Interscholastic Athletic Association, founded on December 29, 1913. What these associations did was establish policies and rules, including uniform standards for all levels of competition.

What many might not know is that the acceptance—or tolerance at that time—of sports was based in scholastic performance and retention. Boys typically didn't do as well scholastically as girls and they dropped out of school more often than girls did; sports offered many of the boys an incentive to remain in school.

Interscholastic sports spread rapidly from the 1930s through the 1950s, mainly for boys—until Title IX voted in 1972 and implemented in 1975 increased sports opportunities for girls. Fifty years later the *Patriot-News* reflected on what it called "The Title IX Generation." The article featured stories of area athletes and coaches affected by this ruling. Included were the following from Lower Dauphin:

♦ Jeannine Lehmer Groff '69, "I would love to have run track. I went to all the boys' track meets and kept thinking it was too bad we didn't have a girls' track team. I'm not sure I was up in arms about it, but I was envious." Groff played tennis and excelled as a majorette, serving as head majorette in both high school and college (Franklin and Marshall). She runs now, winning her age group first time out in the Dartmouth Relay last year. Her daughter Sarah was a competitor in the triathlon in the 2012 Summer Olympics and placed fifth in the women's long distance marathon. Congratulations!

♦ Linda Kreiser '70, "We knew that college players would be practicing at Warwick High School, so we drove there to play field hockey, and sometimes we went to Ursinus. You heard through the grapevine that you're going to play on Tuesdays and Thursdays here and Mondays and Wednesdays there and you'd drive just to play." Kreiser's high school teammates included future Olympian Julie Staver and Karen Shifflet who earned All-American at Lock Haven for basketball and field hockey. Kreiser herself made the U.S. national team pool in field hockey and lacrosse and also was named an All-American at Millersville.

The percentage of boys participating in sports was fairly stable between 24 and 26 percent from 1971 to 2000. The percentage of female athletes increased from 2 percent in 1971 to 18 percent in 1999–2000.

The most popular sport offerings have changed little through the years. Competitive spirit squads replaced indoor track and field for girls. Soccer showed the largest gains over ten years, 99 percent in girls and 42 percent in boys. The same pattern was apparent for golf, 75 percent in girls and 26 percent in boys. With the exception of football (down 5%), all sports showed an increase in offerings over ten years.

Throughout the country football had the largest number of participants among boys, followed by basketball. Over the ten year interval (the first ten years of the new century), the number of participants in the top ten sports for boys increased and several sports changed rank. Baseball and wrestling declined, while track and field and soccer gained. The number of boys participating in soccer increased by about 50 percent in ten years. Other sports for boys that showed significant gains were golf (35%), outdoor track and field (18%), and cross country (17%).

Qualifications for coaches vary among states and school districts. Many states and districts require coaches to have a teaching certificate, but there apparently is a lack of teachers with either an interest in coaching or the necessary credentials. As a result, an increasing number of coaches are not teachers and do not have faculty status.

Lower Dauphin High School is typical of high schools across the country with the increasing number of sports offered through the years. LD has been known for its prowess in wrestling, football, baseball, and field hockey. However the statistics of the most wins might surprise the reader.

Athletic Directors

Name	Years Served
John Goepfert	1960–78
Wilbur Rhodes	1978–87
Randy Umberger*	1987–07
David Bitting	2007–

Coaching History

A special note of thanks for collecting the Coaching History goes to Randy Umberger—coach, athletic director, assistant principal, and an outstanding wrestler in his own career (both interscholastic and intercollegiate), and to Bonnie Toomey, longtime secretary to the athletic director.

In each of the following charts, * indicates Lower Dauphin Alumnus. The sports are listed in order of their year and/or season of origin. In most cases, statistics have been compiled through the end of 2011-12 school year.

Football

Inaugural Season: 1960

Coach	Seasons	Wins-Losses	League Championship
Barney Osevala	1960-61	12-8	1
Bill DeLiberty	1962-65	16-24	
Jim Seacrist	1966-75	61-43 (3 ties)	1
Tom Rae	1976-81	30-35	
Frank Capitani	1982-90	42-51	2
Vince Pantalone	1991-97	54-22 (1 tie)	3
Mark Painter	1998-01	17-23	
Rob Klock	2002-	62-47	2
Cumulative School Record		**294-253 (4 ties)**	**9**

Most Seasons Coached (10): Jim Seacrist, Rob Klock; Most Wins (62): Rob Klock; Best Win Percentage (.701): Vince Pantalone

Wrestling

Inaugural Season: 1960

Coach	Seasons	Wins-Losses	League Championship
Cleon Cassel	1960–73	160-16 (2 ties)	9
Donald Heistand	1973–74	12-2	
Cleon Cassel	1974–78	53-7	1
Cleon Cassel/Randy Umberger*	1978–81	43-7 (2 ties)	2
Cleon Cassel	1981–83	30-2	2
Ed Neiswender*	1983–84	8-6	
Cleon Cassel	1984–87	38-10	1
Ed Neiswender*	1987–89	21-10	
Randy Umberger*	1989–91	11-18 (1 tie)	
Craig Cassel*	1991–96	64-24 (1 tie)	3
Sean Ahern	1996–02	56-27	2
Ed Neiswender*	2002–09	90-22	2
Joshua Lininger*	2009–12	29-12	
Cumulative School Record		**615-163 (6 ties)**	**22**

Cleon Cassel: Most Seasons Coached (25); Most Wins (324); Best Win Percentage (.873)

Boys Basketball

Inaugural Season: 1960

Coach	Seasons	Wins-Losses	League Championship
Jim Bishop	1960–62	16-28	
Frank Capitani	1962–65	28-36	
Wilbur Rhodes	1965–72	68-85	
C. Richard Miller	1972–88	165-216	
Scott Barton	1988–07	277-200	1
Mark Hofsass*	2007–	34-76	
Cumulative School Record		**588-641**	**1**

Scott Barton: Most Seasons Coached (19); Most Wins (277); Best Win Percentage (.581)

Boys Baseball

Inaugural Season: 1961

Coach	Seasons	Wins-Losses	League Championship
Bill DeLiberty	1961–63	26-13	
Jim Seacrist	1964–66	25-22	1
Ben McLure	1967–79	151-82 (1 tie)	3
Ron Gourley*	1980–96	268-109	9
Ken Kulina*	1997–	257-109 (1 tie)	8
Cumulative School Record		**727-335 (2 ties)**	**21**

Ron Gourley: Most Seasons Coached (17); Most Wins (268); Best Win Percentage (.711)

Boys Track and Field

Inaugural Season: 1961

Coach	Seasons	Wins-Losses	League Championship
Gerald Brittain	1961–68	21-42	
Ed Romano	1969–78	48-43	2
Jay Stanton	1979	2-9	
Ed Romano	1980–82	6-21	
Dale Luy	1983–87	19-33	1
Craig Bittenbender	1988–89	5-19 (1 tie)	
Scott Barton	1990–03	47-104 (1 tie)	
Steve Koons	2004–05	7-13 (1 tie)	
Greg Miller	2006–	35-20	1
Cumulative School Record		**190-304 (3 ties)**	**4**

Scott Barton, Most Seasons Coached (14); Ed Romano, Most Wins (54); Greg Miller, Best Win Percentage (.636)

Girls Basketball

Inaugural Season: 1963

Coach	Seasons	Wins-Losses	League Championship
Bea Hallman	1963–67	37-23	2
Barb Atkinson	1967–76	88-51	3
Linda Kreiser*	1976–78	7-32	
Charles Etter	1978–83	47-60	
Linda Donlan	1983–85	13-30	
Allen Moyer	1985–86	9-14	
Scott Delp	1986–90	50-47	
Judy Baumgardner	1990–2001	175-100	1
Bob Heusser	2001–	214-67	6
Cumulative School Record		**640-424**	**12**

Most Seasons Coached (11): Judy Baumgardner, Bob Heusser; Most Wins (214): Bob Heusser; Best Win Percentage (.761): Bob Heusser

Boys Cross Country

Inaugural Season: 1963

Coach	Seasons	Wins-Losses	League Championship
Gerald Brittain	1963–69	44-17 (1 tie)	4
William Bowers	1970	5-5	
Jay Stanton	1971–79	42-53	
Dale Luy	1980–85	24-43	1
Dave Dickson	1986–91	21-50	
Jim Brandt	1992–97	23-46	1
Craig Cassel*	1998-08	48-55	
John Butler	2009	12-7	1
Cumulative School Record		**219-276 (1 tie)**	**7**

Most Seasons Coached (11) and Most Wins (48): **Craig Cassel;** *Best Win Percentage (.710):* **Gerald Brittain**

Field Hockey

Inaugural Season: 1964

Coach	Seasons	Wins-Losses	League Championship
Bea Hallman	1964–77	75-44 (25 ties)	1
Linda Kreiser*	1978–	646-96 (33 ties)	26
Cumulative School Record		**721-140 (58 ties)**	**27**

***Linda Kreiser:** Most Seasons Coached (34); Most Wins (646); Best Win Percentage (.834)*

Golf

Inaugural Season: 1969

Coach	Seasons	Wins-Losses	League Championship
Bill Nixon	1969	3-1 (3 ties)	
Byron Daubert	1970–72	15-28 (1 tie)	
Bob Rath	1973–74	5-26 (1 tie)	
Ed Richards	1975–85	68-105 (3 ties)	
Ron Gourley*	1986–89	52-19	1
Bob Rath	1990–00	249-194	2
Malcolm Garrett	2001–04	93-48	
Terry Bashore	2005–	151-74	1
Cumulative School Record		**636-495 (ties)**	**4**

Most Seasons Coached (13) and Most Wins (254): **Bob Rath**; *Best Win Percentage (.732):* **Ron Gourley**

Boys Tennis

Inaugural Season: 1974

Coach	Seasons	Wins-Losses	League Championship
Vernon Belser	1974–76	11-20	
C. Richard Miller	1977–78	6-10	
Ed Gottwald	1979–83	9-46	
Kathy Keller	1984–86	19-20	
Denise DeShong	1987	9-3	
Jim Hamill	1988–91	32-19	
Carol Miller	1992–94	11-24	
Peggy Steinacker Long	1995–	109-118 (1 tie)	4
Cumulative School Record		**206-260 (1 tie)**	**4**

Most Seasons Coached (18) and Most Wins (109): **Peggy Steinacker Long**;
Best Win Percentage (.627) **Jim Hamill**

Girls Tennis

Inaugural Season: 1974

Coach	Seasons	Wins-Losses	League Championship
Shirley Hollinger Houseal	1974–76	11-15	
Vern Lyter	1977	0-8	
Gail Frankhouser	1978	0-8	
Peggy Steinacker Long	1979-	259-156	3
Cumulative School Record		**270-187**	

Peggy Long: *Most Seasons Coached (31); Most Wins (259); Best Win Percentage (.624)*

Softball

Inaugural Season: 1974

Coach	Seasons	Wins-Losses	League Championship
Jean Walmer	1974-78	25-35	
Linda Kreiser* and			
Peggy Steinacker Long (co-head)	1979	8-6	
Peggy Steinacker Long	1980–94	218-84 (1)	7
Scott Delp	1995–01	97-38	4
Amanda Mease*	2002–05	46-40	
Bret Sparks*	2006–09	80-19	3
Steve Alcorn	2010–	61-15	3
Cumulative School record		**535-237**	**17**

*Most Seasons Coached (16) and Most Wins (226): **Peggy Long**; Best Win Percentage (.808): **Bret Sparks***

Girls Track and Field

Inaugural Season: 1975

Coach	Seasons	Wins-Losses	League Championship
Ed Romano	1975–78	24-13	
Jay Stanton	1979	5-5	
Ed Romano	1980–82	4-23	
Dale Luy	1983–87	24-26	
Craig Bittenbender	1988–89	13-14	
Scott Barton	1990–03	83-69 (2 ties)	2
Steve Koons	2004–05	8-13	
Greg Miller	2006–	37-18	3
Cumulative School Record		**198-181 (2 ties)**	**5**

*Most Seasons Coached (14) and Most Wins (83): **Scott Barton**; Best Win Percentage: (.673): **Greg Miller***

Girls Cross Country

Inaugural Season: 1975

Coach	Seasons	Wins-Losses	League Championship
Jay Stanton	1975–79	38–5	3
Dale Luy	1980–85	24–36	1
Dave Dickson	1986–91	4–36 (*No team '89 and '90*)	
Jim Brandt	1992–97	46–22	1
Craig Cassel*	1998–08	75–30	1
John Butler	2009–	18–1	2
Cumulative School Record		**205–130**	**8**

*Most Seasons Coached (11) and Most Wins (75): **Craig Cassel**; Best Win Percentage (.947) **John Butler***

Boys Soccer
Inaugural Season: 1982

Coach	Seasons	Wins-Losses	League Championship
Al Hershey	1982–87	64–38 (8 ties)	1
Randy Behney	1988–89	11–25 (5 ties)	
Joe Longenecker	1990–00	139–71 (16 ties)	3
Gerry Lynch	2001–	136–74 (12 ties)	2
Cumulative School Record		**350–208 (41 ties)**	**6**

Most Seasons Coached (11): Joe Longenecker and Gerry Lynch; Most Wins (139) and Best Percentage (.615): Joe Longenecker

Girls Soccer
Inaugural Season: 1989

Coach	Seasons	Wins-Losses	League Championship
Randy Behney	1989–2010	303–107 (31 ties)	3
Shellee Copley	2011–-2011	19-6	1
Nic Amici	2012–	12-7	
Cumulative School Record		**334–120 (31 ties)**	**4**

Note: The final Spring Schedule was played in 2012. The first Fall Schedule was played in 2012 when the PIAA moved Girls Soccer from Spring to Fall.

Randy Behney: *Most Seasons Coached (21); Most Wins (291); Best Win Percentage (.687)*

Girls Volleyball
Inaugural Season: 1996

Coach	Seasons	Wins-Losses	League Championship
Sharon Barlet	1996–98	17-34	
Beth Shay Huddy	1999–2000	11-33	
Willie Roberts	2001–03	28-24	
Loretta Ranck	2004–08	38-49 (3 ties)	
David Machamer*	2009–	29-23	1
Cumulative School Record		**123-163 (3 ties)**	**1**

Most Seasons Coached (5) & Most Wins (38): **Loretta Ranck**; *Best Win Percentage (.557):* **David Machamer**

Boys Volleyball
Inaugural Season: 1997

Coach	Seasons	Wins-Losses	League Championship
Mark Painter	1997–98	2-36 (2 ties)	
David Machamer*	1999–	167-112	7
Cumulative School Record		**169-148 (2 ties)**	**7**

David Machamer: *Most Seasons Coached (14); Most Wins (167); Best Win Percentage: (.598)*

Girls LaCrosse

Inaugural Season: 2005

Coach	Seasons	Wins-Losses	League Championship
Cari Brown	2005–08	20-44	
Peggy Barton	2009–11	27-28	
Meredith Thomas*	2011–	10-8	
Cumulative School Record		**57-80**	

*Most Seasons Coached (4): **Carrie Brown**; Most Wins (27): **Peggy Barton**; Best Win Percentage (.555): **Meredith Thomas***

Boys Swimming

Inaugural Season: 2006

Coach	Seasons	Wins-Losses	League Championship
Carrie Zelko	2006-	52-15	3
Cumulative School Record		**52-15**	**3**

Cari Zelko: Most Seasons Coached (6); Most Wins (52); Best Win Percentage (.776)

Girls Swimming

Inaugural Season: 2006

Coach	Seasons	Wins-Losses	League Championship
Carrie Zelko	2006–	31-35 (1 tie)	
Cumulative School Record		**31-35 (1 tie)**	

Cari Zelko: Most Seasons Coached (4); Most Wins (25); Best Win Percentage (.462)

Boys LaCrosse

Inaugural Season: 2009

Coach	Seasons	Wins-Losses	League Championship
Ian Baker	2009–	30-40	
Cumulative School Record		**30-40**	

Ian Baker: Most Seasons Coached (4); Most Wins (30); Best Win Percentage (.429)

Pep, Pep, Hooray:

Pep Clubs, Pep Rallies, and Spirit Sticks

Pep Rallies, as well as Pep Clubs, are loved by many, made fun of by others. With typical fickleness, both students and faculty attitudes can change on a cheer. We likely remember these collections of the masses with greater fondness from a distance than during the actual event. The format of pep rallies has changed little from its beginning and, like the sports for which it is designed, was patterned on collegiate events. However, as colleges became larger and more systemized, pep rallies lost a lot of the spontaneity on college campuses.

High school pep rallies, however, remain in place as a means of encouraging school spirit in a positive way. The rallies include cheering led by the cheerleaders, music from the marching band or a pep band, short rallying speeches by coaches, team leaders and/or principals, and a skit that focuses on the particular week's opponent. Pep rallies are considered successful if most of the students are participating, if an energy is felt, if there are no disciplinary incidents and, in retrospect, if the team wins the game.

The Class of 1962 remembers that "the wonderful Pep Rallies before the football games were awesome." Two years later, the embodiment of the school mascot was first introduced to the students at a fall 1963 pep rally, "dressed in a beautiful falcon costume made by Mr. Fickes and the Home Ec. students."[1] That same year the cheerleaders sent written invitations to the faculty to attend a snake dance on October 31, 1963 to "start at the school, wind through Hummelstown, then proceed to the Borough Park where a Pep Rally will follow."[2] The following year, spearheaded by the newly organized Public Relations Club, advised by Mrs. Beers, Mrs. Ball, and Mrs. Keller, a snake dance was held on November 12, 1964 through the streets of the town, and ended at the Borough Park.[3]

The December 11, 1964 edition of the local paper reported that the South Hanover Township School Board had decided to experiment with "School Spirit" buses for students at the Junior-Senior High School, using township buses to transport pupils home, without charge, from attending extra-curricular activities. It noted, "The directors are deeply disturbed by the definite lack of school spirit at LD and are willing to go out on a limb with this project to start the students on the way to feeling that Lower Dauphin is their school, their alma mater, and not just a place they have to go every day."

In the fall of 1966 a new "tradition" emerged—the awarding of a spirit stick, a practice that had its roots in a cheerleading camp in 1954 when its director was so impressed with a squad that, while not the best performers, had "incredible enthusiasm, dedication, and spirit." He broke a branch off a tree and handed it to the squad, dubbing it the "spirit stick." High schools picked up on this innovation, using manufactured sticks often painted the school colors and awarding them at pep rallies to the class dubbed the most spirited.

That same year there was a great deal of activity because of the newly formed Blue Guard which took school spirit very seriously. There was a rivalry between classes to "win" the spirit stick and the seniors

---

[1]   *Falcon Flash*, November 1963.

[2]   *The Sun*, August 30, 1963.

[3]   "Blue and White" column, *Falcon Flash*, Fall 1964.

were determined to never lose it again after losing in October.[4] The November 28 issue of the Guard's newsletter indicates that "class rivalry was so bad we thought there would be a riot." A letter to the Guard's *Flush Gazette's* editor noted, "Some of the things which the Blue Guard has been responsible for are almost causing a riot during the pep assembly which was held in the auditorium ... and their repeated use of Gestapo tactics in dealing with the students who do not agree with their policy."[5]

A column by student Ann Granzow in *The Sun* described "a new organization has been born at LD, and the school hasn't been the same since.... They call themselves the Blue Guard and can be seen en masse at all school sponsored activities. Their purpose is to support the school and heighten school spirit. Not only have these boys designed and made their own insignia arm bands, but they have given the school paper some hot competition by creating their own "off campus" newspaper!

The Class of 1970 recalls fondly the many football pep rallies in the gym in the fall of 1969; however, two years later (fall of 1971) a mini-editorial in the *Falcon Flash* decried the bad language used in the cheers by the senior football players during a pep assembly. The Class of 1972 remembers pep rallies every Friday when "many students dressed up for the spirit days with hats and buttons sold by the student council or cheerleaders."

In the October 1973 *Falcon Flash* Susan and Sandra Shope co-wrote a tongue-in-cheek review of pep rallies, "...the reversal of classes will once again cancel out the fated seventh period. Another one of L. D.'s notorious pep rallies has intervened on the day's schedule. The cheerleader's uniforms serve as constant reminders of the throat-rasping event. Somehow you still chide yourself for not joining the band in fourth grade. They get out a full twenty minutes early for every pep rally. A buzzing voice from the loudspeakers suggests you return to homeroom to be called to the gymnasium. After a quick stop at the locker, you plod over to the nearly vacant homeroom. The seniors, ruling the roost at L D.'s Falcon farm, flock into the hall. Seconds later the juniors appear on the scene, followed by the eager sophomores. Booming voices boost you into the bleachers and the action begins."

However, no one who was there can forget the Rowdies of '73, the group that reserved its own section at the football, basketball, and wrestling events. They served as a pep squad supporting both the athletes and the cheerleaders. Somewhere they even managed to find their own megaphones and, of course, their own brass section that played prior to the game and at half-time, following PIAA rules of no pep bands *during* the events.

The Class of 1974 writes, "The cheerleaders stoked school spirit. Steve Orsini was our Mr. Touchdown for a fund raiser sponsored by WKBO radio and the cheerleaders collected donations at every pep rally and football game. They also decorated lockers and provided spirit banners in the cafeteria." Spirit was also boosted by the Booster Club and its 75 members during the school year 1973-74.

An editorial on LD Spirit in the November 1974 *Falcon Flash* recalled pep rallies that were almost discontinued because "students were too rowdy, students were almost decapitated by a flying rubber chicken, and 'Battle Cry' almost brought down the roof, leaving one hard of hearing for a week afterward; nonetheless, ...everyone was behind the teams no matter the record."

When the Class of 1975 was poised to be graduated, the June *Flash* noted that one of the things they would miss upon leaving LD was the invigorating pep rallies where the students show their spirit **only** in their attempts to out-scream the underclassmen in the V-I-C-T-O-R-Y cheer.

[4] The *Flush Gazette*, November 7, 1966; [5] The *Flush Gazette*, December 1966.

In the fall of 1976 a Pep Squad was formed with nine members, advised by Miss Spire, to address a need for better support of girls' athletics and to generally improve spirit. Another public call for more spirit came in the December 1982 issue of the *Flash*.

On October 30, 1987 the Flash published an article, "Pep Rally Canceled Due to Lack of Interest." It appears that the students were upset because no early dismissals were being granted to work on the Homecoming floats; the administration purportedly had reason to believe that the disgruntled students were going to cause trouble at the pep rally.

As a result of this issue, Mrs. Witmer, one of the principals, formed a new Spirit Club which held it first meeting in February to plan ways to bring more team spirit to sporting events. A cheering section was formed and attended basketball games and wrestling matches to show more positive support for the Falcons.[6]

Always trying to find new ways to increase student interest, on December 14, 1990, Mr. Appleby, the principal, called the students to the gymnasium during first period where they were told they would be learning the Alma Mater and would be singing it at the end of each forthcoming Pep Rally.

A year later, in the February 6, 1992 *Falcon Flash*, Doug Hofsass wrote a commentary on the new five minute first period that included his description of pep rallies as "where a fifth of homeroom turnout is considered superb." However, this class of 1992 remembers pep rallies fondly, "Traveling to pep assemblies we could hear the band playing its famous repertoire of rally cries as we entered the gym and sat with our class. Cheerleaders boosted our school spirit and impressed us with their meticulously choreographed routines."

This positive outlook continued into the next fall when the October 23, 1992 *Flash* reported a community pep rally held on September 24 in Borough Park to honor high school fall sports as well as the community's Bull Dog team and cheerleaders. Mr. Ronald Zeigler, English teacher, commented that it was "like an old fashioned pep rally." Even the 1993 *Falconaire* viewed this event important enough to devote a full page to it. The 1998 yearbook also mentions a community pep rally held at Shaffner Park.

Into the 21st Century has come an informal group known as the Superfans, later Falcon Nation, students who are in the stands whatever the sporting event is. They participate in every school spirit day and attend many games a week. In addition, LD pep rallies have continued as part of the larger Homecoming Week which has become the highlight of Falcon spirit. However, an article in the November 2005 *Flash* refers to a recent Pep Rally which it was reporting as "the twenty-sixth annual Homecoming Pep Rally." The last we looked, Homecoming Game Pep Rallies  have been held since the fall of 1961 and pep rallies themselves since the fall of 1960.

---

[6] *Falcon Flash*, March 11, 1988.

Booster Club

The Booster Club was described in the November 1963 *Falcon Flash* as "L.D.'s newest club." It is unconfirmed as to whether or not this group was active prior to this date; however, its history is noble. The original purpose of the club was to sponsor spectator buses to away games and dances after home games and throughout the year.

During the summer of 1964, the Booster Club constructed a six-foot tall sign in the shape of a running football player whom they named Mr. Touchdown, LD High.

It is documented that the advisors in 1969 were Mr. Allen Risser and Mrs. Jacquelyn Douglass and that the club met monthly and did no fund-raising. Credit is given to student Sarah Eshelman '74 who reactivated interest in the Booster Club and to Mr. Royal Dimond, who name is almost synonymous with "Booster Club," for it was and is his spirit that provides the fuel that is the Booster Club.

The Club is also credited for purchasing the materials for the first Falcon Mascot costume and it served as the founder of the practice of judging floats at Homecoming, although the members did not serve as the judges. During school year 1971-72 the Booster Club sold football banks, garters, mums for homecoming, jackets, football and basketball pins, and tee-shirts. They also sponsored a car wash, a dance, and a rock concert. They held a parents night for the football, basketball, and wrestling teams, provided a banquet for the cross country team and a buffet dinner for the girls hockey and basketball teams.

Eight years during the 1970s, the Booster Club itself sponsored a prize-winning float, as well as constructing the chariots used for Homecoming in the fall of 1972. In 1973-74 the club boasted 75 members. The Booster Club later operated the school store which provided them with the funds to help with expenses at Homecoming, trophies for special achievements, refreshments, and support for smaller organizations. At Thanksgiving and Christmas, Boosters purchased food and clothing for needy families. They also helped to pay for wrestling jackets for the CAC champs in 1979 and have continued to be LDHS' "biggest boosters."

Varsity Club

Membership in the Varsity Club was open to young men who earned a varsity sports letter. Formed in 1961, Varsity Club members have conducted service projects, promoted good sportssmanship, and fostered school spirit in all Lower Dauphin sports competitions.

Cheerleading

Cheerleading, like most of the traditions of high school, finds it roots in colleges. And like most other sports, cheerleading began as an activity for males. Cheerleading also began a century before Lower Dauphin High School opened its doors. All indications are that it all started at Princeton College where students galvanized school spirit by creating the country's first official football cheer which is said to have been based on a chant delivered by the Seventh Regiment of New York City at the Princeton depot on the way to Washington to fight in the Civil War:

Hooray, Hooray, Hooray!

Tiger Sis, Boom, AAH

Princeton!

This cheer was soon heard at every Princeton game and the first pep club was established at Princeton University in the 1870s. It is likely that a Princeton graduate carried the yell—and the idea of a pep squad—to the University of Minnesota and by the 1890s organized cheerleading was initiated there, as was the first school song. By the turn of the century megaphones were becoming popular. The use of cheerleading spread quickly and being a leader of cheers became a coveted position when the most popular, charismatic, and personable young men on campus won spots on the cheering squad. However, it was not until the 1920s—in both colleges and high schools—that females became active in cheerleading, and by the mid-1920s, coed squads proliferated across the country. In 1927 the first book (*Just Cheers*) on cheerleading was published, signifying the growing popularity of cheerleading.

By the 1940s girls made up the bulk of the cheering squads, particularly when World War II reduced the pool of men. Even so, males remained part of some cheerleading squads well into the 1950s. During this decade cheerleading camps and clinics led to more precision cheering. By the 1960s pom-pons[1] made of vinyl, rather than paper, revolutionized the cheering style.

This was the scene in the fall of 1960 when the first LD cheerleading squad commanded the sidelines with the charge of rallying the spectators—students who had not all previously attended the same school—in their support of the new team. This squad included Linda McGarvey (Captain), Brenda Fackler, Carol Glovola, Kyleen Fisher, Carol Lindsey, Judith Foreman, Elizabeth Smith, Norma Georganakis, and Carol Zinn.

One of the most popular cheers that spans the decades of Lower Dauphin is the following. Readers are welcome to chant this aloud as they read:

For the blue, for the blue, for the blue – fight, fight

For the white, for the white, for the white – fight, fight

For the blue – fight, fight

For the white – fight, fight

Blue – White – Fight

Hey – Hey – Hey!

---

1 The correct term is from the French meaning a decorative ball of fluff, although pompom was sometimes used as early as 1873. A pompom, according to purists, is a type of large gun.

One of the favorites of the 1970s was the Victory cheer:

> Victory, victory is our cry,
> V-i-c-t-o-r-y!
> Are we in it? Well, I guess,
> Will we win it? Y-E-S!

A popular chant began

> Two bits, Four bits,
> Six Bits, a dollar …
> … All for LD,
> Stand up and holler.

A favorite stunt at wrestling matches had the cheerleaders placed around the wrestling mat while the wrestlers were warming up. At the end of the cheer, on cue, the wrestlers all flipped over!

> Hey LD, we're here to cheer
> You're here to win!
> So come on Falcons, let's begin.
> Do your warm-ups — do them right
> Get out on that mat and really fight.
> Just hear our cry — and pin your guy!
> They can't beat us, we're LD High!

Cheerleaders, of course, also do fundraising and decorate the school and the town square prior to all home football games. Recently, cheerleading has been viewed more a sport with its own competitions at various levels. Squads have also greatly increased in number in part to cover more winter sports, particularly basketball and wrestling.

The 1997 *Falconaire* compliments, "The girls' cheerleading squad certainly brought back the meaning of pride to LD this year, and we expect to see more of the same in the future."

The 2010 *Falconaire* notes, "It is no doubt that our cheerleaders have shaped Lower Dauphin Falcon sports into the tradition of pride and excellence they have become today, decorating the halls and the town, planning special pep rallies, and, no matter the weather, nothing stops their enthusiasm. … and still have the energy to participate in various competitions."

Remember the Cheers

The following are favorite remembrances of cheers from Ann Deeney Messner '85, Kathy Imhof Weber '74 and Kathy Saltzer Peffer '73, reminding us these were made to be chanted:

> We, the students from the LD school
> Are gonna take you on a trip that is really cool
> We've got a team that's out of sight
> And we're gonna win this game tonight.

Megaphone routine and song (Mr. Touchdown)

> M-I-S, T-E-R
> Mister Touchdown, LD High
> They always call him Mr. Touchdown
> They always call him Mr. T

Song, often sung on the band bus:

> Cheers, cheers for old LD High
> You bring the whiskey, I'll bring the rye
> Send the sophomores out for gin,
> Don't let a sober freshman in.
>
> We never stagger, we never fall
> We sober up on wood alcohol
> When we win this game you'll see
> It's onward to victory

On the return trip home on the bus we always sang the Alma Mater followed by the Lord's Prayer as we came through town.

Cheerleading Captains

1961	Linda McGarvey		1992	Tonya Meko, Katherine Klinger, and Carrie Stahl
1962	Joyce Keener		1993	Andrea Lelii, Heidi Gray
1963	Joyce Keener		1994	Destinie Smertnick and Michelle Shaffer
1964	Judy Bell		1995	Jessica Whitcomb and Carrie Champ
1965	Fran Fenner		1996	unconfirmed
1966	Terry Witters		1997	unconfirmed
1968	Jane Youtz		1998	Jennifer Harvey
1969	JoAnn Ricker		1999	Brandy Heckman and Cori Grierson
1970	Linda Goepfert		2000	Jill Raffensberger
1971	Annette Basler		2001	Kate Spaulding, Kara Swank, and Tera McCorkel
1972	Karen Fenner		2002	Beth Smolick, Caitie Stoehr, and Renee Hyde
1973	Barbara Verdelli		2003	Lisa Green, Megan Stine, and Nikki Kametz
1974	Linda Poole		2004	Hollyn Harner
1975	Renee Sieg		2005	Jillian Perry
1976	Sherry Paine		2006	Joann Marshbank
1977	Cheryl Wagner		2007	unconfirmed
1978	Susan Reichenbaugh		2008	Abby McCann
1979	Natalie Wagner		2009	unconfirmed
1980	Pam Schug		2010	Maeve Wilson, Alexis Barge, and Angela Olson
1981	Helen Frascella			
1982	Lori Engle and Sandy Fasnacht			
1983	Lisa Hereshko			
1984	Tina Agostino and Kim Allen			
1985	Ann Deeny			
1986	Nikki Henson and Sonya Zearling			
1987	Gail Reichenbaugh			
1988	Tami Swartz			
1989	Janelle Kopopenhaver and Dorinda Norton			
1990	Stacey Dincher, Michele Donnelly, and Gwen Hollenbush			
1991	Crystal Funck			

Five Decades of Sports: September 1960 – September 2007

by Randy Umberger

Despite the rain and the leaky roof, a new era of opportunity and tradition was about to emerge that would identify the Lower Dauphin High School through five decades. Double periods, physical education class, shop, and clubs were all new to a gathering of eighth graders from five different elementary schools. A decision to participate in junior high intramural wrestling would become one of the most important decisions I would make. On that day I met Cleon Cassel and many of the teammates with whom I would spend the next five years helping to establish an athletic program that would serve as a source of community and school pride. This would transcend old geographic boundaries and form a larger new community with a shared source of pride. My first opportunity as a Falcon came that winter at the Hershey Novice Wrestling Tournament. That success gave me confidence to experience more. I accepted invitations from Bill DeLiberty and Jerry Brittain to be part of the football and track and field teams respectively. Each student had their own feelings about Lower Dauphin and what experiences they would embrace to develop who they would become. My motivations were the 1960 championship football team, being a member of undefeated championship wrestling teams, the formation of new friendships, a faculty that cared, and the support of a community that showed concern and became involved. A university education was made possible and became a reality through the encouragement of a faculty, especially Ken Staver and Cleon Cassel, who saw more in me than I saw in myself.

September 1973 brought the same anxiety and uncertainty I felt thirteen years ago in September of 1960. I accepted a position to be part of a faculty that had educated and mentored me as a student. The challenge this time would come from a peer group who would hold me to a higher standard. The acceptance by the faculty was one of guarded optimism. I became involved in many of the school's extra-curricular programs. Coaching wrestling, football and baseball and serving as class advisor gave me an opportunity to communicate and promote the school's tradition and history. I sensed a partnership between the faculty and students to uphold these time-tested traditions. Community pride, tradition and loyalty were the common thread used to promote and sustain the values that unite us as a school community. I will always remember those lessons learned working side by side with dedicated professionals who were always focused on doing their best for each student.

The resignation of Wilbur "Burr" Rhodes as athletic director in 1987 gave me the opportunity and privilege to become just the third athletic director at my Alma Mater. I was proud to assume the leadership role of an athletic program in which I had participated and given credit to for my many opportunities and early successes. Under the early leadership of John "Jack" Goepfert, the athletic department experienced rapid growth and immediate success. From the inaugural year of the school through 1975 athletic offerings grew from five varsity sports for men to a total of eight varsity sports for men and six varsity sports for women. Basketball (1963) and field hockey (1964) were the first interscholastic offerings for women. Burr Rhodes would coordinate the addition of men's soccer in 1982. The decade of the nineties saw an explosion in the expansion of athletic facilities. To address the changing interests of a growing student enrollment, additional facilities were needed. The opening of a middle school campus and the completion of the renovation at the high school gave the secondary schools two full sized gymnasiums for the first time. The addition of two soccer fields, two

field hockey fields, three multi-purpose practice fields, one softball field and one baseball field shifted a multitude of the fall and spring venues to the middle school campus. A field house on each campus was added giving additional locker room space as well as spectator conveniences. In 2003, two years after the renovation of the high school the 1000 wing was added to accommodate an increase in enrollment and academic programming. This new facility would also house state-of-the-art fitness and conditioning equipment and an expanded sports medicine facility. A full time athletic trainer and strength coach was hired to complement the physical education and athletic coaching staffs. This would be the first expansion of athletic facilities since the opening of the school in 1960 with the exception of an adaptive physical education area in 1974. This added area would also serve as the venue for wrestling practice and other after school activities, freeing up valuable gymnasium space. From 1989 thru 2006 I was proud to facilitate, with the assistance of community leaders, the addition of women's soccer (1989), women's volleyball (1996), men's volleyball (1997), women's lacrosse (2005) and men's and women's swimming (2006). Men's lacrosse would be the latest sport to be added in 2009 under the direction of David Bitting. The opening of two lighted turf fields on the middle school campus in 2010 came in response to the social and athletic changes of the student body and the Lower Dauphin Community. A field house which will support the activities at the turf fields is in the final planning stages with the Lower Dauphin Falcon Foundation. Completion of this phase is planned for the fall of 2014.

Lower Dauphin's athletic prowess can be attributed to the dedicated coaches and goal-oriented students who recognized the importance of building and sustaining a tradition. Recruitment and retention of quality coaches have been the underlying ingredients for this continued success. The importance of knowing and showcasing the history, lifting up traditions and adapting to the needs and interests of the students and community will sustain this easily recognized Falcon Pride that began in September of 1960.

Thoughts From a Coach

We are indebted to the coaches who responded to our invitation to reflect on their individual sport and their years as a coach. It was gratifying to hear from nearly every sport. The love of the game, the coaches' devotion to the players, and their respect for Lower Dauphin High School are evident in their own heartfelt words.

The First Sports: The 1960s

(The date listed with each sport is the date marking its first year as a PIAA sport)

Football, 1960   Jim Seacrist, Head Coach, 1966-1975

It was my honor to be a head coach during this time. I admire all the players who worked hard during that time to keep the Falcon tradition at a high competitive level.

I will not mention players, because all the players were outstanding in their contributions. It was a special time having three players selected to participate in the Big 33 Classic.

I will mention a talented coaching staff who were responsible for our success as much as I was. These were Bernie Bernitsky, Frank Capitani, who did a great job with the defense, Buzz Daubert, Dave Erdman, Steve Futchko, and Don Heistand. Also, notable work was done to help the program by Ben McLure and Joe Schan.

During these ten years, the team contended for the league championship for all but two years. The peak was the 1970 team who went 11 wins and no losses. Other teams were as good, but just didn't seem to have that little extra that this team had. However, even during a poor year for wins and losses, LD always remained competitive. For instance, a team winning only one game that year lost to the league co-champions by scores of 7 to 14, and 0 and 10.

More gratifying than just wins and losses, once the game officials starting giving out team sportsmanship awards, we were first in four out of six years.

I thank all the players for their great efforts and hope this experience had a positive influence on their lives.

Wrestling, 1960   Craig Cassel, Head Coach, 1991-1996

I believe that the key to success in the Lower Dauphin wrestling room can be summed up in one word: TRADITION. Since 1960, my father and coach, Cleon Cassel, established a tradition of excellence in the Lower Dauphin wrestling room and our local community. There are few schools that can boast the consistent administrative and community support that Lower Dauphin has enjoyed since 1960. There are many wrestling families and alumni who rally to support our wrestlers and coaches as fans and Booster Club members. This base of support gives our young men a source of pride and motivation. Coaches may come and go, but the tradition of excellence never dies at Lower Dauphin. The challenge as a coach is to rally community support, inspire our athletes, and use our TRADITION to make each individual the best young man he can be.

Returning to Lower Dauphin to take up the head coaching position in 1991 I faced an immediate problem of filling a line-up which had been decimated by injuries and graduation. It was great to have the support of coaches Ed Neiswender, Sean Ahern, Glen Youtz, and Ron Michael to help the team gain knowledge and enthusiasm as the season went on. Once the fun, excitement, and work ethic returned to the LD wrestling room, the rest came easy. As always, there was tremendous school and community support. Principal Landry Appleby, Athletic Director Randy Umberger, and a group of parents worked with me to make improvements that quickly moved the team forward. By my last year the LD pride was back and the 1996 team held a 16-0 record and a District 3 team championship.

Boys Basketball, 1960   Scott Barton, Head Coach, 1988-2007

The challenges of playing basketball in the Mid Penn Conference and in District III are substantial. Our conference and our district are considered to be among the best in the state. When I started in our program in 1988, we established six core values that we wanted to weave through every aspect of our program: (1) WE were going to work harder than any other team in the area; (2) WE were going to become the best defensive team in the area; (3) WE were going to be unselfish in everything we did; (4) WE were going to do everything with class and sportsmanship; (5) WE were going to play as a team; and (6) WE most importantly were going to develop character in young men.

We won more than our fair share of games in our 19 seasons at Lower Dauphin, but more than that, those on our teams have joined the ranks as teachers, coaches, lawyers, doctors, pilots, businessmen, technicians, computer analysts, writers, and so on. Recently, I ran into one of our former players at a local restaurant with his wife and three children. It just doesn't get any better than that.

Baseball, 1961   Ronald E. Gourley, Head Coach, 1980-1996

Coaching Lower Dauphin baseball was a privilege and a joy. The winning records and championships are tangible proof of the quality of the program, but they don't tell the story of the soul of the baseball team. The reputation as a team that played the game "right" and with "class" grew along with the shelves of trophies and medals. Our players were known as good students and model citizens in their school and community. Every year some of our players go on to play college baseball and further their education. Even more of them have joined the coaching ranks in various levels of competition, passing their knowledge and passion for the game on to the next generation.

Like many successful programs, the baseball team develops a familial atmosphere. For many years, I had the unforgettable and rewarding experience of leading fine teams of young men to success on and off the field. They were all my kids for a little while. I loved every minute of it and would have done it for free.

Boys Track and Field, 1961   Ed Romano, Head Coach, 1969-1978

In looking back over my tenure as head coach of the Lower Dauphin Track and Field Team, I fondly remember the accomplishments of the team, the individuals who made up the team, and the coaches who were a part of the team's success. The greatest team accomplishment was the 25 consecutive wins we put together from 1972-1974 and the two Capital Area Conference league championships we won. Indeed, there were many team and individual accomplishments made during those years. I recall sitting in the stands at the Shippensburg Invitational and having my athletes coming up and saying that they won this event or took third in that event until suddenly it dawned on us that we were going to win the meet. I remember the mile relay team of Kevin Patrick, Kim Witmer, Bruce Cox, and Mike Slough winning every time they ran including their heat at States where they eventually came in fourth. I remember the team jumping jacks at the end of every meet and the camaraderie that was built up over the years. I recall going to the Elizabethtown Relays, winning every relay except one and walking to the center of the infield to accept each trophy as we won it. I am also proud that during my tenure as head coach we started the girls' track team.

Many wonderful people were a part of the teams I coached, so many that I don't have the room to list each one of them. I will mention our great miler Steve Spence who won the mile at the State Meet, setting a state record. Steve became an Olympian in the Marathon and an All- American while in college. I can say that it was a pleasure to be the coach of this wonderful group of young people.

Girls Basketball, 1963   Bob Heusser, Head Coach, 2001-present[1]

Lower Dauphin Girls Basketball is about three things: playing hard, playing smart, and playing with class. That's what our coaching staff preaches to our Lady Falcon basketball players. It has been an honor and a pleasure for me to coach at Lower Dauphin. Our female student-athletes have been and are very competitive and strive to do their best on and off the court. They accept and believe in what we are teaching them. They are of high character. We hope our players are learning the game of basketball and what it takes to succeed. The values we teach them regarding basketball are the same values they need to succeed in their lives. I am sure this is what was taught to former Lady Falcon basketball players by previous coaches and what is being taught to all athletes in other sports at Lower Dauphin.

Boys Cross Country, 1963   Jay Stanton, Head Coach, 1971-1979
                                                 Craig Cassel, Head Coach, 1998-2008

Girls Cross Country, 1975   Jay Stanton, Head Coach, 1975-1979
                                                 Craig Cassel, Head Coach, 1998-2008

The LD Cross Country team began under Coach Jerry Brittain prior to the official records being kept in the Lower Dauphin athletic office. Coach Brittain's early teams fielded several fine runners and the team enjoyed moderate success. Later, Bill Bower coached for a year before moving to Lancaster County where he continued his coaching career. When he left, Jay Stanton took the team to a new level of success in the nine years he coached. Official records between 1975 and 1979 don't reflect the outstanding runners like Randy Lehman and Steve Spence who garnered LD's first Gold Medal in the PIAA State Championships. However, the official win-loss record of 38-5 does reflect the excellence that Lower Dauphin Cross Country enjoyed from the start. In subsequent years, coaches included Dale Luy, Dave Dickson, Jim Brandt, and Craig Cassel. Similarly, our competition has changed from power houses like Annville-Cleona to teams like Northern York to today's rivalry with Hershey.

One thing that has not changed in Lower Dauphin Cross Country is the relationship between coach

[1] Throughout the book, "present" means at the time the section of the publication was completed.

and athlete. Because of the combination of individual/team competition, coaches and athletes develop a unique, long-lasting relationship. Recent teams have enjoyed exceptional success under new head coach John Butler who began his coaching tenure in 2009. The future of LD Cross Country looks very bright as we look forward to the future and look back upon our fond memories of the past.

Field Hockey, 1964 — Linda Kreiser, Head Coach, 1978-present[1]

Lower Dauphin Field Hockey was established under the leadership of Bea Hallman. Coach Hallman instilled the importance of work ethic and teamwork in her young student athletes and developed a competitive program, building the foundation of the Lower Dauphin Field Hockey tradition. In 1978, Coach Hallman turned her program over to her former player, Linda Kreiser. Coach Kreiser and her staff strive to provide a supportive and positive experience for their field hockey players.

In forty-nine years of LDFH, the teams have won 25 League Championships, 10 District Championships, and five State Championships (including fall 2012 as this section is being edited). Players have gone on to win NCAA National Championships in all divisions of college field hockey and we have had two Olympians, Julie Staver Pifer and Laurel Hershey Martin.

Our players play with Falcon Pride, "Love the Game," and hold a special place in our LDFH family heart. Loyal fans, Don and Sue Beam, have been with our team for over twenty years. Retired Assistant Coach, Deb McKee, and current Assistant Coach, Kiley Kulina Strohm, are excellent teachers of the game. We now play on our Astroturf "Field of Dreams," thanks to our community and administration. Our Lower Dauphin Field Hockey family is honored to represent our school on and off the field with enthusiasm, sportsmanship, and dedication.

Sports: The 1970s

Boys Tennis, 1974 — Peggy Steinacker Long, Head Coach, 1995-present[1]
Girls Tennis, 1974 — Peggy Steinacker Long, Head Coach, 1979-present[1]

I have been fortunate to coach girls' tennis at Lower Dauphin throughout my teaching career. Tennis is such a great game to teach life lessons. It is a sport of integrity and character as the player must adhere to the rules of etiquette as well as apply the rules of the game. I have been blessed as a coach to have been able to work with talented athletes as well as young ladies of great character. Lower Dauphin girls' tennis teams are highly respected in the tennis community and have had many successful seasons. One of my fondest memories is from moments after our first championship season was realized when the team formed a circle and spontaneously sang the *Alma Mater*.

In 1995, I took over the boys' tennis program. As most of my players could tell you…the challenge of the process of building a team is most rewarding. Over the years with leadership and a commitment to hard work, the boys' team improved steadily and achieved four consecutive championships from 2005-2008. A key component to a successful team is to have leadership. Many young men over the years have stepped up to lead their tennis team and have become leaders in their community.

As I think back on my years of coaching girls and boys tennis, it is the players and their families that have provided me with many priceless memories and have enriched my life.

Softball, 1974 — Peggy Steinacker Long, Head Coach, 1979-1994

I arrived in Hummelstown in January 1979 and began coaching girls' softball that spring. Coming from a small town in western Pennsylvania where sports were such an integral part of the community, I was fortunate to find a home here that was similar. The softball program developed over the years putting out quality teams, season after season with strength from a diverse group of talented players. Strong pitching and catching has been a cornerstone of the tradition of quality fast pitch teams at Lower Dauphin with strong hitting and good defensive players. The seven championship teams that I had the privilege to coach through the mid-80s and early 90s were a highlight for me. I loved those one run games in which you orchestrated how to get that "go ahead" run…how to get that runner into scoring position; steal a base, bunt her over, let them hit away…how exciting it was when the runner crossed the plate. These "teams" of young ladies were true testaments to doing what had to be done at that moment for the team and true and committed athletes representing the Lower Dauphin community. Today, this strong softball tradition continues at LD.

Girls Track and Field, 1975 — Scott Barton, Head Coach, 1990-2003

Weeks before the start of the spring athletic season, I was sitting in the office as Mr. Umberger and Mr. Appleby were discussing the probability of suspending the Track and Field program for a year until they could find a qualified candidate, as the position was still open. We had just concluded our 1989-1990 basketball season, my second at Lower Dauphin. I volunteered to coach for a year until a qualified candidate could be hired. Fourteen years later, I was still coaching Track and Field.

The uniqueness of Track and Field lies in the fact that it is both an individual sport, as well as a team sport. Our first priority was always the team. Our female athletes were hard-working, dedicated, competitive by nature, and just a joy to be around. We were able to put together a tremendous, experienced coaching staff. During our first championship season, we had 16 girls while many of the schools we competed against had 40 or more girls. Our motto was quality, not quantity. Our girls worked overtime mastering the various events each competed in and they didn't back down from any challenge. It was my honor and my privilege to be able to coach these young women for 14 years.

Sports: The 1980s

Girls Soccer, 1989 — Randy Behney, Head Coach, 1989-2010

The Lower Dauphin Girls Soccer Program began in 1989 and played in the Mid Penn League, which was one of the first organized girls' soccer leagues in District 3. The girls' soccer program has been very successful since the beginning, because of the many talented and hard working female athletes that have been part of the program.

There have been many team and individual awards with one of the greatest achievements being a State Championship in 2009. The girl's soccer program will continue to strive for success and maintain the high standards of Lower Dauphin athletics.

Sports, 1996 – 2010

Girls Volleyball, 1996

Dave Machamer, Head Coach, 2009-present[1]

Since the Inaugural season of 1996, the girls teams have seen many changes, from the teams that they have played, through the coaches they have had in charge. Starting a program from scratch is no easy task. We have had a number of all-stars, some girls going on to play at the college level. We have endured many tough seasons competing with teams that have feeder programs. We won the school's only division title in 2010. In 2012, we have begun a feeder program, hoping to develop the skills needed to compete at the higher level. As we look forward toward the future, the sport of volleyball is one that is growing. With the addition of the feeder programs, and the athletes involved with the sport, Lower Dauphin Volleyball will be competitive for years to come.

Boys Volleyball, 1997

Dave Machamer, Head Coach, 1999-present[1]

Since the Inaugural season of 1997, the boys program has seen just a few changes, having very few coaches. Coming into the league with no experience, the first few seasons were not easy to compete. Over the last 10 seasons, the boys team has won seven division titles, winning the first one just six seasons after starting the program (2003), making the district playoffs in 8 of those seasons. After winning their first division, they have had only one losing season. They have competed at the state tournament, having a great number of all-stars, including a few recognized at the state level. They are a top tier team which is known as one of the best programs in the Mid-Penn conference, and one to be competitive with the elite of the sport. Going forward, the boys program continues to strive in competition with the top in the state.

Girls Lacrosse, 2005

Peggy Barton, Head Coach, 2009-2011

Lower Dauphin Girls Lacrosse has provided female athletes with the challenge of participating in a new PIAA sport. The sport of lacrosse demands the ability to make effective game strategy decisions with great endurance and speed. These very talented scholar athletes succeeded in taking a new program to post season competition under each of its first three coaches. Intelligent, unselfish athletes participated in this program. I knew I was coaching the best and the brightest—the leaders of tomorrow. It was an honor!

Boys Swimming, 2006
Girls Swimming, 2006

Cari Zelko, Head Coach, 2006-present[1]
Cari Zelko, Head Coach, 2006-present[1]

Because of student interest and previous participation in an unofficial capacity at district and state meets, and with support of parents, students, and the Hummelstown Swim Club, as well as cooperation with Milton Hershey School to use their facility, Lower Dauphin officially established Swimming as a PIAA sport in 2009. The team grew from a team of 20 swimmers in 2005 to 34 swimmers in 2012-13. The boys' team won the Keystone Division title three years in a row 2009-2011. Lower Dauphin has had swimmers make it to the State Meet since the second year of the team forming.

From the Playing Fields: The First Nine Varsity PIAA Sports at LD

While it is impossible to write about every game or every sport or every season, it might provide the reader with a flavor of students' coverage of some of the sports. While selected excerpts are shown here—many of them summarized—it would be worthwhile for the interested reader to find issues of the *Falcon Flash* as well as the *Falconaires* just to see how well these young writers reported the games.

At the risk of missing some of these talented writers, what can be said is that over the years the school newspaper has spawned some outstanding student sport writers (Early sports writers were not identified by name, and coaches often were asked to write the game reports) beginning with John Neidinger in the mid-1960s. His brother Jim is arguably an even better writer, as he often adds a smidgen of humor and self-effacement. (A *Falcon Flash* editorial of Jim's can be found in the section on Publications). Another example of creative sports-writing is Craig College, who wrote in 1974, "CV's defense was totally obsessed with aiding Fred Shipley's grass count and his quick screen caught CV completely by surprise as Orsini ran for the game-winning touchdown. Thanks to Coach Seacrist, it was a fantastic move and the genius of the play was not lost on understanding Falcon fans." A few other early *identified* sports reporters who wrote particularly well are Greg College, Ray Kennedy, Dave Jones, Jeff Peyton, Brad Fischer, and Brad Kane.

Because there is limited opportunity to describe individual games in the yearbooks, fewer excerpts included here come from the *Falconaires*. What was being sought for this book are snippets that would engage the reader and not just reports of wins and losses. Thus, presentations are uneven in the number of sports represented. Also, some sports had less coverage and simply by the nature of the game don't lend themselves to colorful description.

The main focus of these reports is the earlier years, mainly because of the availability of the *Falcon Flash* collection of Bill Minsker who kept the issues from the mid-1960s through 1992 and from early scrapbooks (with articles not always identified as to newspaper) once retained in the high school library. Sources after that date are sparse. Further, in the interest of the foundation that established the quality of Lower Dauphin High School and its sports program, concentration is placed on the sports with the longest history, particularly those that originated in the first ten years. LDHS's founders and those who followed are to be commended for the many exemplary coaches LD was able to attract.

Football: LD's First Sport

There was no school newspaper the first year of the school's existence. However, those of us who were there when the doors opened to Lower Dauphin High School can still recall the excitement and anticipation of being a part of this new adventure. Faculty and students alike attended the games, although it was an odd feeling to be cheering a team whose members we had not yet met. Because of a delay in the school's opening the first year, the team played its opening game before school began. We all felt the import of building new traditions—and of winning in all ways!

A united team effort was the major factor in the success of the Lower Dauphin Falcons on their first fling in the new Capitol Area Conference in the fall of **1960**. It was this same team effort that acted as the catalyst in welding all these boys from different school districts into Lower Dauphin's first championship team, going undefeated in conference play. Co-captains were Glenn Ebersole and Ken

Epler. Sophomore Mike Shifflet scored the first touchdown ever for the Falcons on the last play of the first game. Barney Osevala served as the first head coach.

♦ November 4: The biggest gain in the advance was a 12 yard pass from Wyld to Emerich. Harry Menear was terrific at center. Broadwater was the leading ground-gainer.

♦ November 12: Led by Broadwater, who figured in the scoring of 16 points, LD defeated Middletown 28-20 to complete a perfect record season with 3,000 frozen fans in the stands.

Patriot News, September 17, **1961**: If Randy Kahler is any indication of what the sophomore class at Lower Dauphin has to offer, the Falcons will roost high in area grid circles for some time. Kahler paced LD to a 32-13 victory over Camp Hill yesterday with four touchdowns.

Flash, Fall **1963**: The Falcons made the greatest comeback effort in their four year football history, getting on the scoreboard with less than two minutes to play and winning 26-13!

Patriot News October 31, **1964:** Quarterback Clayton (Bo) Smith and his hard-running backfield mates packed too many guns for Susquehanna township last night as they scalped the Indians, 20-6.

On Friday, November 11, **1966** 1,000 stunned spectators watched one of the greatest nights in L.D. history as the Falcons destroyed Middletown's hopes of the CAC crown, marching 80 yards in 70 seconds. This was only the second time in L.D. history that the Falcons flew higher than the Raiders. When the last seconds finally ticked off the clock the crowd swarmed their heroes. As *The Sun* wrote, "What a game! What a comeback! In what has to be one of the best high school games ever played, the victory gave the LD area some new fans, many of whom still talk about the great days of the Bulldogs of Hummelstown High. Charlie Yantz said it best when he said, 'I'm a Falcon fan now.' Mike Yancheff had his finest hour, Glenn Snavely played a magnificent game as a substitute for the injured Larry Robertson, and Daryl Lehew turned in his finest performance against the boys from Middletown that he grew up with."

Summer 1967–Spring 1968

Dr. Hughes administered the physical exams and commented on the fine condition most of the players seemed to be in... Lettermen are easily recognized by the LD on their helmets. ...Low cut shoes with white stripes are awarded to last year's veterans... Notice how the rains stopped when practice started ...Practice field is affectionately called The Dust Bowl.... Mountz and Robertson picked by Harrisburg papers as potentially outstanding Pennsylvania footballers. ... Cumberland Valley not picked to win CAC for first time in three years...The Birds have been bothered by a virus all week. ....Season tickets are available... Six home games for the price of five.... A seven man sled has been added to make practice more enjoyable. A schedule in the shape of a football change purse is available from any team member while the supply lasts.

May **1968**: Larry Robertson, who at the time had set more records than any other football player in LD's short history, was honored by having his jersey number (22) retired. (Two years later Mike Orsini's jersey was also to be retired in a ceremony placing the jersey in a trophy case with that of Robertson. Mike needed to leave for football practice at Penn State prior to the ceremony and, according to him, "I don't know what happened after that.")

1968: Tom Weber with 19 tackles and 15 assists made him the best linebacker on the field despite the presence of Big 33 nominee Brown.

May **1969:** Formation of the Lower Dauphin Football Boosters Club.

In the fall of **1969** in a win over East Pennsboro, Mike Orsini, with one touchdown and 93 yards in 16 carries, and Larry Peters, gaining 94 yards in 17 carries with one TD, paved the way to victory. In an earlier game Peters had the biggest night of his career as he reeled off 214 yards on 27 carries.

The first football camp was held in the summer of **1969** at Log 'n' Twig in Pike County; it was very rural with unlevel fields, including pot holes, more like a pasture, and the team was housed in large tents. The following summer the team went to Juniata College with an air-conditioned dining hall and all the milk, Coke, and lemonade one could want. "We roomed two to a room, with my roommate the greatest for several reasons, the most important being that he had brought a dozen and a half *Playboy* magazines."

From Tom Orsini's "A Football Player's Diary," Friday, November 20, **1970:** "A perfect season. The 1970 football team will go down in history as its greatest team."

The **1970** Team was compared to the "great ones of Hummelstown High seasons in 1954 and 1955," capturing LD's first perfect grid season. It was summed up as the result of the finest total team effort, with probably the most underrated offensive linemen whose efforts and improvement played the key role in winning the CAC title.

October **1971:** Jimmy Kulina led the Falcon scoring with three touchdowns.

Fall **1973,** newspaper account: When the Lower Dauphin tailback Steve Orsini stopped as the final gun sounded he was the only man in recent memory to have accumulated more than 300 yards rushing in a high school football game. (Orsini also set a school rushing mark for one season, carrying 234 times for 1,410 yards going into the contest. His final yardage figure stands at 1,712, just 48 yards short of one mile.) Fred Shipley became the first Falcon QB to pass for more than 1000 yards in a season. Also, was outstanding blocking by Jeff Paine, Crawford set a new record for catches, and Scott Mountz hauled in five scoring tosses for the year.

TV Host, insert, November 25, **1973.** All Metropolitan Harrisburg School Football Team:

1st Team Offense	Steve Orsini
1st Team Defense	Steve Orsini
1st Team Defense	Jerry Peacock
2nd Team Offense	Darrell Seaman
2nd Team Defense	Bob Boudreau

Fall **1974:** Jack Basler with seven interceptions broke the old record set by Larry Robertson in 1967. He also tied a record for most touchdown passes in one season. Dale Espenshade broke almost every record involving extra points and field goals and Bob Myers topped the defense with 92 tackles and 53 assists. Jerry Peacock broke seven school records during the season.

October **1983**: At the end of the game, "the excited Falcon crowd of 4,800 stood to applaud both teams as they left the field, honoring a very confident Lower Dauphin team."

Fall **1994**: We improved from game to game with impressive victories over Northern Lebanon, Central Dauphin East, and Red Lion.

2001 *Falconaire*: Stellar performance, defeating Hershey.

2002 *Falconaire*: Victories over rival Hershey 14-13 and winning the Homecoming game against Carlisle were the highlights of the season.

December 19, **2002**: Going into the season the team was expected by many to have a mediocre year. The team proved to everyone that they earned their berth as District 3 Champs.

October 17, **2003**: Susquehanna Township came expecting to pull off an upset, but a stellar effort by the entire team and a long TD run by Matt Ruffner carried the Falcons to a 29-14 victory.

September **2004**: "Falcons ring up a 538-yard night beating the Blue Raiders the way your mama whips the morning eggs, sailing to a 56-14 mercy rule triumph."

November 9, **2004**: Through the first five games, the Falcons were 5-0 and outscored their opponents 233-37! The following week the Falcons met up with undefeated Gettysburg. In what was dubbed as the greatest game in high school football this year the Warriors prevailed over the Falcons, in overtime, 30-24. The squad bounced back the next week and showed their resilience by smacking Susquehanna Township in the mouth to the tune of 42-7. So through seven games the boys in blue were a solid 6-1.

November **2005**: The boys in blue dominated the area and for the first time since 2002 were able to claim solo ownership of the Mid-Penn Keystone Division.

2010 *Falconaire*: One of the best games of the season was the Central Dauphin East game, particularly the second half. The players executed the plays perfectly and cohesively, resulting in a riveting and successful game.

In closing we share excerpts from emails exchanged among the 1970 team members in 2010 as being representative of the camaraderie experienced by most who played on LD teams. Anyone who has ever played on a winning team can identify with these words. The head coach for this team was Jim Seacrist.

"The coaches took a bunch of average athletes, misfits, hard workers, dreamers and believers and molded us into a rather well oiled, smooth-running machine and we became a team before the season ever started."

"I remember the spaghetti supper the evening before the game... and the walk over to the corner church to have a few minutes to meditate and pray before the game. Then, coming back into Hummelstown on the bus after a win... the streets were lined with the fans holding signs, waving, and clapping."

"We almost lost the perfect season...several times...and I remember being in the huddle. Every player was determined. We were not going to lose. No one was going to stop us. And I truly believe we willed ourselves to win those games."

And, as Kirk Lehmer concluded, "You guys have helped mold my life. I have always remembered that if you set a goal, and you 'believe,' and you work harder than anyone else, you can accomplish anything! I still carry that with me today. And, I thank all of you for the great memories!"

Wrestling

When Coach Cleon Cassel arrived at the first meeting with prospective wrestlers at Hummelstown High School in the spring of 1960, there were five boys there to meet with him; then the teacher present told three of the five to leave because wrestling was not for them. The situation was not too promising for this young coach. That summer a well-intentioned member of the community told the new coach that he should take a job elsewhere rather than be responsible for the boys in Hummelstown being injured the way wrestlers on television were. Two years later this same gentleman apologized at the state wrestling tournament after watching Randy Kahler make it to states after only two years in the sport of wrestling.

In the fall of **1960** the new coach found for his use a single 25 square-foot felt mat, smaller than the legal size for the schoolboy sport. The supervising principal said to the coach, "If more than 20 kids come out on the first day of practice, I will buy you a new mat." On the first day more than 150 boys came out for wrestling on both the junior and senior high level.

The first year the gymnasium was not finished for use until the middle of November and the wrestlers were taught only three moves: single leg, double leg, and stand up. Coach Cassel told them, "While you might not learn much, what you learn you will know better than anyone else." Ten days later the team finished third out of twenty teams in the Harrisburg Novice Tournament, finishing the regular varsity season with a record of 6-4. There was no stopping the Falcons under this coach. During the 1960s Lower Dauphin pin records were set and still stand today, remembering that only recently are pins "counted" from tournaments; in the early years, records were based on only the **matches during the regular PIAA season.** Randy Umberger pinned 12 of 14 opponents and Glenn Ebersole pinned his Hershey opponent in 12 seconds, the fastest time ever.

February 6, **1964**: Fifth straight division win and five undefeated wrestlers: Shellenhamer, Sanders, Rhone, Pinkerton, and Umberger who gave an outstanding performance in the 180 lb. class with his unprecedented pin of Joe Laughlin in the third period. This team went on to make a clean sweep at the Section I tourney with Hess, Shellenhamer, Sanders, Rhone, Kahler. Umberger, defending his crown, was the only wrestler in the two-day show to win by consecutive falls in all three matches.

In February **1964** LD hosted the District III, Division I Wrestling Tournament.

Wrestling, always a powerhouse, had seven sectional champions in **1965** with three of those becoming district champs: Randy Umberger, Bill Pinkerton, and Jim Sanders.

Two years later, Coach Cassel was quoted as saying, "In his senior year Umberger had a terrific season. He scored 12 out of 14 falls, nine of them in the first period. He won the Harrisburg Area Division One 180 lb. title. He also was District 3 Champion and runner-up in the Southeastern Regionals. He definitely was the best 180 pounder we ever had at LD.

From November 7, **1966** *Flush Gazette*, the underground newspaper "owned and operated by the Blue Guard": In the summer of 1965 Lower Dauphin was the first school in the U.S. that had three All-Americans and the only team to have five boys invited to train for the 1968 Olympics at Russ Houck's wrestling camp in Bloomsburg, with the 1964 Olympic coach Rex Perry and his son Ed Perry: Jim Rhone, Randy Kahler, Bill Pinkerton, Jim Sanders, and Randy Umberger. (The information regarding the Olympics was also noted in *The Sun*, July 16, 1965 and the Harrisburg paper that reported that Pinkerton, Sanders and Umberger had also been named to the honor roll of *Wrestling News*.)

March 10, **1966**, *Press and Journal*: Randy Umberger, a freshman at U. of Maryland, won the Freshman Eastern Championship at 177, defeating a wrestler from Navy. "Umberger will be recalled as one of Cleon Cassel's all-time greats."

January 22, **1967** *Patriot*: Aggressive Jim Rhone, considered one of the finest matmen in the history of the sport at LD, is handling another honor in flawless fashion as captain of the University of Pittsburgh mat team.

January 26, **1967**: …setting records that make them one of the finest wrestling teams. …they have skill, spirit, and everything it takes for a winning combination, but most of all they possess the greatest factor it takes to win—determination.

Fall **1967**: Craig Tritch voted player of the game against ten-game winning streak holder Susquehanna.

Summer **1969**: Three LD wrestlers participated in the Junior World's Wrestling Championships in Wyoming. Craig cinched a berth on the World Championship team but was unable to compete because of lack of monetary assistance to defray the expenses incurred during the week of qualifying in Colorado. Craig was the first area participant to place in national competition.

March **1970**: The Hershey Chocolate Cup—the award that goes to the team winning the CAC—is again in the LD trophy case.

1970 Season: Ron Michael is the returning District Three Champion, who had a perfect 13-0-0 record last year and scored a team high of 59 points.

1971 *Falconaire*: Wrestling had its third undefeated season.

1972 *Falconaire*: "Wrestlers Close Season Undefeated With Another CAC Trophy!" This makes nine in 12 years of wrestling.

1973: Three wrestlers placed 2nd in the state tournament: Ed Neiswender, Tom Mutek, Mark Stauffer.

1987: The wrestling team dubbed themselves the "no names," but did not become the underdogs as their critics had predicted. Their pride, dignity, and hard work brought this team to an amazing 13 and 3 record.

1992: Falcons end season with 3 straight victories and send 4 to districts: Mike King, Eric Strunk, Brian Moure, and Brad Meloy.

1995 *Falconaire*: The most remarkable of all the wrestling victories this season was defeating Cedar Cliff for the first time in 13 years and accomplishing the first undefeated dual meet season in 23 years.

2002 *Falconaire*: Coach Sean Ahern accomplished a personal milestone winning his 200th dual meet.

2010 *Falconaire*: LD wrestling reached its 600th win.

Basketball

Basketball records for the first season as Falcons:

- ◆ Most points scored: George Emerich, 348
- ◆ Most field goals in one game: George Emerich, 13
- ◆ Consecutive fouls made: Barry Broadwater, 7
- ◆ Most fouls in one game: Barry Broadwater, 8

December 5, **1963**: One of the bright spots of the loss to John Harris was George Chellew who put on a one-man scoring rally that ended with his scoring 32 points.

From *The Falcon Flash*, except where noted:

February **1968**: Lee Seibert was the first player[1] to score 1,000 points on February 20 and was presented with the game ball.

March **1970**: LD concluded its finest game of the year before an unusually large number of Falcon fans who turned out to cheer on the school's most neglected team.

The Sun, February 10, **1971**: WLYH-TV's Bob Keller said the Falcons were the "most nattily attired team I have ever seen."

The **1971** team completed the second half of the season with a sparkling 8-2 record and an overall record of 14-8, the second best record in school history.

March **1971**: The Falcons' number one scorer this season was Jeff Johns with 311; Roger Alleman had 216, and Kim Witmer 212. "Witmer, the Falcons' sophomore sensation, led the team in steals with 71 and free throws converted with 66. He could become the Falcons' next 1,000 point man."

March **1972**: Kim Witmer is high scorer in the CAC league with 464 points and a 21.1 per game average. Thirty-seven points was his high game and a school record. (In December he earned 38 points in a win over Central York.)

A curiosity on the **1972** team was that four players had fathers who had been high school coaches: Mark Osevala, Rick Hivner, Doug Goepfert, and Kim Witmer.

---

[1] Lee is the first 1,000 point player to have spent all of his high school years in LDHS. See "Record Holders."

March **1973**: JV Coach "Knute" Futchko compiled his 100th career win over Red Land. Coach Futchko is probably the most underrated coach at LD and has done a magnificent job in Junior High and later in JV coaching.

The Sun, January 31, **1973**: LD scoring ace Kim Witmer broke the all-time LD scoring record in Tuesday night's contest.

May 28, **1992**: John Botti chalked up 32 points on three treys, 13 free throws and a solid overall shooting performance; Richie Miller iced two free throws with time running out to give the Falcons a 57-55 win. The victory was arguably the biggest in LD history, and certainly the most exciting of the season.

2001 *Falconaire*: The highlight of the season was the packed house against Hershey in a tie and overtime as Paul Knackstedt scored the only 4 points to win.

Baseball

LD won the **1971** Baseball League Championship despite the fact that there were only four seniors. As reported by the *Flash*, "Jim Kulina, who was brilliant all year, won his second game in four days as he fanned 10 Indian batters, not allowing an earned run."

Coach Ben McLure remembers, "We beat CV for the first CAC baseball championship. It was the first year that the CAC included baseball. The CAC replaced the Lower Dauphin Baseball League, and was divided into East and West divisions. We tied with Middletown and beat them in a playoff to win the East, then beat CV to win the **first ever CAC Baseball Title**."

The Sun, August 2, **1972**: Against Palmyra, Jeff Paine paced LD to a 25-0 victory; Don Gourley hit a grand slam and three hits in three times at bat; Dan Paine had three hits and four RBIs; Bill Baum had six hits in six times at bat. Five school records were set, most runs in a game, most hits, most hits by an individual (Baum), most RBIs (Gourley), and most runs (Baum).

1973: Jim Kulina was said to be one of the top school boy pitchers in the country while continuing to rewrite the LD record books. He posted three shut-out wins and chalked up LD's first no hitter while baseball posted a 9-5-1 mark for another CAC East Division title.

April **1976**: Coach Ben McLure reached a milestone with his 100th victory in ten years of coaching.

Todd Eby was honored by Harrisburg Old Timers Athletic Association for the **1977** season. Todd led the CAC East Champions with a .390 batting average and led the club in extra base hits and runs batted in. Previous LD winners were Paul Pintarch in 1970, Don Gourley in 1972, and Jim Kulina in 1973.

May **1986**: The *Flash* reported, "Under Coach Ron Gourley, the Falcon Nine Clinch Mid-Penn Division II Title." In its first game on April 1, a homerun and strong pitching performance by Todd Mostoller lifted LD to a blow-out victory over the Blue Raiders and on April 3 a masterful pitching display by Bob Henry shut down the Hershey offense."

1992 *Falconaire*: At the end of the regular season the Falcons had accumulated a 13-3 league record and were declared co-champs of the Mid-Penn Division II.

2010 *Falconaire*: Baseball had a superb season, advancing deep into the post season with spectacular performances. According to Coach Kulina, "It was all of the little things that made the team what it was." They were the Keystone Division Champions.

Track

Spring **1965**: Falcons win first medal in districts with Steve Schell winning a third in the shot put.

May 28, **1970**: LD concluded its season with a 7-3 record, the best of any track team in the school's history.

May 28, **1971**: The LD track team enjoyed its most productive season ever, finishing with a school record of 8-2. In the Hershey meet, Joe Quigley broke the 12 year high hurdles record with a 16.0 and led the Falcons to a victory over Hershey, 88 ½ -66 ½. In the 1971 conference meet, the foursome of Kevin Patrick, Kim Witmer, Bruce Cox and Mike Slough set a CAC record in the mile relay and came in fourth in their heat at States. The **1972** relay team (known as the "Cinder-ella" team that finished undefeated in LD's first Capital Area Championship) qualified for states but did not go because some girlfriends complained they would miss the prom. Kim went alone to states and medaled in the mile. The **1973** relay team qualified and placed third.

1971-1973 Track Records

440	Kim Witmer	49.7	1973		l j	Julian Mushinski	21-6 1/4	1972
880	Mike Gallagher	1:58.1	1973		h j	Kim Witmer	6 - 4	1972
m	Mike Gallagher	4:38.5	1972		440 r	Jeff Felty,		
2m	Randy Lehman	9:44.1	1973			Kim Witmer,		
120 h	Leo Hydrick	15.0	1973			Jeff Parsons		1973
180 l	Leo Hydrick	20.4	1973		4 m r	Randy Lehman,		
330 I	Jeff Felty	42.5	1973			Gary Witmer,		
880 r	Kim Witmer		1972			Steve Young		1973
m r	Kim Witmer		1971					
2 m r	Steve Young,							
	C. J. Basler,							
	Phil Yancheff,							
	Mike Gallagher	8:17.0	1973					

A headline in the May 1973 *Flash*: 𝔓𝔯𝔦𝔫𝔠𝔢 𝔎𝔬𝔪𝔞𝔫𝔬'𝔰 𝔎𝔫𝔦𝔤𝔥𝔱𝔰 𝔍𝔬𝔲𝔰𝔱 𝔄𝔩𝔩 𝔑𝔦𝔫𝔢 𝔒𝔭𝔭𝔬𝔰𝔦𝔫𝔤 𝔎𝔦𝔫𝔤𝔡𝔬𝔪𝔰 𝔱𝔬 𝔎𝔲𝔩𝔢 𝔏𝔢𝔞𝔤𝔲𝔢 𝔘𝔫𝔰𝔠𝔞𝔱𝔥𝔢𝔡. The team won the CAC for the 2nd year, undefeated and untied, 9-0. Randy Lehman destroyed the school record in the two-mile run and also was the League Meet Champion; Kim Witmer never lost a 440 yard dash and won the League Meet 440 easily; Mike Gallagher also enjoyed an undefeated season in the 880 yard run while winning the 880 League Meet Championship and a school record in the 880. In fact, this team set 12 of the 19 school records.

In the spring of **1974** only one team record was broken when Craig College ran a 40. in the intermediate hurdles to eclipse Jeff Felty's mark of 42.5.

In June **1984** the team held a flawless 10-0 record to claim the Mid-Penn Championship.

2010 *Falconaire:* This year was one of the most thrilling seasons for a very young LD track team. The girls laid claim to the Mid-Penn Keystone Conference Division Championship; long-standing school records were broken.

Girls Basketball

Press & Journal, February 12, **1965:** Karen Shifflet and Darlene Herr are among the top scorers in the league.

1966: In its fourth year of varsity girls' basketball, the team had a 13-1 league championship.

September **1967:** Girls championship basketball teams were honored for 1965-66 and 1966-67.

1967-1968: A 22-game winning streak under coach Barbara Macaw (Atkinson) wrapped up the Lower Susquehanna League title for the third straight year, and with its first undefeated team in 1968.

March **1970:** The girls have proved themselves to be real champions by completing their season with an 8-0 record. The girls now have forty-five consecutive wins in the Lower Susquehanna League competition. Julie Staver, Linda Kreiser, and Beckey Mountz were among those named as outstanding players in a round robin tournament of the Susquehanna League.

Winter **1971** Season: Girls Basketball rules changed from a six-man team (two rovers, two guards, two forwards) to a five-man full court team.

March **1973:** Girls team is unbeaten at home, completing a fine season and bringing winning basketball back to LD. At districts, sophomore Lorraine Heitefuss stole the show with 18 points, several rebounds, and superb offensive and defensive play, but the team lost to Lancaster 36-33.

May **1992:** The girls set a new school record for the most wins in a season with standouts Melinda Schildt (334 points), Sue Holubek, Angie Eifert, and Jen Jones.

1993 *Falconaire:* Girls basketball qualified for districts and defeated Middletown, overcoming a hurdle of three years.

The only girls' basketball team to compete in state competition was the 1994 team (1993-1994).

1997 *Falconaire:* An outstanding year, conquering both Central Dauphin and Central Dauphin East in one point triumphs. The team was named "Quad A school to watch" in the *Patriot News'* state poll.

2002 *Falconaire:* Because of the immeasurable quantity of determination and fortitude displayed on the court, the team was awarded a spot in the play-offs.

2003 *Falconaire:* 14 wins, no losses.

2010 *Falconaire:* Girls Basketball was one of remarkable triumph. Defeating Carlisle, a powerhouse in our district, having a player accomplish a victory that few had done in the past, or having an all-around successful season, the Lady Falcons represented our school through and through.

Boys Cross Country

November **1963**: The Falcons flew across the countryside with the greatest of ease and ran away with all the honors, becoming the League Champions.

October **1964** *Patriot:* Leon Koser, the farm boy from Londonderry Township, captures the Lebanon-Dauphin County X-Country League Crown.

October **1966**: Except for a 27-28 loss to Annville-Cleona (their first loss in four years on their home course), their record has been unblemished. ...Leon Koser, captain and three-year letter winner, unquestionably wins the honor of MVP.

September **1973**: "Cross Country swims to a win in soaking, flooding rain. The team has two practices a day, 6:30 am and 3:00 pm, averaging about 6-7 miles a day, Monday through Saturday. A group of girls, the Gatorettes, are fanatical fans and Kathy Imhof has earned the title of assistant manager in recognition of her hard work."

November **1974**: The first four places were captured by Falcon Harriers with (1) Joe Vought earning a new course record; (2) Greg College, who had held the record; (3) John Snyder and (4) Dave Scholing. This was also the year of the first annual Crystal Pools Invitational. (This year the Girls were District Champs.)

The **1982** spring issue of *Know Your Schools* noted that the Cross Country team had captured the Mid-Penn Division II Championship with a Division Record of 7-0 and overall record of 10-2.

1997 *Falconaire:* The team more than exceeded the expectations of the students, with the boys finishing in an impressive first place in Mid-Penn Division II with an undefeated record with the girls finishing in second place, an equally impressive achievement. Three qualified for the state championship: James Mentzer, Jonathan Coble, and Emily Shertzer.

The **2000** team had a remarkable season led by senior captain Chad Lister: "We always pushed each other and won close meets because of it."

Field Hockey

From an article in *The Sun*, January 17, **1973**: "Julie (Staver) and Linda (Kreiser) named to the U.S. Field Hockey Team. ....juniors at Penn and Millersville and teammates (Class of 1970) on the 1969 championship team of LD." This honor for two high school classmates to be named to the U.S. Hockey Team is likely unprecedented.

A four year hockey player at LD, Julie began her career as a center halfback in her freshman year and went on to become team captain in 1969. At Penn she earned the inner position to become a starter in her first year. She later earned a berth on the US Reserve Team. Julie has also been active in lacrosse at college, and after only two years play she made the US Reserve Lacrosse Team as a sophomore.

Linda has a fine three year record as an LD hockey player, and she has started for three years on the Millersville team as either a wing or an inner. Her team's leading scorer, Linda has competed in the national tourney for three years. Earlier this year she was named to the Mideast I Team. When the Mideast I and Philly I teams met, Linda and Julie found themselves face to face as opponents. Another LD graduate on the Mideast Team with Linda was Karen Shifflet '67. Linda's selection to the U.S. Squad means that she is among the top 44 hockey players in the country.

In commenting on her former players at LD, hockey coach Bea Hallman said, "Both Julie and Linda are natural athletes and beautiful players to watch in a game. Constantly striving to improve individually, at the same time they manage to be the most unselfish team players."

Fall **1984**: This is the "best ever" hockey team, 20-1-0, Mid-Penn Championship, a District III title, "Best Sportsmanship Award" (rare for a successful team) and sent five to the State All-Star Tournament: Kris Eide, Danni Cooper, Becky Hitz, Kim Hurst, and Laurel Hershey.

Fall **1993**: The Falcons clinched the Mid-Penn II Championship. They held the league record of 9-1-2 by battling impressive teams such as arch rival Palmyra who gave the Falcons their only loss in their division.

1997 *Falconaire:* The Lady Falcons' success on the field is best summarized by the *Community Courier.* "And so the Falcons with a 21-4-2 record and 16 shutouts, wrap up a season without one title to their name. But what they achieved as a group could never be measured by the size of a trophy. They are true champions in the spirit of the word. They are determined, they are unselfish, and they are family. They are what teamwork and winning seasons are all about."

Fall **1998**: The team was unscored upon in the state tournament when they gained the State Championship crown.

Fall **1999**: With an immaculate record of 19-0 going into the AAA division playoffs, they fell to Central Dauphin, 1-0. The team was able to perfect a passing game which was almost unstoppable.

2002 *Falconaire:* The team reached a total of 400 victories.

Falcon Flash, February **2003**: ...District 3 Champs who in double overtime with less than a minute to play, Shayna McGeehan passed the ball to Samantha McLenegan who tapped it in the goal.

November **2004**: The girls have been on fire of late and have stormed to second in the division.

November **2005**: In arguably their best game of the year, the Falcons swarmed a hapless Elizabethtown in a dominant 3-1 performance.

2007 *Falconaire:* The **2006** team faced the ultimate test on a cold Saturday morning in November as they faced Mount St. Joseph Academy in the PIAA State Championship Game. It was here they ended their perfect season (29-0) for a championship victory.

December **2007**: A tied score against Hershey drove the game into overtime, when within the first three minutes, Lauren Alwine scored the winning goal unassisted. They continued their winning streak with a 1-0 victory over Warwick with the only goal of the game being scored by the leading scorer in the mid-state, Alwine, who scored with four minutes left on the game clock.

2010 *Falconaire:* Kreiser's **2009** State Title and 600th coaching career win. "It's the most physical game that we've played against Hershey and it's the best feeling in the world to be a part of Coach Kreiser's 600th win and state champs," said Kaitlyn Plouse.

Golf

May **1973** *Falcon Flash* announced that "Golf makes its debut as a competitive sport with Doug Goepfert, Bob Mushinski, Jack Dimpsey, Dave Jones, and Jeff Ebersole. The team thanks everyone for ignoring them, because who could golf with a group yelling, 'Sink that putt, sink that putt!'" (Golf had become a PIAA sport in 1969.)

1990 marked the first time the LD golf team was represented at the state championships.

2001 *Falconaire*: Golf had an exceptional season, the best since 1992.

2002 *Falconaire*: The golf team is one of the top teams in the area with Ryan Burk and Erin Weber advancing to district play.

2003 *Falconaire:* All of the team qualified for the Mid-Penn Tournament, qualifying more players than any other school in the Commonwealth.

2010 *Falconaire*: With only one returning starter the 2009 golf team was well aware of the challenges. They ended up sending five boys to the Mid-Penn competition.

The following smattering comments are included as flavor for some of the sports that began after 1970 or were not originally PIAA sports:

In **April 1966** a tennis team was formed with six boys who were interested.

Winter **1970**: Girls' Gymnastics won the Tri-County Championship for the third successive year.

1993: Girls' Soccer: During their season, the Lady Falcons tried and usually succeeded to clobber almost any team that got in their way.

1995: Coach Longenecker's goals for the season involved getting to double figures in wins, winning more games than last year, and gaining a play-off spot. The team accomplished the first two goals with a 10-6-2 record and narrowly missed a play-off spot.

1997: Volleyball: With the Lower Dauphin gymnasium under renovation, the group overcame many hardships, always playing at the opponent's school.

2001: Boys Soccer: 18-4 Season, 12 games won in a row. A great ending to Longenecker's coaching career. Brian Dell made the all-state team.

2001: Girls Tennis: 13-0, the first undefeated season, Mid-Penn Conference winner. Three gold medals at Mid-Term Tournament.

2002: Girls Tennis: Mid-Penn Championship for the second consecutive year. At # 1 doubles, Sara Marian Seibert and Caitlin Wohlfarth won gold medals.

2002: Boys Soccer: When matched up against the Wilson Bulldogs, one of the best programs in the district, the team won 2-1 in a thrilling match in the Hershey stadium.

2002: In Girls Soccer, led by senior captain Emily Pantalone, the girls had an incredible seven meet undefeated streak.

2002: Girls Volleyball went to Districts.

2010: Girls Lacrosse team can be referred to as nothing less than victorious with one of the best seasons they have had yet.

2010: Boys Soccer was ranked at the bottom of their division at the start of the season. This only motivated the team when they took on Palmyra, the number one state-ranked team. The final score, a one to nothing defeat in overtime, was not at all reflective of the tremendous fight displayed throughout the entire game. This defining game propelled the team into a great season.

2010: Swimming had a remarkable season, particularly with the final meet against Bishop McDevitt and the perfect end to the season when the boys team won Divisions.

In closing we include an excerpt from the *2010 Falconaire* on sports at Lower Dauphin:
"For fifty years athletics at Lower Dauphin have played an integral role in the student life of the high school. On playing fields, gymnasiums, tennis courts, and tracks, blue and white can be seen competing with pride. Whether a 2009 State Championship field hockey player, swimmer on the team's inaugural season, or a football quarterback from 1977, every Lower Dauphin athlete has worked together to define what it means to be a Falcon. The blue banners hanging in the Lower Dauphin gym list our sports teams as District Champs, State All-Stars, Mid-Penn Conference winners, and every other accolade possible. But even if LD were not at the top every year, the Lower Dauphin community knew the individuals representing the team were persevering, demonstrating excellence and pride. The Lower Dauphin community is a key part in the success of our athletics. The administration, teachers, parents, coaches, friends and others have supported Lower Dauphin athletics throughout the generations and have helped them to grow and prosper. All of Lower Dauphin's nineteen varsity sports exhibit commendable qualities on and off the field. And after fifty years, the tradition of excellence will continue to be at the core of Lower Dauphin athletics."

Athletic Training at Lower Dauphin

More recently known as the Sports Medicine Team, the high school began with only a physician who was "on duty" at games and available when needed at other times. The first athletic trainer was Ben McLure who had training in a time before there was a certification; he likely was a volunteer as so many were then. The first identified "team physician" was Dr. E. A. Hughes who was dedicated to local high school sports and was part of its history until his retirement in the mid-1970s. At that time Dr. Glenn Bartlett became the team physician, joining Mr. George "Speed" Ebersole, volunteer athletic trainer who was a fixture at LDHS for as long as anyone can remember and in 2003 was honored by induction into the Pennsylvania Athletic Trainer's Society Hall of Fame. During his service as athletic trainer, Mr. Ebersole, along with Dr. Bartlett, was instrumental in hiring the first part-time salaried athletic trainer, Mr. Mark French. During the mid-1990s Dr. Robert Dahmus, currently with the Orthopedics Institute of Pennsylvania, began his close relationship with Lower Dauphin sports. In 2001, Mr. Paul LaDuke was hired as the first full-time strength coach/athletic trainer, because of Mr. French's desire to spend more time with the high school students, and in 2007 Ashley Moss joined the Sports Medicine Team.

Lower Dauphin Olympians

Among the many very fine athletes to come out of Lower Dauphin High School's sports program are three Olympians. Their respective coaches are Ms. Beatrice Hallman who set the standard high when she created and developed the field hockey program in the 1960s, Mr. Edward Romano, passionate track and field coach who refined the sport by raising the bar at LDHS, and Ms. Linda Kreiser '70, a national seminal figure as a field hockey coach and one of the greatest female athletes in the history of Millersville University.

Dr. Julia Staver '70

Dr. Staver is Lower Dauphin's first widely recognized female scholar athlete, long preceding today's well-used phrase. She played for the US lacrosse team in the 1970s, was captain of the 1980 US Olympic women's field hockey team and co-captain of the 1984 bronze medal-winning US Olympic team. Julia has a thriving veterinary practice in the Reading PA area, specializing in small animals and was one of the four distinguished alumni honored by the Lower Dauphin Alumni Association at the Golden Jubilee.

Steve Spence '80

At Lower Dauphin, Spence won the 1980 Pennsylvania Intercollegiate Athletic Association (PIAA) Class AAA 1,600-meter championship in a then-state record of 4:12. He also won the 1980 PIAA state championship in the mile run with a state record time. A seven-time NCAA Division II All-American, he was a member of the 1992 Olympic team and finished 12th in the men's marathon, marking the best US Olympic marathon finish to that date. He is the cross country coach at Shippensburg University.

Laurel Hershey '87

Hershey was a member of the US women's field hockey team that finished fifth at the 1996 Olympics in Atlanta, Georgia. She competed in two Hockey World Cup tournaments in 1990 and as a member of the USA bronze medal team in 1994. She was named to the 1990 All-America team and earned NCAA all-tournament honors in 1989. She captured a bronze medal at the 1991 Pan American Games and earned a silver Pan Am medal in 1995. She won a bronze medal at the 1995 Champions Trophy and today is the head field hockey coach at Stevenson College.

Sports Record Holders

Lower Dauphin has never initiated a "Hall of Fame" as it is difficult to establish criteria that would not be affected by politics. On the other hand, there are many positive reasons for honoring the best athletes, but to date no action has been taken. However, we have chosen to list the recognized honor of championship teams, sports record holders of note, and those who were drafted by professional teams.

Team Championships of the Decades

1960s: 20   1970s: 13   1980s: 32   1990s: 37   2000s: 51   2010s: 32

District III Team Champions to 2013

These records are not included in the overall records of the teams, as noted at the bottom of page 235.

Baseball: 2005; 2013

Boys Cross Country: 2013

Field Hockey: 1982, 1984, 1993, 1997, 2002, 2003, 2006, 2007; 2008; 2011; 2013

Football: 1995, 2002; 2013

Softball: 2007, 2008

Wrestling: 1980, 1995, 2007

PIAA State Team Champions

Field Hockey: 1993, 1998, 2006, 2009, 2012, 2013

Girls Soccer: 2009

Basketball 1000 Points Achievers

1000 point scores in basketball prior to 1987:

George Emerich '62[2]   Lee Seibert '68[3]

Kim Witmer '73[4]   Bert Kreigh '80[5]

The three point rule went into effect the 87-88 season. The following fall under this category:

Ruth Woltman '89	Chris Kreider '98	Alexandria Bream '05
Richie Miller '93	Jessica Barton '99	Chante Markus '10
MaLinda Schildt '94	Evan Gourley '99	Cody Deal '12
Katie Bogovic '98	Seth Lewis '05	

Wrestling 100 Wins

Jared Kane '07   Nicholas Kristich '08

Track and Field PIAA State Champions

Steve Spence '80: AAA 2 mile/3200 meters, 1980

Michael Brown '09: AAA 300m Hurdles, 2009; 110m Hurdles, 2008; 300m Hurdles, 2008

NCAA Division I, All-American, Collegiate Wrestling

Ron Michael '72, Kent State, 4th place

National/International Field Hockey Honors

Julia Staver and Linda Kreiser both were named to the US Field Hockey Association squad in 1973 and played in the 1975 World Cup competition.

---

[2] George Emerich, the first in LD history to score 1,000 points, should have been honored in the 1962 season for having reached the 1,000 point plateau. George spent his freshman and sophomore years in Hummelstown High School, the birthplace of Lower Dauphin, where he scored a total of 454 points. In his junior year at Lower Dauphin, he scored 348 points and in his senior year, 420 for a grand total of **1,222** career points. LDAA is correcting this oversight; a basketball is being presented to him, and his name is being added to the banner in the gym of record holders.

[3] Lee Seibert was the first 1,000 point scorer who spent all of his years on this squad. He played from 1965-1968 under Coach Burr Rhodes. He scored a total of **1,047** points and was the Harrisburg area leading scorer in his senior season.

[4] Kim Witmer was the next 1,000 point scorer. He played from 1970-1973, and finished with **1,160** career points. He was the Harrisburg area leading scorer in 1972 and was selected to the Big 15 that year.

[5] The highest scorer in LD history was Bert Kreigh who played from 1976-1980 under Mr. Rich Miller. He finished with **1,872** total points. He was selected to the Big 15 in 1980 and was the Harrisburg area leading scorer in the '78-'79 and '79-'80 seasons.

Lower Dauphin Alumni on Professional Teams

Compiled by Ben McLure

Pro Football

- ◆ Mike Yancheff, Quarterback, Philadelphia Bell

Pro Baseball

- ◆ Robert (Meatball) Evans, Detroit, Baltimore
- ◆ Jim Kulina, Cincinnati Reds
- ◆ Greg Patton, San Diego Padres
- ◆ Rich Hay, St. Louis Cardinals
- ◆ Bob Baxter, Los Angeles Dodgers
- ◆ Larry Robertson (drafted, did not sign), Philadelphia Phillies
- ◆ Scott Thompson, San Diego Padres
- ◆ Mark Collier, Baltimore Orioles
- ◆ Ken Kulina, Toronto Blue Jays

Julia Staver and Linda Kreiser were named to the US Field Hockey Association squad in 1973. They went on to play in the 1975 World Cup and Julie was named to the 1980 and 1984 Olympic Teams.

Travers Award

The John A. Travers Award is known as the king of student-athlete honors in the mid-state, awarded to a student who is outstanding in athletics, scholastics, and leadership. Founded in 1982 by Dr. A. I. Garner, the award is named for the former *Patriot-News* executive sports editor. One male and one female senior are nominated by each school district. Lower Dauphin has garnered a total of eight awards since the inception of the honor.

1987 Laurel Hershey	1997 Jaime Tressler	2009 Michael Brown
1988 Tricia Gaudette	2007 Julie Barton	2009 Carrie Diamond
1996 Brian Broadwater	2008 Lauren Alwine	

Lower Dauphin High School Falcons Team Championships, 1960—2010

Note: All championships prior to 1982–83 school year were league championships. In 1982 the Mid Penn Conference was formed and divisional champions were named. In 2005 post season tournaments were instituted to recognize a Mid Penn Conference League Champion in team sports. Also note that this listing covers only to 2010, the first fifty years.

Baseball: 64-65; 67-68; 68-69; 71-72; 80-81; 82-83; 83-84; 84-85; 85-86; 87-88; 91-92; 94-95; 95-96; 96-97;00-01;03-04;04-05;05-06;06-07; 09-10 **(20)**

Basketball (Boys): 04-05

Basketball (Girls): 65-66; 66-67; 67-68; 68-69; 69-70; 93-94; 02-03;03-04;04-05; 05-06;06-07;07-08;08-09 **(13)**

Cross-Country (Boys): 63-64; 64-65; 65-66; 66-67; 82-83; 88-89; 96-97. **(7)**

Cross Country (Girls): 75-76; 76-77; 77-78; 83-84; 98-99; 09-10 **(6)**

Field Hockey: 69-70; 78-79; 80-81; 81-82; 82-83; 83-84; 84-85; 85-86; 86-87; 87-88; 88-89;89-90; 90-91; 91-92; 92-93; 93-94; 95-96; 98-99; 99-00;03-04; 06-07;07-08;08-09; 09-10 **(24)**

Football: 60-61; 70-71; 84-85; 85-86; 92-93; 93-94; 95-96; 98-99; 02-03; 03-04; 05-06 **(11)**

Golf (Boys): 89-90; 90-91; 91-92; 08-09 **(4)**

Soccer (Boys): 84-85; 95-96; 97-98; 98-99; 99-00; 04-05; 08-09 **(7)**

Soccer (Girls): 97-98; 00-01; 01-02; 04-05; 05-06 **(5)**

Softball: 84-85; 87-88; 88-89; 89-90; 91-92; 92-93; 93-94; 94-95; 95-96; 96-97; 97-98: 06-07; 07-08; 08-09; 09-10 **(15)**

Swimming (Boys): 08-09; 09-10 **(2)**

Tennis (Boys): 04-05; 05-06; 06-07; 07-08 **(4)**

Tennis (Girls): 00-01; 01-02 **(2)**

Track and Field (Boys): 71-72; 72-73; 83-84; 05-06 **(4)**

Track and Field (Girls): 90-91; 93-94; 09-10 **(3)**

Volleyball (Boys): 02-03; 03-04; 06-07; 08-09; 09-10 **(5)**

Wrestling: 63-64; 64-65; 65-66; 67-68; 68-69; 69-70; 70-71; 71-72; 72-73; 75-76; 79-80; 80-81; 81-82; 82-83; 83-84; 84-85; 92-93; 94-95; 95-96; 97-98; 05-06; 06-07 **(22)**

Alumni Who Are and Were Head Coaches

Alumnus/Alumna	Sport	Years		Record
Randy Umberger '65	Wrestling (co-head)	1978–81	(3)	43-7-2
Randy Umberger '65	Wrestling	1989–91	(2)	11-18-1
Ron Gourley '66	Baseball	1980–96	(17)	268-109
Ron Gourley '66	Golf	1986–89	(4)	52-19
Linda Kreiser '70	Girls Basketball	1976–78	(2)	7-32
Linda Kreiser '70	Field Hockey	1978–	(32)	600-92-33
Linda Kreiser '70	Softball (co-head)	1979	(1)	8-6
Ed Neiswender '72	Wrestling	1983–84	(1)	8-6
Ed Neiswender '72	Wrestling	1987–89	(2)	21-10
Ed Neiswender '72	Wrestling	2002–09	(7)	90-22
Craig Cassel '82	Wrestling	1991–96	(5)	64-24-1
Craig Cassel '82	Boys Cross Country	1998–08	(11)	48-55
Craig Cassel '82	Girls Cross Country	1998–08	(11)	75-30
David Machamer '86	Boys Volleyball	1999–	(11)	119-95
David Machamer '86	Girls Volleyball	2009–	(1)	2-12
Brett Sparks '86	Softball	2006–09	(4)	80-19
Joshua Lininger '93	Wrestling	2009	(1)	16-5
Amanda Engle Mease '93	Softball	2002–05	(4)	46-40

—includes statistics through end of 2010 year

Legendary Field Hockey Coaches

Coach Beatrice Hallman

Coach Hallman was instrumental in establishing girls' sports at Lower Dauphin High School and was the driving force behind the tradition of excellence on the playing field and in life. When Lower Dauphin first opened in the fall of 1960, there was no interscholastic sports program for girls. All girls' sports were on the intramural level. Miss Hallman provided instruction after school to girls who were interested in learning more about team sports. These teams played field hockey, basketball, and softball.

Girls' interscholastic basketball began in the 1963-1964 school year; field hockey was established that year under the leadership of Bea Hallman, but did not compete interscholastically until the following year. Coach Hallman developed a competitive program and she built the foundation of the Lower Dauphin Field Hockey tradition.

Beatrice Hallman was influential in the lives of many young women and was often the first person to instill pride in high school girls to be a part of an athletic program. An excellent athlete herself, Miss Hallman was also a very positive teacher, coach, and mentor to many. Some of the best athletes, teachers, and coaches had their start under the wings of Miss Hallman. In 1978, Coach Hallman turned her program over to her former player, Linda Kreiser and her influence is still present in every winning tradition of field hockey at Lower Dauphin through Coach Kreiser.

Coach Linda Kreiser

The decision by Linda Kreiser to learn the game of field hockey in the 10th grade at Lower Dauphin High School was a momentous one. With very few choices for women's sports in the late 60s Linda gravitated to this sport. Upon graduation in 1970, she earned her bachelor's degree in education at Millersville University and continued to compete on the field hockey field, making the US national team in the late 1970s as well as the US women's lacrosse team.

Linda Kreiser returned to her Alma Mater to teach science at the Middle School and to become coach of the Lower Dauphin High School field hockey team. Coach Kreiser has earned numerous awards as she herself has continued to play field hockey as well as coach it. She has a legendary reputation for coaching excellence in high school field hockey, including six PIAA Class AAA state championships, and undefeated seasons in 1993 and in 2006.

Just as important to the young women she coaches is the fact that, because of Linda's outstanding reputation, numerous LD graduates have gone on to be awarded scholarships to attend prestigious colleges and universities and play collegiate field hockey. Very few, if any other coaches than Linda, a seminal figure in field hockey coaching, can claim 695 wins and induction into the National Field Hockey Coaches' Association Hall of Fame.

Summit Achiever Jeannine Lehmer '69

A Champion ❖ *A Scholar* ❖ *An Athlete* ❖ *An Artist*

This particular tribute brings long-overdue attention to one who exemplifies overcoming the time in which she lived, a woman who likely would have been an outstanding athlete had she been born ten, or even five years later than she was. Lower Dauphin's 1969 Teen Queen, as well as a Homecoming Queen Candidate the same year, she also was a top student, and was a member of the first freshman class at Franklin and Marshall College to include women. For many, these accomplishments would be redeeming, but for this young woman, these achievements were only the baseline.

In high schools in the 1960s, females were permitted very few avenues in which to compete athletically. There were sports teams for women, but these were limited to basketball (begun in 1963, but not yet recognized by PIAA) and field hockey (begun in 1964, and also not recognized). Like most athletes who excel, Jeannine Lehmer was interested in learning a skill at a very early age when she began to teach herself most of the fundamentals of baton twirling. She came to excel in both the athleticism and the artistry of twirling, although it is likely that her skill in both was taken for granted rather than lauded.

In high school Jeannine served as a line majorette in her freshman and sophomore years, the unstated rule dictating that the head majorette position be awarded to an upper classman. In March 1966, as the only freshman, Jeannine was one of a team of four twirlers to take first place in a national competition.

During her senior year of high school, Jeannine was known as one of the finest majorettes in the state, having been competing and winning honors in baton competitions throughout her entire high school career. In a total of seven contests she collected 21 trophies and earned 12 medals:

★ 5 Single Baton Solo Championship & Fancy Strutting Championships

★ 4 First Places in One Baton Solo

★ 3 First Places in Basic Strutting

★ 3 First Places in Military March

★ 2 First Places in Duet Strutting

A Champion

A Scholar

An Athlete

An Artist

Jeannine Lehmer was not one to assume anything, but there was no question that she would be head majorette in both her junior and senior years of high school. She also was selected in 1966 and 1967 as a twirler in the one baton squad and the two baton squad of the annual Pennsylvania Big 33 Football Game. In 1968 she served as line captain for the performers.

Her last presentation at Lower Dauphin was at the 1969 spring band concert, a baton-dance combination which she herself had choreographed. This was followed by her selection as the solo head majorette for the Sweet 16 and as the featured performer at the half-time ceremonies of the Big 33 game in the Hershey Stadium. Chosen hands down as the best from 18 area schools, Jeannine delivered a flawless performance at halftime which included 1, 2, and 3 fire batons in addition to other routines. She also appeared in "Who's Who in Baton Twirling, 1969." It should also be noted that six years later her sister Denise Lehmer was also a Big 33 half-time head majorette!

Entering F & M in the fall of 1969 Jeannine was heralded as the solo majorette for the F & M College Band, a position she held for four years.

Jeannine Lehmer Groff, a physician's assistant and a tennis player, is also a runner, winning her age group the first time out in the Dartmouth Relay in 2011.

Her daughter Lauren is a prize-winning author and daughter Sarah placed fourth at the 2012 London Olympics in the women's triathlon, finishing 10 seconds out of bronze and 12 seconds out of gold in a race that is a two-hour, full-out effort.

Publications

FIRST EDITION

Merry Christmas

THE FALCON FLASH

Happy New Year

VOLUME I, No. 1   Hummelstown, Pa., Friday, December 22, 1961   Price: Ten Cents

Language Department Christmas Program

A Language Arts Christmas Program has been presented this afternoon in activity period by the Latin, Spanish, French, and German students. Mrs. Yount has directed the German students, Miss Ausmus the Latin and French students, and Mrs. Pratt the Spanish students.

HONOR ROLLS

The Honor Rolls for the first marking period have been posted. There are once again two Honor Rolls, the Distinguished Honor Roll and the Regular Honor Roll. The Distinguished Honor

The Latin students were the first on the program. George Emerich gave a talk about the change in Christmas customs through the years. A group of Latin students sang "Adeste Fideles."

Modern languages were next presented. Students told about Spanish customs in Spanish. Miriam Ramirez explained the portal and the pinata. Judy

MR. CURTIS TAYLOR

1966

Falcon Flash

VOL. 6, NO. 1   HUMMELSTOWN, PA.   SEPTEMBER, 1966

SENIOR ATTENDS EIGHT-WEEK SUMMER SESSION

FE STUDENT ARRIVES AT LD

1967

FALCON FLASH

VOL. 7, NO. 4   HUMMELSTOWN, PA.   DECEMBER, 1967

CONGRESSMAN ESHLEMAN SPEAKS TO SENIORS

N.H.S. Starts Lyceum Program

The National Honor Society will sponsor a lyceum next semester at Lower Dauphin.

The program will bring one or two speakers each month during eighth period to give a twenty-minute talk and lead a twenty-minute discussion. Forty tickets will be available to the first forty students to sign up at the guidance

L.D. Holds Christmas

Janet Kettering, chair publicity manager and accompanist.

1967

FALCON FLASH

VOL. 7 NO. 2   HUMMELSTOWN, PA.   OCTOBER, 1967

VO-AG STUDENTS BRING HOME PRIZE

Vo Ag students represented L. D. well in recent area contests.

On Friday, September 22, the Lower Dauphin Future Farmers of America competed with fellow FFA members from Halifax, Middletown and Upper Dauphin in contests held at the Gratz Fair, Schuylkill County. Two of the Falcon representative winners were Dale Kennedy, senior, and Richard Radle, freshman, 1st in Dairy Judging and 1st in Poultry Judging

1970

MARCH

Falcon Flash

1970

Lower Dauphin

Mr. Filepas

FORUM MEETING TODAY!!

Falcon Flash

April 1973   Lower Dauphin High School, Hummelstown, Pennsylvania 17036   Vol. 12, No. 6

Foreign Studies Scheduled

HOT SHORTS

STUDENTS SUPPORT SAM CAMPBELL 1973

1987 The

Falcon Flash

Lower Dauphin High School

Vol. 27, No. 3   October 30, 1987

Where Do I Park?

By Scott Kucenski

Pep Ra... Du...

The

Member Pennsylvania School Press Association

Falcon Flash 1992

Vol. 29, No. 6, March 12, 1992   Lower Dauphin High School, Hummelstown, PA 17036

Seniors request exemption from finals
By Karen Bolton

LD to enter Envirothon
by Karen Bolton

Mrs. Rist named to delegation

The

Lower Dauphin High School

Falcon Flash

2006

Vol. 44 No. 3 January 23, 2006

LD Student Council leads another successful Food Drive

High schoo... contributes...

2011 Lower Dauphin High School

The Falcon Flash

Four Year Journey
By: Danielle Olson

Vol. 50 No. 5, May 2011

284

Overview of School Publications

Publications have always been a part of Lower Dauphin High School, and later Lower Dauphin School District. Writing for publication, writing to have a voice, writing to critique, writing to share—all are reasons that staffs of the school publications never lacked for student personnel.

The three major high school publications are the newspaper (*Falcon Flash*), the yearbook (*Falconaire*), and the literary magazine (*Media*). There were also occasional newsletters for special programs, such as the *Limestone* from Longitudinal Studies, the underground *Gazette*, the faculty's *The Insider*, and the district's *Know Your Schools*.

The unfortunate circumstance with publications—especially high school newspapers—is that they often are viewed as disposable. The school library does not archive publications; thus, we have only those copies that individuals kept. A major collection of *The Falcon Flash* was donated by Mr. William Minsker whose holdings cover 1968 – 1993. Mrs. Lena Russell loaned the copies she was able to find from 1994 – 2011. Jan Brightbill and Marilyn Menear provided the copies they had kept from high school and the author added the ones from her collection.

The *Falconaire*s came from the author's collection, 1961-2011, as did the early *Media* magazines. Ms. Karen Burk, along with other advisors to the magazine, were helpful in identifying editors for *Media*.

A Free and Noble Press

The first issue of a school newspaper was published in the first year of the jointure in the junior high school under the guidance of Mrs. Patricia Lanshe and was named *The Falcon Flyer*. It continued as such for two years. In the fall of 1961 the *Falcon Flash* was launched in the high school with Gail Walborn, a sophomore, as the editor and Ms. Cynthia Xanthopolos as the advisor. Volume I, No. 1 made its debut on December 22, 1961. Prior to publication the students had voted on the name of the paper, with the winning entry submitted by Donald Green, also a sophomore. His prize was a season pass to basketball games.

The first issue of the *Flash*, as it is sometimes called, reported that of the 487 students in the high school (grades 10-12), **four** reached Distinguished Honor Roll Status: Alice Wiest, Robert Gibble, Anne Wenrich, and Karen Fair. Tenth grade enrollment showed 207 students (114 girls and 93 boys); eleventh grade, 143 (79 girls; and 64 boys) and twelfth grade had only 137 (69 girls and 68 boys).

In the fall of 1964 the newspaper staff announced that because of the volume of information to be published and the difficulty in delivering timely news, the *Falcon Flash* would be following a magazine format beginning with the December 1964 issue. This format continued for three issues, December, February, and April. The following year a decision was made to return to newspaper format.

Initially there was a nominal charge for each issue of the newspaper but before long the publication was offered without charge to its readers.

A high school newspaper always faces challenges, typically of having a place of its own, meeting deadlines and being dependent on having it printed in a short turnaround time, and most importantly, finding fresh material and serving a young readership that often is very critical of peers. It wasn't until the mid-1980s that modern technology helped the newspaper "get on the streets" in a short turn-around time when the Production Printing Class processed and printed the newspaper weekly. According to a fall 1987 issue, "The format is done on a computer, put on a disk, then given to the printers where a series of processes results in the paper."

The *Falcon Flash* encountered its share of criticism, but in December 1986 the 1985-86 issues of the *Flash* were awarded second honors in the 1986 PA School Press Association.

The *Flash* usually had very dedicated staffs who took their work seriously and produced a creditable product. Reviewing the list of *Falcon Flash* editors will reveal some of the high school's best students.

Perhaps the harshest criticism the paper ever faced occurred during the school year 1970-71 when an article appeared that many viewed as being in poor taste when two wrestlers became the brunt of a satiric article that wasn't funny. Because the staff was very talented, it has to be assumed that they just got caught up in the lampoon and didn't know when to rein it in.

As a result of the brouhaha, the entire staff resigned. An entirely new staff was formed for 1971-72 with editor-in-chief, Barbara Saylor '73; sports, Tom Orsini '72; reporters, Mary Zeager '73, Steve Geyer '73, Julie Snavely '73; and photographic editor, Chuck Dowell '73. This staff published an apology in the May 28, 1971 issue, closing with the following remarks, "Our apology extends to you, your family and friends for any embarrassment suffered. We are very sorry."

Among the many letters to the editor over this incident, that written by Donald Bell, a senior, was the most balanced,

> Most probably the article was written for the purpose of humor. I feel it did not achieve this purpose in any sense. If articles of this nature are to be printed, the people which the article is about should be notified. Their approval of the article should be received before the article is finally printed. I do not believe that these two boys would have approved of this article.
>
> I do believe the paper is the best it has ever been in the years I have been at L.D. There are many good articles in the paper and I enjoy reading it. However, for the sake of the individuals being portrayed, please ask their approval of the article when the article is of this nature.

By fall the new editorial team included Jim Neidinger '73 who recalls, "The group (that had resigned) had talented writers but were known for pushing the envelope." Jim himself, as a rookie, rose to the occasion, becoming a responsible, skilled writer and one of the notables of the publication. In his first article in the newspaper he wrote,

> I have found the responsibilities demanding and the work hard, but it is still enjoyable. ... If you personally do not like the quality of the newspaper, why not put forth constructive effort by either suggesting articles or even joining the staff. ... Talent cannot be developed

except by practice. ...If you want a good paper, I urge you personally to help." He adds a postscript: "Despite several rumors, the members of the *Falcon Flash* are all sane and working hard on next month's issue."

The new staff became known for their editorials, inviting letters to the editor and addressing various issues, an example of which follows by Dennis Shope (November 1971):

> A sizable portion of the Lower Dauphin student body attended a science fiction lecture presented by Miss Rose Wolf on October 25 in the auditorium. Although the program was interesting and seldom above high school comprehension, the student audience displayed a surprising amount of disrespect. Miss Wolf was shown no courtesy from a crowd which created a distinct and rude murmur throughout the program. Some viewers even had the audacity to leave the auditorium as the final bell rang and stranded the speaker in a helpless position struggling for attention.
>
> The students, as impolite as they were, are not entirely responsible. The program, planned for approximately 90 English students, received an audience estimated at 250. Where did the extra come from? They came from any class where the teacher wanted to take a period off and simply "dumped" the students into the auditorium and left. They came from the library, science classes, and study halls. Often the students persuaded the teacher into coming by over-emphasis of its importance to them.
>
> What could have been an enjoyable and interesting program was turned into a disgraceful fiasco by a group of impudent students.

The staff aimed for balance with their student journalists who held a very wide spectrum of beliefs. They could even poke fun at themselves describing their two diverse groups of "The Funlovers" and "The Sanctified" whose humor was lost on many. This was an excellent, serious staff of writers and thinkers who were quite objective while maintaining their individual voices, a trait not usually found in school newspapers and should be named herein: Barb Saylor '73 (as an adult in telecommunications), Steve Geyer '73, Mary Oishi (Zeager) '73 (currently a writer, KUNM public radio), Jim Neidinger '73 (musician), Ray Kennedy '74 (cattle farm owner), Dennis Shope '74 (computer specialist), Joe Taylor '74, and Betty Via '74 (accountant).

November 1974 saw the first paid advertisement in the *Flash*.

A slice of school life and culture from the *Falcon Flash* in December 1976 will likely ring true for almost any year. The following list of articles is representative of typical concerns of the time.

▸ Student concerns
▸ Smoking policies
▸ Increasing amount of displayed affection in the halls
▸ Criticism of those who don't participate in events
▸ Chastising of those who don't support the arts
▸ The length of time between classes
▸ A call for school spirit

- A call for more dances
- Complaints about study halls and the cafeteria.

The Class of 1984 found a spokesman for their agenda in Randy Thames '84 who wrote in December 1983, "Is there truly something wrong with the Class of Nineteen Hundred Eighty-Four? Should this class be labeled, as some have done, as the athletic and extracurricular **"rejects"** of Lower Dauphin's past five years?"

Another notable gadfly was Jeff Peyton '85 who in October 1984 wrote a criticism of Student Forums where "no negative comments were to be entertained on the floor."

In May 1987 the editor wrote, "What the *Flash* has become and what it is yet to be, is all due to the complete trust given to us by the faculty and administration. And it is that for which I am most proud and thankful."

Sometime between 2006 and 2009 the newspaper began to be printed in color. And in February 2012 the newspaper became an online publication. Thus, size, formatting, layout, printing processing, even writing styles have changed through the years, but the *Falcon Flash* remains the best record the school has of its daily life and serves as a vehicle for the voice of the students. May it survive—and even thrive—with its move into the electronic age!

Falcon Flash Editors

Because there has been no official or consistent archival retention of issues of the *Falcon Flash*, listed here are editors and co-editors that could be identified. Beginning in the late 1980s there began a trend away from naming an editor-in-chief.

1960–1961	No newspaper	1994–1995	Anita Ketty
1961–1962	Gail Walborn	1995–1996	Multiple division editors
1962–1963	George Hall and	1996–1997	Abigail Martin
	Ralph Espenshade	1997–1998	Abigail Martin and
1963–1964	Kathleen Convery		Megan Gold
1964–1965	Bethanne Bojanic	1998–1999	Megan Gold
1965–1966	Verna Jean Miller and	1999–2000	Multiple division editors
	Elizabeth (Betsy) Sandel	2000–2001	Lindsey Johnson and
1966–1967	Elizabeth (Betsy) Sandel		Charissa Jelliff
1967–1968	Yolande McCurdy and	2001–2006	Multiple division editors
	Joyce Alwine	2006–2007	Chelsea White
1968–1969	Laurie Granzow	2007–2008	Jordan Costik
1969–1970	George Cruys	2008–2009	Shawn Christ and
1970–1971	Beverly Ann Hallman and		Mike Hoffman
	Barbara Saylor	2009–2010	Ashley Errickson
1971–1972	Barbara Saylor		
1972–1973	Barbara Saylor		
1973–1974	Ray Kennedy		
1974–1975	Lisa Kindig		
1975–1976	Lisa Kindig		
1976–1977	Beverly Rife		
1977–1978	A student editorial board		
1978–1979	Tina Taylor		
1979–1980	Elaine Shizkowski		
1980–1981	Cheryl Menges and Lori Engle		
1981–1982	A student editorial board		
1982–1983	Jodie Kramer		
1983–1984	Randy Thames		
1984–1985	Tami Crytzer		
1986–1987	Leslie Price		
1987–1988	Holly Gumpher		
1988–1989	Multiple division editors		
1989–1990	Multiple division editors		
1990–1991	Josh Tison		
1991–1992	Multiple division editors		
1992–1993	Brian Fox		

Falcon Flash Advisors

1961–1962	Cynthia Xanthopoulos
1963–1965	Emily Myers Keller
1965–1968	Patricia Lanshe
1968–1969	unconfirmed
1969–1970	Kathy Taylor and Mel Crook
1970–1973	Ron Zeigler
1973–1987	Nanette Willis (14 years)
1987–2006	David M. Gates (13 years)
2006–	Lena Russell

Falcon Flash Pot-Pourri

As a nod to history, below are limited samples from 1960 to 1992 *Flash* issues which provide a few snapshots of the times.

In the **spring of 1962** Russel Cassel, a ninth grader, won first prize in the Regional Future Farmers of America Speaking Contest at Millersville University with his speech "The Farmer and Fallout."

In **early 1964,** a roving reporter from the *Flash* asked "How do you like the Beatles?"

√ They're tuff (Corinne Davis, Judy Bell, Frank Shandor)   √ I don't like them (Bo Smith)

√ I never heard of them (Jack Musser, Mr. Longreen)   √ They should be stepped on (Mr. Lyter)

√ I get a kick out of watching them (Randy Kahler)   √ I think they're a little wild (Mike Strite)

April 1964 reports that Ron Good was Senior High and Jeannine Lehmer Junior High Grand Champions in the local Science Fair.

1967 notes the beginning of individual scheduling for students using a data processing system. This is also the year of the arrival of Mrs. Emily Keller's student teacher, Andrew Sullivan, the perpetrator of the Carol Channing Hoax (See "Pranks").

October 1967 heralds the Senior Talent Show, self-described as "the most psyched-up, souled-out presentation ever in its history of turned-on shows. The upcoming happening, which will not be a hang-up, is guaranteed to blow your mind." (Note the slang terms of the times!)

December 1967 announces National Honor Society's plans to sponsor a lyceum second semester with one or two speakers each month during last period. Tickets allotted for forty.

January 1968, the *Flash* prints a letter from Dan Dorsheimer, writing from Viet Nam:

> I'd like to give you my praises and the praises of my buddies over here in Viet Nam on the December copy of the "Flash." I'm referring to the article "The Thought of Christmas." I received it from Corinne Davies shortly after Christmas and as soon as I read that article I passed it around the squad. It's really great that you people back home think enough about us over here in a lonely, war-stricken country, to print something like that in your paper. Everything in it was true. When I received it our company was out in the field. We had just dug our fox holes and set up our overnight "hooches." I was reading the Flash by candlelight in my part of the "hooch" when I got to this article. After I read it, I passed it round, and everyone said the same as I; it was really great. The only thing that didn't apply to us was the temperature. It wasn't that hot. In fact, it was rather cool, but everything else is exactly as you described it. I enjoyed the rest of the paper too and was wondering if you could send it over every month. I'd greatly appreciate it. It would keep me informed on the happenings of the school and the sports program, too.
>
> With praise, PFC Dan Dorsheimer

May 28, 1970 offers an editorial highlighting some of the highjinks of the senior class and also announces that Debbie Hummel had signed with the Ice Capades.

Fall of '74 brings with it a new study hall system of honor study halls with students who do not need supervision. Also is the announcement of a system of Senior Release Time by which students with morning study halls can report to school late and with afternoon study halls, they may leave early. There is also the announcement of a school-community production, "Falcon Follies," billed as an old time vaudeville show.

November 1974's edition of *Know Your Schools,* announces the groundbreaking for an adaptive physical education/wrestling gymnasium. In addition, the school library was recognized by the National Library Week Commission, ranking first in the state because of their extensive programming.

1976 tells of a Pep Squad of nine members formed in September by Miss Joan Spire to address a need for better support of girls' athletics and to generally improve school spirit.

The **May 1978** issue reports that Student Council had proposed to the School Board that a drug policy be established. Because of the suspected sale and use of drugs in the school and in the Borough Park area, the Council believes guidelines should be set up to deal with illegal drug offenders. Also, the Honor Study Hall was discontinued because of space and "a few students who left the study hall and ran around the building."

The **June 1978** issue laments the confusing arena scheduling while the **December 1978** issue provides an article on the smoking policy and student smoking passes.

December 1982 announces the arrival of microcomputers.

February 1984 sees seven Gold Keys awarded to LD students, more than in any other area high school.

The **March 1985** *Know Your Schools* notes the recent acquisition of three word processors and four microcomputers that "has enabled the Business Department to begin the transition from manual or typewritten accounting and communicating into the modern electronic era of the business office."

In the **April 1985** *Falcon Flash* Jeff Peyton reminds us that the stage crew, along with costume, make-up, and publicity, will always be the unsung heroes of the musicals.

The **June 1985** issue publishes Jeff Miller's account of the Class Trip to a ski resort.

In **October of 1985,** the *Flash* announces that 109 courses would be dropped the following year, including 62 of the 65 mini and elective courses, because the courses didn't have "courses of study" written and because the high school was preparing for an accreditation evaluation by Middle States Association.

October 30 *Flash* reports that the Hummelstown Borough instituted "Parking by Permit Only" on some streets near the school because residents were tired of kids parking in front of borough residences, particularly when the school recently had built an additional parking lot to hold 55 more cars.

On **November 13, 1987,** a teen club, The Meltdown, opens on Eisenhower Boulevard in Harrisburg.

1988 marks the beginning of the Student Assistance Program, established to provide help to students with substance abuse or emotional problems. **1988** also sees the ongoing debate regarding study halls in general and particularly study halls in the auditorium because of the lack of a way to do homework (no desks or other writing surface) and enough lighting by which to see. The debate about hall passes also continues.

Another issue in the **Spring of 1988** reports the confusion generated when it was decided to denote the days by numbers rather than by days of the week, a popular practice in many schools.

The **December 14, 1990** *Falcon Flash* says that many students do not seem to know the words to the school's Alma Mater.

January 1991 sees the beginning of asbestos removal in the high school.

The **May 1991** issue of *The Insider*, the newsletter of the teachers' union, trumpets that "Four years after the initiation of a teacher mentoring program a New Teacher Induction Plan was introduced to utilize the transfer of the mentors back to the classroom."

The **February 6, 1991** *Flash* comments on the new extended homeroom period of five minutes.

The **March 12, 1992** *Flash* notes that seniors were requesting exemption from final exams if maintaining an average of 90% or better.

We were able to find very few issues of the *Flash* available after this time perhaps because of building renovations, turnover of advisors, fragility of the paper itself, and the nature of a newspaper as a "throwaway."

Yearbooks and the *Falconaire*

The social history of high school life is found in yearbooks and it is said that no matter what you do to escape your past or your identity, someone can find you in your yearbook. Even though information in some yearbooks is sketchy, we all return to the publication, seeking clues to what we think we remember, because information about what we were like back then helps make us understandable to each other now.

Yearbooks are important in that they are both the symbol and the evidence that we participated in something unique to ourselves. What is intriguing is that what is said about a person in the yearbook very likely will hold true throughout the person's life and, other than scrapbooks and diaries, which are individually personal, yearbooks remain the best "snapshot" of a particular school year. These documents are a keen measure of who we are and who we were, where and when we were, and with whom we were. They are also very important in a sense larger than ourselves. They situate us in time and place in both mind and heart.

Yearbooks are singular in that they are the record of a particular collection of young people who by happenstance are placed together. They tell the story of times spent in a hundred different ways in classes, clubs, music, sports, and simply common interests. They showcase clusters of people as well as individuals in their activities, recollecting the wins of a team or a band competition, as well as single accomplishments, such as breaking a record or being honored for a special milestone. Groups of friends are shown in poses with captions that suggest they will never, ever forget this particular moment with this particular set of friends.

The yearbook also serves as a larger social history. Nowhere else can one learn about traditions of a school community throughout the years, such as Class Day, Shelf Day or Senior Day, senior class gifts to the school, or yearbook dedications, and sometimes class officers, team captains and the like. It also is often the best answer to questions such as one that was raised at Lower Dauphin, "Where did the Habbyshaw Award originate?" The answer partially was found in the 1937 *Tatler* which identified the Honorable Mr. William E. Habbyshaw as a member of the school board; further research revealed that in the 1930s he served as a Representative in the State General Assembly.

The first high school yearbook, called "The Evergreen," appeared in 1845 in Waterford, NY. However, it was not until the 1920s that books began to include school activities and teachers, covering more than just the graduating seniors. Sales campaigns began in 1925 both in selling advertising and the yearbooks themselves. Fifty years later, in the 1970s, yearbooks began to break tradition, using more creativity in layout, text, coverage, and themes. Video yearbooks made their appearance in 1980, the 1990s began displaying a stronger journalistic style, and by the new century CDs began to make inroads.

Usually each new yearbook staff spends a lot of time deciding on a theme which should direct the style and content of the book. Sometimes a historical event suggests—or commands—a compelling theme, other times a universally popular song or a movie or a television program suggests the zeitgeist of a class, and occasionally the personality of a particular class is so evident that it becomes the yearbook theme.

For example, "Passing the Torch," as a tribute to John F. Kennedy, was the favorite theme for 1964 yearbooks throughout the nation, much as yearbooks in 1928 honored Charles A. Lindbergh. Yearbooks during World War II featured patriotism, classes of 1949 felt compelled to be "The 49ers," in honor of the original gold rush of 1849; those in 1960 welcomed Alaska and Hawaii to statehood, yearbooks during the Bicentennial were destined to commemorate 1776, while the LD Class of 1987 believed "It's a Jungle Out There," and Lower Dauphin Class of 2010 was expected to make note of the high school's Golden Anniversary.

Yearbook editorial staffs remember the long hours and the checklists and the proofing. Yearbook business staffs recall the sales campaigns and neither staff wanted the responsibilities of the other. Some yearbook themes lent themselves to appealing advertising campaigns, such as the "Bicentennial" edition, "FalconPark" (using HersheyPark), and the Class of 1977 that called itself "77 Up" (as in the soft drink 7-Up):

> The *Falconaire* staff held an un-contest to promote the 1977 yearbook. The promotion matched the theme of "77-Up, the Uncola." The school newspaper described this contest, "The un-winners of the un-contest were un-crowned at an un-pep rally un-ceremony on February 17, 1977. Melissa Noreiga and Dave Nestler became the Un-Queen and Un-King; first un-runners-up were Jean Ball and Mike Habig.

> This same year yearbook advertisements were being offered for the first time to parents with a full page offered at $60 under advisors Mr. Zeigler and Mrs. Witmer.

Then there was the 1978 yearbook campaign with the following announcements in the Daily Bulletins, the first on November 23, 1977:

> The yearbook selling campaign will end on December 2nd. Bring your money and place your order by this date. Don't be left out in the cold without a warm, comforting 1978 *Falconaire*.

> At the projected rate of inflation your yearbook, twenty years from now, should be worth $57.43. Buy one for a great investment. Or buy two and sell one for your twentieth year class reunion. Think of the profit you'll make!

The 1979 staff also had to defend its choice of theme. The December 1978 *Flash* covered the issue:

> "Cleaning Up a Rumor." In an interview with *Falconaire* yearbook editor, Jan Engle, the topic of discussion was "Is Hersheypark the theme of the Lower Dauphin 1979 yearbook?"

> Jan replied, "We would like to clear up this rumor. The yearbook staff used Hersheypark with the intention of bringing back memories of the amusement and challenge pertaining to what has happened during the year of 1978-79. Any suggestions can be given to Jan Engle, Mr. Zeigler, or Mrs. Witmer in room B-1."

Will the staff during the 1980s whose yearbook cover misspelled *Falconaire* ever get over it?

Whether they admit it or not, people remember with uncanny accuracy how many times their picture appeared in their yearbook and exactly what was written under their senior picture. An example is what was written in the 1976 yearbook (which is in the style of a daily journal) the day the 1975 yearbook arrived:

> "September 17, 1975: '75 *Falconaires* arrived today. They're really neat! Cover and color spread are impressive. Tried to count the number of times we appeared in a photograph (I made it 7 or 8 times)."

While yearbooks appear to be all the same, no two are alike. Styles of covers, layouts, and even what content is included changes from year to year, as there is no standard manual for producing a yearbook. It often comes as an unpleasant surprise to find that the yearbooks are not consistent in what is included, as any particular yearbook features what was important to its own class or its editorial staff. Most staffs don't see the importance of being historians as well as artists, causing difficulty to later readers. This, however, is not a new lack. *The Clarionette* (Clarion, PA) of 1925 did not identify anyone in their yearbook, not even the graduating seniors.

Years after graduation, chances are that what is said about a person in the yearbook still holds true. The book helps us remember both the best and the worse—or even the vicissitudes and ironies—of life in high school.

Falconaire Advisors

Mrs. Mary Lewin	1961
Mr. Dennis Musket	1962, 1963
Mr. Vernon Lyter	1964, 1965, 1966
Mrs. Priscilla Schwenk	1967, 1968, 1969[1]
Mrs. Schwenk and Miss Miriam Brandt	1970
Miss Margaret Yakimoff and Mr. Ronald Zeigler	1971
Miss Margaret Yakimoff	1972, 1973
Mrs. Judith Witmer and Mr. Ronald Zeigler	1974, 1975, 1976, 1977, 1978. 1979. 1980
Mr. Ronald Zeigler	1981, 1982, 1983, 1984, 1985
Miss Amy Bodley	1986, 1987
Mrs. Mary Clouser	1988
Miss Amy Bodley and Miss Alicia Imler	1989
Miss Alicia Imler / Mrs. Alicia Imler Morgret	1990, 1991, 1992, 1993, 1994, 2002–2009
Dr. Rudolph Sharpe	1995, 1996, 1997
Mrs. Nanette Willis Singer	1998
Mrs. Belinda Kolmansberger	1999, 2000, 2001
Mr. James Kalos	2010

---

[1] The first year to offer a supplement

Falconaire Editors-in-Chief

1961	No editor named[1]	1992	Tracy Gross and Dania Pazakis
1962	Ann Seaman	1993	Andria Zaia and Jill Trenn
1963	Vivian Lewin and Fred Shope	1994	Stephany Espenshade
1964	Susan Lawson	1995	Jennifer Wolfe and Lori Knackstedt
1965	Kathleen Verdelli	1996	Shanna Plouse
1966	Harold Johns	1997	Michael McBeth and Jaime Bolen
1967	Sandra Mersing	1998	Tony Frascella
1968	Hank Imhof	1999	Sarah McCloskey and Brandy Heckman
1969	Rachel Wywadis		
1970	Cindy Miller	2000	Tracy Thorpe
1971	Mary Frascella	2001	Samantha Carnathan
1972	Rebecca Hughes	2002	Sara Marian Seibert
1973	No editor identified	2003	Tara Russo
1974	Karen Emsweiler	2004	Roberta Murray and Michelle O'Donnell
1975	Suzanne Mader		
1976	Gwendolyn Black	2005	Maggie Boyd and Nina Landis
1977	Pamela Shadel	2006	Becca Snyder
1978	Melanie Boyer and David Early	2007	Megan Chirdon and Melissa Olson
1979	Jan Engle	2008	Kari Skitka and Sara Angle
1980	David Leaser	2009	Maura Sharkey and Marissa Goss
1981	Patricia Early	2010	Erin Cooney and Ellyn Hefflefinger
1982	Coleen Sieg and Cindy Cassel		
1983	Karen Bricker and Michelle Holubek		
1984	Michelle Holubek		
1985	Brenda Stoner		
1986	Deb Holubek		
1987	Lynne Hamann		
1988	Dawn Singley		
1989	Christine Gross		
1990	Corinne Fink and Kerry McGuinness		
1991	Christine Cassel and Erin Sokalsky		

[1] It is likely it purposely was decided not to name or elect an Editor-in-Chief of the first yearbook in a new high school which primarily drew students from Hummelstown Borough and students who would have attended Hershey High School. There was a concerted effort in Lower Dauphin High School to not identify students' home township or borough. In addition, It might be surmised that the faculty advisors also wisely did not want to single out one person since many of the students were still getting to know one another.

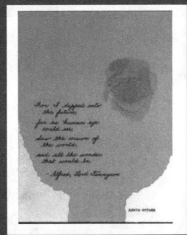

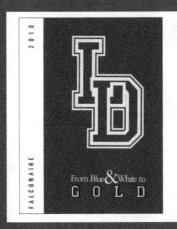

Falconaire Themes

1961	The Flight of the Falcon
1962	The Halls of Ivy
1963	Signs of the Times
1964	Passing the Torch
1965	The Influence of Lower Dauphin
1966	A Day at Lower Dauphin
1967	Keys to Life
1968	Footprints on the Sands of Time
1969	no theme
1970	Snapshots
1971	Symbols
1972	no theme
1973	no theme
1974	The Mind's Eye
1975	Moments and Hours
1976	The Bicentennial
1977	The Comics and Comic Books
1978	Lockers and Caricatures
1979	Falconpark
1980	Tomorrow
1981	The Yearbook as Newspaper
1982	LD Falcon: Private Investigator
1983	Trends, Fads, and Culture Highlights
1984	The Movies
1985	The Way We Were: The Silver Edition
1986	St. Elmo's Fire
1987	It's a Jungle Out There
1988	Destination Unknown
1989	One Step Ahead
1990	Looks At Us Now!
1991	Could You Imagine
1992	The Story of Our Lives
1993	A Time for …
1994	Hold on to the Memories
1995	A Year in the Life
1996	Subject to Change
1997	Together As One
1998	Onward Falcons
1999	The Tye That Binds
2000	Leaving Our Mark
2001	Back 2 Square 1
2002	Many Paths, One Destination
2003	The Difference Between Day and Night
2004	A Life in Lyrics
2005	Imagine
2006	More Than Meets the Eye
2007	Express Yourself
2008	Defining Moments
2009	Making of a Classic
2010	From Blue & White to Gold

Media Magazine

Media, Lower Dauphin's literary magazine, made its official debut in the fall of 1970.[1] Its maiden issue is dated September 8, 1970 and it first editor, as well as its founder, was Kenneth Leskawa '71. This information is memorialized in the October 1970 edition of the *Falcon Flash*:

> The magazine you found lying on your desk the first day of school was "Media." Unlike *Flash*, all articles in "Media" are subjectively written, and anyone may have an article published in it as long as it is signed and in good taste. "The purpose of this publication," according to Ken Leskawa, editor, "is to enable students to express themselves in prose or poetry. We recognize the individual's right to free speech. We will publish any essays, be they criticisms of the school or anything else. We do not support everyone's opinions because we naturally have opinions of our own." "Media" will come out every six weeks and will cost twenty-five cents.

The 1970s saw many innovative programs at Lower Dauphin High School, with this magazine being one that initially met some skepticism. Because a literary magazine was not typical for a public high school at that time, it is fitting to acknowledge the first year's founding staff, who held a belief that publishing a literary magazine had merit.

The Faculty Advisors for the launching issue were Mr. Allen Risser and Mr. William Linnane. Subsequent issues this first year show only the name of Mr. Risser as Advisor. The following are the members of the first staff:

> Editor, Kenneth Leskawa; Assistant Editor and Artwork, R. S. Pierce; Distribution Manager, Douglas Stauffer; Photographer, John Wert; Contributing Writers: Barbara Biessel, Kim Brightbill, Cassie Cally, Charles Hummer, Barbara Larsen, Carol Larsen, Jerry Lesher, Alice Rhoads, and Joseph Popp; Typists: Hope Rhoads and Linda Leskawa

Class[2]	Editor	Art Editor	Advisor
1971	Ken Leskawa	R. S. Pierce	Mr. Allen D. Risser
1972[3]	unconfirmed	unconfirmed	unconfirmed
1973[4]	Sue Eshelman	Warren Nisley	Mr. Charles Cole
1974	Sue Eshelman	Warren Nisley	Mr. Charles Cole
1975	Karen Imhof	Warren Nisley	Mr. Charles Cole
1976	Janet Johnson	Janet Johnson	Mr. Charles Cole
1977	Herb Schaffner	Meg Ruddle	Mr. Charles Cole

---

[1] There was a precursor for this formal date of publication as there is evidence in a newspaper article in September 1970 which identifies Karen Shertzer '70 as "editor of the literary magazine" the previous year. This could not be confirmed nor is *Media* noted as an activity in the yearbook, although at least one other person lists *Media* as an activity in which she participated, Mike Orsini '70 also mentions this magazine; thus, it is very likely there was an earlier launching of some note.

[2] Because some of the information came from individuals without concrete evidence, the years when editors are named may not be their year of graduation; further, editors were not always seniors.

[3] In the fall of 1972, the *Falcon Flash* posted a notice that *Media* was not at present in existence and that the *Flash* would dedicate a page of its Christmas issue to student creative writing.

[4] "The Media staff is still in its [re]organizational stages. Anyone who can write poems or stories, type, or draw and is interested in working on *Media* should contact Mr. Cole in A-12."

1978	Stephanie Hoover	Jeanne Snavely	Mr. Charles Cole
1979	Steve Bobb	Doug Grier	Mr. Charles Cole
1980	Brenda Grimm	Carrie Smith	Mr. Charles Cole
1981	Ann Snyder/Leslie Euker	none	Mr. Charles Cole
1982	Tom Houtz	Erris Moss	Mr. Charles Cole
1983	Jodie Kramer	Mike Lowe/Andrea Sim	Mr. Charles Cole
1984	Catherine Clark	Darlene Snoke	Mr. Charles Cole
1985	Venus Klinger	unconfirmed	Mr. Charles Cole
1986	Ann Schwentker Lori Magaro/Matt Williams	Melissa Fry	Mr. Charles Cole
1987	Matthew Williams/Pam Schwentker	Martha Anderson	Mr. Charles Cole
1988	Pamela Schwentker	Brett Jenkins	Mr. Charles Cole
1989	Holly Feeney/ Rebecca Simmons	Erin Pudlowski	Mr. Charles Cole
1990	Jeremy Fox	Shelagh Dugan	Mr. Charles Cole
1991	Jeremy Fox/Carri Elliott	unconfirmed[5]	Mr. Charles Cole
1992	Beth Grant/Heather Kohler		Mr. Charles Cole
1993	unconfirmed		Mr. Charles Cole
1994	Michael Darowish		Mr. Charles Cole
1995	multiple editors[6]		Mr. Charles Cole
1996	Gretchen Haupt/Lisa Black		Mr. Charles Cole
1997	Daniel Floyd, Jamie Sheaffer		Mrs. Margaret DeAngelis
1998	Jennifer Sheaffer/Jessica Ordich		Mr. Charles Cole
1999	Jessica Ordich		Mr. Charles Cole
2000	multiple editors		Mr. Charles Cole
2001	Abby Snyder/Annie Zaino		Mr. Charles Cole
2002	multiple editors		Mr. Charles Cole
2003	multiple editors		Mr. Charles Cole
2004	Caitlin Downs	Amanda Leer	Mr. Charles Cole
2005	Sara Joyce		Mrs. Karen Burk
2006	Laura Bierbower		Mrs. Karen Burk
2007	Laura Bierbower		Mrs. Karen Burk
2008	Laura Bierbower		Mrs. Karen Burk
2009	no magazine this year		
2010	Chris Pearson		Mrs. Karen Burk
2011	Kayla Stouffer		Mrs. Karen Burk

[5] It appears that after 1991 art editors were no longer designated.

[6] In some of the latter years, there was a different editor for each issue. This list contains names of only those who were editors for the year, not the issue.

Summit Achiever Lynn Taylor '65

Lynn Taylor is a potter of national acclaim. Her interest is porcelain of the 18th and early 19th century with a Chinese influence. Self-taught, she began creating pottery in the mid-1970s and established Kingston Pottery, named for Kingston Plantation in Londonderry Township where her family lives. Her work is greatly admired and considered a specialty, commanding attention of serious collectors and has been commissioned by Presidents Gerald Ford, Bill Clinton, George Bush and George W. Bush, among other luminaries, as well as being featured in national magazines. One of the most recent venues in which her work was shown was "The Gathering of Craftsmen," sponsored by the New England Historical Connections, on September 7, 2012.

A feature article in "The Patriot-News" (February 12, 2012) notes: "Lynn is self-taught and has studied both public and private collections of 17th and 18th century pottery. Her work includes limited editions which are original and one-of-a-kind pieces influenced by historic fine ceramics. Many of her pieces are both functional and decorative. Her trademark reticulated work is meticulously hand cut. Starting with raw materials—clay, pigments, and glaze—each piece of Kinston Pottery is handmade. Lynn's pots are wheel-thrown. Spouts, handles, and finials are hand sculpted using

traditional potting techniques, all with attention to graceful proportion. The painted decoration is freehand and each design has a name that reflects its historic influence: chinoiserie, peacock tail, frigate ships, and wan-li, or bird on rock.

Lynn Taylor creates her work from kalin, a mixture of specific clays. and specializes in four patterns that mostly use cobalt blue and chromium, or green, "steadfast" colors that won't change when fired. She also makes her own paint and glazes.

Last year (2012) Lynn was honored as a Distinguished Alumna of her Alma Mater; she is married to classmate Jim Szymborski which makes them members of the group designated as Lower Dauphin Sweethearts, listed in the Lower Dauphin Alumni Association section of this book.

To view Lynn Taylor's work, please visit **www.kingstonpottery.com.**

School Governance

Student Governance

Student Governance and Policies

Like the student government of most other schools in the country, Lower Dauphin High School's student government is its Student Council. Unlike many other schools, however, Lower Dauphin students were given a lot of leeway in self-governance as early as 1967. Students have continued to have a strong voice in matters relative to school life as will be attested to in the following samples, only a few in the long history Lower Dauphin has held in listening to its students.

1961. The *Falcon Flyer*, May 1961 contained an article about the one-way traffic pattern initiated in C-Wing because of the traffic congestion of students stopping at their lockers between classes.

1967. When a number of new policies were instituted in the fall of 1967, following the lead of Dr. Henry R. Hoerner, the district's first superintendent who took the helm on July 1, 1966, student reactions were reported in the December 1967 issue of the district publication, *Know Your Schools*. We like

- ◆ … that we have greater freedom and responsibility with the reading room available for casual reading with a member of student council in charge and a flexible eighth period.
- ◆ … that the school exhibits new life interest and discussion.
- ◆ … granting students the freedom to execute their own ideas through the Student Forum.
- ◆ … the new eighth period—the best thing that could have happened.
- ◆ … that music is now a credited class and art has become a part of the school just as the sports are.
- ◆ … that students and teachers show pride in each other.
- ◆ … the close connections between the student body and faculty.

Fall 1973. When the band for Homecoming did not appear at the dance, the students made the best of it and the Student Council was commended by the school newspaper for its handling of the situation and its decision to refund all ticket money.

October 1976. A new structure for Student Council was established with four officers and with each class represented by five senators rather than by homerooms. In addition, Positive Concern Sheets were initiated for students to directly convey any concern to Council.

December 1976. During the Christmas Season the Student Council held a homeroom decorating contest, decorated the main hallways, held a Tri-County Children's Party, and collected food for needy families.

October 1977. Student Council and the Adult Booster Club gave the school a huge "Home of the Falcons" sign.

May 1978. Student Council proposed to the School Board that a drug policy be established because of the suspected sale and use of drugs in the school and in Borough Park.

Late 1970s. The ninth grade structure underwent more changes than any other grade in the school district. Initially ninth grade was a part of the junior high, which was housed on the east side of the building in Wings C, D, and E. In the late 1970s into the 1980s the ninth grade was its own entity, with its own principal. It was neither junior high nor senior high, based on the premise that ninth graders would do better by themselves. This entity even had its own ninth grade newspaper, *Hot Line*, which debuted in March 1979.

October 1981. Student Council held one of its many Student Teas for New Students.

December 1982. Student Council installed vending machines in the cafeteria.

December 1982. Everyone talks about the "AEP Room" and everyone—even those who spend no time there—know about this in-school suspension room which most termed "the ape room," an unfortunate nickname for this room originally established to eliminate out-of-school suspension. Alternative Education Program (AEP), established in December of 1982, and officially to open in 1983, according to *The Flash*, was to serve as a means of correcting the behavior of disruptive students.

October 29, 1985 *Evening News.* Mr. Staver, Dean of Students, was named as Student Advocate. Should a student be accused of a crime serious enough for which the question of suspension or even expulsion would be raised, that student would be called before the School Board. Mr. Staver would speak on behalf of the student, to assure his/her student's rights were protected.

October 1987. The Hummelstown Borough instituted "Parking by Permit Only" because residents were tired of students parking on nearby streets even though the school had built an additional parking lot to hold 55 more cars. Council lobbied for more parking spaces.

December 1992. While there were not many articles in the school newspaper about the Alternative Education Program, the *Falcon Flash* wrote, "The AEP Room was designed for any type of student who will not follow classroom procedures or who will not follow student conduct or attendance regulations as specified in the school district printed policies. Due to the fact that new and more rigid policies are being enforced this year, the number of offenses has increased in comparison to last year."

1992-1993 School Year Discipline Policy. During the 1992-93 school year there was a change in the discipline process. If a teacher had a problem with an "unruly" student caught in a Level I or Level II offense, he/she was to handle it in the classroom. If the student's misconduct continued, the teacher was to contact the parent. If the student still did not cooperate, he/she was to be sent to a guidance counselor. This was supposed to impact behavioral change. Instead, it led to confusion.

November 4, 1996. Changes in policies included "enforcement of hall passes, not leaving homeroom before the designated time, not hanging out in the cafeteria, and a stricter enforcement of no smoking, class cutting, or drinks in classes."

December 17, 1999. Plans were formulated for tighter security in the school buildings. These included ID badges, a stricter dress code, new attendance procedures and forms, a "guard" station, television security monitors, a full-time guard on the premises, and building access limited to the front of the building through a designated entrance area for identification verification.

The 2001 *Falconaire* noted that as the school year started the students found that camera and door alarms had been installed as security monitoring.

October 23, 2006. New rules were established on handling absences. Guidelines were published in the school calendar which was distributed to all students and available as well on the district's website. "While the school prefers that students do not miss school for family trips, there is a procedure by which the building principal can approve a trip not to exceed seven consecutive school days. There are specific procedures to be followed when students have been or are expected to be absent, including consequences for chronic absences. In emergency closings the school uses an automatic dialing system to contact parents through landline phones, mobile phones, text messages, and emails." As in most schools, there also were policies in place addressing student behavior such as bullying, weapons, corporal punishment, tobacco, drugs and alcohol, electronic devices, locker searches, and student dress, most of which were not major concerns fifty years ago.

Student Council

Student Councils are defined as the governing body of a high school population. They have as much power as a school administration is willing to imbue. More often than not they are the central committee for planning Homecoming and dealing with issues that the administration may want discussed by a larger representative group of students. It remains an honor to serve, but Student Councils typically have no actual authority.

In the early years of Lower Dauphin High School each homeroom had a representative to the Council; however, in the fall of 1976 a new, more manageable structure was established with four officers, and each class represented by five senators from the class. This number has continued to change throughout the year, more recently to nine. The 1961 *Falconaire* does not provide any information as to the activities of Student Council that first busy year, but the members no doubt had a voice in planning some of the new activities and processes.

A sampling of Student Council's activities includes the following:

- ◆ **1962.** Aided other clubs and organizations, sponsored dances, settled students' problems.
- ◆ **1963.** In addition to the above, published the student handbook, operated the snack bar.
- ◆ **1964.** Promoted Christmas spirit with displays in showcase windows, trees in front of the auditorium, a nativity scene, and a scene of a fireplace and stockings.
- ◆ **1965.** New duties included control of hall traffic and sponsorship of assemblies. On Arbor Day, April 30, 1965, the first tree was planted on the LD campus, an event presided over by Bill Pinkerton, Student Council President.
- ◆ **1970.** Held a summer retreat where the members approved formation of a student-faculty advisory board composed of two parents, two teachers and three students; made plans to register students to vote in school elections, held a faculty tea, dances, a fun night, a car rally, a spring festival, and Homecoming. The Student-Faculty Advisory Board had a meeting scheduled by December. And Homecoming became an extravaganza with the initiation of a parade of floats entered in competition.

- **1971.** The *Falconaire* described Council's primary objective as "better relations between students and faculty." Sometime during the 1970s a new tradition, which occurred annually thereafter, hosted a "New Student Tea" as an evening's orientation for new students and their parents.

- **1974.** Made a call for the return of school spirit along with the establishment of a Student Clinic through the efforts of its President and the guidance of Mr. Kenneth Staver. Council also sponsored a fund-raising basketball game and held a fun night.

- **1976.** In December Council sponsored a homeroom Christmas decorating contest, Tri-County Children's party, and a food drive for needy families. These holiday activities were conducted annually for many years.

- **1979.** Sold T-shirts, sponsored events, and gained "extra privileges."

- **1982.** Took the initiative in the installation of vending machines, both as a school service and as a revenue stream.

- **1985.** Began sponsoring Daffodil Days and coordinating school-wide elections.

- **1987–88.** There was a minor controversy regarding the role of Student Council. This is addressed in more detail under "Student Governance and Policies."

- **1996.** In December Megan Gold wrote in the *Falcon Flash,* "Friday it rained, and I was glad to see that, despite cancellation of the floats, school spirit remained.

- **2000.** In October the *Flash* quoted Missy Kolter, Vice-president of Council and the Homecoming Chair for Decorations at Homecoming, "…this year's theme, 'Reflections of Time,' is more distinctive than in past years." In addition, Council held a food drive, collected bulletins every morning, handled the announcement board at the school's entrance, and sponsored a breakfast for the teachers.

- **2001.** Council President saw as their goal "…to ensure that we leave a lasting impression on the student body."

- **2002.** Council believed their goal was to improve LD and the community and voice the concerns of their peers.

- **2004.** Council was engaged in freshman orientation, food drives, Data Match, spirit week, and pep rallies in addition to their governance responsibilities.

- **2006.** Council led a food drive that filled three trucks and a car with nonperishable food items.

- **2007.** The first Mini-Thon was initiated in March.

- **2009.** Council founded the Mark French Dodge Ball Tournament.

- **2010.** Council noted that "without this beneficial group of students (Student Council), Lower Dauphin would miss out on many fun and exciting events."

Student Council Presidents and Advisors

Presidents	Advisors
1960–1961: Barry Broadwater	Mr. James Burchfield; Miss Kathyrn Zeiters
1961–1962: Ted Eshenour	Mr. James Burchfield; Miss Kathyrn Zeiters
1962–1963: Rick Weaver	Mr. James Burchfield; Miss Kathyrn Zeiters
1963–1964: Michael Farling	Mr. James Burchfield; Miss Kathyrn Zeiters
1964–1965: William Pinkerton	Mr. James Burchfield; Miss Kathyrn Zeiters
1965–1966: Lester Ratcliff	Mr. James Burchfield; Miss Kathyrn Zeiters
1966–1967: David Lidle	Mr. Kenneth Staver; Miss Kathyrn Zeiters
1967–1968: Edwin Laudermilch	unconfirmed
1968–1969: unconfirmed	unconfirmed
1969–1970: Thomas Seaman	Mr. Gary Van Dine
1970–1971: Nick DeRosa	Mr. John Croll
1971–1972: Mark Hughes	Mr. John Croll; Mr. Gary Van Dine
1972–1973: Richard Hivner	Mr. John Croll; Mr. Steven Messner
1973–1974: Steve Rhoads	Messrs. John Croll; Steven Messner; Charles Van De Water
1974–1975: Mark Leaser	Messrs. John Croll; Steven Messner; Charles Van De Water
1975–1976: Robert Hivner	Messrs. John Croll; Steven Messner; Charles Van De Water
1976–1977: Sally Fry	Mr. John Croll; Mr. Steven Messner
1977–1978: Kelly Dibeler	Mr. Steven Messner; Mr. Charles Van De Water
1978–1979: Cheryl Cassel	Mr. Steven Messner; Mr. Charles Van De Water
1979–1980: Patricia Stare	Mr. Charles Cole
1980–1981: Sherrie Sylvester	Mr. John Croll; Mr. Charles Cole
1981–1982: Sherry Reed	Mr. Charles Cole
1982–1983: Carl Law	unconfirmed
1983–1984: Larri Ann Condran	Mr. Charles Cole
1984–1985: April DeMuth	Mr. John Croll
1985–1986: Julia Petrina	Mr. John Croll; Mr. Charles Cole
1986–1987: Amy Wallish	Mr. Charles Cole
1987–1988: Lea Knapik	Mr. Charles Cole; Mrs. Susan Ewing
1988–1989: unconfirmed	unconfirmed
1989–1990: Kerry McGuinness	Mr. James Brandt; Mrs. Rebecca Martin
1990–1991: Nicholas Poppy	Mrs. Alicia Imler; Mrs. Rebecca Martin
1991–1992: Tracy Gross	Mrs. Alicia Imler; Mrs. Rebecca Martin
1992–1993: Amy Petrina	Mrs. Rebecca Martin
1993-1994: Stephany Espenshade	Mrs. Melody Lovelidge; Mrs. Barbara Kuhlen
1994-1995: Anita Ketty	unconfirmed
1995-1996: Michael Slatt	uncomfirmed

1996-1997: Patricia Kelley	Mrs. Anne Bocian
1997-1998: Nathan Barton	Mrs. Anne Bocian
1998-1999: Ryan White	unconfirmed
1999-2000: Caliann Bogovic	Ms. Judy Baumgardner
2000-2001: Chris Stoer	Mrs. Tanya Dreon; Ms. Anne Bocian
2001-2002: Missy Kolter	Mrs. Tanya Dreon; Ms. Anne Bocian
2002-2003: Alisha Cain	Mrs. Tanya Dreon; Ms. Anne Bocian
2003-2004: Joshua Young	Mrs. Tanya Dreon; Ms. Anne Bocian
2004-2005: unconfirmed	Mrs. Tanya Dreon; Ms. Anne Bocian
2005-2006: Joe Skitka	Mrs. Melody Lovelidge; Mrs. Glenda Stahl
2006-2007: Ian Gilchrist	Mrs. Melody Lovelidge; Mrs. Glenda Stahl
2007-2008: Becky Mayes	Mrs. Becky Cassel and Mrs. Darby Fischl
2008-2009: Clay Cooper & Leah Cover	Mr. Douglas Grove and Mr. Scott Payonk
2009-2010: Leah Cover	Mr. Douglas Grove and Mr. Scott Payonk
2010-2011: Shelby Jones & Stephen Mazich	Mr. Douglas Grove and Mr. Scott Payonk
2011-2012: Amie Diamond	Mr. Douglas Grove and Mr. Scott Payonk
2012-2013: Analisa Scott	Mr. Douglas Grove and Mr. Scott Payonk

The Student Advisory Board (later the Principal's Advisory Council) and Spirit Club

The first mention of a Student Advisory Board is found in the March 1970 *Falcon Flash* in an article that begins, "Mr. Osevala, together with his student advisory committee, is starting a new program at LD to reduce the possibility of theft."

In the fall of 1986 following the Superintendent's Forum, Mrs. Judith Witmer, Assistant Principal, established a new **Student Advisory Board** as a means by which students could address academic concerns as well as make recommendations for improved school climate. Its initial charge was to address negative situations in the cafeteria. A representative selection of student leaders was invited to participate and included two students from each grade.

The group's major accomplishment its first year was conducting a smoking survey; the resulting recommendation was that the outdoor area adjacent to the driver's education trailer continue to be used by students with smoking passes or that A-Wing lavatory be designated for smoking. A further recommendation was that harsher penalties be issued to violators. (*Falcon Flash*, January 20, 1987)

By spring the Board had arranged for locks on the stalls in the girls' lavatories and benches for the areas outside the high school, a gift requested of the Class of 1986.

In the fall of 1987 membership to the Board was expanded to include three representatives of the sophomore, junior, and senior classes, one from the freshman class, all four class presidents, the student council president, and the two school board representatives.

In October the Advisory Board sponsored a Halloween dress-up day as part of school spirit and planned for a winter sports pep rally. An article in the *Falcon Flash* (October 16, 1987) reported that the group "tackles issues dealing with problems at the high school and any concerns that students may have about current issues at Lower Dauphin."

In November the Board took on the challenge of devising a traffic pattern for the passing of classes. Because of the narrow halls, traffic flow was a problem. The suggestion of "no stopping at lockers" between classes was met by a cry of "loss of inherent student rights." Discussion of passing outside was not optimal because of potential vandalism to cars. Further suggestions included patio blocks placed between wings, placing benches in the area between the library and A-Wing, and that students with Honor Passes be permitted to use the Class of 1986 Circle in front of the school.

In mid-November a headline in the *Flash* noted "Student Council Seeks Identity," questioning the roles of Student Council and the Advisory Board, asking if Council should be leading the student body or running social events, e.g., Homecoming. "A popular allegation is that the Board has been doing the Council's job," Mr. Appleby said, adding that the Council needed to decide its role because at the beginning of the school year, he had asked them to deal with the assembly and smoking problem but they were too busy planning Homecoming.

Later in November the Board reviewed recommendations from the Student Forum on school assembly programs; members were charged to each come with two suggestions on educating the student body regarding the purpose and expected behavior during assemblies.

In December the Principals' Council (comprised of the three principals) vetoed changes in the recommended hall passing procedure. The Student Advisory Board then reviewed the suggestions for assembly programs, also to be submitted to the Principals' Council.

In late January 1988 because of poor student behavior at the previous week's basketball game, the Advisory Board was faced with a situation regarding their planned Winter Sports Pep Rally. To address this issue Mrs. Witmer formed a **Spirit Club** and by February the Principals' Council noted that student behavior had improved due to organized efforts of the Spirit Club.

Spring 1988 saw the Advisory Board waiting for a response from Student Council for the Board's plan to raise funds for a new falcon mascot costume. The Board also reviewed revisions in the Student Handbook, making a number of positive suggestions. As unrelated student concerns on limited parking continued, student John Talaber met with Borough Council.

The September 1988 *Flash* reported that the "Student Advisory Board is Back in Session," with its focus on academic excellence aligned to the reorganization of the building administrators. This placed Mr. Appleby as Supervising Principal and Mrs. Witmer as Principal for Academic Improvement. In the spring of 1989, Dr. Witmer initiated the formation of a Parent Academic Advisory Board whose purpose was to discuss academic concerns parents had and to make suggestions to the secondary school administration.

The next available written record of the Student Advisory Board is its minutes of January 1990, noting that the recommended changes to study halls being subject-centered (e.g., English, Social Studies, etc.)

had been sent to the Principals' Council. The Board also improved the traffic flow in the cafeteria by changing the direction of the lunch line entrance, ran a Save the Silverware campaign, and revised the Senior Awards System. The Board was then informed of Lower Dauphin's engagement in the planning of the Coalition of Essential Schools project and was asked to review a report "Essential Elements for Effective Schooling" and to recommend which areas should receive initial attention.

By fall of 1990 Dr. Witmer had been promoted to a position at the District Office and Mr. Appleby disbanded the Student Advisory Board. However two years later, the *Falcon Flash* (November 20, 1992) announced that he had formed a **Principal's Advisory Council** to discuss items such as hall passes, school spirit, installation of Channel One, student parking, and the closing of the library during periods when classes were scheduled to use it. Mr. Appleby continued the Advisory as did Mr. Hughes and it continued through 2008 after which it was not re-convened.

In the fall of 2003 Assistant Principal David Weuster convened a large representative group of students to identify problems within the high school and to recommend solutions through a program for student problem identification and resolution of issues together (**SPIRIT**) sponsored by the Dauphin County Human Relations Commission. Students, along with 15 adult facilitators, met for two half days, at the end of which students had identified those problems they had agreed were most important. Plans were made to continue meeting and to enact possible solutions.

Student and Superintendent Forums

1966. In September Dr. Henry R. Hoerner, Superintendent, held a pre-school meeting with selected faculty and student leaders at Dory's to discuss common goals. In September 1967 Dr. Hoerner presided again at a meeting at Meadowbrook; these meetings became the precursor of Student Forums which were formalized in 1969.

1972. Student Forums during this time were held at the Hershey Motor Lodge. The theme was "How the School Could be Improved" through the teachers, course offerings, student attitude, use of public property, and parent reaction to the school.

1974. Forum items for discussion included free time lunch for senior high, junior high student council, smoking area for senior high students, student responsibility, faculty and administrative decision-making, attendance problems, and the importance of athletics.

1975. This year's Forum centered on a new attendance policy. Suggestions included that standard percentages be established for school or class attendance and failure to meet those standards would result in a student's receiving no grade for the course which, in turn, would mean the course could be repeated for credit.

1976. Held at the Towne and Country Restaurant, topics included school morale, discipline, activities, teacher-student rapport, and community-school relations. The *Falcon Flash* editor, Beverly Rife, wrote an editorial on the number of options students have to voice their concerns: "We have Student Council, Student School Board Representatives, student newspaper, and the Superintendent's Forum. Lower Dauphin administrators and faculty are, for the most part, very receptive to the views of students."

1978. This year's topics were leadership, teacher/student behavior, individualized student program goals, attendance policy, and how L.D. can remain "Number One."

1980. Strong student support for strict administration of school attendance and disciplinary policies emerged as a central theme of student discussion at the Superintendent's Forum.

1981. Topics included the school grading system, channels for dealing with student-teacher problems, the new four-year high school program, school trip policy, and a lunch program.

1984. This Student Forum had Falcon Pride as it theme. The following were mentioned as strengths of LD: positive social environment, variety of academic programs, friendly and helpful student population, well-balanced faculty, diverse extracurricular program, fine transportation system. Students especially noted the facilities which add to the success of programs and the opportunities such as work release, field trips, student exchange programs, and the Capitol Classroom Program. An article by Jeff Peyton discussed the above, adding that other items discussed were the development of a brochure to market LD to prospective homeowners, and the preparation of a handout for the orientation of new students. He added, "However, this year's forum included a new dimension. No negative comments were to be 'entertained on the floor.' Instead of a quality forum, where the students could have constructive input into the workings of Lower Dauphin, the end product was the students and faculty members patting themselves on their backs in front of the school board members and administration. Falcon Pride was a poor choice of theme for a Student Forum. One can't find his own mistakes if one isn't humble enough to recognize them."

1986. The Forum topics included class weighting, hall passes (top priority), summoning students via the PA system's loud speaker (it is disruptive), parking passes, required grade point averages for extra-curricular activities, heterogeneous grouping of social studies classes.

1987. Billed as the 20th Annual School Forum, recommendations from the theme "You Can Make a Difference" included the following suggestions: phase out smoking areas, physical education grades not to be included in the GPA, those on sports teams to be allowed a study hall instead of PE, sex education moved from 11th to 9th grade, and keep the same guidance counselor throughout the three years of high school.

1988. Topics for the theme "Stand and Be Counted" included student parking, Second Honors Award, displaying student art in the library, Key Club, and respect for others.

1989. In the spring semester of 1989 a new **Superintendent's Forum** was organized to meet directly with the Superintendent four times a year. Items for the inaugural meeting were commencement speakers, study halls in the auditorium, locker rooms, vandalism, cafeteria, and smoking. The "original" Student Forum was also held in May with a focus on rights and responsibilities.

1989-1990. Items discussed in the fall included impact of CAIU students, LD's image, communication, student parking, fund-raising, cafeteria lunches, building maintenance, team teaching, open campus, pep rallies, revitalizing the Spirit Club, state of locker rooms and restrooms, tennis court lights, wall colors, functions of a school board, sprucing up the school, building program, school desks, writing center, and a recycling project.

1990-1991. *Know Your Schools* noted that the Forum, "has been effective in its goals, including installation of doors on the boys' bathroom stalls, cleaning up graffiti and drinking fountains, and increasing the size of meal portions. However, many of the discussion topics kept resurfacing, revealing that many situations did not change. Some new topics included high school renovations, proposed new middle school, field trips, AP classes, new resource material for the library, mounting student art in the library, seminars and art series, and the method by which GPAs are computed. Arguably the most effective meeting was on February 11 when the students expressed their dismay at their lack of empowerment.

1991–1992. This was a year of change with Mr. Frankford serving as Interim Superintendent for a semester followed by the hiring of Dr. Jeffrey Miller who continued the practice of meeting with students to discuss issues.

Currently there is no Superintendent's Forum/Student Forum.

Student School Board Representatives

Year	Name	Year	Name
1974–75	Debra Glovola, Mark Leaser	1992–94	Stephany Espenshade
1975–76	Gwendolyn Black, Wynn Willard	1993–95	Anita Ketty
1976–77	Marilyn Heffley, Jeffrey Gesford	1994–96	Samantha Barnhart
1977–78	Kristie Myers, Gary Kirman	1995–97	Christopher Rutt
1978–79	Andrea Yannone, Jay Steinruck	1996–98	Abigail Martin
1979–80	Theresa Frascella, Keith Garrison	1997–99	Jonathan Pinkerton
1980–81	Sue Lightner, Kevin Bobb	1998–00	Scott Woodell
1981–82	Craig Camasta, Carol Dillon	1999–01	Amy Schneider
1982–83	Diana Hoover, Lamar Eifert	2000–02	Melissa Kolter
1983–84	Katherine Evans, Steven Ebersole	2001–03	Rachel Myers
1984–85	Susan Borelli, Gilbert Petrina	2002–04	Joshua Young
1985–86	Julie Petrina, Kevin Strawser	2003–05	Casey Stokes
1986–87	Matthew Espenshade and Gregory Hostetter	2004–06	Colin Matichak
		2005–07	Kelly Coupal
1987–88	Jenifer Petrina, Bobbi Jo Strawser	2006–08	Rebecca Mayes
1988–89	Bobbi Jo Strawser, Jodi Pringle	2007–09	Samantha Houck
1989–90	Janay Miller, Jodi Pringle	2008–10	Delia Marks
1990–92	Stephanie Teets	2009–11	Kyle Stauffer
1991–93	Amy Petrina		

While it is not known when the first high school(s) invited students to serve as unelected members of school boards, Lower Dauphin High School likely was one of the pioneers when Dr. Henry Hoerner instituted this position during the 1974–1975 school year. The first student representatives were both seniors; in the school year 1987–1988 the practice was changed to appointing one junior and one senior. Beginning with Bobbi Jo Strawser (1987-88) each representative then served for two years. Student representatives have a voice, but not a vote.

Study Halls, Homerooms, and Scheduling Classes

The issue of Study Halls is a constant. Approaches to them, both philosophically and from the viewpoint of scheduling, wax and wane. Some students view these scheduled periods as a time to study and do homework while others see them as an opportunity to socialize with friends.

As early as November 1966 (and likely even before this recorded date) Judy Williams suggested in the *Falcon Flash* that there be two kinds of study halls, a quiet one for studying and one for socializing.

In September 1967 *Know Your Schools* announced a new method of individualized scheduling based on individual ability and interest rather than being assigned to a particular section. This scheduling would be produced through a data processing system. Mr. Kenneth Staver, Dean of Students, said that under the new system a student's entire range of abilities would be considered and that there could be business students taking academic subjects and vice versa. Mr. Staver said he believed that this system would make school time for the students both more pleasurable and more profitable to them personally.

The November 1969 issue noted how overcrowded the school was and how bad auditorium study halls were in general.

An editorial in the October 1970 *Flash* described a new course selection system, with course offerings increasing from 86 courses to 210. It noted the difficulties and time-consuming task in making course changes. Other problems included students discovering they didn't have enough credits or courses to graduate or the student who had 20 study halls a week the first quarter. The staff writer noted only two advantages to this system, freedom and variety, as the courses are divided into 6, 9, 18, and 36 weeks.

The February 1971 *Flash* polled the students on their views on the course changes, particularly "Mini Courses." The students replied that there were a lot of problems with scheduling and that some course descriptions were misleading.

In February 1973 a new system of activity bus passes went into effect and each student involved in an after school activity was given a pass with his photo and designation. Students were to give the pass to their bus drivers who, in turn, collected them and returned them to the issuing teacher.

In the fall of 1973 a new study hall system was initiated. According to the *Flash*, "Honor study halls are for those budgeting their time wisely and not causing mass riots or even wild disturbances. Study halls in the auditorium or cafeteria would allow a person to talk without bothering the whole of A, B, or H wings. This was followed by an article on October 12 noting that the honor study halls, "unsupervised in the auditorium and cafeteria, seem to be running well."

The fall of 1973 (*Flash*, October 12) also saw the beginning of something called "Release Time" by which seniors with morning study halls need not report until the time of their first class and seniors with afternoon study halls could leave school early. If this worked well, sophomores and juniors might be added. According to student Ray Kennedy, "The educational program here at Lower Dauphin is lending itself more toward the idea of an open school system. As a student body, we must accept new responsibilities and not abuse privileges. If a student has new ideas, he should present them to the administration or take his ideas to student government for action."

Sometime in the mid-1970s arena scheduling was introduced by which students registered in the gymnasium, going from "station to station" to register for a particular course, much as had been the pattern in colleges for years. In June an article in the *Flash* lamented the stress generated by arena scheduling.

By May 1978 the honor study halls had disappeared, the privilege revoked because of lack of space and some students who abused the privilege by using the time to "run around." (May *Falcon Flash*)

The main issue in the 1980s was the ongoing debate regarding hall passes, followed by complaints about study halls, that the auditorium was too dark for studying. The *Flash* noted that classrooms were required to have 30-49 foot candles of light, and the auditorium had only ten.

In the October 1985 issue of the *Flash*, Kevin Strawser wrote a commentary, "Did You Ever Wonder Why?" about the extension of the passing time between classes to five minutes. Mr. Appleby said it was to assure students have enough time to get to their classes. Kevin disputed this, saying it was to comply with the state regulations to assure a 990 hour school year and in so doing the school went from last year's 960 hours to 1008. Kevin then mentioned that Dr. Martin (Assistant Superintendent) was establishing a curriculum council and that 109 courses would be missing from the curriculum guide next year with dropping 62 of the 65 mini-courses because there were no courses of study for them and it costs money to write courses of study. The other 47 courses would be deleted or combined into one because of low enrollment.

Course scheduling, like the system of hall passes, seemed to be in a constant state of flux, with many trends, each more complicated than the last, and LD likely tried them all. In February 1988 the school changed from a Monday through Friday schedule and went to a five day cycle. Later a six-day cycle was instituted. (*Falcon Flash*, March 28, 1988)

Doug Hofsass (February 6, 1992 *Falcon Flash*) offered a commentary on a new five minute homeroom period, termed "extended homeroom period." The writer saw no use for it. "What happens in this eternity of time is in most cases nothing. ...out of all the homerooms in the school there is probably not one that could recognize themselves without the assistance of the homeroom roster. These random combinations of people never see each other except at assemblies where individuals hide in their own separate cultures and at pep rallies where a fifth of homeroom turnout is considered superb."

In the 1992-93 school year a new pass system was initiated, a pass with 40 spaces, replacing what was called "the orange pass." A student was to use a five by eight card until it was full and s/he needed a replacement; however, if the card was lost, there was a three-day waiting period for a replacement. A student was not to be allowed to leave the classroom without the pass. Mrs. Rebecca Martin, a member of the committee who designed the system, cautioned, "Teachers, however, must not abuse the system or it will not be successful."

Drugs and Tobacco

A section on drugs and tobacco may be unseemly in a history of an institution, but these problems are the reality of our times. Further, the Lower Dauphin School District has always worked to make the schools safe for students. That needs to be acknowledged.

No mention was found concerning drugs in the school publications of the 1960s. This is not to say that there was no drug use by Lower Dauphin students, but rather it was not considered widespread enough to note.

In the mid-1960s there had been a growing awareness of marijuana being used in the "big cities" and of some experimenting with LSD, but most teenagers in small towns had very little information about these activities. And at Lower Dauphin, near the end of the 1960s there were more comments being made about miniskirts and dress in general than were being made of illegal drug use.

On March 17, 1970 *The Evening News* reported that the superintendent, Dr. Hoerner, had told the Crestview Manor Civic Association parents that there is "no evidence of drug abuse" at Lower Dauphin. He said that media attention tends to give rise to many rumors on the local scene. While many teachers scoffed at this "head in the sand" response, we were somewhat assured by his belief that there was not a serious problem.

The first editorial in the student newspaper to mention smoking was in the May 28, 1970 issue when Beverly Hallman noted the changes, innovations, controversies, failures, and triumphs of the school year. Among the specifics she mentioned was "smoking in the lavs."

In this same issue the editor, in speaking for the administration, added, "Smoking has neither been condoned nor abolished by the present administration. Smokers are suspended immediately.... I have been assured by Dr. Hoerner that no statement has ever been made by his administration which denied the existence of drugs at LD, although he is quick to add that he has found no evidence of a drug problem as of yet."

By the fall of that year, the story changed when *The Sun* reported in November that "dangerous drugs (were) discovered at a Lower Dauphin dance. A test was run on the apprehended drug and was proved to be a dangerous drug. Further laboratory tests will be run to ascertain the exact contents of the drug." The newspaper also was quick to note that "The youths involved in this drug incident are not now students at Lower Dauphin High School."

The next article available was one found in the March 1972 *Falcon Flash* article, "LD to Host Drug Meetings." The article reported, "To help students and parents become more aware of themselves, their values, and existing drug problems, Lower Dauphin is initiating a program with drug education as its first topic in which it will be possible to discuss and learn from experts how problems develop in society and their possible remedies."

In the October 12, 1973 *Falcon Flash* senior Craig College wrote, "Well, here it is October 12, school has been underway several weeks, the water has been shut off twice (and) the lavs are again unofficial smoking lounges." Four months later the *Flash* quoted a teacher who said s/he thought there should be a smoking area provided for the students and in the March issue a letter to the editor claimed that close to half the students smoke.

The November 1974 issue of *Know Your Schools* notes that among the agenda items for the Superintendent's Forum was a smoking lounge for senior high students.

By spring, the June 1975 issue of the *Falcon Flash* carried a feature on things students would relinquish upon leaving LD. One of these was "The seven smoking breaks a day taken between every class." Whether or not this was true for some students, the point is that smoking definitely was a problem.

Student smoking in the bathrooms was likely the most controversial issue in the school in its fifty year history.

By 1976 students had become more informed about the dangers of drugs and debates ensued, both in classes and out of school. By March 1976 a new smoking policy was proposed that would allow senior high students to smoke in certain areas outside the school so long as they had a pass. In June '76 when the school newspaper took "a creative look at LD problems," it noted that students who smoked refused to yield their positions and to all appearances they were outwitting being caught. The writer added, "Smoking in the girls' lav also continues."

In the December 1976 *Flash*, Kathy Burns wrote an editorial on smoking, particularly in A-wing lav, and called for an alternative place for girls to smoke (to keep the lavs smoke-free). Jenny Jones wrote in the same issue on the benefits of the miracle drug cannabis sativa. This was more indicative of student freedom of expression on an interesting topic than a commentary on a personal choice.

On February 7, 1977, the School Board "handed down the official student smoking policy. This new regulation, which is now operating on a trial basis, permits the use of tobacco by senior high school students in two designated areas of the school." Conditions included the following:
- Must have parental permission
- Outside the auditorium in the area facing B-wing and the porch outside of H-wing
- Must keep it clean
- Three different times: before and after school; during the student's lunch period; between classes.

Before long Student Council proposed that a drug policy be established (*Falcon Flash*, May 1978.) Policies were incorporated into the student discipline code and into the curriculum as part of an educational approach to the dangers of drug use. School publications did not often write about the drug problem and while Lower Dauphin had incidents, drug use in school did not become a major issue.

Nonetheless in December 1978 there continued to be smoking passes and a smoking policy to provide guidelines to smokers.

The next available record from the *Flash* is April 1984's editorial by Randy Thames, "The Great American Smoking Team." Because of misconduct on school grounds a ban was placed on anyone's leaving the building EXCEPT for the smokers. Animosity increased. Finally some of the athletes applied for smoking passes so they could "go outside" under this ruling. The editorial concluded, "This controversy is like a time bomb. The time will come when this bomb is detonated...."

In October 1985 a writer using the pen name of T. J. Mann wrote, "Recently the smoking porch has become the center of some controversy." The writer then recounted the history of the smoking policy, saying that the porch was designated for smoking because it was too costly to provide a smoking lounge. The article continued with pros and cons.

The next year a smoking survey was conducted by the Student Advisory Board which resulted in a recommendation that the outdoor area adjacent to the driver's education trailer continue to be provided for students with smoking passes or that the A-Wing lavatory be designated as a smoking room and that harsher penalties be issued to violators.

The June 1987 20th Annual School Forum made the recommendation to phase out smoking. In the fall of 1987 the outdoor smoking area was closed when the School Board instituted a policy prohibiting smoking on school grounds. The smokers went back to the lavatories.

The headline of an article in *The Patriot-News* (February 23, 1988) announced, "Anti-smoking efforts at LD viewed as unenforceable," based on a report presented to the school board by Assistant Principal Judith Witmer which noted that "the board's policy receives high marks for good intentions, but low grades for realism from the students, faculty, and staff." In February 1987 the board had adopted a policy aimed at banning all smoking in the district by the fall of 1989. Since then smoking has been prohibited and previously designated outside smoking areas were eliminated. However, Witmer reported, "the smoking has not stopped; instead, smokers either hide in the stalls or, forewarned by 'lookouts,' they get rid of the cigarette. Lookouts are also used outside the building. Enforcement is further complicated by smoking in restrooms in more isolated wings of the building which, by chance, are occupied by teachers of the opposite sex. Students do not see that it is their responsibility to report violators and teachers believe that being a bathroom monitor is not an appropriate assignment, that it leads to ridicule by the students. Without seeing the actual act of smoking, there is no definite proof." She concluded her report by adding that the heaviest smoke in the high school seems to come from the faculty lounge," and that the lounge "has become so smoke-polluted that non-smoking faculty have been driven out and have been denied a place in which to do their planning."

In 1989 the district announced that after a two-year phase-in process, Lower Dauphin Schools "are now tobacco free" with its policy banning the use of tobacco products on school property.

By this date the district had also erected Drug Free School Zone signs to alert the public that peddling or using illegal substances within 1,000 feet of school property would bring harsh, mandatory sentences to users and sellers. It also had in place a comprehensive drug prevention education program as part of the regular curriculum and had established a Student Assistance Team comprised of trained staff to identify and help students who use illegal substances.

As a reactionary measure in the spring of 1989, the high school administration locked the lavatory doors in A, B, and H wings in hopes of stopping the smoking. This resulted in a commentary in the May 5 issue of the *Flash*, in which Michele Whitmeyer noted: "Locking the lavs does cut down on smoking, but only at the particular time the doors are locked. Smoking in the bathrooms continues throughout the rest of the day. It seems as though closing the bathrooms is more a form of punishment for those who need to use the facilities in haste than for the smokers who can visit them whenever they want."

The following year, according to the November 1990 *Lower Dauphin Insider*, three new drug and substance abuse policies had been put into place.

The March 12, 1992 edition of the *Flash* reports an incident of selling caffeine pills as "look-alikes" with the young seller claiming the pills were "speeders." The incident was handled by the local police.

Eight years later, the May 1, 2000 issue of the *Falcon Flash* announced a new drug testing policy of "positive peer pressure" which included a mandatory drug testing policy "that has helped control potential negative situations."

On the other hand, smoking by young people has always been a societal issue, and a never-ending battle. Schools have tried many strategies to deter smoking in the schools, even to the point of providing special areas for smokers (a policy hard to believe in retrospect, until one realizes that the smoking areas for students occurred prior to the national move against the use of tobacco in the mid-2000s).

Student Assistance Program (SAP)
Student Problem Identification and Resolution of Issues Together (SPIRIT)

The Student Assistance Program (SAP) was developed in the late 1980s to help students who are experiencing barriers to learning that include one or more of the following: depression and/or anxiety, the use of drugs and/or alcohol, relationship problems, emotional disorders, grief due to separation or death, and/or other disruptive life changes. Designed to be an intervention program, not a treatment program or disciplinary alternative, students are referred to both in-school and out-of-school supports. A student can place a request in locked confidential boxes in Pupil Services or by teacher referral.

In 1991 Mrs. Audrey Conway formed a Community-School-Parent Drug and Alcohol Task Force. This became the successful program in the district known as High on Kids led by parents, teachers, businessmen, clergy, and police officers. A newer program was initiated in 2003 to identify student problems and resolution of issues (SPIRIT) between and among students. (*Falcon Flash*, December 22, 2003)

Alternative Education Program

The Alternative Education Program was originally established to eliminate out-of-school suspension and to serve as a means by which to correct the behavior of disruptive students. Students were and are expected to complete all homework assignments. When first established, teachers were assigned to monitor this room much as they were assigned to study halls. Once it was realized that the program needed a leader—perhaps hero would be a better term—a director was identified to establish the rules, but what he did was change lives. This he did with dignity, honor, and what might be described as "tough love." His job was difficult but many who spent time in what was fondly referred to as "the ape room" first learned to respect this gentleman and the fortunate ones also learned to respect themselves. The program was governed by a list of 13 rules and regulations and by one unwritten rule, "Tell things the way they are, not the way you think they want to be heard." Mr. Mark French, you are sorely missed.

Summit Achiever Craig A. Camasta '82, DPM

Dr. Craig A. Camasta is representative of those who excel in various areas, particularly areas that don't naturally seem to be compatible. In high school Craig was known as a successful athlete, one of the elite wrestlers. What many did not know is that he also had—and still has—an enviable talent as an artist and, as evidence shows, as an architect. In fact, he recently said that he had had to make a choice of which career to pursue as a life's work. Fortunately he has had the opportunity to be not only a highly successful surgeon, but to also serve as the architect of a family retreat known as Hemlock Knob, a building suggestive of the style of Frank Lloyd Wright. A third skill, talent—or perhaps character trait— defines this gentle man. Dr. Camasta is also a philanthropist, generous with his skill and resources.

Dr. Camasta established a non-profit organization, appropriately named Operation Walk, Inc., with the dual mission of (1) providing lower extremity surgery and (2) educating surgeons around the world. His devotion to under-served pediatric patients has taken him to Vietnam and Nepal for annual medical missions where he has performed surgeries that allow the lame to walk. He has developed surgical procedures that have made him the surgeon sought by those who have been turned away by other hospitals. In fact, a prominent Lower Dauphin family was led to him and he was able to perform the needed corrective surgery that made it possible for a young woman to return to the sport she loves.

Dr. Camasta specializes in pediatric and adult reconstructive foot and ankle surgery, and pioneering numerous surgical procedures; he is particularly well-known for treating difficult bone and soft tissue tumors and infections, and specializes in revision surgery. He is a widely sought after international lecturer and teacher in countries including Canada, Australia, Spain, Germany, Vietnam, and Nepal. As a surgical consultant for Helios Hospital Group in Germany, Dr. Camasta teaches reconstructive foot and ankle surgery to orthopedic, trauma, and general surgeons.

As a medical author, Craig Camasta has served as editor and contributing editor to various medical textbooks on reconstructive surgery for the foot, ankle, and leg. His articles on pediatric and adult reconstructive foot and ankle surgery have been published in peer-reviewed journals and textbooks.

Craig has been honored by his Alma Matter in Millersville's *150th Year Anniversary Book* as one of the most influential 150 graduates in the history of the university. In 2007 he served as the Keynote Speaker at Millersville's Winter Commencement. In 2012 was honored by the Lower Dauphin Falcon Foundation as the Honorary Chairman of the Foundation's Blue and White Gala. In 2013 he became the Honorary Co-Chair of the Lower Dauphin Field House Fund-raising Committee and is a spokesman for that endeavor.

Traditions
and
Events

Traditions and Events

Activities and Clubs

Through its long history of engaging students and following their interests, Lower Dauphin has offered numerous special interest activities and clubs. The following is what our research could confirm. Most of the information came from yearbooks; thus, it is possible that activities not noted in the yearbook will not be listed as there is no other reference available. Further, we did not search beyond the 2010 yearbook; any later dates simply reflect that some other evidence was present. Thus, it should not be assumed that any organization ended in 2010. The Activities and Clubs herein listed are school-sponsored. Unofficial or private organizations are found elsewhere in this book. Activities and clubs were sometimes school-sponsored and sometimes independent; a few are featured in other sections of the book as well as in this list. In most cases the year noted is the **fall** year of origin of the activities. In some cases the closing date of the activity or club is also noted.

ACE: 08-10
Advanced Gym: 63
Agricultural Education: 89
American Institute for Foreign Study: 67–92
American Technology Club: 66, 67, 68
Amnesty International: 89–99
Archeology Club: 79
Art Club: 61–64
Arts Magnet School: 92, 93;
  CASA: 01 to present
Art Service: 66
Band Club: 1960s
Band, Marching and Concert: 1960 to present
    Jazz Band: 01, 07–10
    Stage Band: 81–88
    Majorettes: 1960–2010[1]
    Indoor Twirling: 86, 87[2]
    Color Guard: 1960–2010
Falconettes: 61–66
Flags, Guard-on Flags, Flash Flags: 69–79
    Silk Squad: 81–88
    Swing Flags: 81–86
    Rifle Squad: 72–87
    Winter Drum Line, Indoor Drum

    Line: 82–88; 01; 10
  Winter Guard, Indoor Guard: 1980–87;
    01;[3] 10
Bench and Bar Club: 63
Bible Club: 78–83
Biology Club: 66
Book Club: 2007
Booster Club: 60s–86[4]
Bowling: 75
Boys' Club: 65, 66
Boys' Gymnastics: 63, 65
Brain Busters: 03–08 to present
Business Club: 73, 74
Business Internship Club: 06; 10
Business Service Club: 68
Calculus Club: 69, 70
Capital Classroom: 82
Cheerleaders: 1960 to present
Chemistry Club: 66
Chess Club: 66, 68, 69; 77, 78; 00–09[5]
Chorus, Choir, Concert Choir: 1960–2010

[1] In 1984 and 1986 the majorettes were known as Twirlers

[2] and sporadically through the following years

[3] first formed in 1980-81 (FF, Dec. 80)

[4] unconfirmed as to whether or not this was active prior to 1963; in November 1963 *Falcon Flash*, it is described as "L.D.'s newest club."

[5] The class of '01 made an erroneous claim that this was the first year for Chess Club.

Concert Choir: 86–90; 2001
Chorus: 86–90; 2001
    Ensemble: 75, 85[6]
    Falconaires: 1960[7]
    Girls' Chorus: 61
    Girls' Nonette: 63–66
    Horizons: 82, 83
    Imperials: 65, 66[8]
    Vocal Octet: 07, 09
    Women's Select Choir: 09
Civil Air Patrol: 00-01
Class Councils
    Senior: 1972 to present
    Junior: 1972 to present
    Sophomore: 1972 to present
    Freshman: 1980 to present
Coin Club, 65
Communications Club: 97, 05, 06
Computer Club: 85, 86; reinvented 00–05
Cooperative Education, aka Co-Op and
Internship: 90, 93, 99–09
Dance Club: 78; again circa 06–07
Debate Team: 68 – 91; renewed in 2001, 02[9]
Deutsch Club: 06
Diversity Club: 04–07
Dramatics Club: 60, 61, 62, 66;
 new Drama Club: 09–10
Ecology Club: 92–06
Economics Club:
Electronics Club: 66, 82
Environmental Action Club: 78
Envirothon: 05–10 (perhaps earlier)
Falcon Flash: 61–74; 76–81; 83–91;
 2001 to the present
Falconaire: 1960 to present
Farm Mechanics: 62–66

Fashion Board: 68–81
Fellowship of Christian Athletes: 90–93;
 2001 to present
Foreign Language Club: 98–03
Forensics: unconfirmed as an activity
Four Diamonds Club: 08–10
French Club: 64, 69–80; 83–85; 90–97
Freshman Chorus: 80–85
Future Business Leaders: 60–71; 76
Future Farmers of America: 60–93
Future Homemakers: 60–77
Future Nurses: 60–69; 76
Future Secretaries:[10] 65–86
Future Teachers: 60–76
Future Educators of America: 09–10
Gay-Straight Alliance: 09–10
German Club: 60–64; 79–81; 05–08
Girls Athletic Council: 61–75
Girls Club: 62–66; 69
Girls Gymnastics: 63, 65
Golf Club: 69, 74
Good Manners Club: 1960s
Guitar Club: 04
Gymnastics Club: 64, 66, 69, 74
Handicrafts: 69
Health Careers Club: 70–75; 80, 82
Honor Society: 61
Hockey Club: 94–01
Horizons: 1980s
Housekeeping Club: 65
Hunting and Fishing Sportsmen's Club: 66
Industrial Arts Club: 60, 62
Industrial Management Club: 63
Intramural Horseback Riding Club: 67
International Club: 65, 66
Japanese Culture: 07–10
Jazz Club: 60, 61
Junior Classical League: 63
Junior Industrial Development Club: 64, 65

---

[6] There are various combinations of singing groups, not always identified in the yearbook.

[7] mixed vocal ensemble

[8] choral group of eight to nine males

[9] The 01 yearbook erroneously claimed that year as the first year Debate was an extra-curricular activity

[10] Aka Future Secretaries Association, Future Secretaries of America

[11] originated in the 1970s as Student Forum, but not
recognized in the yearbook until 89; in fall of 1991 it was
re-formed from the Student Advisory Board (FF, Sept
27,'91)

Technical Science Society: 69–70

Teen Age Democrats, 1960s

Teen Democrats: 05–10

Teen Age Republicans, 1960s

Teen Republican Club: 03–10

Thespian Society, Thespian Troupe, Thespians: 72–94; 01–10

Tri-Hi-Y: 66, 68

Tri-M (Music Honors): 1992 to present.

Varsity Club: 61, 62, 63, 64, 65, 66, etc.

VolunTEEN: 97–10

Vocational Industrial Club of America: 75

Wallops Island Mariners: 79

Weight Lifting: 06

Wood Maintenance: 63–66

Woodworking Club: 63

Youth Apprenticeship: 93–09

Youth Festival: 69–76

Youth Forum: 67–79

Traditions of Homecoming

Homecoming, like most of the traditions of high schools, originated with colleges in the United States. The University of Illinois claims that the first Homecoming was held there in 1910.[1] The University of Missouri lists its first Homecoming football game as 1911. Homecoming at schools and universities is ostensibly based on the idea of welcoming back alumni of the school and should include activities for current students as well as alumni, sports and culture events, and often a parade through the streets of the city or town. It typically is built around a major sporting event, usually in late September or early October and features a banquet. Very often there is a coronation of a Homecoming Queen (and at some schools, a Homecoming King). The game itself often tries to match the home team against an opponent that is considered easy to defeat. (However, with PIAA rules, this does not happen locally—at least, not by intent.)

Traditions typically include a Homecoming Court of representative students, often voted into this honor, and usually are from the senior class. Classmates traditionally nominate students who have contributed to their school, then students vote for members of the Court from the nominees. Once the Homecoming Court candidates are announced, the entire student body votes for the Queen and King. This latter practice has been replaced in many high schools by presenting each candidate with a boxed rose and the one whose box contains a rose of a different color is noted as the queen. Those schools with kings select that office by voting or by lottery.

Local rules determine when the Homecoming Queen and King are crowned. Sometimes, the big announcement comes at a pep rally, school assembly, or public ceremony one or more days before the football game. Other schools, Lower Dauphin included, select and crown the queen (as described) at the Homecoming football game and the King is crowned at the Homecoming dance. Often, the previous year's Queen and King are invited back to crown their successors.

Many Homecoming celebrations include a parade, particularly in schools in which the high school and its playing field are located in a particular community. Because Lower Dauphin uses the Hershey Park Stadium, in the early days of the school a parade with floats was staged during halftime. In those days every class prepared a float based on the Homecoming theme decided by Student Council. The Homecoming Court takes part in the parade, often riding in convertibles as part of the parade. Activities also include a pep rally (typically at LD held the evening before the game).

At most major colleges and universities, the football game is preceded by a tailgate party. The Lower Dauphin Alumni Association (since 2013 with the Football Boosters) hosts a post-game "tailgate" held indoors, sometimes at the school and sometimes in other venues. Throughout the week, many schools (particularly high schools) engage in special dress-up days, sometimes called "Spirit Week," where students are allowed to wear clothing suitable to the theme. One day is traditionally that of wearing clothing with the school's name, or clothing and makeup of their school's colors.

The Homecoming Dance—usually the culminating event of the week (for high schools)—is a formal or informal event, either at the school or an off-campus location. The venue is decorated, and there is either a disc jockey or a band. In many ways, it is a fall prom. Other events may include a powder puff football game between the junior and senior class.

---

[1] P. 15, the Official Cheerleader's Handbook.

At Lower Dauphin the first Homecoming Dance was held in the cafeteria on October 28, 1961. The ticket price for the 1967 Homecoming was $1.

Mike Skinner '65 remembers Homecoming 1964 (Class of '65): "I was Janie's escort at the Homecoming Game (fall of '64) and Gary Gearhart escorted her during the half-time queen crowning because I was on the football team. He arrived late at the stadium, jumped the fence, and ran down the field to catch up with her so that she would have an escort. The game announcer gave an account of his running progress over the PA system to the enjoyment of the crowd."

Homecoming 1968 (Class of '69) was described thus: "The school cafeteria was transformed into a most attractive ballroom through the efforts of Jeannine Lehmer, Don Frantz, Linda Goepfert, Kathy Schock, Carol Kreider, and others. The pathway to the ballroom led one through two huge stone portals on either side of a drawbridge which opened to reveal a candlelight vision of coats of arms, banners, and a Queen's throne with four attendants' chairs directly out of Camelot."

The first year for floats, according to the *Flash*, was Homecoming 1969 (Class of '70). The band's float was themed "If Music is the Fruit of Love, Play On." The Girls Athletic Council entered one with the theme "Eliminate the Spartans." The winning float "Apollo 11" was that of Student Council. The five queen candidates all appeared in 1969 Corvettes. The record shows that more than 200 attended the dance, themed "Mystic Depths."

The *Flash* thus described the October 1970 (Class of '71) Homecoming Dance, "With the glow of candles twinkling like starlight in the eyes of many young women who are captivated by their handsome young beaus, and with memories of the pomp and pageantry of the Homecoming Game still lingering, LD students should long remember this year's Homecoming Week-end."

The unforgettable Homecoming 1972 (Class of '73) themed its event as "The Olympiad: Ancient & Modern" whereby Randy Lehman, star cross country runner, carried a lighted torch and ran from the high school in Hummelstown to the Hershey Stadium. Upon arrival he ran up the steps in the stands to light the torch therein installed. The Booster Club, after being approached by Student Council, agreed to build chariots in which the queen candidates stood; these were pulled around the perimeter of the stadium by high school males.

In the Fall of 1973 (Class of '74) the Homecoming Dance was memorable for the fact that the band (The Big City Band) hired for the dance didn't show. A record player was used for dancing but the dilemma was what to do about the fanfare for the Queen. Attendees who were members of the high school band excused themselves from their dates, headed to the band room and came up with an impromptu plan to provide something appropriate. According to Ray Kennedy, FF, November 21, "The band members who tried hard to play a fanfare for the crowning of the queen deserve some recognition also. It was suggested that they play since there was no other appropriate music available. Maybe we should thank the band members' dates who were left to amuse themselves while the band went to rehearse." Following the dance the Student Council refunded the ticket price to all attendees.

In the mid-1970s the senior class float collapsed on its way to the stadium and a class that shall remain anonymous was embarrassed that their float had been built backwards (on the wrong side of the carrier) so that the spectators would not be able to view it unless this float would travel in the reverse direction around the stadium; to their credit they reassembled it.

Homecoming 1980 honored Mr. Jack Goepfert, former Director of Athletics for his service and dedication to the school.

The Fall of 1987 is remembered as the time the pep rally was canceled "due to lack of interest." This lack of interest is said to have originated because the students had not been dismissed from school early to work on the Homecoming floats and rumor had it that there might be "trouble" at a pep rally.

In November 1987, in the spirit of the times, Holly Feeney in an editorial in the *Flash* raised the question as to why the choosing of a homecoming queen was still important.

On a more positive note, on November 24, Mr. Randall Umberger, newly appointed Athletic Director and an LD alumnus, made a proposal to Student Council to support a Homecoming Athletic Weekend. This would make Friday evening sports-free for a formal dance, if desired. Saturday morning activities would include a cross country meet and a tennis match followed by a field hockey game and a soccer game at the stadium. The Homecoming Parade and crowning of the queen would be held in the afternoon followed by the football game. The purpose of revamping Homecoming was to make it an actual home coming for the alumni instead of (only) a fall formal for the current students. It also would allow for more time to recognize all the work put into the creation of floats rather than only a twenty-minute halftime.

This suggestion led to a vote to change Homecoming based on some of the proposals made by Mr. Umberger and also to begin the following year to crown a Homecoming King. *(Flash*, December 23, 1987.) Homecoming 1988 saw these suggestions implemented with plans to include more sports, a picnic, a parade of candidates, and alumni.

In the fall of 1996 the senior class donated $1,000 to the Four Diamonds fund at half-time, having raised the money by the entire student body through selling spirit links at ten cents each. The December 13, 1996 *Flash* ran a feature article asking "Where are the floats?" noting the second year of the Homecoming parade being rained out and rumors circulating that the tradition of floats might cease to exist. However, another article "The spirit is still alive" described the evening in the rain: "As I watched the rain soak through each and every one of the spectators' layers of clothing, I was touched, because despite the discomfort, they never ceased to cheer on the team. Students screamed and hollered as blue and white paint dripped from their chins and, even when the score rose against us, they never stopped cheering."

Homecoming 1999 (Class of '00) resulted in perhaps the least-thought-out line in a *Flash* article on the event: "This year's Homecoming Court was made up of girls."

Homecoming Week in the fall of 2000 continued the Spirit Link Challenge as a competition as to which class could raise the most funding for charities, and the Hallway Decoration Competition featured each hallway as reflecting a decade in time. Homecoming saw the Alumni Association included in a community pep rally and bonfire and sponsoring alumni cheerleaders (two dozen with pompon routines from the 1970s and 80s), an appearance by the alumni band, directed by Jim Neidinger, and a celebration of Forty Years of Football.

Traditions continued with hall decorating, pep rallies, and designated days to dress "in the spirit." For example, Spirit Week in the fall of 2000 included "Dress Your Decade." More than a dozen staff got into the spirit and dressed in the decade in which they had attended high school. The December 19, 2002 issue of the *Flash* noted that Homecoming week included a pep rally, spirit links, powder puff football, dress-up days including wacky and wild day, teddy day, patriotic day, pajama day, blue and white day, and hallway decorations. On November 9, 2004 the *Flash* noted a tie-dye day, dress like twins, pajama day, Halloween costumes, and blue and white day.

The 2005 *Flash* describes their day-of-the-game pep rally: "It was a day full of excitement, from blue and white, to pink, to camo, to a pie-eating contest, and a rowdy crowd of students. Opening with a dance by the cheerleaders and the striking up of the Big Blue Band, we were in full swing. Following a pie-eating contest, the real excitement began as the junior boys imitated the cheerleaders and cheered on the girls powder puff team."

2008 Homecoming (Class of '09) saw dressing like twins day, favorite college or pro team, neon dress, and blue and white day. However, this class notes, "The senior class continued the fading tradition of hallway decorating and was the first and last class to win the Hallway Decorating Competition. A new tradition of Spirit Links has slowly replaced decorating; it involves classes buying links and competing to raise the most money for THON."

The 2008 *Falconaire* also reported, "Rachel Stohler organized a tailgate breakfast for a senior activity prior to Homecoming Friday. Students arrived as early as 6 a.m. to set up grills and cook. The upper lot was marked off with caution tape to keep out underclassmen.

The 2010 *Falconaire* described the tradition of spirit days and added their own touch to Spirit Week with a Super Hero Day.

Traditions continue . . . .

Homecoming Themes and Bands
—Homecoming is the Previous Fall of Each Graduation Year

Again, we must rely on the alumni to provide this information. Often the theme was not noted in the yearbook or school newspaper; sometimes the name of the dance was used in the publication and a guess had to be made as to whether or not this was (also) the theme. When disc jockeys became popular, often the name was not used in the program or the publications. Evidence suggests that the first homecoming to use floats was the fall of 1969, with the winning float, entered by Student Council, one honoring the Apollo 11 flight. When the homecoming celebration discontinued the float parade and competition, there also were fewer themes designated. There was no homecoming the first year of LDHS; the first Homecoming dance was held in the fall of 1961, its purpose being to honor the Youth Festival Queen; themes began with the Class of 1966; a queen was first selected by the Class of 1962; the name of the band was first noted by the Class of 1965.

Class Year	Themes	Music
1965	_____	The Del-Chords
1966	Sights and Sounds of Autumn	The DuValles
1967	A Royal Affair	The El Dantes
1968	Midnight Rhapsody	Peter and the Wolves
1969	Ye Noble Knight	The Skyliners[1]
1970	Mystic Depths	The Counts
1971	Boulevarde de Paris	The Del-Chords
1972	Octoberfest	Truth, Justice and the American Way
1973	Olympian: Ancient and Modern	Haji[2]
1974	Mardi Gras	Big City Music Band[3]
1975	The Good Times: America's Golden Years	Favor
1976	Celebrate America	Nickleplate Road
1977	_____	_____
1978	The World of Animation	Skyborn
1979	Lost Horizons[4]	Orion
1980	A Night at the Movies	_____
1981	The Times of Your Life	Joe Hojak Trio
1982	Salute to Pennsylvania	Bondage

1 Suburban York HS Dance Band
2 The *Falcon Flash*, Nov. '72 says the band was "Saturday."
3 The band did not show; students in the high school band quickly organized and were able to play the fanfare. See story.
4 Dance theme: Don't Let the Sun Go Down On Me

1983	A Night on Broadway	Class Act
1984	A Trip Around the World	Off the Wall
1985	Decades	_____
1986	Fairy Tales	The Pros
1987	Cartoons and Comics	_____
1988	Oldies But Goodies	Bill Rivera, DJ
1989	Great Hometown Adventures	Michael Gobrecht, DJ
1990	Decades	Ron Mann, DJ
1991	A Gala of Imaginings	Ron Mann, DJ
1992	Cartoons	Allen Norton, DJ
1993	Around the World	Carl Wagner & Dave Dickson, DJs
1994	Music Styles	_____
1995	Disney Movies	_____
1996	(no floats; rain)	_____
1997	One Moment in Time[5]	Mixed Impressions, DJ
1998	A Night in Paris	_____
1999	Tropical Nights	_____
2000	An Enchanting Evening	_____
2001	Reflections of Time	_____
2002	Treasures Under the Sea	_____
2003	A Moonlight Chariot Ride	_____
2004	Cruise to a Tropical Paradise	_____
2005	Journey Around the World	_____
2006	Dancing Through the Decades	_____
2007	Escape to the Far East	_____
2008	Party in Atlantis	Hot 92 DJ
2009	Sweet Escape	_____
2010	The Golden Years	Scott Payonk, DJ

5 Theme of the dance; no floats this year but they would have been holiday themed

Homecoming Queens and Kings

—Homecoming is the Previous Fall of Each Graduation Year

Class	Fall of	Queen	King
1961	1960		
1962	1961	Mary Ann Grubb	_____
1963	1962	Vicki Fackler	_____
1964	1963	Nancy Fabian	_____
1965	1964	Jane Harper	_____
1966	1965	Carol Gingrich	_____
1967	1966	Sharon Smoyer	_____
1968	1967[1]	Jane Youtz	_____
1969	1968	Bonnie Beissel	_____
1970	1969	Judy Fisher	_____
1971	1970	Donna Gleim	_____
1972	1971	Barbara Higgins	_____
1973	1972	Sherry Cooper	_____
1974	1973	Suzanne Wallish	_____
1975	1974	Jody Reitz	_____
1976	1975	Sherry Paine	_____
1977	1976	Marilyn Heffley	_____
1978	1977	Susan Reichenbaugh	_____
1979	1978	Cindy Heisey	_____
1980	1979	Patricia Stare	_____
1981	1980	Peggy Hoover	_____
1982	1981	Coleen Sieg	_____
1983	1982	Lisa Kurr	_____
1984	1983	Tina Agostino	_____
1985	1984	April DeMuth	_____
1986	1985	Kimberly Cutler	_____
1987	1986	Laurel Hershey	_____
1988	1987	Jenifer Petrina	_____
1989	1988	Kira Jones	Ernie Manders
1990	1989	Jodi Pringle	Michael Pit
1991	1990	Michelle Gaudette	Chris Wallish
1992	1991	Jennifer Pringle	Jeremy Kuhlen
1993	1992	Kim Andrasik	Brett Lovelidge

[1] This marks the first time the queen was crowned at the game.

1994	1993	Jennifer Jones	Jason DeHart
1995	1994	Leslie Miller	Anthony Pazakis
1996	1995	Kristi Templin	Dave Hoopes
1997	1996	Cara Byerly	Forrest Carlough
1998	1997	Rhea Graber	Matt Bolton
1999	1998	Brandy Espenshade	Cody Ebersole
2000	1999	Jena Fulton	Tyler Edmundson
2001	2000	Kellie Kulina	Justin Schildt
2002	2001	Rachel Daubert	Dan Sassani
2003	2002	Jackie Barton	Mike Podrasky
2004	2003	Laura Seesholtz	Carson Parr
2005	2004	Laura Dupler	Alex Sharkey
2006	2005	Alexis Graham	Tucker Berry
2007	2006	Bryn Stevens	Kevin Gearhart
2008	2007	Kari Skitka	William McGee
2009	2008	Marissa Goss	Jared Bausch
2010	2009	Dominique Zegretti	Brandon Desrosiers
Golden Jubilee		Mary Cooper	Brad Ebersole

Traditions of Proms

The term "prom" is derived from the word "promenade," meaning a march of guests into a ballroom to announce the beginning of a formal event or ball. During the Victorian period in the United States, when social class distinctions were much more important than they are today, it was not uncommon for members of the upper class to hold grand balls where each guest was announced before entering. At that time proms were also becoming popular at prominent colleges. By the 1920s high schools were imitating these dances along with most of the other college traditions including Commencement, Baccalaureate, Class Night, class rings and pins, and yearbooks.

However, by the time proms were part of the high school culture in the 1940s, World War II began to put a damper on most social and extra-curricular events, from a reduction of numbers on sports teams and the loss of coaches enlisting to the cancellations of district and regional music festivals. With many young men in the service during their senior year in high school (it was not uncommon for a class to lose half of its males by 1944), the proms during the World War II years found a scarcity of escorts, as well as scarcity of fabric for a prom gown.

Even so, while high school yearbooks during the mid-1940s contained photographs of young women dancing with each other, their prom itself was described in alluring terms, "The quiet charm of a rose garden inspired one of the most glamorous and bewitching proms ever held in Curwensville High School."

By the 1950s, with the Depression and the war behind them, Americans were enjoying more affluence than ever before, and the high school prom started to become more what it is today. Soon many schools, confident in the behavior of their students, began to agree to hold the "after-prom" party at a venue separate from the prom site and with a more informal style.

The first after-prom party for Lower Dauphin was sponsored by the Hummelstown Junior Chamber of Commerce and was announced in the Harrisburg paper in spring 1961: "After lengthy discussion and near altercation, the Lower Dauphin Joint School Board approved."

Then on April 4, 1966, the Joint School Board rejected a proposal from the PTA to hold a post-prom party, saying students should not be encouraged to stay out until 5 a.m. and that midnight was late enough for high school juniors.

The May 3, 1968 *Sun re*ports, "Post-prom activities have been planned with the graduating class, class advisors, and a parent committee. This will be held from 1 to 6 a.m. with movies, games, snacks, and a full breakfast at 5 a.m. The activities are open to the class members with or without an escort."

In most high schools proms still are themed with the invitations, decorations, and even menus planned in the spirit of that theme. The "tradition" of a Prom Queen and Prom King are also relatively recent as attested to by the following lists even in a school as "young" as Lower Dauphin.

While each prom is memorable to those who attend, there is only one (2009) in which the prom-goers had to evacuate because of a fire in the building.

Senior Prom Themes and Bands

Beginning in 1982 the Junior Class and the Senior Class combined their proms. As disk jockeys became more popular, more affordable, or more trendy with disco music, the more unlikely the name of the music provider appeared on the program or was noted in the yearbook.

Class	Themes	Music
1961	_____	Jerry Leffler Orchestra
1962	_____	Mello-Macs
1963	_____	_____

1964	Bon Voyage	Don Weidner and His Band
1965	Dining and Dancing at the Colonial Greens	Gene Soles Orchestra
1966	The Twelfth of Never	Hal Herman's Orchestra
1967	Tender is the Night	Hal Herman's Orchestra[1]
1968	Somewhere	Mello-Macs
1969	Reflections	The Skyliners
1970	Eve of Excalibur	Nicky C and the Chateaux
1971	Xanadu	Truth, Justice & the American Way
1972	Déjà vu	Rich Clare Pentagon
1973	Reflections	Saturday
1974	Days of Future Past	Rich Clare Pentagon
1975	Tomorrow's Yesterday	Favour
1976	Until We Meet Again	Journey's End
1977	We May Never Pass This Way Again	Kicks
1978	The Times of Your Life	Saturday
1979	We've Only Just Begun	Push
1980	Time Passages	High Tide
1981	The End is Just the Beginning	Pair-a-dice
1982	Junior-Senior Prom	Now and Then
1983	Separate Ways	Shark
1984	A Night in Heaven	Maxwell
1985	Take a Look at Us Now	Direct Drive
1986	Almost Paradise	Prime Time
1987	Tropical Getaway	Bill Rivera, DJ
1988	Sun Splash '88	Dan Steele, DJ
1989	Bungle in the Jungle	_____
1990	An Everlasting Moment	_____
1991	Phantoms	Ron Mann, DJ
1992	Candle on the Water	_____
1993	The Sea of Love	_____
1994	Just for Tonight	_____
1995	A Time Soon Forgotten	Pablo, DJ
1996	Wonderful Tonight	Scott Mateer, DJ
1997	The Dance	_____
1998	Time After Time	Mixed Impressions
1999	I Will Remember You	Digital DJ
2000	The Time of Your Life	Soundwaves
2001	Mardi Gras	Soundwaves
2002	A Night Under the Rising Sun	Rico, DJ
2003	A Night Among the Stars	_____

[1] Dinner music by Jeanne Michelle

2004	Caught in a Dream	Soundwaves
2005	Midnight Masquerade	Soundwaves
2006	Classic Hollywood	_____
2007	A Starry Night in Paradise	Mixed Impressions
2008	Arabian Nights	_____
2009	Masquerade Ball	Hot 92, DJ
2010	Big Lights, Big City	_____

Senior Prom Queens and Kings

The tradition of a Senior Prom Queen and King began with the 1984 Prom and continued through the period covered in this history.

Class	Queen	King
1984	Chris Schug	Craig Wallace
1985	Roxanne Hetrick	Shaun Smith
1986	Lisa Filippelli	Kevin Strawser
1987	Laynie Overby	Greg Hostetter
1988	_____	_____
1989	_____	_____
1990	Michelle Pheasant	Brian Bischof
1991	Carrianne Elliot	Elton Nestler
1992	Megan Grubb	Howard Gorberg
1993	Lindsee Bowen	Levin Dillon
1994	Deanna Africa	Ed Gnall
1995	Rosina Spitler	Buddy Long
1996	Heather Rhoad	Brad Lechleitner
1997	Dawn Bedeaux	John Heitsenrether
1998	Natalie True	Al Lundy
1999	Gabby Page	Jarrad Sipe
2000	Sommer Costabile	Chris O'Brien
2001	Nicole Zarefoss	Sam Naples
2002	Missy Colter	Steve Hilbert
2003	Alicia Cain	Brenton Haldeman
2004	Nicole Wolfe	Derrick Halbleib
2005	Kaitlin Santanna	Ryan Bowe
2006	Danielle Cordero	Justin Mack
2007	Melissa Reese	John Gacesa
2008	Chelsea Miller	John Wolgemuth
2009	Sarah Labe	Nathan Kenyon
2010	Kristina Sheibley	Joshua Miller

Additional Traditions and Events
Christmas Window Painting and Homeroom Decorating

Decorating homerooms for Christmas was an annual event for many years. From painting windows and creating special bulletin board displays to a huge hanging gold ball ornament in B-1 and real, as well as artificial, Christmas trees—almost everyone took part in the spirit of Christmas. Perhaps one tree in particular stands out above all of the many other unusual displays: a pine tree so large that it nearly filled the room. Most stood in awe that the giant tree, cut from his back yard by Randy Smink '73, fit through the classroom door of H-2, and then secured in the center of the room. Mr. Messner placed the desks around the tree in a circle. The students drew a manger scene on the blackboard and the day of the judging, the real, live newborn Baby Messner was laid in the manger placed below this scene. The homeroom won first prize.

Also, during these early years students were invited to paint Christmas scenes in the windows of local businesses. Prizes were awarded. More recently, the National Art Honor Society has provided this service.

Field Trips

Many of these "road trips" were events by which students got to know one another better, particularly if they were in the same program, such as Longitudinal Studies or English Enrichment. New York, with its wealth of museums, was often a favorite destination, as was Washington, DC with its Folger Library that houses the largest collection of Shakespeare's printed works. On one such memorable trip English Enrichment also toured Ford's Theatre, as well as seeing the new musical "Joseph and the Amazing Technicolor Dreamcoat." It had not yet been to Broadway, and after its first American production (This Andrew Lloyd Webber-Tim Rice collaboration originated in Great Britain) at Cathedral College, other colleges and amateur groups staged it. We chaperones had read about the show and determined that it would be suitable for the students; however, attendance was optional. We found it engaging and were not surprised at its later success.

Longitudinal Studies (Mr. Thomas Campbell) takes the prize for distance as Longitudinal Studies did an exchange program with students in England. Senior English Enrichment of 1978 (Mr. Ronald Zeigler and Mrs. Judith Witmer) likely took the most unusual field trip when they were invited by Craig College '74 to spend a week-end at West Point, to be lodged at the well-known Thayer Hotel, and to be his guest at a showing of "A Midsummer Night's Dream."

In May of 1973 six science students witnessed the historic launching of SKYAB at the Kennedy Space Center in Florida, one of only two schools to receive an invitation to participate. At the time the SKYLAB was the largest craft ever put into space. The very successful science program and its faculty provided many extended learning experiences for students, including an annual oceanography program at Wallops Island which was initiated in the early 1980s.

Field trips were curtailed during the energy crises of the 1970s and never regained the high numbers they earlier had held. Again in June of 1985 the School Board began a study on field trips because of the expense and volume of fund-raising needed. These trips did, however, serve a high purpose in expanding experiences for many students.

There are field trips and then there were unexpected **field trips (!)** that provided opportunities for LD students that were a gift. Such a one was an invitation from alumnus and Broadway producer Don Frantz '69 who on a Monday morning in September 2008 sent an email invitation to this author to bring a group of students with an interest in music to a pre-opening night performance of his new Broadway musical "A Tale of Two Cities!" Through combined efforts, five days later 70 of us boarded two yellow school busses on our way to New York City where we were guests not only for the show, but for a pre-show dinner with Don and an after-show meeting with the actors and a backstage tour.

Fun Nights

Fun Nights that began in February of 1970 still were being held in the spring of 1977. These were, as they appear, held for the purpose of providing a place for students to gather for various kinds of activities, sometimes a dance, more often games and sometimes both. One is particularly noted in 1973 as a fund-raiser for Sam Campbell at which the band Damascus played.

Halloween

One does not typically associate Halloween with students in senior high school. However, in some years the holiday gained notice at LD. Most students who were in the band remember marching in Hummelstown's annual Halloween parade and others, who were either bystanders or participated in "Witches Watch" during Treat or Treat, escorting the Halloween parade participants to prevent "egging," vividly remember the Halloween activities.

The first *Falcon Flash* to mention the Halloween parade was the Fall 1966 issue. The Class of 1973 band members also write about being in the Halloween parades in their Class Reflection.

The faculty in the early 1960s may have had the most spirited Halloween party in the attic of the then Antonicelli house on E. Main Street where one of the younger teachers was renting a first floor apartment.

Carolyn Sandel '65 writes, "I remember one day (near Halloween) when we entered English class to the music of Mussorgsky's 'Night on Bald Mountain' and had to write a Halloween tale that 'fit the music.'"

For several years in the early 1980s Halloween gained popularity in the high school when contests were held for the best costume. Students (and some teachers, including one with full Darth Vader regalia) came to school in costume and during an afternoon pep rally, the costumes were judged. This idea was later adapted as a part of at least one Homecoming, according to the November 2004 *Falcon Flash*.

Lyceums

Lyceums were offered in 1966-67 as a result of a call for more student-sponsored assemblies. The National Honor Society answered the challenge, sponsoring various topics during the end-of-day activity period.

Majorettes Bikini Car Wash

Ranking among the most unusual fund-raising activities was the Lower Dauphin High School Majorettes Bikini Car Wash held in late summer 1972. As the *Hummelstown Sun* noted in its August 2 issue, "Hummelstown area male residents driving in the vicinity of Lower Dauphin High School last Saturday had to have a will of iron to avoid the temptation to have their cars washed." The workers included Chris Smith, Denise Sieg, Roxanne Sottus, Debbie Kreiser, Candy Tritch, Michele DeRosa, Jeannine Lehmer, Denise Lehmer, Eileen Ferguson, and Tana Goodhart.

Mini Thon

Lower Dauphin is one of approximately forty high schools in the region who hold "mini-thons" as part of one of the largest philanthropic endeavors in the state. The money raised at this high-energy event that includes a marathon dance along with other activities is part of the more than $800,000 raised annually by high schools for the Children's Miracle Network of the Penn State Medical Center.

In 1977, the Four Diamonds Fund, the predecessor to the Children's Miracle Network, became the sole beneficiary of the Penn State IFC/Panhellenic Dance Marathon (THON™), the largest student-run philanthropy in the nation. This year (1977) also marks the first confirmed Four Diamonds 24-hour Marathon in which Lower Dauphin participated, with music donated by three student rock bands of the mid-1970s: Neon, Phoxx, and Full Moon. (*The Fledgling*, May 1977)

New Student Tea

Beginning in the 1970s Student Council sponsored a welcoming event early each fall for new students and their parents to smooth the difficulties often faced by students who change schools. An orientation program included a presentation highlighting the district, the building, academic program, and activities.

See You at the Pole

This event has been a part of Lower Dauphin tradition for about 15 years and is student-initiated, student-organized, and student-led. It is simply about students meeting at their school flagpole, on a designated day in September, to pray—for their school, friends, teachers, government, and nation.

Senior Citizens Prom

The Volunteen Club, composed of more than 60 Lower Dauphin High School students, sponsors an annual Prom for Senior Citizens from the Lower Dauphin Community. Held every April, the event draws a surprisingly large number of attendees who enjoy the dances of their own era as well as trying some of the newer dance steps. Complete with door prizes and the crowning of a Prom King and Queen, most of the prom-goers have such a good time they look forward to returning the following year. Chad Lister, a teacher and alumnus of Lower Dauphin, provides the recorded music.

Senior Last Will and Testament

The publishing of the Last Will and Testament in a yearbook or school newspaper is a tradition that predates Lower Dauphin by many years. The practice seems to have started with the earliest high school yearbooks (early 1920s) and was considered to be part of the humor section of the book. Most of the initial Wills were from the class as a whole, but soon evolved into an opportunity for individuals to select a recipient of any number of items or practices. In hindsight most Wills are trite and in many cases the reader would be hard pressed to find any characteristics in these documents that set them apart from all others. While most of the Class Wills were published in the *Falcon Flash*, some of the more notable ones from LDHS include one from 1962 which wills many things to the faculty and from 1976 which was more cutting and suggestive than usual. The Class of 1970 incorporated theirs into a "Class Night, which featured skits about our years at LD and the reading of the class's Last Will and Testament." The Class of '73 included theirs in their Reflection for this book.

Senior Class Trips (Hightlights of a Few Documented Trips)

The first mention of class trips was the first graduating class which remembers disappointment that they were not to be allowed the traditional senior class trip to Washington, D.C. that the senior classes of Hummelstown High School had always taken. However, the Class of 1962 does make mention of a class trip.

The Class of 1976 noted that previous classes had gone on trips, loading onto buses, driving a couple of hours, touring a city or some historic site and returning the same day. In contrast, the Class of 1976 decided they wanted to go to Disney World and they held continuous fund-raisers to do so. It was the first time for many students to fly, first time in Florida, and first time at Disney World.

In an article in the April 1984 *Falcon Flash* the senior class congratulates themselves for having a good time on their trip, amazed that they were able to work together toward a common goal. As Gaby Maisels noted, "I couldn't believe our class actually got it together, but we did and it was fantastic."

The 1985 Senior Class Trip to the ski resort of Hunter Mountain in New York was less than expected. At their arrival they were told they were too late for skiing. They were admonished not to dive or use the slide in the chlorine-heavy swimming pool. The Jacuzzi was only ankle deep and the skiing, advertised as "just a stone's throw away," was an hour's drive to a small slope.

Senior Day

Senior Day was based on an idea to give the students the opportunity to role play as a teacher, principal, or other staff for a day. There is no record of when this practice started, but it likely occurred in the mid-to late 1960s as it seemed to be a tradition by 1970 in that it was mentioned as part of the May Day celebration that year; this also included a drama festival, a May Day outdoor fair, and a May Day dance. Senior Day is noted in the June 1975 *Falcon Flash*, as the time "when students take the place of teachers, custodians, secretaries, aides, and administrators for a day."

The next year was another article implying this was an ongoing event, confirmed by the Class of 1976. "The other senior day was when students could trade places with a teacher for the day. The student had to follow the teacher's schedule and teach each of the classes." The last article on Senior Day in the possession of LDAA is in the June 1985 *Falcon Flash* which indicates that the Senior Class decided to bring back this tradition of Senior Day.

Talent Shows

Talent shows were more popular in the early years of Lower Dauphin, although they are by no means passé. The first one at LDHS for which there is a record is the Seniors Only Talent Show, produced by the Class of 1965. Their promotion speaks for this: "…is setting a precedent by presenting a special 'seniors only' talent show assembly … given for the entire senior high student body. Featured will be a one-act play, 'The Sand Box,' under the direction of Barry L. Stopfel."

The following year the Service Club, advised by Mrs. Venus Connelly, produced a student entertainment assembly (talent show). This was followed in October 1967 by the self-styled "most psyched-up, 'souled'-out presentation ever in its history of turned-on shows. This being of course the annual LD Senior Talent Show—presented as a live performance. (There) will be two new vibrating groups, two famous singers, and a special attraction straight from its engagement at the band room, one of the greatest world entertainment centers. The two groups are so fresh, so new, so vibrating, so dynamic that both, as yet, are unnamed and will not be named until the right word is invented." The first group included Rod Young, Quinn Barnhart, Dennis Warble, Hank Imhof, Craig Tritch, Scott Finney, and Jeff Wolfersburger. The second group was comprised of Bob Wolfe, Don Saylor, Dave Landis, Steve Keiper, Cy Keefer, Barry Cosey, and Mike Wolfe. Additional attractions included Inez Puzuks and Janice Wenrich.

There either was a dearth of interest or little press coverage for the next 17 years, but it was not until 1984 that there is evidence of another talent show, this one as part of a self-described first of its kind, a Senior Night that also included a covered dish dinner, slide presentation, skits, reading of the Class Will and prophesies.

Sixteen years later, the December 2009 *Falcon Flash* announced a "first ever" talent show.

Winterfest

Winterfest, the major social event of the winter season since 1999, is sponsored by the Fellowship of Christian Athletes. Winterfest is a free mid-winter event to allow students "an evening of food, fellowship, and fun in a drug and alcohol free setting. Activities for the evening include board games, ping pong, volleyball, and basketball, with a lively group normally in attendance; movies are also available." A "whipped cream surprise" pie eating contest has been a long standing tradition of the evening.

Youth Forum

The Capital Area Youth Forum began in the early 1960s. Regional in nature, in 1962 twenty-three area schools, including Lower Dauphin, met on April 10 at Edison Junior High School in Harrisburg. The first representatives from LDHS included Ann Seaman, Sandra Longreen, Alice Wiest, Carol Glovola, Vivian Lewin, Joyce Keener, Gloria Verdelli, Michael Stauffer, Robert Gibble, Frederick Shope, Fred Harner, and Harold Snyder. There is mention of the Youth Forum in the *Falconaire* through 1979.

The purpose of the Youth Forum was to discuss issues of interest to youth and to gain an understanding of the democratic processes of this country. This organization, sponsored by local service organizations, was also the host of the Youth Festival, first organized in 1954 in celebration of *The Patriot's* 100th anniversary as a newspaper. The Festival supported various projects; for example, in 1973 the profits were donated to the Tri-County Crippled Children's Society and the Multiple Sclerosis Society.

The Youth Festival Planning Committee also included students from area schools. In the fall of 1961 Barbara Crumbling represented Lower Dauphin. These events included a formal dance with live bands and each area high school selected a Teen Queen who was the official representative of her school at the Festival. The last year we have a record for this is 1977.

Public Teen Socials

WGAL (Channel 8) Dance Party and American Bandstand

Television joined the teen-age dance movement in the 1950s by initiating dance party programs, helping to popularize dancing even more than the danceable music itself did. Denver had "Teenage Dance Party," Richmond produced "Top Ten Dance Party," and Philadelphia hosted "Bandstand." The first program to go national was Alan Freed's "The Big Beat" in July 1957, followed by Dick Clark's "American Bandstand" in August of the same year. Clark had an advantage in that he appealed to parents because of his clean, good looks and respectable, earnest manner and by making sure his program promoted a wholesome image of teen life.

Because of these programs—and, of course, the music—very likely the 50s, more than any other decade, will be remembered as the golden age of dance in America. While capitalizing on the rock and roll influence, Dick Clark also brought to teenage music what parents wanted to believe was white teen-age tastes: clean, white boy singers who sang about naïve first love, dating, nice girls, cars, going steady, and holding hands. Among these young singers were Fabian, Bobby Rydell, The Everly Brothers, Neil Sedaka, Frankie Avalon, and Paul Anka. Because of Clark's endorsement, most of these young men were successful. In addition to the raft of young male singers, appealing girl groups also were introduced on American Bandstand. These included The Chiffons, Ronettes, and Shirelles. Among the most popular black performers were Ray Charles, Jackie Wilson, Dinah Washington, Nina Simone, the Drifters, Dominoes, and Coasters.[1]

Dick Clark's influence helped to create programs such as WGAL's (Channel 8) Dance Party which debuted on October 14, 1961. As some of the readers here will recall, each week a different Susquehanna Valley high school, including Lower Dauphin in 1964, was invited to send students to the Saturday afternoon program in Lancaster where they danced to pop tunes recorded on 45 rpm records. Those with really good memories may also remember the names of the hosts on the local Dance Party: Terry Abrams and Ginny Lou. And you do remember Justine on American Bandstand, don't you?

WFIL-TV 46th & Market Streets Philadelphia 39, Pa.

AMERICAN BANDSTAND with Dick Clark

American Bandstand is holding a reservation for you to visit the program on WED JAN 2 1962

Dick Clark

NOT TRANSFERABLE · VOID IF SOLD · SEE REVERSE SIDE

No. 19221

234-3005: This was the telephone number for voting in a contest sponsored by WCMB; Lower Dauphin won a dinner and a free night of skiing for the football team and coaches, as well as a dance on January 30 1965 with Gabriel and the Catalinas providing the entertainment.

1 Witmer, *Growing Up Silent in the 1950s: Not All Tailfins and Rock and Roll*, 2012.

Teen Dance Clubs

Just as Hummelstown teens in the 1940s frequented the Dairy Dell's back room which had an area for dancing and those in the 1950s had the Hummelstown Teen Club, so teens in the 1960s were yearning for a place to gather and possibly to dance. In the 1960s the Hob Nob, located across from the high school, served the purpose of a hangout until the highway was reconfigured. To a lesser extent devoted to teens, the Towne &Country, as it was called, also was a popular gathering place following events such as football and basketball games. Both offered standard fare such as hamburgers (with T&C offering more typical family dinner meals). However, dancing was not on the menu.

Enter The Raven, located in Swatara Township and established in the fall of 1965. Housed in a building designed to look like a castle (and sometimes referred to as "The Castle"), the Raven was owned by Carlos Lansa and the Phegan brothers, and was a club especially for teen-agers. On a good night it drew about 2,000 of the 14,000 teens who held membership cards. It was open on Tuesday, Friday, and Saturday evenings in summer and on Friday and Saturday evening during the school year. Would teens today believe that such a place existed that attracted name entertainers such as Little Anthony and the Imperials, The Vibrations, The Ronnettes, The Drifters, Major Lance, Mary Welles, The Impressions, Isley Brothers, Martha and the Van Delles, and The Four Tops?

The *Falcon Flash*, Vol. 27, no. 4 (November 13, 1987) also noted the opening of Meltdown, a dance club on Eisenhower Blvd. that was open Fridays and Saturdays, 8 p.m. to 1 a.m. Other teen-age dance clubs mentioned in various trivia, but not verified, include Odyssey and VIP.

Other General Projects and Events

Channel One

On February 22, 1993 Channel One was officially launched; a television broadcaster, Channel One was the "newest rage" offering a television monitor in every classroom simply by the school's agreement to broadcast its program every morning. The company claimed to bring current events to students, according to the October 9, 1992 edition of the *Falcon Flash*. The fifteen minute news segment, which also included advertising, resulted in passing time between classes being reduced from five to four minutes.

According to Wikipedia, Channel One has been controversial largely due to the commercial content of the show. Critics claim that it is a problem in classrooms because it forces children to watch ads, wastes class time, and wastes tax dollars. A thirty-second advertising spot can cost up to two hundred thousand dollars.

Supporters argue that the ads are necessary to help keep the program running and lease TVs, DVRs (Head-End Units) and satellite dishes to schools, as well as commercial-free educational video through Channel One Connection. In 2006, the American Academy of Pediatrics reported that research indicated that children who watched Channel One remembered the commercials more than they remembered the news. Another criticism is that very little time is dedicated to actual news and that corporate marketing and PR tie-ins promote products and services, furthering consumerism.

Falcon Signage Gifts

The Falcon mural on the gymnasium wall was created by local artist Cig Stroman (father of Brad Stroman '67 who is a former art teacher at LDHS) in the mid-1970s when Dr. Hoerner called Mr. Steven Messner to his office, announcing that he would like something depicted on these walls. While Mr. Stroman agreed he could do this, he questioned how he would get up to that height since there was no access. Mr. Messner, then an assistant principal, went to Mr. Jay Book who was in charge of facilities, including supervision of ladders and all things of a construction nature. Mr. Messner and Mr. Stroman conferred and agreed that scaffolding was needed. For some reason, Mr. Book said no to the scaffolding, so Mr. Messner went to Mr. Charles Van De Water who had been an Army engineer in Vietnam with experience in special building projects. Mr. Van De Water built a ramp up to the area so that Mr. Stroman could create the mural and the Falcon could soar above the players.

In addition to the mural there likely were two additional signs in the gymnasium throughout the past fifty years, one smaller than the other. One of these was a sign sponsored by the Alumni Association and created through the donated talent of Kurt Stoner which proclaimed "Falcon Pride" and was installed sometime after 1989. Others recall a sign above the door through which the players would leave the gymnasium, this one stating "Home of the Falcons."

It is believed that during the renovations of the gymnasium both signs were removed, possibly for repairs or "refurbishing"; however, they were never returned or replaced. New scoreboards filled the area of the one sign, and, in time, most people simply forgot about the "old signs." There also was an exterior sign noting "Home of the Falcons," purchased through the efforts of the Senior High Student Council and the Adult Booster Club in 1977. It is believed that this sign was removed as it had deteriorated in the weather. The blue signage designating District III Championships is the most recent signage.

The Alumni Association recently tried to locate the old signs in an attempt to restore them for use somewhere or simply for archival displays, but without success. Through the research for this publication there now is a fairly comprehensive list of gifts that have been given to the school. It is hoped that a courtesy can be extended to notify the person or group that gave any gift that it is being replaced if such necessity occurs. Perhaps the original donor would want to be a part of the new gift, or at least receive mention when the new sign (or other donation) is installed.

Mock Presidential Nominating Convention

Mr. (now Dr.) Steven Messner, humanities and archeology teacher and later assistant principal, was the impetus for the very successful Mock Democratic Convention held at Lower Dauphin High School in the spring of 1972. As Dr. Messner relates, "The idea came from a mock convention concept that I participated in at Bloomsburg as an undergraduate. Mr. Tom Campbell, also a social studies teacher, supported my recommendations and we started to develop the process. I carefully determined how we would control the flow of the audience with the student body and Mrs. Muriel (Hubert) Humphrey. We started to contact national candidates and their wives that we were doing the convention concept and the response was tremendous. Gerald Ford had done the one at Bloomsburg and we set the entire concept up based on my college notes from that event. Kathy Saltzer was my inspiration because of my belief that she should run for student council president and I believed that women should be leaders. That belief hasn't changed.

"Once Tom Eagleton's issues came into play, Mrs. Humphrey became the key player and keynote speaker for our event, replacing Senator Eagleton. I guess I was the adult in charge, but, actually, Kathy and the other members of H-2 homeroom were in charge. I had already played the Mock Convention game; the game the students were playing was life and I was the pleasant supporter."

According to *The Patriot*, April 22, 1972, more than 600 students participated in the mock convention, complete with nominating speeches and demonstrations. A central committee was formed from a humanities class which, in turn, divided into subcommittees. Joan Hassel noted at the time, "We have the same basic operating committees as a real convention." Each candidate had his own campaign committee and the eleven recognized Democratic contenders were represented by these committees, advised by faculty members. The process followed was that of the actual nominating conventions only with the number of voting delegates reduced to 481 and the agenda condensed into a two-and-a-half hour period.

The student campaign committees were in touch with the real headquarters to secure posters, buttons, policy statements, and handout materials. An economics class was assigned the task of putting a party platform together and several were written to reflect conservative, moderate, and liberal views. A communications network was established, including a mail box area for messages.

Following her appearance on stage, Mrs. Humphrey held a press conference in the home economics suite, emphasizing women's rights and aid to the mentally handicapped. When asked if a woman might serve on a Humphrey ticket as vice president, Mrs. Humphrey replied, "I would say that there is a great possibility that such a thing could occur." During the balloting, Sen. Thomas Eagleton of Missouri, who was supporting Sen. Muskie, made an unscheduled appearance before the delegates.

Summarizing the experience at the time, Mr. Messner remarked, "This has been a tremendous experience for these students. Not only have they seen and heard the wife of a candidate and a U.S. senator, they have also learned how the political machinery works." (It should be noted that LD was among the first—if not the first—high school to conduct a mock convention.)

National Organization for Women Forum

Sometime around 1973 Lower Dauphin High School was host to a forum for the National Organization for Women (NOW) after Dr. Hoerner had received a letter from the organization asking the superintendent to respond to questions concerning the status of women at LD. Dr. Hoerner assigned this project to Mr. Steven Messner who thought it would be appropriate to emphasize the projects that our students were doing and to use the open forum model that Dr. Hoerner used for meetings. Dr. Messner now recalls, "We used the library and invited students and the public. Understandably Mr. Osevala was reluctant to attend and I remember pressing him to do so. He likely was concerned about the possible dangers of what I had created for that evening. As attendees were gathering I asked Mr. Osevala what he would like me to do that evening as I had scheduled him to make opening remarks. He said that I should make the coffee...."

"At any rate, the study groups each had a topic and questions. At the end, the response was very positive about the opportunities we provided for our students, females in particular. The NOW representatives were pleased and their comments were more positive than I had hoped. Mr. Osevala breathed a sigh of relief, seeming pleased with the result."

The irony viewed by some faculty and students regarding this event was that those who organized the event, while quite capable, were all male.

Patriotic Hill

What came to be known as Patriotic Hill—a thirty by forty foot American flag painted on the grass of a sloping rise in front of the high school—was initiated in 2001 by Detective Ryan of the Hummelstown Police Department in cooperation with various student organizations and other volunteers. Students have continued the project annually in remembrance of the terrorist attacks known collectively as "9/11."

The Falcon Mural

As this book was going to press a hugh Falcon Mural had just been completed on the back of the building housing the Subway Restaurant. This mural can be viewed from the new fields at the east end of Hummelstown.

Lower Dauphin Remembers

G. William "Bill" Peck

Lower Dauphin has always been generous in supporting fund-raisers and particularly in raising money to defray the expenses and to express good wishes to support those facing life-threatening illnesses. We were not long into LD history when one of our own was stuck down before he was even thirty years old. Early in 1966, Bill Peck was diagnosed with a disease that was still referred to only in whispers.

Mr. Peck was so confident that he would be able to beat the illness that claimed him, returning to work, even with a cane, during the few times the disease was in remission. It was heartbreaking to see his fortitude. One of the last memories I have of him is his painstaking walk down the hall to his classroom, still well-dressed and as erect as he could manage.

However, there were many returns to the hospital. In December of 1966 a "Mile of Good Wishes," by which students could sign their names to an immensely long roll of paper, was created and delivered to Mr. Peck.

In January 1967 a benefit faculty basketball game on Bill Peck Night was held to help with hospital expenses, all the more poignant because Mr. Peck himself had played on this team when he wasn't officiating basketball games. I wonder now how his teammates ever got through that particular game, because the real motivation for this game was to offer a tribute to the man and his indomitable spirit.

As a local newspaper reported on January 17, "A group of teachers from Wilmington Delaware defeated the Lower Dauphin High School faculty in a basketball game last night, but the winner was a 29-year-old Lower Dauphin mathematics teacher. … a standing room crowd of 1,900 spectators—300 more than the gym can seat—squeezed into the field house to raise $1,152 toward medical expenses and to show support for the man being honored. Mr. Peck, who has undergone three spine surgeries, arrived by ambulance and as he entered the gymnasium, 'a stillness fell over the crowd that sent chills up my spine,' said Student Council president David Lytle."

Glenn William Peck died on Saturday, February 6, 1967.

The Sun, February 24, 1967:

Resolution

Whereas, the great and supreme Ruler of the universe has in His infinite wisdom removed from among us one of our worthy and esteemed fellow laborers Glenn William Peck, and, whereas, the intimate relation held with him in the faithful discharge of his duties as mathematics teacher in the Lower Dauphin Senior High School, as faculty advisor to the Senior High School Boys' Club and as a member of the Lower Dauphin Education Association, makes it eminently befitting that we accord our appreciation of him, wherefore:

Resolved, That the wisdom and ability which he has exercised in the aid of our school district by his service and contribution, will be held in grateful remembrance;

Resolved, That the sudden removal of such a life from among our midst leaves a vacancy and a shadow that will be deeply realized by all the members and friends of the Lower Dauphin School District, and will prove a serious loss to the school district, to the community, and to the public;

Resolved, That the deep sympathy with the bereaved relatives of the deceased we express our hope that even so great a loss to us all may be overruled for good by Him, who doeth all things well;

Resolved, That a copy of these resolutions be spread upon the records of the Lower Dauphin School Board, a copy printed in the local paper, and a copy forwarded to his bereaved wife.

M. J. Mateer, President

Roy B. Brightbill, Secretary

Mark S. French

Mark S. French joined the faculty at Lower Dauphin High School in the fall of 1980 as a teacher of Earth and Space Science and as the first salaried Athletic Trainer. In December 1982 a program, known as the Alternative Education Program, began with its own double classroom configured with study carrels around its perimeter and was supervised by a variety of teachers. By fall Mr. French was asked to head this Alternative Education Program to which he brought consistency and structure. The students quickly took the program's acronym, AEP, and dubbed the area "The APE Room." What they initially failed to realize, however, was that in this room dwelt a very special and caring teacher who, they were surprised to find, would help many of them turn their lives around. Mark French was very serious in his mission to show students a better way to cope. He worked with countless students who had failed and helped them find themselves and to turn bad luck or negative life choices into self-improvement.

In addition to managing what later became known as the In School Suspension (ISS) Program, Mark French was also an athletic trainer, teacher of sports medicine, and health teacher. More than that, he was a good listener and a fast friend to students and faculty alike. Described as being quick with a joke, Mr. Craig Cassel notes that "his witticisms and edge of sarcasm were only one part of what defined him as a man."

In 2008 the unthinkable happened when Mr. French was diagnosed with Amyotrophic Lateral Sclerosis (ALS), better known as Lou Gehrig's Disease, an unrelenting disease that attacks the central nervous system and causes a loss of control of voluntary muscle movements and, ultimately, death.

That winter when Student Council officers and advisors were planning an event that would involve as many students as possible, someone jokingly suggested a dodge ball game. A student remarked, "Mr. French would have loved such a tournament!" All those present simultaneously decided that the money raised in such a tournament would go to benefit Mr. French.

While most of the medical costs and supplies were covered by insurance, there were many expenses that were not. As the advisors, Mr. Scott Payonk and Mr. Doug Grove, noted, "A wheelchair is rather useless if your house is not accessible." Mr. French had plenty of friends willing to help with the changes to the house, but the tournament could provide the funds to purchase materials to build or make what was needed. And so the tournament was born.

The annual Mark French Dodgeball Tournament has continued, as much to raise funds as to honor the memory of a man whose wisdom and common sense approach to troubled students focused on the regard he held for teenagers who needed a strong hand to guide them. While the funds raised now go toward the Mark French Scholarship and ALS research, the tournament is played, according to Mr. Cassel, "to immortalize a man who made a difference and succeeded in changing many lives." He continues, "As Mr. French used to say, 'Fire out.'"

Sam Campbell, Class of 1973

In the winter of 1973 senior Sam Campbell, a wrestler and member of the BOA (a group of young men who had formed an independent organization earlier that year) was diagnosed with cancer. The BOA[1], who, according to one of its founders, "took care of our own," joined forces with Student Council in a combined effort to provide support through fund-raisers to help defray Sam's medical expenses. April was declared as Sam Campbell Month and the two organizations planned a number of activities: a car wash (which the generous public kept in operation for seven hours), an exhibition wrestling match with the Polish National Wrestling team, a raffle, a bake sale (held in cooperation with the Future Homemakers of America Club) and a Student Council Fun Night. At the latter, a film, "The Pit and the Pendulum" was shown and Steve Keefer's band, Damascus, provided musical entertainment.

Council asked for every school organization to "participate and support their efforts which were spearheaded by the Brotherhood of America." Local merchants also donated merchandise for a raffle held in addition to the student effort. $1,787.68 was raised and a check was presented to Sam's father, Mr. Charles Campbell. As Keefer remembers, "It was this partnership that really united our class. It was quite powerful. If only every high school group could do as much…"

There have been a number of fund-raisers for special causes, not recorded but whose efforts reveal the care and support Lower Dauphin gives to its own.

---

1 Formed as Burners of American and aka Brothers of America and the Boys of America. For more see "Unofficial Student Organizations."

Summit Achiever Amy Wallish Hahn '87

Amy Hahn is Vice President and the General Manager of Global Hershey Experience and Licensing in the Hershey Company. In this role, Hahn is responsible for leading and growing Hershey's retail and licensing businesses. She serves as general manager of Hershey's interactive retail attractions in five countries, including Hershey's Chocolate World in Hershey, Pa. and sites in Times Square, Shanghai, and Singapore. She is responsible for multiple e-commerce stores and licensing of Hershey's brands around the globe. While at Hershey, Hahn has held a wide range of leadership positions across the business, including brand marketing, where she built the company's iconic brands, such as Hershey's, Almond Joy and York Peppermint Patties.

In nearly 20 years with Hershey, Hahn has held a wide range of leadership positions. She began her career at Hershey in operations strategy and engineering, leading cross-functional teams in manufacturing planning and margin improvement initiatives. She spent several years working with the U.S. drug channel. Prior to serving as general manager of The Hershey Experience, responsible for retail and e-commerce in the United States, she oversaw the company's e-commerce catalog as director of Hershey Gifts.

Hahn was recently elected to the Board of Director at NEW (Network of Executive Women) at its annual members meeting held during the NEW Leadership Summit in Los Angeles.

Amy has noted, "Be willing to put yourself out there and take a risk; be willing to take on diverse assignments and even "risky" moves. I have developed leadership skills and a deeper knowledge of nearly every corner of Hershey's business model. My work experiences cross several functions and leadership of projects in many business areas, all of which have prepared me for a current role with global span of control, managing several business models and a diverse talent force."

Pranks

Pranks

General Pranks

Fake Bomb Threats of Record

While phoning in fake bomb threats is a serious action, many viewed it as a prank when the action first became prevalent about the same time as school jointures were being formed in the early 1960s. Students rarely thought of the possible dangerous consequences; most bomb threats were made simply to hope that schools would be dismissed for the rest of the day. At Lower Dauphin High School our investigation shows that the first recorded bomb threat was in **1965**. This was followed by one on Valentine's Day in **1966.** There likely were others throughout the years, but the next evidence we have of a bomb threat is that of the **Class of 1978** which, among the many escapades for which they were known, claimed (inaccurately) that it had been the first class to call in a false bomb threat, placing its first call (there were several) in September **1977**.

The next confirmed date for a bomb threat is September 27, **1983** when the **Class of 1984's** Nasty Nine called in a threat "to blow everyone away." This warning "sent all students from the Lower Dauphin School District home to enjoy a beautiful day."[1] The **Class of 1989** remembers this event and mentions it in their Class Reflection, "We were greeted in middle school with our first bomb threat experience where the school was evacuated, and we ended as seniors with another bomb threat."

At 11:30 on March 3, **1989** students were evacuated following a bomb threat call stating, "I have planted a bomb in the high school and it will go off in one hour." Police were notified, students were told about the threat and asked to clear their lockers, leave the lockers open, and report to the far side of the parking lot. A thorough search of the building—including lockers, book shelves, trash cans, and restrooms—was conducted by police and volunteer faculty. By 2 p.m. Hummelstown police had identified four eighth grade suspects who were then charged.

The final verified threat of a bomb in the first fifty years was a report from the **Class of 2009**, "We also took a bomb threat our freshman year and turned it into a wheelchair race."

Auditorium High Rollers

The **Class of 1966** recalls that the year they were juniors, the seniors (Class of 1965) turned a pigeon loose in the auditorium during the Senior Awards ceremony. As Harold Johns (Class of 1966) tells his story, "As the date for our Senior Awards approached, I started wondering what our class could do to make our evening as memorable as last year's. I thought of marbles and began telling everyone to bring marbles and that, when Lester Ratcliffe opened the ceremony, to drop the marbles on the floor. The floor was tile and sloped toward the stage, allowing the marbles to crash down on the floor, making a loud noise as they were dropped, and then rolling to the front of the auditorium.

---

[1]   Recalled in the *Falcon Flash*, June 1984.

"I didn't think I was making much progress until the day of the awards. Upon entering the auditorium, all you could hear was the sound of marbles clacking together in pockets, purses, and even small bags. I did become a bit anxious as there had to be thousands of them.

"When Ratcliffe began, Steve Lower stood up and yelled 'Let 'em roll!' and the sound was almost deafening. The small orbs did just what was expected and more. They crashed to the floor, rolled down hill, bouncing off the metal chair legs and rolled all the way to the stage. A few teachers on stage laughed, some looked puzzled, and some actually looked panicked. It was a success.

"Everyone was careful when approaching the stage to receive awards, some even shuffling their feet to kick the marbles around further. Only later did it become a challenge when some students collected some of the marbles and rolled them down the hallway from the office toward the Senior High wings."

V-Dubs on the Ramp

The **Class of 1968** parked a Volkswagen on the ramp leading from the lobby to the library and B-wing. It is speculated that they brought it in one night after a rehearsal. According to Elaine Bell, "By the way, that car shown in the yearbook was Inez Puzuks' red Karmann Ghia. Not sure why and where we used it but I think it was for "It's a Big Wide Wonderful World."

Pay with Pennies

Early in their senior year the **Class of 1970** proclaimed a "Pay-with-pennies-at-the-cafeteria-day." With the first twenty or so payers the cashier counted each penny, but the lunch line became so backed up that the cafeteria manager brought out a five-gallon bucket. Everyone kept a sense of humor. Then, at the end-of-year awards assembly many class members arrived at the auditorium with pockets full of marbles....On cue, all the marbles were released and began rolling down the sloped floor, ending only when hitting the front of the stage base. The adults did not see the humor.

Vietnam War Moratorium

In the spring of **1971** young men's minds did not turn necessarily to thoughts of love, as attested to by the three seniors who went to Washington, DC to participate in the Vietnam War Moratorium on April 24 of **1971**. As Joe Quigley reported,

"It was really an eye opener. Everywhere we went there were hippies handing out Socialist papers. We had never seen anything like it. The three of us were patriotic and, although hardly anyone wanted the war, we were not anti-American."

Pigeons and Painted Doors

The week of graduation this **Class of 1971** felt unjustly punished when the Awards Assembly was moved to the evening because of what had happened the previous year. A member of the class explained that to get even they wanted a really notable event. When someone mentioned releasing birds in the auditorium, the perpetrator decided he and his friends would do just that. He explains,

"Someone in our class raised homing pigeons and we arranged to pick up four of them. We bought cotton wrapping, wrote **Class of 1971** on the rolled cotton and tied them to the birds' legs, then put the birds in a burlap bag. Very late the night before the awards program we slipped into the rear of the auditorium off the parking lot, silently opening and closing the door.

"With the door closed we were in complete darkness, not daring to use a flashlight. Each of the two of us stumbled, kicking paint buckets immediately after which the custodians' voices were silenced. We waited until the talking resumed and we began to inch our way to the stage curtain sensing the vast emptiness of the auditorium. I threw the first pigeon into the air and heard him flapping his wings as he flew blindly into the total blackness. Then we heard the bird hit the wall and the sound of wings flapping as it hit the floor. We then placed the other three birds on the stage steps and ran out the back door. The next day we checked and the birds were roosting in the ledges on the ceiling. The students noticed them, but the only effect it had was that the teachers did not want to turn the lights on for fear of disturbing the birds.

"Emboldened, we started to think of other pranks to play. We again went to the backstage door, intending to take it off its hinges to paint "**Class of 1971**" on it. While we worked on the door we told the two girls with us to paint "**Class of '71**" on the parking lot. We couldn't get the door open, so we had to be satisfied with the message the girls had decided to paint on the brick wall of the building. The next morning I noticed two small drips of black paint on my sneakers. I spent the rest of the day in fear of someone noticing them."

Pin-ups and Sliding Down Drains

The **Class of 1973** was full of pranks, as well as holding the reputation of being fun-loving, creative, as well as responsible. They enjoyed strong leadership in their class as well as in Student Council; mostly they enjoyed riding the wave of eliciting awe from adults who were fascinated with the changes that were happening in society during this time.

Their practical jokes began in junior high when they taped pin-up photos in the window blinds so that when the teacher lowered the blinds the pin-ups were revealed. They are still talking about the day Ken Mull's voice, full of anxiety, was heard calling for help. The sound was coming from the sink drain, a voice claiming to have been washed down the sink. The teacher did not think to look under the tiny space beneath the sink where the pint-sized Ken was hiding.

The Missing Basketball Uniform

According to stories and confirmed by Jerry Peacock (Class of 1975) in 2010, "During the summer of **1973** before heading into my junior year, Coach Miller coordinated a wonderful trip wherein the basketball team traveled in two vans to Canada, and played exhibition basketball games in New Brunswick, Nova Scotia, and Prince Edward Island. I don't know how Coach Miller funded the tour, but it was a great experience. As players, we stayed with various families at each stop. The trip gave each of us the opportunity to experience different aspects of the Canadian culture. We had a great time, and I don't think we lost a single game.

"As I recall, I didn't forget my uniform, but indeed, I did bring the wrong uniform! Suffice to say, it was not one of my proudest moments. Mr. Futchko and Mr. Romano joined us on the trip to help chaperone and drive the vans. I believe Mr. Romano allowed Mr. Futchko do most, if not all, of the driving…..which over time became quite the source of amusement to all!"

V-Dub on the Steps

On an afternoon in **1974** Mr. Moore found his black VW parked on the steps of H-wing, courtesy of an imaginative senior class.

The Lost Falcon

In October **1976** the Falcon bird mascot costume went missing, whether by accident or design has not been determined as someone just happened to notice that it was not in the closet where it was kept. After a brief search (having no leads), the next day a notice was placed in the daily bulletin asking for information on the missing costume. According to the *Falcon Flash*, "Later that day Mr. Dimond received word that the Falcon head had been found with a major concussion (smashed head) in the girls' locker room. The head was rushed for emergency surgery to F-14 where 'Dr.' Fickes (the art teacher who had created the Falcon head years earlier) carefully mended the Falcon's bruises while Terri Stare 'flew' the bird's body to the dry cleaners."

Homecoming 1982

The very imaginative underground Electronics Club members created and entered their own float in the Homecoming Float Parade. Their subject was the Rocky Horror Picture Show although they wisely announced its theme as "Dracula." Their pranks typically were built on inside jokes and the fact they were not an official club.

Capturing the PA System in the early 1980s

Imagine the surprise to the student body when the music of "Journey" was heard in every room one day after school. This also was courtesy of the Electronics Club in the early 1980s.

1983 on the Auditorium Roof

Probably the most creative and most risky senior prank was carried out in the spring of **1983** by two ingenious seniors who, one crescent moonlit night, set out on a secret mission, ladder and paint in hand. Their target was the roof of the high school auditorium. Access to this roof required climbing two levels. Not wanting to pull the ladder up behind them for fear of losing their grip and being left with no way to leave the scene, the two classmates mounted the ladder—one at a time, taking turns climbing and watching to make sure that (1) no one saw them, (2) no one took their ladder, or (3) the ladder did not topple. Reaching their destination, they were dismayed to find that the roof was made of loose gravel. Not to be deterred, they scraped the pebbles aside to reach a smoother surface beneath the stones. With great care they painted **LD '83** and quickly returned to the ground, one level at a

time. A day or two later they rented an airplane (yes, they really did) and took photos of their handiwork, making the **Class of 1983** the only one to leave its signature in bold lettering on the roof of the high school.

Cycling Down F-Wing

The following spring a motorcycle rider from the **Class of 1984** cruised down F-wing, while a pig waddling through the cafeteria provided entertainment for those who were disappointed with the "dull" spring weather.

The final issue of that year's *Falcon Flash,* recalls "an early Fourth of July was recognized in LD's hallways" when various bombs and firecrackers were set off. Another bomb that almost "ignited" was a controversy going on with the smoking area."[2] Even the perpetrators admitted later that it was not much to be proud of, except for the getting away with it.

I Shot an Arrow

RG of the Class of **1987** admits to shooting an arrow across Route 322 during a physical education class his junior year and during their senior year he, along with friends, "sabotaged the halls of LD with water balloons."

Cafeteria Boycott

On Monday February 6, **1988** many students boycotted the cafeteria lunch line, bringing their own brown bag lunches in protest of an increase in lunch prices. Evidently no clear explanation had been given in advance to the students; rather, only a brief written statement of a price increase, without details, was given to each student to take home the previous Friday. The protest was deemed to have been planned spontaneously and did not disrupt the operation of the cafeteria. The students were said to have behaved appropriately.

Lawn Ornaments

Arguably the **Class of 1996** pulled off the senior class prank that engaged the largest number of persons in class prank history. Acting as a body of the whole, the class members decorated the front lawn of the school with dozens of stolen lawn ornaments, including a goldfish pond.

---

[2] *Falcon Flash*, June 1984.

Beyond Pranks

The Ultimate Prank: the Carol Channing Hoax

The ultimate prank at Lower Dauphin began with the arrival of student teacher Andrew Sullivan in the fall of **1967**. Mr. Sullivan's college roommate was student teaching in Middletown at the same time and was reputed to have some connections to theatre personalities. Early in the second semester, Mr. Sullivan went to his supervising teacher, Mrs. Emily Keller, with what sounded like a very exciting possibility: Carol Channing would be coming to the Harrisburg area and Sullivan said his roommate knew someone who worked for her and could arrange a personal appearance for Miss Channing at Lower Dauphin High School on her way to her next theatrical engagement. With wild excitement, great anticipation, and much flurry, arrangements were made for this visit of Carol Channing, at the time starring in her definitive role in the musical "Hello Dolly," one she played on Broadway for two years and on tour for the next 30.

In readiness for this amazing event, the school administration was given the name of the specific champagne that was Miss Channing's favorite, special flowers were ordered from Early's Flowers in Hummelstown, assignments were readily accepted by some of the faculty, students were vying for a way to be part of the welcoming entourage, and, most important of all, Mr. Seitzinger was scurrying to rehearse his concert band for the thrill of a lifetime: playing "Hello, Dolly" for the star lead in the Broadway musical of the same name! Mr. Seitzinger had played in name dance bands during his own career, but had never served as the conductor for a Broadway star. Of course, it could only be hoped that Carol Channing would perform her signature number.

As the important day approached, a letter was sent by Mr. William Linnane, the designated chairman of the English Department to all faculty, despite cautionary measures being advised by the former chairman who was on maternity leave:

> There is a 90% possibility that Broadway star Carol Channing will perform at Lower Dauphin on Friday, January 12, 7th period. This notice is short because we have not been fully informed ourselves. Her specific arrival time is uncertain so that there may or may not be an assembly called sometime during 7th period. We know that you would appreciate seeing "Dolly" herself and would hate to pass up the opportunity of having her visit our school.

The morning of Miss Channing's expected appearance, most people, except the usual skeptics, were full of excitement. Mr. Sullivan assured everyone that this roommate had confirmed all of the plans and that, yes, Carol Channing would be arriving. As the day wore on, Dr. Henry Hoerner, Superintendent, telephoned Mr. Linnane and asked him to contact Middletown High School to find out the delay and to ask if perhaps Miss Channing was running late. Mr. Brunner, the principal and also a friend of Mr. Linnane, told Bill he didn't know anything about an appearance anywhere. Carol Channing was not expected at Middletown and certainly was not there. Dr. Hoerner went to young Mr. Sullivan and told him this. Totally upset and confused, Mr. Sullivan asked if he could try to reach Carol Channing's agent. Somehow he got through but the agent had no idea what Andy Sullivan was talking about and told him that Miss Channing was not, nor would be, coming to Pennsylvania. It was all a hoax.

Someone (possibly Mr. Seitzinger) had some connections with the Totem Pole Playhouse Theatre and asked the managers, whom he knew, if they could help the school. One of the managers was Jean Stapleton, a relatively unknown actor at the time, who graciously agreed to meet with the students the next day. She sat in the front of the auditorium meeting with any students who wished to talk with her. Mr. Linnane remembers her telling them that she had just shot a pilot for a television series and that she thought it was a funny show and just might be a hit. The irony is that Miss Stapleton would later become more famous than Carol Channing to television audiences as Edith Bunker, the long-suffering wife in the hit television program "All in the Family."

A Prank Gone Wrong: the Falcon Missile

The Falcon missile never was the school mascot, but rather was a gift to the school from the Olmsted Air Force Base in Middletown as a tribute to the power of the falcon bird and the might of the world's first fully operational guided air-to-air missile. Alumni of the 1960s remember that the missile was prominently displayed in the lobby outside of the auditorium.

During the summer of **1970** some of the graduates who worked for the school district took the missile and hid it in the ceiling above the desk of the principal. It was found during the following school year when the ceiling tiles began to sag from the missile's weight.

The following spring the missile was taken by the **Class of 1971** who mistakenly thought it was tradition that the senior class hide the missile. They saw a chance to take the rocket after overhearing a custodian tell the principal they should put the rocket somewhere for safe-keeping until after graduation. Taking it to the projection booth in the auditorium, these seniors entrusted the stage crew with the missile. One class member recently related, "The next day I gave specific instructions to a stage crew member to see to it the rocket was returned after the requisite scavenger hunt or whatever else they wanted to do. I figured they made arrangements to return it but I never knew for sure."

Apparently the stage crew took the missile up to the catwalk and lowered it into the ceiling of the girls' backstage restroom. Records and recollections are unclear as to whether the missile was found 18 months later or much later, perhaps not until 1983. In any event it was then kept in the principal's office.

Tom Backenstose '83 said it is his understanding that the missile was not found until **1983** when he, then a senior and a member of the stage crew, gained possession of it from the principal's office and took it home. There he restored the damaged missile, as well as replacing its nose cone which had not been recovered. As Tom confirmed in September **2009**,

> I took it to my home to clean it and make it whole. …it was in very poor condition when found. The nose cone was missing and most of the orange paint had peeled away. I cleaned and repainted it in gloss white and blue, making every effort to mask and preserve the original decals, warning stickers, and other identifying marks. I also hand-crafted and fit a new nose cone (the Internet didn't exist then, so I had no idea how to find out what the original looked like). I returned it within a week; however, within two weeks it was again taken from the principal's office, recovered, and then stored in the Guidance Office.

In January **1984** the missile was taken from the Guidance Office by a posse of seniors during the school day as part of Senior Hook Day. According to the account in the *Falcon Flash*, some adults were in on what they thought was part of the day's fun and made no attempt to apprehend the culprits. It was further reported that days after the abduction a ransom note was delivered with evidence that the missile had been taken and would eventually be returned to the school.

The missile did reappear several months later, in April, when it was carried across the stage in a scene in the spring musical. This action fit into the scene in "Lil Abner" in which the Dogpatchers carry all kinds of odd items across the stage on their way to sell these oddities to the government who wanted to requisition their town and was purchasing anything as a show of good faith. Of course, the missile being carried across the stage brought the house down as it came as a complete surprise. We expected then to see the missile back in the possession of the school. However, following the show, the falcon missile was never seen again.

There is an unsubstantiated account that the last night of the musical members of the **Class of 1985** staged a sneak attack in the parking lot and captured the missile; however, substantiated rumor, as well as a bold comment in the *Falcon Flash*, has it that the missile was dismantled and that various pieces of it are held by members of the **Class of 1984**. It is a sad commentary that such a special item, that should have been guarded by the students, was, instead, destroyed by them. In 2010, a custodian from LD received an anonymous telephone call one evening and was told to look in the back of his truck. There he found what was to be identified as the missing nose cone of the original falcon missile as identified by Tom Backenstose who had refurbished the missile in 1983.

Protests and Sit-Ins

Lest we forget, there were darker moments in the history of the school which, in retrospect, we might all agree were examples of the American system at work; however, at the time they occurred, they took on monumental importance in the eyes of those affected. As a school, the objective was to minimize the negative effects on the students. The following summaries are being included for that reason as well as to not be charged with reporting life at LDHS only through rose-colored glasses.

In the spring of **1976** the Commencement Program (not Commencement itself) was threatened to be canceled over a protest that escalated into a senior incident when an individual student objected to the graduating class's entering the theatre to a musical processional that was in keeping with the student-produced historical pageant ("The World Turned Upside Down," a bi-centennial pageant that had been written for the occasion). At a meeting held for the senior class an offer was made that if all seniors would learn the words to the Alma Mater and sing this at graduation, consideration would be given to the objection to processioning to anything other than "Pomp and Circumstance." After much stress on all sides, the students processioned to "Pomp and Circumstance." The pageant was a rousing success; however, damage remains with hurt feelings and a division in the class as to what had been a difficult decision for everyone.

In the late **1980s** (with more detail provided in the "Cafeteria Boycott" and in the "Reflection of the **Class of 1992**)," a massive protest was created when the price of cafeteria lunches was raised. Protestors carried their lunches and booed those who continued to patronize the cafeteria. After about two weeks, however, conditions returned to normal.

Also in the late **1980s** there was an outcry over an alleged cheating incident that resulted in a dilemma of whether or not the person who had been deemed the valedictorian would speak at Commencement. A few days before graduation students picketed the District Administration Center. The issue was compounded because of the sensitivity of the matter and the closeness to the date of Commencement. A solution had to be found and was, but one that did not satisfy everyone and would have needed the wisdom of Solomon to mitigate.

Another incident at the end of that decade caused a sit-in, filling the hallway leading to the Senior High wings. It began following an accusation after disciplinary action taken by an administrator at an athletic event in which LD was the guest at the school where the incident had happened. An announcement over the PA system asked the students who were protesting to move to the auditorium where a meeting could be held. Representatives who claimed to have been eye witnesses were identified and the matter turned over to the superintendent. While the situation could have been volatile, acknowledging the anger of the students and assuring an investigation calmed the waters. The situation was resolved and the accused exonerated.

An End to Pranks As We Knew Them

An article in a more recent issue of *Falcon Flash* (Jaclyn Verner, **Class of 2007**) raised the issue of diminishing senior pranks. She noted that new school policies were addressing incidents that in the past would have been viewed as minor. Verner questioned whether the reason was that more recent students were facing the consequences of mistakes made by prior senior classes. She provided this example, "Until last year, it was a tradition at LD for seniors to leave their mark on underclassmen by writing their graduating year on each individual. Without warning, this harmless task was forbidden without any explanation." She concluded, "If little things like this are being taken away, who knows when senior pranks will be forced to come completely to an end." (She appears to have answered her own question.)

Senior Hook Days
Senior Hook Days of Note

In spring, a senior class's fancy turns to thoughts of hook day. While not an approved tradition, "hooking school" is on the mind of most seniors thinking about ways to make a mark in the school's book of memories. At the very least seniors *think about* a reason not to go to school.

While no class has yet proved to be the originators of Senior Hook Day, the **Class of 1966** is the earliest to include mention of it in their Class Reflection. Marty Wrzesniewski Bossler writes, "Does anyone remember wearing an angel blouse, black olives served in the cafeteria, John Knaub and his sweet gherkin pickles, "Are you with me people," Mrs. Mandes and her Civics class, Mike Remsburg's cap gun going off in his pants pocket, and **Senior Hook Day?**"

The **Class of 1971** erroneously has stated that it was they who inaugurated Senior Hook Day. Joe Quigley writes, "During the spring of **1971**, many of us jumped into our fast steeds and traveled to the Gettysburg Battlefield. We picnicked and played softball among the monuments. We were also the first to take part in national Earth Day. In May we entertained ourselves by playing "buck-buck" in front of the school utilizing the flag pole as base of operation."

Senior Hook Day **1976**, according to Pam Sattazahn Zerphy, "was supposed to be a closely guarded secret when seniors were absent from school and met at a pre-determined location for a day of fun. Some teachers always knew about it."

The Absentee Bulletin for March 27, **1980** shows 309 absentees that day in the high school, approximately one-third of the population, and dubbed by science teacher Mr. David Smith as "Water Break Day." Keith Garrison, **Class of 1980**, recalls that several who served on the Commencement Committee were "the only ones in the entire senior class" who did not "hook" school, but remained behind and worked on the program that needed to be completed. That was true dedication. Celebrating their 30th Class reunion in 2010, this group memorialized all the slides from the program and their school year onto a DVD.

On January 13, **1984**, 146 seniors (66%) were absent. According to the *Flash*, "… it was the disease of the '80's, 'sickle senioritis,' caused by classroom fatigue." The few who did come to school were exposed to a disappointed administration. In fact, this incident has received the most support of any of the many plans from the **Class of '84**. This class even admitted that "for once, the seniors felt proud about something they had done."

Following one of several alleged hook days by the **Class of 1984**, a senior wrote a letter to the editor of the *Falcon Flash*, "I am writing this letter in protest of the methods utilized by the school administrators to handle the recent Senior Hook Day…. It is time the officials realize that a majority of the Seniors have a list of priorities that they have set for themselves and attending school for one particular day is not always the top priority."

The Un-Hook Day of the Class of 1973

The ultimate Senior Hook Day celebrant was the **Class of 1973** who rose to the challenge to NOT take a hook day. As they remember: One spring day, Principal Osevala summoned Rick Hivner and Kathy Saltzer into his office and challenged them to come up with an event that would curtail Senior Hook Day. After conferring with classmates, they suggested, "Provide us with a pig roast and concert and we promise to cancel." The deal was struck. For days in advance of the non-hook day, notices were posted and announcements were made by students to not jeopardize this celebration. A roasting pit was dug in front of the school by the flagpole. The entire school benefitted by the picnic treat, followed by a concert in the auditorium by none other than Rich Clare and Pentagon. No class could top that for a school hook day!

Summit Achiever Nicholas (Nick) Poppy '91

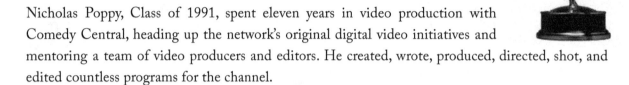

Nicholas Poppy is the holder of an Emmy, awarded for "Outstanding Special Short-format Live-action Entertainment Program" in 2011 for "The Daily Show." Further, he has been a nominee for this award three times (2009, 2011, and 2012).

Nicholas Poppy, Class of 1991, spent eleven years in video production with Comedy Central, heading up the network's original digital video initiatives and mentoring a team of video producers and editors. He created, wrote, produced, directed, shot, and edited countless programs for the channel.

He was also the Senior Producer overseeing Original Digital programming at ABC News. In that capacity he worked with persons such as Bob Woodruff, Katie Couric, George Stephanopoulos, and Christiane Amanpour. He was responsible for the creative and editorial direction of these shows, as well as the development and execution of new series, several of which were named as Webby Award honorees. Nicholas currently is a New York City-based producer, director, and writer.

A graduate of Williams College, Nicholas and his colleague Chris Boebel earned early accolades for their documentary film "Containment: Life After Three Mile Island," receiving the Best Documentary Award at the ArtsFest Film Festival, the Appalachian Film Festival, and the Putnam Valley Film and Video Festival, as well as the Best Over-All Film at the Quittapahilla Film Festival and the Black Earth Film Festival. "Containment" was screened at more than fifty film festivals and several universities, including MIT, Vassar, and Penn State, and was supported by grants from the Puffin Foundation and the Hugh Hefner Foundation.

Other film credits include "Zombie-American," starring Ed Helms, which was screened at more than 75 film festivals where it won several awards. Nick also has written for "The Boston Globe," "The Believer," "BookForum," "indieWire," "Salon," ABC News, and Comedy Central. His interview with author Paula Fox was featured in a recent collection, "Always Apprentices: The Believer Magazine Presents Twenty-Two Conversations Between Writers."

At Lower Dauphin Nicholas Poppy was Student Council President, a National Merit Scholar finalist, participated in soccer and dramatics, and was the founder of the school's chapter of Amnesty International and the Ecology Club. He also attended the Pennsylvania Governor's School for International Studies. At Williams College, Nicholas spent his junior year in England at Oxford University and had the opportunity to travel to the Czech Republic and Morocco.

Nicholas, the son of Jessie and Wendell Poppy, a popular principal at Lower Dauphin elementary schools, is the youngest of our Summit Achievers.

UNOFFICIAL STUDENT
ORGANIZATIONS

Unofficial Student Organizations

Private Societies

While high school fraternities were never a presence at Lower Dauphin High School, there were several organizations that might have qualified for such a designation. All except two (Symposium Society and Culture Creeps) were male-only in membership. In some quarters the organizations were misunderstood because their camaraderie was suggestive of a secret society and, although some students questioned their motivation, all were positive in mission and some even crusaders for the good of their Alma Mater.

Symposium Society

The Symposium Society is the first secret club on record at LDHS. Formed by the **Class of 1965,** its purpose was social with overtones of organized intellectual activities which some thought were a cover for their enviable, but decorous parties, desirable in the sense that everyone else wanted to be invited to these events. This group was class all the way, even issuing coveted membership cards.

They remember the Farm House, the stream, the tug of war, and the white banners created from bed sheets which to this day are brought out upon the occasion of their class reunions and other related special events.

The Blue Guard

The pioneer male covert group at Lower Dauphin was the self-styled Blue Guard, formed under the leadership of John Banks, Mike Yancheff, Steve Sipe, Karl Yankey, and Mickey Demuth. The Blue Guard was LD's version of the Red Guard (only far less political) and was composed of mainly senior boys and lettering underclassmen. This was not an organized club but rather a group of students who wanted to show school spirit. Arm bands were sold for $1.00 and supporters wore these on game day to signify "school spirit." Anyone was welcome to purchase the arm band of which many were sold.

The Blue Guard members sat together at athletic competitions with the avowed mission of increasing school spirit. A fan of the Blue Guard spoke of its success and stated that the sports teams played with more desire and determination knowing that the people in the stands cared about them. Resented by some and envied by others, many of the Guard's detractors didn't notice that in the first issue of the Guard's underground newspaper (tongue-in-cheek named the *Flush Gazette*) they defined themselves as "loyal sports fans who support LD teams."

In the first issue of their countercultural and irreverent underground newspaper, they invited anyone who had strong school spirit and a desire to see LD go for the best to sit with them at the next football game. Perhaps it was the name of this newspaper that bothered some others or perhaps it was a perception by some that the group was elitist. Whatever it was, it took only one issue of the newspaper and appearances of the group at a few games and pep rallies for jealousy to begin, despite the open invitation by the Guard to others to join them.

The next issue of their newspaper thanked the members of the faculty who found the *Flush Gazette* a school morale booster. According to Alan Larsen who recently was asked about his recollection of the publication, "It had the simultaneous virtues of ticking off the administration and ramping up school spirit. The identities of its authors and how the newspaper miraculously appeared in the hallways remain a secret to this day."

Among its varied information, the *Gazette* announced that in wrestling LD was the first school in the U.S. that had three All-Americans in the 1964-65 season at the scholastic level and the only team to have six boys chosen to train for the 1968 Olympics: Rhone, Kahler, Pinkerton, Sanders, Umberger, and Shellenhamer.[1]

The Guard thanked the football players for bringing a winning season back to the school. While the newspaper encouraged attendance at the Senior Class Play, it also noted that there was a sense among some students that the Blue Guard were not welcome to attend the play because they might cause trouble. The *Gazette* disputed the rumor, confirming the Guard's purpose was to organize school spirit, not tear it down, and that they supported the play and would demonstrate that by their attendance.

After criticizing the bonfire at the pep rally for the Middletown game, the *Flush* published this account of the game itself, "...on that night 1,000 stunned spectators watched one of the greatest things that ever happened in L.D. history. For the first time the students—the whole student body— was behind the team. In return, the Birds played their ever-lovin' hearts out. Never showing defeat in their eyes throughout the game, the Falcons set back the Raiders by a score of 27-25, and destroyed their hopes of the CAC crown. ... The student body never gave up hope as many saw the last few seconds of the game from the field's edge. With one minute left on the clock, the Falcons trailed at a score of 25-21, but they wouldn't admit defeat. The crowd went wild as the Falcons marched 80 yards in some 70 seconds. This was only the second time in L.D. history that the Falcons flew higher than the Raiders. When the last seconds finally ticked off the clock the crowd swarmed their heroes."

The Warriors

Unfortunately, there were a few unpleasant incidents from a short-lived group known as the Warriors who seemed to form in an opposition to the Blue Guard. An account of a fight on the parking lot between a member of the Blue Guard and a Warrior was noted in the former's newspaper that also reported that a "brawl resulted after a comment made by the Warriors to the Blue Guard." Some believe that the Warriors were simply those who believed that the Blue Guard took school spirit to the extreme. A letter attributed to a Warrior ends with "I don't like school spirit. I am solemnly against (it) like all the rest of the Warriors. What's even worse, we hate the B.G. because cheering is for sissies!"

Most students and faculty supported the Blue Guard because they seemed to represent what high schools should produce: clean cut young men who supported school activities. Their support, however,

---

[1] The former is unconfirmed, the latter confirmed by the attendees at the training camp.

did not extend to students they dubbed "The Culture Creeps," a quartet who had interests other than sports. (See below.) A purported letter from the editor shows a streak of unkindness, "Dear Editor, My lunch table has been invaded by the Culture Creeps. Not only have they enraged me, but the many others who sit around me . . . . I feel that my life is going to the worms."

There was, however, a backlash: . . ."be kind because we can never really know who another human being might be. ... For example, Clark Kent is a culture creep but he is Superman. So, a word of advice to the wise, don't mess. You may be playing with fire."

Most of the adults believed the Blue Guard held a lot of promise and could have continued as a positive force with some adult guidance. As a letter to the *Falcon Flash* editor from "the hungry i" in December **1966** notes, "... The Blue Guard, under capable leadership, could turn into one of the finest organizations our school has seen. Not that I am particularly for faculty intervention, but for more capable student leaders."

The Culture Creeps

The intelligentsia of **1967**, this group of four friends took most of the same classes and held similar interests, particularly in music and the theatre. They sat together at lunch and, like their peers, talked about their day, their classes, and their activities. Unlike many of their peers, however, they also discussed what they were reading and what music they were listening to. Honor students, they had a keen intellect as well as a good sense of humor. In a word, they were interested in what we loosely describe as "culture." Hence, "The Culture Creeps." They enjoyed one another's company because they shared common interests. At first offended by the title, they came to embrace it.

However, because they appeared to be less interested in athletics, they were targets perceived as being different. For example, during that year music was played in the cafeteria during lunch and all of it was pop music. When these four asked for a variety of music to be played, they were criticized and given the sobriquet of "Culture Creeps." What was different about this small group, when compared to many loner groups to follow at LD, is that they learned an early lesson about individual differences and being true to oneself. (Also see "Reflections from the **Class of 1967**.")

The Rowdies

In the fall of **1972**, a group called The Rowdies was formed.[2] Like their predecessors, the Rowdies emerged in the name of school spirit. Members attended games in a group, always making their presence known. The musicians among them played "Sweet Georgia Brown" at many basketball games, in defiance of the league's ban on musical instruments, but, allegedly with the blessings of Dr. Hoerner, the superintendent, so long as they confined their music to pre-game. The Rowdies, not officially sanctioned as an organization, continued for several years. According to an undated *Falcon Flash* (circa 1976-77) an independent Kazoo Band had formed but did not last long despite their attempts to combine their music with that produced by the Rowdies.

---

[2] *Falcon Flash*, May 1973.

The BOA

This same year the Brotherhood of America (aka Burners of America or simply BOA), led by Steve Keefer, was formed as the anti-Rowdies. While rumor had its headquarters in the B-wing lavatory, the group quickly turned the joke into a serious and noble endeavor, collaborating with Student Council on a fund-raising campaign with service projects including bake sales, car washes, and "Sam Campbell Day" on April 7, **1973**, raising $1,787.68 to help defray the medical expenses of their classmate.

The Midgets

This group formed during the **1977-78** school year with a group of athletes, led by Gary Kirman. It was a novelty act more than anything purposeful with the young men sitting in a row behind a skirted table so that the participants' legs could not be seen. Their arms were covered and their hands covered with shoes so that it gave the suggestion of midgets who sang and imitated dance steps. Highly popular, they made their final appearance at Commencement.

Electronics Club

While Electronics Club was an official school-sponsored activity, it was more than that and needs to be noted in this section. The membership of this elite group typically included those who also served as Stage Crew. Very intelligent and unassuming, they were quite ingenious in the "stunts" they pulled, most especially anything having to do with sound systems and other electronic apparatus.

Rocket Club

The Rocket Club, in addition to its own success in breaking records in competition, will live in Lower Dauphin history as the group who built a replica of the Falcon Missile which had been stolen from the school in **1984**. Contacted in the spring of **2005** by the Lower Dauphin Alumni Association, the young men built and presented the rocket missile to the Alumni who in turn rededicated it at Homecoming **2006**, presenting it officially to Thomas Taylor, son of the late Curtis Taylor who had been principal of Lower Dauphin High School when the original missile had been gifted to Lower Dauphin. Members of the Lower Dauphin Missile Agency who participated in the construction of the Falcon Missile replica are Joe Skitka (in whose workshop the work was completed), Brian Yovoich, Keil Reese, Brian Pagano, Mike Hilbert, Jake Goerl, and Adam Wilson, all **Class of 2006.** The design plans for the missile were drawn by Jaysen Davis '06 from detailed photographs of an original falcon missile.

Music Groups

As long as there are young people there will be music. From banjoes to synthesizers, youth found ways to express themselves. Garage bands, pick-up bands, folk groups, rock bands, heavy metal, and barbershop—LD had them all. Regretfully, few if any are mentioned in yearbooks because these groups were considered "outside of school" activities; thus, there probably were at least twice as many groups whose names were lost to memory than there are names that found their way into the school newspaper. Also because we do not know what "type" some of these groups were and we can find no dates for many, we will list them alphabetically with the dates we have for some of them. We have supplied the names of the members that we could find and regret we were not more successful. The listing is then followed by the two references we found in the school newspaper and two articles that could describe the experiences of many of these young bands by simply changing the names of the young members that appear in the article. Unfortunately, these are the only records we could unearth. The groups with asterisks may be local professional bands.

Names of Groups

Bondage (1981)

Damascus

*DuValles

East (1984)

Ecstasy

Friends of Distinction
   (Barbershop Quartet, 1970s to the present)

Full Moon (1976/79)

Haze (1969-70)

IOI (1986)

Kixx (1982)

Lynch Run Singers (folk-singing, 1964)

*Men in Mourning

Miser (1988) *Falcon Flash*

Montereys (a pop group, 1964)

Neon (1976)

Pink Yard Flamingos (2003-2008)

Phoxx (1976)

Prizoner (1988)

Regatta (1985)

Sand Hill Singers

*Sharks (1985)

Smiling Ape (1980s-1990s)

Spectres (1983)

The Lost Soul (1968)

The Young Troubadors (1964-66)

We Three (folk group)

Xanadu

Additional students groups mentioned in a May **1971** news article are the Hydraulic Peach, the Legends, and September Morn. Another band mentioned in September **1971** is Eden. No other information could be found.

The May **1977** *Falcon Flash* reported: Three school bands performed at the Four Diamonds 24 hour marathon dance: Neon, Phoxx, and Full Moon.

Identified Members

♩ Miser: Don Carson, Mike Royer, Brent Hoover, Dave Sweigert
(from the *Flash* February 12, 1988)

♩ Sand Hill Singers: Inez Puzuks, Dennis Stoner, Hank Imhof, Harry Menear, Bill Orris

♩ The Lynch Run Singers: Bob Jackson, Nevin Jackson, Ralph Espenshade

♩ The Montereys: Ron MacLeod, Ron Wenrich, Ken Espenshade, George Leninger,
Joe Abbondanza

♩ The Lost Soul: Mike Wolf, Bill Swengle, Steve Keiper, Conrad Konecny, Cy Keefer

♩ The Young Troubadors: Ruth Comitz and Linda Kassman

♩ Damascus: Steve Keefer and others

♩ Haze: Jim Kulina and others

♩ Prizoner: Dan Forney, Mike Jennings, D.J. Mowery, and Jeff Mowery

♩ Smiling Ape: Bruce Sacks, Pat McKeever, and Dominic Mariani

♩ East: Dennis Repino, Eric Green, Dave Cladel, Dave Sweigert, Chuck Haas,
Thomas Ball

♩ Regatta: Dave Sweigert, Dave Cladel, Thomas Ball, Doug Rosener

♩ IOI, two members were Lower Dauphin alumni Chris Hadley and Shannon Puglisse

♩ Full Moon: John Fisher, Joe Wilhelm, Kyle Hetzel, Joe Fisher

♩ Pink Yard Flamingos: Justin Hahn, Andy Snyder, Jeremy Robins, Matt Klahre (McDevitt)

The Young Troubadors, Ruth Comitz and Linda Kassman, met the popular folk trio of Peter, Paul, and Mary backstage for a personal interview during the stars' appearance at the Hershey Arena in May **1965**. The Troubadors played occasionally at the Gypsy Rover, a coffeehouse in Harrisburg and appeared at a Hootenanny at West Chester College and at the Lebanon Valley Folk Festival.

Enduring Barbershop Quartet

The best known Barbershop Quartet is one that remained together for a few years after graduation and has reunited for a number of special appearances in school musicals and Commencements. According to Kerry Fies, "The original members were Dave Warfel '73, Jim Neidinger '73, Kent Myers '73 and Kerry Fies '74. The year following my graduation, Chuck Dowell '73 replaced Jim Neidinger while Jim attended Lebanon Valley College. Chuck also sang lead with the quartet in all of the *Music Man* performances since Jim was in the orchestra pit. Recruited at the Barbers Hair Salon, they were often seen singing in the halls, at sporting events, and roundabout. Performances included singing the national anthem at the cheerleading competition and at Central Dauphin High School's annual senior day where they initially were met with boos and cat calls, but after two numbers received a rousing ovation and cries for "More! More!" Dave Warfel strode to the microphone and admitted, "Sorry, that's all we know!" The crowd loved it. The quartet continued, retired, and then resurrected itself over the years to sing for many area banquets, events and notably, to sing the national anthem at several homecoming games. Fies adds, "The original members occasionally get together and try to see if we can remember any of the old songs, even if at a lower pitch."

The Sand Hill Singers

The following is a personal reminiscence from Hank Imhof, a member of one of the most successful groups, *The Sand Hill Singers:* "There were different stories for each person that joined or left the group; perhaps the movie "A Mighty Wind" is a little too close to the truth. Harry Menear and Bill Orris were the mainstays, Dennis Stoner came into the group with a rush of talent and production skill that swept it along maybe to its highest peak. When Dennis left, several others, including Inez Puzuks and I, left also. The album that was finally made was with several original members, Harry, Bill, Sharon, and several new people. I believe the group just lost its steam with the music interest of the times and the other members having families and other interests. It was great while it lasted."

Below are two reprinted articles which chronicle the story of only one of many high school groups who were made up of Lower Dauphin students. What is notable is that these groups were serious musicians and were so viewed by their peers. Jeff Peyton, a feature writer for the *Falcon Flash*, also took them—and his own work—seriously, reflected in a mature result for both the school newspaper and LD musicians.

From *The Flash:*

Summit Achiever Linda Rice '82

Linda Rice is a horse trainer who has won both training and breeding awards. Among her long list of accomplishments are becoming the first female to win the prestigious Saratoga Race Course training title in 2009, defeating Todd Pletcher by one victory, and becoming the first woman in the history of Keeneland to win a Grade 1 race when Tenski took the Queen Elizabeth II in 1998.

Shortly after Penn National opened on August 30, 1972, a 9-year-old Linda moved there with her family. Her father Clyde was the leading trainer multiple times between 1973 and 1982, her brother Kent was the leading apprentice jockey in the country in 1979, and her other brothers Wayne and Bryan were integral to the family's success in the sales ring and in readying young horses for the races.

"Penn National was a great place to grow up," said Linda, who has won more than 1,000 races as a trainer. "My passion for racing started at Penn National, and I learned to gallop horses as an exercise rider there when I was 15. I'm excited about driving down the mountain road and coming back to a place where I spent a lot of time."

At the age of 23, Linda obtained her trainer's license and moved to the New Jersey and New York circuits, saddling her first winner on June 3, 1987 at Garden State Park.

She now maintains a large string of horses in New York and last winter brought a number of them to race at Penn National, considering it as a place to maintain a presence.

"Penn National has some conditions available that meet the needs I am looking for," said Linda. "In addition, it is very accessible from New York, and is familiar territory for me."

Linda was among the industry speakers participating in The New York Racing Association, Inc.'s (NYRA) "New Owners Luncheon" at Saratoga Race Course on Sunday, August 18, 2013.

Faculty, Administration, and Staff

Lower Dauphin School District Administration

School Yr.	Superintendent	High School	H.S. Assistant	Jr. High/Middle	Jr. High/Mid Assist.	Conewago	East Hanover	Hummelstown	Londonderry	South Hanover
1960-61	David J. Emerich	Curtis S. Taylor		H. Victor Crespy		John Fisher	H. Martin Heisey	Richard E. Freeman	John M. Springer	Irvin M. Engle
1961-62	David J. Emerich									
1962-63	David J. Emerich									
1963-64	David J. Emerich			Isaiah D. Bomboy						
1964-65	David J. Emerich					H.E. Wisehaupt				
1965-66	David J. Emerich									
1966-67	Henry R. Hoerner								M. Wendell Poppy	
1967-68	Henry R. Hoerner		Barney J. Osevala				Frank T. Miller			H.E. Wisehaupt
1968-69	Henry R. Hoerner				William F. DeLiberty	Lois K. Miller		Irvin M. Engle		
1969-70	Henry R. Hoerner	Barney J. Osevala	Curtis S. Taylor	Dean R. Steinhart		C. Donald Barbush				
1970-71	Henry R. Hoerner				William W. Linnane					
1971-72	Henry R. Hoerner		Donald E. Myers	William W. Linnane	Jay R. Book / Jere L. Moser					
1972-73	Henry R. Hoerner									
1973-74	Henry R. Hoerner		Stephen P. Messner							
1974-75	Henry R. Hoerner									Jere E. Eckenroth
1975-76	Henry R. Hoerner									
1976-77	Henry R. Hoerner									
1977-78	Henry R. Hoerner		Stephen P. Messner / Jay R. Book	Frank T. Miller	Jere L. Moser	Kenneth B. Allwine	Irvin M. Engle	Frank T. Miller		
1978-79	Henry R. Hoerner		John S. Frankford / Jay R. Book					C. Donald Barbush		
1979-80	Henry R. Hoerner	Barney J. Osevala / John S. Frankford								
1980-81	Henry R. Hoerner		John S. Frankford / Jay R. Book / Jere L. Moser		Paul A. Shirk					
1981-82	Henry R. Hoerner	Barney J. Osevala / John S. Frankford	Jay R. Book / Jere L. Moser	Jere E. Eckenroth						Ronald J. Snavely
1982-83	Henry R. Hoerner									
1983-84	Henry R. Hoerner	John S. Frankford								
1984-85	Henry R. Hoerner									
1985-86	George D. Sauers	John S. Frankford / Landry K. Appleby	Jere L. Moser			C. Donald Barbush		M. Wendell Poppy	Kenneth B. Allwine	
1986-87	George D. Sauers	Landry K. Appleby	Jere L. Moser / Judith T. Witmer	Paul A. Shirk						Robert S. Santarelli

380

School Yr.	Superintendent	High School	H.S. Assistant	Jr. High/Middle	Jr. High/Mid Assist.	Conewago	East Hanover	Hummelstown	Londonderry	South Hanover
1987-88	George D. Sauers	→	→							
1988-89	George D. Sauers	Landry K. Appleby Jere L. Moser Judith T. Witmer	·····	→	·····	H. John Kline				
1989-90	George D. Sauers	Landry K. Appleby Jere L. Moser Paul A. Shirk Judith T. Witmer	·····	Landry K. Appleby Jere L. Moser Paul A. Shirk Judith T. Witmer		→				
1990-91	George D. Sauers	→	·····	→						
1991-92	Jeffrey A. Miller	Landry K. Appleby Kenneth M. Cassell Jere L. Moser Paul A. Shirk	·····	Landry K. Appleby Kenneth M. Cassell Jere L. Moser Paul A. Shirk	·····					
1992-93	Jeffrey A. Miller	Landry K. Appleby	Jere L. Moser	Paul A. Shirk	Coleen R. Heistand		Carol J. Schilling			
1993-94	Jeffrey A. Miller				→					
1994-95	Jeffrey A. Miller		→							
1995-96	Jeffrey A. Miller		Jere L. Moser Randall L. Umberger		Joseph B. Mateer					
1996-97	Jeffrey A. Miller									
1997-98	Jeffrey A. Miller		→	→	→					
1998-99	Jeffrey A. Miller		Donovan L. Mann Randall L. Umberger	Joseph B. Mateer	Sandra Reed					
1999-00	Jeffrey A. Miller									
2000-01	Jeffrey A. Miller				→					
2001-02	Jeffrey A. Miller				Patricia A. Rhine					
2002-03	Jeffrey A. Miller	→	→	→						
2003-04	Sherri L. Smith	Jeffrey D. Hughes	Randall L. Umberger David P. Wuestner	Robert K. Schultz	→			→		→
2004-05	Sherri L. Smith				Rebecca R. Davis			Douglas G. Winner		Patricia A. Rhine
2005-06	Sherri L. Smith		→			→			J. Michael Lausch	
2006-07	Sherri L. Smith		Daniel B. Berra David P. Wuestner			Edward L. Gnall				
2007-08	Sherri L. Smith	→	→	→	→		→	→		
2008-09	Sherri L. Smith	Todd R. Neuhard	David P. Wuestner	Daniel B. Berra	Nadine M. Krempa		Gary R. Messinger			
2009-10	Sherri L. Smith		Justin Hanula David P. Wuestner							Justin Hanula
2010-11	Sherri L. Smith	→	Kathryn I. Ringso David P. Wuestner	→	→	→	→	→	→	→

Superintendents of Lower Dauphin School District

Mr. David J. Emerich
Supervising Principal of the Joint High School
April 28, 1959 – June 30, 1966

Dr. Henry R. Hoerner
Superintendent
July 1, 1966 – December 1, 1985
(Sabbatical December 1, 1984 – November 30, 1985)

Dr. George D. Sauers
Superintendent
December 1, 1985 – December 2, 1991

Dr. Jeffrey A. Miller
Superintendent
December 3, 1991 – August 4, 2003

Dr. Sherri L. Smith
Superintendent
August 5, 2003 – Present

Principals of Lower Dauphin High School

1960–1970	Mr. Curtis S. Taylor
1970–1984	Mr. Barney J. Osevala
1984–1986	Mr. John S. Frankford III
1986–1989	Co-Principals:
	Mr. Landry K. Appleby, Mr. Jere L. Moser, Dr. Judith T. Witmer
1989–2003	Mr. Landry K. Appleby
2003–2008	Mr. Jeffrey D. Hughes
2008–2010 – Present	Mr. Todd A. Neuhard

Lower Dauphin High School Faculty, 1960–2010

A Great Part of the Secret of L.D.'s Success is the Excellent Administration and the Caring, Competent Faculty.....   1982 FALCONAIRE

The following listing contains the names of those who taught at LDHS anytime during the first fifty years. The list includes guidance counselors, nurses, and librarians as well—in essence, anyone in a professional staff position. Names of administrators and support staff are acknowledged elsewhere.

Because the staff directories, first published in the late 1960s, did not always separate junior high and high school and because some faculty held positions in both the junior high and the senior high, there may be some names of persons here who taught only in the junior high; we did not have access to records to determine this distinction. Generally, we did not list junior high school faculty unless they also taught in the senior high school. Further, unless we knew a name was misspelled, we used the name as it appeared in the directory. The names of some women faculty changed during their years of tenure and we made editorial decisions in each case as to how they are herein listed.

Please also note that we have attempted to identify all employees of the district who are Lower Dauphin High School Alumni. This can be found elsewhere in the book.

Marian J. Achenbach	Sharon Eby Barlet	Mrs. Bintliff
Rosemary N. Adusei	Kathleen S. Barlow	James Bishop*
Mrs. Alfred	Anna Barton*	Craig J. Bittenbender
Constance M. Allwine	Peggy Y. Barton	Jon P. Bittenbender
Shirley Allison	Scott A. Barton	David Bitting
Cynthia Al-Qawasmi	Anne Batory	Barbara Blackford
Lawrence Arena	Judy A. Baumgardner	Edward D. Blandy
Charlene A. Arnold	Suzanne Beam	Amy L. Bodley
Stacey M. Atherholt	Mr. Beard	Jennifer Bollinger
Barbara Macaw Atkinson	Lori Beaver	*Isaiah D. Bomboy**
Robert Atkinson	Margaret Becker	Nancy B. Bomboy
Joseph Attivo	*Carolyn P. Bedi*	Frank Bonerigo
Janet Ausmus*	Joan M. Beers*	*Jay R. Book*
Virginia B. Ax*	*Vernon Belser*	Jeffrey L. Bowers
Simon P. Bacastow	Henry G. Benner*	Rosalie Bowers*
Faye L. Baglin	Bernard J. Bernitsky*	Karen Bowser
Christine Bailey	Daniel Berra	James R. Brandt
Harold J. Balmer, Jr.	Nancy Bieber	Miriam E. Brandt
Ana Ravelo Barbush	Mr. Billings	*Jarmila Brinkmann*

Gerald W. Brittain*

Anne W. Broadwater

Christine A. Brown

K. Brown

Stanley P. Bucher

James S. Burchfield

Karen Pennington Burk

Miss Burris

John Butler

William E. Calohan

Gretchen A. Cameron

Roy C. Campbell*

Thomas N. Campbell

Frank A. Capitani

Marjorie Shetler Carlson

Sam Casale

Donna Casey

Cleon Cassel*

Craig S. Cassel

Rebecca Lippart Cassel

Robert A. Censullo

Henry C. Chapman IV

(Dr.) Linda L. Chavez-Wilson

Stephen E. Chortanoff

Mary K. Christ

Peggy Christ

W. Richard Claar

Mary L. Clouser

Charles W. Cole

Laurie A. Coleman

Ron Collier

Elizabeth Colpo

Venus Connelly

Audrey P. Conway

Lynlee R. Copenhaver

Susan E. Copenhaver

Susan Cort-Black

Marsha Reidenbach Costabile

John Croll, Jr.

Melvin E. Crook

Irwin K. Curry, Jr.

James O. Cusick

Jane S. Dalton

Byron R. Daubert

Nancy Daubert

Amy Davis

Kimberly Dean

Margaret Yakimoff DeAngelis

William DeLiberty*

Scott Delp

Louise Kiscaden DeMarchi

Janet Dengler

Jennifer H. Deren

David M. Dickson

Wendi J. DiMatteo

Royal W. Dimond, Jr.

Archie Diveglia

Jennifer H. Doll

(Dr.) Jacquelyn Douglass

Tanya Dreon

Richard E. Dunham III

Jane Durborow

Pamela Eberly

Gary L. Eckenroth

A. Jean Eckman*

Eugene C. Eckroth

Frederick Edwards

Ann B. Ehrhart-Witmer

Richard C. Elliott

David G. Epler

Anita Erdman

David Erdman

Nathan Espenshade

Charles R. Etter

Dodie Lynch Etter

Teri A. Eytcheson

Clinton Fackler

Amy Falk

Richard Falstick

Louis Farina

Robert R. Fickes

Michael A. Filepas

John K. Findley

Lee F. Finkenbinder

Lori A. Fischer

Darby Dimpsey Fischl

Bradley Flickinger

Lori Flickinger

Janet Foreman

Mark S. French

Rebecca Frey

Nancy L. Zazworsky Frist

David L. Fullen

Kathy L. Furin

Stephen N. Futchko

Jean Gainer

Jon W. Gardner

Joseph Garfinkel

(Dr.) David M. Gates

Thomas Gawles

Homer L. Gelbaugh, Jr.*

John L. Goepfert

Roy Gesford, Jr.

Russel Gilbert[1]

Debra Gleim

Margaret E. Gluck

John E. Good, Jr.

Edward J. Gottwald

Linda M. Goudy

David Gourley

Ronald E. Gourley

Susan Dicky Gourley

Michele Glovora

Eileen Graham

Robert A. Gray

Philip N. Green

Sandra L. Green

Ruth Greim

Charles Grenot

Karen Grenot

Jeanne Greisinger

Joan H. Griffith

Doug Grove

Aleda Myers Gruber

Beatrice E. Hallman*

Tom R. Hanninen

Justin M. Hanula

Kelly D. Harbaugh

William Harrell*

Edward Harris

John (Jack) Harry*

Warren Heiss

Coleen Sweikert Heistand

Donald F. Heistand*

Judith E. Heistand/Miller

Carl E. Herr*

Peggy Herr

Julie E. Herring

Al Hershey

Karen Hertzler

Barbara Hess

Nancy Hicks*

Amy S. Hiler

Paul D. Hoffman

Warren H. Hoffman

Jessie Holcombe

Josh Hooper

Despina M. Houck

Linda Houdershel

Shirley Houseal

Warren E. Howard

Patricia Hresko

Jeffrey D. Hughes

David L. Hummel

Linda Whitenight-Hummel

Klaura K. Hunt

Richard D. Hupper

Jean F. Hynicker

Margaret Irizarry

Michael P. James

David Johnson

Jessica Jones

Kathleen M. Jones

Nancy Kachniasz

William Kahler*

James Kalos

Gregory Karazsia

Kermit H. Katzaman

Jason F. Keiner

Emily Myers Keller

Angela Brightbill Key

Elizabeth A. Kirman

Nancy M. Kiscadden

Stephen P. Kistler

Robert C. Klock, Jr.

Molly Knisely

Belinda Kolmansberger

Dawn R. Koons

Helene S. Kramer

Gregory L. Kratzer, Jr.

Stacy Gass Kreitzer

Nadine M. Krempa

Barbara L. Kuhlen

Lynn Kuhn

Andrew Kulp

George Kunkle

Beth Kurtz

Wade D. Kurzinger

Geoffrey D. Kyper

Cynthia W. Laird

Ruby G. Landis*

Thomas G. Lane

Patricia M. Lanshe

Rosemary Lawler

Sandy LeGay*

Mr. Lesher

Mary B. Lewin

Karen Lindeman

Mr. Lingle

Joshua N. Lininger

William W. Linnane

Emilie Lonardi

Peggy L. Long

Ruth Long

Joseph Longenecker

Paul A. Longreen

Melody C. Lovelidge

Dale R. Luy

Vernon C. Lyter, Jr.

David E. Machamer

Heather L. Magness

Miss Magonelli

Marjorie Mandes

James F. Manning

Millicent Maravich

Maureen E. Marks

Sheron E. Marshall

Rebecca J. Martin

Stacey M. Martin

Susan Martin

Anne E. Masorti

Roy L. Maurer

Emilie McAbee

William T. McCardle

Sandra McConaghay

Diane S. McCullough

Keri McCullough

Quinn McCullough

Lori A. McDonald

Faith McGill-Cossick

Michelle A. McGinnis

Debra Rosenberry McKee

Sally A. McKeever

Susan Ewing McLure

W. Benjamin McLure

Lynn McMullin

Donald R. McNutt

Amanda Mease

Susan Meckler

Jane A. Mecum

Kenneth Melchior

Lori A. Mengel Fischer

Cornelia Merwin*

Howard Messick

Laura Shaw Messner

(Dr.) Steven Messner

Ronald W. Michael

*James Middlekauf**

Katherine Mielke

Daniel J. Mikula

Amy Stuller Miller

C. Richard Miller

Edwin R. Miller

Emily Miller

William E. Minsker

Susan E. Morefield

Richard D. Moore

Alicia Imler Morgret

Cynthia Mory

Jere Moser

Kim Motter

Miriam B. Moury

Allen S. Moyer

Ray A. Moyer

Cynthia L. Aldrich Mulligan[2]

Anthony C. Murdocca

Lorraine Yanno Murdocca

James Murdock

Dennis P. Musket*

Frank J. Nardella

Dana Naugle

Ed Neiswender

Frank Neiswender

Charles Nelson

Patricia Neyhart

H. William Nixon

J. Nolt

Joseph L. Nutaitis

Eloise O'Brien

Barney J. Osevala*

Barry C. Oswald

Amy Owen

Kenneth Paden*

Richard Paden

Mark W. Painter

Vincent E. Pantalone

Jeffrey Pascal

Ravi E. Patel

Carolyn Patt

Sandra Paveglio

Scott A. Payonk

*Glenn Wm. (Bill) Peck**

Aimee L. Pellissier Radle

James R. Pelter

Melanie S. Petricoin

Victoria Pine

Jonathan B. Pinkerton

James S.W. Pirtle

Louise Waring Poorman

Aaron Popp

Helen Pratt

Thomas I. Propst

Joan Pruett

Gordon E. Putt*

Thomas R. Rae

Barry S. Ramper

Robert C. Rath

Virginia A. Regan

Dean R. Reigner

Marianne I. Rempe

Wilbur L. Rhodes

*Edward (Max) Richards**

Elizabeth Will Richards*

Kenneth W. Richter

Keri Ricker

Allen D. Risser

Helga E. Rist

Erin E. Ritter

Max V. Ritter*

Laura Robinson

Teri Robinson

Nora Rodriguez

Candace Paice Romano

Edward F. Romano, Jr.

Theodore Roscher

Laura A. Rudzinski

Lena Galicki Russell

Lorraine D. Ryan

Frederick Salomon

*Kathryn W. Sandel**

Dawn E. Sandy

M. Elizabeth (Beth) Santanna

Kathleen Sapanars

Lee D. Savidge

Michael H. Schaeffer

*Louise Schaffner**

*Joseph G. Schan**

Adam Schramm

Priscilla Schwenk

James W. Seacrist

Paula Seacrist

*Prowell M. Seitzinger**

Cynthia L. Shaffer

Molly E. Shank

Robert D. Shankweiler*

(Dr.) Rudolph Sharpe, Jr.

Leslie Shearer

Susan A. Sheffer

Helen Shelley

Tomoko Shimada

Paul Shirk

Paul T. Siegel, Jr.

Barbara Silver

Nanette Willis Singer

Brad Slonaker

Curtis J. Smith

David C. Smith, Jr.

Debbie S. Smith

Jane Mellin Smith*

Mary Smith

Robert Smitley

Nancy Snyder

Judith M. Solensky

Arthur L. Sowers*

Bret C. Sparks

Darlene Wisler Spengler

Joan E. Spire

Glenda M. Stahl

Richard Stahl

William Staman

Carl Stanitski*

Conrad Stanitski*

Christie L. Stankiewicz

Jay Stanton

Douglas Stauffer*

Teresa Galicki Stavenski[3]

*Kenneth W. Staver**

G. David Steffen

Kenneth K. Stehman

Cynthia H. Stewart

Deborah Stoeber

Daniel Stoner

Donald Stoops, Jr.

Larry Strait

*Mary Jane Strite**

Kiley Kulina Strohm

C. Bradley Stroman

Patricia Stroman

Robert Swartley

Susan Swartz

Ruth Greim Sweigart

Susan A. Swicklik

Kathryn Taylor

*Leslie D. Taylor**

Deborah Thompson

Emily L. Trefz

Sally A. Trimmer

Thomas E. Turnbull, Jr.

Carrie Hyla Uhlig

Randall Umberger

Miriam Vanderwall

Charles Van de Water

Gary Van Dine

Marisa Van Zandt

Wilson Veloz

Richard L. Vickroy

James R. Vogt

Jean Vosburg

Jean M. Vuono

Melenie Wagner

Jean Walmer

Mary L. Walsh

Susan Waltimyer

Michelle M. Warner

Carisa Wascovich

Todd C. Wasserman

Marie Bergan Weber

Kim Weber

Kristina Weinken

Carol Lovendusky Weishaar

Melanie S. Wenger

Cynthia L. Wenrich

Jill T. Wenrich

Flora Werner

Patricia R. Wickrowski

Barbara B. Wiegand

Frances Wiggins

Robert Willet

Marian Achenbach Wise*

(Dr.) Judith Ball Witmer*

Shirley A. Witmer

Christina G. Wolfe

Paul Wolfe

Richard O. Wolfe*

Brigitte M. Wolosyn

Farren Woods

Maureen Wylonis

Cynthia Xanthopoulos

Joan L. Yagielniskie

John Yaniger

Steven Yeager

Ronald L. Yerger

Janice B. Yinger

Mark Yocum

Scott T. Yoder

Katherine Young*

*Helen Yount**

Richard Zaepfel

Nancy MacLeod Zeigler

Ronald P. Zeigler

*Kathryn K. Zeiters**

James R. Zeiters

Susan Zerfoss

Richie Zimmer

1 C. Russell Gilbert was a substitute teacher who was so highly regarded that a scholarship in his memory was awarded annually for 28 years sponsored by many, but initiated by faculty members Frank Capitani, Jim Seacrist, Mark French, Burr Rhodes and Dave Smith.

2 The first alumna to return to her Alma Mater.

3 Teresa Galicki Stavenski and Lena Galicki Russell are twins, as are Carl and Conrad Stanitski.

* Denotes original faculty, 1960.

Italics denote deceased, according to our information.

Secretaries and Administrative Assistants

Through the course of high school one realizes that the function of the school greatly relies on indispensable secretaries. These persons dedicate their time for the students in a congenial manner and are interested in easing the students' transition into high school as well as preparing them for college and the work force. Mr. Minsker adds, "Secretaries provide the power for the school, and I think most people would agree, without them the school would not run smoothly."

Secretaries account for student attendance, handling all communications, regulating supplies, as well as many other duties. Mrs. Yost commented, "Keeping the school going is like a business." Mrs. Reichenbaugh added, "Working in a school is never boring." Mrs. Hurst expressed, "Talking to the students and trying to help them work things out is what we do." They all expressed how interesting it is to watch the students grow and mature within their four years here at Lower Dauphin.

1992 Falconaire

As you read through this list of names we can guarantee that you will remember a time (or many times) you hurried into one of the offices in need of help—of any kind—to find that you were greeted with a smile and keen listening skills, then given the right direction.

Joan Bonawitz	Dorothy Huffman	Pat Speraw
Tammy Miller Cogan**	Donna Hurst	Ruth Shope*
Romaine Deimler	Dolores Kuhn	Bonnie Bowerman Toomey**
Lois Dively	Deb Love	Denise Stum Tucci**
Lois Dunkleberger	Terri Frascella (Lutzkanin) Book**	Betty Via
Joan Espenshade	Shirley Meyers	Doris Vickroy
Brenda Fasnacht	Margaret Moore*	Sandy Umberger Wallish**
Brenda Fegley*	Pat Pagano Matincheck**	Kathleen Imhof Weber**
Connie Fenner*	Frances Rathfon*	Lynne Yost
Betty Anne Fry	Marguerite Reichenbaugh	Betty Youtz
Dorothy Hainley	Fay Rhoads	Ruth Zeiters
Dorothy Hess*	Frances Spangler	

Cafeteria Ladies and Custodians

All of us have fond memories of the Lower Dauphin High School cafeteria and custodial personnel, most of whom did far beyond what their job description called for. They are the ones who always were willing to do a favor, act on a special request, or just say good morning. They took care of Lower Dauphin, and, thus, took care of us. Again, there is no central listing of these kind persons who sometimes were shown in yearbook photos but not always with their names. More recent directories do not specify areas of job nor do they indicate those who worked during the day—those whom most of the readers would remember. So, with our usual apology, we may have missed many, naming below those based mainly on collective memory and culling from directories, selecting those whose names appeared more often throughout the years.

Longer Term Custodial Staff

Sam Attick

Connie Baughman**

Charles Berkheimer

Roy Clark*

Bernard Comiskey

James Corsnitz**

Sam Dundore

Eddie George

Arthur Gergely**

Lester Heisey

John Henry

Holly Hess

Roy Hoffer

Carl Hoffman/Huffman

Wanda Huber

Hudson Hughes

Clarence Kromer*

Jim Kveragas**

William Mader

Charles Moore

"Skip" Oakley

Louis Rathfon

Ronald Ream

Warren Reichard

Gordon Riffie*

Robert Sanders

Kermit Seitz

Earl Shaffer

Lisa Shenck

Joseph Shultz

Paul Spitler**

John Stare

Edwin Stauffer

Stanley Tetzloff**

Traci Watts**

Longer Term Cafeteria Staff

Faye Baglin

Sandra Barnhart

Beatrice Boyer*

Patricia Burkholder*

Kathryn Clark*

Martha Cook*

Lois Dean*

Jackie Dean

Edith Epler

Freda Eckenroth*

Jane Freet

Beverly Gipe

Bea Gondek

Brenda Good

Karen Greenleaf

Sylvia Heckert*

Anna Heister*

Barbara Hetrick

Emma Hoke*

Mary Hurst

Florence Kerns

D. Kinley

Grace Kirby

Virginia Koons

Ruth Kugle

Betty Lerch

Mildred Lewis

Dorothy Martin

Ethel Mathias*

Patricia Mattson

Betty Mountz

Mary Olson*

Edith Plouse

Darlene Reichelderfer**

Mary Rhine*

Regina Rhinesmith

Doris Rhoads

Jean Saylor*

Dorothy Seibert*

Betty Smith

Beatrice Snyder

Dorothy Stauffer

Linda Still**

Janet Templin

Jean Wallace

Ethel Walkup*

Marge Wolfersberger

Billie Wright

Elizabeth Zelenak***

*   denotes service the first year of Lower Dauphin

** LDHS alumna/us

*** Mrs. Zelenak has the highest number of service years, according to our records

LD Alumni/Employees to April 2009

Acker, Bathurst, Ann	1985	Aide--Londonderry
Adams, Gwen	1973	School Board Member
Aldrich, Cynthia (Mulligan)	1962	Teacher
Alexander, Heidi	1983	Secretary--EH
Bartholomew, Tim	1976	Teacher--Nye
Beck, Christopher	1992	Teacher--SH/Londonderry
Bell, Sheri	1980	Office Asst.--Nye
Book, John	1980	Maintenance Supervisor--Price
Bowerman, Toomey, Bonnie	1970	Secretary--HS
Brightbill, Patton, Lynn	1975	Nurse--Conewago
Budgeon, Miller, Lee Ann	1994	Teacher--SH
Burkholder, Michael	2000	Teacher--SH
Brubaker, Melody	2004	Teacher--SH, Nye, Conewago
Campbell, Umberger, Teresa	1986	Teacher--MS
Cobaugh, Curry, Susan	1972	Secretary--SH
Cogan, Tammy Miller	1988	Receptionist—HS
Cassel, Craig	1982	Teacher--HS
Corsnitz, James	1990	Custodian--SH
Crawford, Frank	1974	Teacher--EH
Crick, Dave	2000	Custodian--HS
Cruys, Ron	1966	Former teacher--Junior High
Cruys, Lovelidge, Melody	1964	Teacher--HS
Deitz, John	1970	Computer Room Aide--HS
Dennis, Etnoyer, Ann	1976	Secretary--DAC
Dimpsey, Fischl, Darby	1989	Teacher--HS
Eckels, Dana	1983	Food Service--EH
Eifert, Atkinson, Jamie	1995	Teacher--MS
Eifert, Key, Angie	1992	Former employee
Eisenhour, Hoerner, Deb	1979	Aide--MS
Engle, Mease, Amanda	1993	Teacher--HS
Espenshade, Nathan	1994	Counselors—HS
Evans, Lister, Donna	1970	Library Aide--Nye
Etychenson, Terri	1991	Former employee--HS
Fackler, Clinton	2003	Teacher—HS
Fisher, Wells, Susan	1972	Former employee--DAC
Fasnacht, Geesaman, Sandra	1982	Teacher—SH
Frascella, Lutzkanin, Terry	1980	Secretary—HS
Gable, Heary, Deb	1986	Producer Spring Musicals
Gaffney, McGarvey, Barbara	1972	Teacher—SH

Gamber, Nancy	1970	Disbursement/Printing--DAC
Gearhart, Lauren	1989	Counselor--Londonderry
Gergely, Art	1978	Custodian--Londonderry
Gesford, Roy	1987	Teacher—HS
Glovola, Karlin, Debra	1975	Asst. to Business Manager--DAC
Gnall, Ed	1994	Principal--Conewago
Gourley, Ronald	1966	Teacher--HS
Gourley, David	2004	Teacher--HS
Hanula, Justin	1993	Elementary Principal
Hereshko, Michelle	1985	Library Aide--SH
Hess, Ken	1977	Custodian--EH
Higgins, Fasnacht, Barbara	1972	Former employee
Higgins, Kilgore, Lori	1978	Aide--HS
Hilbert, Erica	2003	Teacher--Conewago
Hoerner, Eisenhour, Deb	1979	Aide
Imhof, Weber, Kathy	1974	Guidance AA--HS
Kastelic, Jennifer	2002	Teacher--MS
Katzmire, Wagner, Betsy	1963	Secretary--Nye
Key, Peter	1992	Former employee
Kreiser, Linda	1970	Teacher--MS
Kuhn, Allwine, Eileen	1995	Teacher--EH
Kulina, Kellie	2000	Former employee
Kulina, Ken	1985	Dean of Students--MS
Kulina, Strohm, Kiley	1998	Teacher--HS
Kveragas, James	1986	Custodian
Landis, Kopp, Ann	1965	Teacher--MS
Landis, Richard	1970	Custodian--SH
Lauber, McElwee, Tammy	1979	Teacher--MS
Linderman, Hoover, Bobby	1984	Census & Taxes
Lininger, Josh	1993	Teacher--HS
Lister, Chad	2001	Teacher--MS
Lyons, Fisher, Christy	1992	Teacher--EH
Lutzkanin, Katie	2003	LTS--Nye
Lytle, Chip	1974	Van driver/custodian--DAC
Machamer, David	1987	Teacher--HS
Mader, Mary	1971	Aide--MS
Matesich, Heather	2002	Aide--Londonderry
Mattson, Sean	2001	Teacher--MS
McGarvey, Frederick	1972	Teacher--EH
Meloy, Bradley	1992	LTS--MS
Mentzer, James	1997	Teacher--EH

McCann, Lindsay	1997	Aide--Londonderry
Michael, Ron	1972	Teacher--HS
Miller, Brooks, Deb	1975	Secretary--Londonderry
Miller, Cogan, Tammy	1988	Attendance Secretary--HS
Miller, Hagy, Sharon	1977	DAC Secretary
Monn, Kobielnik, Karla	1997	Secretary--DAC
Mummert, Heather	1998	Teacher--Nye
Neidinger, Jim	1973	Lond/SH,EH, MS,NYE
Neiswender, Ed	1973	Teacher--MS
O'Donnell, Michelle	2004	LTS--Conewago
Oelig, Keith	1983	School Board Member
Phillips, Boyer, Laurie	1982	Aide--Londonderry
Pinkerton, Jonathan	1999	Teacher--HS
Rhinesmith, Smith, Ella	1971	Secretary-DAC
Rothermel, Byers, Nancy	1982	Aide--Nye
Ricker, Keri	2004	Teacher--HS
Saltzer, Peffer (Gottwald), Kathy	1973	Communities That Care
Schan-Bigler, Patti Jo	1985	Teacher--MS
Schauer, Tiffany	2003	Teacher--SH
Schwentker, Waters, Pam	1988	Musical Asst./Substitute Teacher
Shay, Jason	1999	Teacher--Nye
Shope, Darlene	1977	Instructional Aide
Smith, Donna	1971	Retired --MS
Smith, William	1968	Retired --MS
Spitler, Paul	1964	Custodian--HS
Sparks, Brett	1986	Teacher--HS
Still, Linda	1979	Nye
Stroman, Brad	1967	Teacher--HS
Strawser, Kevin	1986	Director, Spring Musical
Tetzloff, Stanley	1987	Custodian--HS
Umberger, Randy	1965	Asst. Principal--HS
Wagner, McCorkel, Natalie	1979	Secretary--MS
Watts, Traci	1982	Custodian--HS
Weaver, Matt	1995	Custodian--MS
Wenner, Mike	1980	Custodian--MS
Wise, Randy	1979	Custodian--Londonderry
Wise, Ron	1975	Supervisor, Maintenance--DAC
Yancheff, Espenshade, Nadine	1974	Teacher--MS
Yohe, Bates, Tina	1987	AA Tech Support--DAC

Faculty Professional Development/In-Service

Scheduling time for renewal, learning, and interacting is important in a profession that is as isolated as teaching. Within the walls of a school building adults often do not converse with another adult from arrival to departure. There is no "exchange of ideas around the proverbial water cooler" because there is no "taking a break" for a few minutes to refresh oneself. Planning periods are not conducive to conversation on curriculum because planning periods in the high school are not, for example, designed to bring together all of the history teachers or all of the tenth grade teachers or any other groups based on similar criteria. The planning periods are scheduled in times that are left over after the scheduling has been completed, and a planning period for an individual teacher is random.

In-service (now referred to as professional development) has been held since at least the mid-19th Century.[1] During the first perhaps ten years of Lower Dauphin High School the teachers attended Institutes generally held in Harrisburg where teachers from all the schools in the County would meet to listen to speakers and attend smaller convocations or planned sessions on various topics on education.

By 1970, most area schools were holding their own "In Service" programs and Lower Dauphin held a two-day conference on October 19-20, 1970 with the theme "To Do, Be Aware." As noted in the Foreword of the program booklet, "This year's in-service committee has attempted to bring before you a beneficial program to be presented in a manner differing from past programs. It is designed to aid you in keeping abreast of new educational methods and materials, as well as the problems and opportunities currently facing our students."[2] The two days were replete with speakers and work sessions, as well as a complete display of the audio-visual equipment used in our district. A sample of the first day's sessions included Why We Are One of the Best (School Districts), The New York Stock Exchange, Drugs and Our Youth, and Are We Preparing Our Students for Junior College.

On the second day of this 1970 program, there were two separate schedules, one for the Elementary and one for the High School Faculty. Morning sessions for the high school featured a student panel of alumni currently in college, a vocational panel, scheduling procedures, and (student) alcohol abuse. The afternoon offered the choice of a bus tour of Lower Dauphin School District, department workshops, or department field trips. The tour was very popular because most of the faculty had no idea of the size of the school district or its rural landscape.

---

[1] Original County Institute programs in this author's possession reflect that in Clearfield County these institutes began in 1863.

[2] This In-Service Committee consisted of the following: Judith T. Ball, Paul A. Shirk, William E. Minsker, C. Donald Barbush.

Faculty Tales In and Out of School

Because the school life of a faculty member is so interwoven with the school, most of the faculty tales are included as part of various sections of *Loyal Hearts Proclaim*. The following are just a few additional examples that reflect some of the views behind-the-scenes.

Teachers in Their First Years

At the beginning of the summer in 1970 I found myself part of the team that was completely overhauling the English curriculum for Lower Dauphin High School. We were given *carte blanche* to design nine-week mini-courses, to order whatever materials we thought appropriate, to shape the presentation of the instruction in literary history, appreciation of literature, and composition in whatever way we found useful. Gone were the lockstep marches through the history of literature in Great Britain and the United States, taught through hardbound anthologies of pictureless pages. *Relevance* was the watchword. As the course selection guide said, "These courses will really blow your mind."

I was assigned to write courses in the short story, creative writing, and "black literature." (Yes, a course in works by African-Americans would be written and taught by a 23-year-old white girl in a school where there were, at that time, no black students.)

For the short story course, I found a snazzy series of paperbacks published by McDougal Littell called *Man in the Fictional Mode*. (There was also *Man in the Poetic Mode*, *Man in the Nonfiction Mode*, and, I think, *Man in the Dramatic Mode*.) I ordered two grade levels, and we were set.

Two Flannery O'Connor stories appeared in those books: "Everything That Rises Must Converge" and "The Artificial Nigger." I don't know if the course blew anyone's mind, but those two stories certainly (in a phrase I prefer) pulled the top of my head off. When O'Connor's *The Complete Stories* was published in 1971, I bought it.

MYD

The fall of 1963 was my first year teaching on an Interim Certificate. Jim Burchfield was my mentor as I had never had a formal student teaching experience. I was just back from Temple School of Dentistry and the US Air Force. Mr. Emerich was my assigned observer and about a month into my tenure he told me he would be coming to my class. I had a good lesson planned on cells with a short 16 mm film midway through the class. During the film I was at the screen pointing out typical cells. When the film was over and the lights were back on I noticed all the film on the floor—it had come off the pickup reel! Mr. Emerich told me I had to pay closer attention to what goes on in the classroom.

At another time in my first or second year, Mr. Emerich said my window blinds were not straight. From that point forward they were straight for the next 34 years. Mr. Taylor also observed me and at the end of the class he asked me to give him a write up on what I did. I mentioned in my note that B-5 was in good condition and the blinds were straight. My evaluation from him was almost verbatim what I had written, including straight blinds!

DCS

As a teacher new to the district in the early 1970s I gained permission from the principal to assign my homeroom students to report to homeroom five minutes earlier than the required reporting time in order to hold homeroom meetings and get to know the students. One of the homeroom members objected and went to the principal and complained, but the principal, who supported my desire to create camaraderie within the homeroom, supported me. The experiment with homeroom worked!

SPM

As a class advisor in the late winter of 1976, I approached the principal asking if it were possible to take a class trip to Disney World. The principal, who was on the telephone dealing with a problem, nodded to me, and continued with the intense telephone conversation in which he was engaged. Weeks later, while out on the archaeology dig, I was summoned by this principal to return to the building where he asked me, "What is this bill for a deposit of $13,000 for a chartered plane?" Then I knew he had not remembered the conversation in which he had merely nodded, not fully realizing the enormity of the request I had made—and to which he had agreed—to charter a jet plane (to land at Middletown Airport, no less, and unprecedented at that time) exclusively for the senior class and its chaperones.

SPM

As the teacher of the new archeology course, I agreed to accept some "problem students" into this program, for which my permission was required, because I thought these two students could benefit from the experience. However, one day I caught one of them smoking on a dig. He was ordered to shovel an area down to its bedrock—down 13 feet. Later, the principal came to the site, viewed the work, and promptly ordered the student to fill it back in. Fortunately the father of the second student was a contractor and the student borrowed a backhoe and the work easily was completed.

SPM

While rumors, both at the time and later, greatly exaggerated the "Annual Faculty Room Christmas Party" in B-wing, perhaps the duration of which ran twenty years, the fact of its existence is true. On the last day of school, long after the last student had boarded the last bus out, a number of teachers stayed and held a social in the faculty room that earlier in the month had been decorated with the main feature—a large gold glass ball hanging from the middle of the ceiling above the round table in the back room which served as the buffet table for Christmas. While the cuisine could not compare to the "special gourmet chili" prepared by the David Smith Club, it was appropriate to the season. Because there were such few occasions for teachers to share any kind of fellowship—or even conversation to any extent—we all looked forward to this "once a year day" and often stayed until after dusk. No questions asked.

JTBW

Women faculty rarely took any risks of "stepping out of character," particularly those who were new teachers in the early sixties, women of "the silent generation" who had been reared to propriety. According to Strauss and Howe (authors of *Generations* which profiled the characteristics shared by generation of birth), the only way we bent the rules was through what Strauss and Howe later called our "cultivating refined naughtiness," indirectly promoted by Hugh Hefner, publisher of the revolutionary *Playboy* magazine. Those of us who occasionally practiced this refined naughtiness did such things as purposely quoting from *Playboy*—although not in front of the students. I also recall once nearly scandalizing the senior high school faculty in the mid-60s when I wore earrings with the Playboy logo. In particular, I will never forget the look on the face of Miss Strite.

That harmless bit of jewelry likely was viewed as only one step worse than my purchasing a twenty-four inch museum reproduction of Michaelangelo's "The David" on an educational conference trip to New York City, so visibly embarrassing two older members of the faculty with whom I traveled that I went back into the store with the reproduction and asked them to ship the item rather than my carrying it back to the hotel. My third foray into notoriety, also in the mid-to-later 1960s, was using a stage name and "moonlighting" as a pianist and vocalist in local supper clubs.

JTBW

There are also back stories of the trust and kindness unheralded between and among faculty such as the following remembrance of Mrs. Jarmila Brinkmann. A colleague recalls, "She had the room across from B-4 where I was, probably in 1990 or 1991. She ran afoul of LKA (as most of us, primarily women, did), I think for speaking critically of the clueless young gum-popping language teacher with Big Hair. Mr. A. began sending Mrs. Brinkmann "nastygrams," and she took to bringing them over to me. She would ask me to read them, and only tell her what they said if she actually had to take an action in response. Looking back now, that seems like an incredible trust she extended to me."

MYD

On the day of the TMI incident, all of the administrators except me, an assistant principal, were attending a meeting at the Pennsylvania Department of Education. Mid-morning the superintendent telephoned and told me to "keep everyone in the building and send someone to go to each teacher's classroom and personally tell each teacher to keep the students in the classroom and not let anyone leave." An hour later a father of three students came into the school office, placed a pistol on the counter, and demanded that his children be dismissed. At that point, still the only administrator in the building, I took matters into my own hands and made the decision that students would be released to any parents who came for them.

SPM

"Teachers' Salaries Are Chief Cause of Lower Dauphin Tax Rise" was the headline in the May 20, 1966 issue of *The Sun*. The article reported that "ten new teachers were needed by the fall of 1966 because of enrollment. Some classes have **42** students while the desired ratio is 30 to1."

In the first few years of operation all of the teachers had to leave their keys in their mailboxes when they left for the day. No one was allowed to come back in later.

In the fall of 1981 a new assistant principal ordained that all faculty had to "turn a tag" upon arrival in the morning and departure at the end of the day. Some refused; he got even; we got our own revenge.

Brief Accolades

♦ Mr. Vernon Lyter was named one of seven outstanding science teachers in PA.

♦ In the fall of 1991, Mr. (later Dr.) Rudolph Sharpe was named Pennsylvania Teacher of the Year.

♦ Mrs. Shirley Witmer was named Pennsylvania Home Economics Teacher of the Year.

What Were They Thinking?

♦ Arguably the most memorable item to be checked on a report card was the following: "Works to the best of his ability."

♦ An English faculty member tells the following, "Sometime between school year 1978–79 and 1980–81, a paperback text was chosen for the Mythology class. I do not know who chose it, nor on what basis, certainly not from an examination copy. When it arrived, someone discovered (fortunately before distribution to students) that some of the myths (or maybe just one) involved castration, described in detail. A decision was made to use the book, but to remove the 25 or so critical pages, by ripping them out of the copies. (They were in the middle of the book.) We told the kids the books had come damaged." *MYD*

♦ I will never forget the note I found in my mailbox the morning following the Challenger disaster: "Please ask for a moment of silence for those people who died in the space shuttle yesterday." I wondered how this principal could possibly think (1) I needed a prompting, (2) I would not have prepared appropriate remarks, or (3) that his own ill-phrased words were fitting. I read the following that I had prepared as the introduction to the morning meditation: "This morning we pause as part of a shocked and saddened nation in mourning the tragic death of seven crew members of the space shuttle Challenger which occurred yesterday. These daring and courageous men and women are representative of a select few who have opened the space frontier. Please join with me in a sincere moment of silent meditation to pay tribute for their sacrifice in the name of their country." *JTBW*

♦ One of the several faculty who earned a doctorate while at LD told this story to the author: After several years of study, including summers in residence at the university from which I earned my degree, I had completed my dissertation on linguistics and was scheduled for what is termed "a defense" of one's research. Because these oral examinations administered by a panel of university experts are always held during the week at the choice of date of the university committee, I requested a day of professional leave from LD. I was told, "This activity has nothing to do with your profession and what you do here," and my request was denied.

RS

Other Lives

Before LD

Following World War II Mrs. Helga Rist, for many years an esteemed teacher of German, was imprisoned in a concentration camp in East Germany. In 1947 as a 19-year-old schoolgirl, she was falsely accused and convicted of spying on the Soviets in East Germany for the United States. She spent eight years in four different East German concentration camps before her release. She once smuggled a letter to her family (out of one of the prisons) in the shoulder of a coat being sent home. She had written this brief message with a sharpened straw and her own blood. (*In Enemy Hands*)

During LD

Mr. Curtis J. Smith's stories and essays have appeared in more than seventy literary journals. His work has been named to the *Best American Short Stories Distinguished Stories List*, *The Best American Mystery Stories Distinguished Stories List*, and the *Notable Writing List of the Best American Spiritual Writing*.

After LD

Mr. Richard Claar, better known by most as the lead in Pentagon, was known to the faculty as a knowledgeable colleague. One remembers an explanation he once provided in the faculty room that, "Sugar in solution keeps it from freezing." Years after he had left Lower Dauphin Margaret De Angelis wrote to him, "I remember the day in about 1972 or 1973, when the Coke machine in the faculty room, experiencing a thermostat malfunction, was delivering frozen Tabs and Frescas, but the regular Cokes were coming out OK, albeit "really" cold. Someone asked why, and you gave the explanation. I have never forgotten that. It is, I say from time to time, the only science I know. I can still see you standing in the B-wing faculty room, explaining to someone holding a frozen bottle of Fresca why she will either have to remain thirsty or give up two more quarters and consume something not laden with saccharine. Those were the days, my friend."

After spending a sabbatical term teaching in Poland in 1989, Mr. William Minsker initiated an exchange teacher program with a university in that country. He later left the district to form a non-profit corporation, Pennsylvania Partnerships Abroad, which places interns from Wroclaw University of Economics in Poland with businesses in the Harrisburg area. Every second semester, Mr. Minsker teaches a conversational English class, the only native English speaker working with the students there.

Mr. Ben McLure, one of the early teachers at LD, resigned in July 1982 to accept a position as Scouting Supervisor with the Toronto Blue Jays Baseball Club.

Dr. Rudolph Sharpe retired from Lower Dauphin to accept a position with the prestigious Lancaster Country Day School where he now serves as Head of the Middle School.

Dr. Steven P. Messner left LD to accept a superintendency, one of several he held and is, as of this writing, interim President of Carson Long Military Academy.

A number of faculty who began their careers at LD later left the district to accept administrative posts in other school districts. These included the following, among possible others: William Linnane,

Dr. Steven Messner, Tom Campbell, Judy A. Baumgardner, Dr. Linda L. Chavez-Wilson, Kelly Harbaugh, Coleen Sweikert Heistand, Karen Hertzler, Warren Howard, and Jeffrey Hughes.

Others left to take positions in colleges and universities or the Department of Education: James Bishop, Ana Barbush, Helga Rist, Jon W. Gardner, Richard Elliot, Michele Glovora, Dr. Kathleen Jones, Sandra McConaghay, Dr. Conrad Stanitski, Douglas Stauffer, and Dr. Judith Witmer.

Dr. Carl Stanitski became an orthopaedic surgeon.

The May 31, 2000 issue of the *Falcon Flash* noted that several long-tenured teachers retired as the new millennium arrived:

- Mr. Kermit Katzaman taught for 35 years and during those 35 years he missed only seven days. He believes the most rewarding part of his job was to see his former students coming back and thanking him. His most memorable event was running into a pole in his chemistry room and his passion for teaching came from his own high school biology teacher.

- Mrs. Elizabeth Richards has at least 20 years of service. She was among the first year teachers at LD in the fall of 1960, took time out to rear a family, then later returned. She was involved with Special Olympics and when the life skills students first came to LD, Mrs. Richards and her ninth grade classes worked with them. She also teaches basic cooking skills to life skills students.

- Mr. Paul Longreen arrived in the fall of 1961 and spent the next 39 years devoted to the students and the challenges they bring to the classroom. He notes that the classes of 1964 and 1965 were some of his most memorable. "Students were much more reliable and harder working when I first started teaching," he said. He spices his lectures with "stories" about assemblies gone wrong and a few ill-planned experiments.

- Mrs. Virginia Regan taught physical education for 25 years, 15 of them at Lower Dauphin. In her youth she had hoped to be a veterinarian but such a profession was not open to women at the time. She speculated that she had taught more than 7,000 students during her tenure and notes that there are many more opportunities open to them than previously.

Following are a few representative notes of appreciation written by exceptional young people who have attended Lower Dauphin:

To my teacher

Over the years you've been refined, tested, and tried by space and by time,
a scar of perfection is each tiny line which loosens your soul and binds your time.

You've loved and learned from husband and friends and then taught it all to your student subjects again and again.

You've been kept waiting which is so agitating and kept a civil grin all the while for the sake of others who could not smile.

You've helped me out when things were bad, lifted my spirits and made me glad, and helped me out along the way with the simple words, "Have a nice day,"

And so to you, my teacher, a valentine's wish: May your heart be full and your joys be rich.

From Jim Brown '85

An extended excuse for being late to a special class

As we lie here on our death beds
It's very important that you should see
That visions of Brit Lit dance in our heads
Along with the nursery rhymes we have read
And thoughts of missing our British tea.

But, alas, never fear,
For there's a plan in this case:
Our friends, close and dear
Are willing it's clear
To come, step in, and take our place.

They will be us just for today,
And if you wait for the start of the week,
When we'll perform without delay,
After school we will stay
And a better performance you'll never seek!

Sincerely yours until the dish comes back with the spoon,
Brian & Rick

Note of Appreciation

This is just a small note to let you know how much I appreciate your friendship, your wisdom and your patience. Sometimes I don't think students realize how much of their lives are influenced by their teachers. I've learned more than readin', ritin', and 'rithmetic. I've learned how to accept responsibility and how to discern fact from fiction. Most importantly, I've gained self-confidence.

Anonymous

Note of Thanks

I'd like to thank you for making my senior year worthwhile. It's not very often a student has a teacher who is enjoyable and also comes prepared to teach. It's hard to admit I learned and enjoyed learning. I wanted to let you know I'm going to take night classes as a beginning. Although you didn't know, you were an inspiration, thank you for everything.

Anonymous

Mementos from the Gang of Ten

David C. Smith, Archivist

We Remember

✓ A newspaper article in **1967** that describes a summer science program (Title I funding) to improve science education. The same clipping announces the addition of eighth period and quotes the rationale provided by Mr. Ken Staver: "The primary purpose of the decision is to give the teacher and pupil a chance to get together on a more favorable pupil-teacher ratio." The article continues that the time will be utilized for all special interest activities such as seminars and research in sciences, advanced studies in math, social studies, English or a foreign language, as well as special interest clubs such as future teachers, farmers, or businessmen. Clubs such as chess club or sports club are also to be conducted. Other uses might be remedial and correctional instruction classes to help students."

✓ An original note providing authenticity to the Carol Channing Hoax in the spring of 1968.

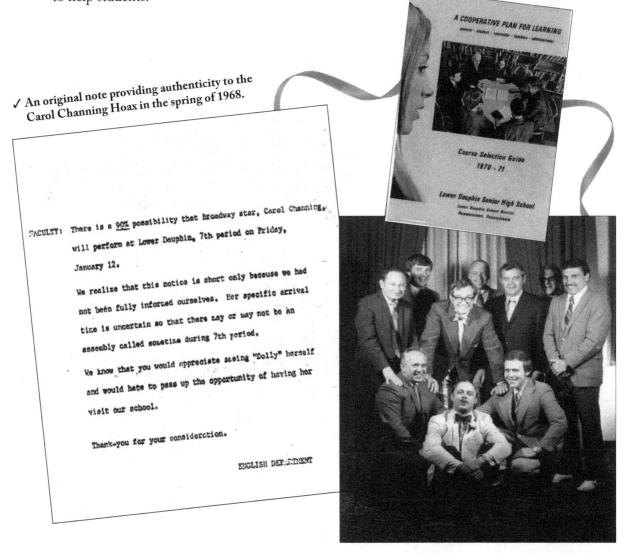

FACULTY: There is a 90% possibility that Broadway star, Carol Channing, will perform at Lower Dauphin, 7th period on Friday, January 12.

We realize that this notice is short only because we had not been fully informed ourselves. Her specific arrival time is uncertain so that there may or may not be an assembly called sometime during 7th period.

We know that you would appreciate seeing "Dolly" herself and would hate to pass up the opportunity of having her visit our school.

Thank-you for your consideration.

ENGLISH DEPARTMENT

Other Clippings

✓ Beverly Hallman's editorial in the February **1971** issue of the *Falcon Flash* called attention to the shortage of assemblies, noting in particular that because there were no class plays there were fewer "previews" and that other assemblies were canceled or rescheduled for a later date. She emphasized, "Student-promoted assemblies have also been scarce because few students and/or organizations have had anything interesting to present."

✓ The **1972** article in *The Patriot* of the comprehensive science electives available to LD students: Genetics, histology, zoology, botany, limnology, organic chemistry, electronics, nuclear science, oceanography, astronomy. Next year to be offered organic chemistry, qualitative analysis in chemistry, anatomy, and physiology.

✓ Japanese teachers with an interest in nuclear education visited LD in Fall **1972**; they observed American educational practices.

✓ In **1973** 50 students signed on for the AIFS trips!!!!!!

✓ An agenda for the Political Rally, October 28, **1976**

✓ Faculty: FINAL REMINDER—All students wishing to go on the November 25 bus trip to the Fiesta Bowl in Tempe, AZ, must have their $2,495. to Mr. Smith in Room B-5 by 2:30 p.m. today. The price includes one end zone seat, an Orange Bowl Shaker, and a map of downtown Miami.

✓ The day the faculty made chili in the faculty room, National Chili Day, January 26, **1979**, 11:45–1:00 p.m. " Note: (1) Nurse Foreman will be on call and (2) It may be necessary to bring a back-up lunch."

✓ The faculty meeting at which a teacher noted that there were too many students in the halls and to which Mr. Osevala replied, "Well, just remember; everyone has to be someplace." (October 16, **1980**, 3:03 p.m.)

✓ Notice from High School Administration to "Teachers Changing Rooms"

Re: Moving of File Cabinets

Date: May 29, **1981**: There has been some concern expressed to us about whether or not file cabinets should be moved from room to room. In the interest of consistency, filing cabinets should not be moved. Please transport only the contents of the filing cabinet. Some teachers have accumulated two filing cabinets. In this case, they may take the second filing cabinet with them. In one or two instances, teachers will find no cabinet in their new rooms. Please notify your respective administrator if this occurs and we will attempt to rectify this situation over the summer.

✓ Notes from Assistant Principal Mr. John Frankford to Mr. Romano, Mr. Zeigler and others on Sept 21, **1981**. Many faculty had been insulted to be told to "turn a tag" when they arrived in the morning and left in the afternoon.

✓Mr. McLure's letter of resignation leaving LD to accept a position as scouting supervisor with the Toronto Blue Jays Baseball Club, July 26, **1982**.

✓The letter from the superintendent ordering daily logs to be kept by the staff.

✓ The day the hazmat team was called to the chemical storage area under H-wing, **1982-83**, because of a chemical spill. A disaster was averted.

✓ The controversy over extending Dr. Hoerner's contract in **1983**.

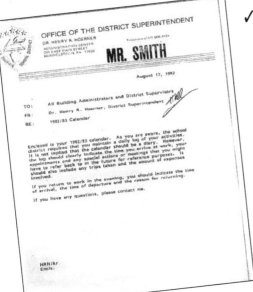

From the desk of:

John S. Frankford III
Assistant Principal

21 Sept 81

Mr. Zeigler:

The check-in board is now in order. Please use it in the morning and before leaving school. Thank you.

✓ The Daily Bulletin, January 28, **1983**: There will be a **mandatory** meeting Tuesday, February 1 in C-7 at 2:40 for those interested in a high school softball team. Please see June Steckler if you cannot attend.

✓ Daily Bulletin, November 19, **1984**, announced a "New Principal, Crowd Behavior."

✓ The following announcement: Your New Avon Man is D. Smith. Orders now being taken.

Updated Flotsum

✓A mimeographed faculty newsletter which welcomes new faculty Anne Broadwater, Tom Campbell, Kermit Katzaman, Tom Propst, Burr Rhoads, Barbara Silver, Maureen Wylonis. Also lists new marriages and new babies as well as other tidbits.

✓Mrs. Sandel removing photos of topless natives from the *National Geographic*.

✓All the men taught in a coat and tie. Women were dressed professionally and rarely if ever wore slacks until pants suits caught on in the 1970s.

✓Men had many more privileges than women did. Two men got extra paid time off to take wedding trips.

✓The cryptic note, "Tell them to get there early." (CC)

Famous Last Words

Can you identify the following speakers?

1. "Now, people…"

2. "Let's fall back and regroup—are there braces on the brain?"

3. "Well (harrumph), what I mean is…"

4. "Deedle Deedle Dumpling" and "Shave and a Haircut."

5. "Best day of my life."

6. "This is why you should never ASSUME anything."

7. "The funniest thing….."

8. "Oh, ferns and creels"

9. "The overall outlook of everything is bad."

10. "You know,"

11. "Nins and peedles"

12. "Go play in traffic"

13. "Working math problems is like eating potato chips! You do one problem, you just have to do more!!" Remembered by Ann Landis Kopp from geometry and trig classes.

14. Rushing in to class, and speaking in a loud tone, "Hellooo. How are YOU today?"

15. "Be Aware!"

Faculty Basketball Team

The "early days of LD," as we later called it, was a time of extensive faculty involvement, the faculty basketball team being notable among the activities. The Junior High Faculty (16 players) played the Senior High Faculty (11 players) and a combined team played against the few school faculty teams in the area, including a combined team of Hershey and Hershey Junior College in a benefit for the new Pennsylvania State Education Association building.

In its first year the faculty team had an almost perfect record. Of the 17 games they played, they won 16, losing to Albright College by only three points.

On January 13, 1962 the Falcon Faculty played the Harlem Satellites sponsored by the Senior High Choir; this event was promoted in the very first issue of the high school *Falcon Flash* on December 22, 1961. The team also went against "a group of barnstorming Baltimore Colt football players" in another benefit game. On November 26, 1963 they again competed against the Satellites as a fund-raiser for the Varsity Club.

What is particularly remarkable about this faculty team is that it was comprised of a number of "former cage stars" including, in addition to Bill Peck from Shippensburg: Jack Goepfert, who had played semi-pro after college; Jim Bishop (who also served as the coach), who had starred for Millersville; ex-Gettysburg athlete Frank Capitani; Bill DeLiberty from Lebanon Valley; and the tall twins, Carl and Conrad Stanitski from Bloomsburg. Also on the team were Dennis Musket, Joseph Schan, Gerald Brittain, Jim Seacrist, Robert Swartley, Jr., Henry Hoerner, and Jim Zeiters. Their games were not open to the public, except when there was a benefit.

This basketball team was such a phenomenon that a faculty cheerleading squad was also formed to cheer the team: Jean Eckman, Betsy Will (Richards), Judith Ball (Witmer), and Mary Lewin (not pictured).

One of their other notable games was a double header as a benefit for the Girls' Athletic Council in which the Junior High Faculty played the Senior High Faculty preceded by a game between two teams of high school girls on January 29, 1963. Officials were Judy Sener, Aaron Neidig and Luke Warble. Cheerleaders were the Junior High Faculty and the Jr. Varsity High School Girls. (To note the importance given this team by the students, an issue of the Junior High's *Falcon Flyer* issued an apology for having omitted the names of three players in its previous issue.) There was also a game in which the Faculty Women opposed the high school girls.

Throughout the years there were other faculty basketball teams who played the Harlem Diplomats and various other groups such as WKBO, but none had quite the cachet or the "following" as the originals.

Rich Clare Pentagon

Yes, this is the same Mr. Richard Claar who taught biology and chemistry at Lower Dauphin High School 1968–1972. He also co-directed the 1970 musical and served as director in 1971.

Claar has been part of various bands since the age of 14 and in college joined the "Soulville Allstars" who in 1967 released two hits which still have a cult following in England and Europe. Claar co-wrote the lyrics to both hits. In early 1971 Claar formed what would become the euphonious "Rich Claar Pentagon," with the name Pentagon based on the original five members who comprised the band. It later came to be known as "Rich Clare Pentagon."

The group went on the road in 1972 after 60 straight weeks at the Driftwood in Harrisburg. During the next twenty years Pentagon became a mainstay in Atlantic City, Las Vegas, and Puerto Rico. In 1991 the band planned to disband following a reunion concert at Hersheypark. However, the attendance was so high that the band decided to stay together and perform locally. Considered Pennsylvania's leading show band, Pentagon marked its 40th Anniversary in 2011.

A Pentagon performance "combines the best of popular music from the 50s to the 90s with a sprinkle of comedy along with serious onstage moving and grooving." They have a devoted following of all ages and backgrounds with many fans from LD and are particularly known for their tribute to rock and roll in a show called "Rico and the Ravens." Viewed as a high energy show band, Pentagon is still going strong, the entertainment never wavering. They also have a fan club, a web page and a book called "Pentagon 40." Rich Claar recently said, "I hope we can rock forever." So do we, dear friend, so do we.

Why I Became a Teacher

When I first decided to write a history of Lower Dauphin High School, one of the "all calls" I sent out was for teachers to tell why they had chosen the profession of teaching. Only one person responded. That in itself was telling, even though it later was echoed (1) when I provided an opportunity for a head coach of each sport to comment on his or her experience and did not receive responses from all and (2) when I asked a representative from each graduating class to write a reflection and received responses from only half of the fifty classes.

What intrigued me about the one response I received is that it is not only forthright, but unexpected. It is both a defense and a confession, expressing sentiments typically not shared. More importantly, it reflects historical research conducted on women who entered the field of education during the 1960s and early 1970s, as well as supports the comments made by Mr. Kenneth Staver and my own lifelong beliefs, observations, and more recent research on the topic beginning in the early 1990s and which has resulted in a number of publications. Typical of the 1950s culture, however, I had never before asked this specific question of anyone except myself.

I debated whether or not to include the following response, but am choosing to do so because it helps to explain the high quality of the female faculty who in other decades likely would have chosen different careers:

> I'm not sure the wonderful story about how I became a teacher is exactly what you're looking for. I became a teacher because it was the only thing my mother would let me be. A guidance counselor at HACC found a program for me that would have meant a full ride to NYU to become a social worker—they wanted to prepare community college grads to go back into their hometowns and work in the social services system to eradicate poverty and end racism, leaving the reforming of education to males. My mother would not even fill out the Parents' Confidential Statement (precursor to the FAFSA), without which I could not be admitted. Instead, I went to Millersville State College to become an English teacher because her boss at the Department of Ed said that was the best place to go for that.
>
> My becoming a teacher was more or less an arranged marriage, and I derived the same benefits women have derived from such for centuries. It gave me social legitimacy and a roof over my head and I learned to live well within the parameters. That it was often not terrible and resulted in many benefits beyond the basics does not change the fact that it was not my choice and, if I were twenty again and had it to do over again, would still not be.
>
> Margaret Yakimoff DeAngelis

Margaret DeAngelis is a novelist and author of short stories, among which is "Take Care," published in *A Community of Writers*. She has been a contributor at the Bread Loaf Writers' Conference and the Sewanee Writers' Conference, and has been a fellow at the Jentel Artist Residency, the Hambidge Artist Residency, and the Vermont Studio Center. Her popular blog, "Markings: Days of Her Life," can be found on her website, silkentent.com.

Summit Achiever Joyce Keener '63

Joyce Keener was graduated from Bennington College in Vermont, with a degree in art. She worked in Public Television for WITF-TV in Hershey, Pennsylvania as editor of the program guide. In 1971 she moved to Pittsburgh, where she worked at WQED-TV as editor of *Pittsburgh City Magazine* and wrote, produced, and hosted a variety of television shows.

In 1975 she and her husband, Tom Cherones (a noted television producer, including the first 86 episodes of "Seinfeld") moved to Hollywood. She had two novels published (*Borderline* in 1979, followed by *Limits of Eden*) and worked on several television shows, among them Knot's Landing, where she was a story editor.

In 1986 Joyce struck out on her own as an independent filmmaker (she served as both Screenwriter and Executive Producer) with "The Silence at Bethany," filmed in Lancaster County. The world premiere of this film was held March 21, 1989 hosted by WITF. The Lower Dauphin High School Band performed as the dignitaries arrived in antique cars while searchlights lit the night sky and the red carpet was rolled out. The production won a Christopher Award. Later Joyce sat on the grant selection panel of the National Endowment for the Humanities where she was instrumental in helping Ken Burns receive funding for his Civil War Project.

In 1988 Joyce and Tom moved to Florence, Oregon. She soon established herself as an artist, showing frequently in local galleries as well as in Portland, Eugene, and Los Angeles. The couple also taught a filmmaking course at the University of Alabama. Joyce's most recent artistic endeavor, a synthesis of her graphic art, photography and writing pursuits, was a limited edition, handmade book, which had its debut exhibition in Tuscaloosa, Alabama.

Remembered as exceptionally creative (and risk-taking as a child of Mennonites heading to *das über liberale* Bennington College in 1963 at age seventeen), Joyce Keener was a friend to her Alma Mater, expressing her fond memories of high school (once even saying that at her death she would like her ashes strewn on the grounds) and supporting fundraising events including the Show Case and the Art Auctions, thus allowing her work to continue to be represented in collections. Joyce Keener died in 2006.

Overview of "The Silence at Bethany"

"The Silence at Bethany" is one of the few feature films to deal with life among the Mennonites. Mark Moses plays Ira Martin, who grew up in a Mennonite community in the 1930s but left to live with out-of-town relatives when his parents were accidentally killed. Returning to his home town in the 1940s, Ira soon demonstrates that he has remained faithful to the religion of his birth, which impresses the local deacon. After marrying the deacon's niece (Susan Wilder), Ira becomes a preacher in his own right. Conflicts arise between Ira and the deacon when the younger man attempts to apply his citified "newfangled" notions to his ministry. Scrupulously avoiding stereotypes and patronization, "The Silence at Bethany" is a well-balanced study of a rarefied (and rapidly disappearing) American lifestyle. Produced by the PBS American Playhouse series, the film was released theatrically before its public-TV debut. The cast also included Tom Dahlgren who has many movie and television roles to his credits.

410

Testimonials and
Tributes

Testimonials and Tributes

"Letters You Wish You Had Written"

Most of us throughout our lifetimes have regretted not keeping in touch with some of those who were influential in our lives either at the time or in reflecting later what shaped us into the persons we are today. As part of the 50th Anniversary Celebration of LDHS, the Alumni Association placed an announcement in *The Sun*, encouraging interested alumni to write a letter, a tribute, or a remembrance of an adult at Lower Dauphin who "had an influence on you, perhaps someone whose class you remember with great fondness or gratitude, the coach who made a difference in your life, the staff person who lent a sympathetic ear, the principal who set you on a better path, the teacher who inspired you, or someone who influenced you and perhaps changed your life."

We offered to send these tributes to the person being noted and to include them in this book, *Loyal Hearts Proclaim*. Contributors were told they could remain anonymous to the person they were honoring, but needed to identify themselves to one of several volunteers to whom they could send their letters. The following tributes are what we received in response to this call, as well as letters that had been sent to individuals or to the association for other reasons, including use in the display case owned by the Alumni Association of Lower Dauphin and located in what is known as the Alumni Lobby.

Tributes from the 1960s

Messrs. Carl and Conrad Stanitski

The two teachers who had the greatest impact on me in our first and only year at Lower Dauphin High School were the Stanitski twins, Carl and Conrad. Carl was my homeroom teacher and Conrad taught us chemistry. They went to great lengths to reach out to our whole class, as we came from several different school districts. They always drew a crowd of students around them as they engaged in their teaching and also tried to enhance camaraderie at our brand new school. I came from Hummelstown High School where all of our teachers seemed older compared to the Stanitskis who were young and fresh. They encouraged us to be all we could be and to go further with our education.

Gloria Shertzer Mader, Class of 1961 Salutatorian

Judith Thompson Ball Witmer

I'd like you to know that when I think back to my days at Lower Dauphin, I remember a lot of fun times in band, chorus, the senior play, etc. But when I think about the classes I took, your English classes come to mind the most. I am particularly thankful for learning correct grammar, sentence diagramming, punctuation, editing—they all helped me the few years I worked at research and editing medical journal articles. Even today I cringe when I hear someone in a television interview say, "My friend and me are going to......." I think the old rules have gone out the window! I'm especially grateful for the love of literature and reading you shared with us that I enjoy even today; I don't go to bed at night without a book in hand. I'm a member of a small book club here that meets once a month, and has been going strong for nine years (that's a lot of books!). So thank you!!

Karen Fair Smith, Valedictorian 1964

Judith Thompson Ball, now Witmer, was our teacher for English I, III, and IV in those early years of Lower Dauphin when students and faculty, too, were young and inspiring. As our instructor, and more importantly as our mentor, Dr. Witmer had an enormous impact in molding our skills and our aspirations. Not once can I recall a negative response to our quests individually and as a class to find new avenues in which to excel. Our Class Motto: "It is better to have tried and failed than never to have tried at all" really typified us well. And she was so understanding as so many of our classmates including my husband and I came to see our lives intertwined—I think it was all that Romantic Period Literature!!! Prophetically Dr. Witmer's inscription in my yearbook happily for me came true: "We've traveled a long road together and though our paths may separate now, I feel sure that they will again cross." I treasure her many years of friendship as one of my life's most wonderful occurrences.

Jean Deimler Seibert, Valedictorian 1965

I could never wait to get to English class, for Dr. Judith Witmer was our teacher for three of our four years of high school. She was a modern Socrates—challenging us, demanding more and better performance, pointing out new perspectives, tickling our brains. Plus she taught me to laugh at myself—the most useful of skills. Her teaching style was far ahead of its time. I remember one day (near Halloween) when we entered class to the music of Mussorgsky's "Night on Bald Mountain" and had to write a Halloween tale that "fit the music." Not exactly your traditional 1960's English teacher. We have remained good friends and even co-authored a book.

Carolyn Sandel Anderson, 1965 Salutatorian

Dr. Judith T. Witmer expected the best from her students so we expected the best from ourselves. It was my blessing to have her as my English teacher in my freshman year and again in my senior year. In my freshman year, she assigned my class a paper on our personal philosophy. My gosh, she wanted us to think! I was terrified! Before the paper was due, I stumbled on Robert Frost, or was that reading another English assignment? I read his poem, "Stopping by Woods on a Snowy Evening," and borrowed the last stanza, "The woods are lovely, dark and deep, But I have promises to keep, And miles to go before I sleep, And miles to go before I sleep." Of course I gave proper credit to the author. It seemed like a good idea, as I was fourteen and did have miles to go. She kept saying how tough things would be in college. I believed her, I wanted to be ready. Then Freshman College English came and after two years with Dr. Witmer, really studying and being inspired to learn, in college I felt I was in grade school again!

Now, these many years later, when someone asks who your best/favorite teacher was, it is always Dr. Witmer who comes to mind. When thinking about this opportunity to offer a tribute to my best/favorite teacher, the "who" is easy but the "why" is difficult. Remembering concrete reasons or events elude me. I think the reason is because she was the best and that encouraged me to give and do my best. I was encouraged by her expectations of me, which made me a better, more confident person. That says what an excellent teacher she is. I use the present tense because she still teaches. Not in the classroom, but wherever she is, whatever project she chooses to lend her talents, I can't separate her from that role. Encouraging and inspiring others comes to her as naturally as breathing; it is who she is.

Dr. Janet Calhoon '66

Dear Dr. Witmer,

Two recent events have brought back memories of you and your classroom. I have found myself marveling at Mr. Obama's skills as an orator. Students in public speaking classes should be required to study both his speaking style and the organizational content of his speeches. Those thoughts morphed into memories of your public speaking class, which was one of my most enjoyable academic experiences in high school.

I've been doing a lot of reading recently and I have found Camp Hill's Fredricksen Library is a wonderful place to spend an occasional few hours. Although many of the books I read are escapist historical fiction or action/adventure with an occasional autobiography thrown in, I decided not too long ago to pick up some 20th century American classics which had somehow never demanded my attention. J. D. Salinger's *Catcher in the Rye* did nothing for me. I was, however, blown away by Steinbeck's *The Grapes of Wrath*. Given our economy, it was certainly a timely read. More than that, I found myself reveling in Steinbeck's use of language, his characterizations, and the overall structure of the piece. I finished it early last week, and still it steps into empty mental spaces at varying times of day. There were many places in the book where I wished I could have stopped and been part of a discussion group. You played a large part in helping to develop my love for language, in helping me to appreciate the power of words.

Jack Brandt '67

Dear Dr. Witmer,

I was recently contacted by a classmate to see if I could get her some information to pass on to you in preparation for the upcoming 50th anniversary of LDHS. While my mind is still wandering through the halls of LD, I thought I'd send you a note directly, to thank you and all of our teachers for a terrific education that really has served me well. After graduation, I went off to Bucknell University. Many of the students were products of elite New England prep schools, or children of NYC lawyers, judges, and power brokers who had received the best education their parents' money could buy. Based on pre-entry merit testing, I was chosen for the Honors English program at Bucknell, where virtually everyone else was a prep school product. I got A's, and after a few weeks of realizing I was as capable as any of them, never felt overmatched or inadequate.

After working for a few years, I went to law school. There, I did quite well also, graduating in the top 10% of my class and being chosen Articles Editor of law review. I worked in one of the largest law firms in the Pacific Northwest, dealing with lawyers from the national power-house firms, writing briefs to the US Circuit Courts of Appeal and even the US Supreme Court. I have published numerous articles for law reviews and professional journals and I am currently in DC as a senior executive and lawyer in the US government. The head of my agency, after seeing my capabilities, directed that I provide "quality control" over every written product of the organization, by editing for clarity, accuracy, and persuasiveness.

Again, I tell you all this to give context when I say, I have been around the best—and I have an ever-growing realization and appreciation, over all these years and in all these contexts, that the education I received from teachers like you, Patricia Lanshe, and Kathryn Zeiters prepared me to run with the best of them. We didn't know it at the time, and many of us who still have no basis for comparison, probably still don't appreciate it. But, the point of telling you about my adventures since LDHS days is that, by now, I have seen enough to allow me to marvel at how fortunate we were to have teachers like you to send us off with the skills to succeed anywhere.

You have touched thousands of lives. I'm sure you haven't heard from many of us thanking you for that. But, you should know that many of us know it, and feel it, and reflect upon it. Thanks, JT (that's what we used to call you, you know!).

Alan Larson '68

Ms. Barbara Macaw Atkinson

The person at Lower Dauphin who had the biggest impact on me was Ms. Barbara Macaw Atkinson, teacher and coach. Ms. Atkinson became the women's basketball coach when I was a junior. Thanks to her, our team was really successful. Not only was she a great high school coach, she became a great friend. In Spring 2009 Ms. Atkinson vacationed in Hawaii, where I live, and we had the opportunity to renew that friendship. Why does she have this impact? Ms. Atkinson always worked well to inspire students to be great athletes, and also to be the best in everything they set out to be.

Wendy Bolton, 1969 Valedictorian

Tributes from the 1970s

Lower Dauphin Faculty

Each us who passed through Lower Dauphin was affected differently by each individual teacher because we each had different needs. All of you can think of a list of teachers who challenged you, made you see something more clearly, or made you aware of something new and fascinating, and that list of teachers is different for each of you. The teachers who gave me the greatest gift were those who demanded more of me than I thought I was capable of. Teachers such as Mr. Campbell, Mr. Gardner, Mr. Grey, Miss Hallman, Mr. Murdocca, Mrs. Rist, and Mrs. Witmer taught me to set high goals, and that in order to reach those goals, I must demand of myself. The motivation to accept a challenge must come from within.

Dr. Julia Staver, 1970 Salutatorian

Mr. William Linnane

Mr. William Linnane taught me things about life that have stayed with me throughout the workplace and home life. He had a gentle way about him, but he could be firm if needed. I knew him as a teacher and a drama coach, having been in two plays where he was the advisor. He once had me over to his house for supper . . . imagine that? A teacher having a STUDENT over to his house! He greeted everyone with a smile and a handshake—met them like he'd never see them again. He made you feel special. It's a shame he left our school district and probably will never read this. I'd thank him for teaching me how to laugh, smile, and greet people like they're the most important person on earth.

Greg (Dino) Warble '70

Mr. William Minsker and Mr. David C. Smith

I had two teachers who made a difference in my life. The first was William Minsker. I first had him for social studies class in 7th grade, and then again in 9th grade, which included one of those "short term" classes from the 1970s, "Man: A Study." He made class interesting and made you think. His classes were never boring. He also cared for the students. He was probably my first exposure to "thinking outside the box."

The second was David Smith. I don't know if I always loved the sciences and he encouraged it, or if he initiated my love of science. I first had him for biology in 9th grade, and then again for parasitology (probably another one of those mini-courses) in 11th. Although I cannot find it on my old schedules, I also had a health careers class, possibly a club, with him. The two science classes were great, and he made them fun, but the health career class/club was the best. We took field trips to the Hershey Medical Center, the Harrisburg State Hospital, and several other places. What a great way to help a student decide what their future career should be! I can give testimony that it helped me. Being in his labs, and visiting these various places made me know that a career in medical technology was perfect for me. I am going on my 33rd year in various labs in the Clinical Laboratories at the Hershey Medical Center.

Sherry Rogers Bement '74

Dear Mr. Smith,

I doubt that you even remember me but I took your human anatomy course in 1978 my senior year. As much as I hated it, I love it now. I attended two years at Millersville State College as a biology major and have transferred to Williamsport College for dental hygiene. I am in a two-year course to earn my BA in dental hygiene and hope to go on for an additional semester for my BS and maybe further for my master's. In any event, I am deeply involved with anatomy here at school. I have oral, head, and neck anatomy as well as human anatomy. I remember, as I look back, studying for hours for your then "difficult tests." It is amazing how much I have retained from your class and I am now using in my classes and will later use in my profession.

I thank you for a basic understanding and detailed background that I am now using. Also, your class was difficult for me. Thank you for pushing me, in your "Mr. Mean Guy" way to achieve and retain all that I have. It is paying off tremendously! We are also, next semester, dissecting a cat, one of my favorite memories of your class. (Ha, ha!) Kathy Sugar and I loved him (our cat) so much that we even named him David Smith.

Sharon Swigart '78

Tributes from the 1980s

Mr. David C. Smith

As their senior year drew to a close, and, along with it, the end of Advanced Anatomy, a group of girls, the self-named "Favorite Five," presented a plaque to Mr. David C. Smith with the following message: "Just remember… if you cheat on a cat lab practical, you will cheat on life's practical."

The Favorite Five '81: Helen Frascella, Barbara Shenk, Lianne Shumaker, Penny Stine, and Sherrie Sylvester

Judith T. Witmer

To Mrs. J. Witmer,

A person who gave me warmth

A person who showed concern

Someone who shared her knowledge

And joy that words cannot tell.

Craig A. Camasta '82

Lower Dauphin Faculty

Excerpt from a letter written to *The Falcon Flash:* One of the reasons I'm writing this letter is because since graduation I've grown to appreciate Lower Dauphin even more. Too often one tends to overlook the opportunities high school provides to prepare for life. Over the years LD has proven itself capable of preparing its students for the challenges which lie beyond graduation. The opportunities do exist. It is just a matter of each of you taking advantage of all the LD has to offer in whatever field you desire.

Ron Orsini, 1982 Valedictorian

Lower Dauphin High School's Production of "Camelot"
——Reflections from a Knight of the Round Table

At Lower Dauphin, I participated in athletics, the school play, and extra curricular activities such as detention and other forms of discipline exercised by coaches and faculty. For me, high school was a rich social experience. Unfortunately, perhaps, I cared more about social exchanges to make favorable impressions on classmates and teachers than I did for my scholastic responsibilities and performance. No doubt, my high school transcripts reflect my priorities of youth! Still, I wholeheartedly believe my cumulative experience as a Lower Dauphin student is a seminal source in my social grounding. Having a graduate degree from one of the most prestigious universities in the world, and now working in Washington DC, highlights the humor in my academic performance at Lower Dauphin.

As an athlete, I worked hard to win, be a team player, and to lead my peers in mischief. Most of the time, as a rampant showoff, I wanted to impress the girls. Though I do reflect on those pursuits with fondness, my prowess was probably less than I imagine. Fortunately, Mr. Cleon Cassell and Dr. Judith T. Witmer taught me that actions have consequences and that I could be more than a class clown.

Going into my senior year in high school I had already enlisted in the United States Marine Corps. Thus, I knew after graduation I would be heading to Parris Island, South Carolina for the rigors of Marine Corps recruit training. Knowing this, my plan for my senior year was to have as much fun as possible. Why do anything more than necessary to graduate? After all, I was going to be a Marine, not an academic! My senior year would be the time of my life! In many ways it was, but in enlightening ways I could not imagine at the start of the school year.

On the first day of my assigned class with Dr. Witmer, prior to its start time, I was sitting in the back of the room with a dear friend who, like me, took pleasure in troublemaking. Though we gravitated to the back of the room, we noticed the vacant desks at the front of the class. "Leave those desks for the smart kids, or other pejorative description," I thought and most likely said.

At the start of the class, Dr. Witmer, took the roll, passed out the syllabus, and began describing the course content. Then, it happened! Dr. Witmer, while sagely pointing to the vacant desk in the front row commented, "Most of the people who have sat in these seats have earned A's, if any of you want to consider that." Without thinking, I jumped out of my seat, took the desk in the front row, and, in fact, surprising everyone, earned an "A" for the course.

This small impulsive move to the front row changed my life for the better and its positive results continue to benefit me, as I was inspired to learn more, do more, and become more. During the year, I learned from Dr. Witmer that a high school education, through the robustness of its opportunities and responsibilities, is a building block for living a fulfilled life. Dr. Witmer introduced me to the intellectual benefits found in art, music, musicals, theatrical performances, dance, literature, and even in doing my math homework. As you can already guess, by the time I left for service in the Marine Corps, my approach and values toward education had changed completely.

As the fall passed, Christmas vacation came and went and I failed to win a state championship in wrestling. September 1985 became March 1986. The talk of spring sports, the musical, thoughts of graduation, future plans, and other activities naturally ruled the hallway conversation. As I recall at Lower Dauphin in the mid-1980s it was common for athletes to have small roles in the musicals. For male athletes, being asked to participate fostered an aura of being popular, possibly because theatre was outside their behavioral norm and often their perception of the norm.

Having decided not to run track, I was excited that Dr. Witmer asked me to participate in the musical. Knowing nothing about the theatre, this was an opportunity for me to step into a new arena of learning possibilities. With Dr. Witmer as both the producer and the director, I knew she would teach me and my fellow athletes all we needed to know to offer stellar performances in our roles as Knights of the Round Table in "Camelot."

As an athlete, it was inspiring to watch the lead characters practice and perform their roles. Most of the lead actors did not participate in school athletics, but these classmates approached their craft of acting with the same zeal with which I wrestled. Having served as a co-captain of the wrestling team and being honored with the Team Award by my teammates and coaches, I know practice, attention to detail, and hard work are essential for performance in any endeavor.

Of course, the teamwork demonstrated by everyone involved in our production of "Camelot" ensured it was an incredible experience for the April 10, 11, and 12, 1986 audiences. For all who served in any capacity of the musical, I hope our production of "Camelot" is not just a fond memory, but remains a life-shaping experience.

Thus, thank you, Dr. Witmer, for preparing me for life beyond homework, school plays, and sporting events. Without your influence, I would not have earned Magna Cum Laude honors in graduate school. Thank you for including me in "Camelot." The indelible experience of my small role as a Knight has facilitated my continued interest in and respect for the arts.

Wade S. Alexander '86

Tributes from the 1990s

Mrs. Nanette Willis Singer

I would acknowledge Mrs. Nan Willis Singer who was my English teacher as having a great impact on my education and career goals. She was wonderful in instilling in me a love of literature, and preparing me to go to college as the next step in my education. Although I majored in economics at Penn, I had enough credits in English courses for a minor. This illustrates the inspiration of Mrs. Singer. I never wrote a book, but Mrs. Singer enhanced my communication skills which are so important in the marketing field.

Andrew Espenshade '90

I had the opportunity to have Ms. Nan Singer both in 8th grade English, and then for AP English as a senior. She was an excellent English teacher who was enthusiastic about the assigned readings and who taught straight-forward writing skills. I also spent several years with Mr. Charles Cole, who always continued to challenge me to write better and think more about the literature that we studied. Because of these two teachers, I have been successful in publishing research articles related to my medical profession. And my bedside stand always has a William Faulkner novel, mixed with the occasional *People* magazine. (Sorry Mr. Cole!)

Dr. Christine Cassel Mackley, 1991 Valedictorian

Mr. David C. Smith

Most tributes teachers receive are written after students have been graduated; however, occasionally students express their appreciation before leaving high school. In the spring semester of 1992, Mr. David C. Smith received the following letter from a student.

> I have only 11 minutes left, so I am not going to try to BS my way through the essay (exam). I am not going to grow up and be a doctor, that you know, but I do want to be successful in life. You have shown me that I am not dumb. That I realize now. When I said I let you down I was also letting myself down. Halfway through the year I stopped looking at you as a teacher, but more as a father or call it what you want. Whatever it was, it had an effect on me. I would just like to thank you for all your love and support through my high school years. I hate to leave, but…I have to grow up now.
>
> Love you always, your son, Joe Wiles '92

Like many students their sophomore year, Joe Wiles was an indifferent student in general biology. However, Mr. David C. Smith, knowing young people well, would not allow students to slack off when they were capable of the work and, as he did with many students, Mr. Smith, in his own words, confirmed that he was "on Joe's case about being lazy." Joe, like most students, was not happy with this "push" and vocalized his sentiments in the hall, although not in class. Wisely, Mr. Smith did not challenge Joe on his anger, choosing to bide his time. Two years later in his senior year, Joe enrolled in Advanced Anatomy and Physiology and on the final cat lab practical he performed in the 90% range, one of the highest scores earned on this exam. Upon graduation from high school in 1992, Joe completed a program at the Culinary Institute of America (CIA) in New York, graduating in 1994. He interned at Hilton Head, followed by a teaching fellowship at CIA. He then returned to the Harrisburg Area where he worked at the Colonial Country Club, then at the Hilton in Harrisburg. Joe is currently head of food and beverage at the Carson Long Military Academy in New Bloomfield, and continues his friendship with his high school mentor.

At Lower Dauphin, Joe served as student manager for both football and basketball. He also was talented to the point that Mr. Smith suggested that he become involved in Thespians. While he didn't take this advice at the time, he now helps his wife Becky, a music teacher in the Newport School District, with the musicals and sets. Mr. Smith smiles as he recalls this. Further, Joe Wiles is a collector of Star Wars memorabilia and an expert in the lore of Star Wars and has been featured on WGAL.

Tributes from the 2000s

Mr. Charles Cole

I acknowledge Mr. Charles Cole as an influential teacher because he always pushed us to go "one step further" so that we would perform to the best of our ability. His approach to teaching has made a difference in so many people's lives.

Amanda Brown, 2002 Salutatorian

Mr. Daniel Mikula

Mr. Mikula, who taught Honors English, was awesome! He challenged you to analyze your answers and to think about why you answered the way you did, and even to reflect on your beliefs. He was not just interested in teaching you knowledge—he wanted you to review what you knew, and to increase your knowledge base by reflecting on what you believe and think you know. Knowledge thus became personal learning. As a student interested in science, it was interesting to be presented all these ideas I had never thought of—and to have discussions about them in class. As a teacher, Mr. Mikula also was interested in helping me develop ways to be a better writer and a thinker. He opened my eyes to different worlds.

Allen Welkie, 2009 Salutatorian

Yearbook Dedications

The formality of a yearbook dedication is rarely seen in more recent editions of high school yearbooks. One likely reason is that the size of high schools today and the individualized program students follow do not allow for a majority of the members of the yearbook staff to easily agree on a person or event that has had special significance for the graduation class. Another is the growing informality of our society which may view book dedications as outmoded, and a third is that yearbook dedications may be viewed as superfluous among pages replete with special recognitions. However, since dedications were once considered serious choices (and often kept secret until the books were presented in an assembly), they are here included in this historical memoir.

Class of 1961:   Mr. Curtis S. Taylor

Class of 1962:   Mr. Douglas A. Stauffer

Class of 1963:   Miss Janet M. Ausmus

Class of 1964:   Mr. Robert R. Fickes

Class of 1965:   Mrs. Judith T. Ball

Class of 1966:   Mr. Gordon E. Putt

Class of 1967:   Miss Aleda L. Myers

Class of 1968:   Mr. James Seacrist

Class of 1969:   Mr. William Linnane

Class of 1970:   Mr. Benjamin McLure

Class of 1971:   Mr. Edward Romano

Class of 1972:   Mr. Stephen Futchko

Class of 1973:   Mr. Steven Messner

Class of 1990:   Mr. Wilbur Rhodes

Class of 1991:   Mrs. Eloise O'Brien

Class of 1974:   . . . to the kaleidoscope of all we have been and the vision of all
                        we hope to be

Class of 1975:   . . . to those who dare to ask of life everything good and beautiful

Class of 1976:   . . . to our parents

Class of 2002:   . . . to the victims and heroes of September 11, 2001

Faculty-to-Faculty Tributes and Eulogies

Mark S. French

Mark French enjoyed a good joke almost as much as he liked going fly fishing, playing with his German shepherds, and working with his students at Lower Dauphin High School. Mr. French, who died of Lou Gehrig's Disease in June 2009, had a knack for "always finding humor, even when things weren't going well," said Mr. Charles Cole, one of his closest friends and a fellow teacher at the high school. "Mark was a joker but had a serious side, too."

Cole, a retired English teacher, said his friend specialized in helping troubled teens. He recalled a problem student who had been suspended several times. "At the beginning of the year, the kid was belligerent," Cole noted. "He started to turn around by Thanksgiving. By the end of the year, he had passing grades, made friends, and was a different kid. Mark gave him tough love and showed that someone cared." Others also recalled Mr. French's joy in "turning around kids with behavior problems. He took pride and joy in seeking kids get their act together." Cole also noted Mark French saying that difficult students needed someone to draw boundaries.

"Teaching was Mark's passion," said Dawn French, his wife of 28 years. "Kids looked to him as a father and mentor because he offered them stability. He was a good listener." A neighbor added, "Mark did the best he could with what was thrown at him. He lived each day to the fullest. We were good friends. I miss him terribly." As do many.

Adapted from *The Patriot News*, October 10, 2009

Glenn William ("Bill") Peck

Glenn William Peck died six years after his teaching career at Lower Dauphin Junior-Senior High School began, the yearbook portrait revealing in his eyes that his illness was winning. I remember the first time I saw him: We were all gathered in the auditorium of this newly-formed jointure. We were an enthusiastic group, many of us in our first teaching assignment. We were open and friendly, ready for this new professional adventure and ready also to spend social time together.

With his congenial personality Bill Peck thoroughly enjoyed the easy banter in C Faculty Room, which was well-used that first year with every classroom filled every period so that a teacher's planning period could not be spent in his or her room. Bill was the first to sign a 1962 proclamation on rules in the faculty room: "It has been recommended that C Faculty Room be "redd out." We members of said room are well aware that our lounge is the least messy of the faculty rooms in the building, but to prove this to certain other parties, let us henceforth adhere to the following rules of good housekeeping" and these were delineated.

And then there were the parties—New Year's Eve at the Lawnton Legion, Halloween in the attic of the Antonicelli house where Betsy Will Richards had an apartment, end-of-school picnics at various places, and Christmas parties, particularly the special traveling "House Hopping Christmas Party" hosted at three different residences.

An athlete and a PIAA basketball official, Bill Peck was a natural working with young boys who needed direction and a friend. A mathematics teacher, he was remembered just as much for the Boys' Club he formed as a means to provide wholesome activities for young men, particularly for those who were not on sports teams or involved in other activities. Many students spoke of Mr. Peck's personal counseling, his ability to relate to kids, and, most of all, his very practical advice. He liked teaching, he liked the kids, and he greatly enjoyed the faculty camaraderie.

During his last days students, such as Ann Landis '65, who then was attending Shippensburg, Bill's Alma Mater, wrote (March 20, 1966), "How is Mr. Peck? I haven't heard any news concerning him." George Nichols, waiting deployment to Viet Nam, wrote (January 18, 1967), "I heard the faculty basketball team raised funds for Mr. Peck's hospital bills. I think that was real nice of the school to do that. How is Mr. Peck getting along?" And at his death, many wept. Comments came from Lois Downes '65 who said (February 9, 1967), "Thank you for relating the news of Mr. Peck's death. I purposely avoided asking it in my letter," and Barry Stopfel '65 commented (February 11, 1967), "Very sorry to hear about Bill Peck. Sure as hell makes me wonder what life is all about." Indeed it did.

Joseph P. Schan

Joe Schan was one of the "originals" at LD, both for the fact that he was a member of the first faculty when the doors of Lower Dauphin opened in the fall of 1960 and for the "character" he played in the classroom. His gruffness hid a kind heart and many students will tell stories of life in math class and the ducking of flying erasers. There was no one, however, more loyal to the sports program, and Joe served as statistician for football, basketball, and baseball. He retired from the school district after 34 years as a math teacher, many of those as math department chairman. The many friends and students of Mr. Schan sorely miss the familiar blue jacket and Falcon cap on the sidelines during the football season.

Mary Jane Strite

Jane Strite, who began her teaching career at Hummelstown High School, which was also her Alma Mater, was principled. Dedicated to the school, she was the matriarch of the Business Department there and, later, at Lower Dauphin. Intrepid on the basketball court, she was a champion before girls' sports were lauded. Zestful in her pursuits, she once rode a bicycle across the United States. She loved traveling, so long as it was not in the air.

Comfortable in who she was, she did not need a chorus of approval. Loyal to both people and causes, once she made a commitment she never strayed. Curious by nature, she often asked why things were what they were and why people acted as they did. Her sensitivity was sometimes misunderstood, as her shyness prevailed in unfamiliar situations with those who did not take the time to know her. With an unwavering inner strength and conviction, the lives she influenced, the friends she kept, the students she assisted, and the athletes she coached numbered beyond measure.

Robert R. Fickes

Bob Fickes left his mark at LD as an art teacher, designer of the Lower Dauphin seal, set designer, lettering and graphic of the Falcon on the original cheerleading megaphones, and as the creator and curator of the original Falcon mascot. One might wonder what we would have done without him.

Mr. Fickes left a lasting impression on all—both faculty and students—who knew him and was the inspiration and first coach of many students who pursued careers in art. His typical demeanor was one of reticence, but when he had reason to be impatient with ineptitude in others, there was no mistaking his passion when he raised his voice. Brilliant and talented, with a rare and very dry sense of humor, he was a unique individual often taking the experimental approach rather than the traditional (in a time when "experimental" had not yet gained the esteem it now holds). His stage sets for the high school musicals were unforgettable, creative works of art, in a time when most high schools did not use full sets. Always striving for perfection, he made a lasting impression in the annals of LD, and, just as in living life, in his leaving of it he quietly and unassumingly went without fanfare.

Prowell M. Seitzinger

The leader of the band is tired
And his eyes are growing old.
But his blood runs through my instrument
And his song is in my soul.

Allegro Con Fuoco:

Prowell Seitzinger was one of a kind. When Lower Dauphin first opened in the fall of 1960, Mr. Seitzinger was faced with all new musicians, students he did not know, coming from various high schools or junior high schools and all having studied under an assortment of music teachers. He was charged with creating a marching band for the high school's first football season. From that uncertain beginning, the foundation for an outstanding music program began.

Mr. Seitzinger in his cream white band uniform, indelible in the mind; memories of students all speaking fondly of him, with respect, a story, and a smile; the delayed recognition of him as the composer of the Lower Dauphin Alma Mater; the obstreperous percussion section ducking his baton, thrown at them in exasperation.

Prowell had no nickname. He didn't need one. His presence was enough, whether it was raising issues at a faculty meeting or, later, writing letters to the editor in the city paper.

Andante Con Moto:

He continued to call his longstanding friends throughout the years after leaving LD, maybe to ask the name or address of a common friend from long ago or to recommend a new movie. To the end he made music, and recently (at the time of this writing following his death) he contracted with one of his former percussionists, one of the many on the receiving end of that baton, to record a private concert so that his family would have a sentient legacy.

Fine:

The leader of the band. No one need say more.

Da Capo al Fine

Patricia M. Lanshe

Mrs. Lanshe was one of the original faculty at Lower Dauphin Junior-Senior High School, arriving as an eighth grade English teacher in the fall of 1960. She later became a guidance counselor in the high school, heading the department following the retirement of Mr. Kenneth Staver. She befriended countless students and many faculty members. Mrs. Lanshe was a person of great integrity and would work diligently behind the scenes to "right" a wrong, whether it involved a student or a teacher. Not many people knew how much the administration counted on her keen insight and wise advice.

Patricia was well-named for she was definitely a patrician, well-bred and stylish even during the lean years when her earnings went toward her children's needs and not her own. I recall how she enhanced her limited wardrobe with costume jewelry that made a statement, particularly large earrings and bangle bracelets, and I will never forget her signature "wedgie" heels.

After being graduated from Harrisburg Catholic High School, Patricia found her niche at St. Joseph's, then a women's college. Her major in journalism led her to New York City during WWII, a time she recalled with great delight, describing the strange exhilaration that such times generated. These years were an exciting time to live, work, and play in New York City for those still in their twenties.

Patricia Lanshe was a mentor before the concept—or even the term—became popular. She was so much wiser than most of us in those early days at Lower Dauphin Junior-Senior High School. (Most of the faculty were "brand new" and looked to the "older ones," including Patricia who was only 37, for direction.) She had an unforgettable giggle. More than that, however, she was a careful listener who provided advice when it was asked for and caution when it was not if she thought one needed to be warned about something or to think more carefully about a decision.

Another term that comes to my mind about Patricia Lanshe is that she was ever so practical, never wasting time on pipe dreams. What she looked for was expediency, not belaboring an issue. Most of all, she did not suffer fools gladly. I believed that Pat knew everything worth knowing. All in all, Patricia was most definitely one of a kind, and we shall not see her like again. The world is less for the loss of this most remarkable person.

Kenneth W. Staver

Shortly after receiving the Award of Distinction from the Lower Dauphin Falcon Foundation, Mr. Staver passed away. His legacy, however, continues, as Ken Staver's life serves as a shining example of meritorious service in leadership in the community, school, professional achievement, and general contributions to the area and the people he loved and served.

Those who heard him speak at the LD Falcon Foundation Gala will never forget his quiet, yet impassioned words as he told why he had spent his life in service. He said that without the help of others he would not have been able to attend college and as one of the few survivors in his military company, he felt an obligation to all of his comrades who had fallen. As one who was spared, he never forgot that those who died in battle never would have the rest of their lives to live as he did.

We mourn his passing and salute him for all he did for so many others, more than any one of us knows.

LD
50

Lower Dauphin Alumni Association
and the
Golden Jubilee

The Lower Dauphin Alumni Association
—Founded 1989

In the Beginning

On August 23, 1988, a group of alumni representing every decade of graduates of Lower Dauphin High School responded to an invitation by Dr. Judith T. Witmer, Principal for Academics, to discuss the formation of a Task Force for Recognizing Student Achievement. The purpose of this task force was to develop a strategy to (1) network with alumni to collect and preserve historical artifacts, (2) design fund-raising projects to support student activities and academics, and (3) plan a program of Lower Dauphin Alumni awareness of their Alma Mater.

By their second meeting the renamed Steering Committee for Falcon Pride was talking in terms of forming an alumni association, and an Alumni Association Kick-Off/Open House was scheduled for April of 1989. Locating 7,000 graduates was a daunting task and key persons from each graduating class were asked to supply names and addresses from class reunion lists. The formidable task of creating a data base of all graduates of the high school began, using a computer program designed by Joseph M. Snavely '83 and further refined by Jesse A. Dillon '79. A general mailing was generated in February 1989. The response from alumni was encouraging, and we were particularly appreciative of a generous donation by **Ann Seaman Grimm '62** to help defray the costs.

At the April 15 organizational meeting the **Lower Dauphin Alumni Association** (LDAA) became a reality with the attendance of more than 200 interested persons. By-laws were approved and officers elected. Special highlights of the event included the singing of the *Alma Mater* led by the Snavely sisters (Julia '73, Jayne '76, Jeanne '78, and Joan '80), accompanied by Prowell Seitzinger, composer of the original score. Elaine Harris Sulkey '63, who had submitted the winning lyrics in a school contest in 1961, was also acknowledged. Featured was a display of memorabilia collected and arranged by Marjorie Park Cassel '65 and Kate Reed Allen '66.

By June 1989 LDAA had 600 paid memberships. That fall the Association participated in the Homecoming Activities, marking the first time that LD's Homecoming was actually a homecoming for graduates.

Other projects initiated that first year included a quarterly newsletter and the formation of a scholarship committee. The newsletter is now published on average three times a year and is sent to all dues-paying (to cover the cost of mailing) alumni.

Every five years a mass mailing is sent to all alumni for whom LDAA has addresses. We are in the process of moving to electronic publication, strongly encouraging our members to provide their email addresses.

In the spring of 1990 *Falcon Pride* had a new logo and format, designed by Cynthia DiEleutoria Miller-Shoemaker '73. The second annual meeting of LDAA featured an alumni chorus and a presentation by members of the original Lower Dauphin Joint School Board. That fall, LDAA took an even broader role in Homecoming with a float entry, "Beauties and the Beast," featuring Homecoming Queens from '65 (Jane Harper), '66 (Carol Gingrich), '72 (Barbara Higgins), '75 (Jodi Reitz), '80 (Patricia Stare), and '83 (Lisa Kurr). An alumni dinner-dance was held at the Tudor Rose Tavern in HersheyPark.

Homecoming 1990 also saw the first appearance of the crowd-pleasing Alumni Band, until recently under the direction of James Neidinger '73, playing the vintage "fight songs." Also appearing on special occasions are the Alumni Cheerleaders who are a great favorite with the sports fans as well as alumni who enjoy the familiar cheers of yesteryear.

Falcon Alumni Trust

One of the major goals of the Lower Dauphin Alumni Association is to acknowledge student achievement in scholarship, athletics, and the arts. In 1990 the Board of Directors established a trust whereby funds would be set aside and invested for the purpose of funding scholarships. The interest from that trust, together with funds raised on a year-to-year basis, have been used to award an annual scholarship to a graduating senior who is continuing his or her education at the post-secondary level. These names are then placed on an award plaque in the Alumni Lobby (See list of winners in this section.) LDAA also serves as overseer of additional scholarships for various organizations and individuals.

In 1992 the Alumni Association Art Show and Silent Auction was established as a fund-raiser for the Scholarship Trust Fund. Alumni artists, friends, and businesses donated works of art, services, restaurant certificates, event tickets, and other items of value, to be bid on at the auction. In addition, monetary gifts in honor or memory of Lower Dauphin faculty, alumni, and friends have been accepted for this scholarship fund.

FIELDS

A major undertaking was the sponsorship of FIELDS, convened by Dr. Witmer, which was a bringing together of interested persons in the community for the purpose of exploring the feasibility of constructing a Sports Complex on acreage owned by the school district. The Sports Complex Committee was an organized response to the need for more playing fields for a sports program which had greatly expanded since 1960. Key to that effort were preliminary drawings by James Szymborski '65 of the Tri-County Planning Commission and architectural drawings rendered by W. Richard (Rick) Glocker, Jr. '64, then a draftsman at TMI.

Falcon Alumni Lobby

Another significant project was the designation of the Alumni Lobby in the high school. This included the installation of a large Falcon mosaic, the gift of the Class of 1988, in the outer lobby at the parking lot entrance at the rear of the school. At the same time LDAA ran a fund-raising campaign to build an imposing Alumni Memorabilia ShowCase. This large walk-in installation is used for exhibits which are staged several times a year. These exhibits are outstanding, museum-quality, themed displays curated by Wade (Kirk) Seibert'65. (See the representative list following.)

Additional Projects

In addition to funding a scholarship and the Alumni ShowCase, LDAA began a number of special projects, many of which continue today. We collected a complete set of yearbooks and began a search for missing items of historical importance. As a result we became the repository of many items that otherwise would have been lost, including programs, photos, scrapbooks, uniforms, pennants, the Lower Dauphin Bible, and class schedule cards, to name a very few.

Another project at that time was a 16-foot square sign placed in the gymnasium under the guidance of Brian K. Stoner '64 for which Kurt D. Stoner '85 donated his services for the sign work with its message: FALCON PRIDE! The Alumni Association also organized the sale of 48 cushioned folding chairs to be used by the winter sports teams. The chairs, royal blue and white, bore the insignia of a falcon on the seat and each chair displayed the name of its individual donor.

Further, we arranged for the Hummelstown High School Alumni Association to install two display cases in the lobby outside the auditorium for the memorabilia of the predecessor school to Lower Dauphin.

In the fall of 2000 LDAA recognized all LD football captains and honored the 1960 Championship football team on their fortieth anniversary, paid tribute to the Big Blue Band at Homecoming 2002, and honored the Field Hockey players and coaches in a Field of Teams celebration at Homecoming 2003.

In 2004 the Alumni Association purchased a field banner to be used for football games, band competitions, and other events. This banner was presented pre-game by Barry Broadwater and Harry Menear, honorary representatives of the first great Falcon football team and Conference Champions in the fall of 1960. The banner is designed to be carried by a runner at the sidelines as a sign of spirit and to celebrate a score.

At Homecoming 2006 LDAA presented to the high school a replica of the original Falcon missile. The Alumni Association paid for the materials and the Lower Dauphin Missile Agency (rocket club) students built the replica.

In the fall of 2009 the 1960 championship football team was honored as our kick-off event for the Golden Jubilee and in 2010 the 1970 championship was celebrated.

Our culminating event to date has been the Golden Jubilee, details of which follow.

LDAA Fundraisers include the following:

- Folding chairs (twice) for use by winter sports
- Silent Auction and Art Show for many years
- Commemorative Crocks with the dates 1960-2010 or year of graduation
- LD Flags
- Brad Stroman note cards with the head of a falcon, special edition
- Brad Stroman prints with the head of a falcon, special edition
- Personalized hats
- Directories
- Above the door/shelf sitter replicas of Lower Dauphin High School
- Sponsorship of a vegetable snack booth at the Hummelstown Arts Festival
- *Loyal Hearts Proclaim: The First Fifty Years of Lower Dauphin.*

Current and Future

On-going work includes the following:

- Helping to locate yearbooks and owners of found class rings
- Keeping lists and records of various honors
- Establishing an archival fund to preserve documents and other memorabilia
- Hosting the annual post-homecoming game tailgate party
- Assisting classes in locating classmates
- Offering assistance for classes holding reunions.

Every five years since 1993 LDAA has published a directory of names and addresses of all alumni. There is no cost to an individual to be included and the book or a CD is available for purchase. The next edition will likely appear in 2015 as we produced the most recent edition in 2010 for the Golden Jubilee.

Through private donations the Lower Dauphin Alumni Association now has a permanent home at the Hummelstown Area Historical Society where our holdings will be kept, catalogued, and protected in a climate-controlled environment.

Lower Dauphin Alumni Association
1989 – 2013

24 Years of Service to the Students and Alumni of LDHS

Founding:

- Convener – Dr. Judith T. Witmer, then Principal for Academics, LDHS, later Asst. to the Supt., LDSD
- First meeting – April 15, 1989
- Founding Members: Catherine Reed Eshenour '66; Marjorie Park Cassel '65; Russel E. Cassel '65; Carl W. Espenshade '62; Nancy L. Hivner '72; Elizabeth Musser Radle '62; Joseph M. Snavely '83; Jean Deimler Seibert '65; Kirk (Wade) Seibert '65
- Current Officers: President Russel E. Cassel '65; Vice President Elizabeth Musser Radle '62; Secretary Kathy Imhof Weber '74; Treasurer George Kline '72
- Additional Current Board Members: Barbara Miller '71, Elaine Mader Royer '65, Carl Espenshade '62, Randy Umberger, '65, Rick Smith, '83. Number of members—technically anyone who was graduated from LDHS; sustaining (paying for a membership) members— approx. 600
- LDAA is an independent organization, not funded by the school district.

Purpose: to collect and preserve historical artifacts, design fundraising projects to support student activities and academics, and plan programs by which alumni continue their involvement in their Alma Mater.

Activities and contributions:

- Meet bi-monthly
- Maintain a database of alumni addresses
- Publish an Alumni Directory – next edition in 2015
- Active in Homecoming
    - 1989 – first participation; 1990 – first Alumni Band and a float featuring past Homecoming Queens and later organizing Alumni Cheerleaders

- ▸ Honor various groups including wrestlers, football teams, field hockey, the first Championship Football Team of 1960, the band, and major half-time program in 2010 honoring the undefeated Championship Football Team of 1970
- ▸ Support an after-game Indoor Tailgate Reception
- ◆ Publish *Falcon Pride* newsletter, initiated in 1989
- ◆ Support the Falcon Alumni Trust Scholarship, twenty-three since the inception of the award in 1990
- ◆ Manage several other scholarships funded by various alumni groups and individuals
- ◆ Honor Distinguished Alumni and LD Supporters
- ◆ Assist Reunion Committes, providing addresses, and serving as a clearing house
- ◆ Serve as trustee for class funds and class gifts
- ◆ Collect and preserve memorabilia and historical archives such as yearbooks, programs, photos, scrapbooks, uniforms, pennants, the LD Bible, class schedule cards, recordings, foootball movies, Commencement speeches, and much more, all to be catalogued as part of our presence as a member of the Hummelstown Area Historical Society
- ◆ Help locate yearbooks and owners of found class rings
- ◆ Keep lists and records of various honors
- ◆ Installed a *Falcon Pride* sign board in the gymnasium
- ◆ Purchased and installed an Award Plaque honoring LDAA scholarship winners
- ◆ Installed a large walk-in Show Case in the Alumni Lobby, which is used for museum quality exhibits that change several times a year
- ◆ Sponsored the creation of a replica of the original Falcon Missile
- ◆ Oversaw installation of a large falcon mosaic, a gift from the Class of '88
- ◆ Sponsored two sets of chairs used by winter sports teams
- ◆ Led a Sports Complex Committee (1998) that brought together former athletes, community leaders and others to support a feasibility study in response to the need for playing fields
- ◆ Assisted Hummelstown High School Alumni Association in gaining permission and space in the high school for two display cases
- ◆ Purchased a field banner to be carried along the sidelines after a touchdown and in band competitions
- ◆ Established an archival fund to preserve documents and other memorabilia
- ◆ Produced the Golden Jubilee, a celebration of LDHS's 50th Year.

Fundraisers:

- Sponsor chairs for use by winter sports
- Silent Auction and Art Show
- Commemorative Crocks with the dates 1960-2010 or year of graduation
- LD porch Flags
- Brad Stroman note cards with the head of a falcon, special edition*
- Brad Stroman prints with the head of a falcon, special edition*
- Personalized hats
- Directories, most recent is the fourth edition, 2010
- Above the door/shelf sitter replica of Lower Dauphin High School*
- Publication of *Loyal Hearts Proclaim: The First Fifty Years of LDHS*
  - See www.ldsd.org/alumni, our presence on Facebook with the name Lower Dauphin Alumni Association and our website, www.lowerdauphinalumni.org.

Contact Kathy Weber, Secretary of LDAA (kweber@ldsd.org) or Dr. Judith T. Witmer (jtwitmer@aol.com) to ask how YOU can help your Alma Mater. There are various committees and special projects through which you can participate as appreciation for the educational excellence you have received and the lifetime of memories you have experienced.

*Items still available for purchase. Contact Kathy Weber, please, for details.

Falcon Alumni Trust Scholarship Winners

The Alumni Association sponsors two scholarships through its Trust, the longest standing of which is the Falcon Alumni Trust Scholarship, first awarded in 1990.

1990	Andrew Espenshade	2002	Abby Snyder
1991	Christine Cassel	2003	Megan Haas
1992	Stephanie Teets	2004	Joshua Young
1993	Renee Hoffman	2005	Erica Bates
1994	Megan Espenshade	2006	Amy Brandt
1995	Jeremy Sharpe	2007	Andrea Leshak
1996	Jodi O'Donnell	2008	Suzanne Cake
1997	Kristen Potter	2009	Clayton Cooper
1998	Abigail Martin	2010	Chase Harmon
1999	Joshua Good	2011	Charles Davis
2000	Margaret Aichele	2012	Amanda Ringenbach
2001	Jennifer Johnson	2013	Kara Kaylor

Distinguished Alumni Award

In 2013 the Alumni Association initiated the Distinguished Alumni Award which is also a scholarship to a graduating senior as a way to honor the Distinguished Alumni and the individual who receives the Distinguished Service Award, usually annually.

The Alumni Association also manages the following scholarships:

Dr. Judith T. Witmer Scholarship (sponsored by the Class of 1965)

LD Class of 1965 Award

Arlene Huss Award

Distinguished Alumni and Friends Honored by the LDAA

In 2008 the Alumni Association began a process by which to acknowledge those who have achieved in career areas and who have been ardent supporters of Lower Dauphin High School. The following are awardees that have been so honored by the time this book went to press.

2008   Randall Umberger '65

2009   Kathleen Imhof Weber '74

2010   Don Frantz '69, Linda Kreiser '70, Dr. Julia Staver '70, Dr. Craig E. College '74, and Dr. Judith T. Witmer

2011   Elizabeth Musser Radle '62, Steve Spence '80, and Sue and Donald Beam

2012   Lynn Taylor Szymborski '65, Glenn Wagner '65, Brad Stroman '67, Barbara Walmer Miller '71, and Bradley Miller

2013   George Emerich '62, Jean Deimler Seibert '65, Sheila Miller '70, Nicholas Poppy '91 Mrs. Ruth Goepfert, and Mrs. Marie Weber

Alumni Band

Thank you to all of the following who have appeared with the LD Alumni Band and a special acknowledgement to graduates of the 1970s who comprise 60% of the members.

61	Jo Ann Eshenour Hale	75	William Bibb
62	Betty Musser Radle*	77	Kyle Myers
66	Ken Espenshade*	77	Tim Gamber
67	Rogie Carroll Fureman	78	Kristie Myers
70	Ed Hershberger	78	Sharon Hoffer Manton
70	Sara Kuntz Sergesketter	79	Richard Stokes
71	Bill Musser	81	Kathy Keiper Vogelsong
71	Donald Bell	82	Marion Rife Zink*
71	Mary Ratcliff Sprunk	82	Tim Brubaker
71	Richard Runkle	85	Tom Rife, Sr.
72	Lois Robertson Menear	88	Tina Sheaffer Alexander
73	Dave Warfel	89	Denise Little
73	James Neidinger*	91	Becky Dixon Brooks*
73	Kent Myers	95	Kelly Runkle
74	Barb Lehman Seibert	96	Terri Seibert Akers
74	Kerry Fies	97	Katie Runkle Boyer
75	David Rhoads*	98	Will Bibb
75	Debra Bechtel Neidinger	08	Tom Rife, Jr.*
75	Ed Shirk		

*Those who have made the most appearances

Lower Dauphin Alumni Association Show Case

The Lower Dauphin Alumni Association has created a huge and unique scrapbook in the form of an outsized display case built with alumni donations to display curated items that provide a platform for remembering the history of Lower Dauphin High School and to provide a legacy for all current high school students. With exhibits being changed several times a year, along with a permanent display, the Show Case has become a focal point for students, faculty and alumni, as well as visitors to the school. Wade (Kirk) Seibert '65 has donated hundreds—if not thousands—of hours serving as curator of these displays.

We encourage all alumni who are looking for a safe home for their LD memorabilia to entrust it to our care. We recently supported renovations of the Hummelstown Historical Society which, in turn, provided storage space in our own Archival Room at the Society for our collection which also will be used for some of their historical displays. This action signifies a partnership, and, more importantly, a permanent home for our memorabilia that will remain in the custody of the Historical Society.

In conjunction with the publication of *Loyal Hearts Proclaim*, we will be starting a major campaign for signage on the Show Case to identify our ownership and management of the case. Along with that we also will fulfill our pledge to earlier donors who supported the building of the case, and they will be recognized as indicated on the original pledge.

Following is a list of our displays since the completion of the Show Case which has stood now for ten years, twice suffering some water damage and once undergoing modifications by our original cabinet maker and artisan, Robert "Fred" Weber '73. The listing of our curated displays is in alphabetical order with notations.

1. 50 Years of Musicals[1]
2. 50 Years of Yearbooks
3. Alumni Art
4. Alumni Friends[2]
5. Barns of LD[3]
6. Board Games[4]
7. Chalk It Up! A List of Firsts at LD
8. Class of 1964
9. Class of 1967 (Parmer Collection)
10. Clocks
11. Coach Kreiser's Field Hockey
12. Commencement Speeches
13. Falcon Book Club[5]
14. Favorite Books of Childhood[6]
15. Fifty-Year Perspective of LDHS
16. Fifty Years of Sweethearts
17. Forty Years of Diplomas
18. Forty-nine years of Field Hockey
19. Golden Jubilee Alumni Honorees & Service Award
20. Golden Jubilee Sponsors
21. Graphics: posters and programs
22. Hats Off
23. Honoring Hummelstown High School
24. Joseph Schan Collection
25. LDAA Founding Members
26. LDAA Golden Jubilee Showcase[7]
27. LDAA Salutes LD: Part I[8]
28. LDAA Salutes LD: Part II:[9]
29. LDHS Staff Who Are Alumni

[1] The display of memorabilia from high school musicals featured props, costumes, libretti, musical scores, programs, tickets, posters, framed photographs, and other items from nearly every musical that has graced the stage at LDHS.

[2] Alumni Friends was a heart-stealer, with a wonderful collection of favorite dolls and bears from the childhood of alumni and friends.

[3] Photographs of many barns of the school district, captured in a display that is both nostalgic and historic.

[4] Past and present games that have been enjoyed by alumni and friends.

[5] Favorite books of various LD bibliophiles.

[6] The books we read and loved.

[7] The Jubilee Time Capsule and memorabilia to be placed in it; also the LD missile and its history.

[8] Clothing from the last 50 years, including sport uniforms, band and cheerleading outfits, and t-shirts, from the high school, middle school and elementary school. This is to display blue and white clothing associated with LD and also to pay tribute to people who make contributions to the school, to the LDAA, or the Golden Jubilee.

[9] The founding members of the LDAA; LDAA officials who have spent over 15 years with the organization; staff from the senior, middle school, elementary schools as well as the administrative office including teachers, administrators, and support staff who are graduates of Lower Dauphin; Golden Jubilee Alumni Honorees & the LDAA Service Award Recipient and Members of the Golden Jubilee Planning Committee.

[10] Pottery from twelve of New Mexico's Pueblos—beautiful in its simplicity and a reminder that beauty should be a part of daily living. High school art students found this display reflective in their own displayed work.

[11] Annual display.

[12] Celebrating the First Graduating Class with many enlarged photographs from the 1961 *Falconaire* (1961).

[13] Acknowledging teachers who had an impact on them.

[14] Special automobile memorabilia collection of Brian Stoner '64, as well as enlarged photos of cars driven by current and past students, toy "wheels," a child size car and tractor, license plates, maps, games, pennants, and nearly everything one could wish to see related to "Wheels of LDHS!"

Showcase Donor Levels

$5,000 (*Distinguished Alumni/Alumna/Donor*) donor(s) name placed on the **face** of the display case.

The names of the following level of donors will be inscribed on **plaques** in the case:

$2,000–$4,999 (*Benefactor)*

$1,000–$1,999 (*Patron*)

$500–$999 (*Platinum Falcon*)

$250–$499 (*Golden Falcon*)

$100–$249 (*Silver Falcon*)

Donors of the following amounts will be recognized in a memory book whose pages will be turned periodically, displaying each set of names in turn:

$50–$99 (*White Falcon*)

$5–$49 (*Blue Falcon*)

Benefactor, $2,000–$4,999

Class of 1965 (donations totaling $4,125)		In Memory or Honor
Jean and Kirk Seibert	$2,100	Dr. Witmer
Jean and Kirk Seibert	$50	Linda Alleman
Jean and Kirk Seibert	$50	Joe Schan
Colonel David and Jane Benton	$250	
Stephen and Susan Schell	$250	Dr. Witmer
Class Donation	$400	Dr. Witmer
Dr. Carolyn Sandel Anderson	$100	Dr. Witmer
Franco & Lauren Cremascoli	$100	
Ruth Ann Graybill	$200	Dr. Witmer
Jack and Dorothy Chilcote Means	$100	Dr. Witmer
Terry and Linda Mumma Mills	$100	
Elaine Mader Royer	$100	
Michael J. Skinner	$100	Coaches
Clayton Smith	$100	Dr. Witmer
Fran Fenner Wood	$100	Dr. Witmer
John Enders	$60	
Jane Benton	$50	Dr. Witmer
Marjorie and Russel Cassel	$50	Dr. Witmer

Dale and Georgia Good	$50	Dr. Witmer
Phillip and Joanne Teets	$50	Dr. Witmer
Linda Paulette Mills	$40	Dr. Witmer
Lawrence and Linda Geesaman	$30	Dr. Witmer
Terry Henry	$25	Dr. Witmer
Virginia Cobaugh Cvijic	$25	Dr. Witmer
R. W. and Carol Knight	$25	Dr. Witmer
Fred and Steph Zeiters Nordai	$25	Dr. Witmer
Dennis Patrick	$25	Dr. Witmer
James and Karen Penman	$25	Dr. Witmer
Susan Petrina	$25	Dr. Witmer
Michael and Brenda Sarao	$25	Dr. Witmer
Cynthia and Ron Teufel	$25	Dr. Witmer
Luke Warble	$25	Dr. Witmer
Bruce and Sharon Williams	$25	Dr. Witmer
George Bonawitz	$20	Dr. Witmer
Maryann Mutek Mull	$20	Dr. Witmer
Evelyn Walkup Nye	$20	Dr. Witmer
Sandra Rowe Gussler	$15	Dr. Witmer
Elaine Mader Royer	$15	Dr. Witmer
Thelma Rhoads Shumway	$15	Dr. Witmer
Mark Brubaker	$10	Dr. Witmer
Maryann Coffman	$10	Dr. Witmer
Linda Boyer Donmoyer	$10	
Patricia Fisher Epler	$10	Dr. Witmer
Judith Lyter	$10	Dr. Witmer

Patron, $1,000–$1,999   In Memory or Honor

Dr. Judith T. Witmer	$1,410	

Platinum Donors, $500 - $999

Dr. Craig Camasta '82	$500	
Joanne Geeseman Uhlig '73	$500	

Golden Falcon, $250–$499

June Steckler '83	$300	
Drs. Doug '73 and Linda Goepfert '70	$250	John Goepfert
Ed Lammando '75	$250	
Ann Seaman '62	$250	
Robert and Kathy Weber, '73 & '74	$250	H. Scott Weber '77
Ron and Sandy Morrow Gold '66	$250	

Silver Falcon, $100–$249

Wally Witmer	$150	Tod H. Witmer '74
Wally Witmer	$150	Kim S. Witmer '73
Helen Yount	$240	
Joyce Potteiger '61	$120	Connie Wolfe Wagner '65
Juanita Warble Ancharski '73	$100	
Florence Bell	$100	Kate Allen '66
Jon Gardner and Sue Ann Campbell '69	$100	
Doley W. Cave, Jr.	$100	Doley W. Cave, Sr.
Tally Fisher Leeper '95	$100	
Ruth Fair Gardiner '62	$100	
Randy Kahler '64	$100	
Joyce Keener '63	$100	
Randy Lehman '73	$100	
Bob and Pam Patrick Myers, '75 & '74	$100	
Mark Osevala '73	$100	
Thelma Park	$100	Marjorie Cassel & Virginia Hoffman
James and Sue Shade '71	$100	Prowell M. Seitzinger
Thomas Strite '66	$100	Mary Jane Strite
Marie Weber	$100	H. Scott Weber
John Williams '66	$100	
Susan Sipe '83	$100	

White Falcon, $50–$99

Roger '75 and Yvonne Calhoon '77	$80	
Dr. Jeffrey Miller '85	$60	
Sherry Rogers Bement '74	$50	
Ted Bauman '82	$50	
Margaret DeGrange '62	$50	
Debra Reed-Gillette '76	$50	Karen Nye

Carl and Connie Keim Holbert '66	$50	
Brian Stoner '64	$50	Cleon Cassel
Thomas '66 and Sheryl Strite	$50	Prowell M. Seitzinger
Katherine Epler Sharpless '80	$50	
Dr. Judith T. Witmer	$50	Linda Alleman '65
Dr. Judith T. Witmer	$50	James Rhone '64
Anonymous	$50	

Blue Falcon, $5–$49

Rick Nester '74	$40	
Tami Butler Cassel '81	$35	
Cynthia Seibert Grove '75	$35	
Kathie Hartwell Kathmann '72	$35	
Carol Larsen Davis '72	$30	
Allison Gault Peacock	$25	
Bryan Rhinesmith '85	$25	
Joyce McNaughton Carbaugh '66	$25	Prowell M. Seitzinger
Jay Kopp '62	$25	Dr. Witmer
Larry Koppenhaver '63	$25	
Carol Poorman Lesser '61	$25	
Amee Lewis Vance '71	$25	William Nixon
Wynn and Patricia Willard, '76, '77	$25	
Wally Witmer	$25	Jean Deimler Seibert
Bob and Kathy Weber	$25	H. Scott Weber
Judith T. Witmer	$25	Linda Lash '66
Susan Nester Moran '75	$20	C. Wallis
Denise Nornhold '81	$20	
Craig Tritch '69	$20	
Lynn Mattern Witmer '74	$20	
Daniel Stokes '76	$19	
Jeffrey S. Calhoon '78	$15	
Jennifer Kerns Horton '80	$12	
Anonymous	$12	
Morgan Williams '03	$12	
Ashley Judy Anderson '01	$10	
Stacy Johnson Lezzer '82	$10	
Denise Little '89	$20	
William Minsker	$10	

Beverly Hallman Overa '71	$10	
Abbie Marie Grubb Shireman '97	$10	
Linda Hetrick Smith '75	$10	
Alisha Cain '03	$7	
Brandy Espenshade '99	$7	
Jared Espenshade '03	$7	
Lauren Dell '09	$7	Evan Gourley
Elnoise Kremer '68	$7	
David Bennetch '75	$7	
Jeff Ebersole	$5	
Katie Leininger Leach '75	$5	
Matt Mallick '99	$5	
Amy Miller '94	$5	
Paula Ross Norton '88	$5	
Samuel Wert '99	$5	

 Lower Dauphin Sweethearts

To our knowledge Lower Dauphin High School is the only high school in the United States to acknowledge alumni who wed each other, what we call Lower Dauphin Sweethearts, graduates of LDHS who have married other graduates of LDHS, not necessarily their own classmates. This list was initiated by Wade Seibert several years ago when a Show Case tribute for Valentine's Day was staged with vases of flowers and the names of alumni sweethearts. This database has been continued by the Alumni Association with the help of those who notify us to add their names. It has generated a good deal of interest and will continue so long as alumni keep us informed. By the nature of such a list, it is fluid and likely not totally accurate at any given time. *Italics indicate confirmed deceased.*

Please let us know if YOUR NAMES should be added to this list and also if we have you listed in error. Thank you. (jtwitmer@aol.com)

March 13, 2013

1961 ♥

John Clemens '61 & Hilda Diehl '61
Roy Henry '61 & Terry Shindler '65
Harry Menear '61 & Lois Robertson '72

1962 ♥

Joe Hosler '62 & Carol Templin '63
Bryce Davis '62 & Barbara Crumling '62
Barry Wenrich '62 & Carole Jane Baker '62
Cynthia Aldrick '62 & Dennis Mulligan '62
Jay Kopp '62 & Ann Landis '65
Fred Harner '62 & Sally Walters '64
Dennis Mulligan '62 & Cynthia Aldrich '62

1963 ♥

C. Richard Weaver '63 & Donna Curry '63
Scott Seibert '63 & Barbara Lerch '69
David L Keller '63 and Barbara Hack '67

1964 ♥

Elaine Fies '64 & Kenneth Bechtel '64
Joe Templin '64 & Janet Smith '64
Byron Wyld '64 & Beverly Walmer '66
Kathy Harman '64 & Bo Smith '65
Linda Heffleger '64 & Dennis Patrick '65
Bruce Williams '64 & Sharon Kennedy '65
Donald Miller '64 & Judy Wolford '65

Craig Pheasant '64 & Patsy Umbrel '68
Bob Strawser '64 & Joanne Pottieger '66

1965 ♥

Russell Cassel '65 & Marjorie Park '65
Wade Seibert '65 & Jean Deimler '65
William Campbell '65 & Donna Reitz '67
David Coble '65 & Sylvia Hoffman '65
Jack Means '65 & Dorothy Chilcote '65
Philip Bentley '65 & Marsha Reed '65
Joseph Hill '65 & Bethanne Bojanic '65
Terry Mills '65 & Linda Mumma '65
Dennis Coffman '65 & Mary Ann Shertzer '65
Robert Hess '65 & Joanne Shenk '65
Michael Hubler '65 & Carol Kauffman '65
Alvin Longreen '65 & Linda Lenker '65
William Martin '65 & Donna Fackler '65
Jim Szymborski '65 & Lynn Taylor '65
Ron Via '65 & Kathy Fawver '65
Stan Wisniewski '65 & Vivian Motter '65
Joseph Heinzman '65 & Sandy Brooks '65
Marty Remsburg '65 & Linda Shuey '66
Sandy Rider '65 & Richard Daniels '66
Ed Neidigh '65 & Veronica Jeronis '67

1966 ♥

Ronald Cruys '66 & Shirley Cooper '69
Kenneth Espenshade '66 & Joan Weirich '66
Connie Keim '66 & Carl Holbert '66
Edward Bechtel '66 & Donna Fetrow '66

1967 ♥

Edward Parmer '67 & Faye Hughes '67
Dennis Carroll '67 & Patricia Jeffries '67
Mike Kreiser '67 & Christine Hoffman '72
Kenton Kreider '67 & Charlene Kolak '67
Roger Berkebile '67 & Carolyn Youtz '67

1968 ♥

Russell Zeiters '68 & Janet Kettering '68
Carol Coons '68 & Tim Grierson '68
Audrey Watts '68 & Kenneth Landvater '68
Bill Smith '68 & Donna Gleim '71
Larry Templin '68 & Kathleen Hoffman '71
Carolyn Hoffman '68 & Dale Parmer '78
Cheryl Curry '68 & Mel Kennedy '68

1969 ♥

Thomas Weber '69 & JoAnn Ricker '69
Lana Eckert '69 & Dale Walmer '69
David Smoyer '69 & Janice Wenrich '70

1970 ♥

Paul Pintarch '70 & Sandra Bair '70
Gary Weaver '70 & Deborah Gilchrist '70
Ben Mader '70 & Mary Frascella '71
John Viselli '70 & Linda Harvey '73
Paul Robertson '70 & Becky Fink '73
Eugene Batz '70 & Dorothy Gamber '75
Robert Ebersole '70 & Roxann Etnoyer '72
Charles Yoder '70 & Marsha Sieg '72
Debra Hummel '70 & Robert Matthews '70
Michael Orsini '70 & Linda Dunkle '70
Randall Eshenour '70 & Cheryl Rozanski '73
Victor Fies '70 & Kathy Watts '76

1971 ♥

Ralph Goss '71 & Deneise Keller '71
Annette Basler '71 & Scott Reichenbaugh '72
Roy Krow '71 & Patricia Hall '73
Thomas J. Wright '71 & Pixie Spacht '73
Ed Thompson '71 & Linda Finch '73
Charles Wyland '71 & Kandy Shope '73
Ella Rhinesmith '71 & Terry Smith '75

1972 ♥

Frederick McGarvey '72 & Barbara Gaffney '72
Don Gourley '72 & Linda Poole '74
Glenn Young '72 & Lori Swartz '76
Bruce Cox '72 & Gwenny Henry '73
Fred Foreman '72 & Pam Burian '76
Jim Forry '72 & Beverly Matincheck '76
Jeff Cassel '72 & Anita Witters '76
Cindy Matincheck '72 & Roger Witmer '74
Carl Holbert '72 & Connie Keim '72
Pam Lebo '72 & Randy Shuey '75

1973 ♥

Mark Osevala '73 & Deborah Aldinger '73
Robert Weber '73 & Kathy Imhof '74
James Kulina '73 & Vicki Finney '75
Luke Ellenberger '73 & Cindy Gumpher '76
Julian Mushinski '73 & Lisa Rhoad '77
Charles Dowell '73 & Ella Lutz '73
Kent Myers '73 & Debra Espenshade '73
Jim Neidinger '73 & Debbie Kay Bechtel '75
William Etnoyer '73 & Wanda Witmer '74
Gary Witmer '73 & Shelley Collins '73
Linda Timmins '73 & Tim McClure '76

1974 ♥

Thomas Christofes, Jr. '74 & Tracy Kling '81
Debra Still '74 & John Dupler '75
Gary Koons '74 & Lynette Rhoad '75
David Walmer '74 & Deborah Johnson '77
Stuart R. Feeser '74 & Crystal Brown '75
Kerry Fies '74 & Helen Frascella '81
David Graybill '74 & Pam Collins '74
Ted Young '74 & Nancy Shaffer '76
Pam Patrick '74 & Bob Myers '75
Brian K. Orwan '74 & Kristine A. Smith '74
Patty Downs '74 and Tom Verdelli '74

1975 ♥

Roger Calhoon '75 & Yvonne Martin '77
Lynn Brightbill '75 & Greg Patton '80
Rhy Coble '75 & MyLinda Kuehnle '75

1976 ♥

Todd Grundon '76 & Jayne Snavely '76
Russ Feeser '76 & Tammy Dempsey '76
Wynn Willard '76 & Patty Hill '77
Steve Noriega '76 & Susan Early '76
Brian Hagy '76 & Sharon Miller '77
Greg Etnoyer '76 & Ann Dennis '76
Mark Lewis '76 & Deb Glass '76
Barry Tonkin '76 & Rae Lynn Scott '77
Roger Olinger '76 & Patricia Lerch '76
Daryl Kreiser '76 & Georgia Finney '77
Tim Bartholomew '76 & Linda Auch '77
Michael Cassel '76 & Tami Butler '81
Mike Yiengst '76 & Julia Hoffman '77
Jeff Reitz '76 & Deborah Fasnacht '79

1977 ♥

John Kiessling '77 & Jill Landis '77
Keith Espenshade '77 & Cristin Pankake '77
Bonnie Graham '77 & Walt Harner '78
Al Fluman '77 & Kristin Cassel '77
Michael Spittle '77 & Donna Capp '78

1978 ♥

Michael Verdelli '78 & Sharon Smith '78
William Aldinger '78 & Sherry Etnoyer '78
John Detweiler '78 & Mindy Grove '79
Douglas Martz '78 & Leslie Scott '78

1979 ♥

Walter Stine '79 & Cheryl Cassel '79
Dick Stokes '79 & Lisa Kennedy '79
Jack Bell '79 & Sheri Vogelsong '80
Michael Kelley '79 & Susan Lightner '81
Dave Bowser '79 & Carol Cassel '82
Mark Pierce '79 & Heather Gearhart '88
John Vigilante '79 & Lena Lausch '80

1980 ♥

Charles Deibler '80 & Tina Cassel '81
Mark Kiessling '80 & Lisa Yohn '80
Gern Haldeman '80 & Debbie Capp '80
Tyler Spitler '80 & Deann Grubb '80
Todd Ruddle '80 & Pamela Schug '80
Victoria Latsha '80 & Greg Denk '83
Mike Hoffman '80 & Brenda Grimm '80
Henry Wilson '80 & Julie Brandyberry '80
Brian Shaffer '80 & Hilda Henry '80

1981 ♥

Thomas Mader '81 & Sandra Plouse '81
Frank Saich '81 & Linda Crater '81
Kathleen Keiper '81 & Bill Vogelsong '83
Jody Stine '81 & *Michael Marsh '82*

1982 ♥

Galen Geeseman '82 & Sandra Fasnacht '82
James Kiessling '82 & Patti Schlegal '82
Glenn Kriner '82 & Diane Dissinger '84
Vicky Swisher '82 & Craig Wallace '84
Coleen Sieg '82 & Jeff Mrakovich '83
Glen Turchin '82 & Janice Zelanak '82

1983 ♥

Mark Hahn '83 & Marialyce Ketrow '83
Bob Alexander '83 & Heidi Jenakovich '83
Greg Jefferies '83 & Lisa Hereshko '83
John Haldeman '83 & Sue Seibert '83
Michael Young '83 & Andrea Sim '83
Laurie Reed '83 & Robert Masino '83
Mike Saich '83 & Michelle Talaber '84
Eric Messner '83 & Ann Deeney '85
Suzanne Martin '83 & Steven D. Hall '85

1984 ♥

Chris Hitz '84 & Karen Beaver '93
Chris Schug '84 & Matt Luttrel '84
Cindy Baker '84 & Pat Junker '84
Deborah Allamon '84 & Ed Huntzberger '84
Bob Benedict '84 & Patricia Sheaffer '84
Jeanine Conrad '84 & Bill Albright '84

1985 ♥

Ed Arnold '85 & Carol Hereshko '85
Edward Fischl '85 & Darby Dimpsey '89
Leah Jones '85 & Sean Ferguson '86

1986 ♥

Eric Burger '86 & Jamie Buck '88
Phil Bentley '86 & Tammy Templin '86
John Saich '86 & Wendy Kellner '86

1987 ♥

David Remsburg '87 & Joy Graeff '93
David Machamer '87 & Michelle Zellers '87
Ron Semancik '87 & Eden Wise '87
James Dodson '87 & Michelle Espenshade '87
Jason Musser '87 & *Tami Swartz '88*
Cory Barber '87 & Cyndi Holtzman '88
Roy Gesford, Jr. '87 & Dawn Wagner '89

Randy Manning '87 & Jen Traino '89
Christine Yohe '87 & Jody "Joe" Bates '88

1988 ♥

Robert Schwartz '88 & Lisa Kireta '88
Kathy Gloeckler '88 & Eric Schmedding '88
Mark Spitler '88 & Tricia Johnson '89
Darrell Gesford '88 & Daniell Witmer '89
Darin Shaffer '88 & Dorinda Norton '89
Bridget Desjardins '88 & Paul Slaybaugh '89
Scott Epler '88 & Jen Baker '89

1989 ♥

Tony Amato '89 & Jennifer Augustine '90
Brian Crow '89 & Janie Barnhart '89
Vince Crone '89 & Athena Amoroso '90
James Carenzo '89 & Suzanne Bendull '90
David Seaman '89 & Kelly Hoke '90
Jack Yeager '89 & Kira Jones '89
Dawn E. Wagner '89 & Don Eldridge '89
Jen Symborski '89 & Grant Castilow '89
Matt Royer '89 & Kerry McGuiness '90
Vickie Studeny '89 & Jeff Geesey '90
Erin Pudlowski '89 & Rance Horton '89

1990 ♥

Barry Shaffer, Jr. '90 & Jennifer Joy Smith, '90
Robert Smith '90 & Stephanie Moure '90
Julie Koch '90 & Curt Hoyt '90
Jennifer Smith '90 & Barry Shaffer '90
Amy Unger '90 & Rob Hess '92
Michele Whitmeyer '90 & Brett Coleman '90
Tricia Shoemaker '90 & Gerald Kreiser III '91
Ryan Woodring '90 & Dania Pazakis '92
Jon Parmer '90 & Darla Wagner '91

1991 ♥

Jason Smith '91 & Michele Shaffer '94
Sean Lingle '91 & Annissa Wells '92

1992 ♥

Peter Key '92 & Angela Eifert '92
Rachelle Maceyko '92 & Neil Beach '93
Lonny Blough '92 & Andrea Hipple '96
Doug Luttrell '92 & Jennifer Meyers '97

1993 ♥

Lynn Berkheimer '93 & Julie Pintarch '95
Justin Hanula '93 & Jessica Strohm '93

1994 ♥

Keith Broadwater '94 & Dianna Stahl '94
William Elliott '94 & Jessica Schwartz '94
Jason DeHart '94 & Jess Lenker '98
Ed Slatt '94 & Jennie Rhoads '99

1995 ♥

Brian Atkinson '95 & Jamie Eifert '95
Mark Bioty '95 and Nora Graber '99
Dylan Paine '95 & Abby Soghomonian '97

1996 ♥

Larry Verdelli '96 & Holly Fletcher '96
Brad Strohm '96 & Kiley Kulina '98
Shawn Benning '96 & Molly Reimer '96
Jana Verdelli '96 & John Woodring '97
Erin Thompson '96 & Jeff Popernack '97
Fiona Kadish '96 & Billy Van Winkle '97

1997 ♥

Zachary Weber '97 & Amy Woodell '97
Levi Blough '97 & Erin Finney '97
Chad Lutz '97 & Kyra Clark '97
Joe Betz '97 & Megan Barto '97
Julie Rhoads '97 & Jeff Toth '98
Chuck Tobias '97 & Joy Cope '97

1998 ♥

Gern Haldeman '80 & Debbie Cap '80
Tyler Spitler '80 & Deann Grubb '80

1999 ♥

Ryan Michael '99 & Brandi Espenshade '99
Brandon Yetter '99 & Kim Crist '99
Jason Eisenhour '99 & Allyson Young '99
Matt Gordon '99 & Courtney Pollock '99
Todd Gutshall '99 & Danielle Fullerton '03

2000 ♥

Justin Fox '00 & Catrina Yohn '00
Drew Lambert '00 & Laura Mushinski '02

2001 ♥

Melissa Deal '01 & Ike Fullerton '02

2002 ♥

Chris Shaffer '02 & Ashleigh Brewer '02
Zac Matinchek '02 & Kelly Ollinger '02
Sara Marian Seibert '02 & Robert Lucking '05

2003 ♥

Troy Espenshade '03 & Lauren Leshak '03

2004 ♥

Colby Brinser '04 & Mallory Haldeman '07
Claudia Rudy '04 & Jared Smalley '04

Sweetheart Stories

Every romance has a story and we had hoped to hear from many of our sweethearts when several years ago we asked our graduates through our newsletter, *Falcon Pride,* to tell us how they met. Most, of course, met at Lower Dauphin, one couple as early as first grade. Here are excerpts from those who were kind enough to share this information with us. In the order of the year of graduation, with each of the first four decades represented, we present "Sweetheart Stories":

Class of 1962

I met my husband Barry at LDHS and we were sweethearts, husband and wife, and business partners for 44 years until his untimely passing on December 14, 2008.

Carol Jane (Janie) Baker Wenrich

Class of 1964

I met my sweetheart in ninth grade, the first year that LD opened. The person who was to become my sweetheart wasn't in any of my classes, but his best friend Bob was in my homeroom. After school one day Bob introduced us. I said "Hi," and continued to my bus. The next day I saw Ken at his locker and again said, "Hi." He asked me if I had a minute and proceeded to tell me that someday we would be married. I told him that we were both too young and that I wasn't even yet allowed to date and certainly was too young to get married. He agreed that we were too young and needed to date other people, but that someday we would get married.

The following year we were in the same English class with Mrs. Pratt. The boys sat on one side of the room and the girls on the other. None of the boys in that classroom ever did their homework except Ken. Mrs. Pratt always went around the room collecting homework from each person; when she got to Ken she would take his homework and without even looking at it she would tear it into pieces and put it back on his desk. Ken never said a word, but, one day Bob asked Mrs. Pratt why she always tore up Ken's paper and why he was failing that class when the other boys who were not doing their homework were all passing the class. She told Bob that it was because Ken wasn't doing his own homework, that Elaine Fies was. Bob told her that was not true and that Bob himself had seen Ken do his homework. Further, Bob told her, I wasn't allowed to date, I didn't have a telephone, and we lived seven miles apart, so I could not be doing his homework. Mrs. Pratt didn't seem to care; she just assumed Ken liked me because he always waited for me after her class and she said we were too young. Ken failed the class and had to repeat the course the following year. Ken did tell his dad, but his dad told Ken he didn't believe a teacher would do that.

His family then moved into Derry Township and he had to go to Hershey High where he was graduated. He was always disappointed to have to leave Lower Dauphin. He and I dated others over the years, but we remained friends and fell in love. After graduation we married and, of course, Bob was our best man. That will be almost 50 years in 2013 and we are still in love.

Elaine Fies Bechtel

Class of 1969

My sweetheart and husband and I have lived our entire lives in East Hanover Township. Officially we first met at East Hanover Elementary School when we were in first grade. We went to school together until 10ᵗʰ grade at which time he went to Hershey in their Industrial Arts program which Lower Dauphin did not offer. I was graduated in 1969 and I am not sure our 42-year marriage would count as sweethearts or not. I was graduated from Lower Dauphin and my husband was graduated from Hershey as part of the Machine Shop program. He would have been a graduate of LD if we had had such a program. We married in 1971 and had three children all of whom were graduated from Lower Dauphin.

Lana Eckert Walmer and Dale Walmer

Classes of 1978 and 79

Mindy and I met in my senior year when we were taking Graphic Arts and the rest is history. We have been married now for many years.

John Detweiler '78 and Mindy Grove Detweiler '79

Classes of 1989 and 90

We met at LD and started dating when he was 16 and I was 15. We were married four years after I was graduated in October 1994. We will be celebrating 19 years together when this book is published in 2013. We have been together now for more than 25 years. We live in Londonderry Township and have two daughters who attend LD. I work for LDSD as a PCA and Vince is in construction.

Athena Amoroso '90 and Vincent Crone '89

Class of 1990

Our friendship began in November of our sophomore year and we married in August of the year we were graduated. We have been married more than twenty years now and have four daughters!

Jennifer Smith '90 and Barry Shaffer, Jr. '90

Summit Achiever Jean Deimler Seibert '65

Integrity and Honor
Stewardship and Dedication
Friendship and Loyalty

If there were to be one ideal Lower Dauphin Alumnus/a, that person would be Jean Louise Deimler Seibert, JD.

If there were one distinguished citizen of Hummelstown to be recognized, it would be Attorney Seibert.

If there were one unsung heroine of the activities and projects supported by the Alumni Association it would be Jean Seibert.

If there were only one generous but very private philanthropist identified from among those we know, that, too, would be Jean,

. . . and if those who know her could have only one friend, that surely would be she.

The co-valedictorian of her high school class, Jean Deimler continued to distinguish herself with academic honors at Gettysburg College, Syracuse University, and the Dickinson School of Law, the awarding of her law degree coinciding with the birth of her son.

She has lent her skills as an attorney and training in the field of economics to community service work in which she is engaged with non-profit organizations that include—in addition to the Lower Dauphin Alumni Association—the Hummelstown Area Historical Society, the Lower Dauphin Falcon Foundation, Gettysburg College, Bethany Village, Bethany Towers Corporation, the Manada Conservancy, the Hummelstown Community Foundation, the Hummelstown Business and Professional Association, Asbury Services, the Lower Dauphin Club Lacrosse, and the Hummelstown Rotary Club.

Preferring not to be singled out, she remains, for the most part, unheralded; instead, she quietly uses her talents, time, and other resources to the betterment of her community and her Alma Mater. Thus, it is difficult to honor someone as unassuming and unfailingly gracious as Jean, one who would prefer not to be praised. And that, indeed, is the ***summit of achievement.***

Lower Dauphin High School's
Golden Jubilee

Plans for Lower Dauphin High School's Golden Jubilee began in early 2008 with the first meeting of an Open Call committee on September 20, 2008. Initial discussion included a review of possible events and an overall focus. It soon was agreed that our Kick-Off Event would be held at Homecoming 2009 and would close with a Gala Week-end during Homecoming 2010. As anyone who served on this committee can attest, it was a daunting task. We were guided by the theme: 50 Years of Educational Excellence and a Lifetime of Memories, with a focus on what has made Lower Dauphin High School unique, highlighted by a sharing of history and fond memories.

Identifying and inviting key people from each graduating class to serve on the committee was a better idea than a reality as we discovered that identifying leaders didn't guarantee that they were interested in helping with the celebration. Despite that initial disappointment, by fall 2009 we had defined our major areas of focus: reflections from each class, fund-raisers, alumni cheerleaders, time capsule, collecting memorabilia, memorializing early administrators, advertising, publicity, and records of sports, the arts, school governance, social events, classes, faculty, mascots, presidents, clubs, and publications, to name only a few areas.

This was an ambitious list, especially considering that we didn't have even a complete set of yearbooks at the outset! Our biggest challenge—and consistent frustration—is the basic fact that school districts don't keep records for most of the areas we wanted to celebrate. Thus finding information to celebrate all aspects of school life, including a written history of the past 50 years, led to a herculean odyssey.

It was fitting that the first public indication of the Golden Jubilee Year was large banners, donated by Carol "Janie" Baker Wenrich '62, hung on the streets of central Hummelstown, and continued with the sale of miniature likenesses of the high school building, a fund-raiser managed by Betty Musser Radle '62. The finale of our huge celebration is this book, *Loyal Hearts Proclaim: The First Fifty Years of Lower Dauphin High School.*

This section of the book you are holding chronicles the record of our work for the Golden Jubilee and perhaps will serve as a guide to future celebrations. As a committee and as a school, we are proud of this exemplary celebration and invite you to review, remember, and relish these events.

Golden Jubilee Committee, 2008–2010

Jubilee Chair

Dr. Judith T. Witmer

Co-Chairs, Alumni Week-end

Susan Petrina '65

Betty Musser Radle '62

LDSD Liaison

Randy Umberger '65

Time Capsule Project

Dr. Jeffrey D. Miller '85

Alumni Show Case Exhibits

Wade Seibert '65

Other Committee Members

Kyleen Fisher Bender '61

Barbara Olson Bowser '62

Carol Jane Baker Wenrich '62

Kathleen Convery '64

Ann Landis Kopp '65

Dr. Janet Calhoon '66

Martha Wrzesniewski Bosler '66

Kathy Saltzer Peffer '73

Kathy Imhof Weber '74

Sheila Pankake Vandernick '88

Denise Little '89

Nicole Cassel '96

Bill Minsker, Faculty

Margaret DeAngelis, Faculty

Major Sponsors ($1,000+)

The Reichenbaugh Family
  In Memory of Tom Reichenbaugh '75

Richard (Rick) L. Smith '83
  Hors d'oeuvres Reception

Special Project Sponsors ($750–$999)

Carol (Janie) Baker Wenrich '62
  Hummelstown Square Banners and
  Framed Portraits of Messrs. David J. Emerich
  and Curtis S. Taylor

K. Wade and Jean Seibert '65
  Various Sponsorships

Special Event Sponsors ($250–$499)

Scott '72 and Annette Basler Reichenbaugh '71
  "Rico and the Ravens"

Class of 1965

Golden Jubilee articles appearing in *The Sun*

  Jubilee Overview
  Do You Remember?
  Class Trips
  Sweethearts
  Falcon Mascot
  Overview of Events
  LD Alumni Assoc.
  One-Day Museum
  Kick-off Celebration
  November 22, 1963
  Tribute to Veterans
  Alumni Chorus
  Letters You Wish You Had Written
  Reflections from 1971
  LD Shield and 1962 Reflections
  Countdown
  Hook Days
  1970 Remembers
  1961 Remembers Falcon Pride
  Blue Guard, Rowdies, Pride
  Three Decades, Four Remembrances
  Yearbooks

2009

The Golden Jubilee One Day Museum

The first Lower Dauphin Golden Jubilee event provided a preview of its forthcoming Jubilee as part of the 2009 Hummelstown Arts and Crafts Festival on September 19, 2009. This Museum was curated by Wade Seibert and housed in the Trefz-Bowser meeting room. The display featured a wide range of items and memorabilia from the 50 Year History of Lower Dauphin High School and appeared only once and on this date. The purpose of the museum display was first to entertain and inform by providing a retrospective of areas of school life in the past half century, second to evoke memories that might be lying dormant, and third to provide a preview of the energy and excitement being generated by the alumni to honor the formation of their Alma Mater.

Homecoming 2009: The Golden Jubilee Kick-Off Event

Homecoming 2009 Committee —

Betty Radle, Kathleen Convery, Randy Umberger, Dr. Judith T. Witmer

Homecoming 2009 served as the kick-off event for the yearlong celebration of Lower Dauphin High School's Golden Jubilee and even an unremitting rain could not dampen the spirit as alumni gathered to celebrate the opening of the Jubilee. Alumni began gathering at 7:30 p.m., enjoying the fellowship of classmates and teammates until all had arrived. With narration by Mr. William Minsker, the original Big Blue Band announcer, the team was greeted by rousing applause

as Co-Captain Ken Epler introduced each team member; Linda McGarvey Rutt, Captain, introduced each member of the 1960 Cheerleading Squad; and Judith Witmer introduced the first Falcon Mascots, Harold Snyder '64 and Susan Petrina '65. The program concluded with remarks from Russel Cassel, President of the Alumni Association since 1994, who recalled that it had been raining the first day of school when LDHS opened in the fall of 1960.

LD's First Falcon Conference Championship

A united team effort was the major factor in the success of the Lower Dauphin Falcons on their first fling in the new Capitol Area Conference in the fall of 1960. It was this same team effort that acted as the catalyst in welding all these boys from different school districts into one championship team. They were described thus:

> The Falcons first tried their wings in a conference tilt in defeating the Eagles of Cumberland Valley, 7-0 in the last second of play. The next week Camp Hill was the second victim as the high-flying Falcons staved off a Lion threat in the final minutes of play. In the following two non-conference games with Cedar Cliff and Steel-High the Falcons got their feathers ruffled for the only times in the season. The mighty birds took to the air against the Mechanicsburg Wildcats to down that squad 19-6. The remainder of the season found that no other conference team could match the Falcons as they went undefeated in conference play. This being the first year for Lower Dauphin High School, the boys had no school tradition to uphold. Rather, they themselves laid the foundation upon which future Falcon teams built.

1960 Championship Team

Don Bashore
Larry Behney
Barry Broadwater
Lew Cobaugh
Pete Costelli
Tom Duck
Robert Eldridge
George Emerich
Bob Engle
Carl Espenshade
William Gaudette

Frank Hawthorne
Bruce Heilman
Craig Heister
James Hertzler
Ross Holbert
Jon Hutton
Randy Kahler
Larry Kopenhaver
Russell Ludwig
John Markey

John McCormick
Jerry McKee
Harry Menear
Frank Neiswender
Dennis Shertzer
Mike Shifflett
Jerry Smith
John Snavley
Rick Weaver
Bruce Wyld

Head Coach: Barney Osevala

Assistant Coaches: William DeLiberty, James Middlekauf, and Frank Capitani

Co-Captains: Glenn Ebersole and Ken Epler

The original Falcon Cheerleading Squad was in full attendance as well and performed their drills, leading cheers between the rain showers throughout the evening. Led by Captain Linda McGarvey Rutt, other members included Brenda Fackler Dove, Kyleen Fisher Bender, Judith Foreman Mease, Norma Georganakis Koons, Carol Glovala Kling, Carol Lindsey Shull, Elizabeth Smith Wille, and Carol Zinn Koppenhaver.

A successful post-game Tailgate Party was hosted by the Alumni Association and held at the Hilton Garden Inn with over-capacity attendance. The Jubilee Committee was pleased with the launch.

SOUVENIR PROGRAM 1960-2010

WON
59-6

LOWER DAUPHIN
Vs.
SUSQUEHANNA TOWNSHIP

Thursday, November 19, 1970   Official Program 25¢

CAC CHAMPS

FALCONS

2010

Lower Dauphin High School's Golden Jubilee
Alumni Week-end, October 1–2, 2010
Schedule of Events

Alumni Homecoming

Friday, October 1   ❖   Hersheypark Stadium, 7:00 p.m.   ❖   Falcons vs. McDevitt

Halftime Celebration

- Welcoming alumni, honoring all LD alumni athletes, special recognition of the 1970 football team
- Alumni band, alumni band front, alumni Falcon mascots, alumni cheerleaders, and alumni homecoming queens
- Golden Jubilee Honorees in academics, leadership, the arts, and sports
- After-game Celebration for all alumni and friends: Hummelstown Fire Hall

Saturday Afternoon, October 2   ❖   Gathering at LDHS   ❖   1:00-2:30 p.m.

- Guided Tours - 1:00–2:00 p.m.
- Display of Time Capsule Memorabilia
- Alumni Association's Show Case Exhibits
- Special Dedicatory Program - 2:00–2:30 p.m.
  - Mr. David J. Emerich, First Supervising Principal, in remembrance
  - Mr. Curtis S. Taylor, First High School Principal, in remembrance
  - Time Capsule Dedication

Saturday Evening, October 2   ❖   Holiday Inn Harrisburg East   ❖   5:30-11:00 p.m.

- Hors d'oeuvres Reception
- Class Memorabilia
- Buffet Dinner and Reminiscing
- Music and Performance (with Rico) by Pentagon

"Howie" Snyder
LD's First Falcon Mascot

LD 50

Friday Night Falcon Lights

Friday Evening, October 1, 2010

50 Years of Friday Night Falcon Lights Honoring Team 70

Guest Announcer: Bill Minsker

Welcome: Dr. Sherri Smith, Superintendent, Lower Dauphin School District

                Russel Cassel, President, Lower Dauphin Alumni Association

Team 70

Forty years ago came the once-in-a-lifetime magical season of the 1970 football season. Fifty-two young men, most having played the game since their days as Hummelstown Bulldogs, came together as a team and provided everyone who ever followed high school football in this area a season to remember. In a moment in time no one will ever forget and will possibly never happen again, the boys were coached by six talented and hard-working men who gave their all to build a championship team. We can only speculate what the team might have accomplished if there had been playoff games in those days.

Marshall Reichenbaugh, father of the team's quarterback and a former star himself for Hershey High School from 1945 to 1949, predicted the team's success as far back as the beginning of the season, "I said they were going to go all the way right from the beginning. This was the greatest Lower Dauphin team that I have ever seen play. It was a great example of an all-around team effort. Hummelstown is steeped in its football tradition." *The Evening News* that fall noted, "There are names out of the past like Wally Witmer, Smoke Warfel, the Seaman brothers, Tony Orsini, Charlie Yantz, and many others who will be remembered as long as pigskins are tossed about. But in the fall of 1970 there was an entire team to remember, one that Hummelstown and Lower Dauphin won't have a hard time remembering."

In summary, the Championship came to the Falcons as the result of one of the finest total team efforts, as every week the TEAM got the job done. The defense carried the Falcons in early games, but the offense got better each week until they were the best in the CAC at rushing. Probably the most underrated troop of people on the team were the offensive linemen whose efforts and improvement as the season went along played a key role in the title. At a lettering ceremony, Coach Jim Seacrist observed that this team set 13 of the 18 LD football records to that date.

While there have been other Lower Dauphin football teams with more wins who also won championships, this team did not have an opportunity to continue their season as there were no playoff games. And so TEAM 70 stands as the first and only Undefeated-Untied CAC Championship Football Team in Lower Dauphin's history.

Friday Night

The evening's Jubilee Ceremonies began at halftime at the football game with the recognition of four alumni representative of the finest graduates from Lower Dauphin in its first half century. The descriptions were written in 2010:

The Arts: Don Frantz '69, who went from creating productions at Lower Dauphin to doing the same at Walt Disney World and for Broadway shows. His Town Square Productions in New York City has expanded to his being CEO of the Beijing Oriental Broadway Company. He is also the originator of the first corn maze in the world, while continuing as a Broadway producer.

Leadership: Dr. Craig College '74, Class Valedictorian, accepted an appointment to West Point, later earning his PhD at Stanford. The recipient of many professional and government awards and honors, Craig recently was Deputy Assistant Chief of Staff for Installation Management for worldwide Army installations at the United States Pentagon.

Scholarship: Dr. Julia Staver '70 is remembered as LD's first widely recognized scholar athlete as Class Salutatorian, and standout in field hockey and basketball. Julia was captain of the 1980 US Olympic women's field hockey team and co-captain of the 1984 bronze-winning US Olympic team. She was graduated in the top 10 of her veterinary class at Penn.

Sports: Linda Kreiser '70 began as a sophomore on the field hockey team under Coach Bea Hallman. She became one of three LD legends to take a place on the US national field hockey team. Returning to her Alma Mater, her coaching record includes perfect seasons in 1993 and 2006, along with six (as we go to press in November 2013) PIAA Class AAA championships and 695 wins.

Lower Dauphin Alumni Association Service Award: Dr. Judith Witmer is being honored as the consummate educator, both as a teacher and administrator, for her service and devotion to Lower Dauphin. She led many innovative initiatives in the high school and in the district. It is her energy and creativity that successfully launched the Alumni Association and the Jubilee Celebration.

When the honorees took their places on the field accompanied by both the Lower Dauphin and Alumni Pep Bands, Bill Minsker announced, "And now I call your attention to the field where Lower Dauphin's Big Blue High School Band and the Alumni Pep Band have taken their place on the fifty yard line."

Mr. Minsker continued by introducing a drum major and 17 majorettes from 1962 to 1982, followed by the alumni Falcon mascots escorted by the current mascot, Luke Adams and led by the very first Lower Dauphin Mascot, Harold Snyder '64. Next welcomed were eight Homecoming Queens, from 1963 to 2009, and **34** returning cheerleaders, representing the years between 1969 and 2010; they later led the cheers during third quarter, joined by the alumni pep band. Five of the cheerleaders were among those who originally had cheered for the team being honored.

Mr. Minsker then introduced the team: **"I am now very proud to introduce the only Undefeated-Untied Championship Football Team in Lower Dauphin's past 50 years; the 1970 Lower Dauphin CAC Champions.** With this, the team ran through an honor tunnel of cheerleaders, majorettes, band, and mascots, just as they had in their glory days and, for a few moments, they were there again.

1970 Team Attendees

Seniors
- 47 Roger Sowers
- 23 Neil Campbell
- 31 Jeff Nester
- 54 Steve Ricker
- 61 Kirk Lehmer
- 62 Dale Goodwin
- 64 Eric Wolf
- 67 Doug Johnson
- 70 Tom Luttrell
- 76 Gordon Weber
- 79 Rick Goss
- 86 Joe Quigley

Juniors
- 5 Jeff Cassel
- 12 Scott Reichenbaugh
- 21 Steve Radanovic
- 41 Paul Quigley
- 50 Tom Orsini
- 60 Kevin Ricker
- 75 Fred Foreman
- 85 Chris Eifert
- 89 Barry Richcreek

Sophomores
- 7 Mark Osevala
- 16 Phil Yancheff
- 25 Mike Gallagher
- 27 Mike Cobaugh
- 36 Jim Kulina
- 55 Greg Luttrell
- 58 Wayne Jockers
- 65 Ed Neiswender
- 69 Mike Rakosky
- 77 Bob Brautigam
- 78 Robert (Fred) Weber
- 82 Lynn Hahn
- 88 Tom MacCormick

Following the game, Falcon Friends and alumni gathered at the Hummelstown Fire Hall with alumni musicians Hank Imhof '68 and Wade Yankey '99 providing the entertainment. Coach Seacrist delivered words of praise for the team and appreciation for the evening's honor, and many, many memories were shared among all in attendance. The winner of the 50/50 drawing, Barbara Bowser '62, donated her winnings to the Alumni Association.

Players unable to attend: Rod Smith, Chuck Shemas, Mike Abraham, Ron Verdelli, Ron Oellig, Doug Aldinger. Bill Mortimore, Greg Schneider, Don Espenshade, Daryl Zerbe, Warren Backenstoes, Elwood Menear, Randy Shirk. Deceased team members as of October 2010: *Chet King, Rocky Thompson. Bill Divel, Rick Kelley, Alex Wolf, Riley Eldridge.*

Coaches: Jim Seacrist, Frank Capitani, Don Heistand, Dave Erdman, Steve Futchko, Ben McLure, Bernie Bernitsky, and *Buzz Daubert* (deceased)

Cheerleaders

JoAnn Ricker '69
Annette Basler '71*
Ruby Day '71*
Karen Fenner '72*
Debora Witters '72
Barbara Verdelli '73*
Kathy Saltzer '73
Joetta Powley '73
Michele Wrzesniewski '73*
Connie Watts '73
Darlene Forney '73
Glenda Gruber '74
Sherry Radanovic '74
Mary Basler '78
Sue Paris '79
Nancy Paul '79
Peggy Hoover '81
Jane Deeney '83
Lisa Mariani '83
Ann Deeney '85
Francine Paul '85
Sonya Zearing '86
Heather Webb '92
Carrie Stahl '92
Tracy Bolden '93
Andrea Lelii '93
Nancy Crow '94
Jennifer Harvey '98
Danielle Fullerton '03
Olivia Henry '08
Shanitta O'Connell '09

Brittney Snyder '09
Melody Herneisey '10

*Members of the 1970-71 Squad

Falcon Mascots

Harold Snyder '64
Susan Petrina '65
Kathy Petrina '70
Becky Hughes '72
Patti Hall '73
Samantha Barnhart '96
Mike Reese '08

Homecoming Queens

Vicki Fackler '63
Judy Fisher '70
Donna Gleim '71
Jody Reitz '75
Peggy Hoover '81
Kira Jones '89
Jena Fulton '00
Kari Skitka '08

Alumni Band and Band Front

Drum Major
Laurie Petrina '81

Majorettes
Barbara Olson '62
Joyce Conrad '62
Rebecca Gluck '64
Ann Landis '65
Sharon Kennedy '65

Maryann Shertzer '65
Linda Shope '66
Barbara Watts '67
Karen Espenshade '67
Sharon Garver '68
Jeannine Lehmer '69
Sherry Rogers '74
Nadine Yancheff '74
Denise Lehmer '75
Michelle DeRosa '75
Kim Kemble '79
Lola Lausch '82

Pep Band

Betty Musser '71
Dave Warfel '73
Kathryn Vogelsong '81
Tom Rife '85
Megan Claar '04
Tommy Rife '08

The Alumni Chorus

One of the many exciting events of the 50th Year Celebration was the Alumni Chorus, representing almost every decade, assembled to sing show tunes from the 47 musicals performed on the Lower Dauphin stage. Four performances were held, including a special showing at the musical's Dinner Theatre. The chorus also sang at the Time Capsule Dedication and later at a community event.

Performing at "Hello Dolly"

A Sampling from 47 LD Musicals in 50 Years

Betty Musser Radle '62, Producer

Judith T. Witmer, Accompanist

Your letter reminded me of the many precious memories about the school, and especially you, Judy Sener, and Barry Stopfel. Happy Fiftieth Anniversary, Lower Dauphin High School. — Jane Mellin Smith (St. John)

While I will not be able to attend to sing in the alumni chorus, I wanted to thank you and Jane and let you know that your love of music inspired me towards a career in teaching and music. — Roberta Espenshade Centurion '63

I still have my costume! — Lena Lausch Vigilante '80

I was in four musicals and I would love to be a part of this. — Darla Ebersole Hoffer '81

I look forward to echoing the auditorium again as my lasting impression of LDHS can be summed up in one word — "Coconuts." — Mark Stare '83, "South Pacific"

The musical was my life in high school and my proudest achievement to that date! — Debbie Gable Heary, '86

For the students who acted the roles of the major and minor characters and for those students who served in the other aspects of the play's production, I hope our performance of "Camelot" is not just a fond memory, but remains a life-shaping experience.

—Wade Alexander, '86, A Knight of the Round Table

Joyce Wolfe Potteiger '61

Barbara Olson Bowser '62

Betty Musser Radle '62

Norma Fink Baum '63

Elsie Badman Daub '64

Susan Petrina '65

Ann Landis Kopp '65

Linda Shope Kerlin '66

Karen Espenshade Elliott '67

Barbara Watts Brown '67

Kandy Shope Wyland '73

Patricia Hall Krow '73

Linda Hetrick Smith '75

John Vigilante '79

Lena Lausch Vigilante '80

Kris Neibert Kiner '81

Darla Ebersole Hoffer '81

Cindy Kerlin Stuart '81

Scott Eisenbise '82

Catherine Germann '01

Mindy Hickson '04

Geralyn Roberts Meacham, HHS '51

Time Capsule Dedication

Dr. Jeffrey D. Miller '85, Chairman
October 2, 2010

Saturday's events began at 1:00 p.m. with building tours narrated by current students based on a prepared script (available to other groups who might want to plan a tour accompanied by descriptions of current and former areas of the building). Items to be placed in the time capsule were on display, and music in the lobby was provided in two areas, one for the

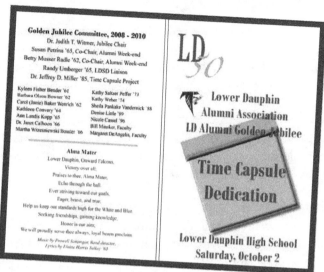

alumni chorus and the other for a string quartette of then current students: Jennie Smith, Lizzy Jackson, Austin Bashline, and Caitlin Hoffman. The stunning Lower Dauphin Alumni Association's Show Case, *Honoring Fifty Years of Our Alma Mater*, curated by Wade Seibert, was a show stopper, even considering the number of items vying for a place in proportion to the size of the case. Masterful!

The dedicatory program itself began at 2:00 with introductions by Mr. Russel Cassel, president of LDAA, followed by remarks from Superintendent Sherri Smith and Principal Todd Neuhard. Glenn Ebersole, President of the Class of 1961, then spoke of behalf of his class.

Janie Wenrich, owner of EGI graphics which donated the framed portraits, presented a portrait of Mr. David J. Emerich, Lower Dauphin's first supervising principal, to his son, George Emerich '62, who then presented the portrait to the school. Mrs. Wenrich then presented a portrait of Mr. Curtis Taylor, the first high school principal, to his son Thomas Taylor who, in turn, presented it to the school. This marked the first formal recognition of these two early school leaders.

Mr. David J. Emerich (1960–1966) devoted himself to building a new community that would become well known in Eastern Pennsylvania with a reputation for scholarship, musicianship, and sportsmanship. He led us in finding pride through a positive attitude and spirit of cooperation.

Mr. Curtis S. Taylor (1960–1970) worked untiringly for the successful start of Lower Dauphin High School and met responsibility with pride. His qualities of friendliness, sincerity, and sportsmanship won a place of high respect, admiration, and affection among the student body.

Next were remarks from Mr. Robert Larsen, a member of the original Joint Planning Board and Mr. Kenneth Staver, former Dean of Students and School Board Member. Remarks from Dr. Henry R. Hoerner, the district's first superintendent, were delivered by Bill Jackson, former editor of *The Sun*. Dr. Jeffrey A. Miller offered comments as the district's third superintendent.

Dr. Jeffrey D. Miller '85, Chairman of the Time Capsule Project, then formally presented the time capsule to the school district on behalf of the Lower Dauphin Alumni Association. Placed in the capsule, among other memorabilia listed below, was a letter from Mr. Ebersole to Lower Dauphin's Class of 2061 to be read at that date.

Items preserved in the capsule included the following: LDHS Dedication Program; 1961 and 2010 Commencement and Baccalaureate Programs; 1961 *Falconaire* and one from each decade of the school; 2010 *Falconaire* with senior signatures; 2010 Alumni Association Directory; front page of the *Patriot News* announcing LD as the 2009 Field Hockey State Champions; signed team photo of 2009 State Champion Field Hockey team; signed coaches photo of "50 Years of Wrestling"; one of the Jubilee Banners that had flown from the light poles in Hummelstown; LD sports letters with sport pins; freshman beanie; copies of the *Falcon Flash*; programs from the school musicals; play programs; FFA patch and pin; class ring; LD mug; and LD Falcon shirts.

Class members of 1961 attending the 50ᵗʰ year Time Capsule Dedication:

Kathryn Bateman Holder	Roy M. Henry
C. Frederick Brightbill	Ann M. Hitz
Barry E. Broadwater	JoAnn Keller Potteiger
Ann Burtner Espenshade	Harry J. Menear
William Calhoon	Marcie Miller Nornhold
John E. Clemens	Janie Porter Lambert
Hilda (Jill) Diehl Clemens	Miriam Roush Haynes
Frances Diffenderfer Light	Victor H. Seesholtz
Thomas L. Duck	Gloria Shertzer Mader
Kenneth R. Epler	Elizabeth Smith Wille
C. Eugene Espenshade	Linda Verdilli Ferretti
Brenda Fackler Dove	Donna Wagner Koons
Kyleen Fisher Bender	Beverly Wiestling Heisey
Barry S. Free	Joyce Wolfe Potteiger
Mildred Gipe Merrell	Carole Zinn Koppenhaver

Welcome to Saturday Night Falcon Fever

The First All-Class Reunion and Celebration

October 2, 2010

Susan Petrina '65, Co-chair, Alumni Week-end

Betty Musser Radle '62, Co-chair, Alumni Week-end

Dr. Jeffrey D. Miller '85, Master of Ceremonies

"I didn't think anything could top Friday night. I was wrong."[1]

And indeed it did top all of the events, special as each one was. Saturday Night Falcon Fever was the culmination to an unforgettable week-end as we celebrated 50 years of Lower Dauphin High School with four major events within a 30-hour timeframe.

Saturday evening saw 300 alumni, faculty, and guests gather at the Golden Jubilee Dinner-Dance, with a Hors d'oeuvres Reception beginning at 5:30 sponsored and hosted by Rick Smith '83.

Arriving guests were welcomed by Greeters representing the first four decades of LDHS: Marty Wrzesniewski Bossler '66, Tom Luttrell '71 and Joe Quigley '71, Sheila Pankake Vandernick '88, and Nicole Cassel '96. Memorabilia Tables with artful displays had been prepared by and were hosted by Kathleen Convery '64.

Following the Invocation by the Reverend Dennis Coffman '65, a buffet dinner began promptly at 7:00. At each table was a Trivia Quiz which served as a conversation starter with the added incentive of prizes for the winning table. (What we had not considered, however, was that cell phones gave the edge to those who had "outside sources" to contact for information.)

Lower Dauphin's perennial favorite band Pentagon took the stage at 8:30. At the band's First Intermission, the Honorees were introduced and each made brief remarks. Dr. Witmer then delivered a Retrospective of the First Fifty Years of Lower Dauphin High School, noting "Distinctive LD Events" and announcing that she would be memorializing the history of the first fifty years of Lower Dauphin High School in a book to be titled *Loyal Hearts Proclaim*.

At 9:30 Pentagon returned to the stage where they played another set for a full dance floor. The Second Intermission offered the introduction of Championship Team 70. The Trivia answers were then provided and the winning table members were presented with small shelf sitters, a replica of the Lower Dauphin High School building as it had been in the first thirty years.

---

[1] Comment from one of the attendees.

Beginning at 10:30 Pentagon's 1950s/60s show band "Rico and the Ravens," sponsored by Scott '72 and Annette Basler Reichenbaugh '71, captivated the audience. A demonstrated reluctance to end the evening led to an encore by the band as classmates and friends closed out this memorable Jubilee.

Those who participated in any of the events will never forget this special tribute to alumni and to 50 years of Falcon Pride. A sampling of comments follows:

- Bravo! What can I say or write that can convey how glorious people said the Jubilee events were.

- The best large scale event I ever attended !!

- A BIG THANK-YOU!!!!! for all the hard and long work/time put into making everything happen this weekend.

- I have always loved LD, and was glad that my children went there as well. In the future I hope my grandchildren will attend and walk the same hallowed halls, so in another 50 years they can share and enjoy 100 years of LD.

- I wouldn't have missed it for the world. I meant what I said—Lower Dauphin gets her hooks in you and, no matter where you've been or where you go, you're always a Falcon.

- Congratulations on a great event—and thanks for causing it to happen.

- All the research, organization, and communication that went into an event of this magnitude was quite impressive.

- Just standing on the 50 yard line brought back a flood of memories.

- This weekend certainly sealed my decision to move back to the area for my children to go to LD for high school.

- I didn't think anything could top Friday night. I was wrong. Saturday night was SUPER!

- It was a huge undertaking getting the players back home to celebrate, but well worth it.

- I have been sitting here for the last hour thinking about how to thank you for one of the BEST weekends I have ever had.

- Long after the weekend is over, people will be talking about LD's 50th celebration!

- What a superb celebration!

Golden Jubilee Sponsors

GOLDEN JUBILEE SPONSOR ($1000+)

The Reichenbaugh Family, In Memory of Tom Reichenbaugh '75

Richard L. Smith '83 (Gala Event Reception Sponsor)

Dr. Judith T. Witmer

SPECIAL PROJECTS SPONSOR ($750–$999)

C. Jane Baker Wenrich '62, Exhibits/Graphics/Interiors (Hummelstown Town Square banners; portraits and framing of photos of Mr. David J. Emerich and Mr. Curtis S. Taylor)

K. Wade and Jean Seibert '65

SPECIAL EVENTS SPONSOR ($250–$499)

Scott Reichenbaugh '72 and Annette Basler Reichenbaugh '71 (Sponsor of "Rico and The Ravens")

Class of 1965 (Jubilee Decorations)

FALCON PRIDE SPONSOR ($200–$249)

Betty Musser Radle '62

Jay Kopp '62 and Ann Landis Kopp '65

Class of 1964

Russel Cassel '65 and Margie Park Cassel '65

Barbara Walmer Miller '71, In Memory of Carol Rhoad '71

June Steckler '83

Dr. Jeffrey D. Miller '85

Barbara Atkinson, Former Faculty

BLUE AND WHITE SPONSOR ($100–$199)

Margaret Friedrich DeGrange '62, In memory of deceased faculty, staff, and classmates

Brian Stoner '64

Donald Deaven '64

Bruce Williams '64 and Sharon Kennedy Williams '65

Jean Alleman, In memory of Linda Alleman '65

Jane Harper Benton '65 and David Benton

Barbara Verdelli Bekelja '73 and Ken Bekelja, In memory of Helen Verdelli from the LD Cheerleaders

Kathy Saltzer Peffer '73 and Rodney Peffer

Dr. Craig College '74

Class of 1985

50 for the 50th SPONSOR ($50–$99)

Pauline Longreen Smith '62

Class of 1962

C. Jane Baker Wenrich '62

Melody Cruys Lovelidge '64, In honor of Classes of 1988 and 1993

Annetta Foreman Buettner '62, In memory of Kenneth "Scottie" Myers '64

Class of 1965

Carol Zerfoss Knight '65

Karen Zerfoss Penman '65

Susan Petrina '65

Brenda Fegley Sarao '65 and Michael Sarao

Randy Umberger '65 and Maxine Umberger

Catherine Reed Eshenour '66

Constance Rhoad '68, Gift Certificate

Connie Watts Barto '73, Gift Certificate

Robert Weber '73 and Kathy Imhof Weber '74

Sherry Rogers Bement '74 and Thomas Bement, In honor of '74 Band Front

Stephanie Bardin Torre '83

Elder Express of Hummelstown

GENERAL CONTRIBUTORS ($5 - $49)

Francine Venneri Bitner '64

Dennis and Maryann Shertzer Coffman '65

Larry and Anita Quigley Peters '70

John Sipe '72, In memory of Charles Rocky Thompson '71

Anita Henson Jeffery '73

Calhoon Family: Yvonne '77, Roger '75 and Melissa '08

Laurie Whitehaus '85 and Jim Gill

Program Advertisers

Betty Musser Radle '62

Class of 1965

Jean Deimler Seibert '65

Dr. Janet Calhoon '66

Karen Fenner Sullivan '72

Dr. and Mrs. Jeffrey D. Miller '85

Lower Dauphin Alumni Association

Dr. and Mrs. Edward Mimnagh

Smith & Kreider Insurance Agency

Stoner Graphix

Stoner Tree Service

Thomas Ball Entertainment

OTHERS (who deserve our appreciation)

Class of 1971 for hosting the Post-Game Gathering

John Bertolette, LDHS Time Capsule

David Bitting, Athletic Director

E. Nan Edmunds, layout design

Rob Klock, Coach

Terry Kugle, Hummelstown Historical Society

Todd Neuhard, High School Principal

Dr. Sherri Smith, Superintendent

The Sun

Trefz Bowser Funeral Home

Trinity United Methodist Church, Hummelstown, PA

Mary Walsh, LDHS Time Capsule

Marie Weber, Faculty

Saturday Night Falcon Fever Attendees

Class of 1961

Glenn Ebersole

C. Eugene Espenshade

Roy Henry

Donna Wagner Koons

Gloria Shertzer Mader

Carole Zinn Koppenhaver

Class of 1962

Elizabeth Gilbert Allio

Barbara Olson Bowser

Linda Landis Doup

George Emerich

Carl Espenshade

Ron Gerlach

Jay Kopp

Ronald Mark

Carroll (Bud) Porter

Betty Musser Radle

Joyce Conrad Weber

Carole Baker Wenrich

Class of 1963

Galen Kopp

Class of 1964

Francine Venneri Bitner

Gloria Verdelli Conlan

Kathleen Convery

Elsie Badman Daub

Eleanor Kauffman Field

Jan First

Jane First

Beatrice Hosler

Bonnie Sassaman Longenecker

Liga Puzuk Neely

Kathy Harman Smith

Brian Stoner

Joseph Templin

Janet Smith Templin

Bruce Williams

Class of 1965

George Bonawitz

Margie Park Cassel

Russel Cassel

David Coble

Sylvia Coble

Dennis Coffman

Maryann Shertzer Coffman

Virginia Cobaugh Cvijic

Linda Gipe Heefner

Terry Schindler Henry

Bonnie Fink Hornberger

Carol Kauffman Hubler

Michael Hubler

Carol Zearfoss Knight

Ann Landis Kopp

Mary Ann Mutek Mull

Stephanie Zeiters Nordai

Karen Zearfoss Penman

Susan Petrina

Brenda Fegley Sarao

Jean Deimler Seibert

K. Wade Seibert

Clayton (Bo) Smith

Randy Umberger

Errol Wagner

Sharon Kennedy Williams

Class of 1966

Marty Wrzesniewski Bossler

Dr. Janet Calhoon

Catherine Reed Eshenour

Class of 1967

Jack Brandt
Barbara Watts Brown
Dennis Carroll
Patricia Jeffries Carroll
Karen Espenshade Elliott
John Seavers

Class of 1968

Sharon Garver Hart
Inez Puzuks Snyder
Patricia Ruhl Taranto

Class of 1969

Jeannine Lehmer Groff
Ann Carlson McCann
Paula Berkebile Wagner
Karl Yankey

Class of 1970

Susan Fink
Nancy Gamber
Virginia Park Hoffman
Linda Kreiser
Linda Dunkle Orsini
Dr. Michael Orsini
Anita Quigley Peters
Larry Peters
Kathy Petrina Rock
Dr. Julia Staver
Russell Walborn

Class of 1971

Sherri Patrick Beazley
Sharon Dowdell Fullerton
Deneise Keller Goss
Ralph (Rick) Goss
Roy Krow
Kirk Lehmer

Thomas Luttrell
Barb Walmer Miller
Joe Quigley
Annette Basler Reichenbaugh
N. Steven Ricker
Nanci Imhof Swistoski
Amee Lewis Vance
Thomas (T.J.) Wright

Class of 1972

Jeffrey Cassel
Kathy Gingrich Hunter
George Kline
Connie Fogleman Lelii
Paul Quigley
Scott Reichenbaugh
Debra Jeffries Rhoads
Barry Richcreek
John Sipe
Karen Fenner Sullivan
Deborah Witters Yankey

Class of 1973

Juanita Warble Ancharski
Connie Watts Barto
Barbara Verdelli Bekelja
Michele Wrzesniewski Crouthamel
Joetta Powley Farner
Anita Henson Jeffery
Patti Hall Krow
Cindy Lewis
Gregory Luttrell
Thomas MacCormick
Darlene Forney Myers
Debbie Aldinger Osevala
Dr. Mark Osevala
Kathy Saltzer Peffer
Sandy Vigilante Reedy
Julia Snavely Seifried

Marian Paul Shireman
David Warfel
Dennis Weaver
Robert (Fred) Weber
Pixie Spacht Wright

Class of 1974
Sherry Rogers Bement
Dr. Craig College
Laura Rogers Graff
Cathy Paul Leese
Sherry Radanovic
Dr. Kenneth Staver
Kathy Imhof Weber

Class of 1975
Roger Calhoon
Rose Hicks Dallago
Steve Hall
Jody Reitz Hatt
Tom Henson
Denise Lehmer Roath

Class of 1976
Anita Witters Cassel
Jayne Snavely Grundon
Todd Grundon
Roy Hicks
Joyce Ann Vigilante

Class of 1977
Judy Vigilante Adler
Yvonne Martin Calhoon
Kim Baumann Iacavone
Jill Landis Kiessling
John Kiessling
Ron Myers
Mary Petrina Smith

Class of 1978
Jeffrey Calhoon
Linda Kerlin Jackson
H. Craig Lehmer
Mary Basler Pugmire

Class of 1979
Nancy Paul Harder

Class of 1980
Lisa Yohn Kiessling
Mark Kiessling

Class of 1981
Laurie Petrina Fleming
Kris Neibert Kiner

Class of 1982
Craig Cassel
Scott Eisenbise
Lola Lausch
Christine Updegraff Matthews
Ron Orsini

Class of 1983
Keith Oellig
Susan Sipe
Rick Smith
Joseph Snavely
June Steckler
Stephanie Bardin Torre

Class of 1985
Laurie Whitehaus Gill
Francine Paul Hawksworth
Dr. Jeffrey D. Miller

Class of 1987
Melinda Rogers

Class of 1988
Sheila Pankake Vandernick

Class of 1989
Brian Crow
Janie Barnhart Crow
Ashley Bossler Derickson
Denise Little

Class of 1990
Michelle Beyer

Class of 1996
Nicole Cassel

Class of 2008
Melissa Calhoon

Faculty/Administration
Barbara J. Atkinson*
Cleon Cassel*
Nancy Paioletti Chango**
Dr. Jacqueline Douglass*
Rosemary Huff*
Dr. Steve Messner*/***
Dr. Jeffrey A. Miller***
Bob Rath*
James Seacrist*
Paula Seacrist*
David Smith*
Dr. Sherri L. Smith***
Marie Weber*
Bob Welsh**
Dr. Judith T. Witmer*/***

*faculty

**former student teacher

***administration

"Time It Was — A Reprise"

General Trivia Questions:

1. What family has had a member of their immediate family—grandparent, aunt, uncle, mom, dad, nephew, niece, etc.—in Lower Dauphin every year of its existence, beginning in 1961?

2. Which class had the largest number of graduates from 1961 to 2010?

3. Which class had the fewest number of graduates from 1961 to 2010?

4. Which class was the first to hold Commencement in the Hershey Theatre?

5. Which class was the only class to hold Commencement in Founders Hall?

6. Which class was the first to hold Commencement in the Giant Center?

7. In what year was the name "Falconaire" misspelled on the yearbook cover?

8. How many seats are there in the auditorium?

9. When was the Rain Garden created?

10. What year did senior pictures in color first appear in the yearbook?

11. What was the last year for Future Farmers of American at Lower Dauphin?

12. In what year did the *Falconaire* first contain photographs in color?

—see answers below

12. 1965

11. 1993

10. 1990s

9. 2008

8. 1,093

7. 1987

6. Class of 2003

5. Class of 2002

4. Class of 1969

3. Class of 1961 with 129

2. Class of 2007 with 332

1. The Snavely family, beginning with Gail Walborn who was in ninth grade the fall of 1960; her nieces and nephew included Julia '73, Jayne '76, Jeanne '78, Joan '80, and Joseph Snavely '83.

Loyal Hearts Proclaim: The First Fifty Years of Lower Dauphin High School

Remember When

» The rubber chicken wouldn't go away

» Silent meditations followed philosophical morning readings

» The total administrative staff at the high school consisted of a supervising principal, high school principal, and junior high principal

» **There were black olives for lunch every day for days in 1962.** According to Dr. Janet Calhoon, "I'll never forget the day at lunch when every tray that came out of the cafeteria had black olives on it, not just one or two olives, but a cupful, enough to probably count as a vegetable. This went on for days and almost every one of us hated these. One day Mike Strite came with large size grocery paper bags, collected the olives from every table and gave the filled bags to the cafeteria staff. We saw fewer olives after that day."

» No street shoes were allowed to be worn on the gym floor

» C-wing was the language wing

» Guns were brought to school for public speaking class

» Tattoos were very uncool.

» In 1973 Mr. Fickes' sculpture class made a plaster man who first entered pupil services, then transferred to the lobby where he drew more attention, then relocated to F-14 where he comfortably occupied a desk, books and all.

» *Falcon Flash*, Editor Barb Saylor, April 1973, commented: "Many of the average LD students resent the special treatment certain people receive at our school. They are allowed to walk into homeroom anytime they wish, to skip classes, to amble aimlessly through the hallways, and interrupt classes demanding to see someone."

» In the spring of 1976 Sue Williams got her finger stuck in a hole in one of the lab tables

» The 1988 yearbook sold for $20

» On March 26, 1991, A-6 was flooded as a result of an eruption of water from pipes under the floor tiles. The water rose to ½ inch within a five minute period.

» When a new all-Mexican, all-the-time line replaced the sandwich line, Sean McCann (*Falcon Flash*, January 2006) questioned the decision. "Just the thought of Mexican every day is enough to make my stomach turn," he said in his case against the overkill. "While the nachos with spicy meat and cheese were always a favorite, it now is losing its allure." Another issue McCann raised is the congestion this causes, particularly at the register. "Should we suggest the return of the Lower Dauphin Dandy and black olives, the scourge of earlier classes?"

We Remember

Sayings and slogans

Just another day in paradise

Lift your knees!

To be or not to be

Out damn spot

Seniors rule!

The juniors are looking forward to next year….

…the season ended without a win, but became a learning experience

We were falcons, seniors, friends

The team hopes for a successful season next year

We are the Falcons, the mighty, mighty Falcons

We sang as one, each to a different tune

The future looks very promising for the team

Something Good is Happening at Lower Dauphin

Quality Education Begins at Lower Dauphin

Falcon Pride, Falcon Power, Falconland, The Pride is Back

Signs

Home of the Falcons

Falcon Pride

Falcons, Class of 1976 — Soar to Victory

Items

Briefolios

Large, white Lower Dauphin Bible

"Hot Line," the Ninth Grade newspaper, first edition, March 1979

The papier-mâché volcano that would not fit through the door

Places

Hershey Junior College

Richmond-Upon-Thames College

The Hob-Nob

STATES!

Designated smoking areas

Camp Hebron

A private movie house, the Wal-Lemar Flicks

Olmsted

Audions, general labs, language labs

The Bunker

People

The teacher who referred to herself in the imperial "We"

The faculty member described in the *Falcon Flash* as the Ayn Rand Libertarian Objectivist

A staff of 80 volunteer student librarians

Audacious stunts generated by Electronics Club

The Out Crowd

Wrestlettes

Falconettes

Percussionists

The Flying Faculty Falcons

The Midgets

Faculty Cheerleaders

The live baby in a creche

Special Privileges

Open lunches and walks to Lynn's Market

Release time for seniors

Smoking passes

Student School Board Members

Special Events

Commencement slide shows, speaking choirs, pageants

Powder Puff football

Exchange assembly program with Hershey

Sit-ins

Be-ins

Picketing the District Office

The informal Christmas Dance named "The Christmas Cushion"

Air Guitar shows in the Middle School

1967 recording of Commencement

Class Nights, Fun Nights, Class Trips

Booster Club Bus

Styles

Long hair, spiked hair, signature hair ponytails (male), earrings, headbands, shorts and sockless shoes all year long, unlaced shoes

Jumpsuits, sideburns, clogs, berets, knickers, peasant skirts, pants suits, mini-skirts

Chinos and madras, teased hair, grunge, preppy

Crocks, UGGS, signature athletic shoes

Hair extensions, mohawks

Awards

Betty Crocker Homemaking

Eras

The glory years of track

The Kreiser championships

The 1964 purchase of the health ball for physical education

Posted announcement: Girls, the White Guard is coming soon so be ready for lots of excitement with the Blue Guard.

The Falcon Nation

▸ **Class of 67's remembrances!** *Do you remember when*

» The Junior Prom menu read "Sweatheart Delight?" rather than Sweetheart

» Dodie Crousor's horses broke loose on April Fool's Day '66 and ran past H-wing

» Ann Granzo immortalized herself in chem class

» Mr. Swartley took a group star-gazing

» Mr. Fickes asserted that the LD doors are painted red so that the custodians can immediately see them when riding their lawn mowers and thus eliminate any unnecessary fatalities

» Mr. Burchfield sat on his prize mutated corn

» The Junior Class Play, *Melody Jones*, was revised and re-written during the performance

» Kool-Aid was put in the football water bucket

» Everybody hid under a tarpaulin at football practice.

Food

Lower Dauphin Dandy, glazed sweets, taco bar

Vending machines in the cafeteria with snack food

Cookies!

Oddities

Extended daylight-saving time and arriving to school in the darkness of night

Locker inspection

Halloween costumes *in school*

Fads

Pac man

LD beanies

LD armbands

Mini rubber wrist bands

Notebook organizers

Daily Bulletin Notices

- February 28, 1976: An encyclopedia was found in the hall. This encyclopedia does not belong to the Lower Dauphin School District. Would the owner please identify and pick this book up in the Senior High Library?

- Early March, 1976: A manila folder containing quizzes and public speaking evaluation forms has been misplaced by Mr. Zeigler. If anyone comes upon this treasure, please inform him.

- Wednesday, March 17, 1976: If you don't buy a yearbook today, all of St. Patrick's Leprechauns will visit you tonight and dash you to pieces upon the Blarney Stone.

- Wednesday, September 16, 1981

    Assigned to Alternative Education Room: Jeff Schildt

    Early Dismissals: Jeff Schildt

Excerpts from a 2010 Essay Contest

The following are excerpts from an essay contest offered to sophomores to describe the building which is Lower Dauphin High School:

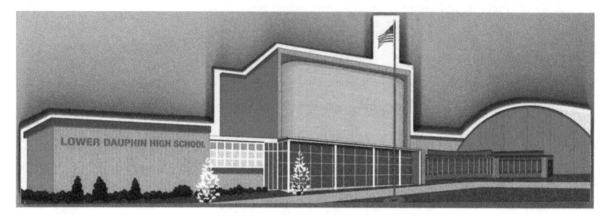

The hallways at LD are unique with the building consisting of a series of smaller hallways conjoined to form the "lightning bolt" shape we all have come to know. This will also make it easier to make additions, perhaps between wings. Inclines complete with guardrails [not present until the 1990s renovations and earlier classes remember occasionally slipping and falling on the ramps] add ease in travel.

Nicholas Diskerud '12

Lower Dauphin has seen tremendous change and growth in the past fifty years and many of the facilities within the school would be completely foreign to past graduates. However, what has remained is a library that serves as a meeting place and common ground, a place for research and a safe haven in a relaxed atmosphere.

Emily Grap '12

Lower Dauphin High School is a beautiful, original building and a place to be proud of. The front of the school stands imposing with the American flag flying atop the pole in the small grass courtyard that is surrounded by pink-flowered trees. Walking through one of twenty doors, you see the office to your left, cafeteria to the right, and the auditorium facing you. Turning left and passing the office, you will pass a display case on your right with pieces from the art classes and, on your right, a major display case that is filled with our history. Take a left and journey down two ramps, then turn to your right where you will see beckoning you with warm yellow lights, my favorite place: the library. Inside is a very special place, a small square alcove with a table and four plush chairs, in a sanctuary which I will miss.

Kelley Gourley '12

The particular class that I enjoy is pottery as it is a way to express feelings without the use of words. It allows the potter to be creative with an open-ended assignment; there are no limits, guidelines, or rules—only your own ideas. While styles of pottery may change in the next fifty years, one thing will remain the same: the opportunity for students to express who they are.

Jenna Flickinger '12

Dear Lower Dauphin Class of 2061

We are now midway through the first one hundred years of the Lower Dauphin School District. Your class will mark the first one hundred years of Lower Dauphin High School unless a major event precludes it from happening. This is stated because it was a major event that took place for the Lower Dauphin Schools to come into being and how our class of 1961 became the first graduating class.

Our class comprised students from Hummelstown High School and the four surrounding townships who attended Hershey High School. Both schools had rich traditions of their own that we needed to forgo in our senior year to become part of a new school with no past. When you hear your great-grandparents talk about the Hummelstown "Bull Dogs" and the "one room school houses," they are referring to our class and our times.

The class of 1961 met for most of its five year reunions the past fifty years where we remembered with fondness our first year at LDHS and the beginning of a new school and making new and life-long friendships. We did not comprehend then that fifty years would pass so quickly and we would be preparing a time capsule for the next fifty years.

We remember the many new and young teachers that first year who blended so well with the teachers from Hummelstown High. Their friendly enthusiasm inspired and helped us to quickly forget what we left behind. I fondly remember being on the first football team and winning the first Capital Area Conference Championship. After fifty years I remember the ride back on the bus from Hershey stadium after winning the championship game against Palmyra High as if it were yesterday. The team cheered give me an F, give me an A, give me an L, give me a C, give me an O, give me an N. What's it spell?—FALCON(S) as we entered the school parking lot to meet a large crowd of students and fans who were also cheering as the team exited the bus. We became united in school spirit and pride that made us feel special and proud to be part of the new Lower Dauphin School District. We were blessed to have head Coach Osevala and a great young coaching staff to bring us together and bring out our best in our short time together.

Our class spirit and enthusiasm was ignited by the band and cheerleaders who had formed for the first time a few weeks before the school opened. Like the coaches, Mr Seitzinger, our band director, brought out the best and inspired all he directed.

As we look back upon this important year in our lives we now know how blessed we were to have so many dedicated teachers, administrators, and coaches to give the inspiration and guidance needed to come together as one class and one school. Our crystal ball will not allow us to see what the next fifty or one hundred years will bring, nor should it.

Take a moment to think about all the classes that graduated before you and contributed to the rich Lower Dauphin High School tradition that you now share. Your class like ours and all the graduates share a common thread with many similar experiences that are only separated by time. We shared the same motto, alma mater, colors, mascot, hallways, classrooms, goals and aspirations.

Sincerely,

Glenn R. Ebersole, President, Class of 1961

Time and Memory

The fingers of insubstantial time close on my wrist,

trying to pull me forward. But I resist. I do not

want to go. Here are my friends, the things

I know. Time tries to tear me through

the misty wall of separated existence,

but I fight it. It fill me with terror,

but . . . there is also beauty. I

realize this now, and loosen

my tenacious hold on

today, to follow

time, but I hold

on with just

one finger,

a memory

of then.

Steve Wilson '80

Legacy

As we contemplate the impact Lower Dauphin High School has had on townships and boroughs joined as one district, as well as the thousands of students and their families, over the last fifty years, we understandably look to the future. What lies ahead? While the future is difficult to predict, what is certain is that the tradition that is Lower Dauphin in terms of scholarship, athletics, the arts, and extracurricular activities will thrive because that is our tradition. Our joy is to watch the ongoing evolution and to revel in the successes that students, faculty, and administration bring not only to themselves but to the entire community that defines itself as Lower Dauphin. **That is the essence of Falcon Pride.**

APPENDIX

Introduction to *The Disappearing Falcon*

We welcome you to 1984 when everyone, it seemed, was reading the newest Stephen King novel, *The Talisman*, of much interest to Lower Dauphin students who two years earlier had attended a writing seminar at Palmyra High School conducted by King himself. Dynasty, Dallas, and the Cosby Show were the favorite television shows being followed by millions of viewers. *Amadeus* nearly swept the Academy Awards, and high school boys everywhere had discovered not girls, but Dungeons and Dragons.

1984 is also the year George Orwell had chosen as the timeframe for his novel of the same name. In this society predicted by Orwell there was no such thing as individualism. "1984: The Prophecy and the Reality" was a natural theme for Lower Dauphin's Commencement program.

There was some trepidation, however, about this year's Commencement because the graduating class was difficult. They already had called in a bomb threat in September, defiantly held a hook day in January during which they had staged a raid, and since that time they had been threatening to finish the year "in style."

There was further controversy because the self-named Senior Mean Team, led by Tom Armstrong, had wanted to do a slide show for Commencement. However, in their typical fashion, they had started late and there was no guarantee they would finish in time, so they had been told by the principal that they could do their slide show Senior Night. Nonetheless, many were angry and vowed among themselves to get even.

Because of the situation, the Falcon Missile had been put under guard in the guidance suite and the Falcon Mascot for the first time in 17 years felt fearful for his safety.

Many seniors joined the Commencement speaking choir which would be wearing clear plastic face masks so that they all looked alike as they chanted T. S. Eliot's "We are the hollow men." This scene was expected to startle the audience as they gazed on the blank faces of the speaking choir.

Because of the masks there was some grumbling among the choir that their friends wouldn't know who was who. In addition, some of the seniors were thinking of how they could swipe a mask or two to use for their own purpose, which was to show everyone that they were a force to be reckoned with.

This was more than enough to put the principal, Mr. Barney Barnum, on edge and he placed the faculty on alert to prevent the graduation event from being sabotaged by the class itself.

This particular Saturday evening was the final dress rehearsal for the program. A covered dish supper was scheduled for 6:00 p.m., followed by rehearsal from 7:00 to 8:30, followed by the Senior Class Night.

A highlight of Class Night, in addition to staying in the school till morning, would be the showing of the class slide show of their fun, their class trip which had been planned at the last minute, and their pranks.

A Saturday night rehearsal was unprecedented. However, because of so many hooky days this class had taken, the advisor believed it was her best chance for getting everyone together for a final rehearsal before Commencement on the following Monday evening. The student rock band "East" was ready, having rewritten the processional Pomp and Circumstance as a rock tune.

The advisor had planned a dramatic climax for the Program that not even the participants would know about in advance. Some suspected this meant including the senior slides, but that didn't seem dramatic enough for what was being hinted at. Not surprising, the group calling themselves the Senior Mean Team announced that they, too, had their own surprise planned. Mr. Frankfurt called for extra security.

To complicate the evening, a television filmmaker, Mr. Willy Silbilly, was producing a documentary of American graduations, and was filming this dress rehearsal. He was fascinated by the fact that Lower Dauphin's graduations still featured student-produced programs. The guidance counselor, Mr. Bac Rhodes, had volunteered to make the arrangements.

Among the chaperones for Senior Class Night were Mr. Cola, Mr. Duke, and Mr. Rhodes—all three men favorites of the Class of 1984, along with their class advisers, Mr. Fudgsicle and Mrs. Attagirl. Two other women, Darling Dulcetta and No-No Nonette, also had volunteered as chaperones, since they had to be there anyhow, Dulcetta conducting the orchestra and No-No helping backstage.

Terry TechCrew is in charge of lights and sound. A most dependable fellow, he knew the auditorium inside and out. He had been trusted by all parties with their separate plans. He felt empowered, but wasn't sure whose surprise plan would gain his favor and to whom he owed the most loyalty.

Also present at this rehearsal was Fred "Whatsit" Matter, best known as the lifetime Falcon Mascot. He didn't know in advance what his role was going to be in the Commencement finale, just that the advisor had requested his participation. While the class was having dinner, he had a trial run-through.

Willy Silbilly had just set his cameras, when he spied Fred in his Falcon Mascot costume. Willy stopped dead in his tracks. "My god," he said, almost aloud. "What a costume! I would love to have it." He then asked himself, "But what is going on here? I thought the school mascot is that imposing Falcon missile I saw in the guidance office!"

At that point No-No signaled to the advisor that the speaking choir members were all accounted for. She then moved off stage left.

The advisor told the choir to follow her direction, to not pay attention to the filming, and to not flinch when the surprise finale occurred for this last rehearsal.

The seniors placed their clear masks over their faces and began. "We are the hollow men, We are the stuffed men, Headpiece filled with straw." It was perfect. Terry was right on target with the sound and lights and didn't even mind that No-No had quietly taken a seat near him in the sound booth. Backstage, Whatsit was confident he would steal the show and that no one would ever forget him again.

Willy smiled to himself, as did Tom, but for different reasons. At the words, "Hail to thee, Blithe Spirit! Bird thou never wert," Tom, standing at the end of the top row nudged the classmate beside him who shared his disdain for poetry, especially from the Romantic Period of British Literature. The next line was the signal for the finale, "When a bird becomes a missile, soaring toward the heavens…"

Across the stage came Whatsit. No one noticed the harness the bird mascot was wearing and it really did look like he was flying toward the sound booth, caught in the spotlight, blue-gelled for the occasion. At that second all the lights went out, including the backstage work lights, the only sound the screech of an acoustic guitar and one thud from a base drum. Suddenly there was a shout from Willy, "It's a wrap!"

A few seconds later, Terry shouted. "I can't find him."

Bac ran to the front of the auditorium, shouting "Everyone stay in your places." Terry turned to No-No, but she wasn't there.

In raced Barney Barnum. "The missile!! Who took it?"

Bac muttered, "Not again."

The advisor looked at both of them. "We can't do the program Monday night without the mascot."

"Which one?" asked Tom. "They are both gone."

"Disappeared," said Terry. Tom smiled at Alma Mater.

So, **who took the Falcon Missile** and **where is the Falcon Mascot?**

Both must be found before Commencement, only two days away …

CPSIA information can be obtained
at www.ICGtesting.com
Printed in the USA
BVHW012129230522
637911BV00004B/49